Monetizing Natural Gas in the New "New Deal" Economy

"Back in 2012, in my book "After the US Shale Gas Revolution", I rightly forecasted that the surge in US oil and gas production combined with the European energy transition would deeply alter the energy and geopolitical landscapes. It is now time to revise our knowledge as energy transition is accelerating all over a post-Covid world that also is de-globalizing! This book provides the latest updates from abundant US upstream supply to global downstream demand, that should increase for at least another two decades thanks mostly to growing economies that need to prioritize economic and human development. A must-read for everyone that wants to grasp the complexity of our energy landscape."

—Dr. Thierry Bros, Professor, *Sciences Po Paris*

"For those readers - experts, beginners and those in between, this book on the natural gas industry will be valuable. Full of historical analysis and also a deep insight into the current fast moving scenario. Gaining insight into the gas sector development is a complex learning experience. Here is a book which covers all different aspects of international gas industry."

—Dr. Bhamy Shenoy

"Through all of my years of knowing and interacting with the lead editor and her colleagues, it has always been about seeing where the facts lead us. And in this fact-laden, realistic look at natural gas supply and demand from a global view over the coming decades, I come away with a strong impression of natural gas as a vital, essential, permanent ingredient in our energy mix. This compelling work should inform our policy debate about how the world best addresses our energy and environmental goals."

—Pat Wood III, past Chairman, *Federal Energy Regulatory Commission and Public Utility Commission of Texas*

Michelle Michot Foss
Anna Mikulska • Gürcan Gülen
Editors

Monetizing Natural Gas in the New "New Deal" Economy

palgrave
macmillan

Editors
Michelle Michot Foss
Baker Institute for Public Policy
Rice University
Houston, TX, USA

Anna Mikulska
Baker Institute for Public Policy
Rice University
Houston, TX, USA

Gürcan Gülen
West Brookfield, MA, USA

ISBN 978-3-030-59982-9 ISBN 978-3-030-59983-6 (eBook)
https://doi.org/10.1007/978-3-030-59983-6

This Palgrave Macmillan imprint is published by the registered company Springer Nature Switzerland AG.
The registered company address is: Gewerbestrasse 11, 6330 Cham, Switzerland

To all energy customers worldwide. May we all get the best deals.

Foreword: The Future of Gas—What Are the Key Issues?

Overview

My collaboration with the lead editor of this book and her associates began in 2003 when I founded the Natural Gas Research Programme at Oxford Institute for Energy Studies (OIES). The dialogue and mutual research support which has continued since then has illustrated how different the energy world looks on different sides of the Atlantic, and how difficult it is—even with virtually limitless availability of information—for each side to understand the relevance of unfolding events.

The two issues we have most actively debated over the years have been the likely impact of climate change policies on energy balances and global natural gas issues. The scepticism around (and at times hostility to) carbon-reduction policies among the Houston energy community in the early 2000s was understandable when it was still uncertain whether the Kyoto Protocol would even be ratified. Fast forward to the start of 2020: the irony of the significant U.S. reduction in carbon emissions compared with far less significant European achievements is not an outcome that any of us could have anticipated. An even greater irony is to see individual U.S. states becoming global leaders in decarbonisation and renewable energy development at the same time as the Administration is withdrawing from the Paris agreement. This is confusing for European observers who tend to believe that presidential announcements are implemented nationally.

As we now know, U.S. carbon reduction is the result of the shale (oil and) gas "revolution"—a revolution which has not been replicated outside of North America. This constitutes a state of affairs that looks unlikely to change. A consequence of the shale revolution is that supply abundance drove U.S. gas prices down to levels that (at the time) was only anticipated by Michot Foss in a 2007 OIES paper. She then followed with another paper in 2011 and a chapter in our book on international gas pricing in 2012.[1] As we now know, low U.S. price levels continued through the 2010s strongly favouring domestic gas demand, but by the end of the decade international gas prices were falling to similar levels causing U.S. LNG exporters to struggle for profitability.

To provide a broad and international context for this book, it is important to bring these three key elements together. The fossil fuel community assumed that decarbonisation would be a development towards reliance on natural gas to meet essential energy needs. But as the lead editor asks in Chap. 1, is this necessarily the case? Decarbonisation as a policy premise, or a policy mandate as many would prefer, may not recognise designating any fossil fuels as "clean". Antipathy towards natural gas can dominate because of the conviction in the climate community that all fossil fuels must be phased out as quickly as possible, contrasting with a consensus in the energy community that these fuels will continue to be relied upon for an undefined period of transition. Affordability and profitability will determine outcomes: the lower the cost of natural gas delivered to end users, the more affordable it is for consumers (voters) and the easier it becomes to prolong its market share as long as it remains a profitable business. If decarbonisation forces up costs this will impact affordability and profitability relative to other energy and technology options and investments. The intersection of decarbonisation, affordability, and profitability will unfold differently in different countries and will be the key issues that determine the future of gas in the 2020s.

The principal proposition of gas companies and "advocacy" organisations in the 2010s was that gas will play a major role in the transition to decarbonised energy markets, up to (and possibly beyond) 2050, because of the carbon reduction advantages of switching from coal to gas, and the role of gas in backing up intermittent renewable power generation. In other words, the proposition that gas could be not just a "transition" but also a "destination" fuel for a low-carbon energy system. But in carbon-centric Europe the policy and environmental communities found these propositions unconvincing.[2]

In 2020, European Union policy makers proposed a law[3] that would require the bloc to achieve climate neutrality ("net zero" emissions) by 2050—the UK (having left the EU) had previously passed such legislation. This significantly more stringent reduction target made clear that to ensure a longer-term future in European energy balances the gas community would need to provide a narrative—backed up by investments—showing how the gas industry intended to decarbonise post-2030.[4] However, outside Europe and other carbon-centric (mainly OECD) countries and regions, the future of gas depends not just on Conference of Parties, COP21 carbon reduction commitments but also, importantly and in many countries more immediately, on its contribution to improving urban air quality and affordability both in absolute terms and relative to alternative sources of energy.

This Foreword therefore is aimed at providing a context for the most important challenges to the future of gas in different countries and regions, and the timescale of those challenges. It is structured in four sections: I first examine modelling projections and scenarios for gas over the next several decades; I then look at the prices and costs—affordability and profitability—of gas, and particularly imported LNG, in different countries and regions. The third section addresses the question of whether countries will be prepared to pay a geopolitical premium for U.S. LNG. In the following section, I look at the extent to which we can expect Asia to change from traditional oil-linked pricing of LNG to spot and hub-based pricing. I close with some conclusions which play out in several of the chapters in this book.

Modelling Projections and Scenarios for Gas

Global energy projections, models, and scenarios published in the late 2010s tend to divide into two categories:

- Those showing how energy balances will evolve in the future, given current and anticipated future trends and policies which governments have announced.
- Those seeking to demonstrate how energy balances must evolve if COP21 carbon-reduction targets are to be achieved.

The International Energy Agency's *World Energy Outlook* (WEO) is the most cited model in publications dealing with gas—not because it is necessarily more accurate than other models but—because it provides a degree of granularity and detail across gas supply, demand, and pricing on a regional level which is not matched by most other studies. Specifically, the

WEO's "Stated Policies" and "Sustainable Development" scenarios provide detailed analysis of these trends up to 2040. The Stated Policies scenario: "incorporates not just the policies and measures that governments around the world have already put in place but also the likely effects of announced policies as expressed in official targets and plans". The Sustainable Development scenario incorporates three major elements: a pathway to the universal access to modern energy services by 2030, a picture that is consistent with the objectives of the Paris (COP21) Agreement by reaching a peak in emissions as soon as possible followed by a substantial decline, and a dramatic improvement in global air quality.[5]

I show future gas demand by region for the period up to 2040 under these scenarios in Figs. F.1 and F.2. The difference is relatively clear: in Stated Policies, gas demand increases in all regions up to 2040 with the exception of Europe, Russia, and Japan, where it stabilises. In the Sustainable Development scenario, gas demand up to 2040:

- Declines significantly in Russia, Europe, and Japan
- Stabilises in Central/South America
- Increases modestly in South East Asia and Africa
- Increases but then peaks and declines post-2030 in North America and the Middle East
- Increases substantially in both China and India

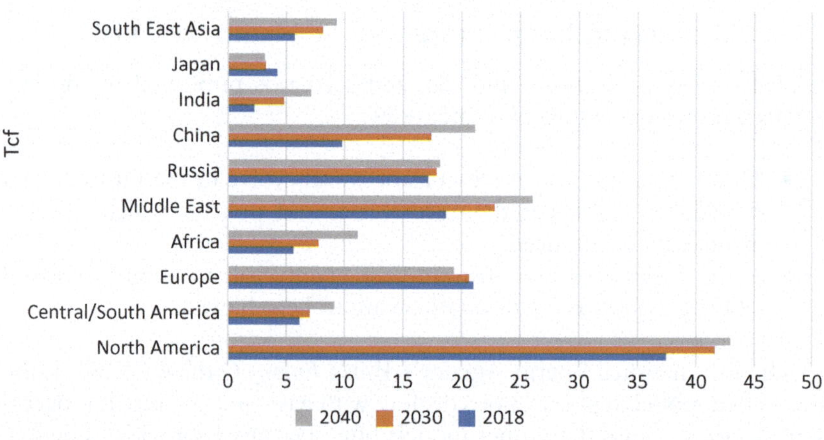

Fig. F.1 Regional gas demand 2018–40 Stated Policies scenario (Tcf). (Source: IEA (2019), Table A.1, pp. 674–5)

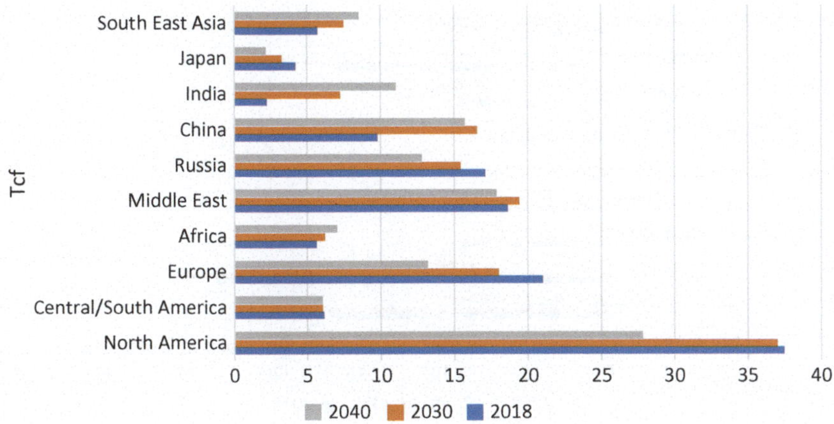

Fig. F.2 Regional gas demand 2018–40 Sustainable Development scenario (Tcf). (Source: IEA WEO (2019), Table A.1, pp. 674–5)

In the Stated Policies scenario global gas demand increases from 140 trillion cubic feet (Tcf) in 2018, to 167 Tcf in 2030, and 153 Tcf in 2040; in the Sustainable Development scenario the corresponding figures for 2030 and 2040 are 151 Tcf and 136 Tcf, respectively.[6] These scenarios therefore suggest that the future of gas is relatively bright; meeting COP21 targets would mean that global gas demand will peak in the early 2030s and then decline sharply, but in 2040 it will only be just below its 2018 level.[7] The only rapidly growing markets over the entire period will be in China and India.

There are interesting contrasts between the IEA and the Shell Sky scenario, which is designed to achieve a "less than two degrees" world (i.e., compatible with the Paris targets) and extends to 2100. The Sky scenario (Fig. F.3) shows outcomes for gas in the period up to 2050. It shows significant gas demand growth outside the OECD up to 2030, followed by some decline (particularly in the OECD) up to 2040. In order to meet targets, there is a 25 per cent decline in global gas demand in the period 2040–50, particularly in China where demand falls by 50 per cent during that decade; nevertheless by mid-century global gas demand is only 7 per cent below its 2015 level.

In Equinor's *Energy Perspectives*, global gas demand increases in all three scenarios up to 2030, but growth in the Renewal scenario is

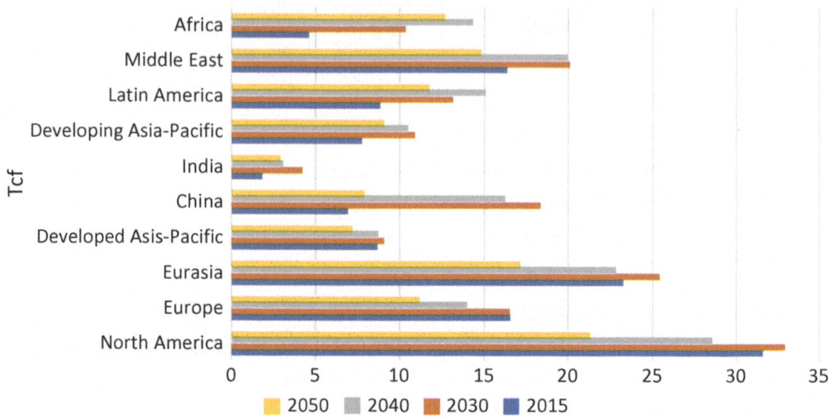

Fig. F.3 Regional gas demand 2015–50, Shell Sky scenario (Tcf). (Source: Shell (2018))

marginal.[8] From 2030 to 2050, global gas demand increases in two of the scenarios, but under Renewal, global demand in 2050 is 10 per cent below its 2016 level, with European and North American demand halving during this period and China having the only substantial increase in demand.[9]

A Grantham Institute/Carbon Tracker study which is critical of what it calls "business as usual" studies by IOCs, tests out the consequences for fossil fuel demand of applying current cost projections for solar PV and growth of electric vehicles and concludes:

> Lower energy demand reduces natural gas demand growth across all sectors, but it is only in our most bullish "Strong PV/Low EV" scenario that we see natural gas demand peak in 2030 and fall thereafter.

One of the study's most pertinent observations is thus:

> In essence, the degree to which natural gas demand grows or not to 2050 could be one of the key factors that determine whether we achieve the 2 degrees C target.[10]

Although many of these studies have scenarios which see a fall in demand post-2030, the only substantial modelling study located by this author which has what might be described a "catastrophic" outcome for gas by 2050 is Greenpeace's (2015) scenarios.[11] Under the Energy [R]evolution scenario:

- Global gas demand in 2030 is above its 2012 level; even in 2040 it is only 16 per cent below its 2012 level, but by 2050 it has fallen to 42 per cent of that level.
- Consistent with that pattern, in North America, OECD Europe, Europe/Eurasia and OECD Asia, Latin America, and Africa, demand does not increase greatly and falls post-2030, but not substantially until the 2040s. In the Middle East, demand is robust throughout the period. Only in China and India does demand increase significantly, peaking around 2040 and falling slightly thereafter.

The Greenpeace Advanced [R]evolution scenario requires fossil fuels to be phased out almost completely by 2050. For that reason gas demand is reduced to negligible proportions by that date:

- Global gas demand in 2030 is very similar to E[R] and is 5 per cent above its 2012 level; by 2040 it is 30 per cent below its 2012 level, and by 2050 it has dropped to 7 per cent of that level.
- Regional demand follows a similar pattern, but it is more resilient across Asia than in other regions up to 2040.

The conclusion of this overview of models and scenarios is that, with the possible exception of Europe, *from a carbon reduction perspective* the future of gas is relatively robust up to 2030 but uncertain thereafter depending on the region under consideration and the speed of decarbonisation. However, an important caveat is that scenarios must take into account the whole of the period up to 2050 because major changes will be needed to meet targets in the 2040s.

Aside from the Greenpeace scenarios (especially Advanced [R]evolution), the consensus is that global gas demand is unlikely to decline *significantly* until after 2030 (and in some regions 2040), although notably in Europe that decline could start in the late 2020s and must accelerate post-2030 to meet net zero targets.[12] From a global perspective, a 20–25 year horizon prior to significant decline could be viewed as an acceptable definition of gas as a "transition fuel", but very far from fulfilling the role of a "destination fuel".

The focus of the majority of all current energy studies is to illustrate the constraints that carbon (and other greenhouse gas) emissions impose on fossil fuel use over the next several decades. Given the consensus of 196 parties at the 2015 COP21 Paris conference, this is completely understandable. A major proposition of OIES research is that other factors may impose more important, and significantly more immediate (although potentially related), constraints on gas demand. The most important of these constraints are the affordability and profitability of gas in relation to the development and delivery costs of pipeline gas and LNG in the late 2010s.

Affordability and Profitability of New LNG Projects

Regional and National Wholesale Gas Prices 2005–19

Figure F.4 shows data for wholesale prices of gas by region for the period 2005–19, from which it can be seen that, aside from Europe, Asia Pacific, Asia (post-2009), and North America (before 2009), the price of gas has seldom approached $4/MMBtu and, in most other regions, has been significantly below that level.[13] This presents a clear differentiation between what could be deemed the historically "high-price" regions (Europe, Asia Pacific, and since 2010, Asia) and "low-price" regions (Latin America, former Soviet Union, Africa, and the Middle East).

The Asia-Pacific region had sustained price levels in excess of $8/MMBtu for the first half of the 2010s (Fig. F.4) due to the linkage of

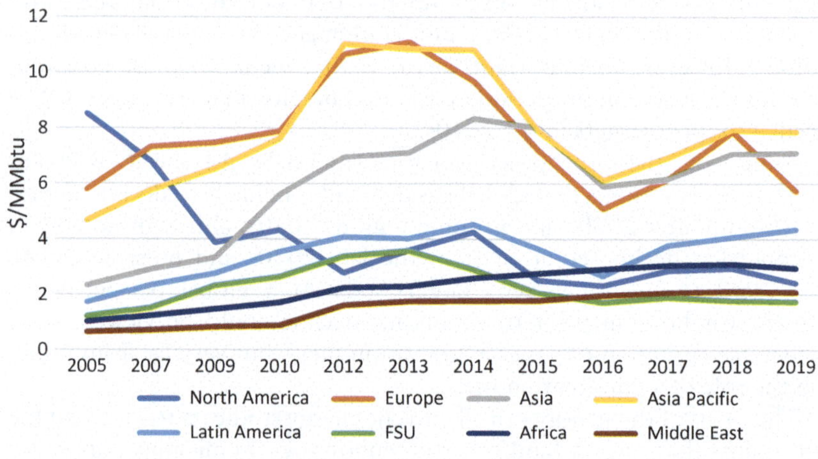

Fig. F.4 Wholesale gas price levels by region 2005–19. (Source: IGU (2020), Figure 2, p. 7)

gas—and specifically LNG import—prices to those of oil. European prices were at similar for much of the period but fell below Asian levels in the late 2010s. All other regions, Latin America, Middle East, former Soviet Union, and Africa, have sustained price levels below $4/MMBtu throughout the period. The exception is North America, which, due to the shale gas revolution, moved from prices in the $8–10/MMBtu range in the mid-2000s to $2–4/MMBtu thereafter.

Comparing the gas price scenarios in Table F.1, to the IEA scenarios in Figs. F.1 and F.2, the potential disconnect is clearly evident. If we take the EU, China, and Japan as proxies of global LNG price levels, then LNG importers will need to pay $7.5–8.8/MMBtu for gas during 2025–40 in the Sustainable Development scenario and $8.00–10.2/MMBtu in the Stated Policies scenario. For regions that have been paying only around half of those prices for the past decade, it is questionable how much gas they will be able to afford at these prices, which raises questions about the demand scenarios in Figs. F.1 and F.2.

This is particularly important in relation to projections of LNG trade since, with the exception of pipelines from Russia to Europe and Asia, the vast majority of the increase in international gas trade in the period up to 2040 is expected to be LNG.[14] The OIES Gas Programme has published substantial research on the costs of new LNG projects and how these might be reduced in future. Figure F.5 shows cost estimates for delivering LNG from new projects to northwest Europe, Fig. F.6 shows the same for delivery to high-price Asian markets (Japan, Korea, Taiwan, and China), and Fig. F.7 for delivery to low-price markets in India, Pakistan, and

Table F.1 Natural gas price scenarios 2025–40[a] (real 2018 $/MMBtu)

	Stated policies				*Sustainable development*	
	2025	*2030*	*2035*	*2040*	*2030*	*2040*
U.S.	3.2	3.3	3.8	4.4	3.2	3.4
European Union	8.0	8.0	8.4	8.9	7.5	7.5
China	9.1	9.0	9.3	9.8	8.6	8.7
Japan	10.0	9.7	9.8	10.2	8.8	8.7

Source: IEA, WEO (2019), Table B4, p. 756

[a]U.S. figures reflect the wholesale price prevailing in the domestic market; EU and China figures reflect a balance of pipeline and LNG import prices; Japan figures are LNG import prices

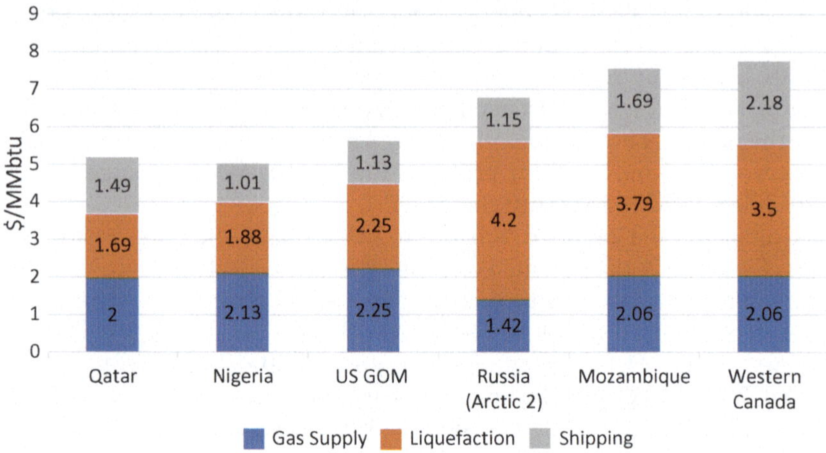

Fig. F.5 Cost of LNG from new projects delivered to northwest Europe in 2025. (Source: Stern (2019), Figure 14, p. 27)

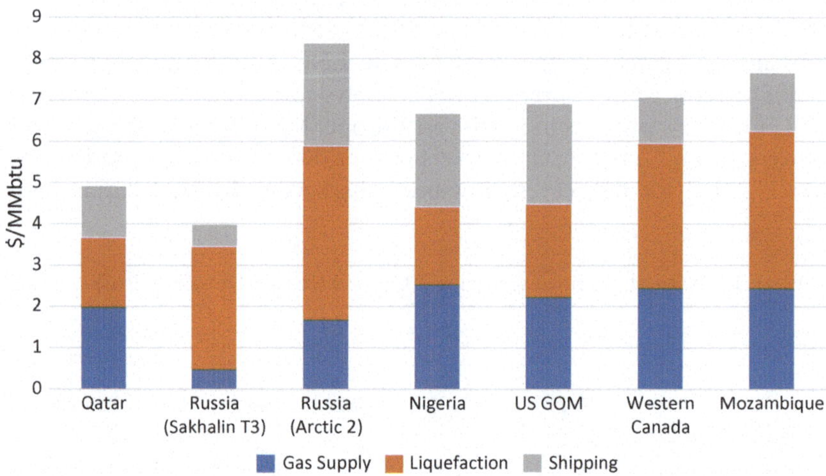

Fig. F.6 Cost of LNG from new projects delivered to Japan, Korea, Taiwan, and China in 2025. (Source: Stern (2019), Figure 15, p. 28)

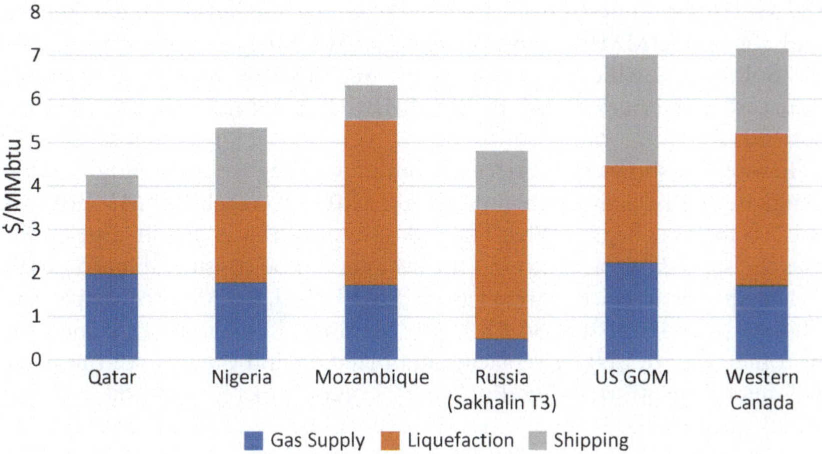

Fig. F.7 Cost of LNG from new projects delivered to India, Pakistan, and Bangladesh in 2025. (Source: Stern (2019), Figure 16, p. 28)

Bangladesh.[15] The differences in costs are largely accounted for by shipping, but the Nigerian, Canadian, Mozambique, and Arctic 2 projects also have differences in supply costs. Figure F.5 shows that all projects can be delivered to northwest Europe at less than $8/MMBtu, although Western Canadian projects are close to that level.[16]

For high wholesale price countries in Fig. F.6, the findings are similar to those of Europe. Steuer's estimate of Russia's Arctic 2 costs is substantially higher than that of the project developer Novatek (2017) at $5.71/MMBtu.

I must stress that these are cost estimates for new projects. They are in many cases significantly below the delivered costs of projects that started production in the 2010s, particularly for Australian projects that ranged from $10 to 15/MMBtu.[17]

This opens up a larger issue for suppliers of LNG to Asian markets where traditionally more than two-thirds of global LNG is sold, and all projections show as having the fastest growing future demand. Figure F.8 shows average wholesale gas prices for Asian countries for the period 2005–19; this provides important country granularity that is not apparent from averaging prices across a region (Fig. F.4). Asia divides into three price groups: Japan, Korea, Taiwan, and Singapore, which have paid above

$8/MMBtu (and up to twice that level); China and Thailand, which have paid above $6/MMBtu (and up to $10/MMBtu); and other Southeast and South Asia, which have paid below $6/MMBtu. India is an intermediate case with prices as high as $8/MMBtu but falling below $6/MMBtu post-2015.

Figure F.8 shows that prices in some countries are increasing rapidly: Bangladeshi prices more than doubled in 2019 to reach $6/MMBtu and as LNG imports began. What Fig. F.8 does not show is that in large countries the spread of prices around the average can be considerable. In 2019, Indian domestic prices ranged from $3.23 to 9.29/MMBtu, while the Chinese price range was $6.87–9.69/MMBtu. This can be explained for customers where LNG is replacing imported oil and the price of the latter will determine affordability. But where LNG is not replacing oil, or once oil substitution has been exhausted there will be significant limits on what is affordable which may depend on subsidies from government (or government-owned utilities). So a key question—in relation to future demand projections—is whether LNG will be affordable in importing regions in terms of domestic wholesale prices and, if not, the level of subsidies which governments will be willing and able to support.

For LNG sellers, this suggests that an increasing volume of their exports needs to be sold to counterparties that may not be regarded as “investment grade”. In addition, profitability may be a problem for the higher cost projects in Figs. F.6 and F.7 for exports to some of the south and southeast Asian countries. Only Qatari, Nigerian, and Russian (Sakhalin) costs are below the $6/MMBtu cost level which may be required to deliver LNG to India, Pakistan, and Bangladesh; North American exports prices may need prices of $7/MMBtu or above if they are to achieve profitable sales. Figures F.5 through F.8 suggest that U.S. LNG exporters (assuming liquefaction cost of $2.50/MMBtu and a Henry Hub price of $3/MMBtu) require a delivered price of at least $5.70/MMBtu in Europe and at least $7/MMBtu elsewhere to make a return on their investments.[18]

Other key judgements for U.S. LNG exporters are whether European importers will prioritise U.S. imports over Russian pipeline gas imports for geopolitical reasons, and for all exporters whether Asian LNG importers will continue to pay oil-linked prices. The following sections examine these questions in more detail.

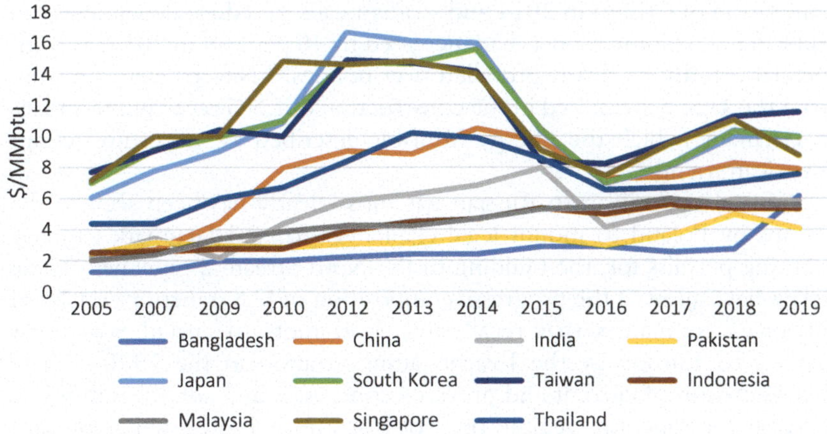

Fig. F.8 Average wholesale gas prices in Asian countries 2005–19 ($/MMBtu). (Source: IGU wholesale gas price survey (various years))

Is There a Geopolitical Premium for US LNG in Europe?

Are European countries willing to pay more for LNG—and particularly U.S. LNG—in order to reduce (and in some cases completely eliminate) imports of Russian pipeline gas? Thus far Poland and Ukraine have shown they are definitely willing to do so, while Lithuania (and possibly other Baltic countries) has suggested a similar preference. Because gas industries in these countries are controlled by governments—or majority government-owned utilities—they can implement such policies, irrespective of the costs of new import infrastructure, or the LNG required to fill it.[19] While creating an alternative supply source to Russian gas was previously an essential element in a commercial bargaining position with Gazprom, that requirement largely disappeared. This was a consequence of the spread of hub-based pricing in Europe and Gazprom's commitment to EU competition (antitrust) authorities that European gas buyers be offered a competitive price whether or not they are able to physically access a hub market.[20] Nevertheless, the Polish government has taken steps to eliminate the need to import any molecules of Russian gas post-2022 (although these will continue to transit across the country), and Ukraine is declining to make any direct gas purchases from Gazprom.[21]

There is no sign that any other European country is willing to pay more for non-Russian gas supplies, as evidenced by the fact that, following the annexation of Crimea in 2014 and strident calls to reduce dependence on Russian gas, volume exports had increased by 40 per cent in 2019, as commercial conditions clearly prevailed over politics.[22] Nevertheless, pressure from the U.S. has resulted in the construction of LNG receiving terminals in Germany, which the Energy Minister described as "a gesture to our American friends".[23]

Political opposition to Russian gas most clearly has been seen in the actions by Poland to mount legal challenges to, and Denmark to delay granting permits for, the building of the Nord Stream 2 pipelines. These delays have allowed the progressive imposition of U.S. sanctions on Nord Stream 2 companies that recall similar attempts to curtail Soviet gas exports to Europe by the Reagan administration in the 1980s.[24] The determination of current and previous congresses and administrations to increase the sanctions regime on Nord Stream 2 has caused significant irritation in the western part of Europe as it seems to be aimed as much at increasing sales of U.S. LNG as protecting Europe and Ukraine from the economic and security implications of Russian gas imports and transit. Protection of Ukraine has become a somewhere less urgent issue following the (somewhat surprising) five-year extension of the Russia-Ukraine gas transit agreement which guaranteed Kiev significant flows and associated revenues until 2024.[25]

Few outside (and even within) Europe have recognised that a major cause of increased Russian gas imports has been the sudden demise of Dutch gas. In five years, 2013–18, the Netherlands moved from being a net exporter of 1.5 Tcf of pipeline gas to Europe to becoming a net importer of natural gas.[26] Falling European gas production (everywhere except for Norway) will mean accelerating import dependence despite the fall in demand.[27]

Many European governments see the geopolitics of natural gas and LNG supplies in two ways. One relates to the dangers of becoming overdependent on Russia (a country which continues to invest in multi-billion-dollar infrastructure to deliver gas to Europe). The other is the political stability of countries supplying (and transiting) pipeline gas and LNG in north and sub-Saharan Africa and the Middle East. Concerns about U.S. LNG may have increased due to the perceived unpredictability of the Trump administration on trade and tariff issues, but there is general confidence that the administration wants to promote LNG exports and would not jeopardise their expansion principally because of its own political agenda to replace Russian pipeline gas with "freedom gas," that is U.S. LNG.

The past two years have seen a surge in European LNG imports to their highest-ever levels, after a period when more than 7 Tcf of European regasification capacity had only been utilised around 25 per cent.[28] That share nearly doubled in 2019 and may be slightly higher in 2020.[29] In 2019, 38 per cent of U.S. LNG exports landed in Europe accounting for 15 per cent of imports. In 2020 problems emerged for U.S. LNG due to the lack of a sufficient price spread between U.S. and European (but also Asian) markets (Fig. F.9), which resulted in many offtakers being unable to cover even their operating costs and led to the cancellation of a significant number of U.S. cargoes despite having to pay the liquefaction fee.[30] Should the price spreads between Europe and Asia that were seen during much of the 2010s recur, then Europe will once again lose a significant share of its LNG, as exporters seek the highest prices and become more dependent on pipeline gas.

The Pricing of LNG in Asia

How long this surge of LNG into Europe continues will depend on developments in Asia, specifically gas demand and pricing. The traditional method of pricing LNG in Asia has been linkage to crude oil with the Japan crude cocktail (JCC) as the dominant methodology.[31] At the beginning of the 2010s, the first U.S. LNG contracts introduced a new methodology of Henry Hub plus liquefaction+shipping+regasification, with the buyer having the option to deliver the gas to the liquefaction plant in a pure tolling arrangement, or for the plant owner to source the gas and deliver the LNG to loading dock.[32] The innovative elements that U.S. LNG exports brought to Asian contracting were, first, that they introduced a pricing alternative to crude oil and, second, that they were destination-free. Japanese LNG buyers had been trying to obtain more destination freedom for many years.[33]

Figure F.10 shows that during the period when the first wave of U.S. LNG contracts were signed (2011–14), Henry Hub-based prices were substantially cheaper for Asian buyers than oil-linked prices. However, when oil prices subsequently collapsed around 2016–17, the latter fell below Henry Hub prices (although the difference was not significant). With the increase in oil prices in 2018 to $70–80/bbl, U.S. LNG once again became both attractive and profitable in Asia. The collapse of hub gas prices in 2019 (Fig. F.9) followed by ultra-low oil prices in 2020 has

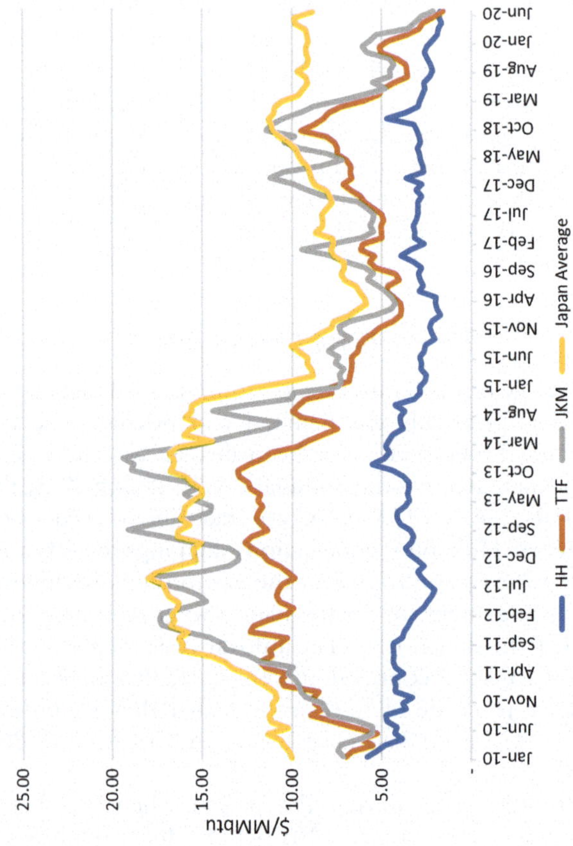

Fig. F.9 U.S., European, and Asian Hub, spot and oil-linked prices 2010–20. (Source: Platts)

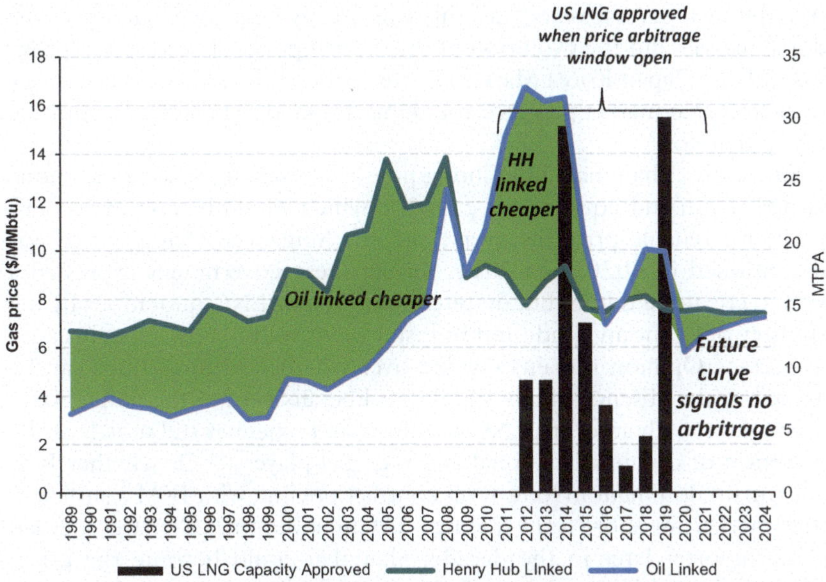

Fig. F.10 Prices of oil-linked and Henry Hub-linked LNG delivered to Asia. (Source: Beveridge (2018) updated; used with permission)

resulted in a lack of arbitrage opportunity and, as already noted, price levels which by 2020 were too low to cover even operating costs.

A basic question for Asian (and indeed all) buyers of U.S. LNG is whether it makes sense to sign 20-year contracts on the basis of a price determined by the fundamentals of the U.S. gas market, rather than the fundamentals of the energy market where the gas is being sold. There has been a significant amount of speculation about the development of Asian LNG prices over the past several years.[34] The logic expressed by those arguing for a move away from JCC pricing is straightforward and echoes what has happened in North America and Europe over the past several decades: prices should reflect supply and demand conditions for gas in the markets where the commodity is being sold. Linking the price of LNG to crude oil had a logic when it was introduced many decades ago, but that logic is no longer tenable.

Supply and demand are reflected in the competitive markets of North America and Europe through price discovery at market hubs, and this is therefore what is suggested should happen in Asia. Moreover, the volume of LNG that is not dedicated to long-term contracts will grow significantly over the next several years, and this will greatly help the liquidity of the global market and the evolution of short-term prices. The very fast progress of JKM (Japan Korea Marker) swaps—offered by Platts—is testimony to the fact that market players are seeking this kind of product to optimise their portfolios.[35]

Singapore, Shanghai, and Chongqing have exchanges, although none has the depth and liquidity for gas trade which would be considered sufficient for reliable price discovery, and the Singapore "Sling" price was discontinued in 2020.[36] In 2014, the Japanese government expressed a wish to create a gas hub, but despite monthly spot LNG quotations by the Ministry of Economy Trade and Industry on its website, there has been no progress.[37] Opinion remains divided over whether regional hubs can be created in the absence of any significant liberalisation of the major Asian gas markets, with access to LNG terminals and pipelines still mostly at the discretion of dominant national and regional players.[38] Or whether JCC will remain dominant in long-term contract pricing, with JKM a sufficient price marker for short-term trading. As China becomes the largest Asian LNG importer later in the decade, Shanghai could become the price-setting hub for LNG in Asia, and this could finally force other Asian governments to create similar market arrangements.

Conclusions: Two Future Time Horizons for Natural Gas

For energy outlooks based on meeting the COP21 objective of limiting global warming to below 2 degrees Celsius target, modelling exercises focus on reduction followed by phasing out of fossil fuels.[39] These studies—whether by energy companies, international organisations, NGOs, or academics—show gas demand either stable or growing in almost all regions in most scenarios for the period up to 2030. For the post-2030 period, the outlook for some regions is flat or declining gas demand, but others show growth or only modest decline up to 2040. Only post-2040 does gas become progressively globally "unburnable" if COP21 targets are to be met. Regionally, nationally, and in large countries sub-nationally, the picture will be very different, and this level of granularity is crucial for any kind of detailed appraisal of the future of gas. This is particularly the case in Europe, where the adoption of legally binding climate neutrality ("net zero" emissions) by 2050 will require natural gas phase-out to start by the late 2020s. Despite these reservations, in the opinion of this author, a

20-year horizon prior to *significant global* decline qualifies gas to be regarded as a "transition fuel".

Key Issues to 2030: Affordability, Profitability, and Market Pricing

The period 2011–14 did a great deal of damage to the future of gas due to very high international price levels that made the fuel either unaffordable in absolute terms or uncompetitive in relation to other energy sources. In addition, cost escalation had investors struggling to recoup their investments in many large LNG export projects that came on-stream towards the end of the 2010s. By 2019–20, international spot and hub price benchmarks had fallen to historically low levels below (and for some periods well below) $6/MMBtu (roughly equivalent to €18/MWh at mid-2020 exchange rates), with the only exception being Asian LNG contracts still linked to oil which were significantly above that figure.

In relation to affordability it is not useful to try to generalise; in all regions—and indeed all countries—conditions will be different. It would be wise to imagine that, even with significant increases in GDP, a future ceiling price for substantial gas imports into Latin America, Africa, and large parts of Asia would be in the range of $5–6/MMBtu. There are limited numbers of countries outside the OECD which can be expected to pay import prices of $6–8/MMBtu and above, which may be needed to remunerate delivery costs of large volumes of gas from new LNG projects. Prices towards, and certainly above, the top of this range are likely to lead to progressive demand destruction. What is uncertain is whether at these price levels, there will be substantial numbers of new—and particularly greenfield—pipeline gas and LNG projects which will be sufficiently attractive to investors.

This affordability context means that it is likely that all regions will progressively move to a price which reflects supply and demand conditions in their markets, and that eventually this will lead to the establishment of national and regional hubs where these do not already exist. The longer this takes to happen, particularly in Asia, where the major increase in global gas demand is expected over the next two decades, the more expensive gas is likely to be and the more likely that the fuel will fail to penetrate (or be squeezed out of) energy balances, as the cost of lower carbon energy technologies falls (or, as the Chap. 5 authors point out, coal continues to be used).

In this context, geopolitics will become a less relevant factor in gas trade in terms of favouring one source of gas or LNG over others. To the extent that the international economic (trade and tariff) and political (regional stability and conflict) environment deteriorates, this will curtail international gas trade to the detriment of its future. Moving from pipeline gas to LNG has already allowed some of the political risks to be reduced by switching exports or imports away from problematic countries. However, the fungibility of LNG allows for rapid switching between suppliers and markets as commercial conditions change, and this could become a problem for import-dependent, price-sensitive countries when the global supply/demand balance tightens.

The Post-2030 Future

Ultimately however, the future of gas—as with all fossil fuels—will depend on the progress of decarbonisation and the determination of governments to meet the greenhouse gas emission reduction targets to which they have signed up. Although it seems likely to fare better than either oil or coal in terms of its longevity, not least because of the possibilities of conversion to hydrogen with carbon capture, storage, and utilisation, the global future of *natural* gas post-2040 in most countries will be a story of accelerating decline.

Oxford, UK Jonathan Stern

Notes

1. Michot Foss (2007, 2011, 2012).
2. For details of advocacy propositions and the European response see Stern (2017a, b).
3. The EU Climate Law was passed by the Council in December 2020.
4. To be specific, and in order to make the distinction between natural gas and other gases, whether methane could decarbonise.
5. Details of these scenarios are provided in the IEA (2019), p. 35 and 751.
6. IEA (2019), Table A.1, pp. 674–5.
7. It is very important to know how a scenario develops to 2050 to see the extent of the reduction which would be needed in the 2040s to meet targets.

8. The three scenarios are Reform, Renewal, and Rivalry with policy and the geopolitical environment being the major differences between them.
9. Equinor (2019), p. 33.
10. Grantham Institute (2017), pp. 28–9.
11. Greenpeace (2015). Energy [R]evolution (E[R]) is a 2 degrees C scenario (similar to the IEA's 450 scenario which was the Agency's 2 degree scenario prior to WEO 2017) with the additional aim of phasing out nuclear energy. Advanced [R]evolution (ADV E[R]) "needs much stronger efforts to transform energy systems of all world regions towards a 100% renewable energy supply … a much faster introduction of new technologies leads to a complete decarbonisation of the power, heat and especially the transportation sector".
12. This consensus is for energy models, not on studies which make the assumption that natural gas (and other fossil fuels) must be phased out to meet targets. See, for example, Anderson and Broderick (2017), p. 3, which concludes that, "By 2035 substantial use of fossil fuels, including natural gas, within the EU's energy system will be incompatible with the temperature commitments enshrined in the Paris Agreement".
13. This data is from surveys published annually by the International Gas Union (IGU), most recently IGU (2020). For the methodological limitations of the IGU data see Stern (2017b), Box 1, p. 11.
14. IEA (2017), Figure 8.11, p. 362.
15. The data in Figures 5–7 embody a great many assumptions. Readers wanting further detail should consult the original source, Steuer (2019).
16. The Arctic 2 figure is significantly higher than the operator's estimate of \$4.84/MMBtu for delivery to Europe. Novatek (2017).
17. Songhurst (2018), p. 33.
18. And even these levels may not fully remunerate their investments. For European readers, \$5.70/MMBtu was equivalent to €17/MWh at 2020 exchange rates.
19. For details of the Polish example see Yermakov and Sobczak (2020).
20. Stern and Yafimava (2017).
21. Although Ukraine is undoubtedly importing Russian gas molecules, which transit the country and are then sold back by European gas traders.
22. Following the COVID-19 pandemic and the fall in European gas demand, Russian gas exports to Europe declined by nearly 20 per cent in the first quarter of 2020 but recovered somewhat in the second quarter. Gazprom has confirmed that exports will be at least 17 per cent lower in 2020 at 5.9 Tcf (167 bcm) compared with 7 Tcf (200 bcm) in 2018 and 2019. Interfax (2020), p. 7.
23. These terminals will not be operational until 2023–24 at the earliest. EuroActiv (2018).

24. For details see Pirani et al. (2020) and Gas Strategies (2020).
25. Pirani and Sharples (2020), Pirani et al. (2020).
26. Honoré (2017).
27. In 2020, the fall in gas demand associated with COVID-19 pandemic may result in a reduction of import dependence, but this is expected to be temporary.
28. IGU (2017) p. 49.
29. GIIGNL (2020), pp. 6–33.
30. For details of US LNG pricing and problems which have emerged see Stern and Imsirovic (2020). Data available up to August 2020 suggest that offtakers had cancelled lifting more than 100 US LNG cargoes.
31. For the history of JCC pricing see Stern, 2012, pp. 68–72.
32. The early US projects contained "modified tolling" contracts where Cheniere sourced the gas and delivered the LNG to the customer's ship; later contracts were "pure tolling".
33. In June 2017, an investigation by the Japan Fair Trade Commission concluded that requests to change destination of cargoes "should not be unreasonably refused", but it is unclear whether this has led to any significant changes. Japan Fair Trade Commission (2017), Chap. 4.
34. For early analyses see Rogers and Stern (2014), Stern (2016), Palti-Guzman (2018).
35. Stern and Imsirovic (2020).
36. Ason (2020).
37. http://www.meti.go.jp/english/statistics/sho/slng/index.html
38. Ason (2020).
39. The COP21 goal is limiting the average global temperature increase in 2100 to 2 degrees, or "well below 2 degrees", Celsius above pre-industrial levels.

References

Anderson, K., and J. Broderick. 2017. *Natural gas and climate change*. Tyndall Manchester: Cemus and Teesside University, 17 October 2017.

Ason, A. 2020. *Scenarios for Asian long-term LNG contracts before and after COVID-19*, OIES paper, NG160.

Beveridge, N. 2020. Does the world want US LNG. *Bernstein energy and power*, March 2018 (updated).

Equinor. 2019. *Energy Perspectives 2019 Report: long term macro and market outlook*.

Euroactiv. 2018. Germany to build LNG plant in 'gesture' to US drive to sell more'. September 18, 2018. https://www.euractiv.com/section/global-europe/news/germany-to-build-lng-plant-in-gesture-to-us-drive-to-sell-more/

Fulwood, M. 2018. Asian LNG trading hubs: Myth or reality?. Centre on Global Energy Policy, Columbia University, May 2018.

Gas Strategies. 2020. US Threatens to Sanction Shell, Uniper, Wintershall, Engie, OMV for Funding NS2. 16 July 2020.

GIIGNL. 2020. *The LNG industry: GIIGNL annual report 2020.*

Grantham Institute/Carbon Tracker. 2017. *Expect the unexpected: The disruptive power of low-carbon technology*, February 2017.

Greenpeace. 2015. Energy [R]evolution: A sustainable world energy outlook report, 5th edition world energy scenario 2015.

Honore, A. 2017. The Dutch gas market: Trials, tribulations and trends, 2017. https://www.oxfordenergy.org/wpcms/wp-content/uploads/2017/05/The-Dutch-Gas-Market-trials-tribulations-and-trends-NG-118.pdf

IEA: International Energy Agency. 2017. *World energy outlook 2017.* Paris: OECD/IEA.

IEA: International Energy Agency. 2019. *World energy outlook 2019.* OECD/IEA: Paris.

IGU: International Gas Union. 2017. IGU *World LNG report, 2017 edition.*

IGU: International Gas Union. 2020. *Wholesale gas price survey 2020 edition: A global review of price formation mechanisms 2005–20.*

Interfax. 2020. *Russian and CIS oil and gas weekly*, July 9–15, 2020.

Japan Fair Trade Commission. 2017. *Survey of LNG trades.* https://www.jftc.go.jp/en/pressreleases/yearly-2017/June/170628.html

Ledesma, D., and K. Yafimava. 2017. *The DG competition investigation of Gazprom's sales to Central and Eastern Europe: A detailed analysis of the commitments and the way forward.* OIES paper NG 121.

Michot Foss, M. 2007. *United States natural gas prices to 2015*, OIES, NG18.

Michot Foss, M. 2011. The outlook for US gas prices in 2020: Henry Hub at $3 or $10, OIES NG 58.

Michot Foss, M. 2012. Natural gas pricing in North America. In *The pricing of internationally traded gas*, ed. J.P. Stern. OUP/OIES, Chapter 3

Novatek. 2017. *Transforming into a global gas company: From 2018 to 2030.* Corporate strategy report 2018. http://www.novatek.ru/common/upload/Strategy30ENG(1).pdf

Palti-Guzman, L. 2018. The future of Asia's natural gas market: The need for a regional LNG hub. *Asia Policy*, 13(3, July).

Pirani, S., and J. Sharples. *The Russia-Ukraine gas transit deal: Opening a new chapter.* OIES Energy Insight 64.

Pirani, S., K. Yafimava, J. Sharples, and V. Yermakov. 2020. *Implications of the Russia-Ukraine transit deal for alternative pipeline routes.* OIES Energy Insight 65.

Rogers, H.V., and J. Stern. 2014. *Challenges to JCC pricing in Asian LNG markets.* OIES, January.

Shell. 2018. Sky – Meeting the goals of the Paris agreement (2018). http://www.ourenergypolicy.org/wp-content/uploads/2018/03/shell-scenarios-sky-1.pdf

Songhurst, B. 2018. *LNG plant cost reduction 2014–18.* OIES paper NG 137.

Stern, J. 2012. The pricing of gas in international trade – An historical survey. In *The Pricing of Internationally Traded Gas*, ed. J.P. Stern. Oxford: OUP/OIES.

Stern, J. 2016. LNG pricing: Challenges in the late 2010s, Chapter 8. In *LNG Markets in Transition: The great reconfiguration*, ed. Corbeau, A.-S., and D. Ledesma, 468–501. OIES/OUP.

Stern, J. 2017a. *The future of gas in decarbonising European energy markets: the need for a new approach.* OIES paper NG 116, January 2017.

Stern, J. 2017b. *Challenges to the future of gas: Unburnable or unaffordable*, OIES paper NG 125. December 2017.

Stern, J. 2019. *Narratives for natural gas in decarbonising European energy markets.* OIES paper NG 141.

Stern, J., and A. Imsirovic. 2020. *A Comparative History of Oil and Gas Markets and Prices: is 2020 just an extreme cyclical event or an acceleration of the energy transition?* OIES Energy Insight 68.

Steuer, C. 2019. *Outlook for competitive LNG supply.* OIES paper NG 142.

Yermakov, V., and K. Sobczak. 2020. *Russia-Poland gas relationship: Risks and uncertainties of the ever after.* OIES Energy Insight 70.

Preface

How do we think about natural gas today, and with what meaning for the future? We know, and can demonstrate, that the resource base is abundant (industry business models and technology always evolving). Decarbonization, "decarb", is a concern in the Old World but not so much in the New World (roughly OECD, the Organization for Economic Cooperation and Development, and non-OECD, respectively, but see Chap. 5 for important nuances). Despite lip service in the New World countries (most importantly China and India, rooted in ancient civilizations and their philosophies), economic and human development needs eclipse climate any day. Local benefits associated with access to, and use of, natural gas are huge. Even climate benefits are significant when gas replaces coal. China, India, and other countries seem to understand the priority of local benefits. They cannot build alternatives in sufficient capacity with high performance and reliability in target time horizons to meet growing energy needs. As well, the environment, social, and governance (ESG) footprints of alternatives are growing rapidly as their market shares increase. For all of that, monetization of natural gas remains a challenge given supply chain costs, diminishing profit margins as costs are absorbed to create value, unestablished "commercial frameworks" in many parts of the world, geopolitics, and much more.

We can discern that New World countries do not need the Old World as much, and alignments are changing. As we completed our book manuscript, on November 15, 2020, 15 countries in Asia-Pacific signed the new Regional Comprehensive Economic Partnership, RCEP. Although we will not see the full impacts until member states ratify it, the RCEP covers almost a third of world GDP and population, both of which will grow faster than the Old World, and includes OECD countries such as Australia, Japan, and South Korea while India and the U.S. continue to evaluate. Climate politics creates new alliances of interests. Companies of all sorts from various energy supply chain segments along with financiers are lining up to enjoy guaranteed returns, highly valued in stock markets, courtesy of government subsidies as countries position for perceived competitive advantage on sensitive materials and technologies. These conditions are not likely to change because of shifts in scientific views and advances. Rather, the flavor of climate politics in place at the end of 2020 risks implosion from fiscal strains as the world emerges from the COVID-19 pandemic, and/or because costs of climate mitigation, as transparency improves, become unbearable for most people.

We make all of these points—at least to some extent—in our book. A focus is the emergence and sustainability of open, competitive markets with supporting commercial frameworks for natural gas resource development and use, including the evolution of natural gas as a distinct commodity. The U.S. with its large and liquid marketplace and nimble industry is, of course, a unique model of competitive supply and monetization to such an extent that the rest of the world is benefitting in myriad ways. Global energy customers are enjoying a substantial comfort zone with respect to both oil and natural gas prices. Supply-demand imbalances and fluctuations in price are inevitable. The pandemic disruptions of 2020 have been record setting but crucially, as we went to press in spring 2021, recovery was being manifest. In the U.S. oil and gas production has recouped and exports are close to or exceeding pre-pandemic peaks. Prices are more robust—after widespread beliefs that oil would not creep out of the $30s until well beyond 2021, the U.S. index is roughly double that, as are international oil prices. Deep pandemic cost-cutting and new practices are providing better profit margins. These improvements are reflected in valuations of U.S. oil and gas shares, providing breathing room and better encouragement for still-needed consolidation. Except for aviation, demand for petroleum fuels remained mostly intact (all of those home deliveries and "see the USA" road trips). Domestic natural gas demand also had not registered much in losses. Long-time observers of the natural gas industry in all of its forms know that interesting times always lie ahead. These lie mostly within the endless questions and speculation swirling around energy choices ahead.

The timing for a book of this scope is fortuitous. We began work before the COVID-19 pandemic, and before oil and gas business conditions deteriorated in the first half of 2019, a consequence of exuberant U.S. production and an inconveniently timed oil price war among members of the Organization of Petroleum Exporting Countries (OPEC) and Russia, with an eye to the U.S. Prior to the pandemic, U.S. gas supply was setting historical records, with billions of dollars of capital inflows targeted for expanding already dense pipeline and distribution networks, capturing molecules for industrial and power generation use, and penetrating the global marketplace with LNG exports. Yet even without pandemic ructions, numerous challenges existed, ranging from shifts in industry organization and finance to public antipathy toward development and use of a fossil fuel widely regarded as most favorable for addressing myriad environmental concerns. Many of the challenges reside in the nature of the commodity itself—the energy content of delivered gas (the methane component) is lower than liquid fuels, which makes capital cost of infrastructure per equivalent Btu expensive. The same feature that makes methane attractive as a lower emission fuel for power generation (its gaseous state) encumbers the ability of methane to compete against liquid fuels in key applications such as vehicle transportation or to penetrate easily, given capital cost hurdles, international markets in liquefied form.

The underlying economics of delivered natural gas—methane, with which the vast majority of consumers are most familiar—affects perceptions and reality. For one, the value of liquids (oil, condensates and natural gas liquids captured in processing and refining) tends to be greater and thus the attractor for upstream capital investment with methane often a byproduct. Off and on in the history of U.S. domestic production, mainly during low crude oil price periods, methane sales yield insufficient revenue to support drilling, eventually setting up price volatility at Henry Hub and across the major indexes. For another, worldwide, infrastructure intensity across the full natural gas value chain creates persistent public relations dilemmas. This is especially true of long-distance, large-diameter pipeline networks for transmission of methane to large population areas (load centers), sometimes across national boundaries, and small diameter, dense, local distribution networks that connect households and commercial users. Pipeline bottlenecks have long been disruptive to natural gas value creation. The old mantra of "it ain't supply, it's deliverability" remains true in spite of the push in recent years to expand pipeline capacity for field-to-market linkages. Options to use liquefied natural gas, LNG, where it makes more economic sense than pipelines can mean more expensive, delivered natural gas. The U.S. has abundant underground, or geologic, storage, mostly depleted oil and gas fields but also salt caverns that have much higher injection and withdrawal rates, critical for short-term market balancing. Other countries have little or none. Natural gas storage, especially geologic storage, is a key enabler of gas market development. It is no myth that large-scale, rapid-response underground storage has been critical to fostering market depth in the U.S. and Canada, and will play a role in helping the Mexico market to expand (mainly via the convenience of U.S.-based salt cavern storage developed with Mexican customers in mind). Few, if any, countries have the salt cavern resource endowment, or even other underground storage options, deployed so successfully in the Lower 48. In sum, on many occasions, for all infrastructure and all locations, too much capacity is never enough, unless there is too much.

The title of our book reflects the role of natural gas in a world in which beliefs are widespread that energy technology needs to keep pace with broad shifts in consumer tastes and preferences and prevailing views on energy and environment. In a greenhouse gas–sensitive political environment, methane carries an advantage over other fossil fuels. Yet, conflicts have surfaced over the meaning of "clean", and natural gas has become encumbered by new emphasis on displacement of all fossil fuels, even the cleanest burning. In his Foreword, Jonathan Stern lays out these tensions and their implications for affordability and pricing. In other chapters, authors provide points that complement and counter those in the Foreword, demonstrating the complicated context for natural gas business economics, policy, and regulatory regimes, across regions and countries that have dramatically different profiles and priorities when it comes to energy development and use.

In Chap. 1, lead editor Michelle Michot Foss lays out the complexities of the U.S. upstream revitalization, which has had such impact on natural gas markets and prices worldwide, and lays out fundamentals that must be recognized as upstream sets the tone for U.S. and global value chains. In Chap. 1 the results of ten years of producer benchmarking by Michot Foss and her colleagues affords an in-depth analysis of U.S. producer economics as the shale era took hold and progressed. A clear message is that U.S. upstream businesses must find business models for profitability, and the upstream/midstream interface is a crucial piece. Chapter 2 by co-editor Gürcan Gülen provides a definitive analysis of natural gas in the U.S. electric power mix and suggests a widening cone of uncertainty for gas burn. Countervailing forces continue to battle within a dynamic and geographically diverse political environment: cheap domestic natural gas, retirement of aging coal and nuclear plants, and expansion of locationally low-cost, yet almost universally subsidized, renewable energy. In Chap. 3, Michot Foss, Gülen, Barbara Shook, and Danny Quijano examine monetization of natural gas in the broad expansion of the U.S. petrochemical base. The authors draw on a database of projects that illustrate motivations, timing, costs, and related strategies for what many hope is a U.S. "renaissance". The general messages across these chapters are cautionary but somewhat optimistic. The natural gas endowment in the U.S. and all of North America is substantial, and geography and internal trade linkages and flows are an enormous advantage to suppliers and customers. That said, the realities of retaining competitiveness for natural gas are not ignored.

The U.S. natural gas market does not exist in a vacuum, of course. Over the years, internationally traded gas has grown, and even more, internal gas market development has expanded across a variety of countries and economies. We incorporate two perspectives in our book. First is the more obvious push to monetize U.S. methane, along with the variety of natural gas liquids, NGLs (and light oil), through international trade. The spate of liquefaction developments has been headline news. Most of these are at brownfield sites that were in the mix during the import terminal expansions of the early to mid-2000s. Long-time collaborator Andy Flower covers treatment of U.S. LNG export prospects in Chap. 4 along with a global view of LNG supply and commercial strategies.

Our second perspective is on the evolution of internal gas markets in critical consuming countries. Chapter 5, by co-editors Anna Mikulska and Gürcan Gülen, encompasses the large, dominant markets of China and India, both of which are magnets for international gas trade and investment, as well as emerging issues in Europe/Eurasia and other regions. Importantly, Chap. 5 captures tensions not typically reflected in publications on natural gas or even energy in general. These reflect "Old World, New World" schisms, whether political, economic, or otherwise, that characterize natural gas development and use. To a large degree, these incorporate distinctly different priorities when it comes to energy and environment (including but not exclusively climate) tradeoffs that we feel will dictate terms and conditions for gas markets around the world going forward.

To these core subjects, we add observations in Chap. 6 from the many other market locations investigated and worked in over the years by Michot Foss and Gülen. These incorporate experience from projects and case studies undertaken during formative years at the height of the "Washington consensus" model for economic liberalization and energy sector reform. Chapter 6 includes a "decision tree" approach intended to foster awareness of key ingredients for successful gas/power linkages. The authors derived the conceptual model for the dual purpose of fostering project development due diligence and, importantly, for communicating to host governments the critical nature of enabling commercial frameworks. The decision tree tool reflects lessons from a number of locations. The authors are cautious on the inference of the U.S. experience for other countries. Yet, U.S. customers, consumers, and suppliers have tested so rigorously the distinctions of natural gas components as fuel and materials feedstock, and implications for economics of robust infrastructure systems, that inference for other countries should not be ignored. Key conclusions on the importance of infrastructure, transparent pricing, and, not least, institutional governance capacity are addressed throughout the book.

Increasingly, energy opinions and decisions in the Old World do not hold fossil fuels, in general, in the same regard as renewable energy. Often, these views exist apart from emissions and other environmental considerations as well as economic and human development needs (e.g., mitigating energy poverty), becoming belief systems. Delivered methane is the only modern, distributed energy form from which consumers can derive the heat value of an energy fuel directly. Methane also provides needed reliability and flexibility in electric power generation, to back up growing intermittent and variable wind and solar capacity. This reliability is critical for visions of economic transition based on information technologies. Battery storage and the desire to push the envelope on and exploit advanced battery technologies are emerging as the main competitor to natural gas for reliability and flexibility. While these and many other prospects are exciting to consider, highly visible efforts to achieve rapid scaleup of alternatives may impose stress on infrastructure, systems, market performance, and other aspects of their own value chains that are worth more attention. We the editors look ahead to these strategic concerns along with potential future pathways for natural gas in the concluding Chap. 7.

Finally, a detailed Appendix provides readers with background information and details on the U.S. and North America policy and regulatory experience.

In our book, with our collaborators, we explore many aspects of and considerations for natural gas market development. We hope our effort illuminates some questions and raises many others. A particular goal is to map out lessons learned and demonstrated for those countries, customers, and consumers that aspire to build effective natural gas markets and to expand natural gas development and use.

Houston, TX, USA — Michelle Michot Foss
Anna Mikulska
West Brookfield, MA, USA — Gürcan Gülen

Acknowledgements

My co-editors Anna Mikulska and Gürcan Gülen performed yeoman's duties to help me bring this book to fruition. I conceived the idea as I was preparing to retire and exit the University of Texas at Austin (UTA), Bureau of Economic Geology's Center for Energy Economics (CEE). My notion was to prepare a memoir of work. Much of the content featured in our book occurred under my direction and the auspices of BEG-CEE and previously at the University of Houston. Chapters 1, 2, 3, 6, and the comprehensive Appendix represent the overall body of research undertaken by my team and me over nearly 30 years. During our tenure, contributing authors Jonathan Stern, Andy Flower, and Barbara Shook provided significant insights and input on key topic areas and geographies. A number of peer reviewers, long-time colleagues, and friends helped with the book effort: Thierry Bros, Jacqueline Campos, Les Deman, Blake Eskew, Peter Hartley, Bhamy Shenoy, Rick Smead, Terry Thorn, and Bob Tippee.

I am indebted to the long and loyal support from corporate donors to the research team and program I led for about 30 years, first at the University of Houston and then at the BEG. Our donors brought not only crucial funding to help solidify our research and program activities, but also insights, information, and access to the array of commercial and business economic realities that I feel are vital for any solid energy research program. I especially thank EY, Frost Bank, Toyota Motor North America, ExxonMobil, Haddington Ventures, and McKinsey & Company for their final donations in 2018 as I was retiring from UTA and preparing to undertake this book project. I also thank Chevron Overseas Petroleum Inc. for their final donation that year to help close our Mexico research effort—a legacy of the research program I built over the years. We had many other corporate supporters. Indeed, the changing demographics of our corporate support were a good mirror for the constantly changing U.S. energy scene.

I thank the BEG for support from the State of Texas Resource Recovery (STARR) program, which helped to underwrite much of our electric power and gas-power analysis over the years, and the Jackson School of Geosciences Endowment for the support of my research team during our time at UTA. The BEG graphics and editing team, Cathy Brown and her staff of Travis Hobbs, Jana Robinson and Jamie Coggins, helped initially with production before Springer Nature/Palgrave Macmillan took over publication. Ian Duncan, Michael Young, Eric Potter, and Mark Shuster all provided guidance; Ian and Jay Kipper helped facilitate a unique move of an ambitious, natural gas and power-focused research team with international project commitments from University of Houston to BEG. Ian also provided excellent input over the years from their work on gas pipeline risks. Scott Tinker, head of BEG, was the reason for my team becoming part of BEG and UTA, roping us into a variety of adventures, not least the Gulf Coast Carbon Center, Texas FutureGen, STARR, and the shale resource studies. What a learning experience!

I thank all of my former research team, some of whom contributed to this book. Gürcan Gülen generously joined as co-editor as well as author and co-author. Miranda Wainberg prepared an initial draft of Chap. 5. Fisoye Delano and Dmitry Volkov (along with Sara Vackshouri) wrote discussion papers that helped shed light on Africa, Russia/Eurasia and Middle East. Chen-Hao Tsai spent quality time on the gas and power modeling captured in Chap. 2. Deniese-Palmer Huggins never failed to serve as a great sounding board on financial markets and risk. Daniel Quijano (our analyst for the petrochemicals database in Chap. 4) and Rahul Verma helped update the producer benchmarking featured in Chap. 1, which Miranda and I launched in 2010. Laura Martinez, our final program coordinator, had the additional responsibility of helping me to wind down our research program as I prepared to retire from BEG and UTA.

Over the years, I benefited hugely from advisors who never failed to react to what we were doing and provide additional insights, and who continue to do so. Thanks go to Vicky Bailey, Les Deman, Juan Eibenschutz, Herman Franssen, Robert (Bill) Gilmer, Luis Giusti, Sheila Hollis, Edward (Ed) Kelly, David (Dave) Knapp, Donald (Don) Knop, Benigna Leiss, Ernesto Marcos, Rae McQuade, Edward (Ed) Morse,

Hisanori Nei, Bhamy Shenoy, Robert (Bob) Skinner, Andrew Slaughter, Bruce Stram, and Terence (Terry) Thorn. I especially recognize Herman, who passed away in January 2020. I cannot even count the number of conversations I had with Herman over the years as we talked and debated the state of the oil and natural gas industries and "all things energy". I also acknowledge a former employer, Matthew R. Simmons. Matt's energy and constant motion were widely known, and his passing in 2010 left big shoes empty for the industry. As with Herman, and I know like many others, I cannot count the conversations, arguments, debates I had with Matt. His presence looms as his many former colleagues and friends work to sustain the oil and gas industry through this latest set of challenges. Another friend to all of us who with Juan was my second "Wise Man" in Mexico, Pablo Mulás, passed away in March 2021. He would have enjoyed this massive book.

I thank Ken Medlock, senior director, and my colleagues at the Center for Energy Studies, Rice University's Baker Institute for Public Policy, where I currently reside as a fellow. Ken championed my effort to close up work on this book, not least by supporting my co-editor Anna Mikulska. The CES gang have added fresh views and fodder to my long-time curiosity about natural gas and the vital role of this fuel.

Finally, my husband Deane Campbell Foss always helps to keep me honest on my many opinions about the upstream business. His career, professional interests, activities, and excellence in geoscience provide the unique opportunity for my direct, personal observation of the oil and gas industry at work.

Michelle Michot Foss

When Michelle first mentioned to me that she was writing a draft of a new book on this topic, my immediate reaction was that it needed to be published, and published quickly, and that I would do whatever I could to help. The topic could not be more current, and at the same time, more difficult to conceptualize as world energy transformation has captured global attention. Economic growth and energy access have been often juxtaposed against clean energy and climate goals, with natural gas evaluations ranging from savior to villain depending on the assessing party. A comprehensive volume that touches upon those assessments in a systematic way, devoid of bias as much as possible, would be a great addition to current literature on the subject, and something I would be happy to assign to my students in the graduate energy policy seminars I have taught at the Kleinman Center for Public Policy at University of Pennsylvania. In fact, the book is something I would reach for as a reference when I research and write on my favorite subject of geopolitics of natural gas.

Michelle's book is all that and more, and I cannot thank her enough for bringing me onboard and giving me a chance to be a part of the final product. As we worked on finishing the volume, Michelle's input and depth of professional experience has been invaluable, as was the contribution of our co-author, Gürcan Gülen. Working with Gürcan, a brilliant and friendly economist with deep understanding of global affairs, has been political scientist's dream come true. Discussions with him and Michelle on conceptualization of Old and New Worlds of gas have been enlightening, thought-provoking, and have hopefully resulted in a well-rounded assessment of current gas markets.

I would like to thank both institutions that support my research by giving me the freedom to engage in projects like this book. In the Center for Energy Studies at Rice University's Baker Institute, under the wonderful leadership of Ken Medlock, who has fostered atmosphere of diversity and inclusiveness of views and experiences based on solid foundations of data and excellence in scholarly research, I feel I have found my scholarly home. The Kleinman Center for Energy Policy at the University for Pennsylvania, with Mark Allan Hughes and Cornelia Collijns at the helm, has generously co-funded my research endeavors via annual grants and has given me the opportunity to stay in touch with both the scientific community and students after my family and I relocated from Houston to Philadelphia.

My husband, Ali Soleymannezhad, as always, has been the source of my strongest support and encouragement. An avid business person and engineer by training, he keeps me grounded and committed to quality and balance, both personally and professionally. Together with my kids, my family has been more than patient whenever deadlines call for after-hour work and when work travel takes me away from home. And for that, I am truly grateful.

Anna Mikulska

Having worked in Michelle's research teams for over 20 years, it should come as no surprise that my biggest thanks go to her for her leadership and mentoring over the years, and inviting me to be a part of this book. I will not repeat the long list of sponsors and advisors that she acknowledged already but clearly I know what I think I know thanks to all of their selfless input to the research, training, and technical assistance work we have done across many geographies over many years. I also owe gratitude to the leadership of the Bureau of Economic Geology—Dr. Scott Tinker, Mr. Mark Shuster, Mr. Eric Potter, Dr. Michael Young, and Mr. Jay Kipper—for their support over the 13 years I spent at the Bureau, which has provided me with a whole new understanding of geologic foundations of natural gas resources and their impact on economics of gas. Finally, I thank my other co-editor and co-author in Chap. 5, Anna Mikulska, for her diligent work and patience with an economist as a co-author.

Gürcan Gülen

Contents

Notes on Contributors

Andy Flower has been working as an independent consultant since May 2001 specialising in the LNG business, where his areas of expertise include: strategy, marketing, project structures, shipping, pricing, supply and demand, and project economics. He retired from BP in 2001 after thirty two years of service, including twenty two years working in the company's LNG and natural gas business units where he managed BP's interests in LNG projects in Abu Dhabi, Nigeria, Australia and Qatar and negotiated LNG sales and purchase agreements with buyers in Asia, Europe and the USA.

Daniel Quijano is a global energy consultant with Berkeley Research Group. He works on U.S. electric power sector issues, data management, renewables, nuclear power, and pricing mechanisms. He has previously engaged in research covering broad areas of the global energy value chain including analyses of U.S. and national oil company (NOC) upstream costs, demand for natural gas in the U.S. industrial sector, Mexico energy reform, international commercial frameworks/best practices, global gas demand, energy storage (critical minerals), and various issues in the mid/downstream sectors. He holds an MS in Business Analytics with a background in energy research at the University of Texas at Austin and a BBA in finance from University of St. Thomas.

Barbara Shook was a widely recognized energy reporter for decades, specializing in oil, natural gas, and the downstream industries. She began her career in 1971, and was Chief Energy Reporter for the Houston

Chronicle during the 1980s. Her 22 years at Energy Intelligence Group included service as Houston Bureau Chief and Senior Reporter-at-Large. She received the Award for Journalism from the Organization of Petroleum Exporting Countries (OPEC) at the group's gala dinner in Vienna in 2018.

Jonathan Stern is a distinguished research fellow and founder of the Natural Gas Research Programme at the Oxford Institute for Energy Studies (OIES). He holds professorships at the University of Dundee and Imperial College, London, and fellowships at the Energy Delta Institute and the Institute of Energy Economics, Tokyo, Japan. He is the author and editor of several books published by the OIES, including *Natural Gas in Asia*, *The Pricing of Internationally Traded Gas*, and *The Future of Gas in the Gulf*; and author of two chapters in *LNG Markets in Transition: The Great Reconfiguration*. His papers on "Narratives for Gas in Decarbonising European Energy Markets", and "Challenges to the Future of LNG: Decarbonisation, Affordability and Profitability", can be found on the OIES website. He is working on a study of methane emissions from natural gas.

Michelle Michot Foss is Fellow in Energy, Minerals & Materials at Rice University's Baker Institute for Public Policy-Center for Energy Studies, USA. She has contributed widely recognized research on the natural gas and LNG industries. Foss has nearly 40 years of experience in senior positions in energy and environment research, consulting and investment banking. Her professional engagements have entailed more than 20 countries, more than 40 with capacity building. She has numerous professional recognitions and awards. She is a past president of U.S. Association for Energy Economics (USAEE) and IAEE, and is a USAEE Senior Fellow.

Anna Mikulska is a nonresident fellow in energy studies at Rice University's Baker Institute for Public Policy-Center for Energy Studies, USA. She is also a senior fellow at University of Pennsylvania's Kleinman Center for Energy Policy. Mikulska's research focuses on the geopolitics of natural gas within the EU, former Soviet Bloc and Russia. Her interests include the potential use of natural gas as a geoeconomic tool and ways in which U.S. LNG exports could bolster European energy security.

Gürcan Gülen is an energy economist with 25 years of experience in research on oil, natural gas, and electric power value chains; related technical assistance; and customized capacity building in numerous countries. After 9 years at the University of Houston and 13 years at the Bureau of Economic Geology (UT-Austin), he is now an independent consultant and continues to instruct in executive education programs. Gülen is a USAEE Senior Fellow.

Units and Conversions

Natural gas quantities in cf, Btu, cm	A cubic foot, **cf**, of natural gas is the volume per cf at standard (normal) temperature (60 degrees Fahrenheit) and pressure (sea level). A cf of natural gas that is entirely methane gives off about 1011 British thermal units (**Btus**) per cf. Energy (heat) content varies with natural gas composition. Natural gas heat values can range from 950 to 1150 depending upon molecular composition (see http://www.engineeringtoolbox.com/heating-values-fuel-gases-d_823.html). Natural gas volumes in metric are expressed in cubic meters or **cm**. Natural gas volumes in this book are measured in thousand (**M**), million (**MM**), billion (**B**), trillion (**T**). Average throughput associated with natural gas facilities (the volume of natural gas moved through facilities such as pipelines, underground storage and LNG trains, storage and regasification) is expressed generally as volumes "per day" or "cf/d" or for metric "per annum" or cma. One billion cubic feet or Bcf of natural gas converts to metric, one billion cubic meters, or Bcm, using a multiplier of 0.028. The BP Statistical Review of World Energy, http://www.bp.com/en/global/corporate/energy-economics/statistical-review-of-world-energy.html includes useful conversion factors and data.
LNG quantities in t, tpa	Tonnes of LNG, **t**, a measure of LNG facilities' capacity and tonnes per annum, **tpa**, a measure of throughput from LNG facilities. LNG facility capacities and throughput are most commonly expressed as million tonnes, **mt**, and million tonnes per annum, **mtpa**. A Bcf of natural gas converts to 1 mt of LNG with a multiplier of 0.021 (rounded). A Bcm of natural gas is converted to 1 mt of LNG with a multiplier of 0.74 (rounded).
Bbl, BOE	Standard 42-gallon barrel, or **Bbl**, of crude oil, liquids, or oil equivalent (expressed as barrel of oil equivalent or **BOE**).
Electricity in W, Wh	Electric power generation capacity in watts, **W**, and delivered in watthours, **Wh**. Units for both are thousand (kilo, **K**), million (mega, **M**) and billion (giga, **G**).

See EIA Glossary for more information. https://www.eia.gov/tools/glossary/

See BP Annual Statistical Review for typical conversions. http://www.bp.com/en/global/corporate/energy-economics/statistical-review-of-world-energy.html

Abbreviations

AC	Alternating current in electricity
AEO	Annual Energy Outlook, the U.S. EIA flagship publication
AFE	Authorization for expenditure in oil and gas drilling
API	American Petroleum Institute
ARO	Asset retirement obligation
BOE	Barrel of oil equivalent (per day, BOEPD or BOED)
CBM	Coal bed methane
CCGT	Combined cycle gas turbine
CCS	Carbon capture and sequestration
CEO	Chief executive officer
CNG	Compressed natural gas
CO_2	Carbon dioxide
CTO	Chief technology officer
DD&A	Depreciation, depletion, and amortization
DE	Distributed energy
DER	Distributed energy resources
DES	Delivered ex-ship
DG	Director (directorate) general
DOE	U.S. Department of Energy
DOI	U.S. Department of Interior
DOL	U.S. Department of Labor
DOP	Deliver or pay
DOT	U.S. Department of Transportation
DQT	Downward quantity tolerance (in LNG contracting)
DUC	Drilled (through horizontal lateral) but uncompleted
EBITDA	Earnings before interest, taxes, depreciation, and amortization

EIA	U.S. Energy Information Administration. IEO is EIA's International Energy Outlook.
EOR	Enhanced oil recovery
EPA	U.S. Environmental Protection Agency
EPC	Engineering, procurement, and construction (in project contracting)
ERCOT	Electric Reliability Council of Texas (U.S.)
ESG	Environment, social, and governance
ETD	Electricity transmission and distribution
ETF	Exchange traded funds
EU	European Union
EUB	Energy utility board (Canada)
EUR	Estimated ultimate recovery (of oil and gas resource)
EV	Electric vehicle
FEED	Front-end engineering design
FERC	U.S. Federal Energy Regulatory Commission
FF	Fossil fuels
FID	Final investment decision
FLNG	Floating LNG
FOB	Free on board
FPC	U.S. Federal Power Commission (now FERC)
FRB	U.S. Federal Reserve Bank
FSRU	Floating storage and regasification unit (for LNG receipts)
FTA	Free Trade Agreement (Canada-U.S.)
GAO	U.S. Government Accountability Office
GCC	Gulf Cooperation Council (Middle East)
GDP	Gross domestic product
GHG	Greenhouse gases
GOM	Gulf of Mexico
GOR	Gas-oil ratio
GTD	Gas transmission and distribution
GTL	Gas to liquids
HBP	Held by production (in U.S. oil and gas leasing)
HDPE	High-density polyethylene
HFCV	Hydrogen fuel cell vehicle
HH	Henry Hub (U.S.)
HOA	Heads of agreement
IAEE	International Association for Energy Economics
ICE	Intercontinental Exchange
IEA	International Energy Agency. WEO is IEA's World Energy Outlook.
IEEJ	Institute for Energy Economics Japan
IGU	International Gas Union
IMO	International Maritime Organization

INGAA	Interstate Natural Gas Association of America
IOC	International Oil Company
IOU	Investor-owned utility
IP	Intellectual property
IPO	Initial public offering
IPP	Independent power producer
IRP	Integrated resource plan (planning)
ISO	Independent system operator
IT	Information technology
ITC	Investment tax credit
JCC	Japan crude cocktail
JKM	Japan Korea Marker
JLC	Japanese LNG Cocktail
JV	Joint venture
LCOE	Levelized cost of energy
LDC	Local distribution company (for natural gas or electricity)
LDPE	Low-density polyethylene
LLDPE	Linear low-density polyethylene
LMP	Locational marginal pricing
LNG	Liquefied natural gas; mainly methane, chilled under atmosphere pressure, to -256 °F (Fahrenheit). See CEE's Introduction to LNG, http://www.beg.utexas.edu/energyecon/INTRODUCTION%20TO%20LNG%20Update%202012.pdf.
LOE	Lease operating expense
LPG	Liquid petroleum gas, mainly propane; may have butane present.
LT	Light oil
LTO	Light tight oil
MA	Moving average
MARAD	U.S. Maritime Administration
MENA	Middle East-North Africa
MLP	Master limited partnership
MOU	Memorandum of understanding
MTG	Methane to gasoline
MTO	Methanol to olefin
MVC	Minimum volume commitment
NAESB	North American Energy Standards Board
NAFTA	North American Free Trade Agreement
NAG	Nonassociated gas
NAM	North America
NBER	National Bureau of Economic Research (U.S.)
NBP	National Balancing Point (UK)
NDRC	National Development Reform Commission (China)

NEB	National Energy Board (Canada, now Canadian Energy Regulator)
NG	Natural gas
NGLs	Natural gas liquids, including C_1–C_5 (methane, propane, butane/isobutane, pentanes)
NGO	Nongovernmental organization
NGV	Natural gas vehicle
NOAA	U.S. National Oceanographic and Atmospheric Administration
NOC	National oil company
NO_x	Nitrogen oxides
NPV	Net present value
NYMEX	New York Mercantile Exchange
OCS	Outer Continental Shelf
OECD	Organization for Economic Cooperation and Development
OFS	Oilfield services (companies)
OIES	Oxford Institute for Energy Studies
OPEC	Organization of Petroleum Exporting Countries
OSHA	U.S. Occupational Safety and Health Administration
OTC	Over the counter
PPA	Power purchase agreement
PPI	Producer price index
PSC	Production sharing contract
PTC	Production tax credit
PUC	Public utility commission (U.S.)
PUD	Proven undeveloped production
PV	Photovoltaic
ROI	Return on investment
RPS	Renewable portfolio standard
RTO	Regional transmission organization (U.S.)
SD	Standard deviation
SEC	U.S. Securities and Exchange Commission
SEE	Southeastern Europe
SLO	Social licence to operate
SOE	State-owned enterprise
SPA	Supply purchase agreement
SSA	Sub-Saharan Africa
SSHE	Safety, security, health and environment
SSP	Shared socioeconomic pathway
SWOT	Strength, weakness, opportunity, threat (analysis)
TOP	Take or pay
TPA	Third party access
TTF	Title transfer facility (Netherlands)
UGS	Underground storage

UGSS	Unified Gas Supply System (Russia)
USD	U.S. dollar
USGS	U.S. Geological Survey
USMCA	U.S.-Mexico-Canada Agreement
VPP	Virtual power plants
WEO	World Energy Outlook (IEA)
WTI	West Texas Intermediate (light sweet crude)
ZEC	Zero emissions credit

List of Figures

List of Tables

CHAPTER 1

All Value Chains Begin Upstream

Michelle Michot Foss

"The Art of the Long View"[1]

The rule of thumb for long-term scenario thinking: first, understand the present.[2] This stands to reason. If we cannot separate noise from signals in today's reality, we face a good chance of getting things wrong on down the road. This rings true even more in these "virus times". A great deal of noise, positive and negative, has surrounded the natural gas industry overall, U.S. upstream in particular, since the "shale era" took hold in the early 2000s. Even more noise surrounds the fate of natural gas and other energy fuels and technologies as societies and their governments around the world grapple with Covid-19 and chart a recovery. For this chapter, which covers the crucial building block of upstream, my main goal is to survey current state of knowledge and, more complex, perceptions about the upstream business.

Before doing so, and as a backdrop to the excellent Foreword to our book, it is worthwhile to contemplate briefly our understanding of the present when it comes to our energy sources and the role of natural gas in

M. Michot Foss (✉)
Baker Institute for Public Policy, Rice University, Houston, TX, USA
e-mail: michelle.m.foss@rice.edu

M. Michot Foss et al. (eds.), *Monetizing Natural Gas in the New "New Deal" Economy*,
https://doi.org/10.1007/978-3-030-59983-6_1

that mix. In doing so, I must grapple at least indirectly with any number of beliefs, ideologies and dogmas that permeate polite conversations about energy in today's world.

Within the global milieu of some 278 million barrels of oil equivalent per day (MMBOED) of total energy use, oil and gas consumption stands at about 162 MMBOED (based on BP's 2020 Statistical Review of World Energy,[3] 2019 data). The share for hydrocarbons of about 58 percent (using Our World in Energy[4] for fuel mix) has barely budged since 1970, the year of Earth Day, fluctuating between about 56 and 61 percent around the long-term average. The use of oil has diminished—each price shock exerted a demand response—from a peak of about 45 percent in the auspicious year of 1973 (when the Arab Oil Embargo occurred) to roughly 334 percent in 2019. Meanwhile, natural gas increased share steadily, year after year, from 15 to about 25 percent. All expected, to be sure, but overall not as profound a shift to gas as some might think. And therein lies the rub.

When natural gas use is looked at more closely (Fig. 1.1), the enormous baseload consumption comprised by North America stands out. From that tradition comes a great deal of industry know-how with demonstrated market penetration, power generation and resurgent petrochemicals constituting plentiful growth examples. The North American experience also offers many lessons, for those who care to take them, from the (very) arduous and involved adventures with policy and regulation and how they affected industry organization (see Appendix). The attention-grabbing headline comes from the very rapid escalation in demand in the Middle East and Asia. These regions are driving new investment and expected to account for much of the natural gas story at least through the decade. Europe offers incremental opportunities for any intrepid liquefied natural gas (LNG) exporter who wishes to go toe-to-toe with Russia, Europe's largest supplier. Africa and the remainder of Latin America appear as laggards and explain much of the lackluster outcome in the shift to gas globally. Africa has its own numerous continental challenges but also tremendous opportunities for natural gas to play a key role in economic modernization. South America, in particular, has been a disappointment. From visions of continental pipeline networks and intra-region trade during the 1990s until today, the ability for gas to make steady advances has been fraught with any number of disruptions, not least uneven commitments by governments—creating inconsistency in policy and regulatory

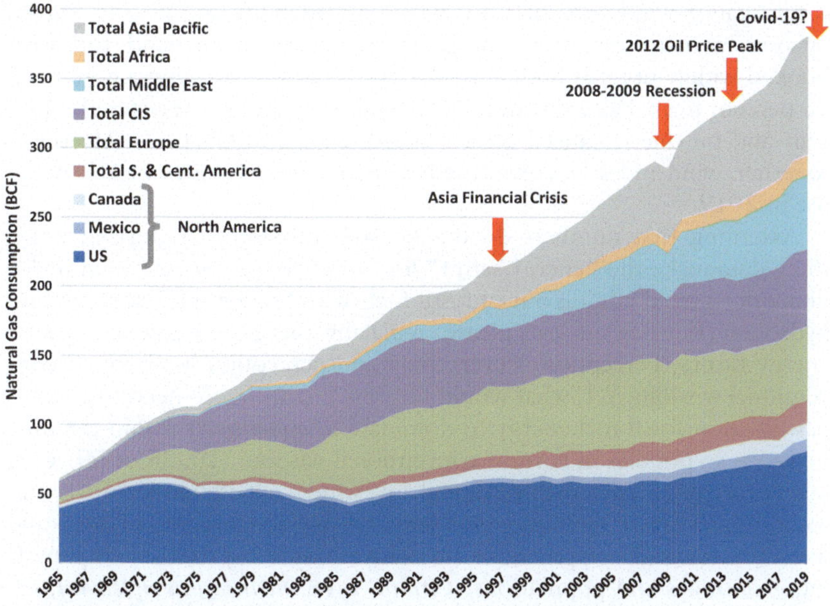

Fig. 1.1 Worldwide natural gas consumption by region. (Source: BP Annual Statistical Review of Energy, https://www.bp.com/en/global/corporate/energy-economics/statistical-review-of-world-energy.html)

approaches—and political and economic turmoil in a pattern that has become all too familiar across the region.

These data reflect the conundrum for natural gas—affordability and pricing—that is at the heart of this book. Price sensitivity can be deduced from three episodes—the Asia financial crisis, onset of the 2008 recession and the 2012 peak in oil price (the Covid-19 effect is unfolding in 2020). Where pricing for natural gas does not exist, the tendency is to link delivered natural gas to oil, making gas expensive for price-sensitive customers.

The incursion of natural gas in the United States, Europe and other locations has come, of course, mainly at the expense of coal. Use of coal since 1970 has kept that fuel at a rough 27 percent share of worldwide energy consumption. When gas is relatively expensive coal wins out in many parts of the world, in particular Asia (see Chap. 5 for many nuances on natural gas demand and pricing) but also, from time to time, in the United States (see Chap. 2). Increasingly, natural gas for power generation is set against wind and solar, for which affordability and pricing remain opaque in many countries and markets. Energy from wind and solar booked widely noticed high annual growth rates—averaging a combined 25 percent from 1990 through 2019 while coal and gas registered 2 percent and oil one (financial returns are discussed in Chap. 7). However, together, wind and solar constituted about a *3 percent* share of total energy use in 2019.

Assuming that numbers do not lie, and mindful of reporting error, these data make the "energy script" for our energy prospects seem melodramatic: a rapid edging out of fossil fuels with "renewable" sources[5] and hydrogen (but not nuclear, please) replacing them for a greener, cleaner energy future. Perception is everything and perception has become conventional wisdom. Yet, what would future scenarios *really* need to encompass for non-fossil fuel energy to dominate *as aggressively* within the time horizons so popular in current conventional wisdom (10, 25 or 50 years, take your pick)? Meanwhile, capital investment in established fuels and technologies must continue, not least to provide sources of cash and wealth to foster development of alternatives much less to sustaining existing economies and populations. *Capital investment begins upstream, setting up the order of value chains.*

Which Version of Conventional Wisdom on Resources and Supply?

If we take the view that the progression in natural gas use shown in Fig. 1.1 will not end any time soon—slowing growth in established markets being offset by rapid growth in emerging ones—then the upstream block of natural gas value chains is crucial.

It is a truism, an established fact, that how upstream investments are shaped will influence the remainder of the value chain in an industry. A great deal of thought, countless case studies, any number of prominent books in economics and business have been dedicated to the organization of industries. In particular, certain questions have been hotly debated for generations. For instance, what is the contribution to profits of linked segments? Classic views of industry value chains tend to illustrate a tidy accumulation of profits once all is done. That is, a company runs its value chain cash register every day, and computes profit and loss at the end.[6] In truth, of course, different segments can be winners and losers at different times, presenting any number of dilemmas. (A glance at the natural gas system depicted in our Appendix will help ground the reader.) How should companies position—in one part of a value chain as specialists or across multiple segments? Which style of positioning works best for creating and preserving shareholder value? The oil and gas industry alone has seen dramatic cycles. Large corporate entities controlling all aspects of their value chains. Corporate breakups with business segments spun off almost as fads (packaged as a search for improved shareholder return or often in response to changes in tax codes). Re-combinations into integrated wholes as corporate managements struggle to accommodate shareholder pressures or respond to strategic imperatives.

In oil and gas—the extractive industries in general—value chains initiate early with ideas about where and how resources occur and how to capture and monetize them.[7] Commodity price provides the occasional lure for risk taking "prospect generation"—the latest concept of where to hunt for and harvest resources. Technology usually is a great enabler, fostering new frontiers and helping companies survive the inevitable downside. The oil and gas industry has continually replenished itself while, crucially, extending the lives of legacy assets. One might think of the process as an oil and gas technology pathway (Fig. 1.2), not smooth but persistent. The tendency toward replenishment has continuously defeated naysayers, including some within the industry, who crop up periodically to declare the "end of oil and/or gas as we know it". Those who experience only one frame of the ongoing saga and form opinions accordingly are likely to suffer from biases, sometimes acutely. A test of patience is required to fully appreciate, and place into proper context of human development, the long path of the industry.

Hydrocarbons carry great allure, as stores of energy and materials with molecules and now atoms that we can combine and recombine in countless ways. Modern oil and gas supply chains have considerable fungibility. This is tough to beat, especially when stacked up against competing options. Advances in materials science enable hydrocarbons to penetrate new applications and markets and, in fact, may ensure that oil and gas are environmentally and financially sustainable. Many other factors, not least the needs of world economies and populations, make it hard to see an end in sight. Even the pressures of decarbonization, which I allude to in the book Preface and that we cover in the Foreword and elsewhere, are just one more competitive driver. A commercial "peak" almost certainly exists, on either side of supply and demand, beyond which the technology challenges and cost hurdles simply are too much to bear and against which substitutes and alternatives look much better. The modern industry has

Fig. 1.2 An oil and gas technology pathway. (Source: First developed by the author in early 2000s based on industry and corporate histories and technical and industry trade publications [I was director of research at Simmons & Company International when Baker Hughes acquired Eastman Christensen in 1990, one of the significant, early transactions to spawn the advanced unconventional drilling businesses. The SPE JPT series on R&D Grand Challenges (Judzis et al. 2011–2012) is an excellent compilation of thinking on the oil and gas technology pathway into the future. The challenges were defined as increasing recovery factors; in situ molecular manipulation; carbon capture and sequestration; produced water management; higher-resolution subsurface imaging of hydrocarbons; and environment. The last mainly focuses on above-ground risks—how companies interact with communities and societies on operations.]. U.S. oil and gas production data based on U.S. Energy Information Administration, EIA. "3-d" and "4-d" are 3 dimensional and 4 dimensional; CH_4 is methane, H is hydrogen, C is carbon. The general permeability descriptors reflect darcy units or millidarcies. Treatment to enable extraction of hydrocarbons increases as permeability reduces from conventional to unconventional to "nano". Treatment for unconventional production mainly entails hydraulic fracturing ("fracking" or "fracs") along lateral well bores, with complex "superlaterals" or "superlats" and multiple "frac stages" at very high pressures and with more proppant (almost always sand) as permeability deteriorates toward nano. IT is information technology and AI is artificial intelligence)

conquered many commercial peaks over the course of its history. Picking the timing of an ultimate end to oil and gas as a business proposition is not of much use beyond cocktail conversations. No one can say what the end game might look like. Far better to learn the lessons for how they might apply to other industries and businesses that incorporate similar complexities and aspire to global reach.

The U.S. Factor

Where does the United States reside within these pictures of global natural gas consumption and the oil and gas technology pathway? In fact, the United States has been the icon for oil and gas industry reinvention and replenishment—the cumulative production curves included in Fig. 1.2 show no sign of abating, yet. In that auspicious year of 1970, U.S. oil production hit a modern peak with average output of more than 11 MMbpd, nearly one-quarter of total world output. The collapse in oil price in 1979 and then again, more seriously, in 1984–1985 drove U.S. production to its low of about 6.8 MMbpd during 2006–2008. By 2013–2014, with robust oil prices and the technology pathway at work, U.S. combined oil and gas production returned to where it stood in 1970. In 2019, with global oil market ructions forming and Covid-19 waiting in the wings, the United States stood as the single largest producer of crude oil in the world at more than 17 MMbpd, well ahead of Saudi Arabia and Russia, both nearly 12 MMbpd.

Who would've thunk it? Hardly anyone, as it turned out. The natural gas story follows a similar trajectory. Natural gas output peaked at an average of roughly 56 billion cubic feet per day or Bcfd during 1970–1973, commanding 55 percent of global gas output. In 2005, U.S. gas production plateaued at a bit more than 47 Bcfd, about 18 percent of global supply. In between those periods lay the 1990s, a time of large surpluses in both the United States and Canada, much of it policy driven (see the Appendix), saturating markets, pushing prices below every corporate target deck. The "gas bubble" or "sausage" era was characterized by low prices for both oil and gas. Some worried that low prices would so cripple upstream investment that the industry would be unable to meet demand (OGJ 1995a provides a classic take from the International Energy Agency, or IEA). By 2010, following the natural gas price adventures from 1999 to 2009, U.S. gas production had regained its output level of the 1970s. With a more diverse portfolio of global suppliers (again, the technology pathway at work) the United States stood at just over 18 percent of the global total. By 2019, U.S. natural gas production averaged 89 Bcfd, swamping Russia, the next largest, at about 65 Bcfd. Iran was a distant third at about 24 Bcfd.

How did all of this happen? Relative to the rest of the world, the U.S. domestic upstream, in particular, remains a cradle of opportunities, Schumpeterian creative destruction[8] and new life, altering the size and scope of its oil and gas industries. Industry players never are assured of commerciality, at least at the time of prospect generation. Many ideas for the next hot new oil and gas play are relegated to round dustbins of history, only to be dredged up later and demonstrated (which is why "success rate" is such a faulty measure of upstream pursuits). Many fumbles made in building field-to-market linkages get new life (U.S. bankruptcy courts being the ultimate cure for sunk cost and the ultimate lever for regeneration). Generally speaking, oil and gas resource development reflects waves of progression of play concepts that reflect the constant interplay of new and revisited ideas and the introduction of technology to facilitate entry and achieve exploitation. In the continental United States, these waves ranged from (Fig. 1.3; see the Appendix for discussion of terminology for types of plays):

- Early conventional reservoirs, onshore (Appalachians, Midwest) to offshore (Gulf of Mexico shelf and then deeper)
- Early tight plays (Pinedale—Jonah field where multiple-well pads were deployed) and other unconventional types (coal bed methane in Powder River, Black Warrior, San Juan)
- The more recent shale or "resource play" pursuits (first the Barnett, then back to Appalachia for the Marcellus, on to Haynesville, back to South Texas for the Eagle Ford and below the prolific Permian fields of oil history lore)

Infrastructure followed the distribution of people and economic activity. When companies achieved resource development far from population and industrial market centers, new field-to-market connections had to be built.

Two aspects of the U.S. hydrocarbon resource endowment and its development deserve emphasis.

First, much of the natural gas production that has been proved up over several generations has accompanied petroleum, with black oil the

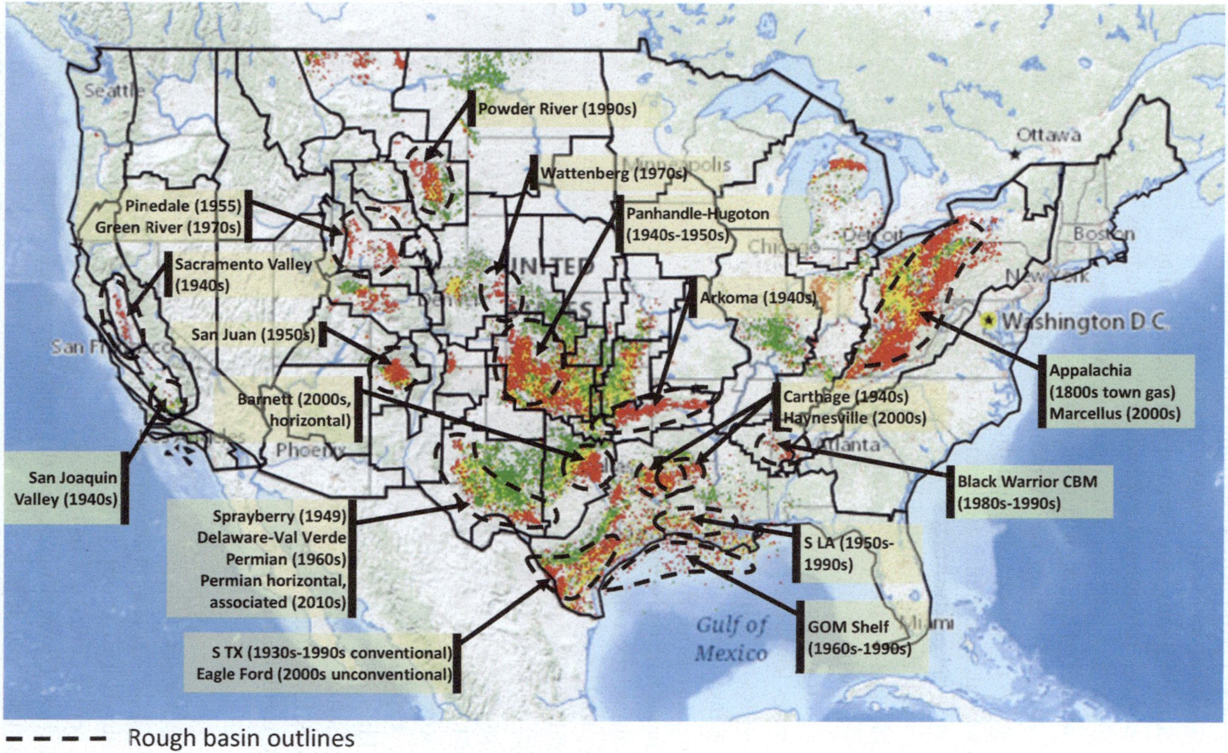

Fig. 1.3 Major U.S. natural gas basins and development eras. (Sources: Base map from USGS, https://certmapper.cr.usgs.gov/data/apps/noga-drupal/, approximate initiation of activity in various basins and plays from USGS and industry information)

premium target and natural gas liquids, or NGLs, and sometimes methane helping to boost well and field values (hopefully). In the current generation dominated by unconventional activity, with shale resource plays as the primary targets, natural gas byproduct, "associated gas", is the dominant feature of play economics. This dynamic will remain in place for the foreseeable future. The opportunities and challenges presented by that dynamic constitute most of my treatment of the upstream businesses and monetization in this chapter and much the book.

Second, oil, petroleum fuels and natural gas liquids for industrial and energy uses have advantages over piped methane in that suppliers and customers can deploy many different modes of transportation and storage and build clusters for processing, fractionation, refining and chemicals. Certainly, pipelines for oil/condensate, NGLs and refined products are attractive and necessary but until companies can build and place into service pipelines for these products, they can make use of trucks, rail and even inland barges to alleviate bottlenecks. Historically, as the natural gas—delivered methane—industry extended its reach, long-distance pipelines to handle variations in natural gas quality and local distribution networks for methane had to be built and expanded. In more recent years, natural gas pipelines, the only reasonable mode for long-distance transportation of cargo that is mainly methane, continue to be a main impediment to monetization. Because of oil's fungibility, it has been easier (relatively speaking) to cure strong differences in price, basis differentials, between the light crude oil, West Texas Intermediate (WTI) index set at Cushing, Oklahoma, and a large supply location such as Midland, Texas. It has been much more difficult for the industry to achieve expansions of methane pipeline capacity and thus close strong price differences between the Henry Hub index (Erath, Louisiana) and supply locations in West Texas or Appalachia. These differences associated with fungibility and their consequences for value chains are striking in how they affect operating and financial results, as I illustrate later.

Will U.S. Natural Gas Remain Cheap?

Nothing quite captures the essence of prevailing long views, and the conventional wisdom about U.S. natural gas, as the conviction that natural gas will remain cheap, if not forever then for quite some time. The rationale for these convictions lies in the upstream block, in the U.S. domestic oil and gas "patch", in the remarkable turnaround in oil and gas production growth I described earlier. As always, a fundamental aspect of the technology pathway is the shift in sovereignty from producers to consumers as new slugs of supply work to lower the price signals that attracted upstream investment in the first place. *Must "cheap gas" for customers always imply financial losses for producers?* That seems to be the other side of the sovereignty coin, considering lessons from experience. The definition of "resilience" for U.S. producers—producers worldwide—is survival in the face of inevitable diminishing returns. More times than not, companies are monetizing production into a falling price environment. The same challenges exist along value chains as capacity expansions for midstream assets, LNG, refining and chemicals are commissioned and increased supplies from monetization filter into markets. *Consequently, profitability upstream (and through the value chain), relative to supply largesse is a crucial bookend for long-view stories.*

In the current psychological milieu surrounding "cheap gas", the richness of the continental U.S. resource endowment and dynamic attributes of the U.S. upstream businesses are enough to convince many people that cost of gas is not an issue. This holds not least for the companies undertaking vast midstream connections (touched on in this chapter), those vested in natural gas power generation (Chap. 2), petrochemical expansions (Chap. 3) and LNG export developers and their customers (Chap. 4). By exporting our surplus oil and gas, U.S. market players have added to a growing global price pipeline that is carrying the U.S. competitive cost structure to other countries, like it or not.

To a considerable degree, whether U.S. gas can remain cheap for end users is the central question for the fate of gas as a preferred option, at least for mid-term, current project planning periods of 15–20 years. Affordability and competitiveness are joined at the hip. The latter is contingent on the industry's ability to resolve upstream profitability shortcomings, cure existing field-to-market gaps, address environmental challenges for operations and all at a delivered price customers will still be willing to pay (see the Appendix for a U.S. example). Since many international customers access natural gas via LNG, the cost of LNG value chains is crucial. LNG is an expensive option without breakthroughs in business models and/or generous economies of scale to amortize capital expenditures. If market participants link gas price to oil, keeping gas cheap for importers can be difficult. This largely explains the slower than might be expected growth in natural gas consumption over the past decades, as I highlighted above. Ergo the attention in recent years to "de-linking" gas/LNG from oil and the lure of the U.S. Henry Hub index for price-sensitive customers worldwide. This approach has its own shortcomings, not least the vagaries of the U.S. domestic marketplace. Given the state of the world, the irony for the competitiveness of gas, including that of U.S. production abroad, remains the cost advantages of coal in key markets like Asia.

As with any commoditized industry, price is the defining element. Even though market participants are price takers, how price signals are formed and transferred, how they influence prevailing profit margins and how price risk is mitigated exert considerable influence over industry and market organization. The main commodities, crude oil and methane, are traded in the United States with multiple trading points that capture physical locational differences and transmit information about supply-demand balances, available capacity for delivery to markets and quality (Btu content, extent of treatment required, lighter and heavier oil—see later discussion in What's in YOUR Barrel? Part I—Re-tooling Company Portfolios). The worldwide venue of traded products has grown over the years as modern energy finance evolved, but the WTI and Henry Hub indexes remain the primary price indicators used in the United States and abroad, increasingly so for Henry Hub.

The visual in Fig. 1.4 depicting price dynamics to 2030 reflects conclusions from an extensive review and analysis of U.S. natural gas conditions over the years (Michot Foss 1995, 2007, 2011, 2012, 2015). The nature of natural gas commoditization being what it is, and the natural gas value chain system functioning as it does, extreme price events below $3 MMbtu and above $6 MMbtu have happened even during long periods in which the customer cost for natural gas is quite moderate. A "target" price of $3 is not unreasonable given the producer benchmarks I show later. A price signal of $4 is even more interesting for producers and, as the increment of associated gas plays out, has a greater possibility of occurring. The lower the oil price for longer, the sooner customers might see higher price events for natural gas demand, ceteris paribus.

Throughout a long history, natural gas supply is more responsive to oil price (see later section "Growth or Profitability Revisited: Rigs, Drilling and the Future of U.S. Production"). As detailed through the remainder of the chapter, the prevailing pattern for the U.S. upstream is methane capture mainly associated with liquids rich acreage. The captured and monetized value of liquids provides essential, material "uplift" for producers while methane prices remain low (Chap. 3). The uplift value from condensates and NGLs is contingent upon midstream capacity. Outside of

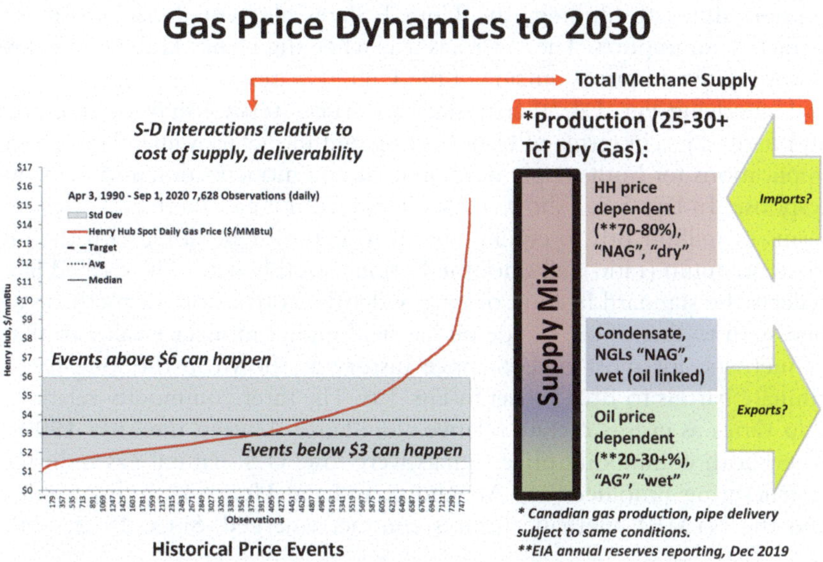

Fig. 1.4 Natural gas price dynamics and scenarios through 2030. (Source: Developed by the author and used with permission. *AG* associated gas, *NAG* non-associated gas, *HH* Henry Hub, annual average, nominal price)

natural gas associated with higher value liquids, nonassociated gas (which may have small concentrations of ethane) and dry gas (methane, perhaps with other constituents like CO_2) are the targets for methane recovery, and require a Henry Hub price with wellhead netbacks sufficient to support gas-directed drilling and production. How long producers can rely on liquids uplift to drive or boost wellhead value is contingent upon oil price and the value of condensates and NGLs relative to oil (Chap. 3). Another critical ingredient—attractive and accessible acreage for resource exploitation—is essential. Acreage opportunities for domestic natural gas and methane supply are nearly entirely onshore, at least for the near- to mid-term horizons. Deeper water offshore locations are prospective for oil, but problematic for methane capture and monetization as they require costly infrastructure solutions (deep subsea pipelines or floating systems). As U.S. and North American import and export capability expands, the interface between price attraction for drilling and trade balance will remain dynamic. If, or when, upstream players need a higher "HH" price to support domestic drilling, the United States also could become more attractive for imports. The reverse is true when the Henry Hub price index is low relative to prices outside of the United States.

Underlying Fig. 1.4 "thermostat" are crucial relationships between oil and natural gas in terms of both heating and monetary value. These bear implications for both supply development and monetization and demand response. In Fig. 1.5, I show crude oil and natural gas (methane) prices in terms of million Btu to equilibrate oil to natural gas, along with the oil price premium (ratio), all smoothed using monthly data. The dashed line reflects the standard heating or energy density conversion for methane of one-sixth to that of oil. Crude oil has held higher monetary value to that of methane for most of U.S. price history as shown in the long-term, annual "barrels to Btus" chart in Fig. 1.6. The inter-commodity relationship varies as events dictate relative abundance. During the early 1990s, when both commodity price signals were low, U.S. natural gas industry restructuring unfolded (see Appendix) and the Henry Hub price index and the NYMEX methane futures contract emerged. Since 2012, both

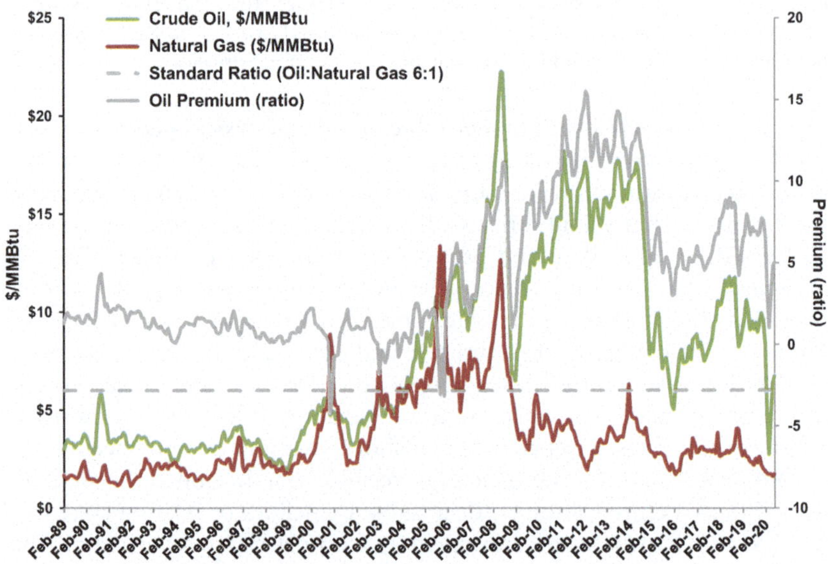

Fig. 1.5 Oil and natural gas prices and oil price premium. (Sources: CME/NYMEX as reported by EIA; author calculations and depiction)

commodity markets have been dominated by the more attractive price of oil for drilling in shale plays, the resulting oil supply abundance and the flood of associated gas.[9]

Shale and other tight rock plays have features that tend to exacerbate the intrinsic disparities of oil and gas values. Larger molecules do not pass easily through rocks that have nano porosity and permeability. Shale plays tend to be over-pressured. The initial release of pressure with well completions results in the by now, well-known steeply declining production curves and often high or rising gas-oil ratios (GORs), especially in gassy locations. Financial performance follows. High initial peak production rates allow producers to quickly amortize well costs, an attraction for investors. Tails constitute profitability. When prices are lower, production rates must be higher or capital cost recovery takes longer, cutting into profitability.

The bottom line, of course, is exactly profitability. Attaining oil-denominated pricing is nirvana for methane suppliers even while HH pricing is sought by buyers. The LNG industry was built upon the stability of oil-indexed pricing, in particular for the long-distance Asia-Pacific markets. The stronger signal from oil prices relative to natural gas favored U.S. LNG export project development in recent years. The difficulty, of course, is that those same customers who traditionally offered and relied upon oil-indexed contracts are happy to add HH-priced cargoes to portfolios. (Chap. 4 covers LNG commercial agreements.) In effect, international trading has communicated the U.S. price for natural gas worldwide via exports of LNG and, ironically, coal given its rivalry with natural gas and HH influenced price tag.

Apart from LNG, converting methane and other natural gas constituents to a middle-distillate equivalent puts gas more directly into the petroleum value chain. (Chap. 3 incorporates gas-to-liquids, GTL and methane-to-gasoline, MTG projects.) These are expensive processes, particularly GTL. Most often, GTL developers like to see an oil-gas price ratio of at least 20 to support project economics.[10] Methane and NGLs also can be monetized through chemicals—methane to methanol, NGLs into the array of intermediate products with natural gas feedstock output competing with oil (naphtha and gasoil; see later sections and Chap. 3).

Demand response exerts balancing forces and much of demand response centers on substitutability. Other chapters in our book provide an in-depth analysis of price-sensitive demand response in power, LNG and petrochemicals. When the HH index rose above \$2/MMBtu in mid-1999,

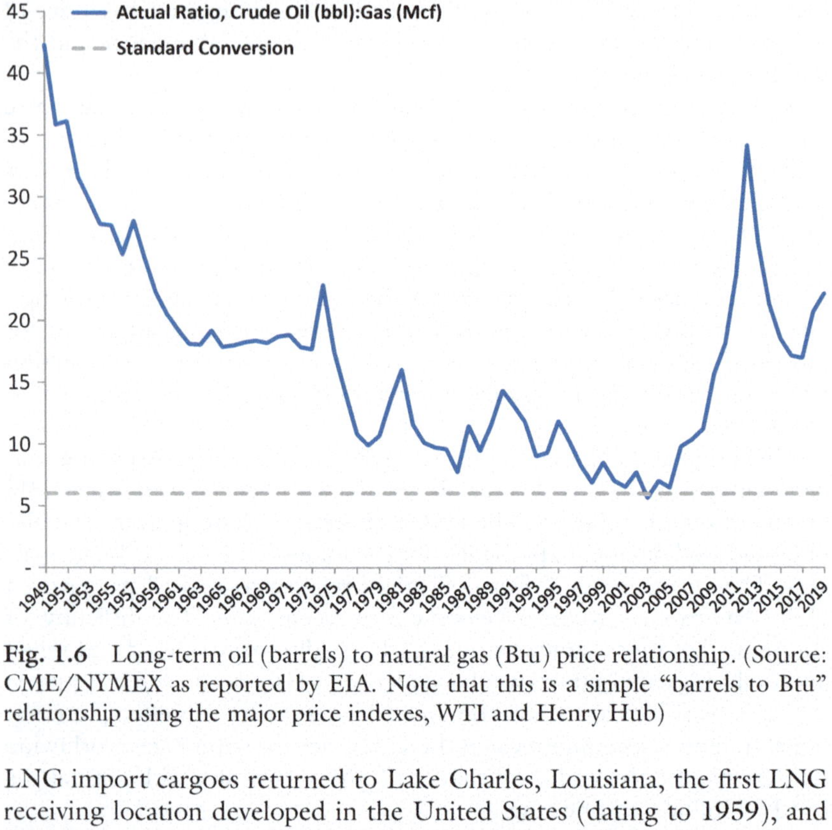

Fig. 1.6 Long-term oil (barrels) to natural gas (Btu) price relationship. (Source: CME/NYMEX as reported by EIA. Note that this is a simple "barrels to Btu" relationship using the major price indexes, WTI and Henry Hub)

LNG import cargoes returned to Lake Charles, Louisiana, the first LNG receiving location developed in the United States (dating to 1959), and the location that proved the concept of liquefying and shipping methane. The Lake Charles terminal had been inactive during the 1990s. Interest in building new LNG receiving capacity soared with the HH price until 2007. At the same time, methanol plants built during the 1990s to use low-cost methane feedstock were shut down and, in some cases, dismantled and shipped out of the United States. When the HH index collapsed in 2007, strategies shifted again. The methanol plants returned and LNG promoters set new goals of monetizing U.S. natural gas in European and Asian markets where oil-denominated cargoes were selling for $12–19/MMBtu. And so it goes.

Of Attributes and Caveats

Clearly, the richness of continental U.S. endowments and persistence of the oil and gas technology pathway combined in fortuitous ways to alter, at least for some period of time, both perceptions and realities for the domestic, Lower 48 onshore oil and gas industry. The shift in fortunes have had wide-ranging impacts across the U.S. energy sector and internationally. It is easy to see why expectations grew to embrace the United States not only as a dominant supplier of oil and gas—from dead zone to live broadcast—but as an influential exporter. We also can appreciate, in hindsight, how unprepared myriad actors were for the blowback. These included politicians, geopolitical partners and rivals, environmental groups, the research and university communities, and even the oil and gas industry itself.

The blowback was rapid and multi-dimensional. The Foreword to our book reflects some of those tensions. Reactions on geopolitical inferences were immediate with endless scrutiny of how a resurgent United States might exploit its advantage, or whether we would simply exit. The high-speed upward ratcheting of opposition (to drilling and fracking, pipelines, exports, fossil fuels, natural gas as a fossil fuel—a “bridge to nowhere”[11]) with compelling, “viral” imagery (night skies bright with gas flaring) has only proven that with success comes many other things, not all of them pleasant. Along with abundance came a relentless “treadmill” that constrains upstream profitability and induces investor agitation. Each period of price appreciation induces new supply, quickly eroding commodity prices, as companies must keep drilling to combat the fast-depleting nature of shale wells. I shall say a great deal more about this as we go on. The contradictions between resource wealth, business challenges, vast economic benefits and environmental unhappiness have been, in word, astounding.

The “shale iteration” of the U.S. oil and gas technology pathway, as it has unfolded so far in this century, upended widespread beliefs about how we understood the present. In the old paradigm, the United States was a large and perhaps problematic net importer, competing for supply, driving up prices, creating and/or exacerbating geopolitical tensions. The end of that paradigm tore through investments that reflected bets on the script playing out as intended (not least for LNG import developers; see Chap. 4). Low-priced natural gas means less expensive fuel for power generators, enabling expansion of gas-fired generation. It also reduces electricity prices and thus revenue for every form of generation, including both legacy plants (coal and nuclear) and renewable energy developers. These realities add to competitive tensions (overall, coal has been the loser; see Chap. 2). Environmental opportunism and geopolitical power plays were rooted in the old paradigm. The more expensive oil and natural gas, the easier to push arguments in favor of shifts away from these and other fossil fuels. Agitation on "climate emergencies" almost certainly is coincidental with cheaper fossil fuels and energy in general. Internationalists previously worried about use of oil as a political weapon. In the new paradigm, their concerns became that a net exporting United States would so disengage from the world scene as to threaten post–World War II geopolitical balances and institutions.

These schisms and the competitive interests embedded in them underlie opposing viewpoints about whether companies and investors should continue to plow capital into hydrocarbons-related businesses that could, should, might or might not be on the way out. Often relegated to lower status are benefits derived from "affordable, safe, secure" and, especially, domestic, "made in America" energy (all well-trod ground in wording) that can supplement hard currency earnings through exports. Indeed, greater sympathy to these views can be found among citizens in vast parts of the world where economic development is a priority and natural gas is a prize.

All together, the long-view storyline for oil and gas is one of the more interesting in the pantheon of business histories. Which version of wisdom is conventional—the transition away from hydrocarbons or their continued dominance given properties inherent in these resources and the technology pathway that has kept them and the industries at the forefront? How critical is U.S. supply in cementing natural gas as a fuel of choice, not just for temporary "bridging" convenience and not just for our domestic markets? If U.S. gas has to remain "cheap" for all of this to happen, what does that mean in terms of gas price, in particular relative to oil? Can the adaptive, inventive U.S. upstream patch continue to deliver, and prosper? And, if it can't, what then?

We have thoughts elsewhere in the book on competitiveness of natural gas, including NGLs components, at given prices. To frame, artfully, a longer view of the future, our understanding of the present must get at oil and gas upstream fundamentals in spite of forces impinging upon the here and now. Up to this point, I have alluded to two conditions and caveats that will be critical in determining possible forward pathways.

- One is the key role of oil as the driver for upstream investment and commensurate availability of low-cost-associated natural gas. *What happens if/when oil price is not attractive?*
- Another is upstream industry profitability and funding. Both are linked inherently to views on commodity markets. Profitability, or lack of, was a distinct constraint as the U.S. and global oil and gas industry completed 2019. The pandemic has introduced stresses that are unusual in the history of the industry. For the core analysis in this chapter I use results from ten years of industry benchmarking that illustrate the treadmill effects and capture the impact of shifting commodity values on positioning (from gassier to oilier plays and acreage portfolios) and monetization (to improve upstream economics). In the maelstrom of 2019 oil market share battles and Covid-19 demand destruction key questions are: *How many companies will survive? In what organizational form? With what business models? And with what impacts on aggregate U.S. supply and exports?*

I will continue to touch on these for the remainder of the chapter. I add a number of key features that explain a great deal about the U.S. upstream and its performance. All of these attributes also have caveats. I will explore these in detail as we proceed.

The Lure of Private Lands and Minerals

A prime U.S. attribute is private land and minerals ownership. Many observers have associated the ability to quickly mobilize and prove up production to "fee" land and minerals. However, *upstream deal terms drive value creation*. And fee minerals can be expensive.

Private land and minerals ownership are a major, distinguishing feature of the United States as compared to other countries. I have noted that upstream deal terms drive value creation. By "deal terms" I mean not only bonuses for drilling options and leasing and royalties on production, but also performance requirements (drilling activity and achievement of production), length of lease and so on.

The bulk of oil and gas production in the U.S. today, at the time of publication, comes from privately owned land and minerals. Private lands contribute more than half of U.S. output.[12] Lack of activity on public lands onshore along with declines in the federal offshore and Alaska has contributed to the prominence of private minerals production. Natural gas monetization from Alaska's North Slope, even with the State of Alaska's involvement, has never been accomplished. In the minds of many, the rapid development of shale plays was due in large part to private land and minerals holdings in the major basins and states where production growth has been most significant. For the most part, private land and mineral owners have been willing to host activity. The ability to negotiate with private owners affords a degree of flexibility not typical of public lands, which are subject to political oversight.

Initial deal terms, no matter whether land ownership is private or sovereign, including U.S. federal and state domains, have a great bearing on the financial success of upstream projects. Unlike federal and state auctions, which tend to use sealed bids, private leasing is open, activity is visible and news gets around. Pay too much at the outset, with deal terms that are too onerous, and these obligations will come back to haunt during the inevitable price cycles. A well-known "slippery slope" exists; during highly competitive lease acquisition phases, once one company accepts stringent deal terms these tend to become known in the marketplace and resource owner expectations shift in that direction.[13] During tough times, lack of demand for acreage eventually induces deal terms that are more attractive for producers and investors. Mineral leases contain myriad provisions that allow flexibility during low price periods. Exits (through sales of properties, "farm outs", sales of whole companies) and, even more important, the option to exit are highly sought after. I touch on these in later sections.

Private land owners can be notoriously savvy about industry activity and market conditions. It is customary for companies to face expensive per-acre land acquisition bonuses and royalties of 20 percent or more in "hot" plays. High costs of entry and royalties, paid on gross production before expenses, can burden well economics and create a drag on net present value especially as commodity prices fall. Land strategies can have undue influence on producer behavior, drilling activity and ultimately production and supply. In the early 2000s, a huge, initial wave of intensely competitive leasing occurred as companies and backers built land blocks large enough to accommodate the dense well patterns needed to drain shale plays effectively. Companies faced the twin challenges of attracting investment and managing costs associated with a surge in drilling activity needed to test and achieve production in order to hold land blocks. Drilling to achieve "HBP"—held by production—led to the early glut of gas, just in time for a robust U.S. recession, and consequent collapse in the Henry Hub index.

To the point about flexibility: Leasing on private lands and minerals enables producers to implement a variety of entry strategies and tactics in emerging plays over relatively short time frames. Access to private lands and minerals supports robustness of the U.S. domestic industry through longer time horizons and repeated commodity price cycles. Outside of the United States, sovereign negotiations and agreements can encumber the ability of operators to achieve commercial flexibility for extent and timing of investment commitments and exits. Field-to-market linkages typically are made worse by government ownership and/or control or influence over oil and gas infrastructure.

For unconventional plays of all types, the size and scope of acreage requirements and scale and scope of development drilling and logistics are important. A key difference in pursuit strategies between "conventional" and "unconventional" oil and gas lies in acreage typically leased for testing. Because conventional targets involve exploration risk—the chance that hydrocarbons are absent—companies lease as little acreage up front as possible. If an exploration well is classed a "dry hole", the acreage is typically condemned, no further acreage will be obtained, and the leased acreage will either be written off and returned to the market or sold.

Finally, the happiest companies could be those operating on private lands with very low or even no royalties. These are rare exceptions, but they do exist.

The Role of OFS

Compared to other countries, the United States has enormous oil and gas field service (OFS) support. OFS equipment and manpower is integral to the technology pathway. The tough industry conditions at work as our book goes to press are pressuring OFS companies even more than upstream operators. The interactions between cost of OFS support and "headroom" between exploration and production or E&P expense and commodity price are compelling: *rapid cost escalation on the upside of cycles can squeeze producers; collapsing day rates on the downside can deplete service companies.*

The size and scope of the U.S. oil service segment is one that many countries would like to emulate, for economic development reasons as much as to attract and sustain industry interest. The U.S. upstream segment is all about "location"—the hunt is always for the best, prime geology that can yield hydrocarbons in commercial quantities. Difficulties in building workable logistics for all of the supply and service requirements associated with bursts of and shifts in upstream activity can mean precious delays and higher costs for vital resource inputs. From an operating company perspective, the risk is that delays and cost escalations eat so much into early years on projects that net present value is destroyed. From an OFS company perspective, contracted day rates must support mobilization, and in "real time".

When upstream strategies migrated to deeper water offshore during the late 1980s and early 1990s as I illustrate in the technology pathway (Fig. 1.2) OFS contractors had to expand and extend the performance of drilling rig systems and the reach of supply boats. As onshore unconventional plays unfolded in the 1980s and shale in particular in the late 1990s and early 2000s "frac spreads"—the available equipment and supplies for complex horizontal well completions and hydraulic fracturing—had to increase in number and evolve in sophistication.

OFS day rates (as indicated by the producer price index, PPI, Fig. 1.7) tend to follow oil price but usually are faster on the upswing and sticky on the downside. Rapid escalation in demand for OFS as plays heat up and producers push for new capacity and technology can propel day rates beyond where they might be otherwise. On the downside, lags in OFS cost reductions burden producers as they struggle to sustain or find profit margins with falling commodity prices.

Any number of advances were made to accommodate the new surge in shale drilling.[14] New drill bits with metallurgies suitable for chewing through tight rock in corrosive subsurface environments were developed. OFS companies improved availability of larger drilling rig systems and trained service crews for superlat and superfrac well completion designs. Superfracs require much more pressure pumping and water to force that much more proppant (sand used to prop open fractures) into host rock. OFS companies made large investments in pressure pumping trucks that could deliver on the superfrac well designs.[15] Supplies of suitable frac sand and water and larger pump trucks and equipment to force sand, water and chemicals into harsh (electron) microscopic pore spaces and fractures all must appear on time and OFS equipment and workers must perform with few, preferably no, lost time incidents. To meet shortened "cycle time" drilling goals, OFS companies and some operators invested heavily in depots to centralize supplies and services as drilling migrated across locations and around basins. Sensing equipment advanced in order to guide precision drilling through narrow benches. Better understanding of fracture systems and frac results remains a Holy Grail to reduce well costs. Constructing and executing drilling of multiple wells on supporting

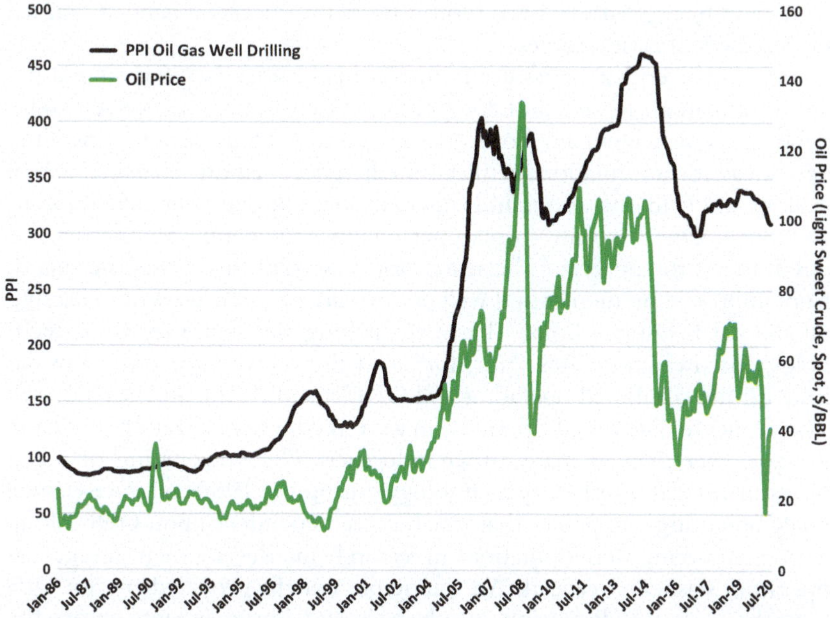

Fig. 1.7 PPI for oil and gas well drilling (primary). (Source: U.S. BLS, producer price index [PPI] for oil and gas well drilling, primary, not seasonally adjusted. https://beta.bls.gov/dataViewer/view/timeseries/PCU213111213111P)

"pads" minimized environmental footprint and facilitates logistics. These and many more adaptations, borrowed intact from experience or recombined with new inventions, enabled the shale plays to progress in similar fashion to previous eras of upstream advancement.

At the end of 2019, the OFS segment on the whole was in worse shape than producers but this is par for the course. It has always been difficult for OFS companies to generate the cash that investors push for. While many of the strategic cost reductions across the domestic industry, offshore and on, revolve around actions taken by OFS segment leaders, they all are subject to capex spending by producers. OFS companies have few options for diversifying or otherwise shielding themselves from spending reductions. The highest margins for OFS are earned offshore and the combination of low prices and attraction of onshore unconventional plays undermined offshore capex considerably. Meanwhile, onshore, the cost of sustaining frac spreads to be as responsive as producers demanded drained OFS coffers of cash reserves.

One of the critical issues going forward is health of OFS if oil and gas are to remain affordable and competitive for customers. Labor remains a large cost component for both operating and OFS companies, instilling new ideas for automation, artificial intelligence, remote management of drilling and field operations and other advances dominating industry conversations. One has only to scan petroleum engineering and geoscience publications to appreciate the search for new solutions across the board, from improved prediction and well performance to new ways of managing oil and gas field operations. The search is long and ongoing, as the technology pathway intimates. Nor, for all of the reinvention and rejuvenation, do the combined operating and OFS legs of the oil and gas industry adapt quickly. The time horizon from idea to commercialization in oil and gas is slower than in many other industries. The outsourcing of much operator-owned proprietary technology during the 1980s oil price crunch made operating companies that much more dependent upon OFS. Along with outsourcing were reductions in research and development budgets as operators slashed overhead. An intangible benefit provided by the OFS segment is in the dispersion of advances and improvements across the upstream businesses. This dispersion has considerable reach but proprietary concerns for operating companies and the propensity to free-ride adds to the long time horizon.[16]

The desire for innovation to manage cost includes SSHE costs, a growing component of opex. Heightened scrutiny of the fossil fuels industries could add to cost pressures and cost management complexity. Companies face the veritable rock and hard place—managerial caution about integrity of assets and SSHE metrics in the post-Macondo age on one side and the pressure from investors for cost management and improved margins and free cash flow on the other.

Getting from Field to Market: Midstream

The United States hosts a vast complex of midstream infrastructure for field-to-market linkages and monetization. I have already emphasized the critical role of midstream. The majority of capacity is independently owned and financed as opposed to residing within vertically integrated organizations. *There can be big lags in responsiveness, delaying vital field-to-market linkages.* Midstream operators also are tested when production declines affect "throughput" and thus revenues. The same treadmill characteristics of shale plays have made planning and execution of field-to-market linkages that much more complicated.

A number of midstream assets developed by producers were spun off into master limited partnerships or MLPs (see later and Chap. 3). Pipeline companies separated assets into MLPs and new midstream businesses were formed as MLPs. The income tax advantages associated with MLP structures (no federal taxes at the company level) created a strong demand for ownership of units and moving assets into MLPs was enormously popular.[17] When the tide turns against the businesses and assets in question, or if the subsidiaries become a burden on the parent, clearly disposition becomes a challenge. Midstream and MLP assets declined in value (Fig. 1.8) with falling commodity prices, disappointing utilizations or other factors, including oil and gas falling out of favor with investors (see later discussion). In some cases, the MLP structure itself became awkward for growth. MLP structures work best with mature assets, and not so well for raising and funneling capital into new projects. This constraint resulted

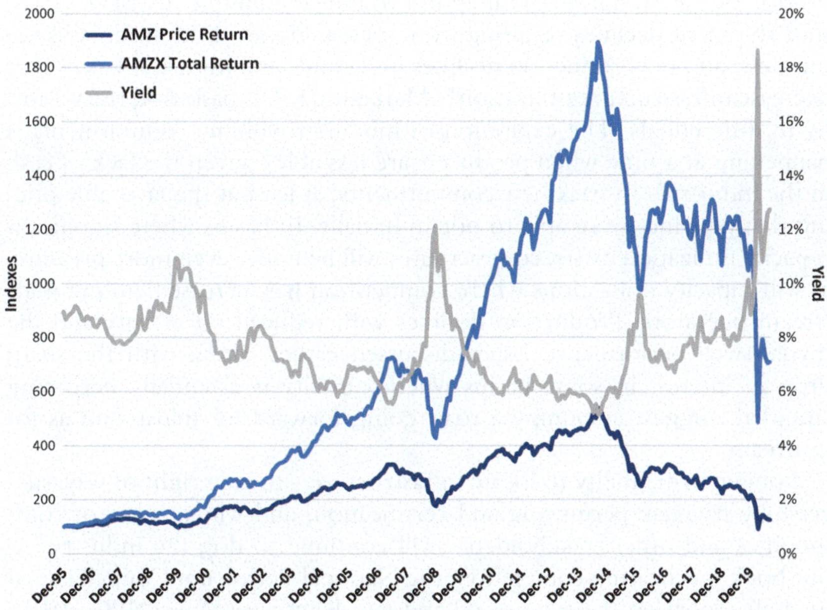

Fig. 1.8 Shifting picture for midstream. (Source: Alerian, https://www.alerian.com/. Author depiction)

in a decision by a leading midstream MLP to restructure back to a corporate entity.[18] While funding continues to be pursued and raised for midstream ventures, the investment environment has changed for midstream as significantly as it has for upstream. Energy infrastructure businesses are currently less attractive for investors. The consequences continue to play out in field-to-market gaps.

Midstream is a feeder to downstream. New volumes of NGLs required new fractionation and processing, sometimes bundled with downstream refining and petrochemical expansions, but all leading to the final combination and recombination of intermediate materials that underlie the vast majority of industrial and consumer goods. The "industrial Renaissance" detailed in Chap. 3 illustrates the end game for field-to-market links and concentrated value capture from hydrocarbons.

Biracree (2020) identified "four major sources of headwinds that will have widely varying effects on midstream companies, depending on their specific assets. These are: (1) marketing risks for companies that contract and ship volumes on their own or third-party pipelines; (2) contract roll-off risk, or the expiration of minimum volume commitments (MVCs); (3) spot shipment declines resulting from increased competition for walk-up business; and (4) production declines in second- and third-tier basins that decrease infrastructure utilization". Marketing risk is basis risk, the volatility in differentials. The expiration of minimum volume commitments is happening at a time when producers are less able—given the lack of cash in the industry—to back new commitments, at least at the favorable pricing that pipelines were able to obtain initially. In basins where significant capacity utilization exists, contract rates will be under even more pressure, as will capacity utilizations where competition has increased among midstream operators. Production declines with reduced rig activity and the myriad well performance issues discussed earlier, along with the sharp drop in interest in some basins where capacity is essentially becoming stranded, suggest as bumpy a road going forward for midstream as for upstream.

Longer term, ability to locate infrastructure—to gain right of way, successfully navigate permitting and certification, and win support of communities and other stakeholders—will continue to dog the industry. As our book was nearing completion, the National Petroleum Council issued its draft report on the state of oil and gas delivery systems (NPC 2019). Distinct bottlenecks that are widely known—pipeline access to deliver more Appalachian gas into New England and New York, congestion in the

Houston Ship Channel and export capability—were touched on. Other, more difficult and contentious issues were raised and acknowledged. These included: work force adequacy; resiliency (optionality in the delivery system); complexity of permitting (with growing attention to the National Environmental Policy Act or NEPA process); stakeholder engagement (including with tribal governments); the climate overlay (the incidence of flaring as midstream lags persist did much to make the natural gas industry a target of criticism during 2019); cybersecurity; safety assurance and the need for investment in technology R&D for monitoring and risk mitigation.

For upstreamers, there is never enough capacity in the right places, and it is always expensive. For midstreamers, it almost never fails that capacity additions are put into service just in time for down cycles.[19] For integrated companies as well as independent producers, the distinct challenge is dilution of upstream profits through their field-to-market links, no matter whether producers own them outright in vertically integrated corporate organizations or engage in "virtual" integration through contracting and other arrangements.

Structure and Financing of the Patch
Three attributes and their qualifications round out the list.

- The U.S. oil and gas patch is quite diverse[20] with different motivations and limitations across industry demographics *and thus many implications for business strategies and funding.*

The oil and gas money story is quite distinct when it comes to large, vertically integrated majors relative to the smaller, "scrappy" independents, terminology that originated to distinguish companies outside of the Standard Oil Trust ("juniors" tends to be the favored terminology outside of the United States and Canada). Tradition holds that smaller, often privately held, independents tend to be the "wildcatters", opening up new plays, while the integrated majors tend to keep their powder dry until development, more conducive to their large value chains. To some extent, this separation of duties occurs worldwide.

Investors prize having large, publicly traded international integrated majors in portfolios for their dividends. The integrated structures are key to balancing upstream and downstream risks, the natural hedge for the free cash flow to support dividends and dividend boosted returns to shareholders. Returns on equity among integrated majors tend to be lower than for independents even during peak commodity prices. Independents ("secondary" oil and gas in equity trading parlance) offer a "pure" exposure to production performance and commodity prices, for the obvious reasons. Larger independents that pay dividends offer a blend of exposures but their dividends can be challenged during tough times. Investors have long considered the largest integrated majors as blue chip stocks and view their dividends to be sacrosanct.

The upshot is that motivations of companies and investors differ according to where they sit. Investors have been attracted to "pure play", "shale specialist" independents especially for the possibility of "deal flipping" and commodity price appreciation. Equities analysts liked pure play companies—especially, in recent years, producers gravitating to and emphasizing Permian holdings—for the ease of research.[21] Entry of the integrated majors into tight rock plays reflects the established penchant to optimize deployment of their internal integration by building large value chains. Ability to export from the United States and to slide U.S. assets into global trading portfolios offers crucial "optionality" for these strategies.

- Barriers to entry into and exit from U.S. oil and gas upstream businesses are relatively low *but shifting business conditions can complicate things*, especially the ability to exit.

The U.S. domestic oil and gas industry has always flourished from the buying and selling of drillable prospects, land holdings and producing properties, using a variety of approaches. A well-trod path for emerging plays—accelerated in the shale-dominated era—has been private equity backing with credit access for existing companies and new ventures to acquire land holdings and engage in large vertical well pilot drilling programs to prove up production. A critical feature of the U.S. business is disposal of interests and assets through "farm outs" and sales, including acquisition and divestiture (A&D) and merger and acquisition or M&A strategies and tactics. Private equity backers exit through acquisitions or initial public offerings (IPOs) in new upstream enterprises or new share issues in existing publicly traded operators. Rising prices and parallel rising valuations for stocks grease transactions and exits. Falling valuations during low price periods stymie exit strategies.

From 2014 through 2019, a prominent debate was how and whether shale play exits could be engineered as part of a long-awaited consolidation, and whether pullbacks in drilling, and their commensurate effects on commodity prices, might improve netbacks and valuations enough to support exit ramps. With Covid-19, many of those bets are off. As we complete this book, companies and their investors along with analysts all are looking to find signals in the maze of conflicting data on demand recovery and price. Without doubt, the U.S. domestic industry will "right size". The main questions, as I stated earlier, are in what form and to what extent.

- Last, the U.S. oil and gas ecosystem is characterized by vast financial liquidity *but it is never enough and external capital often is not there when upstream companies need it most.*

The predominance of private land and minerals holdings and abundant financial liquidity explain much about U.S. investment patterns and entry/exit, including the ability to mobilize capital even when competition for minerals is fierce and land prices are at a premium. The presence of privately owned and controlled U.S. producing businesses, with access to the capital markets for credit and private equity, bolsters the industry platform. Relatively liberal rules apply to foreign direct investors through U.S. affiliates, including companies owned or controlled by their home governments. These entities targeted both private and public (usually federal offshore) minerals. Both operating and OFS companies benefited from the waves of diversified funding as the shale plays opened up. Much of the investment that flooded into specialized services and technologies in recent years was foreign sourced. A driver may have been post-2008 financial recession low interest rates that pushed investors into riskier businesses, with the domestic oil patch an attractive destination given U.S. standing as a relatively stable regime.

Constraints on external capital have been increasingly visible since the 2014 oil price collapse. Capital constraints will play a major role in post-2020 recovery. The tug-of-war of conflicting opinions about energy, environment and economics is, largely, about money and funding flows.

Resource, Resource Everywhere

Since the late-1990s, shale sources have come to comprise more than 60 percent of total U.S. domestic oil production and serve as the main engine of supply growth (Fig. 1.9, bottom). The bulk of shale output derives from major basins in the key states as indicated in Fig. 1.9. These are the Permian and Eagle Ford in Texas; Haynesville in northeast Texas-northwest Louisiana; Marcellus and Utica in Pennsylvania, Ohio and West Virginia. The Williston in Montana also produces natural gas (see Fig. 1.3). Texas alone accounts for 24 percent of total U.S. supply while Pennsylvania contributes 17. New Mexico and Wyoming are the main sources for CBM production (San Juan, Powder River). Wyoming and Utah constitute the bulk of "Rockies" supply, a much-diminished source, and Alaska rounds out domestic onshore inventory (Fig. 1.10).

The extent of drilling to test other onshore basins and plays beyond the majors—Permian, Eagle Ford Haynesville and Marcellus—cannot be underestimated. The flood of external funding since the early 2000s enabled companies to cast wide nets in the search for the next emerging shale plays. At the time of writing, the four basins remain the main sources for light, sweet "black" oil, condensates, natural gas plant liquids and

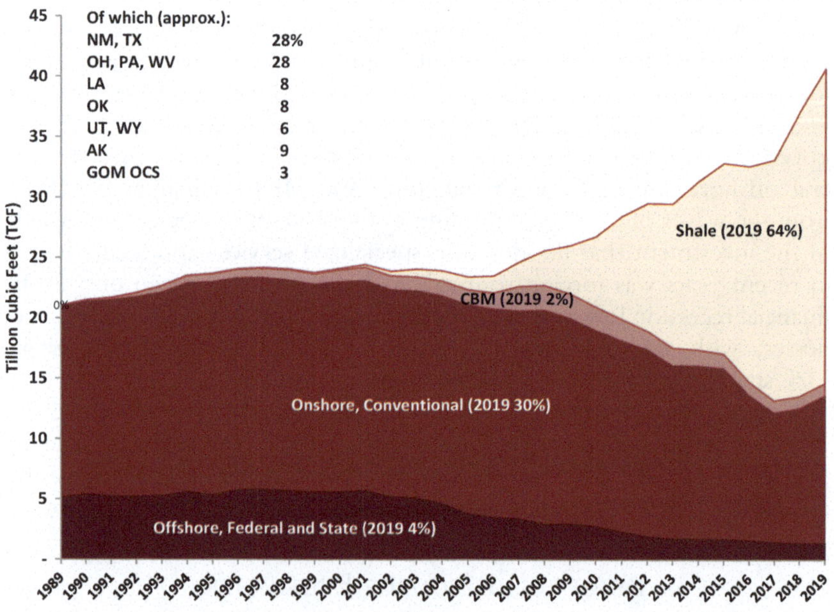

Fig. 1.9 Major natural gas gross withdrawals sources in the United States by type. (Sources: EIA; author estimates for 2019 based on state data and proprietary drilling and production information)

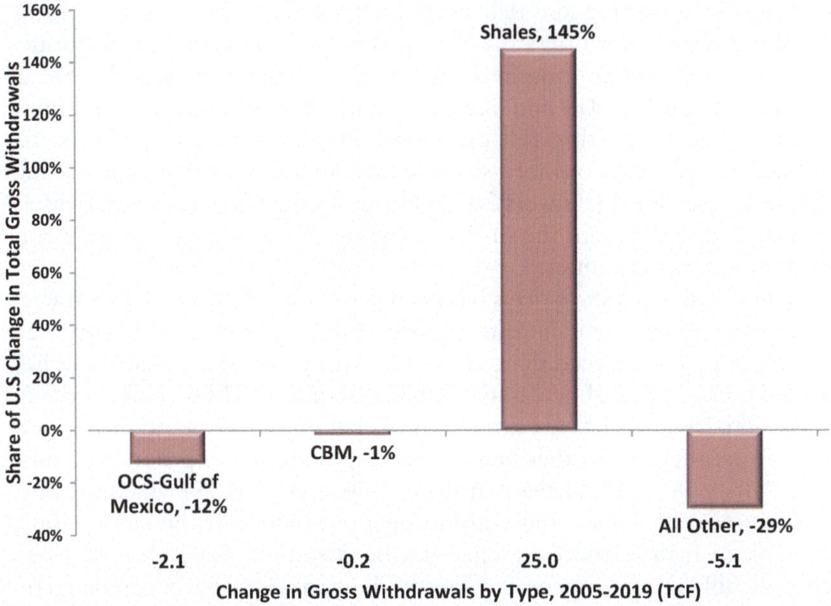

Fig. 1.10 The 2005–2019 shares of change in gross withdrawals by type. (Sources: EIA; author estimates for 2019 based on state data and proprietary drilling and production information)

methane. With lower commodity prices, other notable unconventional plays have struggled to sustain investment. These include the dry gas portions of Louisiana-Texas Haynesville, an early "shale rush"; Fayetteville (Arkansas, also dry gas) and new entrants like Oklahoma's "SCOOP" (South Central Oklahoma Oil Province) and "STACK" (Sooner Trend, Anadarko, Canadian and Kingfisher counties) plays in the venerable and huge Anadarko Basin, once a mainstay of mid-continent onshore production.

Against onshore gains in the major shale basins and plays, the offshore Gulf of Mexico (GOM) has paled in comparison. U.S. natural gas supply has shifted away from older, declining, shallow water production to the Outer Continental Shelf, or OCS, also a federal government domain and now the prime location for offshore lease blocks. Risk, cost and SSHE (safety, security, health and environment) effects, the last a hangover from the April 2010 Macondo spill, are largely to blame along with the difficulty of capturing and delivering methane from deeper water blocks. Offshore deep water offers the lure of very large hydrocarbon accumulations that can sustain long-lived, legacy oil production assets. Before oil market ructions in 2019 and onset of Covid-19, cost reductions and innovations were supporting full cycle returns for deep water projects that seemed on par with onshore shale. Expectations were that capex would return to the GOM (Flowers 2019) but prolonged effects from Covid-19 and deep dislocation in the offshore drilling businesses have created substantial new uncertainties.

The bias toward shale plays has been pronounced. Shale plays attracted external funding from the outset, in particular private equity, corporate bonds and bank-sourced debt associated with young, well-placed publicly traded companies and new initial public offerings or IPOs. This is because shale, in particular, has the attraction of enabling investors to avoid, or at least think they avoid, that bane of the exploration and production business, "dry hole cost". Shales constitute "resource plays" in which the original source rock underlying conventional production is the target. But if the risk of hydrocarbon presence has been settled, shale plays still bear considerable uncertainty with respect to how much resource can be recovered at what cost and price. These uncertainties flow into huge and ongoing capital commitments that companies and their backers must be able to bear.

Elsewhere in North America (NAM, Fig. 1.11), Canada and Mexico face distinct challenges. Canada still provides about 10 percent of U.S. total dry gas supply. Natural gas production has been declining in the Western Canada Sedimentary Basin, or WCSB, long an important source of gas supply for Canadian customers and the Lower 48 states.[22] WCSB conventional field declines were a dominant theme underlying "re-plumbing" of the main, TransCanada trunkline (Canadian Mainline) that delivers gas eastbound from the Alberta Basin and Foothills and across the U.S. border. A portion of the underutilized system was proposed for conversion to carry oil from Canada's oil sands operations, helping those producers to unlock market access for their commodity. Public opposition to the Energy East and Eastern Mainline projects resulted in those applications being terminated.[23] Although shale gas production is growing, severe bottlenecks exist for Canadian shale producers. The Montney and Horn River in the far north of Alberta Province, the two basins in the forefront of Canadian shale activity, will require much in enabling infrastructure if they

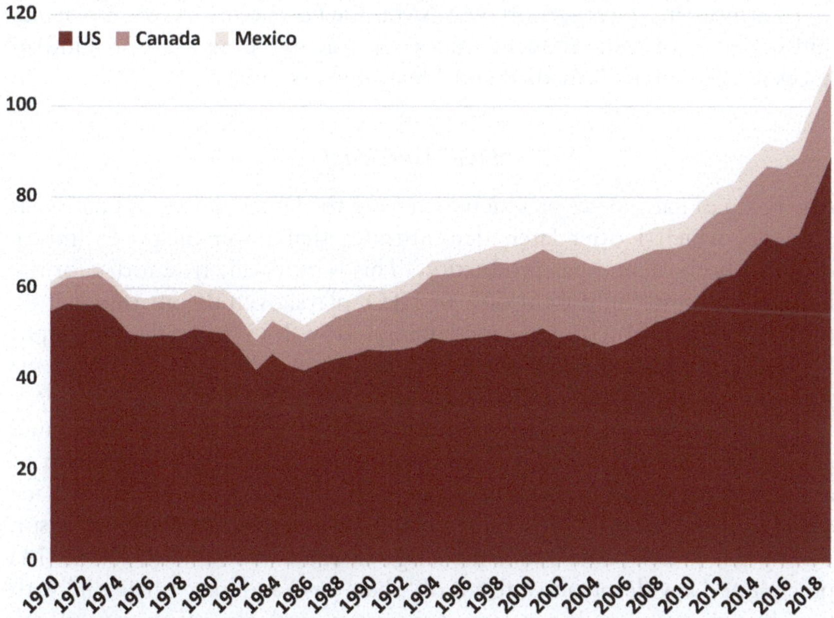

Fig. 1.11 North America natural gas production. (Source: BP Annual Statistical Review of Energy)

are to be fully developed. They also are being positioned for LNG export destinations (see Chap. 4 and later in this chapter).

Meanwhile, Mexico's oil and gas production has foundered amid near collapse of that country's major asset, the Cantarell complex offshore Mexico's Yucatan (Bay of Campeche), and uncertainty about Mexico's upstream regime (see Appendix to book). In the early 1990s, some believed that, with reforms and diligent investment, Mexico could grow its natural gas production such that it could export into the Lower 48.[24] Mexico's national oil company Pemex tested onshore tight rock basins (principally Chicontopec and Burgos), using service contracts to tap into international expertise, but with mixed results. Low natural gas prices, security issues in northern Mexico and other impediments have limited industry interest in building shale and other unconventional production capacity.

I say more in a later section on NAM trade flows but U.S. gas is playing, and will play for some time, an important role in curing locational imbalances in the eastern Canadian and Mexican gas systems.

"Free" Gas. Yay!

Any recap of natural gas production among the largest states and nation as a whole, which I offer later, demonstrates that lower oil prices induce drops in both oil and gas production. This is especially true today for the lightest, tightest "light tight oil", or LTO, plays given the intrinsic nature of the resource. Much of the incremental growth in domestic gas output comes from the gassiest, highest GOR locations. *In effect, the lowest net present value production streams have outsized effects on natural gas supply.*

I illustrate the importance of incremental production from associated gas yields relative to domestic consumption in Fig. 1.12. The wealth of associated gas supply is a byproduct of the hunt for liquids, primarily black oil and, in the most recent years, mainly in the enormous Permian Basin. Falling gas prices (2007) and the surge in crude oil value (2009–2014) precipitated a widespread shift out of "shale gas" and into "shale oil" with liquids rich acreage dominating new capex and abundant natural gas byproduct. We will see this demonstrated in the producer benchmark data. Lower oil prices (since 2014) induced companies to hone those portfolios. But while getting "oilier" was the goal, the result has been more gas output. The "typology" of shale plays exerts an over-sized effect. Solution gas drive reservoirs serve as enormous "engines" to accelerate production of hydrocarbons as drilling and hydraulic fracturing release pressures inducing gases to come out of solution. Over time, gas-oil ratios (GORs) can increase as remaining reservoir pressure moves the smaller NGLs and methane molecules more easily. Rules among state oil and gas regulators vary a bit when it comes to determining GORs. EIA classifies natural gas wells as those exceeding 6000 cubic feet per barrel (EIA 2017).

I note that as we approached publication, EIA data for year-end 2019 oil and gas reserves was not yet available, but I expect these patterns to hold for some time. The initial growth in NAG production from 2000 reflects the pursuit of shale gas opportunities. From 2011, the rapidly developing wedge of AG production and flatter output from nonassociated gas sources are outcomes of the preference for oil and liquids rich locations for upstream economics "uplift" (see Chap. 3). The growing surplus in supply is mainly from AG output and has been driving the

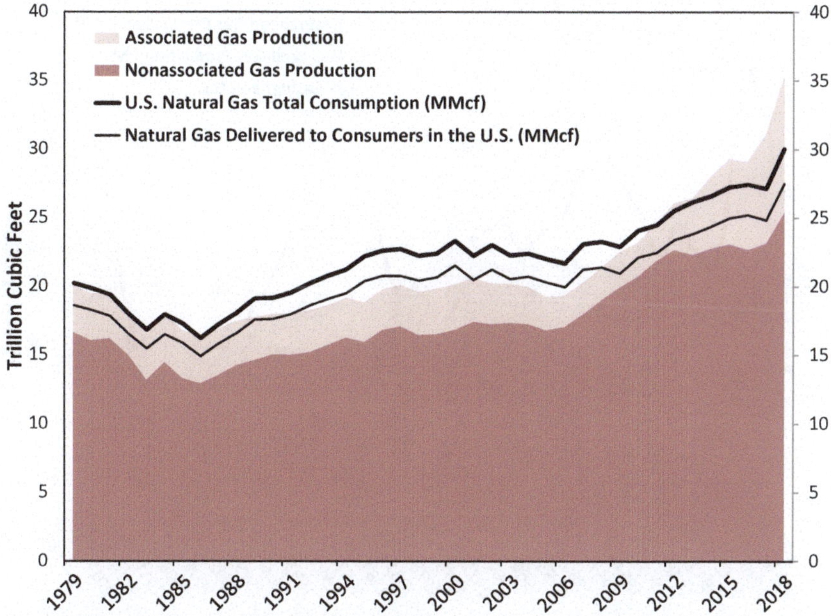

Fig. 1.12 Associated and nonassociated U.S. natural gas production. (Source: EIA with author calculations and estimates)

commercialization strategies detailed in this book, in particular petrochemicals (Chap. 3) and LNG exports (Chap. 4). NAG production grew 2018, mainly a result of drilling in gassier locations such as the Haynesville.

Within these broad national trends are distinct winners and losers among the large producing states, across basins and plays and across companies. Texas, the largest contributor to national gas supply with 24 percent of output, logged roughly 21 percent of the 2005–2019 gains depicted in Fig. 1.10. Texas also reflects, in fact is, the big story in the move away from gas-directed investment and drilling and toward oilier, liquids rich portfolios with gas as an abundant AG byproduct. Even more, Texas data acutely capture the long slog from the 1970s peak until the 2005 recovery described earlier (Fig. 1.13). The Texas Railroad Commission, the state's oil and gas regulator, reports gas production from natural gas wells generally classified as those wells producing 100,000 cf./bbl (cubic feet per barrel; EIA classifies gas wells as those with gas-oil

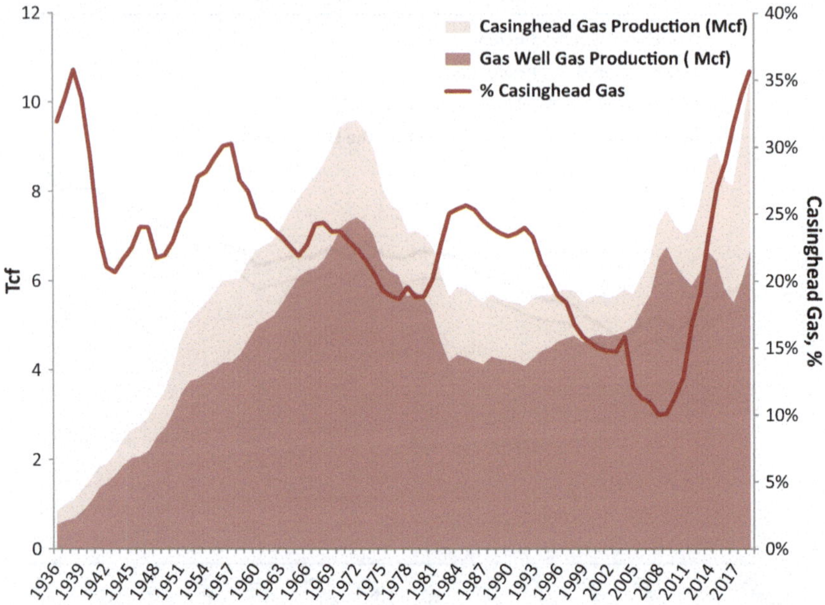

Fig. 1.13 Texas natural gas production by source. (Source: Texas Railroad Commission, author calculations and depiction)

ratios or GORs of 6000 cf./bbl). Casinghead gas, produced with crude oil (dissolved and/or associated), in Texas has grown 440 percent since 2005, matching Texas oil production growth of 434 percent.

Black oil is scarce in the Appalachian region, but portions are strong in NGLs. Activity shifted accordingly. Ethane is the main target (or problem, depending upon one's viewpoint) and can be extracted in portions of the Marcellus-Utica complex (western Pennsylvania, West Virginia, eastern Ohio). Overall, as drilling and midstream expansions progressed, gross withdrawals of natural gas surged 3586 percent since 2005 in Pennsylvania, which accounts for 17 percent of U.S. supply. Pennsylvania commanded 44 percent of the national increase larger than Texas and a rival for top producer. Ohio clocked in with a nearly 2800 percent increase; and West Virginia with more than 700 percent (all using EIA data). Famously, Marcellus and Utica production continued to grow even as Appalachian producers have had to take occasional negative netbacks to Henry Hub, a condition that Texas producers later came to enjoy (refer to The Vagaries of Commodity Markets and Prices). Because of a lack of offtake and markets, producers in many parts of the region still must "reject" ethane (usually by leaving it in pipeline sales, if it constitutes a small enough percentage; see Chap. 3) rather than monetize it for additional value. In effect, *Marcellus producers have traded production growth for profitability*, a situation that spread to the Permian and has come to exemplify the broader condition in the U.S. domestic upstream business. Development of ethane export capacity in Pennsylvania (Marcus Hook) and the Gulf Coast, the latter supported by reversals of large gas pipelines to provide transportation access to the huge Gulf Coast downstream complex, is helping to soak up ethane and other NGLs (refer to Chap. 3 for detail).

Gross withdrawals from Oklahoma's light tight oil and liquids plays increased by 80% and that state contributes 8 percent of U.S. production. In North Dakota, natural gas gross withdrawals increased more than 1400 percent since 2005 as Williston basin (Bakken and Three Forks) oil drilling escalated. North Dakota only constitutes 2 percent of U.S. supply and so is excluded it from Fig. 1.9 (remoteness, lack of pipelines and relative lack of natural gas resource in the Williston can be deduced from Fig. 1.3—the Williston is denoted by oil accumulations north of Powder River).

In all of this, losers have been those states and locations that primarily contain conventional oil and gas fields, and are thus on the wrong side of the current, shale archetype or where producers lacked possibilities for value added from NGLs. For instance, from 2005 to 2012, natural gas production in North Louisiana, dominated by the huge Haynesville basin, grew by 375 percent and then declined by 43 percent as the Louisiana portion of the Haynesville, without liquids to attract, fell out of favor. Drilling results reversed the pattern with production doubling. Companies deployed larger scale well completions in order to improve unit costs, making "H'ville" a prime example of what many expect to see in technology gains for shale plays. Production from South Louisiana, which had been a major source of gas supply, collapsed during the 1990s bubble and never recovered. That part of the state is characterized by conventional fields, with early unconventional pursuits in the Austin Chalk; efforts to prove up the Tuscaloosa Marine shale play, which gained much attention, never succeeded.

In Wyoming, a large supplier of gas during crucial periods in times past, production has fallen 14 percent since 2005. NGLs occurring with oil and condensates in the Powder River Basin helped to dampen somewhat declines from the huge, deep, challenging Rockies Overthrust fields commercialized during the 1970s. In one of the ultimate ironies of disruption and "re-plumbing", aggressive Marcellus output forced abandonments and reversals of major pipelines and pipeline projects that were to feed Rockies gas to Midwest and Northeast markets and provide relief for producers. Rockies producers suffered low and negative netbacks long before shale gas players. New Mexico also has been an important contributor of natural gas supply at crucial times. The wave of tax policy–encouraged CBM investment in the San Juan basin (see Appendix) was one of the early unconventional gas pursuits. New Mexico production has dropped 8 percent since 2005, its portion of Permian Basin supply being insufficient to cover losses elsewhere.

"Ten Cents and a Bowl of Chili"[25]

U.S. domestic producers, more than any other cluster in the global oil and gas businesses, have demonstrated a great ability to deploy the technology pathway tool-kit through long periods of adverse business conditions. The phenomenal success of the U.S. shale plays influenced how people think about the future of oil and gas resources and businesses, the bigger picture of supply-demand balances and trade and even U.S. international relations and foreign policy. The great puzzle for many outside observers has been: *why can't U.S. shale players make money*? This is a crucial question for our times. It is much more difficult to challenge strong, profitable industries than financially weak ones.[26] The pushback against hydrocarbons, as I summarized earlier, is much less effective when business conditions are robust, share valuations are high and investors are satisfied.

In fact, making money in the oil and gas businesses has always been tough, and it will ever be thus. An important lesson from the past 20 years is that many old lessons are still valid.

The oil wars of the early 1900s provided a classic case of capital destruction, in those days courtesy of uncoordinated production from common pools. My title above reflects that Texas experience—a time when the cost of a standard meal exceeded what producers were selling. Famously, the Texas Railroad Commission eventually pro-rationed production after some very rough politicking and only after then Governor Ross Sterling deployed the Texas National Guard in 1931 to save unwieldy East Texas producers from themselves. For a time, of course, the Commission was de facto price setter; pro-rationing later provided a template for OPEC to borrow. The past returned to haunt during debates in 2020 about whether, in light of the twin effects of oil market share battles and pandemic, the Texas Railroad Commission should limit producer output (Blackmon 2020). The prevailing view that "by allowing the free market to work, producers can determine for themselves what level of production is economical" (Christian 2020) puts the onus squarely on the nature of the beast and business models.

To a very large degree, the attributes that make the U.S. upstream patch so attractive contribute to imbalances (if providing windfalls for customers). In every era of U.S. oil and gas production and replenishment, producers have had to deal with "margin squeeze"—diminishing returns as revenues shrink with falling commodity prices. Since producers cannot influence price, the prime response is to increase volumes and reduce unit costs. The saga of shale plays, thus far, is no different in this regard. A relevant question is *whether intrinsic characteristics of shale plays exacerbate producer tendencies.*

Shale plays entail thousands of acres and dozens of pilot wells for proper evaluation; "off ramps" or exits can be difficult to achieve (Haskett and Brown 2005). The large amounts of land under lease, substantial up-front expense of pilot programs and midstream (gathering and transportation) field-to-market costs create large pools of sunk costs. These sunk cost pools exacerbate producer behavior to continue drilling and development even if pilot test results suggest otherwise. Indeed, producers might even "deliver volumes below marginal cost"[27] implying falling commodity prices along the way.

As I mentioned earlier, shale plays present a central upstream business model challenge in the need for constant spending on drilling to replace very fast declines common among these tight rock, low (nano) permeability plays and wells. By 2014, it was widely recognized that U.S. shale players were trading off profitability for growth—the more acreage that could be demonstrated to be productive, the greater the value that could be commanded at sale; the more reserves that could be booked, the greater the value of the underlying asset. There is the attendant problem of running an enterprise—sustaining production at a level, given price, that can keep the doors open. Investors and analysts have disparaged production growth strategies since the 2014 oil price collapse. In 2019, companies came under increased pressure to improve profitability and, especially, generate free cash flow, as oil and gas valuations plummeted against other assets, most notably technology stocks but increasingly, a sore point, stocks of emerging energy businesses that compete with legacy energy industries. By end of 2019, the hope was that producers could restore profitability through increased "discipline" on capital spending and industry consolidation with commodity prices responding in kind.[28]

"Frankelnomics"[29] in Theory

The early oil wars served as the backdrop for Howard Hotelling's theories on economic rents and questions about producer behavior and Paul Frankel's later thinking about the oil industry's inability to self-adjust.

Resource economics, as a school of thought, leans heavily toward thinking about economic rents. Hotelling (1931) defined rent as the difference between price of the exhaustible natural resource good and the marginal cost of capture plus opportunity cost (with prevailing price and technology). Assuming a prospector's idea has merit and drilling indicates hydrocarbons that can be extracted, the problem becomes how much to produce and over what time frame in order to optimally deplete the exhaustible endowment. Hotelling's treatment of opportunity cost was specific—a barrel of oil equivalent produced today is a barrel gone from production tomorrow. The expected result *should be* behavior in which an operator holds back production in order to preserve future Hotelling rents. The obvious corollary is that if the operator holds back enough production, the price of the resource good should appreciate. In theory, a monopolist, such as a sovereign-owned or sovereign-controlled enterprise, should have substantial advantage in this manner.

Hotelling's main concern was how best to avoid destruction of natural resource assets.[30] His idealized version of optimal depletion has largely fallen out of favor being rarely, if ever, applicable. However, he also thought that producers would be inclined to restrict production in order to increase prices and rents, especially as they neared ultimate depletion of the resource. In any case, he thought that *producers would not act in ways that pushed prices below a profit maximizing equilibrium.*

Paul Frankel, founder of Petroleum Economics Limited, authored perhaps the most influential publication, *Essentials of Petroleum*, to shine light on the oil and gas industry conundrum of adjustment (Frankel 1969; originally published in 1946). In a widely quoted observation he maintained that what "matters most" to the petroleum industry is its inability to "self-adjust", that is, to attain that Hotelling equilibrium. The lack of self-adjustment meant a "continuous crisis" with oil (raw feedstock and refined products) always in a state of surplus even though periodic or eventual (when the resource is finally exhausted) shortage was an "undertone" (p. 67 and 69).

Frankel associated the lack of self-adjustment with three features (p. 67). First was drilling, marked by high costs of exploration (capex) but low costs of exploitation (opex) thus fostering the inevitable scale up of volumes. Second was the "unwieldy" combination of fixed (demand) and variable cost in midstream and downstream segments, the field-to-market linkages. Third, in his time, was a pricing structure for oil, pre-OPEC (Organization of Petroleum Exporting Countries) that fostered "ups and downs which fail to bring relief from dearth or glut".[31]

For all of his concern about "dearth or glut" Frankel held a dim view of producer associations, like OPEC, as price managers, emphasizing the tendency for members to behave in ways that undermine cooperation (for a classic take on OPEC in this sense, see Rattner 1981). Rather than market organization, it was his observations on the business dynamic that constituted his main influence. Kemp (2016)[32] brought Frankel's complaint that "there is always too much or too little oil" into the 2014 oil price cycle by noting that: "Economists and policymakers are enthralled by the concept of equilibrium but experience as well as the theory of complex systems suggests the oil industry has never actually been in equilibrium. Oil markets are in a perpetual state of disequilibrium; at any given point they may be moving further away from equilibrium rather than towards it". Priddle (2014)[33] channeled Frankel on persistently low natural gas prices, observing that "factors on the supply side of that equation include the petroleum industry's long-observed tendency to neglect sunk costs and frequently to produce at less than full cost because of the typically low ratio of its operating costs to total costs" (p. 14). He elaborated (quoting Frankel directly): "Owing to the unorthodox character of crude production, the aggregate cost of achieving production is seldom borne in mind and, therefore, not always recovered" (p. 14 footnote as cited).

Most of *Essentials of Petroleum* was focused on midstream and downstream. Frankel viewed all hydrocarbon compounds as not only byproducts but also coproducts. Producers cannot achieve any single component without investment in the whole and the price of any individual product is subject to the market. These were not simply problems for oil refiners. Frankel had plenty to say about natural gas pipelines. Natural gas processing, fractionation and the ultimate yield of dry gas (methane) are part of the mix (Chap. 3). The inability to isolate costs associated with producing individual components creates price-taker conditions across the board, with supply-demand fundamentals shifting continuously.

England and Mittal (2014) noted that for Frankel, the transfers of products across linked business segments were "essential" for maximizing profit, reducing risk and creating stability in an inherently unstable system. In other words, value creation downstream of the wellhead is crucial for upstream attainment. In their view, the greater the ability of companies to participate across value chain segments, the better they will be able to survive and prosper.

In the persistent low natural gas/NGLs price environment, profits from gas production may continue to shift downstream to LNG and petrochemicals so long as markets exist for U.S. supply. Meanwhile, gas producers remain price takers with the Henry Hub index defining general market conditions and netbacks from HH to wellheads driving realized revenues and margins. Likewise, if oil producers face steep discounts to WTI, which sets the general market tone for oil, they effectively shift profits to refiners. Refiners are able to convert the discounted feedstock into products that, in many U.S. (and international) markets, correlate with Brent, a higher value oil index given the surplus of WTI quality crude in the U.S. mid-continent (see later section "Effect of Infrastructure Bottlenecks"). This "margin migration" (England and Mittal 2014, p. 11) could result in too much investment in some segments while undermining profitability elsewhere.

A first-order improvement for producers, therefore, is to achieve Henry Hub or WTI pricing if they are not already getting paid the index—that is, the netbacks to their particular production locations are less than the price index. Gluts of production trapped behind pipeline or other midstream bottlenecks and gaps have been the bane of producer existence in the shale plays. Any improvement in HH or WTI helps producers even with poor netbacks. Higher HH and WTI pricing can undermine LNG and petrochemical competitiveness, relative to global conditions. Vertically integrated companies are best able to capture variation in profitability across value chain segments and to adjust as margins cycle between upstream and downstream business segments—the classic "natural hedge". Non-integrated companies are left with building virtual integrated structures, "an interactive community of value chains". England and Mittal further described this community as a collaborative ecosystem that links "pure play" shale producers with myriad midstream and downstream partners and offtakers such that the created value is diffused across the marketplace

(p. 16). The level of cooperation among independent, specialist upstream companies required to create such a value ecosystem entails transactions costs that almost certainly exceed the direct benefits to any individual participant.

"Frankelnomics": In Action

U.S. domestic oil and gas producers have accomplished amazing feats along the oil and gas technology pathway, enabled by a large OFS segment and any number of attributes unique to the U.S. scene. Yet, "Frankelnomics" describes an industry that ignores its sunk costs, tends to produce below full cost and even deliver volumes below marginal cost, brings down its commodity price, must absorb expensive field-to-market obligations with output that incorporates numerous byproducts and coproducts and is always in disequilibrium. How should we analyze such an industry?

Beginning in 2009, colleagues and I undertook an effort to benchmark U.S. domestic producer operating and financial results.[34] Our goal was to build an understanding of domestic oil and gas business performance using financial reporting to the U.S. Securities and Exchange Commission (SEC). The Notes on Research Methodology section to this chapter provides details. In general, our main objective was to scrutinize performance on a "full cycle" basis, meaning inclusion of all capital expense associated with finding oil and gas (leasing and initial drilling to explore and evaluate reservoirs). Many observers advocate "half cycle" or even "quarter cycle" (only or mostly opex) assessments. These leave out the very large capital expenses associated with entry costs. However, in light of the propositions about behavior of producers and other industry segments with substantial sunk costs we felt the full cycle approach to be a more accurate analysis.[35]

We concluded our benchmarking with the 2018 reporting year. Due to M&A activity during 2019, and with continued consolidation, adding that year or subsequent years to our data would entail restating all prior years. As 2019 closed and business conditions deteriorated in 2020, many research houses suspended or ended their coverage of mid-size and smaller publicly traded domestic producers, in particular the shale "pure players" that had captured so many imaginations. Nevertheless, I will show that our ten years of data collection yields observations that demonstrate upstream fundamentals for the onshore domestic shale plays, allowing isolation of business model challenges from the larger context of market conditions. These fundamentals will apply regardless of where the industry pursues shale plays, with locational differences mainly deviations from the U.S. attributes I have identified.

Our sample of 16 companies consists of independent producers with prominent positions in the dominant basins. This means considerable exposure to the Permian, with other basins (Eagle Ford, Haynesville and Bakken) represented. By the end of our ten-year data collection, Marcellus assets are held only by the gassiest members of our club. We interacted with and compared our work with several organizations. We also regularly sought reactions and feedback from industry peer reviewers.

Why take this approach? Plenty of research houses evaluate exploration and production costs in basins and plays of interests. That information provides baselines for entry and operation. All companies are affected by changes in operating conditions across basins and drilling locations, mainly shifts in OFS day rates and other logistics expenses. They also all face changes in costs for business inputs that are driven by overall economic conditions in the United States or globally (interest rates, tax policies, including those among producing states, trends in costs of materials etc.). Labor costs will fluctuate with demand for the skills needed by domestic producers and by competing career opportunities in a healthy economy. As these influences migrate around the industry, so do new practices, shifts in technical approaches, new technology and new information. Companies vary considerably in management style and their essential land portfolios; land positions are an important determining element in oil and gas overall and shale plays in particular. Thus, while economics across basins may seem compelling, the ultimate measure of how demanding and sustainable a business might be is how well, or not, companies are able to act upon the available opportunities and soundness of strategies and managements.

There is the added consideration of entry and exit. Considerable debate surrounds how best to account for capital costs that ultimately become sunk. Taking a full cycle approach necessarily incorporates the initial capital expenditure, which is extremely lumpy. As stated in the Notes on Research Methodology, we used a typical, three-year moving average to evaluate acquisitions and divestitures and associated changes to booked reserves, the underlying inventory for the industry. We also used three-year moving averages for these substantial capital expenditures, which affect depreciation and amortization and thus operating cash flow and so are important to understand.

To re-phrase my initial question: *Why can't best in class U.S. domestic companies, those that have become the pure players that analysts and investors prefer, make money*? By "making money" I mean the ability to generate sufficient cash flow from operations to pay dividends, for those companies in our sample that pay them, as well as to cover annual capital expense obligations. Without sufficient cash flow to support these burdens, companies must rely on external funding sources, a critical point and one that I elaborate upon in later sections. In building our cash flow waterfalls, we attempted to isolate and incorporate revenues and costs that were associated with midstream and other commitments. These are essential to a company's ability to market its production as incorporated in "Frankelnomics" and thus central to our analytical approach.

In the consolidated cash flow waterfall for the full ten years of results, midstream-related sales and expenses are reflected in the "Production and Marketing Revenues" stack, "Production Costs" (for companies that include their midstream commitments in that category) and the "General, Administrative and Marketing" cost bucket. From our calculated revenues and costs we compute a "Net Income" for comparison with "Reported Net Income" in company filings. The "Difference in Net Income" patterned bar, *about $10/BOE*, is, we believe, a primary indicator of the financial and operating challenges for our sample companies and the larger population. In effect, companies are not achieving the net income we expect or model, based on business structure, revenues and costs. We then take the company's Reported Net Income and add back "Depletion, Depreciation and Amortization" and "Other Cash Flow Adjustments" to reach the commonly reported "Cash Flow from Operations" against which we can balance annual "Capex". For the entire ten years, on a weighted BOE basis, our cluster of companies spent *more than $5/BOE* beyond what they reported in operating cash flow. Across millions of BOEs, the combined lower net income and capex in excess of cash flow translates into quite a pull on external capital sources (Fig. 1.14).

A great deal more is going on, of course, that we also can identify in explaining performance. Volumes produced should meet, hopefully, expectations given the amount of capital expenditure. If they do not, capital is destroyed. The realized price for company production streams, including company strategies and outcomes for hedging to manage price risk, should be close to the main commodity price indexes. If not, then revenues will not exceed costs and the company incurs losses. Price fluctuations matter in any case and explain much about the ten-year snapshot. A company's cost management for its businesses is a crucial factor. Our sample reflects all of the diversity in the business—larger and smaller

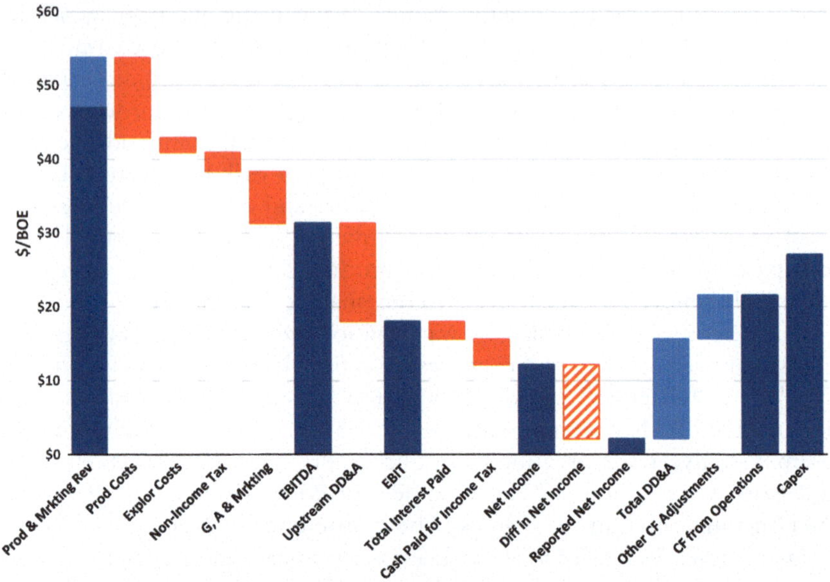

Fig. 1.14 Consolidated annual cash flow waterfall, all companies, all years 2009–2018. (Source: Based on data collection and analysis by the author and others using U.S. Securities and Exchange Commission annual financial reports for 16 companies. Hereafter sourced as "2009–2018 producer benchmarking". See Notes on Research Methodology: Producer Benchmarking)

companies, oilier and gassier ones, companies that have greater field-to-market bottlenecks to contend with and those that do not. "Location" is a dominant theme. All of our companies, like the industry overall, have worked and spent heavily to "high grade" their land and drilling portfolios. This means the best acreage in terms of hydrocarbon potential and recovery rates for producing wells and the most liquids rich, preferably black oil rich, land under lease. The vagaries of the business extend from drilling wells that are not equal in performance (but cost the same to drill), to drilling into gassier locations than originally thought, to the rising GORs already mentioned, to logistics. The distances in shale basins, especially west of the Mississippi, place onerous demands on people and equipment to service and supply drilling locations. Companies have had to spend heavily to bolster their supply chains and design the most efficient, low-cost logistical management for operations. These and other observations are dealt with in the following sections.

Considerable debate surrounds the use of earnings before interest, taxes, depreciation (and depletion) and amortization (EBITDA). It has become widely relied upon as a screening metric, the idea being that all of the expense items beyond capital and operating expenses can vary considerably across companies, even within the same industry and so EBITDA is a fairer lens through which to evaluate performance. One of the main shortcomings in use of EBITDA is to project cash flow. EBITDA is a particularly poor base from which to evaluate cash flow, as the following three charts illustrate. Especially when "cash is king" for investors, capital-intensive businesses in commoditized industries can struggle to generate sufficient cash flow to pay dividends and reinvest in core businesses. Commodity price cycles tend to drive up costs faster than revenues as lags prevail across markets (Fig. 1.15, using total costs—capex plus opex). A component of operating cash flow is DD&A (depreciation, depletion and amortization), credits that are returned in conformance with accounting practices. Figure 1.16 highlights the variability of EBITDA relative to operating cash flow across the ten years of analysis. It also illustrates the extent to which DD&A can dominate operating cash flow and capex, using the percentage component of DD&A in each, during times of stress, in this case the years 2015–2017 when oil prices were unfavorable. From our monitoring of quarterly reports, the proportion of DD&A in cash flow and capex rose again in 2019 to 90–100 percent, suggesting that, if our benchmarking had continued 2019 would mimic previous years. Finally, I highlight the problem of lack of cash for reinvestment with Fig. 1.17 in which I net capex from operating cash flow. Other analysts and researchers have observed and commented on this measure of cash flow to capex as a gauge of U.S. upstream performance.

Across a much larger and more varied population of companies under coverage (50 as of the last quarter, 2019), Bernstein Research has profiled quarterly cash flow and capex patterns that provide a useful backdrop to our own analysis.[36] From the beginning of 2004 through 2019, the Bernstein sample of companies outspent their operating cash flow in 48 of the 64 reporting periods. The reality is worse considering that financial performance is not equally distributed among the 50 or so companies. Because our sample is smaller and dominated by the larger shale pure players, overall performance is actually better than the larger Bernstein group, which also includes a handful of Canadian companies (including oil sands

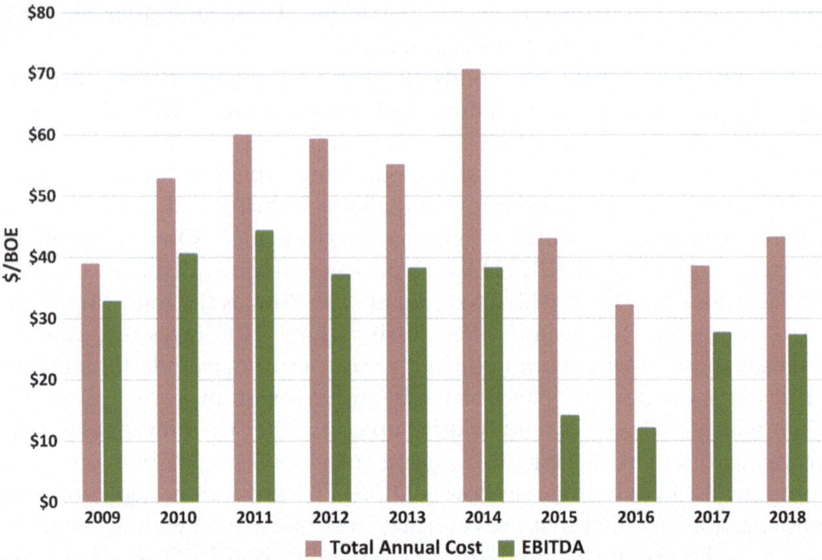

Fig. 1.15 Total annual costs and EBITDA by year. (Source: Based on 2009–2018 producer benchmarking. Costs and EBITDA are as stated by companies)

and refining). The quarters and, in our case, years of negative cash flow to capex included times when commodity prices were more generous. As usual, price attracts investment, but costs also are higher. The cash flow to capex relationships parallels the surge in capex from 2010 as companies spent heavily to high-grade acreage positions in order to improve oil and other liquids production and the loss of revenue during 2014–2016 as the oil price collapse played out.[37]

Much has been written and said in the public domain about the treadmill of shale plays and the continuous spending by companies to sustain their businesses. Companies tend to drill their best locations first, moving into less attractive targets over time at the same (or even higher) costs but with mediocre outcomes (Zeller 2014). This is true of the oil and gas upstream business in general—opex rises as assets mature; drilling costs increase on a unit basis as the industry pursues less attractive targets and with lower production volumes. Again, the nature of shale plays with their accelerated decline curves heightens what is already the bane of industry

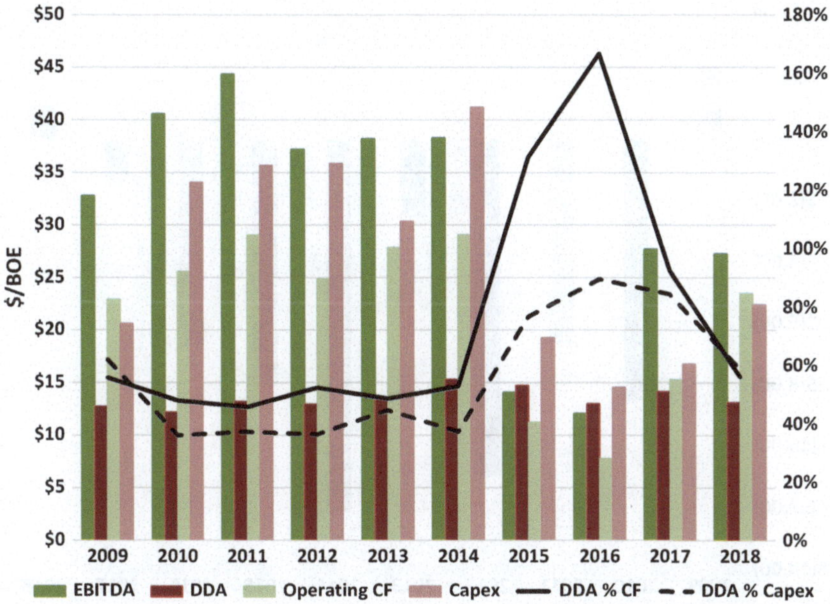

Fig. 1.16 Costs, EBITDA and cash flow by year. (Source: Based on 2009–2018 producer benchmarking)

existence. The treadmill effect is evident in continuous outlays of capex, largely funded by accumulated depreciation and external capital.[38]

With respect to cost trends, Fig. 1.18 provides an indication of variability by highlighting the lowest-, average- and highest-cost producer from among our sample, for each year. As before, we computed costs on a full cycle basis and used the three-year moving averages for capex (land acquisition and major facilities plus drilling) and reserve bookings to determine finding and development, F&D, costs per BOE. F&D costs include the net of acquisitions and divestitures and other adjustments. I show the results using weighted barrel of oil equivalent for ease of comparison across different corporate production slates. In this depiction, the surge in capex to accumulate oil and liquids rich acreage stands out for the years 2013–2015. Following the collapse of oil prices in 2014, companies sold off and wrote down the value of booked reserves, thus the negative F&D outcomes for 2015–2017. Figure 1.18 also shows the stubbornness of costs; the average producer each year does not vary much in total cost.

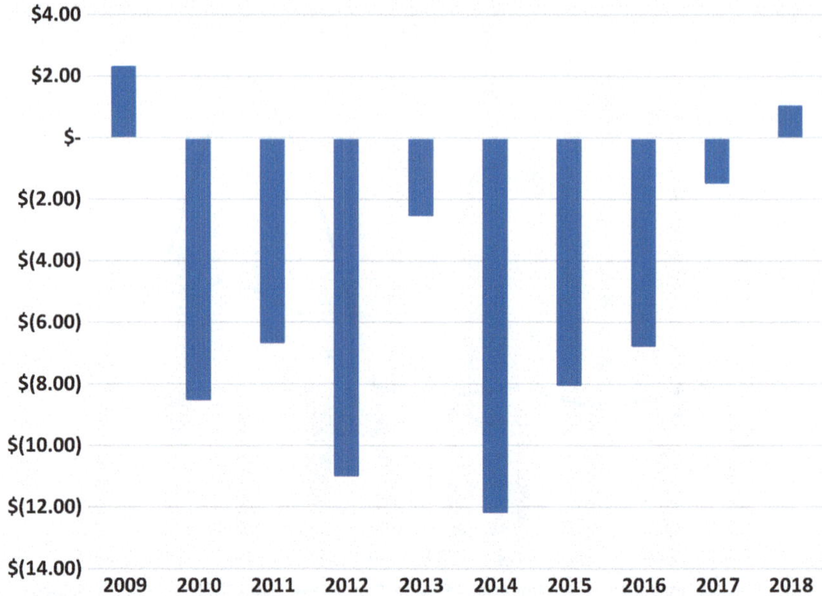

Fig. 1.17 Cash flow minus capex by year. (Source: Based on 2009–2018 producer benchmarking)

By 2018, there is a decided reduction in capex with spending even lower than during the oil price collapse as companies worked to respond to investor pressures. As 2019 reached a close, and 2020 opened, the pace of write-downs and divestitures accelerated beyond what we captured thus far. I include oil prices as data labels above the high-cost producer columns. Clearly, higher cost producers have faced the toughest business conditions, no matter how much moral support they receive for acquisitions and other strategic moves. As explained below the lowest-cost producers are gassier. As I discuss later, they are also less profitable. In any one year, of course, the positions change quite a bit. Companies winning confidence in a good year can undertake expensive acquisitions and/or drilling programs which, if they don't pay off, undermine confidence and burden the enterprise.

To the crux of the matter—producers' dependence upon outside capital—the difficulty of generating sufficient cash flow from operations to support capital spending means that dependence on outside funding grew

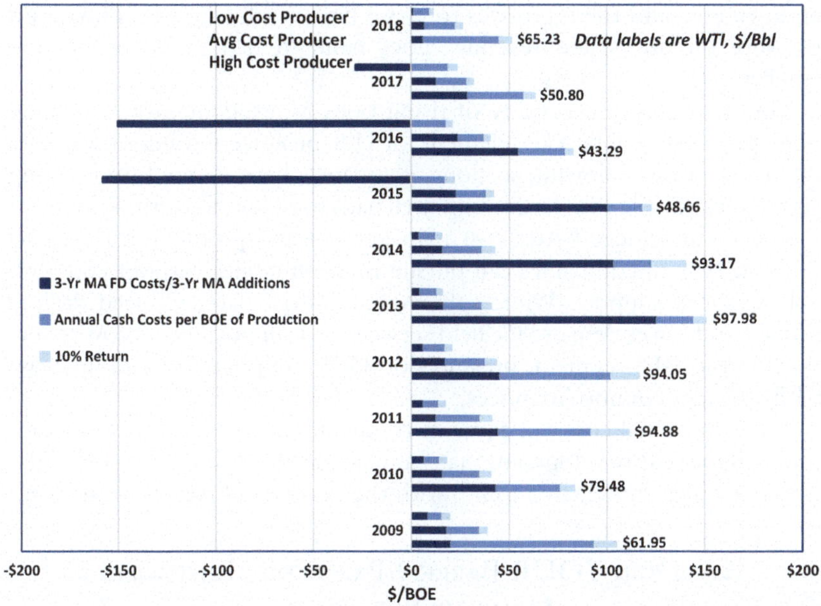

Fig. 1.18 Distribution of low-, average, high-cost producers by year. (Source: Based on 2009–2018 producer benchmarking)

commensurately. One estimate was that more than 80 percent of U.S. oil and gas production growth between 2008 and 2018 was a result of outside capital infusions (Kimmeridge Energy Management review of 90 companies as reported by Denning 2019a, b). The compound annual growth rate for production without outside help was 2.7 percent; with external funding it was 10.2 percent.

Pushed by their backers, U.S. companies have worked to keep spending in line with cash flow in the face of price challenges and reduce the large contribution of depreciation to cash flow funded spending. The harsh reality noted by Hotelling, Frankel and every keen observer since remains the central question: what is the rationale for supply coordination and could it ever be achieved (legally)? I described earlier the 2020 debates on pro-rationing in Texas. Even if regulatory authority were clear, political pressure, including resistance within the industry, encumbers ideas about supply coordination. Especially given the vagaries of shale resource endowments and the incentives to chase higher-value liquids, downward pressure on prices and revenues goes hand in hand with production profiles.

Given the historical reality of rising opex as assets mature, managing operating costs will be a key element for U.S. producers going forward. As discussed in the following sections, companies have focused on building economies of scale with large multi-well pads to reduce footprints, improve logistics and achieve better cost management and production results all around. Not all companies can pursue these strategies without considerable financial support. While softer commodity prices, reduced drilling activity and lower demand for field services and support forces cost reductions in the OFS segment, pressures on OFS components build up again with stronger commodity prices.

Shifts in capital cost will come as companies pursue larger, more complex drilling and development plans and acquisitions. Industry consolidation is a widely anticipated trend, with the Permian of particular interest.

What's in YOUR Barrel? Part One: Re-tooling Company Portfolios

The most important "innovation" for improving upstream margins has been the re-tooling of company portfolios. With a persistently low HH index, the diminishing appeal of gassier portions of basins and profound shift into more liquids rich and oily acreage fostered the surge in LTO and associated gas production and spurred the downstream renaissance detailed in Chap. 3. In that chapter, Part Two of the barrel composition story elaborates on petrochemical investment trends, one of the more interesting and possibly profound developments in recent years.

As commodity and market conditions changed dramatically from the early 2000s, producers responded in tandem. Along with the switch in capital spending to liquids rich acreage, producers pursued "core of core" positioning to increase holdings in "sweet spots" where drilling results and resource recovery often are best, a logical tactic given the very large capital spending commitments required.

When black oil is not present, producers have tried to derive as much value as possible from NGLs. These efforts have been heavily constrained by midstream infrastructure bottlenecks and downstream capacity for petrochemicals. Producers often face eroding NGLs prices, a result of abundant supply. As shown in Chap. 3, some NGLs remain attractive options relative to methane (see Chap. 3, Fig. 3.8). The enormous build-out of U.S. NGLs-based petrochemical capacity pits those abundant intermediate products against naphtha- or gasoil-fed output in the global marketplace. For producers, shifts in relative prices for oil, NGLs and methane feedstock (methane also is an important raw material for refining and petrochemical facilities; see Appendix for value chain flows) can mean swings in margins and profitability and shifts in competitive acreage positions.

LTO production is another story. The quality range of the U.S. crude production slate extends from light sweet crude with API (American Petroleum Institute) gravities of about 30 to 45 degrees to high API gravity condensates that can test above 60.[39] U.S. refineries had only recently expanded to accommodate large supplies of heavy crudes—including Mexico's Maya, Venezuela's extra heavy crude from the Orinoco Belt and Canada's oil sands. The widespread belief was that the future of refining feedstocks would entail lower API gravity crudes. The abundance of LTO production upended that paradigm and encouraged an influx of LTO production handling responses. LTO producers are able to move production using liquids transportation modes, including trucks serving tank batteries that store lease production and rail cars, which dominated trade reports for several years because of several high-profile safety incidents.[40] Natural gas requires pipeline transport to exit production from leases.

What did, and does, all of this mean for the portfolios of domestic producers? On the whole, domestic producers in our benchmark sample spent heavily to re-orient acreage portfolios to liquids. For 2014, when most of the repositioning took place, our group of 16 companies spent nearly $95 billion in total annual capex (Fig. 1.19). Companies spent about one-third of that on proved and unproved property acquisitions, with the rest devoted to drilling to prove up and hold acreage. Industry-wide spending exceeded our total by an estimated three times (based on comments from equity analysts and investment bank research staffs). For instance, in their proprietary reporting, Bernstein Research estimated total capex in 2014 of $203 billion for their coverage of 56 companies, largely driven by portfolio shifts to dispose of dry gas acreage and/or acquire oil and liquids rich positions. Given that this spending was on the cusp of the oil price collapse in 2014, investor hindsight kicked in especially given the subsequent (if temporary) erosion of asset values.[41]

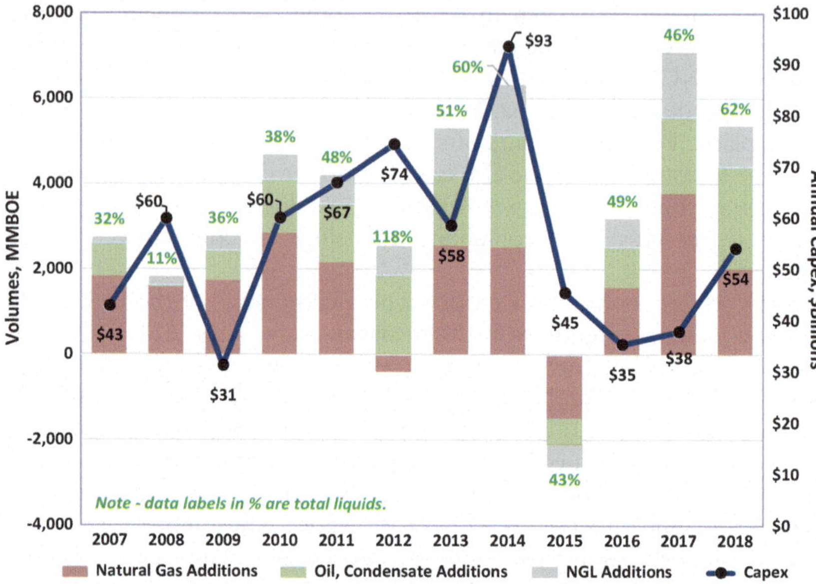

Fig. 1.19 U.S. all source additions (net of revisions) and capex by year. (Source: Based on 2009–2018 producer benchmarking. Note that annual capex includes spending for all sources [proved and unproved property acquisitions, exploration and development])

The upshot for our benchmark group of producers has been a decline in natural gas production and increasing oil and NGLs output, using weighted, barrel of oil equivalent conversions (Fig. 1.20). Importantly, our sample of companies includes those who had financial resources, borrowing capacity, market capitalization and/or sufficient private equity investor backing to fund these expensive portfolio shifts. While the share of natural gas production declined for our benchmark sample (and much of the domestic patch) total volumes have grown especially for liquids rich producers (see Fig. 1.24 later) and thus aggregate associated gas output. Operators that are less well positioned, especially those that retain gassier acreage (Appalachia and the gas windows of other major basins), have had no choice but to increase production volumes (with midstream field-to-market constraints) to compensate for lower per unit prices in terms of both market indexes and netbacks to production.

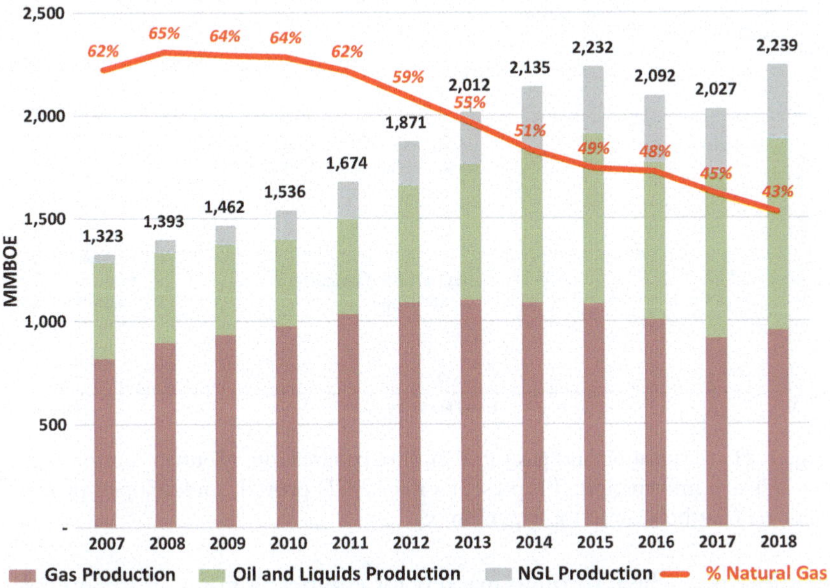

Fig. 1.20 Annual production slates. (Source: Based on 2009–2018 producer benchmarking)

We (Were) in the Money

Conceptual Basics

The shifts in land portfolios went hand in hand with availability of outside capital. Capital market responses coincided with an evolution in "learning" about shale plays. It is a long and complex, but vital, story for those wishing to understand better development of the U.S. shale plays. Two simple overview diagrams may help readers not steeped in the arcana of oil and gas business terminology, in particular in the shale era. Figure 1.21 illustrates a typical progression in value capture, with rewards highest in the earliest, riskiest, land acquisition, proof of concept stage with flipping to capture returns. These transactions are highly visible and effective investor magnets. As plays and projects are "de-risked" rewards (returns) diminish. Value is created through drilling to establish proven undeveloped production (PUDs, the "currency" of the oil and gas business). For ongoing operations, value is captured through sales of production and, as

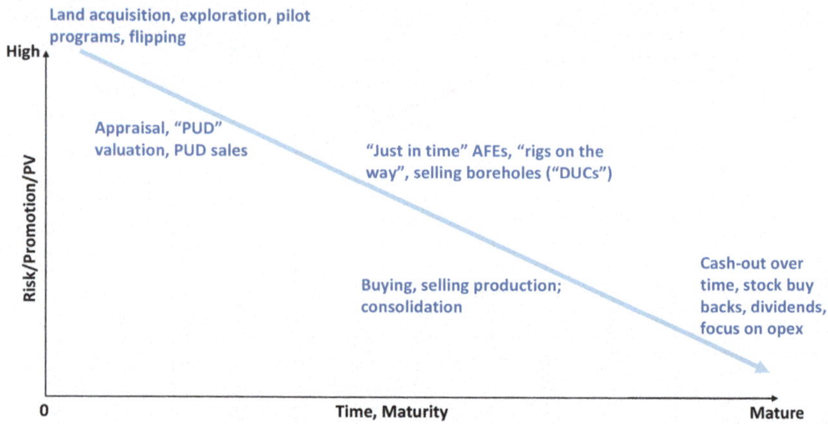

Fig. 1.21 Typical oil and gas value capture progression. (Source: Author, based on industry information. *PV* present value, *PUD* proved, undeveloped production, *AFE* authorization for expenditure)

maturity is reached, through markets for equities. A going upstream concern will have any number of value capture efforts underway, with varying risk weightings, in its portfolio. A conceptual shale learning curve is show in Fig. 1.22. Complexity of shale plays, variability in well performance, initial reliance upon (perhaps over-reliance upon) and later reduced importance of, "type curves" (used early on to estimate resources and recoveries)—all parallel the overall decline in value with maturity. I provide a context for actual maturity and time along with underlying commodity price dynamics using the oil price premium highlighted in Fig. 1.5. Were type curves, upon which so many investment decisions based, inflated? I offer thoughts from published accounts and other sources in the following paragraphs (and associated endnotes). As with any other investment opportunity, due diligence separates wheat from chaff. When opportunities become exciting—HH averaging above $6 and WTI at $100 or above—pressure to enter increases accordingly and due diligence can be tested.

Historical View

During the early 2000s, initial waves of leasing and pilot drilling to prove up concepts attracted investors and led to new company formations with successful IPOs that later fed the first round of acquisitions by the larger,

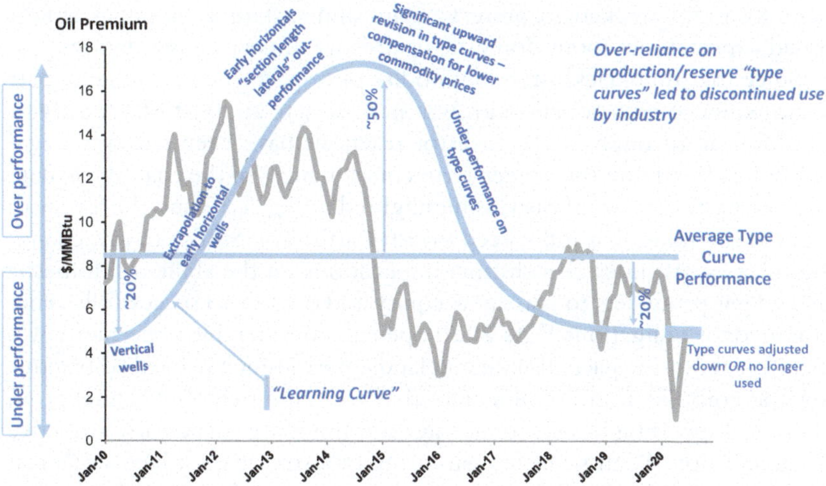

Fig. 1.22 Shale era learning curve. (Source: Author, based on industry information)

major integrated corporations during 2008–2011.[42] By 2010, some U.S. shale gas production leaders were sending signals that even in the best locations costs were too high to sustain their businesses with Henry Hub below $4 per MMBtu. These companies built early strategies to exit gassier locations in order to focus on oil and NGLs where they perceived returns to be better.[43] As the Henry Hub gas price index crashed through the psychologically important $3 price threshold during 2011–2012 the shift to oilier opportunities accelerated.[44] Following the 2014 oil price collapse, many fewer transactions were registered during the 2015–2016 timeframe for a variety of reasons but primarily large gaps between what asset owners felt the value of their holdings and companies were relative to willingness to pay (in industry parlance, the "bid-ask" spread). Many more bankruptcies occurred, given the financial challenges of the times and debt burdens and "junk" status of some debt issues that had permeated the industry. In 2016, the funding landscape shifted toward private equity, offered flexibility over public placements but with increasing engagement by private equity managers. With improving outlooks on oil prices, existing and new entrants and their backers "doubled down" and, in some cases, "tripled down" mainly on Permian assets.[45] Producers in liquids rich shale locations worked to preserve gains and sustain asset values amidst broad expectations about domestic upstream industry consolidation.

Since that time, lackluster commodity price performance, in large part a consequence of production growth necessary to support M&A activity, set the tone through 2019. Investor reactions have been strongly negative[46]; I elaborate on the longer-term consequences in the chapter closing. In large part, the lack of cash, as highlighted in Fig. 1.17 and the legacy of years of spending, has influenced investor attitudes. Suffice to say, changing investor attitudes bear distinct implications on the ability of domestic oil and gas producers to issue new equity and debt or to successfully renegotiate debt obligations.[47] As 2020 opened, considerable uncertainty was manifest about the pace, timing and landscape of much needed restructuring and consolidation.[48] Companies that are "land rich" but capital poor, a result of spending heavily for acreage positions, are particularly attractive for acquisition. With so little cash in the industry, many M&A deals rest on exchanges of stock. All-stock transactions are rarely attractive to investors and raise any number of issues, from questions about value to conflicts over roles of buyer and seller and how the enterprise is to be managed going forward (Rappaport and Sirower 1999).

Funding Entries and Exits

Through all of the waves of capital infusions and commodity cycles, a constant question was: ***how could producers remain so resilient with production growing almost without pause?*** Answer: external capital coupled with price risk-management practices that producers had adopted, in no small part, because financial backers required them. The prevailing style of hedged shale drilling and production in order to win or preserve support from capital markets prolonged the lag effects between drops in price and industry activity and output. With their cash flows sheltered companies responded to pressure from investors to perform on growth. They continued to drill and prove up production, both to hold private minerals leases and to attract potential buyers and support IPO strategies. They did so—reminder—even as their actions undermined their core commodity price signals.[49] Hedging has been a key part of oil and gas producer strategies almost since inception of commodity trading and its importance to sustaining activity has been well demonstrated in past. In the shale era, the role of hedging was heightened given the rapid escalation of activity and dependence upon capital markets. I will say more about hedging relative to performance of our benchmarked companies.

I have highlighted features of unconventional plays that have come to define the domestic industry and altered the onshore OFS businesses. Too often, even keen observers do not fully appreciate the interaction between key characteristics of these plays and financial and operating inputs and outcomes (see Allan 2011, for a good illustration using Marcellus experience).

Earlier, I have noted that companies and their backers absorb a great deal of expense for large land blocks, larger than what is typically optioned and/or leased for conventional exploration, and expensive pilot drilling programs to prove up acreage. I also noted the dilemmas associated with defining exits. With the accumulation of sunk cost (returned as depreciation, if sufficient revenues are generated) producers may put some wells and acreage into production that probably should have been condemned based on pilot drilling. In drilling unconventional wells producers must spend much more before declaring success or failure (well abandonment with commensurate strategies for offloading acreage).[50] In conventional exploration, declaration of commerciality comes once wells are drilled vertically, cased, perforated and tested. Although producers may be able to utilize vertical well bores from pilot drilling, unconventional wells must be drilled laterally to their full extent, completed, fracked and then tested before commerciality can be established. This means larger capex budgets and perhaps tendencies, given sunk costs, to put wells on production that have weaker production profiles (producers do not commonly declare "dry holes" in unconventional plays). If companies engage in this behavior across enough across wells and locations, they can compromise operating and financial results.[51]

Vagaries of Type Curves

A notable, perhaps too often dwelled upon, characteristic of tight, overpressured shale plays and wells is the type curve of large early production volumes followed by rapid and steep declines as well pressures deplete (Fig. 1.22). The petroleum engineering community has captured well the debates on type curves and how to appraise unconventional plays (Haskett and Brown 2005, 2010; Gouveia and Citron 2009; Haskett 2011; Willegers et al. 2017). Investors and other observers came to rely too heavily upon type curves of wells that are on production as predictors of future results, a point I take up below. The feature of high initial volumes, fast declines and long tails have direct bearing on revenue streams. From a financial point of view, initial capital expense (capital return) is paid back from early (usually the first 18 months to two years) initial production or IP. Over time, tails provide profit (surplus). The higher the early production volumes, the faster the pay back. The lower are commodity prices, the higher IP volumes must be to achieve pay back. Because of these characteristics, unconventional wells can provide “fast” positive net present values or NPVs and returns to investors. I have already mentioned that investors like shale plays for the absence of exploration risk. Because shale plays are resource plays targeting remaining hydrocarbons that usually underlie existing conventional oil and gas fields, the presence of hydrocarbons is accepted. Producers are reaching for remaining hydrocarbons from low reservoir quality conventional lenses as well as shale source rocks themselves. Initial data must demonstrate high enough organic content to indicate hydrocarbons but recoverability is uncertain. Substantial heterogeneity exists across and within shale basins and plays, with considerable variability in total organic content and subsurface conditions, recovery rates and production per wellbore. Expected ultimate recovery (EUR, the primary hurdle) can be quite different from well to well and across basins and sub-basins.[52] Companies drill plenty of non- or sub-commercial wells but managements generally do not include these in investor presentations nor do analysts in their research.[53]

All of this can make for considerable risk and uncertainty in development (exploitation) cost and performance. A further attribute of onshore unconventional oil and gas business models is that although well opex remains low relative to capex, companies must drill wells almost continuously to counteract the steep production declines. Operators try to drill denser well patterns in order to optimize recovery of hydrocarbons from dense, tight rocks. The best locations will have multiple opportunities—the benches I alluded to previously—creating stacked drillable zones. In previous sections I mentioned the advent and progression of horizontal drilling, lateral completions and multi-stage hydraulic fracturing with multiple-well bores drilled from common pads. Multiple-well pads help to counter the number of (and surface impacts of) vertical wells that marked past rounds of industry activity in unconventional plays. Superlaterals and superfracs requiring more, and more expensive, OFS support and larger, more complex, well pad designs are all geared toward generating larger volumes to speed pay back and improve profitability. Business models for unconventional plays require ongoing outlays of capex to fully exploit opportunities and achieve sufficient volumes to sustain companies. These larger volumes require more midstream capacity and market depth.

For investors and companies, capital recovery is quickest from the best acreage and drilling locations, ergo the pressure on land portfolios. Producers have been able to improve early production volumes by targeting drilling expenditures to the best locations, and not only to the best basins but to sweet spots within basins.[54] This has put portfolio optimization—high grading acreage positions—at the forefront of improvement in unit cost and performance. Once producers drill, complete and frac wells, they can deploy a operational tactics to enhance cost management and performance. For example, in some gassier locations producers have been able to choke back initial production to flatten production declines. Slower declines means ability to defer capex for new drilling to replace production. The tradeoff is reduced revenue and lower NPV.

Given variability across and within basins and plays, individual well, leasehold and company operational and economic performance can be quite different. As shale plays have matured, performance—productivity of wellbores—has become one of the main concerns, creating contrary views to those that emerged early on around well productivity gains with superlat and superfrac approaches (McDaniel 2010[55]). In their search to define and harvest sweet spots, producers may add costs that they may not be able to balance with improved well productivities. That may seem a contradictory statement. A host of issues congregates around well interference. In tight rock environments, initial "parent" wells can drain hydrocarbons away from proximal "child" locations. Well interference bears serious implications for well spacing and field planning, undermines the benefits from superlat and superfrac approaches, and undermines company performance.[56] It can even cause pressure depletion across substantial portions of, or even entire, basins, a much bigger threat (see King et al., 2017; Rainbolt and Esco 2018 for detailed treatment of well interference issues). An irony is that better porosity and permeability makes for better fracs, which is saying a lot given the tight rock nano native fracture environment. A possibility is that the better the native fracture environment, the worse the well interference.

A concept for managing the wide-ranging risks and uncertainties around well interference productivities is the larger-scale, industrialized "cube" which includes drilling and completing all planned wells in a bench simultaneously. Cubes with multi-well pads incorporating the longest laterals and largest number of frac stages can cost from "$120 million to $250 million" depending upon number of wells, facilities and other factors, "a price tag that for many smaller shale producers is simply out of reach" (Jacobs 2018, p. 6).[57] Clearly, producers and their investors would much rather see expensive wells and cubes that yield strong results. A number of recent evaluations of drilling and well data indicate that this too often is not the case.[58]

An observation on shale development is that one-third of wells make money, one-third break even and one-third lose money. This is a variant of the venerable "West Texas" rule of thumb of three times finding cost for profitability; finding cost includes, of course, unsuccessful efforts. An earlier commentary (in a déjà vu sense) was that a $1 MMBtu cost for gas wells needed a $3 Henry Hub price for profitability (1990s money of the day). In sum, much of the "missing money" in our benchmarking is likely associated with production challenges and performance. Midstream bottlenecks and costs and effects of commodity prices and netbacks simply round out the difference.

A Barrel Full (of Something)

How did our companies fare in their efforts to optimize portfolios and solve the vagaries of tight rock drilling and completions? The bottom line has been harsh. We have learned that gassier companies are lower cost but also less profitable, largely explained by the rapid build-up of surplus and erosion of commodity price. Gassier companies are more exposed to the bigger problem of monetizing gas production streams. The larger volumes associated with "industrialization" of tight rock plays damaged commodity prices faster than companies could adjust in cost management, minimizing margin improvement. Operating and financial results also reflected the technical challenges prevalent across the shale plays summarized above—well interference and productivity plateaus or losses undermined improvements associated with productivity gains. In a recap at the start of 2020, Rassenfoss (2020) culled a variety of sources that question whether reliance on core acreage (see the previous discussion on sweet spots) with superlat and superfrac well designs is sufficient to improve productivity and profitability. The very high degree of variability contributes to a population of underperforming wells that, in the prevailing price environment, continue to stymie efforts to boost results.[59] The continued experimentation with well designs also suggests capex deployment with no surety of acceptable outcomes. Yet ideas about how to improve predictability using artificial intelligence applied to-ever-more-granular well datasets have not paid off.[60] These observations apply to oily basins, and particularly basins like the Permian. Natural gas is easier to move through tight rock and so volumes per dollar spent can be higher, but profitability lower because the natural gas molecules are less valuable.

Over the ten years of our benchmarking, 11 companies among our 16 evolved from gas production comprising more than 50 percent of total (the typical criteria for categorizing "gassy" companies) in 2007–2009 to only four by 2017–2018. The changes we capture are a fair reflection of the portfolio dynamics that played out across the industry at large. In the following charts, Fig. 1.23 left column, I show the pattern of production and costs over time for all companies for which gas production is 50 percent of their total slate each year. By 2017–2018, that group reduces to the four companies that were primarily shale gas players from the outset, mainly in the Appalachians. In the right-hand column of Fig. 1.23, I provide the historical production slates and cost structures for these four organizations for comparison (gas pure players). Wherever they could, these four companies added liquids volumes (the growing NGLs output, Fig. 1.23, top right) while the other seven companies phased out of gassy plays in search of black oil.

The barrel equivalent costs in 2018 (Fig. 1.23, bottom row) were $2.57 in natural gas, billion cubic feet equivalent, or Bcfe, terms, with an assumed 10 percent return. This equates to about $15 per BOE. Note that the 2017 and 2018 costs are the same in both columns, given that only the four gas pure players remain in our sample. The lowest-cost producer averaged less than $2 per Bcfe ($1.89 in total cost with 10 percent return); natural gas comprised 85 percent of production. The highest-cost producer averaged about $3.49 per Bcfe (but with larger, more expensive to acquire, oil and liquids holdings). Natural gas was 73 percent of production. Henry Hub averaged $3.15 per MMBtu for all of 2018. In the Fig. 1.23c and d cost charts, I also show an additional, patterned bar. This represents the additional return, above the typical 10 percent, that our companies would have to generate *if they were going to cover all of their capex commitment in that year*. Isolating gassy and gas pure players provides a hint for where the cash flow problem comes home to roost—*the cost stack with the additional return to cover the balance of annual capex exceeds market price in every year even for the gas pure players.* The lowest-cost producer in our sample (indeed, the entire 16-company benchmark) beat Henry Hub for reporting years 2016–2018. That company—let us call it "Company A"—is the most profitable of the gassy companies including, no surprise, companies that exited gassy plays and acreage. Company

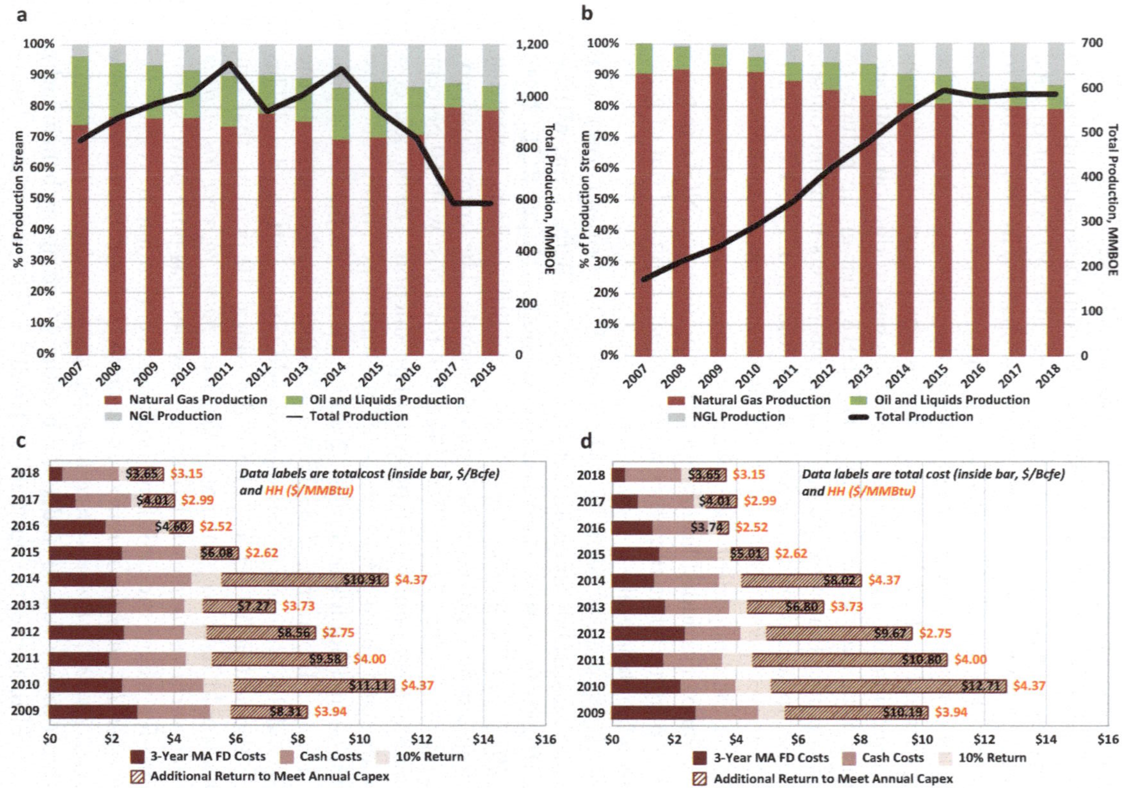

Fig. 1.23 Equivalent barrels and full cycle costs for "gassy" companies and gas pure players. (**a**) Equivalent barrels, gassy. (**b**) Equivalent barrels, gas pure players. (**c**) Full cycle costs, gassy. (**d**) Full cycle costs, gas pure players. (Source: Based on 2009–2018 producer benchmarking)

A now operates only in the Marcellus (having divested of non-Marcellus assets, including in Texas). Company A produces nearly 100 percent gas, has maintained fairly steady volumes of NGLs, and is advantaged by a major pipeline for exiting methane from the Marcellus for which it executed capacity agreements (15 and 20 years) and firm sales contracts (15 and three years). Company A also has a component of fee minerals in its holdings.

Land holdings for the oilier producers (Fig. 1.24 top), including the seven companies that divested out of gassier plays over time, mainly are in West Texas (Permian, where the richest premiums have been paid) and North Dakota (Bakken). There is some Alaska and Gulf of Mexico production in the sample—it is difficult to impossible, at the corporate reporting level, to exclude certain operations. However, over the years this group has steadily moved toward shale oil "pure play" strategies, effectively becoming specialists in onshore light tight oil exploitation. On a BOE basis, oilier companies are more "expensive" than gassier ones. The 2018 total cost of about $25 per BOE including 10 percent return compares with the $15 average for our gassiest companies mentioned previously. This is true for all years in our benchmarking. Along with the premium prices per acre these companies paid to hone land portfolios and improve black oil recovery, oilier companies have spent more aggressively to cure transportation bottlenecks and seek export outlets. The pattern of costs in Fig. 1.24 reflects the shift to oilier acreage and associated midstream expenses during 2011–2014. All of the producers in our sample sell their gas production to the market; none have internalized petrochemical or LNG value chains, nor are they affiliates to integrated majors as noted previously. This stands in stark contrast to oilier integrated major producers and their pure play affiliates who have participated in capacity to facilitate oil and condensate transportation and who are monetizing production through their internal refining, petrochemical and LNG export value chains. The lowest-cost producer—"Company B"—averaged about $22 per BOE for 2018. The highest-cost producer had a significant offshore commitment, pushing that company's cost structure to more than $51 per Bbl. Our second-highest-cost producer, at almost $47 per Bbl, is a Permian pure player that was, at one time, lauded for its land holdings and drilling proficiency. Once that company initiated large-scale cube development, both cost management and well performance have disappointed. The most consistent oily company in our sample has been the most profitable over the ten years and is a low-cost, *but not* the cheapest, producer. This

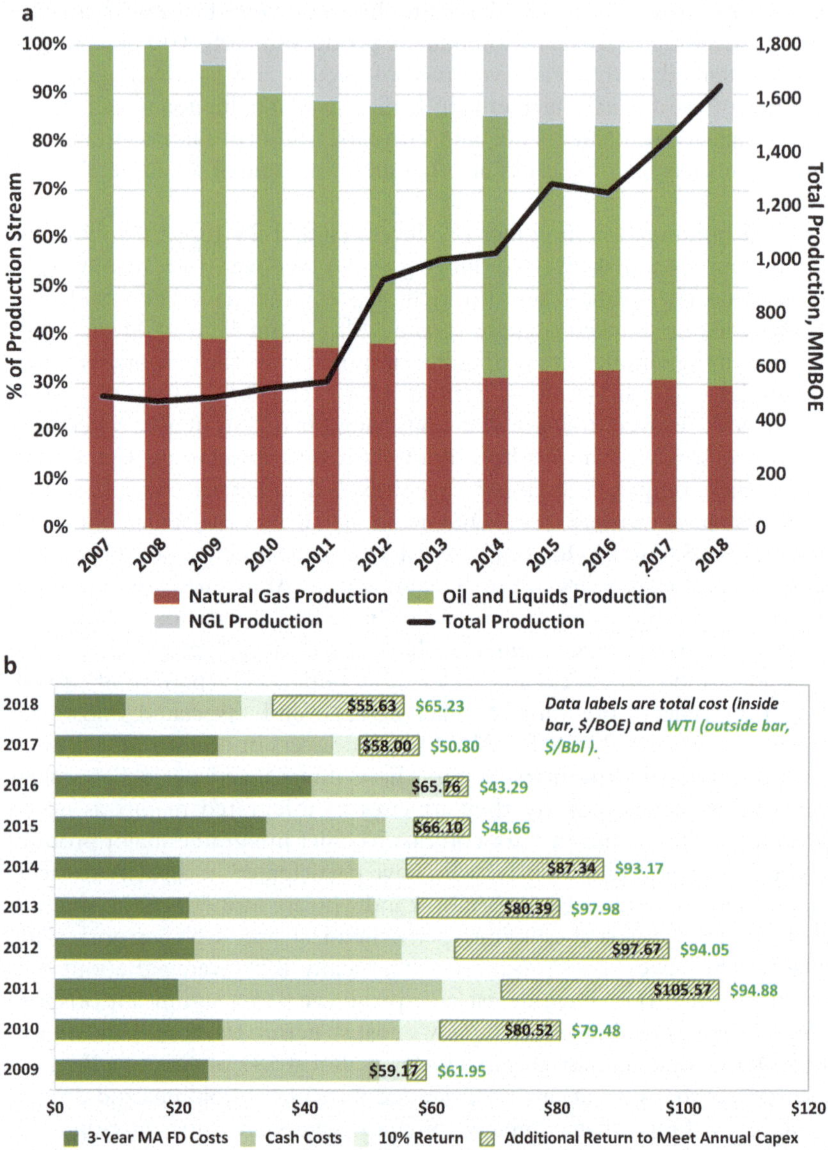

Fig. 1.24 Equivalent barrels and full cycle costs for "oily" companies (all BOE), (**a**) Equivalent barrels, (**b**) Full cycle costs. (Source: Based on 2009–2018 producer benchmarking)

company exited shale gas plays early but successfully paid down associated debt, is primarily a Permian player but with strategic interests elsewhere, has honed its supply chain and executed early midstream arrangements for production handling.

As with the gassy companies, in Fig. 1.24b I show a hypothetical additional return that would be required if our companies tried to cover all of their remaining current year capex. On the whole, as a group, oilier companies have come a bit closer to recovering their remaining annual capex; their full cost stacks with additional return exceed market prices (West Texas Intermediate) in six of the ten years. Again, I am only using the broadly traded price of oil as my barometer. The six years in which total costs with additional return exceed average WTI match the widening spread between the U.S. WTI and international Brent prices as shown later in Fig. 1.31. This comparison provides a nice encapsulation of the impact of widening differentials on the industry as producers added more volumes than could be effectively monetized.

Of course, in all of my examples using the hypothetical additional return for annual capex recovery, the rollover in depreciation on cash flow statements absorbs some unamortized capex but the essential point remains. On average, overall, the industry simply has not been able to keep up; pressure builds on commodity prices faster than companies can recover costs. Moreover, for this experiment I use market prices (Henry Hub and WTI) and not netbacks to production or realized prices, covered in the following section. Thus, my results *understate* the predicament that the industry has faced, especially companies producing mainly or only natural gas and mostly methane without supporting transportation access.

Results expressed in the broader financial metrics of EBITDA, net cash flow to capex and DD&A relative to cash flow and capex flow logically from the preceding discussion. These metrics are captured in Fig. 1.25 for (a) gassy companies (again, only four companies remain in 2017–2018) and (b) oily companies. I provide depreciable finding and development costs or capex as a percent of total costs, excluding returns, in data labels above the capex columns in each chart. Because, overall, oilier companies have had more headroom with respect to the price of traded WTI—even with periodic deep discounts in netbacks from price indexes to locations of production sales—they are more profitable relative to the gassier companies each year. This also occurs in spite of generally lower costs for companies that mainly produce gas in a given reporting year. EBITDA, earnings before interest, taxes and depreciation, depletion and amortization

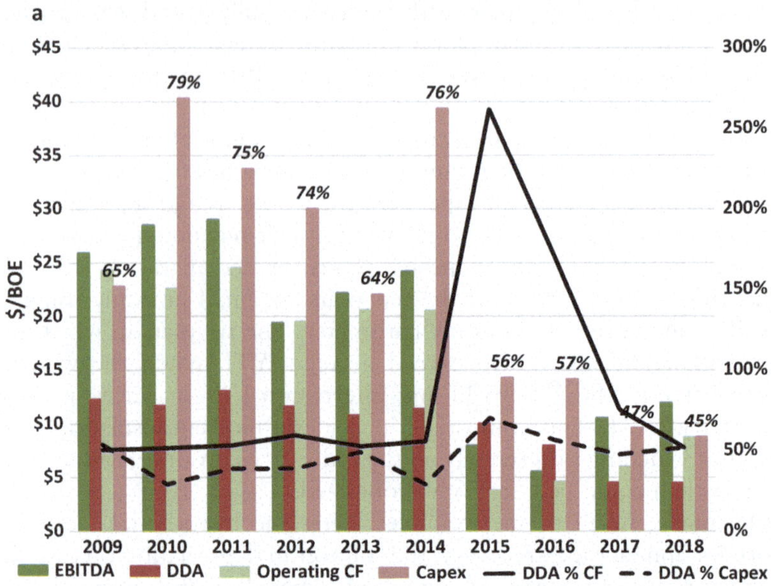

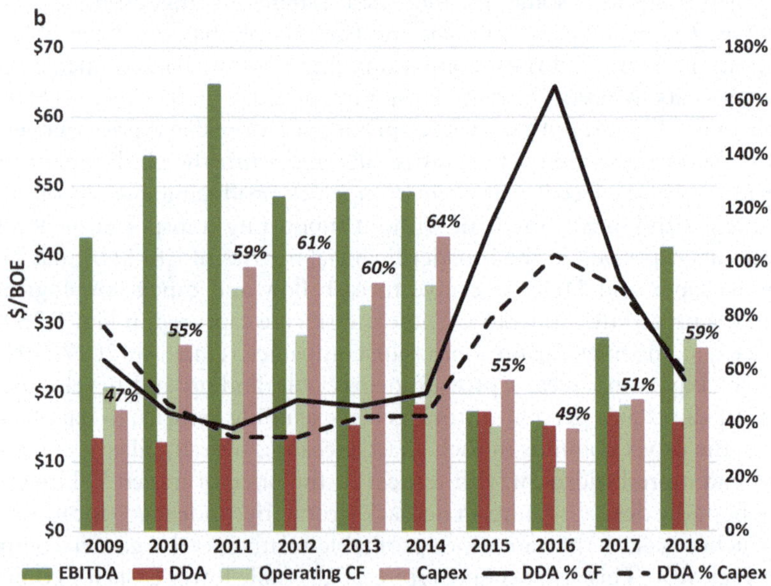

Fig. 1.25 Costs, EBITDA and cash flow for gassy and oily companies by year. (**a**) Costs, EBITDA and cash flow for gassy companies. (**b**) Costs, EBITDA and cash flow for gassy companies. (Source: Based on 2009–2018 producer benchmarking)

(DD&A), for oily companies was about $41/BOE in 2018, as opposed to $12/BOE for gassy companies. For oily companies, 2018 EBITDA improved by about $13 per BOE over 2017 results. For gassy companies, the improvement in EBITDA 2017 to 2018 was about $1.40 per BOE, a stark difference. After spending about the same during 2015–2016, gassy companies achieved capex reductions in 2017 and 2018 while oily companies increased spending for 2016–2018, along with EBITDA and an improvement in cash flows relative to capex. As a group, gassy companies achieved parity between operating cash flows and capex in 2018, the first time since 2009 and after being cash flow negative during the intervening years. The oilier group generated net positive cash flow for the first time since 2010; for all years, oily company cash balances were better than for gassy companies. DD&A for gassy companies zoomed to more than 250 percent of cash flow in 2016. It has been on a gently rising trend as a percent of capex since 2010. After rising rapidly during the worst years of oil price adjustment, DD&A as a percent of both cash and capex has been declining for the oilier companies.

In the end, in a business that is exciting but demanding on all fronts, the case for companies exiting from strong gassy positions—as did the seven companies in our coverage during the past ten years—is well illustrated by the charts of Fig. 1.25. The much larger capex commitments relative to earnings and cash flows for gassier producers stands out clearly in Fig. 1.25a. The much more robust EBITDA results during strong oil price years (Fig. 1.25b), the greater upside potential even when oil prices fell, were too compelling. The tradeoff lies in the cost and capex commitments for implementing strategies to re-engineer portfolios, the drilling and completion strategies for execution, and attendant expectations of investors as laid out in the previous section. The two companies that I singled out as examples, A and B, have, in many respects, "stuck to their knitting", shedding assets that did not fit the primarily gas (Company A) and oil (Company B) positions, once those were achieved in the case of Company B. Neither of these companies ended the full ten years with positive net cash flows (cash flow to capex). Only two companies of the 16 held that honor, and neither of these were low cost relative to others. One has non-shale production and the other a significant legacy oil position in the Permian. In all, producer portfolios explain much about company cost structures and ability to optimize portfolios explains much about company performance.

Field-to-Market Monetization (or Not)

Clearly, the price paid for production is a crucial variable in producer revenues. As I noted earlier, the United States is advantaged by a vast complex of midstream infrastructure, the majority of which is independently owned and financed at risk, *but there can be big lags in responsiveness, delaying vital field-to-market linkages.* To reiterate, midstream "field-to-market" linkages often are never enough, even more often are not in the right places, and are always expensive (from a producer point of view).

Given the realities of the predominant shale plays—"gas drive" reservoirs that yield large volumes of light tight oil and natural gas and deplete rapidly—along with midstream bottlenecks and constrained offtake as downstream, export and other end uses expand, the impact on prices and spreads has been an adventure. "Frankelnomics" shows strongly in the deviation of realized prices to market indexes.[61] Realized price is what a producer actually is paid, on average, for volumes. Producers hedge to shelter cash flows and so realized prices also are a reflection of hedging programs. The difference or spread between the expected market price and actual, realized price is a succinct indication of market conditions. Positive spreads mean that producers are realizing prices that are lower than the expected market price. This most often is an outcome of inadequate midstream capacity. With insufficient midstream capacity, netback prices to production become discounted to the traded commodity index. The greater the supply build relative to takeaway for markets, the worse the discount. Clearly, investments in midstream capacity will help to close spreads. Companies also try to close gaps with judicious hedging strategies. The more supportive the strip of prices going forward into the future, the greater the chance of success in hedging. Notably, companies can get their hedges "wrong", that is, outcomes do not exceed opportunity costs.[62] Increasingly, companies have used a variety of approaches such as collars given the uncertainties in forward prices.

Because we necessarily rely on company reporting of their realized prices and hedging positions, our dataset does not extend to all 16 companies in our coverage. On a quarterly basis, 15 of our benchmark companies reliably report realized prices for production and nine report impacts of derivatives along with NGLs volumes, enabling evaluation of that portion of their production streams. We used Henry Hub, West Texas Intermediate or light sweet crude oil and the EIA's composite NGLs price to capture value companies could have earned if they were able to monetize production at least at the market price. In Fig. 1.26, I use all 15 companies to compare reported realized prices to the market. From the zero line on right vertical axis, companies spreads are negative (market price was less than realized price) or positive (market price exceeded realized price). In all, producers have faced unconstructive price environments for their volumes. The high and rising trend for natural gas (mainly affected by methane) generally coincides with Fig. 1.32, basis differentials at the Waha Hub in West Texas, while the spreads for oil parallels Fig. 1.31, the WTI discount to Brent, in the section "Effect of Infrastructure Bottlenecks".

For all quarters and years, our benchmarked companies earned about 11 percent less than the Henry Hub market price, with a mean of 16 cents below HH and a standard deviation of 36 cents. For oil, our companies earned about 4 percent less than WTI, with a mean of $1.46 per barrel less than the WTI and a standard deviation of $2.86. NGLs is toughest for realizations, given the lack of open trading and deep liquidity for commodities such as ethane, propane and butane extracted in processing and fractionation. Our companies earned about 86 percent less than the EIA composite market price, with a mean of about $11 and standard deviation of $5.64. Readers should take results for NGLs with a grain of salt. While the pattern has been for values of NGLs to rapidly diminish as production volumes swamp offtake (see Chap. 3), the EIA composite is only a very rough indicator of the basket of molecules that producers have the potential to sell.

If I split our sample into the gassiest and oiliest companies, the weighted averages are 16 percent, 0 percent and 54 percent relative to market HH, WTI and EIA composite, respectively, for gassy companies and 7 percent, 4 percent and 46 percent for oily producers. Our findings are broadly compatible with what many other groups have observed. While these differences may not seem large, losses of $0.60 to $0.80 per MMBtu of methane and $8 to $10 per Bbl for oil are significant across production slates, volumes, revenues and EBITDA.

The Vagaries of Commodity Markets and Prices

The ability of producers, or any market participant, to mitigate commodity price risk and ensure businesses can survive and thrive is complicated by the nature of commodities. All participants are price takers, and prices move in both long- and short-term patterns. Prices of commodities reflect

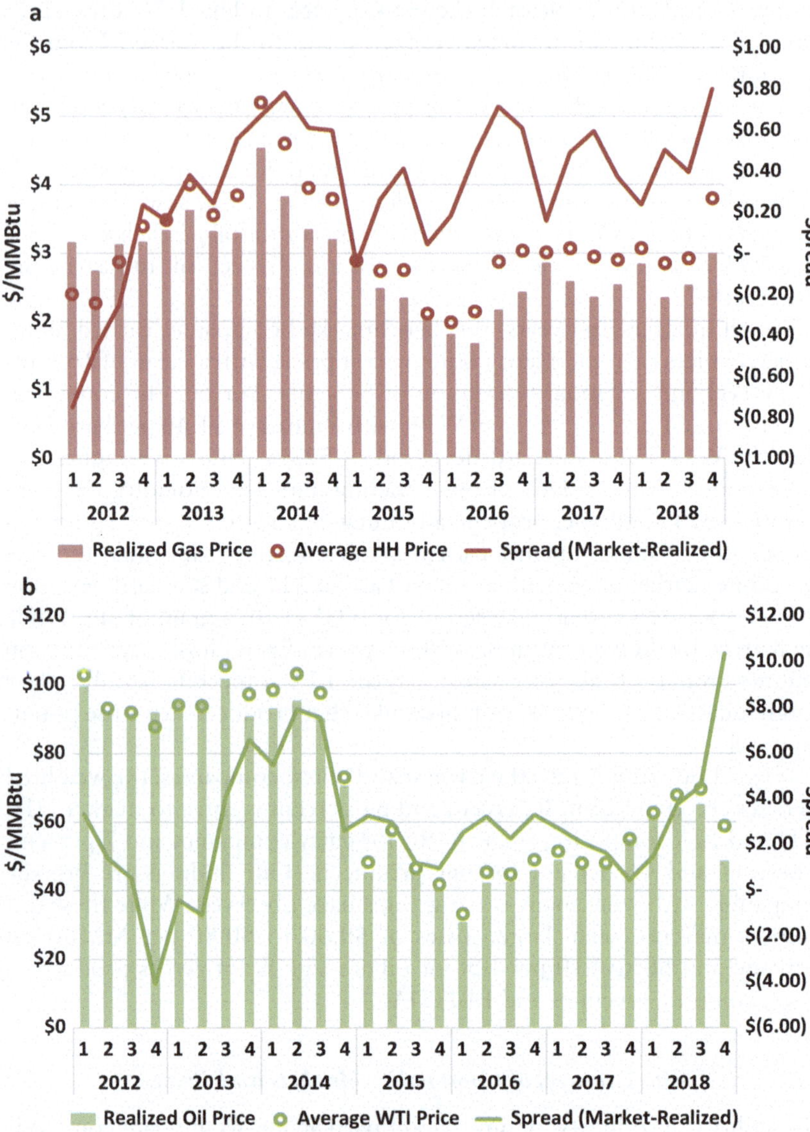

Fig. 1.26 Realized gas, oil and NGLs prices relative to market (traded price). (**a**) Natural gas. (**b**) Oil. (**c**) NGLs. (Source: Based on 2009–2018 producer benchmarking. EIA and CME/NYMEX prices)

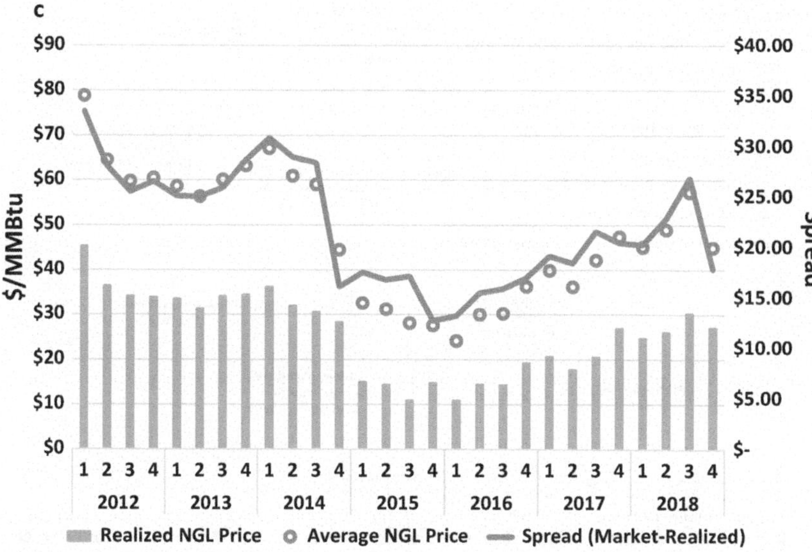

Fig. 1.26 (continued)

supply and demand balances that are constantly shifting (seasonally as well as over longer periods); weather and economic events; influence of outside groups as in the case of oil with OPEC's members positioning around production quotas.

How physical and financial markets are developed, meaning the organization of physical and virtual infrastructure and pooling points (market centers and hubs); the rules and norms and associated regulatory oversight that apply; the extent of financial participation (number of participants and money brought to the table) all have bearing on price formation, transmittal, transparency and reliability. Oil is a global commodity. The physical and financial trading of oil entails deep pockets whereas natural gas is most widely traded in the United States and Canada, with Canadian market locations well-integrated, and widespread use of U.S. derivatives and financial markets. It has been a long and bumpy road for U.S. natural gas market evolution (see Appendix to this book), especially as compared to Europe and Asia, the other large regions where trading of natural gas occurs and is growing (see Michot Foss and Palmer-Huggins 2016).

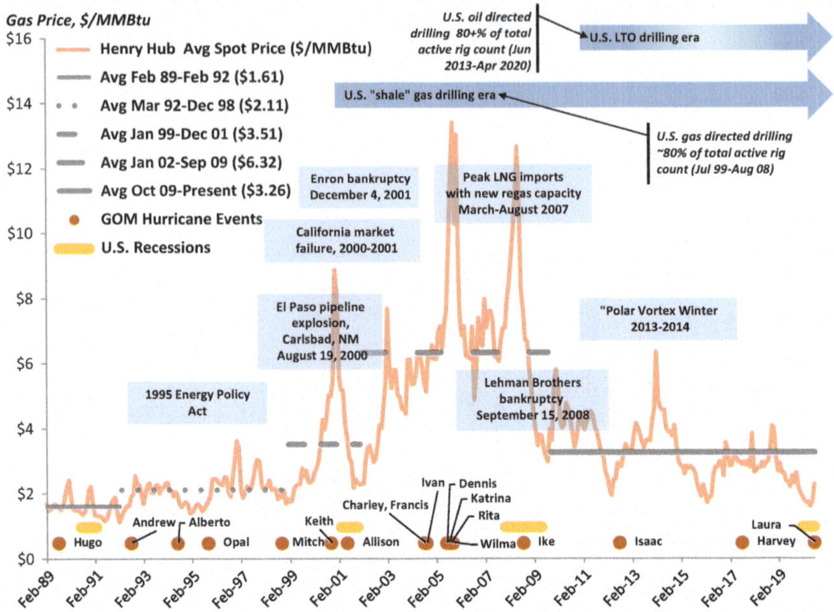

Fig. 1.27 Henry Hub history. (Sources: CME/NYMEX as reported by EIA; NOAA; NBER; various news outlets for events. Start of traded natural gas data January 13, 1994)

The Henry Hub longitudinal price series (Fig. 1.27) reflects the history and evolution of the U.S. natural gas system and marketplace (see Appendix to book). Until onshore gas production saturated the Lower 48 marketplace, traders generally looked to hurricane events and the purchase of gas for winter storage or, increasingly, to supplement gas-fired power generation for summer cooling, for price movements. Price swings mark key moments in natural gas industry and market transformation, up or down depending upon the nature of the event. With the onset of the unconventional gas drilling era supply growth already was pressuring price before the onset of the 2008 recession. The onset of the LTO drilling era and influx of associated gas volumes has prolonged the price pressure. The mean since October 2009 post-recession is very likely to drift down, possibly through 2020 and even 2021.

Sovereign crude oil producers are paid, and oil is traded, in U.S. dollars. This gives the global oil marketplace the added complexity of

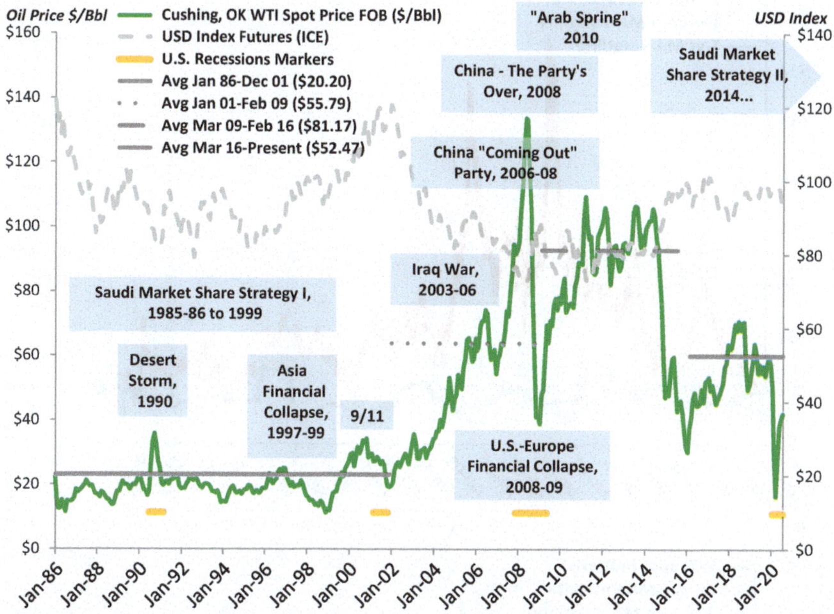

Fig. 1.28 WTI history. (Sources: CME/NYMEX as reported by EIA; Federal Reserve Bank of St. Louis; NBER; various news outlets for events. Start of traded crude data January 2, 1986)

currency effects. I show this in Fig. 1.28 by including a U.S. dollar index. When the dollar is strong relative to other major currencies, lower oil prices can be accommodated. A weak dollar tends to encourage OPEC decision making toward reduced quotas in order to prod oil prices higher and meet sovereign fiscal budget targets. Oil and economic growth are closely linked. Crude oil prices typically are a first-line indicator of stress as demand for oil products falls with slowing economic activity. Likewise, oil price shocks are usually associated with recessions (other factors can mitigate severity). A feature of the oil market since 2014 has been OPEC's institutional response to U.S. domestic production growth. With so much oil supply in the global system, geopolitical events that would have moved oil prices only a few years ago now have a dampened effect.

I compare natural gas and crude oil price volatility in Fig. 1.29 and Table 1.1. Differences are reflected in the realized price results I reported earlier. In Fig. 1.29, I show price volatility using different periods for

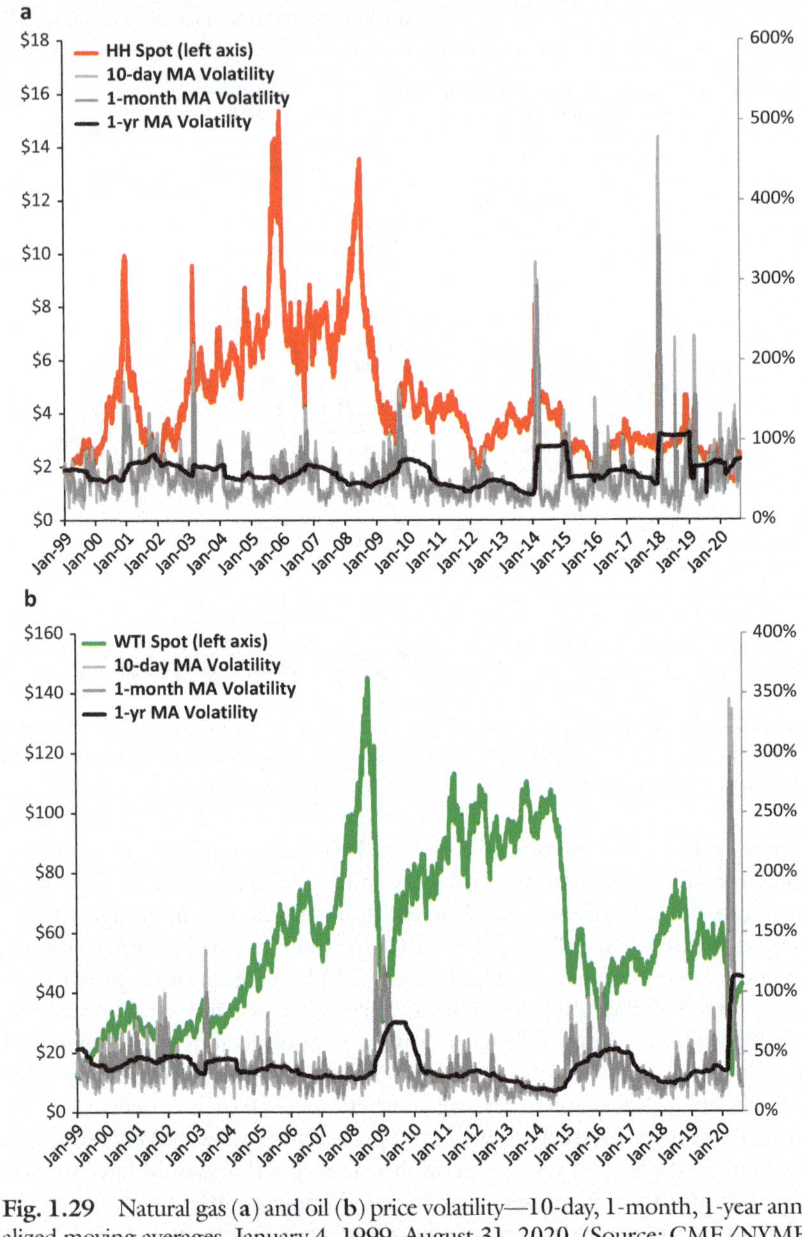

Fig. 1.29 Natural gas (**a**) and oil (**b**) price volatility—10-day, 1-month, 1-year annualized moving averages, January 4, 1999–August 31, 2020. (Source: CME/NYMEX as reported by EIA; author calculations and depiction; as developed by Gülen (see Gülen and Michot Foss 2012). NOTE—on April 20, 2020 light sweet crude oil settled at –$36.98 and on April 21 at $8.91. These dates are excluded from the calculated volatilities. The previous historical minimum was $10.25 March 31, 1986 but oil prices had already deteriorated from the then-historical high of about $37)

Table 1.1 Trading volatility measures, natural gas (HH) and crude oil (WTI)

	10-day MA volatility annualized, %	*1-month MA volatility annualized, %*	*1-year MA volatility annualized, %*
Natural gas			
Max	479	356	109
Min	8	16	31
SD	36	32	16
Mean	53	55	61
Crude oil			
Max	345	296	113
Min	5	10	17
SD	27	25	15
Mean	36	37	39

Source: Based on CME/NYMEX as reported by EIA; author calculations; as developed by Gülen (see Gülen and Michot Foss, 2012). See previous note for Fig. 1.29 regarding treatment of 2020 data

smoothing and summarize volatility measures in Table 1.1. Even with the extreme volatility in oil prices during 2020, natural gas remains the more unpredictable commodity. The greater volatility is mainly due to disruptions associated with weather. While seasonal patterns exist in oil markets—summer driving demand for gasoline, for instance—they are less prominent. The main impacts on oil derive from economic and geopolitical events and the periodic market share battles among major producing/exporting countries.

Liquidity—financial participation in these commodity markets—has grown steadily for both crude oil and natural gas. Growth in market participation means more counterparties engaged in trades and greater liquidity. More liquidity implies greater ease in building monetary value around physical assets like MMBtus of gas and barrels of crude oil. The multipliers of volumes of natural gas and oil in the front (or first, which roughly equates to spot price) month contracts relative to physical production and sales provide an indication of the amount of liquidity in these markets.[63] For 2019, on average, volumes in NG1 traded contracts exceeded physical combined output from the United States and Canada (where most trading in natural gas derivatives occurs) more than 39 times. For oil, the multiplier is more than 102 times physical supply.[64] Uncertainty about commodity price increases into the future, and so activity across different traded contracts declines. The NG1 contract volume exceeded NG3 by four times, NG6 nine times and NG12 65 times. By comparison, for oil the CL1 contract volume exceeded CL 3 ten times, CL6 26 times and CL12 103 times. While liquidity has grown overall, trading in futures and other derivatives fluctuates with markets and business conditions, dropping when prices are falling and low and increasing when prices are rising and high. For example, with the extreme volatility in crude oil during 2020 (Fig. 1.29b), average CL1 contract volume for January–August fell 20 percent from the same period in 2019. At the same time, however, it is important to point out that volatility attracts market participation, especially by counterparties who are looking for exposure to these commodities and treat the derivatives as an asset class. This segment has grown, adding crucial liquidity, but also complicating the dynamic since their motivations and strategies may be quite different than commercial interests (producers, for instance).[65]

The challenge of ascertaining fundamentals underlying commodity prices (Figs. 1.27 and 1.28) and the volatility that results (Fig. 1.29) explain much of the spread between market and realized prices that I estimate and show in Fig. 1.26. What about broader market performance—do thousands of participants do any better than the 16 companies we benchmarked?

I demonstrate market trading "error"[66] in Fig. 1.30. These charts do not include the more volatile and exceptional conditions of 2020. The question is how well market participants anticipate the future (answer, not much, but that is actually the point). In these charts, I compare current spot price to what market participants expected it to be when each contract trade settled. In other words, I am comparing the current spot natural gas or crude oil price in a period to the settlement price in the futures contracts that traded 3 (NG3 or CL3), 6 and 12 months prior to that spot price (a truncated futures 12-month "strip" for ease of analysis). Because contract volumes and open interest tend to drop into the future, the contracts that tend to have the greatest activity are three and six. As with the realized price results for producers, there is much more market error for natural gas than for oil. Natural gas error rates increase further into the future; many more misses are evident for contracts 6 and 12 than for 3. Most of the misses are on the high side; that is, the futures contract settlement price was higher than the actual spot. When compared to the realized price results for our producers, this suggests that companies are, indeed, able to protect themselves somewhat from price risk and are, to some extent, able to use hedging to offset losses associated with business conditions, specifically the severe discounts in their netbacks. When misses

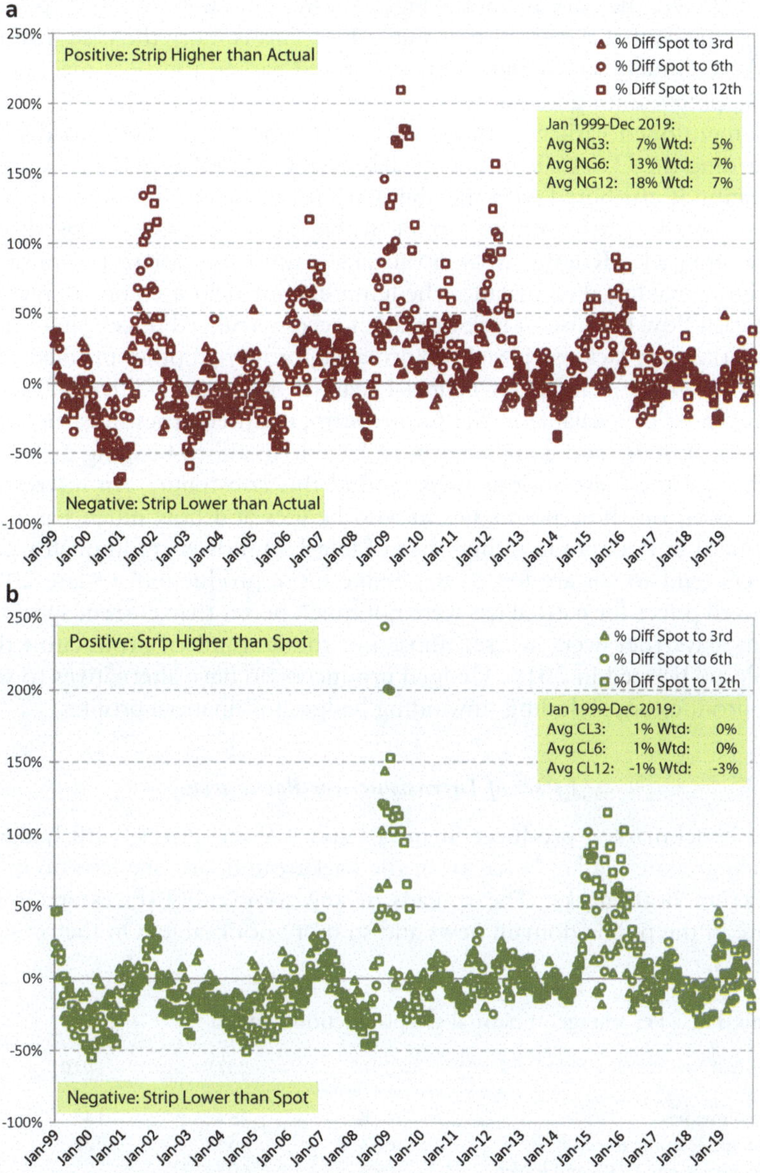

Fig. 1.30 Market trading "error"—natural gas and oil differences, forwards vs. actuals. (**a**) Natural gas. (**b**) Crude oil. (Sources: CME/NYMEX accessed via Quandl; see footnote 67 for attribution; author calculations and depiction)

are negative, the current spot is higher than prices were in the strip; market participants have given up some value. This is more the case with the CL12 contract, on average, and, as I noted earlier, can be a magnet for unhappiness among investors.[67]

I mentioned earlier in this chapter that one of the vigorous debates regarding the U.S. shale businesses has been the "resilience" of producers. Hedging is attributed with the ability for producers to not only continue operations but to continue drilling when, by all measures, they should have stopped. Hedging is by no means a substitute for sound business decision making. For instance, hedging cannot help a company recover lost cash flow because of lack of market access (realized prices discounted to market), or lackluster well performance, or myriad other problems. As well, given the features of financial markets for commodities, attractive prices must be available in the futures strip, counterparties must be available for trading, and companies must be able to afford hedging programs (although there are various ways around this constraint). An interesting dimension on these points lies in who hedges and how much based on Standard & Poor credit ratings data (Table 1.2). Lower credit quality producers tend to (or are forced to) hedge more production. In late 2018, forward prices for natural gas were not much better than current spot. For many days they were worse, impacting the amount of production that could be hedged in 2019. Hedged producers do have alternatives to selling production, including unwinding hedges for financial profit.

Effect of Infrastructure Bottlenecks

Our benchmarked producer financials and realized prices, with hedging and aggregate market behavior in the background, are one lens on infrastructure bottlenecks. The spreads in key commodity prices are much more in the public domain news and so more noticeable. On the oil side,

Table 1.2 Percentage of natural gas production hedged

	2017	*2018*	*2019*
All companies	47%	38%	13%
Spec-grade companies	66%	56%	22%
Companies rated "B" and lower	67%	60%	17%

Source: S&P Global Ratings, as of December 2017. Analysis by Denise Palmer-Huggins with global implications, the main indicator has been the fluctuating differential between WTI and the UK Brent index (Fig. 1.31). The Brent price index is widely used by producers and customers outside of North America but refinery buyers of crude oil in the United States also make purchases on Brent. The WTI futures contract is located in Oklahoma, and so reflective of market conditions in the mid-continent L48. Since the late 2000s, the volatility in that spread reflects the surge in light tight oil in the mid-continent onshore resource plays, improvement in oil midstream capacity by the mid-2010s and a widening spread again toward the end of the decade. The latest widening reflects drilling in response to oil price recovery post-2016, including the portfolio shifts out of gassier assets covered above, and the widely expected arrival and escalation of activity by the large integrated majors. While a narrowing spread can mean improvement in WTI and more revenue to U.S. producers, in an open, global market it also makes U.S. crudes less attractive to some overseas buyers (a premium of WTI to Brent could render U.S. exports uncompetitive for some customers). Figure 1.31 also shows the spread between the Midland, Texas, sales point and the WTI futures contract. The WTI Midland index is an indicator of the price producers actually receive at their Permian locations. The sharp drop into negative territory explains much of the difference between market (WTI) and realized prices for producers (Fig. 1.26). Again, the volatility reflects bottlenecks and new midstream capacity that helped to cure the basis spread and enable Permian oil producers to achieve a sales price closer to WTI.

Less well known, but with bigger consequences for producers and growing global effects, has been the spread between the main Henry Hub index and other prominent natural gas market centers and hubs. Most notable of these has been the Waha Hub which serves West Texas (Fig. 1.32). The rapid expansion of activity in the Permian and the flood of associated gas pushed the Waha to HH spread into negative territory. Affected producers have had to pay pipeline operators to exit gas production from leaseholds, a most unhappy situation given the limited number of options (oil producers were able to use alternative transportation modes such as truck and rail to move oil production out of the glutted midcontinent). Unlike the oil differential, the natural gas spreads widened strongly into 2020 as gas production exceeded even capacity additions. Should the Permian continue to anchor U.S. oil production activity, spreads are likely to remain wide until gas pipeline operators are able to obtain commitments for projects.[68] The Marcellus market area has

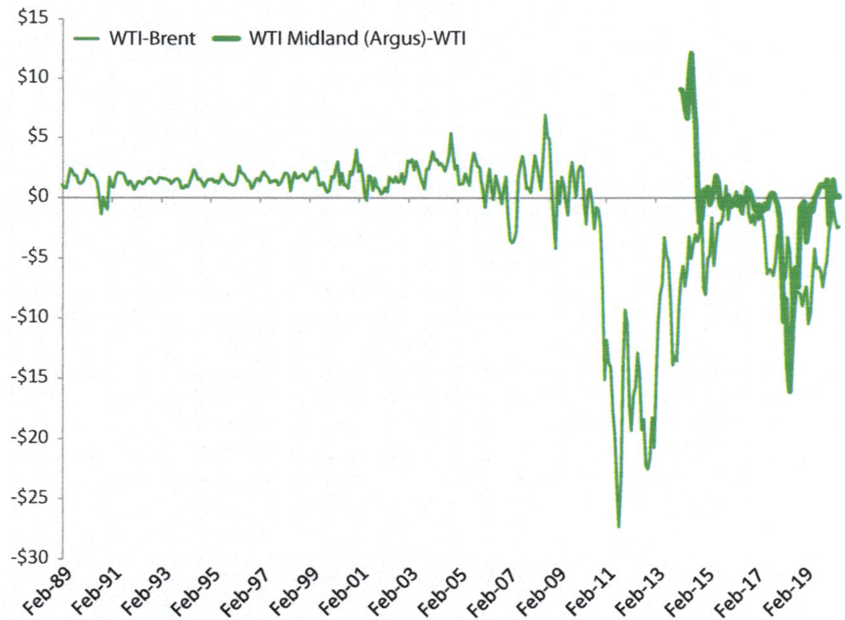

Fig. 1.31 WTI Midland (Argus)-WTI and WTI-Brent spreads. (Source: Author calculation of WTI-Brent based on CME/NYMEX as reported by EIA; Argus data accessed via Quandl. See https://www.argusmedia.com/en/methodology/key-prices/argus-wti-midland for information on the Argus index and EIA's treatment of Permian spreads, https://www.eia.gov/todayinenergy/detail.php?id=31132)

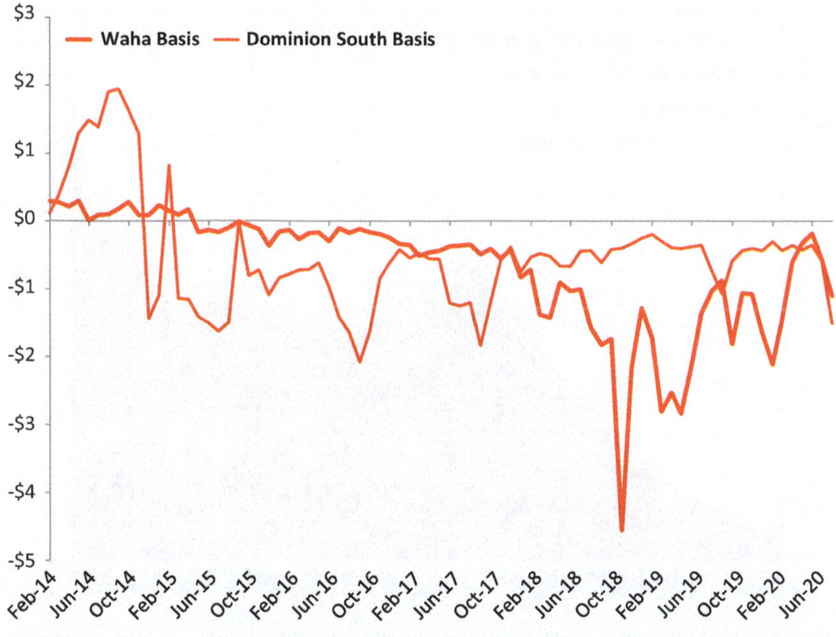

Fig. 1.32 Waha Basis (Platts/IFERC) and Dominion South Basis (Platts/IFERC). (Sources: Platts/IFERC indexes accessed via Quandl. See EIA's commentary on the Appalachian region bottlenecks and spreads at https://www.eia.gov/todayinenergy/detail.php?id=18391)

experienced similar fluctuations, affecting realized prices for producers operating in that region. Using the Dominion South hub benchmark for Appalachia supply, pipeline capacity additions generally narrowed the spread with Henry Hub to less than a dollar (the plummet back to more than a dollar in September 2019 reflected Dominion's Cove Point LNG being offline for maintenance). The cancellation of the Atlantic Coast pipeline in July 2020 served to highlight continuing challenges achieving exits for Appalachian natural gas production (Ridder 2020).

When it comes to NGLs, the rapid growth in plant output is shown in Fig. 1.33, an increasing proportion of gross withdrawals. NGLs must be removed from production streams to meet specifications for pipelines which handle dry gas, methane. Previous charts (Figs. 1.19, 1.23 and 1.24) illustrated the responsiveness of producers as they increased drilling

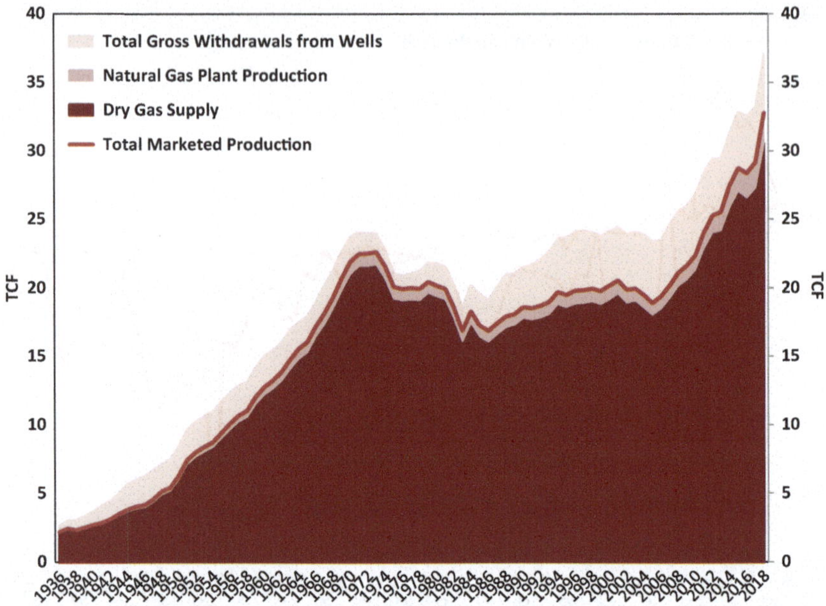

Fig. 1.33 U.S. natural gas supply stack. (Source: EIA; author calculations and depiction. Gas production is shown using EIA accounting: Gross withdrawal of all hydrocarbons and other compounds; marketed production post consumption in the field and after processing to extract NGLs; dry gas production, ultimate consumer/pipeline grade)

and production in locations rich in NGLs and recovered NGLs out of condensate (the lightest of light tight oils). The rapid increase in NGLs volumes has challenged monetization and pricing, as I note previously and as can be seen in Fig. 1.26c.

Who Pays to De-bottleneck?

The establishment of production in oil and gas shale basins and plays pushed the upstream segment beyond the limit of existing midstream "plumbing". The large number of wells required for optimal drainage of unconventional pads and fields means larger gathering systems to aggregate production and connect production to pipelines. Aggregators and pipelines typically conduct business as separate segments, facing their own risk-reward decisions about entering service in new plays and growing to accommodate new production volumes. We have seen that delays in building field-to-market midstream linkages can result in strong disparities or differentials between wellhead locations and market sales points. The often deeply discounted netbacks mean that producers that cannot get their supply to market face steep discounts in the prices and sales revenues that they actually realize. The longer it takes to cure gaps, the worse the potential losses for upstream businesses.

Spreads—as painful as they may be for producers and customers—send important signals into the marketplace, luring investment into capacity additions where the low basis helps to amortize the cost of infrastructure. Once investors respond, and new field-to-market capacity is built, the spreads disappear. If the differentials are in place long enough, the new capacity may be partly or even fully amortized. This is rare. What investors hope to avoid are spreads that diminish too quickly, lowering revenues such that payback lengthens or the midstream business cannot meet its financial targets.

I have mentioned in several places the shifting style of financing pipelines and consequences for producers. With "demand pull" high prices in locations that are under-served provides incentives for investment with customer backing (gas utilities, industrial and/or electric power). In some situations, pipelines and other needed infrastructure can be developed with the pipeline company taking some of the risk, given price conditions in receiving markets. In the "supply push" environment that has prevailed in recent years, many producers have had to fund midstream infrastructure. Most often, this has been in the form of producer commitments for new capacity, financial guarantees for minimum throughput using take or pay conventions, thus making midstream projects "bankable". In some instances, producers invested in midstream infrastructure directly, forming affiliates sometimes through joint ventures to speed up capacity additions. With all of these diversifications, the issue is whether to keep them on the books or, if not, when and how to dispose of them. If the businesses are attractive on their own, the parent companies can benefit from monetizing them.

When producers participate in gathering and pipelines directly, capex is affected, of course. Producers back long distance, risky pipelines by contracting for minimum volumes. We account for these costs in opex. The G&A and Marketing cost component can be highlighted by looking at sources of non-depreciable cash cost or opex as shown below in Fig. 1.34. G&A and Marketing costs eased as a proportion of total opex after natural gas prices collapsed in 2007 and the recession commenced in 2008. It was

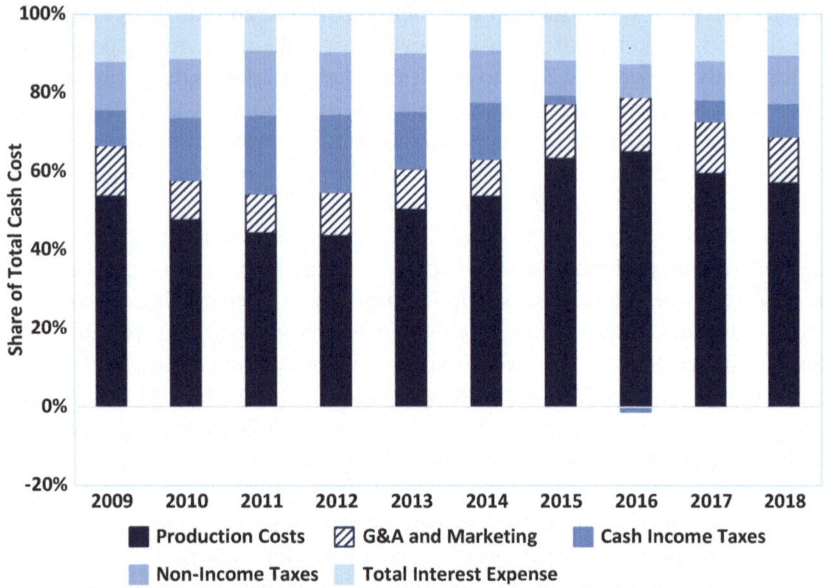

Fig. 1.34 Components of cash cost (operating expense). (Source: Based on 2009–2018 producer benchmarking)

a smaller component of opex during years when producers were more focused on land portfolios and investing heavily in drilling to prove up that acreage. It grew again since 2015 as companies work to solve midstream and especially transportation bottlenecks. Figure 1.34 also illustrates shifting obligations for upstream companies over time, as leverage increased (interest expense), oil prices collapsed (negative income tax obligations) and, in some cases, as states adjusted production taxes (severance or other taxes that constitute the non-income portion of opex in Fig. 1.34).

Growth or Profitability Revisited: Rigs, Drilling and the Future of U.S. Production

The uneven transition from growing volumes to prove up plays and satisfy investors that the unconventional businesses were "real" to achieving sustainable profitability that investors demand raises significant questions about U.S. oil and gas supply going forward. Profitability, while keeping production at current levels much less attaining new growth, means continuing to push the envelope on drilling and well completion efficiencies and costs while curing midstream gaps. Few, if any, of our 16 companies can fully maintain their businesses on production "tails". Shale and other tight rock dynamics being what they are, the industry needs to engage a great deal more work to wrestle with pressure depletion in order to balance revenues. Otherwise, producers in shale plays have no choice except to drill to remain in business. In light of, or perhaps in spite of, these realities, a consensus among analysts emerged that rig activity no longer is a reliable guide to the future.

Generations of analysts and researchers have built models to forecast U.S. oil and gas output using active drilling rig counts as a key input and indicator. More rigs meant more wells and eventual production. This long-established view of rig activity as a key leading indicator came under challenge as shale plays evolved. Initially, lag effects between declines in oil price, drilling activity and oil production raised an assortment of questions about whether shale fundamentally altered commodity market dynamics. Rig contracts are sensitive to operator expectations about price. In recent years, hedging clearly enabled producers to continue drilling when price signals otherwise would not warrant. Changes in drilling strategies—the dominance of longer horizontal well bores and completions, multiple frac stages, multiple wells drilled from common pads—have made the simple metric of total rig activity a less reliable predictor.

Figure 1.35 illustrates oil price as a driver for rig activity and eventual growth in gas production (compare to Figs. 1.12, 1.13 and 1.33). From 2007 on, given the lack of a gas price attractive to gas-directed drilling, and without the benefit of a recovering oil price to boost drilling, rig owners likely would have seen activity flatten around an average of 900 working rigs. Had that been the case, the story today on natural gas supply abundance and perceptions about the future would be completely different. U.S. gas supply would look nothing like it has after 2009. With the influence of higher oil prices and higher value of oil relative to natural gas, especially methane rich gas–producing locations, producers put rigs under contract in tight oil plays. The share of rigs under contract to drill in oily plays has fluctuated around 80 percent, excluding the low oil price years of 2015–2016. The rapid growth in incremental associated gas production followed.

Conventional wisdom has it that a lower rig count is less important in the just-in-time shale-dominated upstream business. Drilling practices

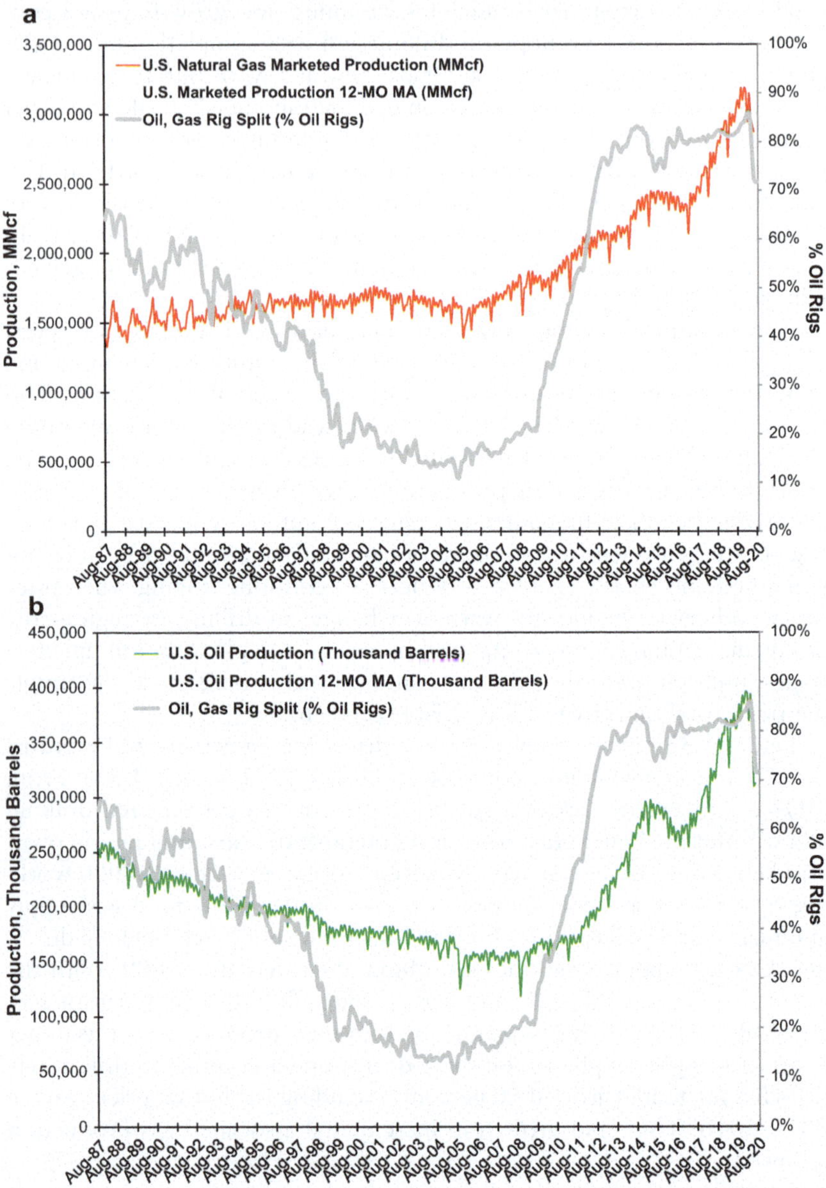

Fig. 1.35 U.S. gas and oil rig split (percent share of rigs targeting oil) and production, monthly and moving average. (**a**) Natural gas. (**b**) Crude oil. (Sources: EIA, Baker Hughes, author calculations and depiction)

reduced the number of rigs needed. Multiple laterals drilled from single well pads, an approach driven by desires to manage both costs of building well locations and the environmental "footprint" associated with the intense extraction needed in these tight rock plays, means fewer rigs in total (but rigs on contract longer at pads).[69] The number of wells and footage drilled per rig clearly has increased substantially given well design. Drilling "cycle times" shortened as operators and OFS vendors became more proficient. Shorter cycle times mean a rig can drill more wells over a contract period. These and other steps to improve drilling efficiencies altered thinking about the significance of rig activity, and about metrics used historically to evaluate oil and gas industry performance. Price is perhaps the most significant enforcer of discipline. We know that drilling efficiencies decline during high price periods when drilling budgets are robust and companies can sweep the occasional miscue under a commodity price rug. In general, across shale plays and basins, production per rig has grown, sometimes dramatically. This mainly is a consequence of operators drilling more wells per rig at multi-well pads and deploying bigger frac jobs.[70] The tradeoffs I identified earlier have bearing on performance across companies and locations. Similar dynamics are at work in well completions. Analysts now are learning how to track frac spreads as a clue to activity.[71] Ability of frac crews to complete more stages during the well completion phase improves efficiency. OFS companies have been able to achieve improved efficiencies even as the number of frac crews has declined with declining drilling activity.[72]

Total rig count more than doubled from the 1990s–early 2000s' trough (below the then psychological marker of 1000 rigs working) to pre-2014's peak (nearly 2000 rigs in operation, on average). This enabled U.S. L48 oil production to increase by nearly 90 percent and gas production to grow almost 40 percent from the 2008 lows (Fig. 1.36). Any time that rig count must increase substantially, following price declines or long periods of inactivity, imposes a "call" on inventory of available drilling locations and OFS equipment, supplies and crews. Clearly, some level of drilling is required to sustain, much less grow, oil and gas production. *As I completed this chapter, U.S. total rig count had fallen to 250, a historical low since 1949.* Going forward, drilling intensity must increase just to keep U.S. oil and gas production at their previous, 2014, highs. But to what level?

For all of the views about the importance, or not, of historical and current rig activity the desire for indicators for activity, recovery and growth will beat out any realities underlying available data. *The question becomes:*

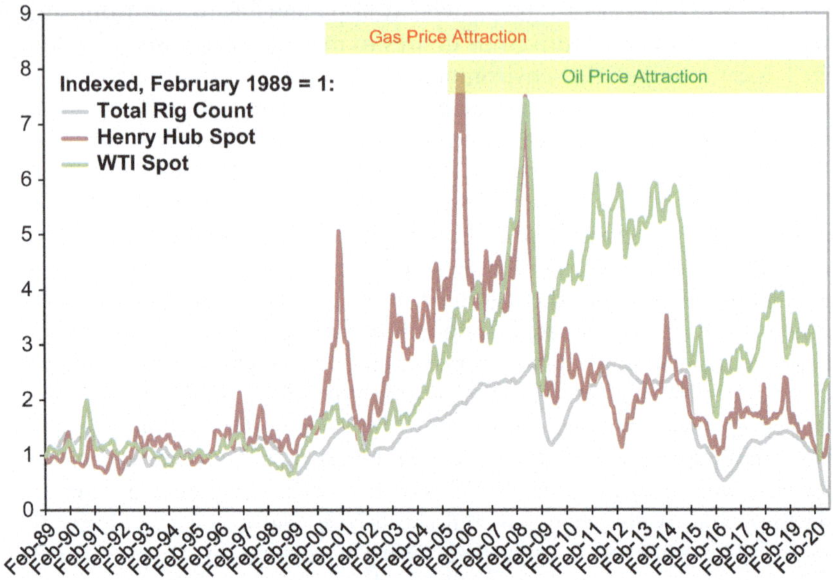

Fig. 1.36 Prices and rig activity, indexed. (Sources: CME/NYMEX as reported by EIA, Baker Hughes)

what measures will best capture and predict the next phases of development in onshore plays? Under the right market conditions, demand for rigs in the future could be as strong, if not stronger, as in the past as operators work to sustain shale output (given accommodating price signals), even if moderated by shale-led drilling strategies and efficiencies. As I show in Table 1.3, the relationships among price, rig activity and production are not straightforward. Commonly used correlations, typically deployed by analysts who cover the OFS segment, illustrate the difficulty in building robust predictors of activity. In general, and following from above, oil price is the strongest motivator for reaching spending decisions and putting rigs on contract. Oil price correlates strongly with U.S. gross domestic production, or GDP, a longtime handle for oil traders. Neither oil nor gas production is responsive to their respective prices. *Even more, the correlations are mildly inversely related, a function of industry tendency to explore when prices are high, but exploit and monetize when prices are lower.* Gas-directed drilling is responsive to gas price, but gas production is more sensitive to oil price and oil-targeted drilling, reflecting the dominance of

Table 1.3 Key relationships: correlation coefficients, monthly, February 1989–June 2020

Variables	*Correlations, %*
Total drilling (rigs working) to oil price	83
Total drilling to gas price	58
Oil drilling to oil price	64
Gas drilling to oil price	32
Gas drilling to gas price	79
Oil production to total drilling	-30
Oil production to oil drilling	46
Oil production to oil price	1
Oil production to year-over-year oil price	-27
Marketed gas production to total drilling	9
Marketed gas production to oil drilling	53
Marketed gas production to gas drilling	-43
Marketed production to oil price	40
Marketed production to gas price	-14

Source: Author calculations using EIA data

associated gas. Different slices of time can produce different correlations, of course. Over the long annual history since 1949, oil production negatively correlates with oil price (-16 percent), while gas correlates positively with gas price (43 percent) but more with oil (61 percent). The bottom line reinforces the relationships in my gas price thermostat (Fig. 1.4), emphasizes the importance of oil price for the foreseeable future and buttresses the Frankelnomics nature of the business.

Previously I addressed the question of producer resilience as downward pressure on commodity prices persists or worsens with drilling activity and production growth. The idea that U.S. producers, in particular shale players, are immune to lower oil prices has been another bit of conventional wisdom to emerge in recent years. This all is a matter of speculation regarding "break evens" which, as I have observed, tend to be focused more on basins and plays rather than resilience and sustainability of operating companies. Those defending producer resilience typically point to "lower cost", a perspective rooted in observations that rig activity and oil and gas production hung on at higher levels than expected during periods of commodity price stress (2007–2009 and 2015–2016). A related view is that shale producers are quicker to turn on or off with price signals. I indicated from our benchmark data that financial losses are real and realized prices, including hedging, provide insulation. As well, the powerful links between oil price and oil drilling to gas supply have deep implications for a more pronounced or, worse, extended low oil price period. Shale plays have enhanced the impact of associated gas from oil and liquids production. However, the historic oil-dependency of U.S. gas production likely has been more pronounced than indicated here, largely because the intrinsic value of gas has been more difficult to build and endure as compared to oil.

As to whether enough is enough and for how long, key questions revolve around the length of time in which oil price provides sufficient attraction and robustness of oil and liquids rich opportunities.[73] Shale players face rapid consumption of drilling locations in the best acreage blocks and wide variability in quality (organic content, resource in place and ultimately recovery rates) in the next, lower tiers of shale acreage. One option is infill drilling, as producers seek to coax more molecules out of established leases, but the well performance issues outlined previously will impinge on those approaches. The U.S. and North American shale oil and gas industry eventually will be on a new page as the world learns whether companies can coax hydrocarbons from very tight source rocks once those pressures are depleted. It is difficult to anticipate the extent of success in repressurizing unconventional reservoirs (enhanced recovery) based on the very few experiments thus far. As with conventional fields, the ability to breathe new life into existing well bores and facilities makes the idea alluring (Jacobs 2019).[74] If the industry proves able to move forward on that front, the size and scope of U.S. shale basins could help sustain domestic production longer, staving off the need for new frontier resources.[75]

Summing Up

By this time, a reader might wish for that famous one-handed economist. Yet, it is the caveats, provisos, warning flags and qualifications that trip up the best-formed scenarios, strategies and plans. One could also argue that the United States is just too different to matter in the greater scheme of things. In spite of our country's uniqueness, we can draw many lessons from U.S. experience again, for those who care to take them. To close this chapter, I offer three perspectives—on myth and mythology in the U.S. upstream business, on how that mythology played in capital markets and bridging from understanding the present to thinking about future prospects. My perspectives should be read in the context of where things stand as our book went to press. U.S. crude oil output shed roughly 2.5 MMBD on average during May-June 2020, a 20 percent drop from the start of that year. Since July 2020 to early 2021, production has recovered to average just over 11 MMBD, regaining about a third of lost supply. A smaller effect played out for natural gas. By June 2020, marketed gas production had declined 10 percent. Since October 2020 and through January 2021, marketed gas has averaged about 83 BCFD, recovering about 6 percent of lost output.These trends parallel commodity prices. The negative settled price for light sweet crude of –$37.63/BBL on April 20, 2020 sent shock waves through the global industry. At the time, few thought WTI could climb out of the $30s—the 12-month forward contract traded at just over $34. Yet, in February 2021 WTI breached $60. Spot trading since then has ranged between $58 and $65. Pre-pandemic, natural gas had been selling for close to $3/MMBtu, which many view a more "normal" valuation (see Fig. 1.4). During 2020, natural gas was often below $2. From October 2020, gas had largely been above $2.50. However, Henry Hub soared above $6, and then $10 and then 20 during February 11–18, 2021, as a Siberian freeze gripped the U.S. mid-continent, with Texas as "ground zero". Natural gas likely will remain priced between $2.50 and $3.00 or slightly above until post-pandemic patterns become clearer. As before, the influence of shale oil drilling on associated gas largesse is manifest in both lower price and, except for those seasonal adventures, lower volatility Henry Hub since 2010. U.S. exports of crude oil and other liquids dropped more than production—nearly 3.2 MMBD by May 2020, more than one-third from the pre-pandemic peak of almost 10 MMBD in February 2020. Petroleum exports have recovered to average close to 9 MMBD in January 2021. By June 2020, U.S. gas exports, mainly via pipeline to Mexico and as LNG, fell almost 34 percent from the pre-pandemic peak of nearly 1.4 BCFD in January 2020. LNG (nearly half of total gas sold externally) collapsed more than 60 percent. By January 2021, gas exports returned to a new peak topping 1.7 BCFD with LNG soaring 217 percent to a new high from the June 2020 low. And so it goes.

Myth and Mythology

I opened this chapter by invoking the art of the long view in scenario building. Scenario practitioners have long been relied on "myth"; it is an integral part of the "art" of building long views. Myth and mythology are as important in the business world as in human culture. Indeed, the use of myth to define management or business culture is a venerable topic of study. Personalities of business leaders, distinct styles of decision making that companies tend to adopt, almost to cult-like extent, and the socialization of work forces all go in tandem with notions about reputation, "brand" and how best to "warehouse" reputational and brand risks. The shale era has had a formidable impact on attitudes and politics—of that there is no doubt. It also has its share of myth and mythology.

- **"Manufacturing wellbores and making widgets".** The idea that shale plays can be, are becoming, "industrialized" has included a tag line that all shale wells can be pretty much the same. In fact, the high degree of variability that I point to, and that is replete in industry literature, undermines the idea that all dollars spent on all wellbores, pads, and cubes can yield consistent results. Manufacturing efficiency thrives on production of repeated models, honing assembly lines so that asset managers can minimize imperfections and faults. Shale plays are natural resources. The industry needs either much more R&D spending to hone the assembly lines or companies must figure out "bespoke" approaches that are amenable to cost management. It could be that some of the ideas in circulation, in particular to improve data capture and analytics or to employ machine learning or artificial intelligence, can make a difference. The big hurdle is predictive quality. So far, that remains out of reach.
- **"No dry holes".** I have mentioned that an attraction of shale plays was the absence of exploration risk, that is, "no dry holes". That said what should we call uncompleted or underperforming wells, which operators would in any other circumstance plug and abandon for lack of commerciality? A particular failing of due diligence among competitors and capital providers has been deeper scrutiny of what producers report. Likewise, the industry would benefit from increased transparency in how companies report and discuss their results.
- **"Shale plays can be throttled up or down".** Perhaps the most widespread myth is that shale is "throttleable". Producers have experimented with choking back production in order to flatten decline curves. We could consider decline curve exhaustion the dark side of resource play largesse. It certainly is the downside, quite literally, of shale assets. The problem of discerning the throttle goes well beyond decline curves. One is counting DUCs. I argued that the

tendency to rely on DUCs as evidence of drilling readiness overstates the case. Producer resilience is another example held up as proof. If resilience means apparent activity and production growth in the face of adverse conditions that ordinarily would encourage more and better discipline, then it is a false messenger. Companies have substantial tool kits for managing assorted risks and uncertainties, and they certainly should use them. However, to conclusions I shared before, if a business is not operating on solid profit-loss grounds then these tool kits can only do so much. Altogether, management of declines, the fascination with DUC inventory and the notion of resilience combined to give shale plays the reputation of being "just-in-time" businesses. Companies, their investors and bankers, their customers and their governments in all jurisdictions—all would benefit if they took perspectives that are more reasonable on the demands of these plays. Along with that, a better sense of the full upstream cycle—entry, development, optimization and exit—and associated timing would help educate views. The "just-in-time" bias largely is an artifact of the distinctive, highly visible rushes into waves of shale investments. In many respects, the loss of confidence in domestic producers by capital markets could be the best thing that happens if the industry is to evolve more robust business models. Producers need true resilience, the internal financial wherewithal to support reinvestment.
- **"Geoscience is less important than engineering".** Forever, these two disciplines have locked horns over the soul of the oil and gas industry. Fundamental geoscience understanding of the subsurface environment grounds most, if not all, of what we have learned about well performance. We often describe pounding away with superlats and superfracs as a "brute force" method. To date, as I note, and with plenty of evidence, financial results are very much suspect. Geoscience is essential if the new concepts in data analytics are to prove reliable. Companies will either re-build the "exploration shop" to reflect the nature of the resource or suffer the consequences. From what I have been able to deduce through our benchmarking, the more successful producers are the ones who seem to have a good sense of how to balance disciplines and tool kits.
- **"Companies can continue to drive down costs".** The effects of innovation and competition are very tangible and can help monetize lower-quality acreage, no matter the target opportunity. This is the technology pathway at work. In the shale era, beyond the deploy-

ment of the main enabling technologies—long used in other ways for other oil and gas plays and projects—most technical improvements are incremental. Investments to optimize land portfolios and chase better geology have been much more significant. Analysts have been able to detect diminishing returns as they picked apart and scrutinized the superlat, superfrac, cube and other drilling strategies. More interesting than the next incremental improvement in shale is to consider what could happen if strategies and approaches from shale plays were applied to conventional fields and opportunities where reservoir quality might lend itself to the same kind of pursuit. Bringing interesting conventional plays into the mix could be a more correct interpretation of a widely used phrase, "making the unconventional conventional".

- **"The major companies will industrialize the shale plays".** The jury is still out on whether this particular notion is myth or reality. By the end of 2019, and from early indications in 2020, the majors had certainly entered shale plays, in some cases as a second or even third round and with some announcements of aggressive drilling and production targets that almost certainly had the effect of dampening price expectations.[76] The major companies also must perform or risk losing investor confidence, in spite of their dividends. For all of the power of major company integrated value chains, they face distinct challenges in upstream cost management, while achieving economies of scale and preserving their safety records, and staying ahead of downstream and LNG margins as they monetize.

The size and significance of unconventional resources are not mythical—they are very real, with very real complications and challenges. We have always counted shale basins in the U.S. resource endowment, but our math mainly was through assessment of technically recoverable resources and booked reserves in overlaying conventional fields and from early unconventional forays such as coal bed methane. As companies and prospectors pushed into shale resource plays as a distinct asset for upstream portfolios, they deepened our understanding of the U.S. and Canadian endowment.[77] The trick, as always, is how best to capture resources that are technically recoverable while surviving, and thriving, in the process.

The Patch and Money

Outcomes and stresses from "Frankelnomics" show up in a variety of ways, in company operating and financial results along with historical drilling and production trends. Considerable deviation among companies exists, depending upon location of production and field-to-market connections. Producers can face considerable price discounts from the traded commodities (lower netbacks to the wellhead and lower realized prices). Operating cash flow serves as the piggy bank that helps to fund continuing operations as well as organic capital spending and crucial acquisitions for growth. Producers have outspent that piggy bank for most of the quarters and years that shale plays have dominated strategies. Producers spread sunk cost accumulations over time in DD&A charges against revenue. Those DD&A charges return in the form of credits, comprising a portion of cash flow from operations, sometimes overwhelmingly. The more generous and flexible the tax rules (U.S. tax treatment tends to fit that description) the greater the availability of depreciation credits. The prevailing characteristic of shale and other tight rock plays—type curves with sharp and rapid declines in production and ongoing drilling to counter declines—implies a large inventory of depreciation credits, so long as producers have income. Clearly, producers need a next iteration of viable business models if they and their customers are to continue to harvest from these resources. A place to start could be acknowledging the shortcomings embodied in some of the beliefs about shale plays and strategies I lined out above.

Profitability and cash flow stresses that emanate and persist from "Frankelnomics" realities run counter to capital market expectations. A pronounced business risk for shale plays, so dependent upon external capital, is that capital markets would close to them. We cannot underestimate the importance of the powerful capital market funding conveyor belt for the role it has played in empowering the size, scope and rich potential of the U.S. shale basins. Following the onslaught of the 2008 recession, oil and gas emerged as "must-have" assets for investment portfolios hammered by low interest rates, a consequence of the Federal Reserve Bank's "quantitative easing", and collapsed values for alternative investments that had been popular, namely real estate and bank holdings. To a large extent, the ability for oil and gas upstream companies to survive the 2007 natural gas price collapse, the 2008 recession, the 2014 oil price collapse and persistently low realized prices and revenues from midstream bottlenecks was all due to the continued attractiveness of oil and gas equities and debt relative to competing opportunities.

The conveyor belt of funding for shale plays topped past metrics for investment in the U.S. oil and gas businesses by far. Funding sources were diverse. Traditional bank debt, private equity, hedge funds, exchange traded funds, or ETFs, linked to the oil and gas equities and other avenues—these and more vastly enlarged the pool of potential market participants in the “shale gale”.

Over the course of 12 years, our sample of 16 domestic producers spent, on average, about $55 billion per year in capex (Fig. 1.19). The larger industry sample of roughly 50 companies covered by Bernstein Research totted up capital spending in excess of $100 billion per year, on average, for domestic U.S. assets.[78] Neither the Bernstein samples nor ours include integrated major companies. Capex spreads liberally throughout the oil and gas ecosystem. Companies paid many billions initially to land and mineral owners and OFS providers for drilling and field management support. Beyond upstream, billions more were spent on field-to-market links and expansions. Capex surged into the midstream plumbing needed to hook everything together, with funding sourced both from midstream specialists and their backers and from the operators in the form of those capacity guarantees. Billions have flowed into the domestic power expansion described in Chap. 2. For the first time in many years, U.S. (and foreign) commitments expanded for oil and gas downstream, refining and petrochemicals, particularly for export capacity. As noted in Chap. 3, companies have plowed almost $150 billion into downstream petrochemical investments to soak up supply abundance. Tens of billions more flowed into LNG export projects described in Chap. 4.

Oil and gas holdings are longstanding components of institutional and individual investment portfolios, mainly as dividend-yielding equity shares and commercial debt issues of companies. Depending upon business conditions, investors also may include OFS enterprises and smaller, non-dividend-paying independents.

To use a much over-used phrase, “at the end of the day”[79] the issue is what investors see that makes them unhappy. Today, oil and gas, OFS equities and midstream are out of favor, moving in that direction since 2014 as lower commodity prices and inability to achieve and sustain profitability eroded investor confidence. Commodity price cycles are a gatekeeper for industry funding, and investors are fickle. At the end of the second quarter 2019, total market capitalization for the Bernstein sample of 54 companies I referred to earlier was about $457 billion. This is roughly half of the value of their slightly smaller, 52-company industry

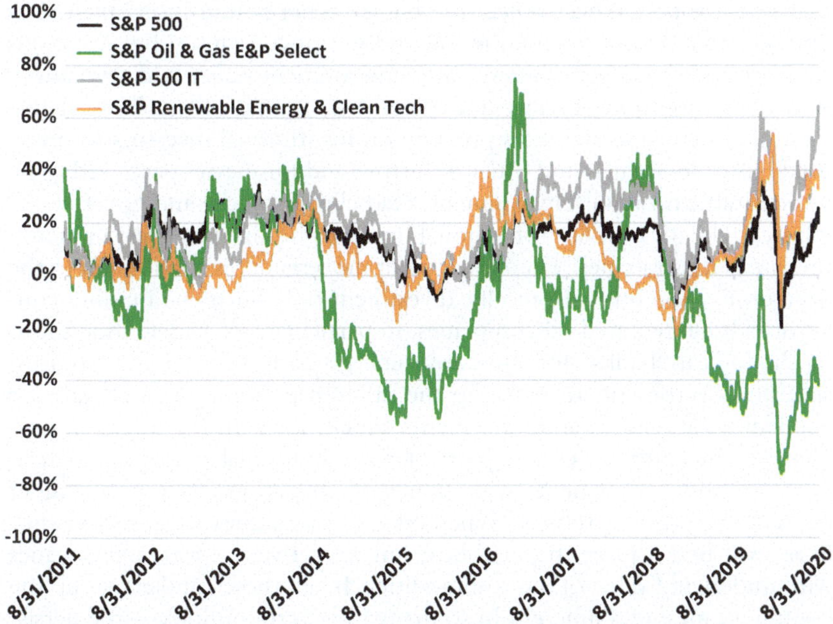

Fig. 1.37 One year returns on S&P indexes. (Sources: Standard & Poor indexes (access required), author calculations. *E&P* exploration and production, *IT* information technology)

sample (about $864 billion in market cap) at the end of the second quarter 2014 before the bottom fell out of the oil market.[80]

Falling valuations and equity investment returns for oil and gas complicated the competitiveness of oil and gas businesses with alternative opportunities. Figure 1.37 illustrates the waxing and waning fortunes of oil and gas relative to other key sectors in the S&P 500 index. Investors have diverted attention to technology shares, in particular during the pandemic markets. Returns on "clean energy" have been widely publicized with many arguing that more is going on than cyclical variations made extraordinary by the pandemic. However, actual valuations of alternative energy enterprises remain low unless coupled with traditional businesses that have greater EBITDA potential.[81]

Shifting perceptions about future viability of the oil and gas industry and its assets at a time of historically low valuations makes it easier to claim that investor preferences reflect the bigger "energy transition" picture as opposed to reactions in the low oil and gas price regime. Big questions swirl around the effect of energy and environment policy and regulation, as noted in the book Preface and Foreword, among other places. A distinct, and new, uncertainty is pressure on institutional investors to divest holdings of fossil fuels and other industries and businesses perceived to be less desirable on ESG (environment, read climate, social and governance) metrics. The idea is that institutional investors in turn will exert influence on corporate strategies. The "divestment movement" is a follow-on to the decarbonization push. Ironically, divestment only hurts the funding conveyor belt—integrated oil companies, in particular, are widely thought to be the logical "banks" for alternative energy projects—and adds to pressure on governments to make up the difference. Some shifts already are happening, at least in announcements, albeit not with the intended outcomes.[82] In truth, investors, particularly institutional managers such as pensions and endowments with fiduciary obligations, face even bigger pressures to produce returns. When oil and gas equities are attractive they likely will find a place in portfolios, but attractiveness waxes and wanes with underlying value of the commodities. In all, these conflicts set up the contrarian messages inherent in so many long-term outlooks—the persistence of oil and gas as dominant energy sources even as market shares of electric vehicles and renewable energy increase.[83]

IT is heavily embedded in the oil and gas technology pathway and Silicon Valley has taken note of the push for more as companies utilize remote management and surveillance for drilling and ongoing operations. Along with interest in data science and AI to improve decision making, the IT components of the technology pathway have expanded rapidly since 2014 and in the face of pandemic operational challenges.

The prevailing "buzz" words for oil and gas—"digitization", "data analytics" and so on—reflect the rapid adoption of IT strategies seen as crucial for everything from cost reductions in shale plays to optimization of complex global value chains, for market intelligence and monitoring and for improving and reporting on environmental management. Oil and gas companies are embracing the marriage in order to beef up credentials in a world in which honing "reputation" and "brand" are nearly everything. If all of this has a familiar ring, one need only look to healthcare in general and biotech and pharmaceuticals in particular. The latter has long been my favorite analogy for traditional oil and gas exploration—large outlays of capex for, essentially, research and development (R&D) in search of blockbusters.

Many of the bigger names in the tech space also are investing in energy for their own facilities and operations and to create new businesses—notably electric vehicle and renewable energy components that are expected to replace traditional transport, fuels and electric power value chains. The large IT firms have been guarantors for clean energy projects through power purchase agreements (PPAs) and other mechanisms.

Using the S&P market indexes, one can easily see that, for the past year oil and gas producers have been in negative territory for valuations (-45.9 percent total return) while clean energy equities have been positive (+52.9 percent).[84] These differences have received abundant press coverage and commentary from fund managers, private equity groups, investment banks and others. A more fair comparison shows annualized five-year returns of -10.6 and 16 percent for oil and gas and "clean tech", respectively, while ten-year returns are -3.6 percent and 2 percent. In fact, ups and downs in the clean tech space are notorious, as one would expect for new sectors and industries in general, news coverage notwithstanding.[85] A good question is how attractive returns might happen for renewable energy businesses, in the first place, given the nature of the business—the value lies in the components and the energy generated and dispatched, rather than intrinsically in a physical commodity. The role of public support, encompassing everything from local tax abatements for renewable energy projects to federal production tax credits and other forms of support, cannot be ignored (Chap. 2; Gülen et al. 2017, 2018). This sets up one of the more interesting conundrums. Large oil companies, under pressure to diversify capex and to help speed the growth of renewable energy, will do so only if the opportunities look financially sustainable in the end. Thus, any number of industry leaders have offered pointed remarks on the difficulty of moving beyond public support in order to facilitate the transition to renewable energy on a commercial basis[86] while, seeing the writing on the wall, defending vigorously the role of natural gas.[87]

Flash forward to spring 2021. Improved profitability (see my update in the opening to this chapter) and, crucially, reductions in massive debt loads accrued by shale players – a function of brutal cost adjustments but also improved oil prices – are showing up in public company share valuations. The U.S. oil and gas industry today is nearly three times as valuable as the March 2020 low (coincident with that amazing price collapse). It remains a fraction, more than one-third, less valuable than in June 2014.

Importantly – crucially, in so many ways – while oil and gas industry share prices are below the broader S&P 500 index, they now exceed both high tech (by almost 40 percent) ***and*** "renewable and clean tech" indexes (by ten times). The latter captures a psychological point. Pre-pandemic, "clean energy tech" companies had soared more than 1.5 times in worth as speculation took hold that these businesses would be favored as "pandemic cures". News was rampant that many governments, including the U.S., would target public spending to "clean tech" as a "green" economic boost. Instead, the pre-pandemic assertion that investors would forevermore turn against the oil and gas industry, a "decarbonization" "peak demand" thesis, seems, at least at present, a figment of imaginations. Indeed, news reports that major banks had directed more than $750 billion toward fossil fuel investments during 2020 definitely went against the grain of expectations (Nauman and Morris, 2021). In any case, going forward the funding conveyor belt is crucial for natural gas to remain cheap and affordable and, therefore, competitive. That surely is a bottom-line lesson for these times and the next decades.

U.S. Energy Abundance, Security and International Trade

In Fig. 1.38, I estimate "excess supply" including storage injections and withdrawals for the United States. Net imports via pipeline and LNG mirror the amount of excess supply after domestic use. Looked at this way, it is easy to deduce that the absence of generous U.S. supply would imply a much different future than many have envisioned for U.S. natural gas exports.

In Fig. 1.39, I provide context for U.S. exports while also highlighting the pronounced shift in internal, Lower 48, natural gas flows and trade within North America. The re-plumbing of the U.S. interstate natural gas system has been nothing short of profound. The mighty Marcellus disrupted the long-established exit of natural gas from the Gulf Coast "HH region" to the upper Midwest and northeast. Lack of other options for gas sales, especially natural gas rich with NGLs, caused a reversal of pipelines that originated from the Gulf Coast to carry gas northward as producers sought monetization in the vast Gulf Coast hydrocarbons processing complex. As I remarked previously, Appalachian production also upended newly built pipelines that originated to carry Rockies gas eastward. LNG import capacity built during the early 2000s investment wave is being redeployed for export strategies along with new export projects, as detailed

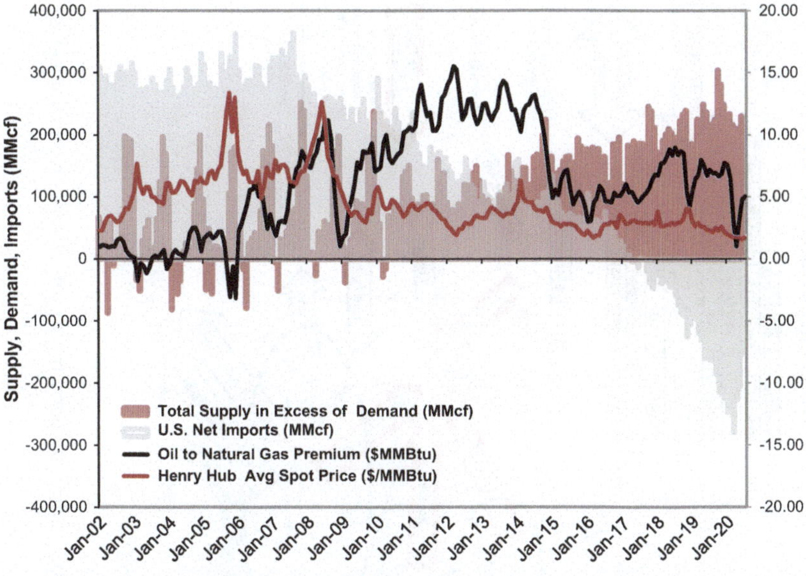

Fig. 1.38 U.S. total supply in excess of domestic demand. (Source: EIA, author calculations and depiction)

in Chap. 4 and summarized in the inset table. The expansion of oil and gas downstream especially along the U.S. Gulf Coast, detailed in Chap. 3, will be equivalent to building out a third to half again as much capacity as previously existed for some NGLs products. All of this represents a great deal of "iron in the ground" that will not be easy to dispose of if underlying strategies prove incorrect or a transition away from oil and gas is more rapid.

How important is natural gas to U.S. energy security and foreign policy? That is a debatable question. I remarked previously on the plethora of opinions and discernible shifts in attitudes as the position of our country in global energy balances evolved. For all of the influence U.S. exports, both oil and gas, have had on world views about energy there is no real consensus on U.S. energy "independence"—a loaded term. Nor is there any real consensus as to how energy independence would impact geopolitics and international relations. Nor would it be possible to definitively research and ascertain U.S. political influence, given all of the other historical and cultural characteristics that impinge on international trade and politics.

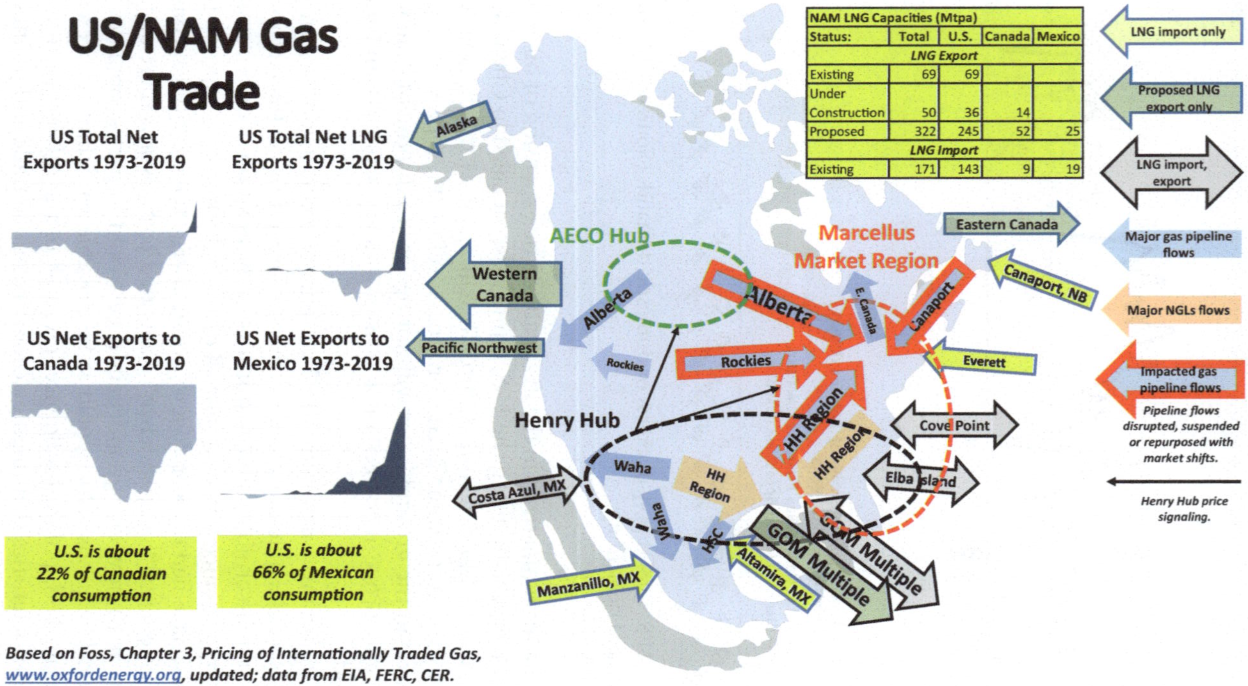

Fig. 1.39 North American natural gas trade. (Sources: EIA; FERC; various industry trade publications on pipeline flows)

The United States is extraordinary in energy resource endowments of all types, an artifact of how the continent formed. Could some combination of energy sources and technologies render the U.S. truly energy independent? Possibly, if we also make decisions to repatriate components of alternative energy technologies for which we rely on foreign suppliers. This is a pronounced weakness of new, new things like new green deals and undermines debates about natural gas bridges. For all of the big news on U.S. exports and the implications for geopolitical balances, U.S. positioning abroad and global energy markets, the United States still imports energy. We take receipts of electricity from Canada, with potentially more to come from that country's huge Labrador hydropower potential. Receipts of natural gas from Canada have reduced dramatically, but not completely.[88] Receipts of LNG remain critical for New England seasonal needs. Heavier oil continues to enter the U.S. refining segment to balance our LTO production. Any number of disruptions could alter the trade balance picture. Should natural gas supplies become tighter, U.S. customers would essentially be bidding against international buyers, with both market and political ructions. Alternatively, the competitive forces lining up against natural gas in the electric power sector could preserve the "long gas", supply surplus conditions for some time to come.

The moral of the long view story? Building paradigms always is a risky business.

Notes on Research Methodology: Producer Benchmarking

In 2010, I and my research team at the Bureau of Economic Geology's Center for Energy Economics initiated benchmarking of a select group of U.S. operating companies considered best in class. The sample underlying the data in this chapter included Anadarko, Apache, Cabot, Chesapeake, Concho, ConocoPhillips, Continental, Devon, Encana (Canadian-based), EOG, Hess, Marathon, Occidental, Pioneer, Range and Southwestern.

In 2018, this group of companies constituted almost 25 percent of U.S. crude oil and liquids production and about 18 percent of U.S. marketed natural gas production based on EIA.

My decision that we should undertake benchmarking and our methodology were influenced by investor presentations from EOG and communication with then-CEO Mark Papa and other EOG personnel regarding the state of the business relative to natural gas market conditions (Fig. 1.40).

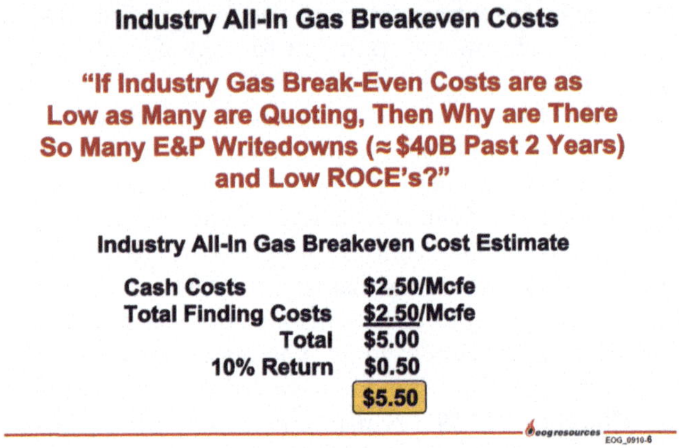

Fig. 1.40 Breakeven cost estimate, EOG resources. (Source: EOG investor presentation, September 2010)

U.S. Producer Calculation Methodology

In order to most appropriately portray the cost structure of companies in the U.S. E&P sector, we categorized the full cycle, all source, average, breakeven costs of the sample of 16 producers into two categories on a $/boe basis. We calculated a three-year (beginning with 2007 reporting) rolling average of finding and development capital expenditure weighted against the number of barrels added to reserves. We computed cash operating costs weighted against production. Comparing F&D with reserve additions shows us how well a company is able to convert dollars into reserves while cash operating costs allocated to production is a representation of the company's operational efficiency. In other words, by implementing this methodology, we may properly examine how efficient our sample is at proving up reserves and producing those barrels as independent functions of a company. When taken together, these two figures demonstrate what it costs a company to find and produce a single barrel of oil equivalent in a year. To complete the picture, we add two return scenarios, discussed below. We use data only for U.S. activities from audited annual reports filed with the SEC (10-ks for the domestic companies in our sample and form 40-f for Encana). All figures related to additions and production are on an equivalent basis (6 Mcf of gas = 1 barrel of oil).

Finding and Development (F&D) Costs per Barrel of Additions

The F&D category is composed of costs incurred for the acquisition of proved and unproved properties, exploration and development. We averaged these costs over three years in order to match them more accurately with the benefits managements and investors expect them to yield. The rationale behind using a weighted average rather than the current year F&D flows from the concept that capital expenses incurred in one period are expected to yield results in future periods. It is common practice to use between three- and five-year averages when considering capital expenses. Taking a rolling average also has a smoothing effect on spending over the years, as capital expenditures tend to be lumpy in nature. As mentioned above, these costs are allocated to the increase in reserves booked over the corresponding years to come up with a $/boe figure.

As our interest was in examining the efficiency of dollars spent to prove reserves, we have excluded some line items from F&D costs and net changes in reserves. Specifically, we omit sales, asset retirement obligations (AROs) and expenses associated with unevaluated acreage that are suspended or excluded from the full cost amortization pool.[89] On the additions side of the calculation, financial statements have six line items involved in accounting for changes in reserves: sales, production, revisions, purchases, improved recovery and additions (extensions, discoveries and other). The first two of these are not included in our analysis because while they are, of course, material and ordinary actions done by companies, they are unrelated to the process of finding reserves.

Cash Operating Costs

Cash costs are a bit trickier than F&D. This is because much of the financial data in this cost category is not allocated to the different business segments to which they correspond. Therefore, it is necessary to allocate certain line items to the upstream segment when applicable. The best method for allocating these costs is to prorate them based on segment revenues (which *are* presented in the statements). The components of cash operating costs are lease operating expense (LOE), general and administrative (G&A) and marketing, income tax, non-income tax (usually production taxes) and interest. We take cash costs against barrels produced over the same period.

Calculating Returns

Our view was that incorporating a return for investors is an equally important component of the situation for companies (no one is in business with the intent of breaking even). We devised two return scenarios. The first is a standard 10 percent return on investment or ROI based on current year F&D and cash costs. The second is a return equal to current year F&D, with our assumption that any business would want to produce a return at least equal to its annual capex. A 10 percent return is a typical screening rate. Setting returns equal to current-year F&D yields larger amounts. Because we became concerned about the ability of U.S. producers to generate free cash flow for reinvestment, calculating the alternative return allowed us to explore the consequences for capital requirements if companies generated insufficient cash flow to continue and/or expand operations.

Notes

1. Borrowing the title of the classic book on scenario thinking by Schwartz (1996).
2. See footnote 1.
3. See https://www.bp.com/en/global/corporate/energy-economics/statistical-review-of-world-energy.html for downloads.
4. See https://ourworldindata.org/energy for data set and sources.
5. It is important to note that the concept of renewability refers only to the energy source itself, such as wind, solar, tidal and wave (marine) and biofuels (crops). Most inputs to renewable energy sources are nonrenewable.
6. That classic view is, of course, from Porter's (1980) influential work.
7. *Oil Is First Found in the Mind: The Philosophy of Exploration*, compiled by Norm Foster and Ed Beaumont and published by the American Association of Petroleum Geologists in 1992 as number 20 in a petroleum geology series, makes the point succinctly. The book title was drawn from phrasing by Wallace Pratt, "Where oil is first found, in the final analysis, is in the minds of men" in another classic, Pratt's 1952 paper "Towards a Philosophy of Oil Finding" in the AAPG *Bulletin*, volume 36.
8. In this phrasing, I refer to the classic work by Joseph Schumpeter from his classic work (Schumpeter 1942).
9. As explained in the book Appendix, gas (piped methane) delivered to customers requires considerable capital investment to dehydrate and separate from other hydrocarbons (to satisfy pipeline quality specifications) and build the necessary pipeline infrastructure. The larger capital investment relative to oil implies a price discount inherent in methane. See section "The Lure of Private Lands and Minerals".

10. Based on communications with Barbara Shook, Chap. 3 co-author, regarding discussions with GTL developers.
11. It is hard to put a finger on exactly when critiques surfaced regarding natural gas as a "bridge" fuel for energy transition. A rough timeline is available in this link, https://grist.org/natural-gas/natural-gas-a-bridge-to-nowhere/
12. Estimate based on U.S. government data for federal production as compared to total output and accounting for production from state and tribal lands. For a view of the main federal oil and gas domain—the OCS—see https://www.api.org/oil-and-natural-gas/energy-primers/offshore.
13. The concept of "obsolescing bargains" for extractives industries, mining as well as oil and gas, is well-trod ground. From the original idea, widely attributed to Raymond Vernon (1971). The notion, focused on multinational enterprises and their negotiations with resource-owning host governments, is that sovereign resource owners "learn" and bargaining power shifts away from the enterprise and to the sovereign. The same is true in open, competitive, private land and minerals markets and leasing. Companies may have the initial advantage in terms of knowledge about the resource endowment and commercialization potential. Private land and minerals owners come up to speed very quickly.
14. Ailworth (2017) provided an excellent case study of the gamut of improvements, including those I mentioned, with emphasis on logistics and inferences for OFS companies.
15. Operators now are moving toward "e-fracking" or fracking using electricity fueled by field gas. This has the advantage of soaking up gas production that operators might otherwise flare and providing substantial cost savings. The downside is faced by OFS companies who must pay to retrofit diesel pumpers (Hampton 2019).
16. In a proprietary review of E&P innovation (2001), McKinsey & Company found that the timeframe from idea to prototype to commercialization (50 percent of market penetration) tended to be more than 30 years. This compared to about 15 for broadband, about 12 for medicine and about 7 for consumer products. The study identified a number of inefficiencies, including those mentioned in the text.
17. See the Alerian website for excellent information and background on midstream, energy infrastructure and MLPs. https://www.alerian.com/
18. Kinder Morgan was the notable exit from its MLP arrangement. Other large midstream partnerships have not followed. See Steffey (2014) for a good overview.
19. The quick turnabout of business conditions in the Permian is a case study in midstream business challenges. Having finally achieved new pipelines, producers in the Covid-19 world are using substantially less capacity than midstream developers planned for (Elliott 2020).

20. See Michot Foss (2020b) for an overview on U.S. domestic upstream organization.
21. A prominent upstream equities analyst once referred to the often mentioned "shale factory" as the equity research shop strategy of covering pure play companies explaining that it was easier for "generalists". Analysts typically hired by equities research groups could build valuation models for unconventional players as opposed to conventional, exploration risk (personal communication, November 30, 2011).
22. In fact, during the 1990s, Canadian producers and pipeline operators struggled mightily with the problem of how to get more gas into the Lower 48 in order to gain some relief from large surpluses and low prices. Prior to the wave of LNG import projects—including projects proposed in Eastern Canada to serve northeast U.S. markets—Canadian gas export pipeline expansions were the most closely watched and discussed gas industry news topic (OGJ 1995a, b, 1997).
23. See the newly named Canada Energy Regulator for status, https://www.cer-rec.gc.ca/pplctnflng/mjrpp/nrgyst/index-eng.html.
24. The author participated briefly in a Canadian Energy Research Institute report initiated in 1993 that argued Mexico could become a large gas supplier and exporter, sending output from its northern basins into the United States and competing with Canadian deliveries. That report is no longer publicly available. However, other coverage from that period provides snapshots (see OGJ 1993a, b; Norton 1993).
25. Based on a quote in historical treatment of the Texas oil and gas industry. From *Hazardous Business, Industry Regulation and the Texas Railroad Commission*, Texas State Library Archives Commission online exhibit, https://www.tsl.texas.gov/exhibits/railroad/oil/page6.html. To wit: "Hell, I sell a barrel of oil at ten cents and a bowl of chili costs me fifteen!"
26. New lessons are emerging on this front as Big Tech punches its weight. See Foer 2020.
27. From a proprietary Bernstein Research report, July 24, 2015. Bernstein analysts have consistently questioned whether "sunk cost fallacy" permeates the unconventional play operators.
28. Summary based on a number of industry reviews and retrospectives and author analysis of company financials and proprietary analyst reports. See section "We (Were) in the Money", for details on various phases of the emerging shale gas and oil businesses.
29. I derived the term "Frankelnomics" in Michot Foss (2020a).
30. In Hotelling's time, oil wars in California paralleled events in Texas.
31. See also Verlager 2007 for his review of Frankel's views and idea on oil markets and pricing going forward.
32. Kemp also updates theories about oil prices moving beyond Verlager's 2007 treatment.

33. Priddle's comments are part of his independent review of a natural gas market analysis submitted to support the proposed Bear Head LNG export project in Nova Scotia. The project was never developed and was put up for sale in July, 2020 (Beswick 2020).
34. The producer benchmarking effort entailed a number of researchers in addition to myself: Miranda Wainberg, Daniel Quijano, Deniese Palmer-Huggins and Rahul Verma. See Notes on Research Methodology for more detail. An initial paper (Michot Foss and Wainberg 2012) included methodology and reasoning. See also http://www.beg.utexas.edu/files/energyecon/think-corner/2015/CEE_Snapshot-Producer_Benchmarks_Part_Deux-Mar15.pdf, http://www.beg.utexas.edu/files/energyecon/think-corner/2016/CEE_Snapshot-Producer_Benchmarks_2016-Mar16.pdf; http://www.beg.utexas.edu/files/energyecon/think-corner/2018/CEE%20producer%20benchmarks%202017.pdf
35. For an overview of breakevens and the various considerations, including components of full and half cycle economics, associated with the emergence of unconventional plays, see Kleinberg et al. (2018). The many definitions of breakeven points cloud use of those measures when assessing industry activity and response to different current and expected commodity price signals. Assessing breakevens of wells, plays and projects without consideration of overall enterprise sustainability can be misleading.
36. I acknowledge Bob Brackett, who has led E&P coverage at Bernstein Research for many years. We used their quarterly State of the Business reports, 2011–2018, for comparison with our benchmarking, among other research.
37. After initial publication of our results, we provided input to Liam Denning for a review of producer performance at Bloomberg (see Denning and Molla 2016), who cited our work.
38. Denning (2018a) commented on the distortions created by sunk costs and depreciation. "Shale's treadmill of spending every dollar earned (plus some more if capital markets obliged) has been fantastic for U.S. oil and gas production, but less so for returns ... As companies have shifted from basin to basin, learning by doing and driving down costs per barrel, so the sunk capital in older positions has become a drag on returns...as the legacy of the earlier land-grab and drilling frenzy fades, so depreciation charges should moderate, bringing them closer to finding and development costs and making earnings multiples more meaningful".
39. API gravity is a measure, in degrees, of how heavy or light the petroleum product is when compared to water—the specific gravity of petroleum relative to water. Oil with an API number less than 10 (which is the degrees API of water) has a high specific gravity; that is, it is heavier than water and will sink, while oil with a high-degree API is lighter than water and will float. Lighter crude oils are valued more in the market as they will refine

more easily into "light ends" like gasoline, diesel, kerosene and naphtha. In a market surplus of very light oils, the value of heavier crudes can appreciate as larger, more complex refineries will demand those crudes in order to optimize refinery runs.

40. Long lags in securing new oil pipeline capacity meant a surge in demand to transport oil by rail. See RBN Energy for news and research coverage (https://rbnenergy.com/, subscription required). The volatility of LTO led to specific challenges in tank car safety. Information on incidents, preparedness and response can be obtained from the Pipeline and Hazardous Materials Safety Administration (PHMSA), https://www.phmsa.dot.gov/safe-transportation-energy-products/safe-transportation-energy-products-overview
41. David Einhorn's critique of shale oil producers received considerable attention. See presentation at Sohn Investment Conference, May 15, 2014, https://www.greenlightcapital.com/926698.pdf
42. In notable deals, BP engaged in several acquisitions of interests and joint ventures with Chesapeake (Fayetteville, Haynesville, Marcellus), an early leader in deal making, 2008–2010; ExxonMobil acquired Crosstimbers (XTO) in 2009 (mainly Texas plays); BHP acquired Petrohawk in 2011 (Eagle Ford); after several transactions in the Marcellus in 2010, Statoil acquired Brigham (Bakken and Three Forks in Williston Basin); Chevron acquired Atlas in 2010 (Marcellus/Utica); Shell acquired East Resources in 2010 (Marcellus/Utica). Petrohawk and XTO were early inclusions in our producer benchmarking.
43. EOG was the early leader in exiting shale gas acreage. In Notes on Research Methodology: Producer Benchmarking, I source an EOG investor presentation from September 2010 that was widely reviewed. EOG's announced exit from its shale gas acreage positions to focus more on oil-rich plays and its accumulation of $5.1 billion in debt to finance that strategy (Womack 2010) triggered strong reactions. See Moody's, 2010, press release, https://www.moodys.com/research/Moodys-changes-EOGs-outlook-to-negative%2D%2DPR_209537 (registration required). As I clarify in the Notes section, the 2010 announcement of EOG's strategy and coverage of that announcement spurred our benchmarking concept.
44. Notable deals in that phase included acquisition by Shell, Chevron and EnerVest, a private equity group, of Chesapeake's Permian upstream and midstream assets.
45. Notable deals in that phase included Noble's purchase of Rosetta in 2015 (Permian and Eagle Ford liquids window, all-stock transaction); EOG's acquisition of Yates in 2016 (widely viewed as a shift in emphasis from Eagle Ford, added New Mexico Permian and included cash in the transaction); the acquisition of Memorial by Range Resources in 2016 (an all-stock transaction for Louisiana liquids rich production).

46. See Dezember (2019), Matthews (2019a, b). The blogosphere is replete with bad reviews on oil and gas shares at the close of 2019 and opening of 2020 (Brower 2020).
47. Producers considered shale bonds, securitizing individual assets such as oil and gas wells (Matthews 2019a). For other treatments of producer debt, see Matthews et al. (2019a, b; lackluster well performance triggers tighter requirements on credit lines provided by banks), Dezember (20; push by producers to use improvement in revenues from higher oil prices to pay down debt rather than re-invest), Ambra Verlaine and Goldfarb (2020; rally in riskier bonds enabling some producers to refinance). It is not clear the extent to which shale bonds could apply with continued deterioration of business conditions in 2020.
48. The most prominent transaction during 2019 was Occidental's acquisition of Anadarko after a brief competition with Chevron, widely credited for its discipline in walking away from a bidding war (and earning a $1 billion break-up fee). Other transactions, mainly among smaller companies who most need consolidation but where all-stock deals have been prevalent, have been highly criticized for providing low or no premiums. These include Parsley's acquisition of Jagged Peak and Callon's acquisition of Carrizo, considered a prime example of Permian bottom fishing. All content in footnotes related to transactions from public domain financial news reports.
49. Producer behavior is evident to the markets now (see Matthews et al. 2019a, b; Denning and Molla 2016; Denning 2010a, b, 2017, 2018a, b, 2019a, b) just as it was evident then (Denning, April 8 and 20, 2010a, b).
50. See Haskett and Brown (2005) for typical off ramp decision points in conventional and unconventional play development.
51. Raymond James analysts acknowledged that: "The untold reality is that the industry still drills a small amount of "problem" wells that have officially started the drilling process but are failed wells that will never be completed. These failed wells could be due to tools lost in the hole, sidetrack problems, lost circulation issues, stuck pipe, or a myriad of other real world problems". Proprietary report, December 2, 2019. The Ray James report was focused on the inventory of uncompleted wells called "DUCs" (drilled, uncompleted) that observers have viewed to be most responsive to increased prices but which include wells that will never be completed. See following section "Growth or Profitability Revisited: Rigs, Drilling and the Future of U.S. Production" for views on future U.S. supply. See footnote 53 below for related comments on failed wells.
52. EURs factor into how companies report on hydrocarbons to the U.S. SEC or other financial regulators. The Petroleum Resources Management System (PRMS) was created to improve consistency in hydrocarbons

reporting, using project-based guidelines. Information on PRMS is at https://www.spe.org/en/industry/reserves/.

53. Bernstein Research estimated that publicly traded companies in their coverage report roughly 3 percent of the wells drilled and generally the best wells (proprietary report and personal communications). The presence of sub-par wells and ongoing discussions about "type well" and "type curve" definitions and how to properly evaluate unconventional plays are reflected in Freeborn (2016) and Freeborn et al. (2012). They caution that expected ultimate recovery (EUR) can be inflated when forecasts from older type wells are used for newer, less productive wells given that companies tend to drill their best wells first in order to optimize NPV. They note that the reverse can happen during times when operator knowledge is improving with experience. In an influential paper, Fulford (2016; see also Carpenter's 2016 excellent summary) goes further to explore sampling error, point to false positives and widespread practice of excluding underperforming wells from sampling for type curves (see Freeborn 2016) and many other risks and uncertainties associated with unconventional plays that undermine success from pilot drilling through development.
54. Are sweet spots all they are cracked up to be? Emphasis on sweet spots is prevalent in oil and gas exploration and exploitation, but for unconventional plays in particular. In a rejoinder to widespread beliefs that reliance on sweet spots is the solution to variable well production, Haskett (2014) offered up an interesting critique of the approach. While defining sweet spots can improve efficient in development, the frequency of false negatives and positives causes producers to make decisions that later prove incorrect and thus to incur costs, including missed opportunities. Most of all, the sweet spot focus shortchanges well completion learning curves: "If by chance or skill, a company has been successful in defining or drilling a real sweet spot, the science may stop as the exploitation team revels in the high productivity and then falls behind on drilling and completion techniques for the vast majority of wells that are not 'sweet'. While no team would likely admit to such a thing being possible, the reality is that once we believe an answer is found, it is sticky and we slow our drive for efficiency and solution" (p. 6).
55. In his review of the superlat and superfrac "horizontal shale completion" (HSC) model, McDaniel noted: "Economic success achieved in only the past 2 to 4 years in shale reservoirs in North America has fired a 'shot heard round the world' for the oil and gas industry. Although a few high profile shale plays have caught the limelight, in a more complete picture, we should really say that it has been the production…fueled mostly by multi-stage hydraulic fracturing of extended lateral completions" (p. 1).

56. Quoting from Jacobs (2018): "an executive with Range Resources was even more exacting when he told analysts that underperforming wells in the company's Louisiana shale asset and 'corresponding frac hits to offset production' amounted to a financial loss of $75 million per day". In a proprietary report, Raymond James analysts evaluated well interference and suggested that well productivity gains could slow but with uncertain timing (April 15, 2019).
57. For example, a 12-well cube cost $150 million based on information from proprietary projects in the Permian-Delaware Basin. Companies can vary starkly in costs for wells and pads that should otherwise seem comparable. For the cube in question, an adjacent operator was able to drill, complete and frac comparable well laterals for upward of $2 million less per well.
58. Jacobs (2018) noted that Encana credited cube development with increasing well productivity in a Permian field by 70 percent. Olson (2019a) reported that Encana's largest cube would yield about half of the oil the company predicted in 2017. Financial reporters have tracked shale company results with an eye to financial implications. See Olson et al. (2019), Elliott and Matthews (2019).
59. Rassenfoss (2020) quoted from a Deloitte review: "Over the past 3 years (2016–2018), the industry's productivity was flat despite a 25% increase in proppant and fluid loading", the report said. Wells with big fracturing jobs can produce more, but the amount of increase may fail to justify the expense. The data Deloitte analyzed showed many such instances where the added production of a well was not economic. In those cases, Bonny said, "maybe that was not always the right decision".
60. Rassenfoss (2020) also quotes from published results of attempts to map breakeven oil prices for well locations that demonstrate the difficulty of extrapolating from small samples to large areas, which many have been inclined to do in tight rock plays. It is useful to consider that certainty about recovered volumes is strongest at end of life of producing assets. A substantial constraint to improving predictability lies in the fact that wells must be drilled, completed and put on production before results are known which means considerable capital destruction in the process.
61. Many analysts use realized revenues against modeled revenues using expected market prices.
62. The acquisition of Burlington Resources by then ConocoPhillips was widely thought to have been hastened by shareholders unhappy with a large missed hedge in which Burlington was too conservative in selecting future Henry Hub contracts (based on communications with ConocoPhillips personnel at the time, 2004–2005).
63. The CME Group, which operates the largest energy exchange, holds the NYMEX futures contracts and other derivatives for oil and gas and other

energy products. Each crude oil (CL) contract is in units of 1000 barrels; CL futures contracts are based at Cushing, Oklahoma. Each natural gas (NG) contract is in units of 10,000 MMBtu; NG contracts are based at Henry Hub in Erath, Louisiana. See https://www.cmegroup.com/ for information on energy derivatives and trading.

64. For both multipliers I use production from the BP Annual Statistical Review and trading volumes reported by CME, as aggregated by Quandl, www.quandl.com.
65. A great deal of concern about who participates in financial markets and for what purpose, including whether markets could be manipulated, arose out of the 2008 recession. We considered the implications of non-commercial interests participating in financial trading for commodities (Michot Foss et al. 2009). That paper was a precedent to the work by Gülen and Michot Foss (2012).
66. I adapted this terminology and the methodology from David Pursell, then at Tudor Pickering & Holt, now at Apache Corporation, and used in a presentation to the Independent Petroleum Association of America (IPAA) supply-demand committee meeting in Houston, Texas, November 7, 2008. A broader, more fundamental, topic is how well commodity markets perform when it comes to trust and motivation. We explored the shifts in financial markets following the 2008 recession and the onset of new regulation (Michot Foss et al. 2009), concluding that financial and physical markets had become intertwined and that demand for financial products (derivatives) as an asset class could be influencing prices of the underlying physical goods. We also raised concerns about non-commercial participants seeking exposure to financial derivatives, such as private investors (as individuals or through funds) whose behaviors and motivations are quite different than commercial participants. I surveyed the state of literature on commodity trading since 2000 and drew several observations. Researchers realize that behaviors and motivations of market participants are different. Attempts to model behavior are fraught with complexity and lack of knowledge (within the academic research community) about how commercial market participations, including producing companies, operate and function. An age-old question of whether futures and spot prices are co-integrated is unsolved, although they can react simultaneously to new information. I first used the market error approach adapted here in Michot Foss (2020a).
67. Hedging by Pioneer resulted in losses of almost $8 per barrel during the third quarter of 2018 as crude oil spot prices during that quarter were higher than the value of the company's hedges. Pioneer's quarterly reporting also provided a lens on how hedging has offset losses from differentials associated with oil pipeline bottlenecks. The company's hedging program

through 2017 added $1–2 per barrel in income while netback discounts resulted in losses of $2–3 per barrel—Pioneer's realized oil prices were lower than market due to the bottlenecks (Denning 2018a, b). Periodically over the years, commodities markets and prices and their regulators and policy overseers have been enveloped in debates about speculation (market participation for profit) as opposed to hedging (market participation to reduce price risk and volatility and their impact on revenues and cash flows) and potential for manipulation. See Pirrong (2017) for a useful survey of manipulation, the role of hedgers and speculators, and legal and regulatory considerations.

68. Pre-pandemic, various analysts expected Permian gas production to grow from about 13 Bcfd in the first half of 2019 to 10–12 Bcfd with high cases of 24 and sometimes even 30 Bcfd. Appalachian production was about 31 Bcfd; the back room chatter was that opposition to pipe projects would cap Marcellus output. The total U.S. market at the time was about 83 Bcfd delivered to customers, including exports. Two Permian gas pipes had reached FID and appeared to be one to two years away from entering service—Gulf Express, backed by XTO/Exxon Mobile with Apache, Pioneer and others. Gulf Express would add 2 Bcfd of capacity at a total cost of about $2 billion. The second was Permian Highway—again backed by XTO/Exxon Mobil and Apache. PHP also would add 2 Bcfd of takeaway and also at a total cost of $2 billion. Both projects were undertaken by Kinder Morgan. The PHP has been under continuous, intense pressure from opponents. These projects would contribute 4 Bcfd of the high case 24–30 Bcfd of output requiring transportation. Even the more conservative outlook of 10–12 Bcfd of production growth would need substantial pipeline takeaway capacity. Six projects were under discussion, none near FID. All of these projects need financial backing; prevailing assumptions were that the major companies were most likely sponsors.
69. See footnote 29. The Raymond James analysts noted the widening gap between monthly well completions and the average number of rigs working, attributing this to greater productivity per rig for all of the reasons I outline.
70. See the EIA Drilling Productivity Report for public domain tracking of activity and developments in the major onshore unconventional basins, https://www.eia.gov/petroleum/drilling/#tabs-summary-3.
71. An SPE JPT news item, "Analytics Firm: Permian Fracturing Work Underreported by 21 percent in 2018", July 24, 2019 covered remote tracking of frac spreads developed by Kayrros. Subscription or other access required.
72. Based on Westwood evaluation of frac crew efficiency in a public domain posting, February 11, 2020, https://www.westwoodenergy.com/

reports/us-unconventionals/stages-per-frac-crews-increase-by-26-across-shale-plays?utm_source=ActiveCampaign&utm_medium=Email&utm_campaign=Frac_Efficiency&utm_content=ReadMore.

73. See footnote 29. The Raymond James analysts argued that viable DUCs were substantially lower than EIA's count, by about 15 percent. The analysts' consensus is for a drop in oil production near term: "Investor fears that a falling rig count will not translate into reduced completions, on account of ample supplies of drilled but uncompleted wells is based on the incorrect assumption that DUC inventories can return to lows of 2016. They cannot, for one thing, U.S. onshore completion activity (shown by the red bars in the graph above) is at an all-time high. As a result, operators are going to naturally require more inventory to continue running efficiently at an expanded pace. Adding to this, the near ubiquitous adoption of pad drilling, increasing wells per pad, and frac crew optimization have raised the 'months of inventory' required for efficient operations to four months from the historical level closer to two months of inventories. Making the situation all the more perilous, the EIA DUC data overstates the true amount of DUCs due to the inclusion of hundreds of 'lame DUC' wells that were drilled years ago and are never likely to be completed in the future. We estimate that the EIA DUC data is overstated by almost 15% (or about 1200 wells). Even assuming the EIA count is correct, the current disconnect between completion activity and drilling is the biggest we've ever seen and cannot be sustained through next year. Using what we believe to be the correct count, DUCs reach critical levels by February. At that point, frac crews will need to be idled or dropped as their simply won't be enough slack (DUCs) to operate at today's rapid pace, supporting our below consensus oil growth forecast next year". Balancing their enthusiasm is the question of producer discipline—whether companies will rein in spending in order to focus on profitability and improved cash flows, and the extent to which industry consolidation will re-shape the landscape.
74. The most prevalent experiments reported and cited are in gassier locations, with Eagle Ford most often mentioned and documented. A big question is whether enhanced recovery can be repeated across multiple locations so as to support economics and availability and cost of equipment for high-pressure "huff and puff" applications.
75. Readers can look to the EIA for views on basin production and drilling trends (Drilling Productivity Report, https://www.eia.gov/petroleum/drilling/) and future supply and demand (Annual Energy Outlook, https://www.eia.gov/outlooks/aeo/).
76. Olson (2019b) is a good example. See footnotes in section "We (Were) in the Money" for major company deal making. Chevron, in particular, and Exxon Mobil have advantages in legacy land holdings.

77. The Bureau of Economic Geology has made distinct contributions to the understanding of shale and tight oil plays. See http://www.beg.utexas.edu/research/programs/shale and http://www.beg.utexas.edu/tora; individual research consortia make additional contributions. The U.S. Geological Survey provides ongoing resource assessments for the United States, https://www.usgs.gov/centers/cersc/science/united-states-assessments-undiscovered-oil-and-gas-resources?qt-science_center_objects=0#qt-science_center_objects, and rest of world, https://www.usgs.gov/centers/cersc/science/world-oil-and-gas-resource-assessments?qt-science_center_objects=0#qt-science_center_objects. The EIA compiles and reports year end oil and gas reserves, https://www.eia.gov/naturalgas/crudeoilreserves/.
78. Based on Bernstein Research proprietary reports. Bernstein covers mostly "pure play" companies. The sample is based on reporting as of second quarter 2019.
79. Phrasing most often associated with Tom Wolfe and bonfires of vanities.
80. See footnote 5. A few differences exist between time periods with respect to companies under coverage but the populations are substantially the same. Most of the differences can be attributed to bankruptcies and M&A.
81. A survey of alternative energy investments gaining attention through first half of 2020 indicates that many are held by corporate entities that also hold legacy utility businesses including power generation assets in states where cost of service ratemaking still is used.
82. To considerable fanfare, BP announced it would phase out its core oil and gas businesses. BP stock dipped to a historical low as investors reacted. See Hurst (2020) for typical treatment and Kennedy (2020) for a more nuanced view.
83. See previous footnote 14. Pyper (2019) observed: "For one thing, greater levels of electrification threaten to weaken their core business, and oil majors investing in cleantech could be cannibalizing their own profits. Whether shareholders see this as a risk or as a new opportunity amid an undeniable shift within the industry is another related issue".
84. I used https://us.spindices.com/indices/equity/dow-jones-us-oil-gas-index and https://us.spindices.com/indices/equity/sp-global-clean-energy-index, access required.
85. Smith and Eckhouse (2019), in typical reporting, reference prevailing views that industry maturity will reduce volatility, in coverage of one of the most prominent exchange traded funds, Invesco Solar.
86. For instance, in his keynote remarks at the 2019 Oil & Money conference, Shell CEO Ben van Beurden stated that "Governments can provide regulation and consumer signals…as well as incentives, like grants to help buy electric cars". https://www.shell.com/media/speeches-and-articles/2019/embracing-evolution.html. Pyper (2019) noted: "The power gen-

eration business in particular is known for having relatively low returns, [Shell's Marten] Wetselaar said. But that could change too. Subsidized solar and wind have attracted a lot of cheap capital. But as subsidies start to phase out, cheap money will begin to disappear, and as risk levels in the generation business rise, the returns are expected to be higher. 'So I do think we'll find serious pockets of value,' said Wetselaar. 'But ... it won't be easy; because if it were easy, then everybody would be doing it' ".

87. Outgoing BP CEO Bob Dudley's remarks at the 2019 Oil & Money event were telling. https://www.bp.com/en/global/corporate/news-and-insights/speeches/gas-in-a-net-zero-energy-system.html
88. Les Demand, Consultant, notes that "Canadian production and infrastructure development has been retarded due to the U.S. shale explosion. Their large resources base might act as a ceiling on medium term U.S. prices". (February, 2020)
89. Costs excluded from the full cost amortization pool are discussed separately in our full report found in Michot Foss and Wainberg (2012).

References

Ailworth, E. 2017. Fracking 2.0: Shale drillers pioneer new ways to profit in era of cheap oil. *Wall Street Journal*, March 30. All WSJ cites require subscription or other access.

Allan, P.D. 2011. Stochastic analysis of resource plays: Maximizing portfolio value and mitigating risks. *Journal of Economics and Management, Society of Petroleum Engineers*: 142–148. (Earlier citation, SPE 134811, SPE annual technical conference and exhibition, Florence, Italy, September 19–22, 2010.) All SPE publication cites require membership or other access.

Ambra-Verlaine, J., and S. Goldfarb. 2020. Energy companies seize the day with bond refinancings. *Wall Street Journal*, January 14.

Beswick, A. 2020. Bear head LNG for sale. *The Chronicle Herald*, July 22. https://www.thechronicleherald.ca/news/local/bear-head-lng-for-sale-476413/

Biracree, T. 2020. Against the wind – Assessing midstream company performance after a decade of record investment. *RBN Energy*, January 28. All RBN Energy cites require subscription access.

Blackmon, D. 2020. Texas railroad commission will consider an oil production cut that is too late to matter. *Forbes*, April 30. https://www.forbes.com/sites/davidblackmon/2020/04/30/texas-railroad-commission-will-consider-an-oil-production-cut-that-is-too-late-to-matter/#31baa43a7c99

Brandily, T. 2018. 2H 2018 LCOE update, global. *BloombergNEF*, November. All Bloomberg cites require license or other access unless provided by open sources.

Brower, D. 2020. U.S. shale producers bleed cash despite slashed spending. *Financial Times*, September 15. Subscription or other access to FT required.

Carpenter, C. 2016. Unconventional risk and uncertainty: What does success look like?, *Journal of Petroleum Technology, SPE*, December, p. 49–50.

Chari, V.V., and L.J. Christiano. 2014. The optimal extraction of exhaustible resources. *Economic Policy Papers*, Federal Reserve Bank of Minneapolis. https://www.minneapolisfed.org/research/economic-policy-papers/the-optimal-extraction-of-exhaustible-resources

Christian, W. 2020. Opinion: Texas capping oil production? Chairman Wayne Christian picks a side. *Houston Chronicle*, April 29. https://www.houstonchronicle.com/opinion/outlook/article/Opinion-Texas-capping-oil-production-Chairman-15235207.php

Denning, L. 2010a. EOG's rational exuberance for oil. *Wall Street Journal*, April 8.

———. 2010b. Gas bears should try smoking pipes. *Wall Street Journal*, April 20.

———. 2017. The one commodity frackers can't do without. *Bloomberg*, August 8.

———. 2018a. Drilling some discipline into the shale frackers. *Bloomberg*, October 24.

———. 2018b. Pioneer casts a shadow over Permian earnings. *Bloomberg*, July 31.

———. 2019a. Chevron-Exxon Texas showdown spells trouble for frackers. *Bloomberg*, March 5.

———. 2019b. EQT's battle is over but the shale war goes on. *Bloomberg*, July 10.

Denning, L., and R. Molla. 2016. The big cracks in shale's resilience. *Bloomberg*, October 5.

Dezember, R. 2019. Energy stocks fall faster than oil prices. *Wall Street Journal*, October 16.

———. 2020. Energy producers' new year's resolution: Pay the tab for the shale drilling bonanza. *Wall Street Journal*, January 1.

EIA. 2017. The distribution of oil and gas wells by production rate, December, https://www.eia.gov/petroleum/wells/pdf/full_report.pdf.

Elliott, R. 2020. America's top oil field was desperate for pipelines, now it has too many. *Wall Street Journal*, September 22.

Elliott, R., and C.M. Matthews. 2019. As shale wells age, gap between forecasts and performance grows. *Wall Street Journal*, December 29.

England, J., and A. Mittal. 2014. *U.S. shale, a game of choices*. Deloitte University Press, 32 p.

Flowers, S. 2019. The edge: Deepwater investment bounces back. *Wood Mackenzie*, June 20.

Foer, F. 2020. What big tech wants out of the pandemic. *The Atlantic*, July/August. https://www.theatlantic.com/magazine/archive/2020/07/big-tech-pandemic-power-grab/612238/

Frankel, P.H. 1969. *Essentials of petroleum*. London: Frank Cass, 208 p.

Freeborn, R. 2016. Two vital secrets for building reliable type wells. SPE Distinguished Lecture.

Freeborn, R., B. Russell, W. Keinick. 2012. Creating analogs, fact and fiction, SPE 162630, presentation at SPE hydrocarbon, economics and evaluation symposium, Calgary, Alberta, Canada, September 24–25.

Fulford, D.S. 2016. Unconventional risk and uncertainty: Show me what success looks like, SPE-179996-MS, presentation at SPE/IAEE hydrocarbon economics and evaluation symposium in Houston, Texas, May 17–18.

Gouveia, J., and G.P. Citron. 2009. A statistical approach to effective economic modeling and portfolio selection of unconventional resource opportunities, SPE 121525, presentation at SPE EUROPEC/EAGE annual conference and exhibition, Amsterdam, Netherlands, June 8–11.

Gülen, S.G., and M. Michot Foss. 2012. Factors impacting oil price. BEG/CEE Think Corner Research Note, June. http://www.beg.utexas.edu/files/energyecon/think-corner/2012/Think%20Corner%20factors%20impacting%20oil%20price.pdf

Gülen, S.G., M. Michot Foss, and C.-H. Tsai. 2017. Competitive electricity markets: What future? BEG/CEE Paper, March. http://www.beg.utexas.edu/files/energyecon/think-corner/2017/CEE_Research_Note-What_Future_for_Electricity_Markets-Mar17.pdf

Gülen, S.G., C.-H. Tsai, D.P. Huggins, and M. Michot Foss. 2018. Competitiveness of renewable-generation sources: A review of the role of system integration costs, regional differences and externalities. BEG/CEE report, April. http://www.beg.utexas.edu/files/energyecon/CEE_Research_Note_Competitiveness_Generation_Apr18.pdf

Hampton, L. 2019. Low-cost fracking offers boon to oil producers, headaches to suppliers. *Reuters*, September 5.

Haskett, W.J. 2011. Unconventional type curves: Useful or Sirens of destruction?, SPE 147059, presented at annual SPE conference and exhibition, Denver, Colorado, October 30–November 2.

———. 2014. The myth of sweet spot exploration, SPE 170960-MS, presentation at SPE annual technical conference and exhibition, Amsterdam, Netherlands, October 27–29.

Haskett, W.J., and P.J. Brown. 2005. Evaluation of unconventional resource plays, SPE 96879, paper presented at annual SPE conference and exhibition, Dallas, Texas, October 9–12.

———. 2010. Pitfalls in the evaluation of unconventional resources, SPE 135208, presentation at SPE annual technical conference and exhibition, Florence, Italy, September 19–22.

Hotelling, H. 1931. The economics of exhaustible resources. *Journal of Political Economy* 39 (2): 137–175.

Hurst, L. 2020. BP hits 25-year low a week after unveiling climate strategy. *Bloomberg*, September 25. https://finance.yahoo.com/news/bp-drops-25-low-week-172458895.html

Jacobs, T. 2018. In the battle against Frac hits, shale producers go to new extremes. *SPE JPT*, August.

———. 2019. Shale EOR delivers, so why won't the sector go big?, *SPE JPT*, May.
Judzis, A., R. Felder, D. Curry, B. Seiller, G.A. Pope, D. Burnett, T.A. Torp, J. Neal, C. Krohn, J.M. Karanikas, R.L. Arscott, C. Fairhurst, L. Lake, R.A. Liroff, and A. Poddar. 2011–2012. The five grand challenges plus one. Journal of Petroleum Technology series, Society of Petroleum Engineers, SPE-163061-MS for entire compilation.
Kemp, J. 2016. Persistence of instability in the oil market. *Reuters*, September 15, https://www.reuters.com/article/us-oil-global-kemp/persistence-of-instability-in-the-oil-market-kemp-idUSKCN11L1H9
Kennedy, S. 2020. Lost in transition: Big Oil searches for purpose as peak demand looms. *Energy Flux*, August 10. https://energyflux.substack.com/p/lost-in-transition-big-oil-searches
Kleinberg, R.L., S. Paltsev, C.K.E. Ebinger, D.A. Hobbs, and T. Boersma. 2018. Tight oil market dynamics: Benchmarks, breakeven points and inelasticities. *Energy Economics* 70:70–83. Open access, https://www.sciencedirect.com/science/article/pii/S0140988317304103
Matthews, C.M., 2019b. Tapped out: As investors ditch the energy industry, producers try to keep above ground. *Houston Business Journal*, November 29. All HBJ cites require subscription or other access.
Matthews, C.M. 2019a. Frackers float shale bonds as traditional investors flee. *Wall Street Journal*, October 20.
Matthews, C.M., R. Elliott, and B. Olson. 2019a. Shale companies, adding ever more wells, threaten future of U.S. oil boom. *Wall Street Journal*, March 3.
Matthews, C.M., B. Olson, and A. Prang. 2019b. Banks get tough on shale loans as fracking forecasts flop. *Wall Street Journal*, December 23.
McDaniel, B.W. 2010. Horizontal wells with multi-stage fracs provide better economics for many lower permeability reservoirs, SPE 133427, presentation at SPE Asia-Pacific Oil & Gas conference and exhibition, Brisbane, Queensland, Australia, October 18–20.
Michot Foss, M. 1995. U.S. natural gas in the 21st century: Adjusting to the new reality. Ph.D. Dissertation, University of Houston, 395 p.
———. 2007. North American natural gas scenarios and United States prices to 2015, Natural Gas Programme, Oxford Institute of Energy Studies, NG 18, January. https://www.oxfordenergy.org/publications/united-states-natural-gas-prices-to-2015/?v=7516fd43adaa
———. 2011. The outlook for U.S. gas prices in 2020: Henry Hub at $3 or $10? Oxford Institute for Energy Studies working paper, NG 58, December. https://www.oxfordenergy.org/publications/the-outlook-for-u-s-gas-prices-in-2020-henry-hub-at-3-or-10-2/?v=7516fd43adaa
———. 2012. Natural gas pricing in North America, Chapter 3. In *The pricing of internationally traded gas*, ed. J.P. Stern, 85–144. New York: Oxford University/Oxford Institute for Energy Studies.

———. 2015. U.S. natural gas update and outlook, private report prepared for Cedigaz, September, http://www.cedigaz.org/products/Cedigaz%20 Insights/u-s-natural-gas-update-and-outlook.aspx (Cedigaz membership required).
———. 2020a. Forward: Seeking less uncertainty. In *Beyond market assumptions: Oil price as a global institute*, ed. A.V. Belyi, v–xiii. Cham: Springer Nature Switzerland AG, 166 p.
———. 2020b. U.S. shale goes viral. *Forbes*, March 19. https://www.forbes.com/sites/thebakersinstitute/2020/03/19/us-shale-goes-viral/#20f019f165a8
Michot Foss, M., and D. Palmer-Huggins. 2016. European and Asian natural gas market developments – Swamped by the present?, Chapter 6. In *Managing energy price risk*, ed. V. Kaminski, 4th ed. London: Risk Books.
Michot Foss, M., and M. Wainberg. 2012. Upstream attainment, producer challenges. BEG/CEE working paper, June, http://www.beg.utexas.edu/files/energyecon/think-corner/2012/Think%20Corner%20-%20Producers.pdf
Michot Foss, M., L.-K. Choo, G. Gülen, and B. Shenoy. 2009. The future landscape of energy trading. BEG/CEE Research Note, June 17. https://www.beg.utexas.edu/files/cee/legacy/2009/Energy_Trading_Foss.pdf
National Petroleum Council. 2019. Dynamic delivery – America's evolving oil & natural gas transportation infrastructure, December 12. https://dynamicdelivery.npc.org/downloads.php
Nauman, B., and S. Morris, 2021. Global banks' $750bn in fossil fuel finance conflicts with green pledges. *Financial Times*, March 23. https://www.ft.com/content/c1e31c6f-6319-4bfcbde3-3ace80b46a2b
Norton, P. 1993. Pemex predicts 50% drop in U.S. gas exports to Mexico. *The Oil Daily*, September 30. Oil Daily cites require subscription or other access.
Oil & Gas Journal (OGJ). 1993a. *OGJ Newsletter* 91 (27): 2. OGJ cites require subscription or other access.
———. 1993b. Tight fit seen for Canadian gas exports, demand. 91 (41): 38.
———. 1995a. *OGJ Newsletter* 93 (41): 2.
———. 1995b. Canadian gas producers, pipelines cope with weak prices, oversupply. 93 (25): 20.
———. 1997. Canadian natural gas export pipeline race heating up. 95 (34): 29.
Olson, B. 2019a. Chevron, Exxon Mobil tighten their grip on fracking. *Wall Street Journal*, March 5.
———. 2019b. A fracking experiment fails to pump as predicted. *Wall Street Journal*, July 4.
Olson, B., R. Elliott, and C.M. Matthews. 2019. Fracking's secret problem-oil wells aren't producing as much as forecast. *Wall Street Journal*, January 2.
Pirrong, C. 2017. The economics of commodity market manipulation: A survey. *Journal of Commodity Markets* 5: 1–17.
Porter, M. 1980. *Competitive Strategy*. New York: Free Press, 396 p.

Pyper, J. 2019. Shell new energies director on investing in clean energy: 'It's about survival'. *Green Tech Media*, April. https://www.greentechmedia.com/articles/read/shell-new-energies-director-on-investing-in-clean-energy

Rappaport, A., and M.L. Sirower. 1999. Stock or cash?: The trade-offs for buyers and sellers in mergers and acquisitions. *Harvard Business Review* 77 (6): 147–158.

Rattner, S. 1981. Oil price pact called unlikely. *New York Times*, May 11. https://www.nytimes.com/1981/05/11/business/oil-price-pact-called-unlikely.html. NY Times cites require subscription or other access.

Ridder, K. 2020. The end of Atlantic coast pipeline. *The Appalachian Voice*, July 21. https://appvoices.org/2020/07/21/the-end-of-the-atlantic-coast-pipeline/

Schumpeter, J. 1942. *Capitalism, socialism, and democracy.* New York: Harper & Bros.

Schwartz, P. 1996. *The Art of the Long View*. New York: Doubleday, 272 p.

Smith, M., and B. Eckhouse. 2019. Best returns of the year lure 'believers' to clean-energy ETFs. *Bloomberg*, October 1.

Steffey, L. 2014. Kinder Morgan eats its own: Will other MLPs follow its lead?, *Forbes*, August 10. https://www.forbes.com/sites/lorensteffy/2014/08/10/kinder-morgan-eats-its-own-will-other-mlps-follow-its-lead/#6d8957bb18a1

Verlager, P.K., Jr. 2007. Market structures and price policies in the oil and gas industry: The case of oil, Chapter 4.1. In Vol. 4, Hydrocarbons: Economics, Policies and Legislation, Alberto Clô and Piero Bernardini scientific coordinators, of the Encyclopedia of Hydrocarbons, Instituto Della Enciclopedia Italiana, Fondata da Giovanni Trecanni.

Vernon, R. 1971. *Sovereignty at bay: The multinational spread of U.S. enterprises.* New York: Basic Books, 336 p.

Willegers, B.J.A., R.B. Bratfold, and J.E. Bickel. 2017. Maximizing the value of unconventional reservoirs by choosing the optimal appraisal strategy. *SPE Journal of Reservoir Evaluation & Engineering* 20: 502–512.

Womack, J. 2010. EOG Resources shifts its focus to finding oil. *Wall Street Journal*, April 8.

Zeller, T. 2014. Is the U.S. shale boom going bust? *Bloomberg View*, April 22.

CHAPTER 2

The Gas-Power Nexus

Gürcan Gülen

Introduction

The first draft of this chapter was written in early 2018. It is now end of summer 2020, when the COVID pandemic continues to present a range of uncertainties for the global economy. But there have been other developments since the first draft that will have more structural impact on the use of natural gas for power generation than the COVID pandemic, the response to which may strengthen some of these recent trends.

To start with, installed wind and solar capacity increased much more than previously predicted. The developers built 34 gigawatts (GW) of wind instead of 18 GW and 20 GW of utility-scale solar instead of 12 GW. The 2016 extension of tax credits (production, PTC, and investment, ITC) and growing state, city, and local mandates and corporate procurement certainly played a role but the cost declines, especially for solar, have been substantial. Battery storage seems to be following a similar path of mutually reinforcing trends: declining costs and increasing policy support.

G. Gülen (✉)
Independent Consultant, West Brookfield, MA, USA
e-mail: gurcan@g2eis.com

M. Michot Foss et al. (eds.), *Monetizing Natural Gas in the New "New Deal" Economy*,
https://doi.org/10.1007/978-3-030-59983-6_2

Also relevant are baseload capacity retirements. Coal-fired plant closures between 2018 and early 2020 have been 10 GW larger than previously planned levels. Most of the lost baseload generation was replaced by gas-fired combined cycle units but wind and solar generation also played a larger role than in the past. The future of many coal-fired plants is bleak, but there is now reason to expect more nuclear plants to continue operating longer. In early 2018, many nuclear plants were expected to retire in the 2020s because they had been unable to generate enough revenues in wholesale markets with historically low electricity prices. Only one operator had applied for a license extension to 80 years by early 2018. Then courts supported state efforts to save nuclear plants with zero emissions credits (ZECs) or other mechanisms. Following the court decisions, more states instituted policies to keep nuclear plants online. Now, there are 11 units with about 11 GW of capacity that either received an extension of their operating license to 80 years or are in the process of applying and having their applications reviewed by the Nuclear Regulatory Commission.

In the meantime, challenges to environmental advantages of natural gas as compared to coal have increased. Methane leaks along the oil and gas supply chain infrastructure are the main concern but flaring and venting of associated gas across the low-permeability resource plays around the country also attracts considerable attention. The industry is investing in reducing methane leaks and flaring. There are innovative companies that started deploying 24-hour monitoring equipment. But until these practices become standard for all operators and positive outcomes are transparently and effectively communicated to the wider public, opposition to natural gas will likely spread. In certain parts of the country, local opposition, often organized and supported by national environmental groups, has been able to delay or force cancellation of pipeline projects with increasing success in 2019 and 2020. Prominently, there have been several court decisions that curtail regulatory initiative in permitting and encourage more opposition filings.

In the meantime, a few cities around the country started banning new natural gas infrastructure, including the connection of new homes to distribution networks. These actions are so far limited to only a few locations and several states took action to stop cities from implementing such bans but they have the potential to spread in parts of the country with ambitious decarbonization goals. A central tenet of decarbonization is electrification of energy services commonly provided by natural gas such as space and water heating, cooking, and drying laundry. One might expect electrification to induce demand growth but electricity demand has been fairly stable since the Great Recession of 2008–2009. Electrification is still in its infancy in most areas but the expansion of energy efficiency and conservation programs may also be masking the scale of electrification. As such, higher utilization of gas-fired plants cannot count on load growth. The lack or contraction of gas demand will undermine economics of gas distribution utilities as well as pipeline and storage operators with attendant implications for gas supply contracts of power generators.

These anti-gas trends should be seen as part of the wider issue of climate change, which increasingly influence investors and corporate decision makers. Although not yet dominating their investment decisions, the promotion of environmental, social, and governance (ESG) standards by an increasing number of investment banks and major management consultancies advises caution around bullish power sector gas burn prognostications.

The growing opposition to natural gas, legal barriers to developing gas infrastructure, and rising prominence of ESG also undermine gas use as feedstock for hydrogen. Popular color coding of hydrogen classifies it as gray if derived from natural gas (or blue if associated CO_2 emissions are captured and sequestered) as compared to green if obtained from electrolysis that uses electricity from renewable energy or nuclear. Hydrogen is expensive and energy-intensive to separate from carbon or oxygen, to transport, and to store. Hence, its large-scale penetration is decades away if it is to occur. But the current hype supports a momentum of sorts behind the technology. From the perspective of the power sector, however, hydrogen's role may be worth a closer look. Major gas turbine manufacturers have been able to mix hydrogen with natural gas in power generation with a hydrogen ratio of fuel ranging from 5 to 95 percent. Increasing the share of hydrogen in the mix requires design modifications but seems doable. Already, hydrogen is available as a byproduct of refining and petrochemicals operations; most of it is used within that industrial complex but some can be made available for power generation at a relatively low cost. Still, these conditions exist only in a few locations, which should limit the use of hydrogen in the power sector.

It may be difficult to focus on these trends since the recent growth in gas-fired generation conceals some of their impacts. In 2019, 38 percent of utility-scale generation was from natural gas as compared to 23 percent from coal.[1] As a result, electric power sector natural gas burn increased nearly 50 percent between 2008 and 2019. Nearly two-fifths of the natural gas consumed in the United States[2] is burned for electric power generation, which is now the largest gas market.

However, considerable uncertainty exists about the future gas use in the power sector. Although I acknowledged these uncertainties in early 2018, I was confident about the growing role of gas-fired generation across the country through at least the 2030s and, likely, beyond. Today, I am not as confident about nationwide growth although gas burn growth is still the most likely scenario in many regions. Other regions will continue to move away from all fossil fuels, including natural gas. For example, between 2008 and 2019, gas burn declined 44 percent in California, 14 percent in the New England region, 17 percent in New York, and 16–58 percent in wind-rich Idaho, Kansas, and Nebraska. These trends reflect a combination of factors highlighted above. Any speculation on the future role of natural gas utilization for power generation, certainly beyond the mid-2020s, needs to take the evolution and spread of these factors into account across different regions.

This chapter is an attempt to provide such a holistic analysis. I start with a historical perspective on how and why natural gas became the dominant fuel for power generation. I then provide a SWOT analysis in order to put a structure around the issues highlighted in this introduction. Then, I depict the multiplicity of scenarios for future gas burn in the power sector as defined by four key drivers mined from the SWOT analysis. The rest of the chapter provides details on each driver and trends that influence them. I conclude with an outlook to demonstrate the range of uncertainty.

Resurgence of Natural Gas in Power Generation

Power generation was not always the primary consumer of natural gas. Only about one-fifth of marketed natural gas was used for power generation in the early 1990s. Since the beginning of the twenty-first century, gas-fired power generation has been increasing rapidly building on the momentum gained in the second half of the 1990s (Fig. 2.1). Unlike in the 1990s, when growing demand for electricity encouraged more generation from coal and nuclear as well, the growth of the gas-fired generation fleet has been phenomenal in the new century (Fig. 2.2). The share of gas-fired generation increased from about 12 percent in 1990 to nearly 16 percent in 2000, 24 percent in 2010, and 38 percent in 2019.

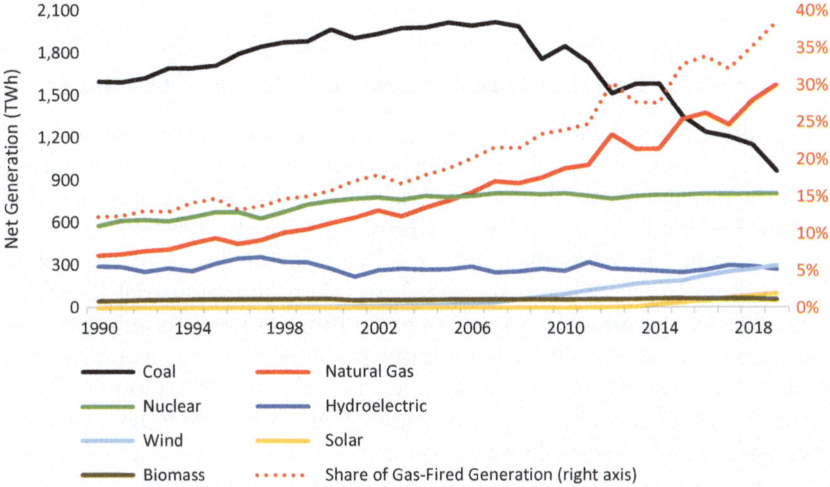

Fig. 2.1 Electricity generation by fuel/technology. (Source: U.S. Energy Information Administration (EIA) data for generation from all sectors. Solar includes the EIA estimate of small-scale solar since 2014. Excludes fuels with minute shares of production (<0.5 percent): petroleum liquids, petroleum coke, other gases, geothermal, and other. Altogether, these fuels account for less than 2 percent of total annual generation since 2008 and less than 1 percent since 2017)

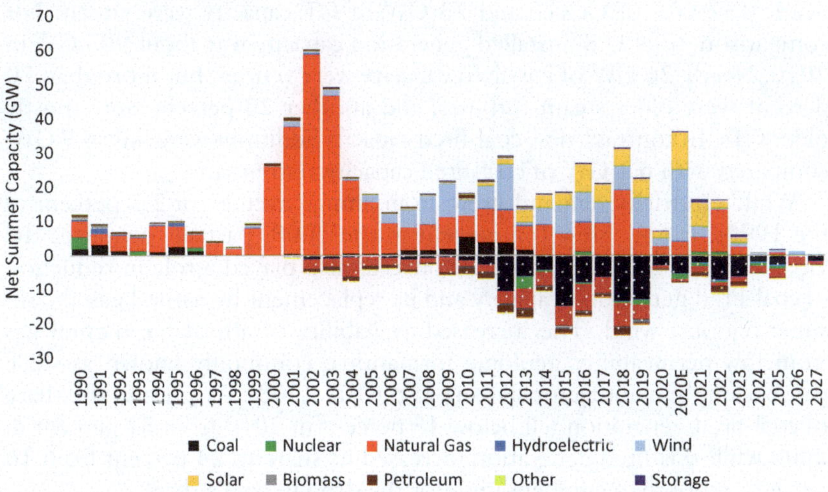

Fig. 2.2 Actual and planned generation capacity additions and retirements by fuel/technology. (Source: Compiled by author from EIA-860 data. Expected capacities for 2020 and beyond include construction completed but not commissioned, under construction, regulatory approval received or pending. Data set for retirements before 2002 is incomplete)

Drivers of Gas-Fleet Transformation and Increased Gas Burn

Three drivers of gas-fired generation growth are worth highlighting. First, the deregulation of natural gas wellhead prices and markets, which started with the passage of the Natural Gas Policy Act in 1978 and continued with various Federal Energy Regulatory Commission (FERC) orders, increased the availability of affordable natural gas by the 1990s.[3] Second, the Public Utility Regulatory Policies Act and Powerplant and Industrial Fuel Use Act of 1978, encouraged nonutility generation, either as combined heat and power facilities built by large industrial consumers, or as new plants built by merchant generators. Finally, natural gas turned out to be a favored fuel for technological and commercial reasons. Merchant generators could build large-scale gas-fired plants cheaper than the avoided cost of regulated utilities and quicker than other thermal plants fueled by coal or uranium. Combustion turbine (CT) plants provided the capabilities to follow load and quickly ramp up or down, valuable features in competitive electricity markets. Improvements in gas turbine efficiencies and combined-cycle gas turbine (CCGT) plant designs rendered natural gas the most efficient fuel to burn for baseload generation.

The restructuring of regulated, vertically integrated utility models into competitive electricity markets fueled much investment in the 2000s: nearly 157 GW of CCGT and 73 GW of CT capacity were added. For comparison, total U.S. installed generation capacity was about 905 GW in 2010. Nearly 26 GW of gas-fired capacity were retired, but more than 70 percent were older steam turbines, and another 20 percent were mostly older CTs. In contrast, new coal-fired capacity additions were only 6.7 GW, compared with 6.1 GW of coal-fired capacity retirements.

While electricity demand grew at an annual average of 2.2 percent in the 1990s, it only grew 0.7 percent in the 2000s partially owing to the Great Recession. Environmental concerns also played a role in reduction of coal-fired generation capacity and its replacement by natural gas and, in some regions, wind. The increased availability of affordable natural gas from low-permeability geologic formations, commonly known as shale gas, became a major factor starting in the late 2000s. As a result, the share of coal-fired generation fell below 45 percent in 2010 from 52 percent in 2000 while gas-fired generation increased its share to 24 percent from 16 percent, more than compensating for the drop in coal's share.

In the 2010s, when electricity demand remained flat, coal lost market share to wind and utility-scale solar in addition to natural gas. Between

2011 and early 2020, operators retired nearly 82 GW of coal, 46 GW of gas, and about 6.8 GW of nuclear capacity while building 90 GW of gas-fired capacity, 67 GW of wind, and 38 GW of utility-scale solar (Fig. 2.2). A lot more wind and solar capacity are expected to be completed before the end of 2020. More than 70 percent of gas-fired retirements were older steam and combustion turbines, nearly 90 percent built before 1980. About 13 GW of other capacity were retired during the same period. Almost all of these "other" plants burned petroleum products. As a result of these changes, the share of coal-fired generation fell to 23.3 percent in 2019 while the shares of gas-fired, wind and solar (inclusive of small-scale) generation increased to 38.2, 7.2, and 2.6 percent, respectively.

Regional differences are important to note for possible implications on natural gas supply chain infrastructure. More than half of the gas retirements since the early 2000s occurred in Texas and California but for different reasons. Lower gas and accompanying low electricity prices drove retirements of older, less efficient steam and combustion turbines as well as some CCGTs in markets already dominated by gas-fired generation, such as Texas. The addition of large wind and solar capacity in California played a major role although wind capacity additions were also a factor in Texas.

A handful of regions hosted most of the new gas-fired capacity built since 2000 led by Texas (13 percent), Florida (10 percent), California (8 percent), and Pennsylvania (6 percent). The Southeast, including Florida, hosted about 30 percent of the new gas-fired capacity. Most of the additions (especially CCGTs) in Texas, California, and the Southeast occurred in the 2000s. In contrast, the states in the largest organized market, PJM Interconnection (PJM), hosted more than 20 percent of new gas-fired capacity, about 50 percent of which were built in the 2010s fueled by the availability of cheap natural gas from the Marcellus shale and the need to replace retired coal-fired capacity.

In summary, the natural gas-fueled generation fleet in the United States has undergone a significant transformation since the early 2000s with new, more efficient CCGTs and CTs replacing older, less efficient CCGTs and steam turbines. The rejuvenation of the gas fleet continues. Nearly 33 GW of new gas-fired capacity are expected between 2020 and 2025 (Fig. 2.2). The majority of future gas builds will occur in the PJM and Southeast regions. About 10 GW of mostly steam turbines are planned to be retired by 2025. As a result, the average capacity-weighted age of the U.S. gas-fired power plant fleet will be around 20 in 2025. But one needs to distinguish between capacity additions and how they will be utilized. In Midwest, California, and New York, many additions are CTs intended for backing up intermittent renewables. Even CCGTs will likely be used more for reliability purposes as coal-fired plants are pushed out and renewables are added rather than consistent baseload generation. In essence, this is the scenario where natural gas is a "bridge" fuel.

Gas-Fired Versus Renewable Energy Capacity Additions

Wind and solar capacity additions have been more than double the amount expected in early 2018. At the time, planned wind and utility-scale solar additions between 2018 and 2020 were 18 GW and 12 GW, respectively. Instead, 34 (20) GW of wind (solar) was built since 2018 with another 6.5 (4) GW expected to be completed by the end of 2020. In contrast, more than 38 GW of gas-fired capacity was expected online between 2018 and 2020 but only 34 GW will be completed by the end of 2020.[4]

Despite the recent surge in wind and solar capacity expansion, the near future is still gas-heavy (Table 2.1). Nearly 29 GW of gas-fired capacity is expected between 2021 and 2023 as compared to 8.7 GW of wind and 15.7 GW of solar. In terms of capacity under construction and with regulatory approvals, gas-fired capacity has a bigger advantage.

However, permitting and construction are faster for wind and solar than natural gas. Given lower costs, more projects are likely to be developed in good resource locations such as the Southwest for solar and east of the Rockies for onshore wind. An extension of federal tax credits, more generous state programs, COVID stimulus targeting clean energy, or, more likely, a combination of these approaches will promote renewables across the country.[5] Probably reflecting these policy drivers, other data sources suggest a more bullish renewable future than the EIA 860 data,

Table 2.1 Expected gas, wind, and solar power plant capacity, GW (2021–2023)

	Natural gas	*Wind*	*Solar*
Under construction	3.9	2.7	2.7
Regulatory approvals received	8.1	<0.1	4.0
Regulatory approvals pending	7.6	2.2	3.9
Planned	9.4	3.8	5.2

Source: EIA 860 March 2020

which are based on surveys and EIA research. For example, American Public Power Association (APPA; Zummo 2020), using the ABB Velocity Suite database, reports nearly 15 GW of gas, 20 GW of wind, and 10 GW of solar capacity as under construction, some of which already came online in the first half of 2020. But Zummo (2020) also reports 18 GW of gas, 13 GW of wind, and 10 GW of solar as permitted; and 14 GW of gas, 24 GW of wind, and 28 GW of solar with pending applications. The shift toward wind and solar is even stronger with the proposed plant data: 66 GW of wind and 64 GW of solar versus 27 GW of gas. Much of the proposed capacity will not be built any time soon, if at all. Still, as compared to previous APPA reports, the shift in these numbers away from gas toward wind and solar deserves to be taken seriously.

The capacity in interconnection queues of system operators provides another perspective on intentions of developers. In 2019, total capacity in queue was 265 GW solar, 215 GW wind, 97 GW solar with battery storage, 9 GW wind with battery storage, 48 GW standalone battery storage, and 76 GW natural gas.[6] Again, most of the capacity in queue will not get built right away, if at all, even if they receive their interconnection permits. Most importantly, new transmission infrastructure is needed in many locations. But the large discrepancy between gas and renewable energy capacities is strong evidence of energy transition in the power sector. These trends also signal that utilities and regulators are becoming more focused on low capital cost projects that can be developed relatively quickly rather than long-lead, capital-intensive projects.

Coal Retirements

Nearly 90 GW of coal-fired capacity has been retired since the early 2000s, 90 percent of which occurred in the 2010s.[7] Environmental regulations such as Mercury and Air Toxics Standards (MATS), increasing belief in a sustained period of low natural gas prices, and rising penetration of wind and solar all contributed to decisions to retire uneconomic plants. Actual retired capacity has consistently surpassed planned retirements throughout the 2010s but 2019 was still a surprise (Fig. 2.3). The early 2020s are promising to be another period of large coal-fired capacity retirement.

The increased supply of natural gas from low-permeability resources has been the main cause of low electricity prices, as gas-fired generation is often the marginal generator setting the price in competitive electricity markets. Figure 2.3 depicts three series of natural gas prices for power

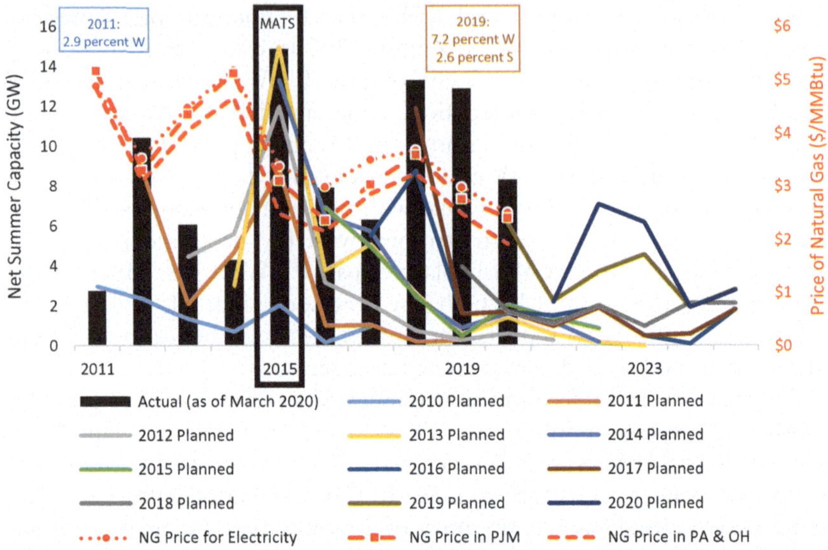

Fig. 2.3 Actual and planned coal-fired plant retirements (net summer capacity). (Source: Compiled by author from data reported in EIA-860 monthly spreadsheets except for the natural gas price for power generation from EIA natural gas price data. MATS: Mercury and Air Toxics Standards. Percentages for wind (W) and solar (S) in 2011 and 2019 are national averages of generation inclusive of small-scale solar PV in 2019. 2020 retirements are the sum of 2.94 GW already retired and about 5.4 GW expected to retire in EIA 860 March 2020 report)

plants: an average U.S. price, an average of prices in six states that make up the great majority of the PJM market (home to a third of the coal retirements), and an average of prices in Pennsylvania and Ohio, where more than 21 percent of the coal retirements occurred. The PJM territory covers all gas production from the Marcellus shale. On average, gas prices in the PJM region have been 5–10 percent lower than the U.S. average price; the gap is much larger for the Pennsylvania–Ohio region. Nearly 40 percent of the coal retirements in 2018 happened in the Electric Reliability Council of Texas (ERCOT) market, where natural gas prices have also been lower than the U.S. average.

Increasing penetration of wind and solar lowered prices further in some markets. The low dispatch cost of renewables will continue to put downward pressure on wholesale electricity prices, which has become a concern for all generators, including operators and developers of renewable energy facilities (see the "Clean Technology Penetration" section for details).

Although MATS was the most influential environmental regulation driving retirements through the 2015 compliance year, other regulations targeting regional haze (ozone), cooling-water use, and coal-ash and combustion-residual management have played a role in decisions to retire particular plants. Some utilities made the necessary investments to render some coal-fired plants compliant with MATS and other regulations. Others could not justify investing in equipment to comply with these regulations in a low-price environment. In essence, these environmental regulations expedited the exit of older, less efficient units. More than three-quarters of coal units retired in the 2010s were built before 1970 and had historically low or declining utilization.

SWOT

With a young fleet of efficient plants ready to replace retiring baseload generation with low-cost electricity fueled by a relatively clean-burning fuel with a low price, the power sector is primed to burn more natural gas in the future. But a SWOT analysis is useful to balance the fuel's technical and economic strengths that laid the foundation for its current dominant position in the generation portfolio with its weaknesses—mainly environmental in nature—that lead to threats in policy, regulatory, and public acceptance space. Yet, the natural gas industry also has opportunities that can be realized primarily, albeit not uniquely, by proactively abating environmental risks (Table 2.2).

Table 2.2 SWOT—Natural gas burn for power generation

Strengths: *Cheap, efficient, baseload, dispatchable, scalable, fits existing grid, much cleaner than coal*	**Weaknesses:** *Methane leaks, flaring, combustion emissions, hydraulic fracturing impacts, price uncertainty and volatility, too much competition among generators*
Opportunities: *Reducing methane leaks and flaring, remaining low-cost, improving efficiency, feedstock for and co-firing with hydrogen*	**Threats:** *Expanding policies & local opposition to block gas infrastructure, growing financial & public support for wind, solar, storage & other alternatives*

Strengths

Natural gas burns much cleaner than coal. The fuel offers a tremendous improvement over coal in terms of local emissions that cause many illnesses: no mercury emissions, negligible emissions of sulfur dioxide and particulates, and lower emissions of nitrogen oxides. There is also no solid waste such as coal ash. Also, combusting gas for power generation emits up to 50 percent less CO_2 than combusting coal, which can be reduced further with carbon capture and sequestration (CCS) but at a considerable cost.

The natural gas price has been low enough to generate baseload electricity cheaper than coal since the mid-2010s. Some regions benefited from even lower prices (e.g., the Marcellus region). Given the abundance of the resource not only in North America but also globally, the price of natural gas should remain in a range that makes it attractive for power generation for the foreseeable future. The gas turbine technology is advanced, but improvements in turbine and combined cycle power plant designs can raise conversion efficiency that allows for the cost of electricity to remain low even at higher natural gas prices.

Plants can be built relatively quickly at reasonably low capital cost in locations fit for replacing retired baseload units without significant, if any, investment in grid expansion. Importantly, existing capacity is sufficient in most regions for years to come. Increasing the utilization of existing CCGT plants by a few percentage points should suffice to compensate for lost generation from 28 GW of coal and nearly 6 GW of nuclear capacity scheduled to retire by 2025. All regions have flexible gas-fired plants such as CTs that are currently best resources to provide backup generation to intermittent wind and solar facilities.

It is difficult for wind and solar to replace retirements one-to-one for mainly three reasons. First, the locations of coal and nuclear retirements and the locations of best wind and solar resources do not overlap in most cases. Second, availability of wind and solar generation does not overlap with load profiles in most regions. Third, once adjusted for intermittency, depending on location, their utilization of nameplate capacity decreases to roughly 35–55 percent for wind and 20–35 percent for utility-scale solar. Taken together, these shortcomings necessitate the building of two to five times more capacity than the dispatchable thermal plants being replaced. Moreover, to maximize their utilization and to increase their match to load profiles, the facilities should be geographically distributed, which requires additional investment in the transmission grid. All of these additional investments increase the unit cost of renewable energy delivered to customers, often above the cost of competing technologies such as CCGTs (see the "Potential Potholes for Further Expansion of Renewable Energy" section for a more detailed discussion of system integration costs).

Weaknesses

Large amounts of installed capacity and rising share of generation does not mean high utilization of all plants. In a previous rapid expansion period, a large wave of construction added many new gas-fired plants. At the peak construction period between 2000 and 2005, nearly 206 GW of new gas-fired capacity were added. But in following years many gas-fired plants struggled commercially in many locations. A growing number of state and federal programs encouraged the expansion of renewable energy technologies and undermined the market share of gas-fired plants. Low natural gas and, hence, electricity prices in competitive markets worsened the profitability of many plants.

But the most important reason for commercial difficulties faced by gas-fired power plants was the intense competition among generators that caused lower utilization of even the newest plants, some of which often did not receive proper compensation owing to poor market designs (e.g., energy price caps). In hindsight, capacity expanded too much in the 2000s, encouraged by the low-interest-rate environment, expectation of continued load growth, encouragement of generous capacity compensation schemes, or some combination of these factors in competitive wholesale electricity markets. The low electricity prices since the early 2010s have caused bankruptcies and consolidation in the merchant sector.

History may repeat itself. Electricity prices remain low partially due to low price of natural gas but also because of excess generation capacity in many markets. The retirement of much of the baseload capacity offers an opportunity for newer gas-fired generation to fill the gap, but there is too much capacity being built in some regions. One driver of this potential overbuild is the confluence of capacity mechanisms that encourage some older plants to stay online while also inducing new builds, and government incentives to promote wind and solar farms and to prevent retirement of uneconomic nuclear plants.

The tensions over market design issues and out-of-market policies among various stakeholders in organized electricity markets have been rising for some time. Federal and state policymakers and regulators are increasingly at odds with each other. Some states threaten to leave organized markets. I expect generation portfolios in most regions to be determined increasingly by state policies rather than markets. State mandated portfolios will exclude gas-fired units as long as they are not needed for supply security and reliability.[8]

Although the price of natural gas is forecasted to be low for years to come, its history is one of volatility. The boom-bust cycles are common for natural resources. Low prices encourage demand but discourage upstream investment to prove up more reserves. This cycle eventually leads to supply constraints and higher prices. However, the cycle may be broken in the United States because of associated gas. Since the early 2010s, the price of natural gas remained low despite decreased drilling for dry gas because the supply of associated gas from low-permeability plays rich in liquids has been significant once midstream infrastructure was developed to allow market access. As such, oil prices have become a key influencer of the natural gas supply and hence its price in North America (see Chap. 1 for extensive treatment). Oil prices have been even more volatile than natural gas prices. The mitigation of this price risk has been a key justification of utilities for signing long-term power purchase agreements (PPAs) with wind and solar developers at prices above wholesale market prices. Long-term stability of electricity costs provided by PPAs has value to utilities and their customers. Such PPAs are increasingly seen as a better way of securing sufficient generation capacity in power systems than ill-designed and oft-challenged capacity compensation schemes.

But there is a more pervasive reason why states, cities, utilities, and corporations are willing to announce net-zero targets within the 2030–2050 timeframe and sign 100-percent renewable energy contracts. Nominally, that reason is climate change but other environmental and local economic concerns are pertinent from the perspective of public opinion that doubtless informs policy and influences companies' public relations messaging. For example, the labor intensity of wind and solar installations as well as energy efficiency retrofits and the fact that these jobs are local have been instrumental for garnering support of more state representatives to pass aggressive clean energy targets. Similarly, some nuclear plants are saved by state initiatives partially to preserve economic benefits they provide to host communities.[9]

Although not always observable in their investment decisions, the promotion of ESG standards and decarbonization by an increasing number of investment banks signal potential difficulty of financing fossil fuel projects, including natural gas infrastructure, in the future.[10] There is a movement toward developing standards to include emissions in traditional financial reporting of publicly traded companies.[11]

In short, the main weakness of natural gas is that it is a fossil fuel that causes climate change. The fact that it releases about half as much greenhouse gas emissions as coal when combusted for power generation is not satisfactory to a growing portion of the public and, as a result, policymakers. Increasingly, methane leaks along the supply chain and flaring of associated gas concern the environmental community. Risks of groundwater contamination, earthquakes, increased truck traffic, local emissions, and other environmental and social impacts associated with hydraulic fracturing are still relevant although they are not the headline nowadays. These environmental concerns establish the foundation of main threats to natural gas.

Threats

The social license to operate (SLO) is becoming harder to obtain for natural gas infrastructure, including gas-fired power plants and pipelines, in many locations. Some states have been able to block new pipelines using a variety of tools at their disposal, often challenging FERC, and ban new gas-fired power plants or force the retirement of older units, replacing them with renewables, energy efficiency and conservation, battery storage, or a combination.

Local opposition can also cause costly project delays and may have become more impactful as a result of a D.C. Circuit Court of Appeals ruling from mid-2020 that forces FERC to end its decades-long practice of delaying decisions on rehearing requests by landowners or other stakeholders regarding infrastructure projects such as pipelines under the Natural Gas Act. Some legal experts consider this decision a milestone with potential implications for power sector projects under the Federal Power Act. This ruling is just one of the many recent court decisions that make getting permits for natural gas infrastructure such as pipelines more difficult.

This growing anti-gas movement gains in significance when seen within the context of energy transition. There are now examples of utilities cancelling permitted natural gas projects. Instead, utilities focus on technologies mandated by states. Utilities' ability to include the state-sponsored assets in their cost base for regulatory approval is a catalyst for such transformation of utility portfolios. This strategy also appears to shelter incumbent utilities from smaller competitors implementing more distributed technologies.

But also important are declining costs and increasing popularity of alternative technologies. Years of incentives, technological advances, and globalization of supply chains brought down the per-MWh cost of new wind and solar farms to beat the cost of new gas-fired generation in locations with good wind and solar resources and ready access to transmission and distribution (T&D) grids. The cost of battery storage seems to be following a similar decline curve. Cost declines make it easier for states to mandate even larger shares of these technologies. Continuing federal tax credits make these resources even more palatable. This feedback loop among cost declines, public opinion, and policy is critical for future expansion of clean technologies.

Distributed resources add more complexity to energy transition. Some customers seem to be showing more interest in rooftop solar and battery storage for their homes or businesses but also in smart appliances and ability to respond to price signals. More than 30 states have renewable portfolio or clean energy standards (RPS and CES), ranging from 10 to 60 percent by 2030 (80–100 percent by 2050 in several states). Despite its now well-known cost-shifting and other regulatory problems, 40 states have mandatory net metering rules to promote rooftop solar. More states are expected to follow in the footsteps of seven states with energy storage targets, which also offer financial incentives for storage installations. Overall, there are several thousand policies and incentives across different levels of jurisdiction that support utility-scale or distributed renewable energy (with varying technologies eligible as renewable energy in different jurisdictions), storage (mostly battery), energy efficiency, electrification, and other clean energy projects.[12] All of these changes signal a fundamentally different electric power system, in which the role of gas-fired generation will change and gas burn will likely shrink.

But adding a large amount of intermittent and variable resources into electricity grids either in utility scale or as distributed energy resources (DER) brings about system integration costs from building T&D facilities to compensation of units that can provide backup and grid reliability services. Even energy efficiency programs show up as a cost in customer bills. These costs have been rising, which may offer an opportunity for natural gas.

Opportunities

The retail cost of electricity, inclusive of all charges in a bill (energy, T&D, renewable, energy efficiency, etc.), has been rising in many states in a widening path of divergence from wholesale electricity prices, which have been declining since the early 2010s. The decline was driven mainly by low natural gas prices and, in some markets, low-cost, subsidized wind and solar generation. Generally, retail costs increased more and fastest in some of the states with large renewable energy mandates and other clean energy programs while they remained flat in states with low clean energy targets or none.

The increasing cost of energy transition started to attract more attention in political discussions with a particular focus on energy justice implications. Low-income consumers, for whom the share of energy bills in disposable income is high, are voicing their concerns via consumer organizations. It is not clear, however, whether this issue will gain sufficient traction in policy debates. Even if it does, the cross-subsidization of utility rates—a common regulatory practice for decades—may be a relatively easy solution to protect low-income customers. Public support for energy transition is strong and has been rising. The lack of pricing environmental externalities of fossil fuels has been a successful counterargument in the past in response to higher cost of integrating intermittent and variable wind and solar technologies to power systems. Enough customers may be willing to cross-subsidize low-income consumers as long as the transition does not jeopardize reliable delivery of electricity. Hence, whether the mass media coverage of rising energy costs, if it ever happens, will lower the support for energy transition policies enough to matter is unclear.

On the other hand, the goals for energy transition are becoming greater in many regions. Adding more wind (especially offshore), solar (especially rooftop), battery storage, and charging infrastructure for electric cars, and implementing more energy efficiency programs in a more compressed timeline will add to the costs more visibly. Similarly, a carbon fee will raise the cost of electricity right away. In the absence of alternative ways of paying for these costs, rising customer bills will certainly induce more consumers calling their representatives.

However, the natural gas industry cannot and should not wait for these external developments to result in its favor. The industry needs to change the perception of natural gas as an environmentally harmful fossil fuel with proactive elimination of its externalities. There is already movement in detecting and stopping methane leaks across the supply chain. These efforts must continue with demonstrable results. Operators should continue to reduce flaring without waiting for regulations. Hydraulic fracturing and its limited environmental impacts are better understood by more of the public as a result of outreach campaigns but work is not finished. Similarly, the industry should not shy away from promoting the substantial benefits of natural gas in reducing local pollution (mercury, particulate matter, sulfur dioxide, nitrogen oxides, coal ash) when it replaces coal. Critically, the communication of best industry practices, self-regulation efforts, and fuel's benefits has to be honest, transparent, and constant.

The low-price, low-demand environment caused by the COVID pandemic created a survival instinct for many companies and probably pushed mitigation of environmental impacts down the list of priorities. But mitigation is not optional if the industry is to enhance its public acceptance across wider geographies. Inherent strengths of natural gas as a cheap and versatile fuel that is cleaner burning than coal are not sufficient to guarantee its future share in power generation. The electric power sector has many alternatives, albeit often costlier, and is experiencing a significant transition not only in terms of utility-scale generation technologies that garner more policy support every day but also on the consumer side with a growing demographic of prosumers adopting modern technologies to generate, store, or manage their electricity.

Drivers of Future Gas Burn for Power Generation

Will the share of gas-fired generation continue to increase as it has over the last three decades? It is tempting to extrapolate the upward trend seen in Fig. 2.1. However, four drivers extracted from the SWOT analysis may stimulate or hinder future gas burn: natural gas price, baseload capacity retirements, penetration of clean technologies, and difficulty of obtaining SLO. The first two are straightforward but last two are composites that require some explanation.

- Clean technologies include the usual suspects such as wind, solar (utility-scale and distributed), and energy storage technologies but also demand side technologies such as smart thermostats and appliances, heat pumps, and others that are mostly leveraging advances in digital technology. The collection of these technologies allows for visions of micro grids and virtual power plants (VPPs) that signal a more efficient system with control of more distributed resources to optimize generation and consumption of electricity in real time.

- Difficulty of obtaining SLO is meant to capture all kinds of environmental regulations at different levels of government that does not directly impact the price of natural gas,[13] legal and regulatory changes that increase the cost of the permitting process, and local opposition to infrastructure.

In Fig. 2.4, I offer an admittedly limited 2-D visualization of the combined influence of these four drivers on future gas burn relative to 2020

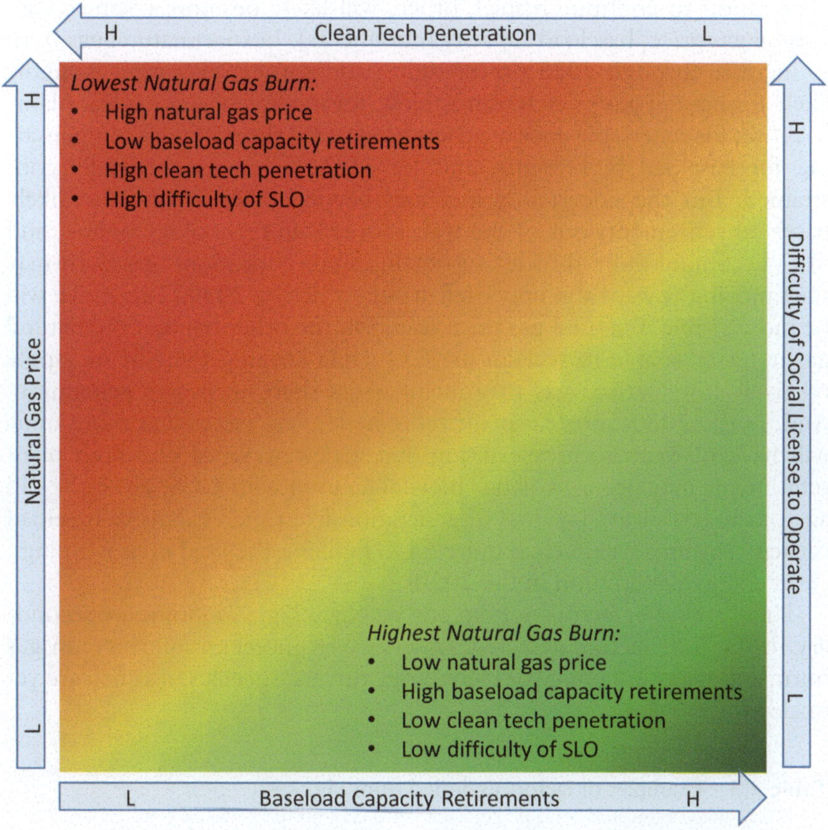

Fig. 2.4 Key factors driving natural gas burn for power generation. (Note: Arrows indicate direction of increase from low (L) to high (H), all relative to current state (2020). See discussion of internal dynamics and external forces throughout this chapter)

level. These drivers are interdependent. For example, higher natural gas prices would likely encourage deployment of more clean technology, especially utility-scale wind and solar generation facilities. Somewhat counterintuitively, higher natural gas prices may also help economics of baseload plants, including CCGTs, to generate more revenues from higher wholesale electricity prices. All else being equal, lower gas prices would produce opposite effects.

The graphic can be interpreted for any point in future. Although one might expect some drivers to follow recent trends (e.g., clean technology penetration to continue rising), others will likely be more volatile (e.g., natural gas price, baseload capacity retirements). I expect natural gas burn to increase through 2025 (lower right-hand corner) because it is highly likely for natural gas price to remain low, for more coal and nuclear plants to retire, for renewable energy penetration to fall short of fully compensating for baseload retirements, and for SLO to remain regionally constrained. But the uncertainty increases beyond 2025. With most likely baseload retirements out of the way, more clean technology online, and SLO becoming more difficult to obtain in more locations, gas burn may start moving toward the upper left-hand corner by 2030. This move will be more visible if natural gas price rises. On the other hand, if the natural gas industry is able to reclaim its SLO while keeping the cost of supply relatively low, natural gas may maintain its share in power generation. And, in the 2030s, nuclear plant retirements may increase as more units will have 60-year licenses expiring and a new wave of coal-fired plant retirements may occur, which is inevitable, even with CCS, given the old age of the coal fleet. The loss of generation from such extensive baseload capacity closures will likely require CCGTs filling the void even with high clean energy penetration in the 2020s.

There are other factors not directly visible in Fig. 2.4. Some are secondary to the four factors depicted; others exert uncertain influence on gas burn; and many are policy or technology drivers, specifics of which are yet unclear (Table 2.3).

Table 2.3 Examples of factors excluded from Fig. 2.4

Secondary	Oil price, environmental regulations that increase cost/price
Uncertain influence	Distributed gas-fired generation
Unclear external policies	Electrification (load growth)

- Oil prices high enough to encourage liquids-directed drilling increase associated gas production and put downward pressure on natural gas prices and upward pressure on drilling costs, both of which disadvantage operators in dry gas plays. At the time of writing, the COVID-19 pandemic is leading to a significant decline in upstream activity in the United States. This lower level of activity is reducing associated gas production that may eventually lead to a recovery in the price of natural gas once the demand starts increasing. On the other hand, a recovery in oil price may encourage liquids-directed drilling and associated gas production once again.
- New environmental regulations on water or chemical use in, or an outright ban on, hydraulic fracturing will increase the cost of natural gas production.
- A CO_2 price should help gas replace more coal-fired generation, but it will also increase the cost of gas-fired generation and the cost of natural gas production and delivery due to methane leaks along the supply chain unless the leaks are prevented.
- A ban on flaring and venting of associated gas can push natural gas price higher or lower depending on capacity of midstream infrastructure. If there are no midstream bottlenecks, more associated gas will reach the market, putting downward pressure on the natural gas price.
- Distributed gas-fired generation via microturbines or reciprocating engines could change the dynamics of gas burn, but its net impact is uncertain, as distributed gas-fired generation can reduce the need for gas-fired peakers.
- U.S. electric-power demand has remained fairly flat since the early 2000s, albeit with significant regional differences. Energy efficiency and conservation measures, along with increasing penetration of behind-the-meter generation and storage, will continue to temper load growth for wholesale generators. On the other hand, electrification of transportation and building use (e.g., space and water heating) could reverse the downward trend of load growth. The specifics of how load growth will influence natural gas use in power generation will depend on energy versus peak load growth, impact of new technologies on power systems and traditional load profiles, and cost and policy trends of technologies such as battery storage and heat pumps.

Before I provide a detailed discussion of the drivers in Fig. 2.4, a brief discussion of some modeling results is useful to highlight not only the importance of input assumptions but also relevance of drivers that are not easy to include in models.

Results from Long-Term Capacity-Expansion and Economic-Dispatch Modeling

Between 2011 and 2017, we have analyzed numerous long-term scenarios via economic-dispatch and capacity-expansion modeling for the ERCOT market and nationwide (e.g., Gülen and Soni 2013; Gülen and Bellman 2015; Tsai and Gülen 2017a).[14] Consistently, our modeling resulted in more gas-fired generation capacity in the future, about two-thirds CCGTs and the rest CTs. Generally, business-as-usual scenarios led to large coal retirements with additions of small amounts of new wind and solar and more CCGTs. We also developed scenarios with large amounts of hard-wired wind and solar because federal tax credits and state mandates continued to encourage their development. In some cases, we also assumed declining capital costs for wind and solar. These scenarios yielded more CTs and fewer CCGTs than the business-as-usual scenarios but still more CCGT capacity than renewables. Importantly, gas-fired generation did not always increase at the same rate as gas-fired capacity, depending on load-growth assumptions, natural gas basis differentials, and, to a lesser extent, the share of other generation sources, including coal and nuclear.

Figure 2.5 is a version of Fig. 9 in Tsai and Gülen (2017a). This version includes the impacts of CO_2 prices. The wide range of gas burns reflects our particular focus on four drivers (consistent with those in Fig. 2.4): capacity and pace of wind and solar buildout, natural gas price paths, large nuclear retirements, and CO_2 prices that would result from the implementation of Clean Power Plan (CPP) starting in 2022. The lower gas-burn levels result from scenarios with faster penetration of larger quantities of renewables (57 GW of wind and 20 GW of solar hardwired to be online by 2022) and higher natural gas prices [$4–$5 per million British thermal units (MMBtu) in real terms] but without CPP and new nuclear retirements (bottom of patterned bars). Lower natural gas prices ($3–$4/MMBtu in real terms) and lower wind and solar buildout (11 GW of wind and 7 GW of solar hardwired) encourage more gas burn.

The most significant jumps occur with CO_2 price increases, which induce coal retirements, and hardwired early nuclear retirements. Nuclear

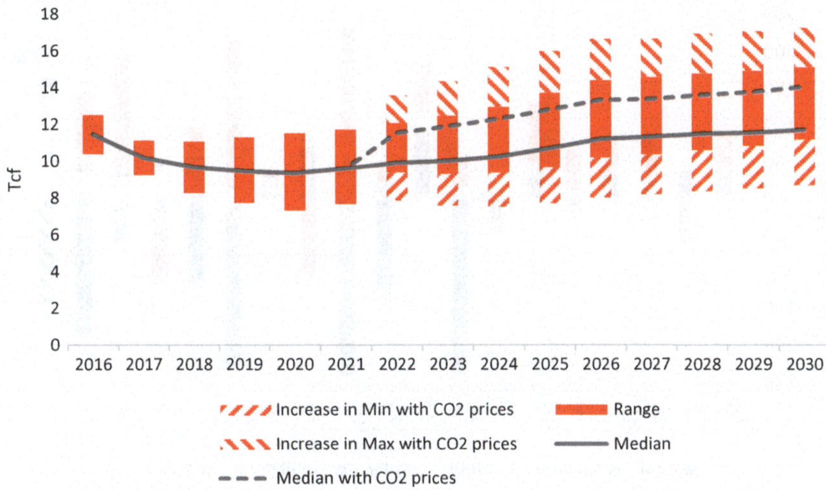

Fig. 2.5 Scenarios of natural gas burn for power generation. (Source: Summary from long-term capacity-expansion modeling using Energy Exemplar Aurora software. Modified from Tsai and Gülen 2017a)

retirements push gas burn to the tops of the red bars in Fig. 2.5. CPP-induced CO_2 prices would force more coal retirements and further increase gas burn to within the range covered by the top patterned bars.

The real world supports our ranges. In 2019, nearly 11 trillion cubic feet (Tcf) of natural gas was utilized for power generation, higher than the median (9.5 Tcf) of our modeling but lower than the top of the range (11.3 Tcf).[15] This larger natural gas burn is due to much larger coal-fired capacity retiring between 2016 and 2019. However, since 2015, replacement of coal-fired generation by gas-fired generation has been less than one-to-one (Fig. 2.6), with wind and solar claiming some of the market share lost by coal because a lot more wind and solar capacity were added. Actual and expected wind capacity additions between 2016 and the end of 2022 are 63 GW for wind and 50 GW for solar as compared to 57 and 20 GW in our modeling.

Recall the discussion of anticipated large renewable capacity adds in the "Gas-Fired Versus Renewable Energy Capacity Additions" section. Wind and solar will compensate for a growing share of retiring baseload capacity. Some simple calculations, albeit ignoring power system realities across regions,[16] is illustrative. Based on the planned coal and nuclear retirements

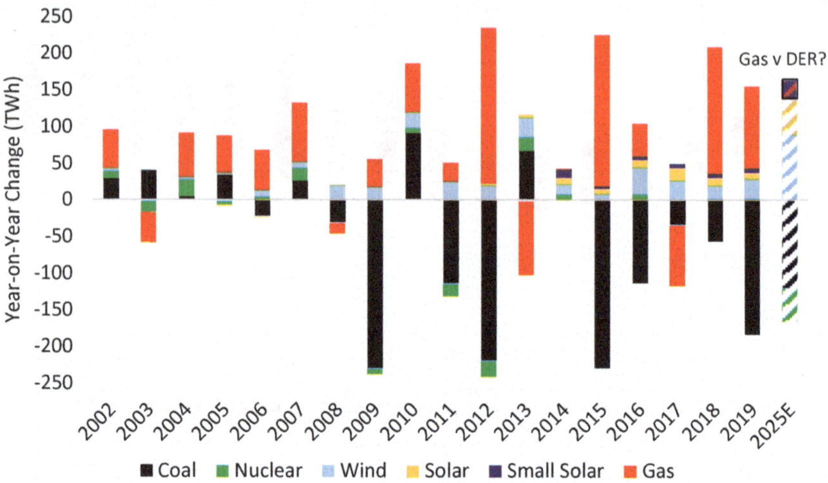

Fig. 2.6 Change in generation. (Source: Author calculations based on EIA net generation data downloaded from EIA data browser. For 2020–2025 see the discussion associated with Table 2.4)

between 2020 and 2025, using recent average capacity factors for each type of facility, coal and nuclear generation will decline by about 119 and 46 TWh respectively.[17] Increasing the capacity factor of CCGT fleet existing at the end of 2019 by only 4 percent will compensate for this loss of baseload generation (165 TWh). This would translate into an additional gas burn of 1.2 Tcf, or an increase of over 10 percent from 2019.

However, expected utility-scale wind and solar facilities, some of which are already under construction, can generate 90 and 49 TWh, respectively, using recent national average capacity factors of 35 and 24 percent (Table 2.4). If all wind and solar expansion were to occur in regions with coal and nuclear capacity retirements (a crucial but unrealistic assumption), the need for additional gas-fired generation would be only 26 TWh (Fig. 2.6). There is no reliable data on planned distributed solar capacity but according to EIA data, small-scale solar has been adding about 5 TWh a year since 2015. If this trend continues, small-scale solar may add 25 TWh by 2025, which would negate the need for additional gas-fired generation, again assuming that small-scale solar will get developed in locations with baseload retirements (see patterned boxes on top of the last column of Fig. 2.6).

Table 2.4 Replacing coal and nuclear generation retiring in 2020–2025 (TWh)

	Coal	*Nuclear*	*Gas*	*Wind*	*Utility solar*
2019 generation	964	809	1579	299	72
2025E change in generation	-119	-46	26-165?	90	49

Source: Author calculations from EIA net generation data downloaded from EIA data browser and EIA 860 data

Clearly, the locations of wind and solar additions and coal retirements will not be a good match. As discussed before, most coal retirements are occurring in regions without great wind and solar resources but with access to cheap gas (e.g., Pennsylvania, Ohio). In contrast, largest solar and wind additions were in locations with better resources such as Arizona, California, Florida, North Carolina, and Texas for solar; and Iowa, Kansas, Oklahoma, and Texas for wind. Also, from the perspective of system balancing in real time (i.e., generation matching load at all times), the intermittency and variability of wind and solar do not allow for a one-to-one replacement of baseload coal-fired capacity even if they are connected to the same grid. On the other hand, tax credits and state mandates continue to encourage the development of wind and solar facilities in sub-optimal resource locations, including regions with baseload retirements. This is especially true for distributed solar. Although these facilities have even lower capacity factors than the national average, grid expansion is making more of wind and solar generation available across larger regions that undermine gas-fired generation.

Overall, gas-fired generation should still replace a considerable share of lost baseload generation in most regions. The existing fleet can replace lost generation simply by raising utilization of existing plants by a few percentage points. However, nearly 33 GW of new gas-fired capacity is expected to come online by 2025, mainly in the same regions as retirements. If the load remains flat as it has in the 2010s, there is a risk of excess capacity just like the experience in the 2000s. As a result, some gas-fired plants may be challenged to generate sufficient revenues.

In addition to wind and solar expanding much more than we modeled, our nuclear retirement scenarios now appear to be premature. Some of the expected nuclear retirements are likely to be postponed beyond 2030 since states save plants with out-of-market compensation (see "Nuclear Revival?" section). In contrast to renewables and nuclear, gas-fired plants depend on market price signals or utility planning.

It is difficult to capture the evolution of this policy space or the growing anti-gas movement and ESG activism in modeling exercises. But it is important to acknowledge that other modeling exercises demonstrate the technical feasibility of reliable grid operations almost exclusively with today's renewable energy technologies. There is much debate about the practicality of such model results and the cost of such systems; most models focus on power system technical capabilities and avoid total cost calculations. But their existence influences policies and regulations that attempt to accelerate the transition to a decarbonized electricity grid.

With this background on key drivers and what modeling suggests about their impact on future gas burn, it is time to deepen the discussion on key drivers, their interactions, and secondary or tertiary factors that can influence their future evolution.

A Wide Range of Uncertainties

It is necessary to set the context for discussing drivers of gas burn by acknowledging regional differences across electricity systems. To begin with, although gas deliveries for power generation increased at the national level, there are several regions where they declined. For example, in California, they declined nearly 50 percent since 2008 as a result of strong policies and regulatory programs favoring alternatives. Many states mimic California in their pursuit of decarbonization. These changes have been forcing organized markets to tweak their designs to ensure proper compensation of resources for the services they provide to maintain grid reliability and resource adequacy.

The developments in regulated utility territories appear more orderly and predictable than developments in organized markets, where the dynamic environment of market design changes has the feel of whack-a-mole, because new adjustments are constantly needed as earlier modifications lead to distortions and complaints by market participants. For example, California programs targeted higher shares of renewables, including distributed generation, gave customers more choice in self-generation and demand response, and encouraged electrification of the transportation sector.[18] For some time now, state regulators have been concerned about another energy crisis (similar to the 2001 meltdown) resulting from the collision of uncoordinated policies. This portfolio of policies has been forcing thermal generation, including natural gas facilities, out of the market. But, California Public Utilities Commission (CPUC) raises concerns about the negative impact on reliability of retiring gas-fired plants and opposition to new fast-ramping gas-fired units (Colvin et al. 2018). Concerned, CPUC is pursuing new policies to require all load-serving entities to hold three- to five-year capacity requirements, which can be met jointly via a central buyer structure. With these policies, CPUC is hoping to keep some thermal plants online in locations critical to grid reliability and resource adequacy until alternatives are in place (e.g., see Randolph 2018).

Other concerned regions started to save some plants (mostly nuclear) with out-of-market support mechanisms (see the "Baseload Capacity Retirements" section). This multijurisdictional policy and market-design space has been evolving over the 2010s. It is setting states against FERC and, in some cases, against each other. Most states prefer mandating specific capacities of specific technologies to reach their decarbonization goals rather than saving markets by pricing various attributes of different technologies such as environmental externalities and reliability. The role of natural gas in this transition is highly uncertain in some regions. Is it a "bridge" fuel, mostly as a supporter of intermittent renewables? Or, will it play a longer-term role as a baseload generation fuel? I remain mindful of this electricity market context as I turn to several factors that will determine gas burn for power generation through 2035.[19]

Natural Gas Price

The natural gas price remains the major determinant of gas-fired generation in the short-term. Historically, coal price has been stable and natural gas price has been volatile. This difference has led to constant switching between baseload coal and gas-fired units to minimize total cost of electricity in real-time operations. There are regional, real-time operation considerations but roughly speaking, as long as the cost of gas delivered to power plants remains below \$3.8/MMBtu, CCGTs generate electricity at a lower average cost than coal-fired plants (see ovals in Fig. 2.7). CTs always cost more than coal or CCGTs but do not compete with baseload plants, as they are needed for load following and real-time balancing of demand and supply (see "Disruptive Technologies" section for a comparison to battery storage costs).

Another driver of CCGT's competitiveness is its lower fixed operating and maintenance cost. Finally, the improvement of average efficiency of the gas fleet as more-efficient plants replaced older units played a role. The average heat rate—a metric of power-plant efficiency measured in heat content of the fuel burned to generate one unit of electricity—for the natural gas fleet (inclusive of CCGTs and CTs of all ages) declined from about 8.5 British thermal units (Btu) per MWh in the early 2000s to about 7.7 Btu/MWh by the mid-2010s. Modern CCGTs have design heat rates of below 7 Btu/MWh. In contrast, the coal fleet average heat rate is about 10 Btu/MWh.

Regional Differences

However, regional fuel costs, average capacity factors, and heat rates may deviate from the U.S. averages represented in Fig. 2.7. The rate of wind and solar penetration also matter for decisions regarding which generator to run at any time during the day across the seasons. A closer look at generation data from ERCOT reveals the complexity of coal–gas switching

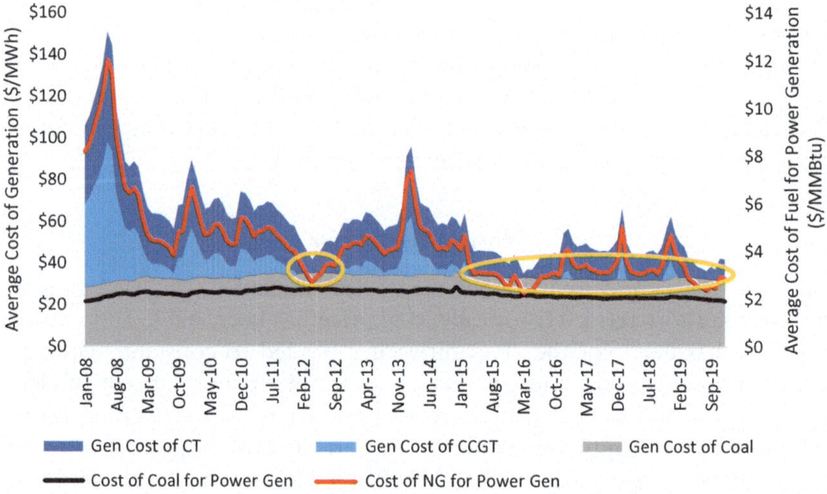

Fig. 2.7 Average coal and natural gas cost to power plants and generation costs. (Source: Generation costs are calculated by author using average fuel costs for power generation from EIA data browser, average capacity factors from various issues of EIA's Electric Power Monthly, average heat rates from EIA-860 Annual Electric Generator Report, and fixed and variable operating and maintenance cost estimates within the ranges provided in Lazard (2019a). CT: combustion turbine. CCGT: Combined-Cycle Gas Turbine. Ovals highlight periods when CCGT generation cost is lower than coal-fired generation cost)

dynamics due to the increasing share of wind and availability of local and cheap gas and lignite supplies. For example, the increasing price of natural gas in the early 2010s reduced the share of gas-fired generation while boosting coal-fired generation (Fig. 2.8). In contrast, the declining price of natural gas from early 2014 appears to have forced the share of coal-fired generation to decline. But the share of gas-fired generation stabilized although the price of natural gas continued to decline. Certainly, changes in electricity demand across seasons, locational considerations for grid reliability, and transmission grid congestion play a role in generation decisions. But, rapid expansion of wind generation after the Congress extended PTC in 2016 has eaten into potential market share of gas. Without the declining natural gas price, gas-fired rather than coal-fired generation could have been reduced. As the natural gas price started to rise in April 2016, coal regained market share.

But revenues were still not sufficient to prevent the retirement of more than 4 GW of coal-fired capacity in early 2018. The share of gas-fired generation increased from 38 percent in 2017 to 47 percent in 2019 while the

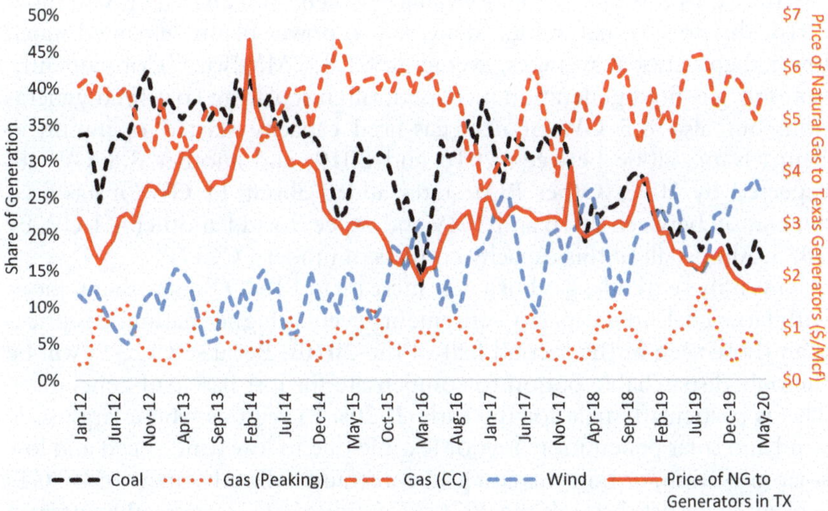

Fig. 2.8 Share of fuels in ERCOT generation (January 2012–May 2020). (Compiled by author using ERCOT fuel mix data (http://www.ercot.com/gridinfo/generation). Natural gas price to generators in Texas from various issues of Electric Power Monthly of EIA)

share of coal declined from 32 percent in 2017 to 20 percent in 2019. Most of the increase came from CCGTs that replaced lost coal-fired generation. The switching in 2019 is driven by continuing decline in natural gas price. The share of wind generation increased to 19 percent in 2018 and 21 percent in 2019, which is probably contributing to increasing utilization of gas-fired peaking, or load-following, units, the share of which reached 7 percent in 2019.[20] Notably, the increase in gas-fired generation came almost exclusively from existing gas-fired plants increasing their capacity factor.

Nationwide, the share of total natural gas delivered to power plants fluctuates seasonally. The correlation between the natural gas price and gas delivered to power plants between January 2002 and March 2020 averaged -0.5 with some seasonal volatility (e.g., lower correlation in summer months). In summer months, the share of gas in generation reaches 50 percent then falls to the 20- to 25-percent range during winter. But regional differences matter. For example, the 2014 "Polar Vortex" increased heating demand for natural gas by residential and commercial customers and reduced gas availability for power generation in parts of the Northeast. In contrast, in Pennsylvania between April 2015 and November 2016, the price of natural gas delivered to power plants remained much lower than national averages, averaging $1.83/MMBtu.[21] Consequently, not only gas-fired generation increased, often replacing coal-fired generation, but also 8.5 GW of new gas-fired capacity started operating in Pennsylvania alone between 2016 and 2019, and another 3.8 GW are expected by 2022. Other PJM states added about 11 GW of gas-fired generation between 2016 and 2019 and expect to add another 4.1 GW by 2025. Almost all of this capacity consists of modern CCGTs.

Given these trends, gas burn may increase in ERCOT and other regions with large coal-fired capacity retirements even at higher natural gas prices than those seen in the second half of the 2010s. Because CCGTs will be the only dispatchable option to compensate for lost baseload generation. This is particularly true for the early 2020s. In regions where large-scale wind and solar penetration are not feasible due to low wind speed and low solar insolation, or transmission grid constraints, the advantage of CCGTs is likely to persist through the 2030s. Existing CCGTs can readily increase their utilization from the current mid-50-percent range by a few percentage points where needed.

Natural Gas Demand in Other Sectors
The future path of natural gas price also depends on demand from other sectors, including exports. Competition from heating customers, who often get priority access to natural gas during tight market conditions such as extreme cold fronts, may occasionally constrain how much gas can be burned by power plants. Although these impacts are seasonal and mostly limited to a few regions (Northeast in particular), restrictions on new natural gas infrastructure (often in the same regions) may increase the frequency of gas shortages for power plants. On the other hand, decarbonization and electrification efforts may reduce the residential and commercial sectors use of natural gas, which has been flat. Such reduction, while freeing gas for power generation, also supports decarbonization efforts. Hence, there is little prospect for gas demand growth from residential and commercial consumers.

The industrial sector's demand for natural gas has been inching up toward 30 percent of total consumption since the development of low-permeability resources increased supplies and lowered prices. While there are alternatives to gas-fired generation such as coal, nuclear, and—increasingly—wind and solar, the alternatives to natural gas as industrial feedstock are limited, at least for certain processes such as methanol and fertilizer production. Nevertheless, industrial gas demand growth in the 2010s has been relatively small (less than 1.7 Tcf—see Chap. 3) and the potential for future growth remains constrained by competing petrochemicals capacity build-out in other parts of the world as discussed in Chap. 3.

In contrast, increasing availability of sizable liquefaction and pipeline export capacity offers a potential outlet for up to 10 Tcf by the late 2020s (EIA 2020). Pipeline exports to Mexico and Canada reached nearly 8 Bcf/d in 2019. Since most natural gas sold outside of North America is indexed to oil price, it may be possible for U.S. liquefied natural gas (LNG) exports to compete globally at prices too high for competitive domestic power generation. As discussed earlier, gas deliverable to power plants below $3.8/MMBtu renders gas-fired generation competitive. In some systems and certain times of the year, even higher prices are acceptable to power plants. These higher prices could still attract global buyers of U.S. LNG and petrochemical products depending on the price of oil and competition from other LNG and petrochemical capacity developers.

However, global natural gas market conditions change rapidly as new resources and markets are developed. Furthermore, in many of the emerging markets gas competes with coal and renewables in power generation, and with liquids in industrial uses. So, U.S. LNG exports may be challenged at times. The COVID pandemic, though unprecedented, demonstrated the competitive weakness of U.S. LNG in a global market with excess supply of natural gas and low oil prices. Despite the availability of 10Bcf/d of liquefaction capacity, U.S. LNG exports fell to 2–3 Bcf/d range by mid-2020.

Natural Gas Price Outlooks

Modeling by the EIA considers the complex interactions among the sectors discussed above as well as various energy and environmental policies, and provides us with ranges of future natural gas prices. For example, 30 scenarios included in the EIA 2018 Annual Energy Outlook (AEO) (2018a) forecast the price of natural gas delivered to electric power plants in a range from about \$3.8/MMBtu to \$7.0/MMBtu in 2019 dollars between 2020 and 2030. The low end of the range (lines in green tones) follows a fairly flat trajectory, while the high end (lines in orange tones) follows a rising path (Fig. 2.9). Lowest prices occur in four scenarios, all with high oil and gas

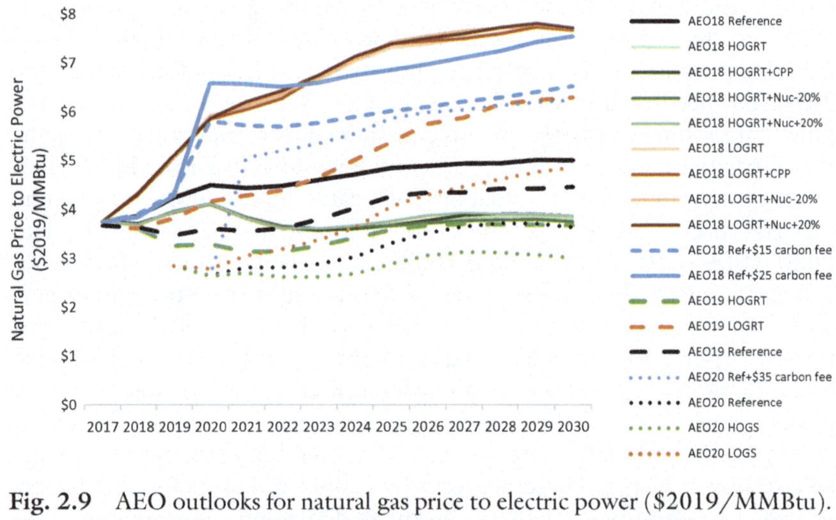

Fig. 2.9 AEO outlooks for natural gas price to electric power (\$2019/MMBtu). (Note: Not all AEO scenarios and all years are represented. LOGRT = low oil and gas resource and technology; CPP = Clean Power Plan implemented; Nuc-20 percent and Nuc+20 percent = 20 percent lower or higher nuclear costs, respectively; Ref = reference; HOGRT = high oil and gas resource and technology; HOGS = high oil and gas supply; LOGS = low oil and gas supply)

resource and technology (HOGRT) assumptions. In contrast, highest prices occur in four scenarios that assume low oil and gas resource and technology (LOGRT). The scenario with a $25 per ton carbon-allowance fee yields a price path similar to ones from these LOGRT scenarios even with gas resources higher than levels assumed in the LOGRT scenario.

Markedly, natural gas price forecasts in AEO 2019 (EIA 2019) declined from comparable scenarios of AEO 2018 and AEO 2020 (EIA 2020) registered further decreases. These declines reflect primarily the improved understanding of natural gas supply from low-permeability plays. They are so substantial that the AEO 2020 low oil and gas supply (LOGS) price for 2030 is lower than AEO 2018 reference-case price. Even a $35 carbon allowance fee scenario in AEO 2020 leads to prices around the AEO 2019 LOGRT scenario.

One does not have to take these price outlooks literally; but the range of natural gas price forecasts do highlight the importance of the oil and gas resources and the technological ability of the industry to deliver those resources.

However, there are many uncertainties on the supply side. Shale operators have struggled with profitability, almost since inception of these plays and through the 2010s. Associated gas production from liquids-directed drilling suppressed natural gas prices and curtailed drilling for dry gas. As detailed in Chap. 1, "gassier" operators—those for whom natural gas is 50 percent or more of production—tend to be lower cost but less valuable based on earnings (expressed as earnings before interest, taxes and depreciation, depletion and amortization, EBITDA). During 2018, EBITDA for gassy players ranged from $1 per thousand cubic feet of natural gas–equivalent (Mcfe) to $2.70/Mcfe.[22] Their annual costs ranged from about $1.60/Mcfe to $3/Mcfe, placing inordinate pressure on hedging (as described in Chap. 1) and other sources of revenue (NGLs uplift, as discussed in Chaps. 1 and 3, and midstream operations, as discussed in Chap. 1). It has become more difficult for operators to find cheap capital. If interest rates rise or oil and gas assets remain less attractive to investors, the cost of capital may rise further. The difficulty of raising external capital, upon which so many producers depend, will curtail capital investment. A combination of factors could push the breakeven price that operators need to support new natural gas-directed drilling to above $3/Mcfe, to $3.50/Mcfe, and perhaps even higher.[23] Since gas-fired generators can access the fuel with only a small premium above these breakeven prices in resource regions (e.g., PJM that sits on top of the Marcellus play, ERCOT in Texas with its large portfolio of plays, and the Southeast in close proximity of several plays), gas will remain very competitive. Even in regions where the cost of gas to electricity generators can be 20–30 percent above these breakeven levels, gas-fired generation looks attractive.

However, beyond the next several years, the price outlook is less certain. If the natural gas prices to end-users rise high enough, higher-priced electricity would encourage investment in alternative technologies. The timing of these demand-supply cycles is central to future gas burn for power generation. For example, rapid rise in natural gas price could delay some baseload capacity retirements and encourage federal and state support for CCS. On the other hand, higher electricity prices can also help gas-fired generators that currently suffer from low revenues, especially in some regions, to increase their earnings even if they generate the same amount. But the current near-term price outlooks do not support such a scenario.

Baseload Capacity Retirements

At the time of writing, nearly 26 GW of coal-fired and 5.7 GW of nuclear capacity are planned to retire by 2025 in addition to more than 80 GW of coal-fired and 6.8 GW of nuclear capacity that retired in the 2010s (Fig. 2.3). Planned coal retirements have been increasing; 2020 announcements are even larger than 2019 announcements which were already significantly larger than previous years. The average age of the remaining coal fleet is about 45. Average age of capacity retired each year has been around 50 since the 2000s. There is already 40 GW of coal-fired capacity that is older than 50 with an average of 9 GW to be added to the 50+ club every year through 2035 (Fig. 2.10). The nuclear fleet is younger but by 2030, 60-year licenses will start expiring for a growing number of units.

The location and utilization of a plant are important factors in retirement decisions. But, in an environment of low natural gas price and growing penetration of wind, solar, and energy storage, aging coal-fired plants are more likely to lose market share and revenues. There are also more environmental concerns with aging plants, especially if their owners did not invest in state-of-the-art emission controls. Hence, I expect the 2020s to witness at least as many coal retirements as the 2010s. However, there are efforts to delay retirement of baseload capacity.

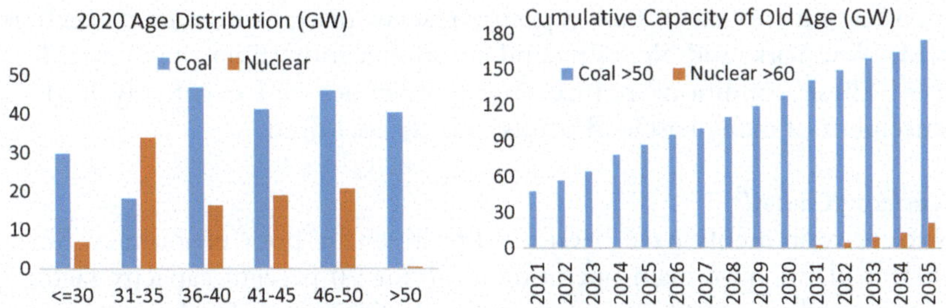

Fig. 2.10 Aging coal and nuclear fleets. (Source: Author calculations from EIA 860 data)

Coal-Fired Capacity Beyond Saving?
Efforts to save coal-fired plants have faltered so far. For example, Ohio regulators approved PPAs for the existing coal and nuclear assets of FirstEnergy and AEP Ohio, but FERC blocked the PPAs in early 2016. In 2017, the U.S. Department of Energy (DOE) asked FERC to devise a mechanism to value "resiliency" of baseload plants that could store fuel on site. FERC rejected the DOE proposal, which was opposed by many market participants. The Administration came back with a bailout of select coal and nuclear plants based on Section 202 of the Federal Power Act. This plan called for the federal government to buy electricity directly from specific generators for two years. The plan was stillborn due to strong and widespread opposition from market participants and other stakeholders.

Despite the failures so far, battles continue in different fronts. In summer of 2020, Wyoming regulators initiated an investigation of the utility plans to retire some coal units. The conflict seems to be between saving local jobs and out-of-state corporations. PacifiCorp—parent of the local utility—also operates in California, Oregon, Washington, Idaho, and Utah, most of which have ambitious decarbonization and renewables goals.

There is also a more pseudo-market approach to saving baseload plants rather than any specific unit owned by a specific utility. Organized markets have been revising their capacity market schemes to provide sufficient compensation to baseload units. But these technocratic fixes by system operator staff have been mired in an environment of conflict between states that want to add wind and solar to their grid and FERC that wants to maintain a resemblance of competitive markets.[24] These capacity markets have been keeping too much existing capacity online while encouraging too much new capacity: reserve margins in markets such as PJM, New York, and New England are significantly larger than target levels.[25] These conditions reduce energy revenues and eventually lead to retirement of many baseload plants, mostly coal-fired.

Nuclear Revival?
Nuclear retirements have been mostly driven by poor economics. Since nuclear plants have been operating at about 90-percent capacity factor[26] and supplying nearly 20 percent of electricity in the United States (Fig. 2.1), they are most easily replaced by CCGTs, as our dispatch modeling confirmed when we assessed retiring 43 GW of nuclear capacity by 2030 (Fig. 2.5). Our scenario was supported by many studies. For example, PJM (2016) forecasted 14 GW of nuclear retirements by 2026 under their low gas price–sensitivity case. Szilard and others (2017) concluded that 63 (36 merchant, 19 regulated utility, and 8 public power) out of 79 units would have lost money in competitive markets in 2016, but additional revenue of $15/MWh would have returned all but ten units to profitability. Market developments supported these studies' findings. In the 2018 PJM capacity-market auction, 7 GW of nuclear capacity did not clear the market.

In response to the retirement risk of zero-emission generation facilities that also create a lot of jobs and sustain local economies, states started developing initiatives to save them. First movers, New York and Illinois, created subsidies for some nuclear plants scheduled to retire in 2017 or 2018. These states felt it necessary to offer credits ranging in value from $10/MWh to $17/MWh (consistent with the findings of Szilard and others 2017) to prevent the premature retirement of nuclear plants. While competitive generators and ratepayer groups challenged these initiatives, courts upheld 2016 initiatives by New York and Illinois. FERC claimed that it, rather than the courts, had the authority to assess whether ZECs were consistent with "just and reasonable" rates in wholesale electricity markets. So far, FERC did not challenge these programs. New Jersey, Connecticut, Pennsylvania, Ohio, and other states either created similar support mechanisms or are considering them.

Perhaps encouraged by such support initiatives by states, more nuclear operators applied to the Nuclear Regulatory Commission (NRC) to extend their operating licenses to 80 years. As of mid-2020, NRC renewed licenses for 4.1 GW in two plants, and was reviewing another application for 1.7 GW with three more applications expected for a total of about

5.3 GW. More plants may pursue license extensions to 80 years. But current market conditions challenge the financial viability of these plants, especially if their license extension requires large capital investments (e.g., due to aging equipment) to qualify. Luckily for these plants and their operators, many states pursuing decarbonization policies are realizing nuclear plants' value as generators of large amounts of baseload, zero-carbon electricity, without which they are unlikely to achieve their decarbonization goals. Subsidizing existing nuclear plants is a cheaper way to keep emissions low than building a large amount of new wind, solar, and storage capacity and investing in the T&D network to accommodate these facilities.

Also, despite significant delays and cost overruns with associated regulatory battles, new nuclear capacity of 2.2 GW will come online in the early 2020s. But this expansion has to be contrasted with the mid-construction cancellation of a major project in South Carolina and cancellation of other projects over the last decade. These experiences highlight the difficulty of a nuclear revival: very high capital cost, 10–15 years from planning to operation, lost capabilities of big engineering firms due to lack of nuclear construction in decades, and shortage of public acceptance.

There is some optimism about the advanced nuclear technologies. For example, NuScale's small modular reactor is expected to receive its NRC license in 2020 and its first plant is reportedly on track for operation in 2027. There are other advanced nuclear designs. Most promising ones are small units that can be deployed much quicker than the traditional nuclear units without the same level of safety and waste concerns. Some can be fit for distributed use in mini grids. There are also federal tax credits available to new nuclear capacity; and Congress has been considering other initiatives to support nuclear technology research, development, and deployment. However, it is highly unlikely for advanced nuclear to play a significant role before the late 2030s.

Overall, multijurisdictional and multipronged efforts to save nuclear and, to a lesser extent, coal-fired plants continue. To the extent these efforts are successful, they will lead to less gas burn. Some gas-fired assets in regions with delayed retirements and low electricity prices may become stranded even if they are relatively young. Nevertheless, aging baseload capacity, especially coal-fired plants, cannot be saved forever. Unavoidable retirements present an opportunity for CCGTs that will only grow toward 2030 and beyond. However, clean technologies have significant potential to undermine this opportunity.

Clean Technology Penetration

Clean technology penetration is complex because it is a composite of multiple drivers, including the usual suspects of wind, solar, and storage but also many technologies to empower consumers to produce their own energy and respond dynamically to prices by managing their consumption, and other technologies that can help utilities improve their management of the T&D grid. Overall, they have the potential to change the electric power industry fundamentally from the model of large generation facilities connected via an expansive T&D network to one where smaller generation and demand-side resources in mini grids are managed by prosumers. Examples can be found around the world. Clean energy portfolios implemented via integrated resource plans (IRPs) propose systems without any gas-fired or any other thermal generation (e.g., Dyson et al. 2018). Their collective impact on gas burn is negative.

Nevertheless, this transition is slow and full of obstacles (see the "Disruptive Technologies" section). For the purpose of this analysis, focusing on wind and solar should be sufficient to highlight the risk to gas-fired generation's market share. About 31 GW of wind and 23 GW of solar was built between 2016 and 2019; and 32 GW of wind and 27 GW of solar are expected to come online by the end of 2021 (Fig. 2.2). Also, more than 29 GW of distributed solar were installed (more than half of it on homes) as of the end of 2019 according to the Solar Energy Industries Association.[27] These additions are much larger than what many expected only a few years back.

The influence of solar and wind on electricity markets and systems are already significant in some regions. Wind generation accounted for 7.2 percent of total U.S. generation in 2019, but reached 21 percent in ERCOT, which has nearly 29 GW of installed capacity and another 6 GW expected by the end of 2021. Utility-scale solar accounted for only 1.7 percent nationwide, but in California, about 14 percent of 2019 generation came from solar facilities. Including EIA estimates of small-scale solar (mostly as DER), the share of solar is about 2.6 percent.

Increasing wind and solar output has been eating into gas-fired generation's market share. This impact has been masked to a certain extent because CCGTs replaced most of the baseload generation lost to retirements. However, there is no guarantee that gas-fired generation will replace as much of the lost generation from future baseload capacity retirements given the expected large wind and solar expansion. That renewable energy will be able to replace baseload generation in larger scale is also supported by a couple of other trends. First, there is significant investment by the utilities in transmission grids across the country, partially to accommodate remote wind and solar resources. And, demands for larger investments to clear the hundreds of GWs of renewable capacity in interconnection queues are becoming louder. Second, many utility-scale solar projects are increasingly coupled with battery storage, which allows more of their generation to be supplied to the grid throughout the day.

Potential Potholes for Further Expansion of Renewable Energy
Still, renewable energy technologies face several challenges, which grow along with the scale and visibility of wind and solar facilities. **First**, despite the recent impressive record of expansion, the continued large-scale development of wind and solar capacity as well as the emergence of battery storage remains dependent on strong incentive mechanisms such as federal tax credits and state mandates. The expansion of tax credits by Congress in early 2016 led to a boom in wind and solar investment, particularly where state incentives or mandates supplemented federal tax credits. This wave has been much stronger than previous expansion periods because of lower cost and higher efficiency of wind and solar technologies. Encouraged by these trends, more cities and corporations are announcing renewable or clean energy targets, many as high as 100 percent within years (some by 2030), and are willing to sign long-term PPAs, which are essential for securing attractive financing. Batteries seem to be the next technology benefiting from a similar feedback loop.

Nevertheless, it is important to recognize that the plethora of incentives makes the wheels of clean energy investment turn. A good illustration of this dependence on incentives is the history of PTC. Every time Congress allowed PTC to expire, wind-capacity additions fell significantly the next year (Fig. 2.11). Despite cost declines of recent years, the history may repeat itself: capacity expansion is expected to fall after the PTC expires in 2020 based on planned projects. Some outlooks are more bullish but the average annual new builds are less than the average since 2016. Still, bullish outlooks are consistent with data reported earlier from Zummo (2020) and Berkeley Lab interconnection queue database.

If borne out in coming years, the decline in wind build-out suggests that wind costs are not expected to decline sufficiently to render wind competitive against alternatives across all geographies without federal tax credits. At least some customers who are willing to sign long-term PPAs

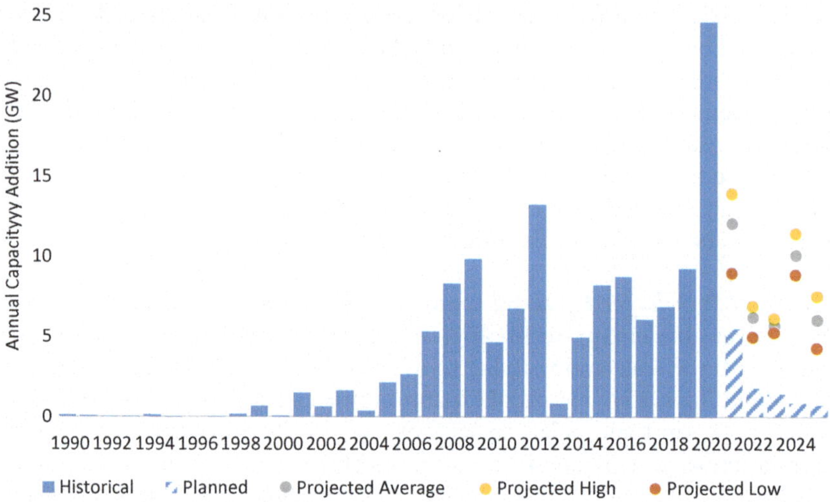

Fig. 2.11 Historical, planned, and projected U.S. wind-capacity additions. (Source: Historical and planned capacity additions are from the same EIA 860 data used in other figures in this chapter. 2020 data includes 18 GW that started operating in 2020 and another 6.5 GW that is expected online before the end of 2020. Projected figures are analyst projections as reported in Fig. 65 of Wiser and others 2020)

do so because of the attractive prices they receive. Prices are lower than a price that would allow for capital cost recovery with an acceptable rate of return to lenders and developers because tax credits allow them cash flow security, which facilitates financing with attractive terms. On the other hand, collectively, state, city, or corporate incentives may be adequate substitutes for PTC. It is also possible for Congress to extend PTC as part of the COVID stimulus package or separately.

We must also consider the global supply chains for wind and solar. The current level of renewables penetration would not have been achieved without the incentive mechanisms across the supply chain. Importantly, subsidies and mandates in the West encouraged China to invest in and subsidize solar panel manufacturing way beyond the country's own needs. About 40–45 percent of solar modules in the world are supplied by Chinese manufacturers. This still considerable market share is lower today owing to expanding manufacturing capabilities in North America, Japan, and elsewhere. Trade wars and the COVID pandemic demonstrated how supply chains can be disrupted. Recent resurgence of economic and political nationalism across the globe suggests further trade wars and disruptions to supply chains. A similar geopolitical threat is emerging for battery manufacturing. China is trying to control the supply of critical minerals and investing in Li-ion battery manufacturing although South Korean and a few Western companies are competing in the same space. The geopolitics of supply chains can push costs of solar panels, batteries, and windmills higher, which will likely necessitate the extension of government subsidies and incentive programs.

Regardless of how this complex geopolitical drama evolves, one observation stands: the demands of the renewables industry for continued policy support are contradicting the simultaneous claims that wind and solar are already competitive with conventional generation technologies based on levelized cost of electricity (LCOE) estimates. One reason for this incoherence is that generic LCOE estimates do not account for regional variations of the inputs of the LCOE formula, especially the capacity factor of wind and solar, which is determined by the quality of wind speed and solar irradiance and insolation of the location. But LCOE is also problematic for other reasons.

Second, wind and solar generation impose electricity system integration costs. These costs are not captured by generic LCOE estimates but electricity customers, taxpayers, and shareholders of mostly competing assets but also of renewable energy companies pay these system integration costs. See Gülen (2019) for a more detailed discussion with more references but most important of these costs can be summarized as follows:

- ***Intermittency:*** Wind and solar farms are not dispatchable by a system operator because the generation depends on availability of wind and sunshine. They get dispatched when resources are available. Resource adequacy necessitates real-time balancing and backup generation. Conventional thermal generation resources—mostly burning natural gas—provide these services. These plants must be compensated properly to remain available even if their annual generation declines. If the compensation is not adequate, some generation assets may become financially stranded.
- ***Variability:*** Wind and solar are also variable. Meteorological conditions (e.g., clouds and storms) and technical difficulties (e.g., equipment malfunction) can cause unpredictable variability in very short

time frames and increase system balancing needs. For example, at high wind speeds, operators shut down the turbines to prevent damaging them. A recent report by kWh Analytics[28] points out systemic underproduction by solar facilities due to optimistic irradiance assumptions, inadequate modeling that ignore intra-hour variability due to cloud cover, installation errors that lead to degraded cells and modules falling offline in first year of operation, and inverter failures. Such issues impact the ability of system operators to accurately predict wind and solar farms' generation in time frames ranging from minutes to hours and raise the cost of emergency balancing services.

- ***Cost of intermittency and variability:*** The literature estimates for balancing costs mostly range from \$1/MWh to \$5/MWh depending on the resource, penetration levels, and load profiles. Estimates for adequacy (i.e., backup) costs range from \$5/MWh to \$9/MWh for penetration levels less than 30 percent but can be as high as \$20/MWh at higher penetration levels.[29]
- ***Remoteness of best resources:*** One way to mitigate the intermittency and variability of wind and solar is to build them in best resource locations to maximize their capacity factor and their ability to complement each other[30] via expanding the transmission network. Utilities invested more than \$200 billion in new transmission capacity in the 2010s partially to facilitate renewables penetration (EIA 2018b). More T&D investment is required to accommodate growing utility-scale and distributed renewable energy capacity, much of which are waiting in the interconnection queue. Overall, the literature provides a wide range of \$2/MWh to \$22/MWh for grid costs, depending on the system characteristics and penetration levels.
- ***Overproduction:*** New transmission lines offer transitory relief. As more generation capacity is built in areas of high-quality resource, transmission capacity becomes insufficient and congestion costs rise again. Often, excess generation is curtailed. For example, in the early 2010s, new transmission lines were built to accommodate wind in West Texas. They reduced congestion costs for a few years. But, according to Potomac Economics (2020), congestion costs in ERCOT started to increase again in 2017. Constraints in moving wind-generated electricity out of wind areas is one of the main drivers and wind generation is increasingly curtailed. These costs and curtailment will continue to increase without new transmission capacity expansion. System operators in California and Germany

have also been curtailing renewable generation due to what Ueckerdt and others (2013) call overproduction. Wind generators in Texas bid negative prices to collect their PTC.[31] California pays Arizona to take its excess solar generation. Similarly, Germany sends its excess renewables generation to neighboring grids. Overproduction costs are negligible until the system achieves relatively high levels of penetration (e.g., roughly 25 percent for wind and 15 percent for solar in Germany, according to Ueckerdt et al. 2013). Overproduction costs increase at a fast pace after reaching these levels: \$10–\$20/MWh depending on the market for an additional 5-percent increase in share of generation.

- ***"Full-load hour reduction."*** As a result of subsidized renewables eating into their market share and lowering average prices, existing generators lose revenues.[32] During restructuring of regulated utilities, they were granted stranded cost recovery because utilities argued they made investments under the regulatory compact and restructuring to allow competition posed a threat to their cost recovery at allowed returns. Similarly, merchant generators made investments under the competitive-market construct, but renewables, and increasingly battery storage, are imposed on competitive markets by mandates and subsidies. Ueckerdt and others (2013) present "full-load hour reduction" costs that are akin to stranded costs and estimate them at \$10–\$20/MWh at 5- to 10-percent penetration of wind or solar.[33]

In short, as renewables penetration levels increase, these system integration costs become more visible. Notably, there is growing realization of the declining market value of wind and solar once their share of generation reaches a threshold, which is dependent on characteristics of each power system.[34] It is increasingly likely that, in order to recover their capital investment, wind and solar will become perpetually dependent on long-term PPAs, prices for which would have to increase[35] unless tax credits and mandates also continue.[36]

Some of the system integration costs are explicit in retail cost of electricity, which has been increasing across the Unites States despite historically low wholesale electricity prices. Increased T&D, renewables, energy efficiency, or other charges related with state clean energy programs add to customer bills. Barbose (2019) provides rough estimates of RPS compliance costs, which average 2.6 percent of retail electricity bills in 2018 with a range from 0.3 to 5.8 percent across states with RPS. This wide range is a reflection of differences of RPS programs across states but the higher shares are more likely in states that pursue wind or solar despite the poor quality of the resource in that state.[37] Importantly, Barbose (2019) omits the following costs: balancing costs ($1–10/MWh), T&D network upgrades ($2–20/MWh of costs versus $4–50/MWh of benefits), wholesale market price suppression ($30/MWh of consumer benefits that, as discussed earlier, becomes a stranded cost once generators are compensated for selling less power at lower prices or early retirement), and declining market value of renewables ($5–15/MWh for wind, $10–30/MWh for solar).[38]

However, RPS is not the only policy that matters. According to the Clean Energy Technology Center at the North Carolina State University, there are several thousand programs on supporting renewables, energy efficiency, battery deployment, and other clean energy applications across the United States.[39] A look at the average cost of electricity to end-users in comparison to average wholesale prices across many states depicts a picture of additional costs associated with all clean energy programs not just RPS. Perhaps the first observation from Fig. 2.12 is that residential costs of electricity[40] are much higher in California, New England, and New York. Also, residential costs diverged from wholesale prices faster, especially after around 2012 in first two regions.[41] Costs are expected to increase in these and other regions that pursue increasingly ambitious targets for not only established utility-scale wind and solar but also offshore wind, battery storage, electric vehicle (EV) charging infrastructure, and more technologies that will likely show up in customer bills as separate charges on increased T&D, renewable/clean energy, energy efficiency, and other programs.

The top row of states in Fig. 2.12 have an RPS or CES target of 50 percent or more by 2030. In the case of California, the striking divergence between the average cost of electricity to residential customers and the wholesale price of electricity is a reflection of the costs associated with roughly 150 programs California has in place in pursuit of its decarbonization goal.[42] Other states on the top row have been able to maintain residential costs relatively flat after 2010. There are many factors that determine the cost of electricity to consumers, including ratemaking approach followed by the regulators. But it seems safe to postulate that average residential cost of electricity remained flat in New Jersey and Maryland thanks to low price of natural gas from the Marcellus shale and

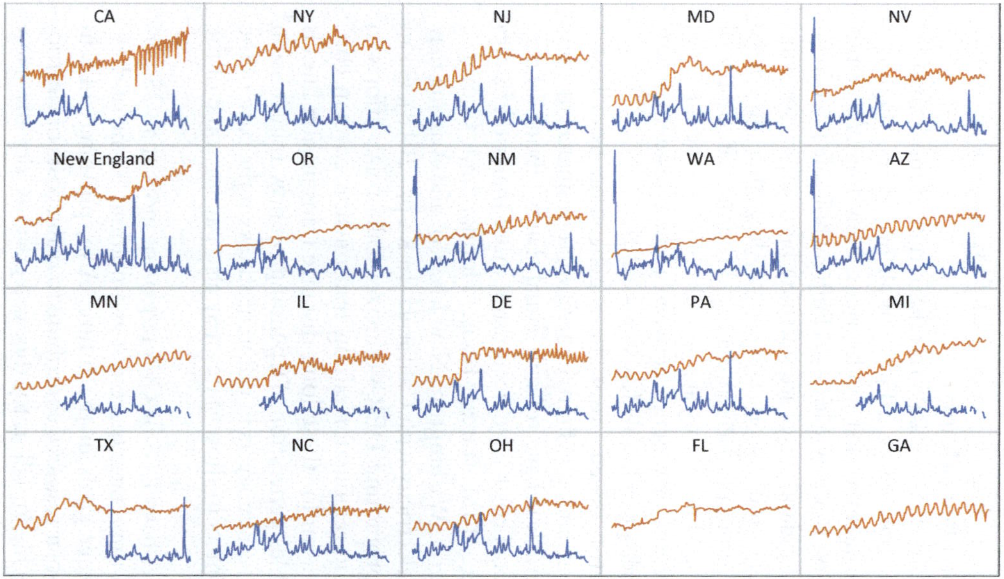

Fig. 2.12 Residential cost of electricity and wholesale electricity prices across the United States (January 2001–April 2020). (Average retail prices (costs) of electricity are from EIA Electric Power Monthly as reported in EIA's interactive data browser. Wholesale prices are from EIA's Wholesale Electricity and Natural Gas Data (https://www.eia.gov/electricity/wholesale/) except for Texas, for which I used average ERCOT energy price as reported by the independent market monitor, Potomac Economics. There is no wholesale market that is relevant to Florida and Georgia. For all other states, I used the wholesale price from the region closest to each state. In all charts, the left vertical axis is the average residential cost (orange line) with a maximum of ¢25 per kWh, and the right vertical axis is the wholesale electricity price (blue line) with a maximum of $300/MWh. States are grouped in rows relative to the RPS and/or CES targets. From first to last row, they represent: more than 50 percent by 2030; more than 50 percent by 2040–2050; more than 25 percent by 2025; and less than 12.5 percent)

the excess capacity resulting from compensation of generators from the generous PJM capacity market. Nevada's traditional utility regulation is probably the driver for relatively flat costs. New York continues to benefit from its nuclear plants and imports from the neighboring PJM market but still experiences significantly higher prices than PJM neighbors such as New Jersey, Maryland, and Pennsylvania.

The second row of states have an RPS or CES target of more than 50 percent by 2040 or later but before 2050.[43] In all five states, there is a sharp upward trend in residential cost of electricity. New England stands out: it is the only region on this row with a declining wholesale price in an organized market. New England states are pursuing high targets for wind and solar but also storage and energy efficiency. Altogether they have about 250 programs in support of clean energy. Programs are not well coordinated across states. Many states are actively blocking new natural gas infrastructure. Hence, the divergence between average residential cost of electricity and wholesale price has widened since 2013.

Oregon and Washington benefit from cheap generation from legacy hydroelectric assets. Coal and gas-fired generation dominates in New Mexico. Gas, coal, and nuclear have roughly equal shares (about 30 percent) in Arizona. Still, retail costs have been rising more than other states dominated by gas (e.g., PJM states, Texas, Florida, and Georgia). Wholesale prices in Oregon, Washington, New Mexico, and Arizona may reflect the large trade of electricity with California. In Karpa (2018), Clean Coalition—a nonprofit promoting DER—criticizes California's efforts to connect with neighboring regions for raising transmission costs in consumer bills. The main reason for these long-distance transmission lines is to import more renewables generation. Depending on how transmission costs are distributed across ratepayers in different states on the path of the transmission lines, customers in those states may also pay for some of the transmission costs.

The third row of states have RPS or CES targets of more than 25 percent by 2025. Although these targets are not as ambitious, some of these states are indicating bigger goals in the future. Also, pursuing solar in states with poor quality solar resource contribute to rising costs of electricity. Minnesota and Michigan fall into this category as do the New England states.

The last row of states either have low targets they have already achieved or do not have any targets. Texas stands out because of several factors. The competitive ERCOT market kept wholesale prices low thanks to several factors. Cheap natural gas produced in the state certainly played an important role but the state is also home to the largest installed wind capacity in the country, which has been expanding since the late 2000s. Retail choice also kept residential costs in check. All states on this row experienced somewhat rising electricity costs in the 2000s which stabilized in the 2010s thanks to mostly large gas-fired capacity expansion and the low cost of natural gas. All had average residential costs below the U.S. average in the 2010s.

Finally, renewables too have environmental and geopolitical impacts. A fundamental challenge is their large footprint given the low capacity of individual units (windmills or solar panels) and low capacity factor. As renewables scale up to capacity levels that are necessary to replace conventional generation technologies, environmental impacts are becoming more visible such as clear-cutting of forests or damage to desert ecology. The most notorious example of local opposition to a renewables project is probably the Cape Wind offshore wind farm that, after 16 years, was cancelled because of opposition from "wealthy property owners like the Kennedys, Mr. Koch, and Rachel Lambert Mellon" and economic concerns of many local officials, businesses, residents, Indian tribes, and environmental activists due to high cost of offshore wind power or impact on the local environment (e.g., Seelye 2017).

However, similar groups, mostly local but also some national environmental NGOs, objected to solar farms in Joshua Tree National Park and Mojave National Preserve, offshore wind farms along the Texas Gulf Coast, wind or solar facilities in New York City, and many more. Transmission projects are also blocked. For example, New Hampshire blocked a high-voltage line from Québec to bring hydroelectricity to Massachusetts. Environmental justice activism that has been successful in re-routing or forcing cancellation of fossil fuel projects such as pipelines, storage facilities, or LNG terminals is also looking into siting of large-scale renewable energy projects to prevent unfair treatment of disadvantaged communities. Increasingly, recycling of solar panels, batteries, and windmills that reach the end of their useful life or break down is attracting attention because they contain toxic minerals. As larger capacities get old, the renewables industry and its observers are realizing that recycling has to scale up and be done in a responsible manner. Otherwise, public backlash is guaranteed.

Finally, the supply chain of minerals necessary for manufacturing of clean energy technologies is global. As such, environmental and social impacts associated with minerals mining, processing, and transportation as well as manufacturing and shipping of various pieces of equipment multiply as demand for these technologies grows. Also, geopolitical and economic competition for resources that is already evident will increase. O'Sullivan and others (2017) call this emerging dependence on minerals for clean energy technologies the "new" resource curse.

In short, these three challenges will grow in significance as footprints of clean energy technologies increase. Nevertheless, it is unclear whether opposition to renewables will ever reach the same high pitch as refusal of fossil fuel infrastructure. A lot will depend on each industry's ability to find and successfully implement publicly acceptable solutions to their externalities.

Harmonization of Natural Gas and Power Systems

In systems with increasing share of intermittent and variable resources that are being better connected across larger geographies via expansion of transmission networks, gas-fired plants are needed less for baseload generation and more for balancing and resource adequacy. Even those roles are challenged as some regions seek alternatives such as battery storage to provide these backup services.

These shifts in utilization of gas-fired plants raise some issues regarding the co-optimization of natural gas and electric-power infrastructure and markets that function on different time scales and economic parameters. For example, increased cyclical use of gas-fired plants has implications for pipeline deliverability of gas. Changes in how much gas is required where, when, and at what pressure force changes to utilization of natural gas infrastructure. Reserving capacity in pipelines may have to change into shorter time periods (e.g., measured in hours) and may have to be done in very short notice or none at all. Storage needs will likely increase and diversify, perhaps necessitating the use of unused capacity of pipelines as storage (linepack). Since pipeline throughput is likely to go down in a power system with more variable resources, room for linepack should be larger. But, such utilization will likely increase the wear and tear on equipment adding to the cost of maintenance. FERC and the North American Energy Standards Board have been working on these issues since the early 2010s but gas–power harmonization remains a challenge.

Disruptive Technologies

Many technologies—especially consumer technologies—have been altering the electric-power landscape and fueling visions of micro grids, smart grids, and VPPs. Indeed, demand-side technologies such as rooftop solar, programmable thermostats, remote-controlled appliances, and others have the potential to empower consumers into prosumers. The emergence of this power ecosystem is certainly posing risks for central generators as well as utilities but it will take some time for large-scale impact to be visible and it is too complex to cover here. Instead, I will focus on battery storage because it is one technology that is promoted heavily to mitigate problems associated with intermittency and variability of wind and solar and is also integral to future visions of mini grids and VPPs.

The Berkeley Lab interconnection database included 48 GW standalone battery storage in queue in addition to 97 GW solar with battery storage and 9 GW wind with battery storage. California accounts for 15.5 GW of battery storage, 17 GW of solar-storage, and 5 GW of wind-storage projects. According to the EIA data, nearly 4 GW of storage are expected between 2020 and end of 2023. In contrast, CTs built since 2000 have net summer capacity of nearly 89 GW. The total gas fleet capacity is more than 500 GW.

However, batteries remain expensive and pose technological challenges, such as depletion of capacity and deterioration of charge–discharge cycles, that reduce their value to the grid. Even the solar–storage combination is more expensive than other alternatives without ITC and state support of solar facilities. Lazard (2019b) reports a levelized cost range of $165/MWh to $325/MWh for in-front-of-the-meter storage, which declines to $102–$139/MWh when combined with solar PV. Standalone storage used by T&D utilities or commercial and industrial facilities are more expensive, often costing more than $1000/MWh. In contrast, an existing CT can supply electricity at less than $100/MWh, even at $5/MMBtu natural gas and 10-percent capacity factor. The average cost of gas peaking since 2016 (2008) from Fig. 2.7 is $46 ($61) per MWh.

Forecasts of EV demand are more bullish than grid-scale battery-storage forecasts. Rapid growth of lithium-ion battery demand for grid-scale storage and EVs will have repercussions on minerals markets. We have already seen lithium and cobalt prices triple between 2015 and 2018. Unsurprisingly, these price signals induced new investment in mining, processing, and transportation capacity, thus reducing prices. As natural resources in increasing but variable demand, it is reasonable to expect this volatility to be a permanent future of these markets just as they have been for other natural resources. The cost of minerals is usually a small part of the cost of a battery but disruption of access to these minerals critical to battery manufacturing and performance can have implications along the supply chain.

Researchers assert new battery chemistries will be needed not only to eliminate geopolitically or environmentally undesirable minerals such as cobalt, but also to reduce battery degradation, to store more power, to extend discharge time at rated power, and to improve safety.[44] Byrne and others (2018) highlight the need for regulatory consistency to develop energy management systems and optimization tools that can accommodate different technologies serving different energy and power functions. Similarly, Sivaram (2018) argues the current solar PV technology based on silicon is not sufficient for solar to claim a much bigger share of the energy space; he states the industry must invest in "technological innovation to harness the sun's energy more cheaply and store it to use around the clock," and "redesign systems like the power grid to handle the surges and slumps of solar energy."

These and other challenges have the potential to curtail smooth expansion of batteries. Nevertheless, batteries and other emerging technologies will continue to complement already established wind and solar to disrupt the traditional power systems. For example, Dyson and others (2018) argue "the current rush to gas in the U.S. electricity system could lock in $1 trillion of cost through 2030…clean energy portfolios are cost-competitive…" The portfolios are based on an IRP approach and consist of energy efficiency, demand response, battery storage, and distributed and utility-scale renewables. I find some of their assumptions unrealistic. For example, they assume a natural gas price higher than the most recent EIA outlooks in Fig. 2.9; and assume away difficulties faced by cross-jurisdictional transmission lines (e.g., see Walton 2018). In Trabish (2018), the head of Integrated Innovation and Modernization at Southern California Edison, which pursues a DER-heavy strategy and looks at storage to replace gas peakers, calls the scale and scope of portfolios and changes necessary to achieve them "unprecedented."

Nevertheless, it is possible to see IRPs around the country that mimic portfolios from such studies. Their influence is strengthened by industry developments such as the Aliso Canyon natural gas–storage leak and pipeline explosions (especially those near population centers). Following the Aliso Canyon leak, California has more aggressively pursued battery storage as an alternative to natural gas peakers. Seven states already have targets for energy storage deployment and New England is pursuing a clean peak standard. More states are expected to follow their lead. FERC issued Orders 841 and 845 to remove barriers to storage's participation in energy, capacity, and ancillary-services markets. Some jurisdictions, such as Arizona, have placed a moratorium on new gas builds until alternatives such as solar-storage combinations are explored. Many customers demand storage to be added to their solar farms (hence the 97 GW in interconnection queue). PPAs for solar-storage projects have been priced as low as $36/MWh at the time of writing. In short, despite its challenges, battery storage will have significant impact in certain regions.

Social License to Operate

Gas-fired generation has a large advantage over coal with respect to local emissions and land impact (e.g., coal ash disposal) but also with respect to carbon dioxide (CO_2).[45] The FUTURE Act, included within the Bipartisan Budget Act of 2018, increased the tax credit "incrementally over ten years from $10 to $35 per ton of CO_2 stored geologically through enhanced oil recovery and from $20 to $50 per ton for saline and other forms of geologic storage" and may help some coal-fired plants, especially if the cost of CCS also improves. Although accepted as necessary to combat climate change by many energy experts, CCS does not seem to have much public support.

The CPP was stillborn but a growing number of states and cities are pursuing decarbonization policies to comply with the Paris Agreement on climate change. The public perception of what clean technology penetration can achieve influences these policies and difficulty of securing social license to operate for natural gas infrastructure. Efforts to block gas infrastructure—including power plants and ways of delivering gas to power plants, such as pipelines and upstream operations—act as proxies to a CO_2 tax and may increase the cost of natural gas, especially if the price-suppressing effect of associated gas supplies recedes. Adding to the challenges of the natural gas industry operations are the resolutions by cities around the country to ban gas connections in new homes. Whether these relatively few cases will turn into a trend is uncertain but it is yet another component of a growing anti-gas movement. In some regions, it is certainly part of a long-term goal. For example, Massachusetts Attorney General followed on the examples of New York and California and called for an investigation of the gas sector to ensure "safe, reliable and fair transition away from reliance on natural gas and other fossil fuels" (see reporting in Walton 2020).

As discussed in "Weaknesses" and "Threats" sections, financial institutions and management consultancies are also putting pressure on companies to decarbonize. Some of these pronouncements may not have much teeth, at least not yet, but they certainly contribute to public discourse against fossil fuels. If standard reporting of environmental impacts or simply GHG emissions or exposure of assets and operations to climate risks becomes a requirement by governments, investors may have to scrutinize fossil fuel companies and projects more closely.

These developments influence federal regulation as well. Although its centrality ebbs and flows with the changing mix of commissioners, FERC commissioners debate whether to consider climate impacts of new natural gas infrastructure up the supply chain while evaluating midstream and downstream projects. Methane emissions along the supply infrastructure and flaring at the wellhead are two visible challenges the oil and gas industry must mitigate in order to counter growing opposition to the cleanest burning fossil fuel. In the meantime, communication of massive benefits of natural gas in reducing local pollution when it replaces coal should continue.

Conclusions

The power sector is primed to burn more natural gas. Nearly half of installed capacity in the United States will be fired by natural gas and the capacity-weighted average age of the CCGT fleet will be less than 20 years by the mid-2020s. With more coal and some nuclear plants slated to retire, more gas burn for power generation seems certain, at least in the early 2020s. Predictably, new gas-fired capacity has been expanding the most in regions with most baseload capacity retirements such as the PJM, Midwest, ERCOT, and Southeast region. All of these regions also happen to be either home or in close proximity to shale plays with relatively easy access to low-cost gas. However, there are headwinds even in these regions.

Decarbonization policies are spreading across the country, promoting renewables, both utility-scale and distributed, as well as demand-side measures to increase efficiency, conservation, and demand response. These efforts build on the momentum gained since the 2008 Great Recession with the help of a large set of support policies at federal, state, and local levels. At the same time, a growing anti-gas movement raises questions about the financial and physical health of the natural gas industry and infrastructure, which is reaching the age of replacement in certain parts of the country.

Consumers and regulators are increasingly aware of system integration costs, many of which are reflected in higher customer energy bills, associated with the penetration of intermittent and variable resources. But lower costs and rising concerns about climate change sustain the momentum behind decarbonization efforts. More wind, solar, and energy storage but also geothermal and biomass will certainly be added in the future and will continue to take market share away from gas-fired generators.

The argument that gas-fired generation is the perfect complement to intermittent and variable wind and solar generation is problematic. Although technically accurate, shifting gas-fired plant use away from baseload to balancing and backup will burn less gas as the share of renewable energy increases. A better integrated grid and storage will reduce the need for load-following units further. Even baseload generation will be lost to wind and solar. After all, eliminating fossil fuel-based generation is a goal of energy transition. This gradual shift in utilization of the gas fleet will require proper compensation of units forced to cycle more. However, reforms of organized markets to fix compensation schemes have been contentious. While there is policy and public support for wind, solar, and nuclear, which lays the ground for out-of-market compensation of those generators, natural gas is taken for granted as the "bridge" fuel. The "length and width" of the bridge is a policy risk to financial sustainability of even newer CCGTs. Building too much gas-fired capacity in certain markets adds to the risk of cash flow security for all generators in that market. Regions where utilities pursue IRPs with the approval of regulators offer a more predictable yet still changeable future for utilization of gas-fired plants.

This complex set of drivers for gas burn are captured in four dimensions of Fig. 2.4 and discussed in some detail throughout the chapter. This discussion can be summarized in Fig. 2.13 that demonstrates the wide range of uncertainty around gas-fired generation over the next 15 years. The wide range results from the balancing of four dimensions' possible movements in pushing gas burn higher or lower. I distinguish between the near future (roughly through 2025) and the more uncertain long-term (beyond 2030). I provide AEO 2020 low and high envelopes for comparison purposes. Importantly, I assume flat load, mimicking the 2010s. If substantial

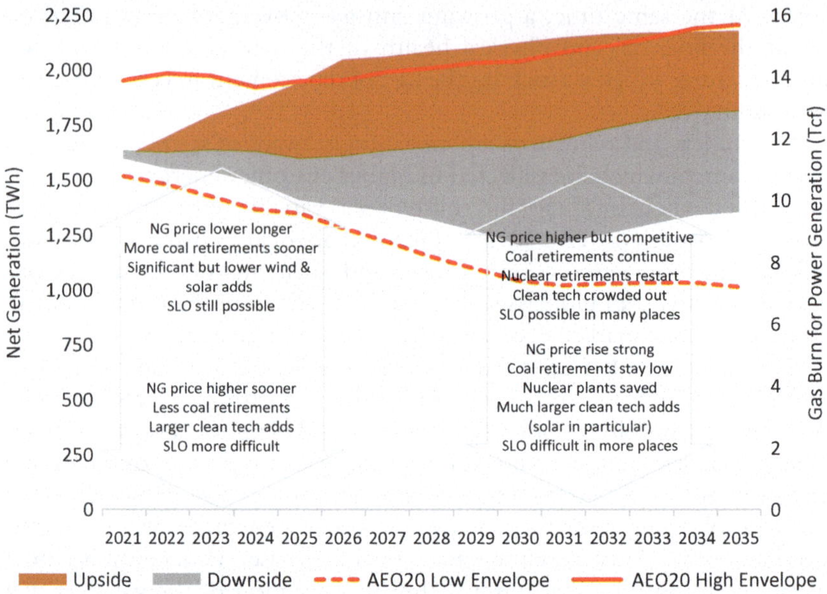

Fig. 2.13 Wide range of the future gas-fired power generation. (Source: Author estimates. EIA AEO 2020 envelopes capture lowest and highest gas-fired generation for each year across all AEO 2020 scenarios)

load growth occurs, say due to rapid electrification, gas burn should benefit from it within the time frame of this analysis.

The existence of a young, efficient, and dispatchable gas fleet along with relatively abundant cheap natural gas provides an advantage to gas-fired generation to replace retiring baseload capacity. Coal and nuclear fleets are aging. Large-scale retirements of coal-fired capacity should continue through the 2030s in an environment of low electricity prices. Subsidized CCS may save a handful of coal-fired capacity but not the great majority of old coal plants with declining utilization. Nuclear plants are being saved by state initiatives mainly due to their zero-emission attribute and local economic benefits. However, by the 2030s, states may not be as inclined to save plants with expiring 60-year licenses.

A regional bifurcation must be recognized. Roughly speaking, baseload coal and nuclear retirements occur in regions where gas resource is available, renewable resource quality is weak, and cost of electricity to end-users is an important political consideration. These conditions help natural gas. But other regions of the country, without ready access to low-cost gas but with better wind and solar resources, will double down on their decarbonization targets. This divergence is important to track, in particular for the fate of existing and for the purposes of siting new mid-stream infrastructure. A gas-fired plant is valuable only if it has access to reliable supply of natural gas.

This regional divergence is not unqualified. Even the former regions are home to many states pursuing energy transition despite the availability of low-cost gas. To the extent the transition proves successful in terms of reliability, affordability, and acceptability, it can spread to other states. The success, however, is contingent upon continued policy support in the form of tax credits, mandates, and other measures at federal, state, and local governments for investment in renewable generation, storage, and T&D enhancement. Such support appears set to grow in many regions building on the momentum gained in the 2010s but the size and scope of it is dependent on federal and regional politics that will have to balance the pros and cons of the dimensions discussed in this chapter.

Notes

1. Halfway through 2020, gas-fired generation continues to grow year-on-year at the expense of coal-fired plants, signaling more coal retirements.
2. Throughout this chapter, the United States refer to continental 48 states, excluding Alaska and Hawaii.
3. Secondary to this deregulation of the natural gas market, years of DOE funding to hydraulic fracturing and horizontal drilling research, Nonconventional Fuels (Section 29) Tax Credit that went into effect in 1980 and other programs helped the eventual development of low-permeability resources in the late 2000s.
4. These nameplate capacities are not one-to-one comparisons due to intermittency of wind and solar. When adjusted wind summer peak availability, which is, for example, 14 percent for noncoastal wind and 58 percent for coastal wind in Texas, dispatchable gas-fired capacity is much higher than available wind capacity. Solar peak availability is much higher (e.g., 77 percent in Texas), but accounting for it would still widen the gap between gas and solar capacities.
5. For example, offshore wind projects along the northeastern seaboard are getting mandated by states while states in Southwest pursue stronger solar and solar-storage mandates.

6. Based on Berkeley Lab Electricity Markets & Policy Group database: https://emp.lbl.gov/generation-storage-and-hybrid-capacity
7. Some of the retired coal-fired capacity was replaced with CCGT plants in the same location (roughly one-fifth). In roughly equal amount of capacity, boilers were converted to burning natural gas. In this chapter, I simply refer to all of these options of stopping coal burn as retirements of coal-fired capacity.
8. There are many issues with competitive electricity market designs, which vary across regions and over time. I will highlight some of the issues with direct impact on gas burn later in this chapter but interested readers can find a more in-depth discussion of key market design issues in Gülen (2019).
9. There is an emerging view among economists and other social scientists that rejects neoclassical economics that sees labor as a cost. This socioeconomic context is fully woven into the fabric of public support for energy transition. These trends induce growing bipartisan support for bringing local manufacturing and jobs back.
10. For example, Energy Intelligence developed a Vulnerability Index to assess "which oil and gas companies are best placed to survive the energy transition."
11. For example, Task Force on Climate-related Financial Disclosures is developing standards for reporting climate-related financial risk exposure to investors, insurers, and other stakeholders. The Partnership for Carbon Accounting Financials lists 69 institutions with financial assets estimated to be worth $9.7 trillion (as of July 31, 2020). Most are non-U.S. institutions and many are small, but the list is growing and includes Citi, Bank of America, and Morgan Stanley.
12. NC Clean Energy Technology Center has been maintaining a database of these programs: https://www.dsireusa.org/
13. For example, a carbon tax will increase the natural gas price whereas banning new gas connections in certain regions has an indirect, if any, effect on the natural gas price across the country.
14. We used a commercial software also used by utilities, merchant generators, and system operators. Every user can adjust the database of existing fleet of generators, their operational characteristics, planned additions and retirements, and so on. The model's algorithm is a good reflection of how power systems operate to meet demand and supply reliably in real time (known as security-constrained economic dispatch and unit commitment). The model also does a good job of estimating least-cost expansion of generation capacity to meet the needs of any demand outlook.
15. Roughly speaking, 1 Tcf is equivalent to an average of 2.7 billion cubic feet per day, or Bcf/d.

16. Ideally, a dispatch model is required to assess the contribution of each type of generation in each power system.
17. In fact, plants announced to be retired, especially coal-fired, may already be generating below the average capacity factors.
18. According to the NC Clean Energy Technology Center, as of July 2020, California has 148 programs across city, utility, state levels that cover rebates, grants, building energy codes, permitting standards, tax incentives, and other mechanisms to promote clean energy projects (https://www.dsireusa.org/).
19. See Gülen (2019) for a detailed discussion of electricity market uncertainties that dominated the 2010s. Market designs continue to evolve with attendant risks to power sector participants.
20. Wind generation in ERCOT peaks in the spring (often March or April). In addition to switching due to relative competitiveness of coal and gas generators, their share is also impacted in the shorter term by seasonal availability of wind.
21. Natural gas prices in the Marcellus region suffered from significant basis differential due to increased production stranded without sufficient pipeline capacity.
22. Mcfe rather than MMBtu is used because this metric captures the value of not only methane but also other molecules produced at the wellhead. If production is dry gas (i.e., almost all methane), Mcfe and MMBtu prices will be roughly the same.
23. Many analysts have published forward natural gas price decks approaching \$3/MMBtu during 2021 with some suggesting \$3.50 or higher. Most of these views hinge on the reduction in associated gas yield with lower oil output as softer prices for crude oil discourage drilling in oilier plays, as explained in Chap. 1.
24. See Gülen (2019) for a detailed discussion of some of these design changes.
25. According to North American Electric Reliability Corporation (2020).
26. In contrast, average capacity factor for the U.S. coal fleet has been declining and reached 47 percent in 2019. As a result, CCGTs will have to increase their utilization more for every GW of nuclear capacity retired as compared to coal-fired capacity retirements.
27. Note that the installed capacity of distributed solar is reported in direct current (dc) by the SEIA and not as net summer capacity as reported by the EIA for utility-scale solar. As such, 29 GWdc is not readily comparable to other capacity figures in this chapter.
28. 2020 Solar Risk Assessment: https://www.kwhanalytics.com/solar-risk-assessment (accessed July 28, 2020).
29. Estimates are mostly from Heptonstall and others (2017) and Ueckerdt and others (2013).

30. Generally speaking, wind is available in early mornings and evenings while solar reaches its maximum during midday to late afternoon.
31. Tsai and Eryılmaz (2018) find in ERCOT, "for every additional 1000 MW of wind generation in a Real-Time 15-minute Settlement Interval, nodal prices at non-wind resources would be suppressed by \$1.45/MWh to \$4.45/MWh, with considerable heterogeneity across time and space."
32. For example, Tsai and Gülen (2017b) show that in ERCOT, high wind penetration correlates with gas-fired units (CCGTs as well as CTs) cycling more as well as ending up with lower capacity factors and revenues.
33. Incidentally, the state incentives to nuclear plants have been in the same range.
34. For example, Sivaram and Kann (2016) report that when solar reaches 15 percent of generation in a system, its value falls by more than one-half. See Gülen (2019) for additional references.
35. As quoted in Penrod (2020), a VP at LevelTen, developer of PPA Price Index, sees prices leveling off or possibly increasing driven by expiring tax credits, supply chain bottlenecks, and other factors. These increases reduce renewables' competitiveness but are not irreversible with more economies of scale and technological advances in the future. Still, they highlight the irrationality of expecting recent pace of cost declines to continue.
36. An alternative is a return to integrated resource planning (IRP) where generation portfolios are determined by regulators and utilities. Gülen (2019) provides an outline of a competitive IRP construct.
37. Page 43 of Barbose (2019) lists six studies published between 2013 and 2019, all of which report from low single digits to up to 17 percent of rate increases, with increases higher than 10 percent seen in states with most aggressive RPS policies.
38. See page 39 of Barbose (2019), which also lists some benefits. Note, however, that most benefits are conceptual (e.g., global benefits of reduced carbon emissions) whereas most costs find their way to electricity bills. Also note that cost estimates reported in parentheses are consistent with literature ranges provided earlier.
39. For details, visit http://www.dsireusa.org/
40. EIA calculates this cost by dividing the electricity providers' operating revenues by sales of electricity to different customer classes. Revenues include energy charges, demand charges, consumer service charges, environmental surcharges, fuel adjustments, other miscellaneous charges, and taxes (state, federal, other).
41. For example, according to Barbose (2019), the share of RPS compliance costs increased from less than 8 percent in 2016 to almost 12 percent in 2018 in Massachusetts.

42. See Griffiths and others (2018) for an attempt to quantify costs of some California clean energy programs.
43. The regulatory staff in Arizona proposed a 100-percent CES by 2050 in July 2020.
44. For example, American Chemical Society publication, *Chemical Reviews*, dedicated a full issue to the topic of "Beyond Li-ion Battery Chemistry": https://pubs.acs.org/toc/chreay/120/14
45. Following common practice, I use carbon dioxide to represent all greenhouse gases, which also include methane, nitrous oxide, and fluorinated gases. All tons are metric tons.

References

Barbose, G. 2019. U.S. renewable portfolio standards—2018 annual status update. https://eta-publications.lbl.gov/sites/default/files/rps_annual_status_update-2019_edition.pdf

Byrne, R.H., T.A. Nguyen, D.A. Copp, B.R. Chalamala, and I. Gyuk. 2018. Energy management and optimization methods for grid energy storage systems. *IEEE Access* 6: 13231–13260. https://doi.org/10.1109/ACCESS.2017.2741578.

Colvin, M., D.I. Fellman, R.L. Rodriguez, and A. LaBonte. 2018. *California customer choice: An evaluation of regulatory framework options for an evolving electricity market.* San Francisco: California Public Utilities Commission (CPUC), 112 p.

Dyson, M., A. Engel, and J. Farbes. 2018. *The economics of clean energy portfolios: How renewable and distributed energy resources are outcompeting and can strand investment in natural gas-fired generation.* Rocky Mountain Institute, 59 p.

Griffiths, B.W., C.W. King, G. Gülen, J.S. Dyer, D. Spence, and R. Baldick. 2018. *State level financial support for electricity generation technologies—An analysis of Texas & California*, Energy Institute Full Cost of Electricity white paper series. The University of Texas at Austin, 73 p.

Gülen, G. 2019. *Net social cost of electricity: Policy smog and waning competitive markets, lack of consumer participation, importance of the grid, and scalability challenge*, Udden series no. 7. The University of Texas at Austin, Bureau of Economic Geology, 86 p. https://doi.org/10.23867/US0007D.

Gülen, G., and D. Bellman. 2015. Scenarios of resource adequacy in ERCOT: Mandated reserve margin, impact of environmental regulations and integration of renewables. *The Electricity Journal* 28 (2): 89–100. https://doi.org/10.1016/j.tej.2015.01.011.

Gülen, G., and M. Soni. 2013. The impacts of raising the energy price cap in ERCOT. *The Electricity Journal* 26 (7): 43–54. https://doi.org/10.1016/j.tej.2013.07.002.

Heptonstall, P., R. Gross, and F. Steiner. 2017. *The costs and impacts of intermittency—2016 update: A systematic review of the evidence on the costs and impacts of intermittent electricity generation technologies.* London: UK Energy Research Centre (UKERC), 73 p. https://doi.org/10.13140/RG.2.2.17246.02888.

Karpa, D. 2018. Exploding transmission costs are the missing story in California's regionalization debate. *Utility Dive.* https://www.utilitydive.com/news/exploding-transmission-costs-are-the-missing-story-in-californias-regional/526894/. Accessed 7 Aug 2019.

Lazard. 2019a. Levelized cost of energy—Version 13.0. https://www.lazard.com/perspective/lcoe2019/

———. 2019b. Levelized cost of storage analysis—Version 5.0. https://www.lazard.com/media/451087/lazards-levelized-cost-of-storage-version-50-vf.pdf

North American Electric Reliability Corporation (NERC). 2020. 2020 summer reliability assessment, June, 37 p.

O'Sullivan, M., I. Overland, and D. Sandalow. 2017. *The geopolitics of renewable energy.* Columbia University, School of International and Public Affairs, Center on Global Energy Policy Working Paper. https://energypolicy.columbia.edu/sites/default/files/CGEPTheGeopoliticsOfRenewables.pdf

Penrod, E. 2020. Renewable energy prices begin an upward trend, LevelTen data shows. *Utility Dive.* https://www.utilitydive.com/news/renewable-energy-prices-begin-an-upward-trend-levelten-data-shows/583110/. Accessed 7 Aug 2020.

PJM Interconnection (PJM). 2016. *EPA's final clean power plan—Compliance pathways economic and reliability analysis.* Norristown, 117 p.

Potomac Economics. 2020. *2019 state of the market report for the ERCOT electricity market.* Fairfax, 170 p.

Randolph, L.M. 2018. Assuring grid reliability in California—A view from Commissioner Randolph. *Utility Dive.* https://www.utilitydive.com/news/assuring-grid-reliability-in-california-a-view-from-commissioner-randolph/526696/. Accessed 7 Aug 2019.

Seelye, K.Q. 2017. After 16 years, hopes for Cape Cod wind farm float away. *The New York Times,* December 19. https://www.nytimes.com/2017/12/19/us/offshore-cape-wind-farm.html

Sivaram, V. 2018. *Taming the sun—Innovations to harness solar energy and power the planet.* Cambridge, MA: Massachusetts Institute of Technology, 392 p.

Sivaram, V., and S. Kann. 2016. Solar power needs a more ambitious cost target. *Nature Energy* 1 (4). https://doi.org/10.1038/nenergy.2016.36.

Szilard, R., P. Sharpe, E. Kee, E. Davis, and E. Grecheck. 2017. Economic and market challenges facing the U.S. nuclear commercial fleet—Cost and revenue study. Idaho National Laboratory, Nuclear Economics Consulting Group, and Grecheck Consulting, report prepared for the U.S. Department of Energy (DOE) Office of Nuclear Energy under DOE Idaho Operations Office contract no. DE-AC07-05ID14517, 63 p.

Trabish, H.K. 2018. End of the 'gas rush?' Renewables, storage reaching cost parity, report finds. *Utility Dive*. https://www.utilitydive.com/news/end-of-the-gas-rush-renewables-storage-reaching-cost-parity-report-fin/524840/. Accessed 7 Aug 2019.

Tsai, C.-H., and D. Eryılmaz. 2018. Effect of wind generation on ERCOT nodal prices. *Energy Economics* 76: 21–33. https://doi.org/10.1016/j.eneco.2018.09.021.

Tsai, C.-H., and G. Gülen. 2017a. Natural gas use in electricity generation in the United States: Outlooks to 2030. *The Electricity Journal* 30 (2): 15–24. https://doi.org/10.1016/j.tej.2017.01.012.

——— 2017b. The ERCOT experience with integrating renewables. IAEE Energy Forum, third quarter, pp. 42–45.

U.S. Energy Information Administration (EIA). 2018a. *Annual energy outlook 2018—With projections to 2050*. Washington, DC: EIA, 74 p.

———. 2018b. Utilities continue to increase spending on transmission infrastructure—Today in energy. EIA.gov. https://www.eia.gov/todayinenergy/detail.php?id=34892. Accessed 8 Aug 2019.

———. 2019. *Annual energy outlook 2019—With projections to 2050*. Washington, DC: EIA, 83 p.

———. 2020. *Annual energy outlook 2020—With projections to 2050*. Washington, DC: EIA, 81 p.

Ueckerdt, F., L. Hirth, G. Luderer, and O. Edenhofer. 2013. System LCOE: What are the costs of variable renewables? *Energy* 63: 61–75. https://doi.org/10.1016/j.energy.2013.10.072.

Walton, R. 2018. DOE terminates partnership with Clean Line Energy Partners. *Utility Dive*. https://www.utilitydive.com/news/doe-terminates-partnership-with-clean-line-energy-partners/519995/. Accessed 7 Aug 2019.

———. 2020. Massachusetts attorney general urges state examine shift from natural gas heating. *Utility Dive*. https://www.utilitydive.com/news/massachusetts-attorney-general-urges-state-examine-shift-from-natural-gas-h/579277/. Accessed 2 July 2020.

Wiser, R., and others. 2020. Wind technology data update: 2020 edition. Berkeley Lab, Electricity Markets & Policy. https://emp.lbl.gov/sites/default/files/2020_wind_energy_technology_data_update.pdf. Accessed 21 Aug 2020.

Zummo, P. 2020. America's electricity generation capacity, 2020 update. American Public Power Association, March, 22 p. https://www.publicpower.org/system/files/documents/Americas-Electricity-Generation-Capacity-2020.pdf. Accessed 13 July 2020.

CHAPTER 3

Petrochemicals: An Industrial Renaissance?

Michelle Michot Foss, Gürcan Gülen, Danny Quijano, and Barbara Shook

Introduction

Historically the industrial sector has been the largest consumer of natural gas in the United States (35 percent to 40 percent in the late 1990s), most methane being used as an energy source (i.e., to generate heat and power). However, large users of methane as feedstock, such as methanol and fertilizer producers, also contributed to natural gas demand in the industrial sector. Heavier molecules associated with "wet" gas, that is, NGLs, serve

M. Michot Foss (✉)
Baker Institute for Public Policy, Rice University, Houston, TX, USA
e-mail: michelle.m.foss@rice.edu

G. Gülen
Independent Consultant, West Brookfield, MA, USA
e-mail: gurcan@g2eis.com

D. Quijano
Berkeley Research Group, Houston, TX, USA

B. Shook
Sugar Land, TX, USA

M. Michot Foss et al. (eds.), *Monetizing Natural Gas in the New "New Deal" Economy*,
https://doi.org/10.1007/978-3-030-59983-6_3

as feedstock in petrochemicals and refining industries. We discuss the uses of methane and NGLs in more detail in the section on "Methane and NGL Use in the Industrial Sector."

Synergy exists between different types of facilities, and access to byproducts of certain processes (e.g., hydrogen from petrochemical facilities to refinery operations or associated gases and propylene from refining to petrochemicals) aids in the economics of downstream assets, providing some facilities the flexibility to switch feedstock in response to market-price signals.

Natural gas liquids (NGLs) are hydrocarbons that have condensed from a gaseous into a liquid state. They include ethane (C_2H_6), propane (C_3H_8), butane (C_4H_{10}), pentane (C_5H_{12}), and heavier molecules. Pentane and heavier molecules are often bundled and referred to as *natural gasoline*. Condensation may occur naturally at the wellsite when pressure is reduced or at the surface. Today, because most NGL production occurs at gas-processing or fractionation plants or refineries via distillation and refrigeration, some have begun to refer to *natural gas plant liquids*. Methane (CH_4), which is lighter, remains in a gaseous state. In most parts of the world with well-established natural gas systems, small, noncommercial amounts of ethane are left in the gas stream (so long as tolerances for infrastructure are not exceeded). This "ethane rejection" occurs until or unless sufficient steam-cracking capacity is developed to absorb ethane volumes.

And yet, following a period of rising natural gas prices in the early 2000s, many gas-intensive industrial facilities in the United States closed or moved overseas, where feedstock and other costs were lower. For example, between 1999 and 2006, nearly 90 ammonia plants closed so that U.S. nitrogen fertilizer production declined by more than 40 percent. Similarly, most methanol plants in the United States had shut down by the mid-2000s. Ethylene capacity also declined in the late 2000s, although not as significantly as other segments.

Even when methane was not a feedstock, increasing costs of natural gas as the source of heat and power had a negative impact on industrial operations, and petrochemical facilities that depend on NGLs suffered because of increasing oil prices. NGL prices have historically correlated highly with the price of oil, with the exception of ethane, the price of which has followed that of natural gas owing to "ethane rejection" (see box and discussion later in this chapter).[1] Overall, the U.S. manufacturing sector was in decline, owing to a lack of competitiveness in an increasingly global economy, and the higher cost of energy and feedstock was the final blow for many facilities. As a result, U.S. industrial gas consumption declined by 30 percent between 1997 and 2009, the power sector surpassing the industrial sector as the largest consumer of natural gas (Fig. 3.1). In Chap. 2, we provide a detailed discussion of power-sector trends and scenarios of future natural gas burn for electricity generation.

Increasing natural gas prices destroyed some demand but along with low interest rates encouraged investment in the upstream sector, especially in new domestic tight oil and shale gas plays. (See Appendix for classifications of and discussion on hydrocarbon sources.)

By the mid-2000s, production of natural gas from the Barnett Shale in North Texas had proved successful. Service companies and operators

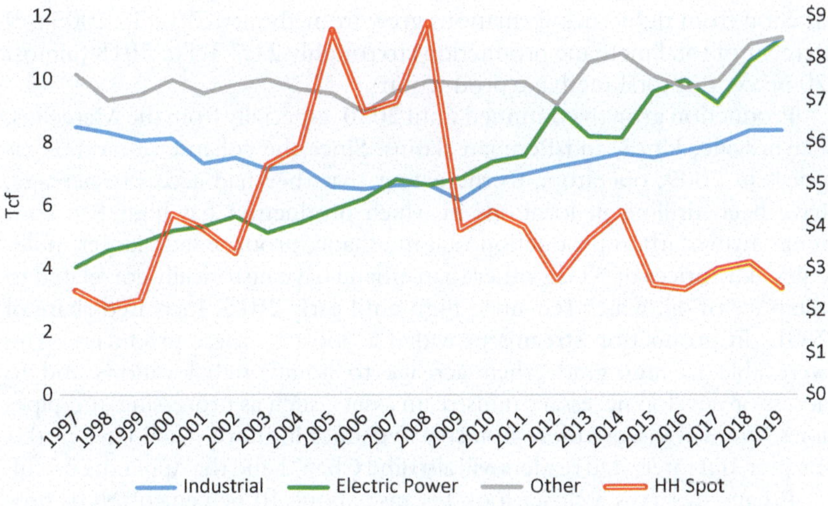

Fig. 3.1 Natural gas price ($/MMBtu) and consumption by end use (Tcf). (Source: Based on EIA data on natural gas use; CME/NYMEX prices; HH is Henry Hub)

quickly ensured that the new processes spread throughout the industry and across various low-permeability formations around the country. The decline in natural gas production in Texas that began in the early 1970s at first slowed, then reversed, and the fall of natural gas prices in the late 2000s encouraged many operators to drill in the western Barnett Shale, yielding more NGLs. New operators entered the industry who started drilling more wells in Fayetteville, Haynesville, and Marcellus, thus continuing to add to natural gas production. Associated gas production from tight oil liquid-rich plays, such as the Eagle Ford, Bakken, and Permian, supplied the market with even more natural gas and NGLs. Locations of tight oil have been especially prolific for NGLs by virtue of associated gas production (see Chap. 1).

As a result of this new intensive drilling, U.S. natural gas–marketed production, including dry gas and NGLs, grew significantly from 18.9 trillion cubic feet (Tcf) in 2005 to 32.7 Tcf in 2018 (see Chap. 1 for extensive treatment of U.S. supply). Perhaps more impressively and more relevant to the petrochemical sector, NGL production doubled over the same period from about 0.9 trillion cubic feet equivalent (Tcfe) to almost 2.3 Tcfe. Activity in tight-rock plays has been the key driver as production from conventional plays has declined in most locations, and methane production from tight-rock formations grew from about 1.7 Tcf in 2005 (~9 percent of total methane production) to roughly 21.7 Tcf in 2018 (almost 70 percent of total methane production).

Production growth continued until 2020, especially from the Marcellus, Haynesville, Utica, and Permian Basins. Since the collapse of natural gas prices in 2009, operators, to the extent that they had access to acreage, have been drilling in locations in which production has high Btu content—hydrocarbon production rich in ethane, propane, and larger molecules. The prices of NGLs other than ethane have historically correlated to the price of oil, which remained high until early 2015. Increased share of NGLs in production streams provided a boost to these producers, who were able to high-grade their acreage to liquids-rich locations and to access or develop necessary midstream assets, such as processing and pipelines. We will discuss these industry dynamics in more detail later in this chapter, but interested readers will also find Chap. 1 and the Appendix useful.

Ethane deserves a closer look because about 40 percent of NGL production has been ethane. But the ethane market is limited. Historically the most obvious use of ethane has been in steam crackers in the production of ethylene as the building block in many products, particularly plastics. As ethane production has increased, supply has exceeded demand by a large margin, especially in certain regions such as the southwest Pennsylvania part of the Marcellus play. By late 2012, ethane prices began to follow the price of natural gas more closely, and, as a result, a good deal of ethane was left in the natural gas stream—a practice known as *ethane rejection*.

The increased availability of cheap methane and NGLs, especially ethane, fueled interest in expanding industrial capacity to convert these feedstocks into valuable products and export them. By 2012, seven world-scale crackers had been proposed, six on the Gulf Coast and one in the Marcellus shale play, and so much ethane and propane were being produced that export terminals were in development. Ethane is exported in liquefied form, which was a novelty for the global NGL trade, and the first liquefied ethane export facility of the United States began exporting Marcellus ethane to Europe from Marcus Hook in early 2016. Ethane from Marcellus is also exported to Canada via pipeline, whereas some NGLs are shipped to the Gulf Coast. Later in 2016, another ethane export facility came online on the Texas Gulf Coast. According to the U.S. Department of Energy (2018), the U.S. Energy Information Administration (EIA) estimates ethane exports growing from about 180,000 barrels per day (bpd) (~13 percent of production) in 2017 to more than 330,000 bpd (~17 percent of production) in 2019.

Only a few years earlier, the United States had been a major importer of liquefied petroleum gas (LPG), the main ingredient of which is propane or butanes. By 2012, with about 200,000 bpd, the United States became a net exporter of LPG and, at the time of writing, has become the largest LPG exporter in the world, averaging 1.2 million bpd in 2017 and accounting for almost one-third of global seaborne supply.

Across the country, interest in new nitrogen-fertilizer capacity began to increase, with more projects always seemingly under consideration than actually under construction. The Gulf Coast attracted investment in the olefin cluster (ethane crackers for producing ethylene and propylene and the C4 stream for supplying downstream sectors in the manufacture of ingredients for everyday products such as polyethylene), as well as in methanol plants. Refining and petrochemical clusters around the Texas and Louisiana Gulf Coast have been key to the renaissance of the industry, and most industrial sector investment has taken place in that region. Reasons include the synergy afforded by the proximity of existing refining and petrochemicals facilities, access to export facilities along the coast, and availability of midstream infrastructure (fractionation, processing, and pipelines) connecting the facilities to the Eagle Ford, and—increasingly more important—Permian production. As such, the Gulf Coast region has seen the largest increase in methane and NGL consumption in the industrial sector. A significant part of investment in the region is in ethane-only steam crackers to take advantage of the low-cost ethane in the United States, most facilities also including derivatives plants (e.g., polyethylene).

By 2018, excitement had begun to wane, although some continued to predict a second wave of investments in the early to mid-2020s because (1) U.S. producers are expected to continue drilling and supply sustained amounts of methane and NGLs and (2) global demand for petrochemicals products is forecast to go on growing. We define *second wave* as a repeat of the large projects (>$1 billion) that have been under development since 2016 or so and are expected to come online by 2022. We exclude smaller projects, including expansion and debottlenecking projects. Many such projects are under various stages of development and more will likely come.

The concentration of hydrocarbon processing along the U.S. Gulf Coast raises the inevitable question of hurricane risk. Hurricane Harvey (late August 2017) was often suggested as a key reason for construction delays in many facilities. Even under normal circumstances, large, complex, and capital-intensive projects tend to experience cost overruns and schedule delays. Regardless, most facilities that were under construction are operating as of this writing. The uncertainty of extreme weather events could certainly raise the cost of future facilities and spur additional capital investment in existing facilities to render them more resilient.

More commercially relevant was the low level of oil prices in 2015 and 2016 that raised questions about sustained competitiveness of U.S. exports of ethylene, its derivative products, and methanol. The competitiveness of U.S. facilities, after all, depends on relative prices of oil, refinery products, methane, ethane, and heavier NGLs, as well as other countries' industrial strategies. With liquefied ethane exports increasing and startups of new ethane crackers, U.S. ethane prices began to increase, squeezing ethylene margins. In a world of tightening cost advantage and lower profitability, a distinct question is whether U.S. ethylene and derivative producers can compete against Saudi Arabia's resource endowment and China's capital cost efficiency. These and other countries are pursuing expansion of domestic petrochemicals capacity, often backed by their governments, and are utilizing byproducts of existing refining and petrochemicals complexes at nonmarket prices.

Covid-19 has clearly introduced new and complex puzzles regarding economic recovery and resumption of demand for key petrochemical products. Until onset of the pandemic, global demand for ethylene, methanol, and other products from the petrochemical value chain was strong and expected to be robust over the next several years, barring a global economic crisis. However, even in the absence of economic malaise across the world, U.S. exports face threats. For example, the trade war that erupted between the United States and China cast a shadow on the viability of accessing the Chinese market—one of the largest and fastest growing today. Pre-pandemic, U.S. tariffs on Chinese goods and retaliatory tariffs by China were impacting billions of dollars of chemicals and plastics. LPG exports to China fell after China imposed a 25 percent tariff in late 2018, and future tariffs or sanctions on Chinese or other countries' products, including nonpetrochemicals, could further undermine the competitiveness of U.S. petrochemical exports (e.g., steel tariffs raised the cost of U.S. oil and gas operations across the value chain). Similarly, the renegotiation of the North American Free Trade Agreement (NAFTA) created jitters. As reported by the American Chemistry Council (ACC), Canada and Mexico, at $23 billion each, accounted for almost two-thirds of U.S. chemical exports in 2018, followed by China ($12 billion) (see ACC 2019a). Although NAFTA's replacement, the United States–Mexico–Canada Agreement (USMCA), seems to be a satisfactory solution and has the support of the ACC (see ACC 2019b), USMCA's impacts on the chemical industry will only become apparent over time.

Bullish demand outlooks combined with the forecast of strong U.S. production keeping ethane relatively cheap seem to be driving some investment. Notably, ExxonMobil and Saudi Arabia's SABIC formed a joint venture to build the largest ethane cracker project in the United States, a complex with derivative plants near Corpus Christi in South Texas at an estimated cost of $10 billion. These experienced partners have advantages that other companies may not possess. The JV partners are positioned with pipeline capacity for NGLs from the Permian and Eagle Ford, as well as storage capacity near the facility. The site will also house polyethylene and monoethylene glycol plants to take advantage of integration across the petrochemical value chain. The companies are well-connected with many markets around the world, providing further internalization of transaction costs via integration across the global value chain.[2]

Likewise, Shell's $6-billion complex under construction in Pennsylvania[3] will have three polyethylene units to remove ethylene from the ethane cracker and convert it to low- and high-density polyethylene, which is used in the manufacture of many everyday products. Shell has access to relatively cheap NGLs from the wet-gas region of the Marcellus Shale. In southwest Pennsylvania, parts of Ohio, and West Virginia, the Btu content of produced volumes is high, ranging from 1050 to 1350 Btu per cubic foot in rich or wet-gas regions, and exceeding 1350 Btu in super-rich areas. Up to about 15 percent of wellhead production can be NGLs, depending on the Btu content.[4]

Location of the complex lacks easy access to global markets, as well as synergistic opportunities with other facilities that stand along the Gulf Coast. The value of synergistic opportunities among different types of facilities is difficult to quantify and beyond our scope but nonetheless significant by all accounts. In fact, the lack of such infrastructure has been a handicap to petrochemical investment in the Appalachian region.

Overall, with much more capacity on the way, not only in the United States but around the world, the sector may suffer from excess capacity by the mid-2020s, raising questions about the viability of an anticipated second wave of ethane-only crackers and other facilities in the United States, as well as the long-term profitability of existing facilities. The second wave becomes more questionable if global demand does not materialize as expected. Before the onset of Covid-19, global demand implied by some economists' concerns regarding economic growth, with growth slowing in emerging economies (China, Brazil, India, Turkey, and South Africa, among others). If anything, the Covid-19 pandemic has only exacerbated these concerns.[5]

Methane and NGL Use in the Industrial Sector

The EIA's Manufacturing Energy Consumption Survey (MECS) provides a detailed breakdown of natural gas consumption by the manufacturing sector, which accounts for about 80 percent to 85 percent of total industrial gas demand (Fig. 3.1). The remaining 15 percent to 20 percent is consumed primarily in agriculture, construction, and mining.

Just two industries—chemical and petroleum and coal products—accounted for 57 percent of total U.S. manufacturing natural gas demand of about 6.4 Tcf in MECS 2014 (Fig. 3.2). This share was about 46 percent in 2006 after the shut down or exodus of many gas-intensive industries from the United States. The chemical sector accounted for almost all natural gas use as feedstock (~9 percent of total), same as in the years past,

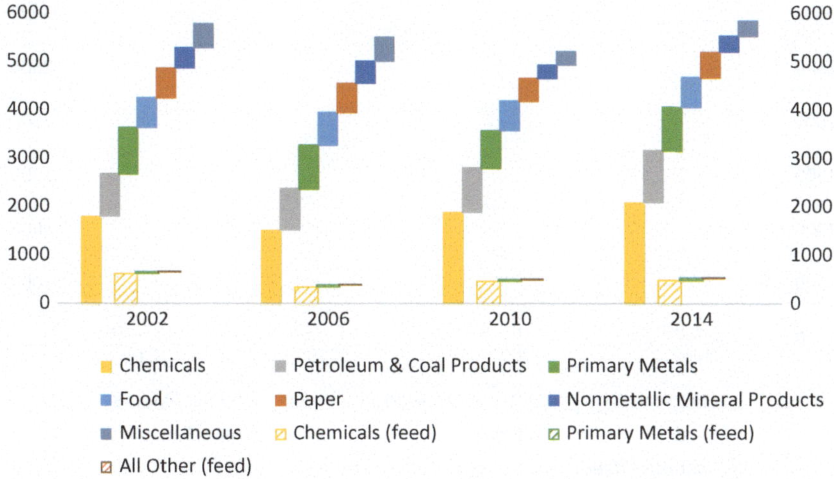

Fig. 3.2 U.S. consumption of methane for fuel and feedstock by industry (trillion Btu). (Source: Authors' calculations using data from MECS 2002, 2006, 2010, and 2014 (EIA 1991–2014). Note that we separate feedstock use for chemicals, primary metals, and other. All other bars represent natural gas use as fuel)

followed by the primary metal sectors, a distant second. In terms of using natural gas as fuel (~91 percent of total natural gas use), the chemical sector remained the leader by a wide margin (35.7 percent), followed by petroleum and coal products (18.3 percent), primary metal (15.5 percent), food (10.5 percent), and paper (8.9 percent) sectors. Feedstock uses of NGLs in the chemical industry accounted for 97 percent of NGL use throughout history (Fig. 3.3). However, amount used declined significantly from about 3000 trillion Btu in 2002 to about 2000 trillion Btu in 2010, before rising to 2361 trillion Btu in 2014. With the significant capacity additions of ethane crackers and other petrochemical facilities since 2014, NGL consumption in the chemical sector has certainly increased. We expect the 2018 MECS data to at least return to 2014 levels.

EIA's *Annual Energy Outlook 2019* (AEO) (EIA 2019a) reference case projections serve to indicate that growth trends in industrial natural gas use are expected to continue (Fig. 3.4, top). In addition to the chemical sector, which is expected to increase its use of natural gas, both as fuel and as feedstock, refining and a few other sectors will increase their use of natural gas for their fuel, heat, and power generation needs. However, the

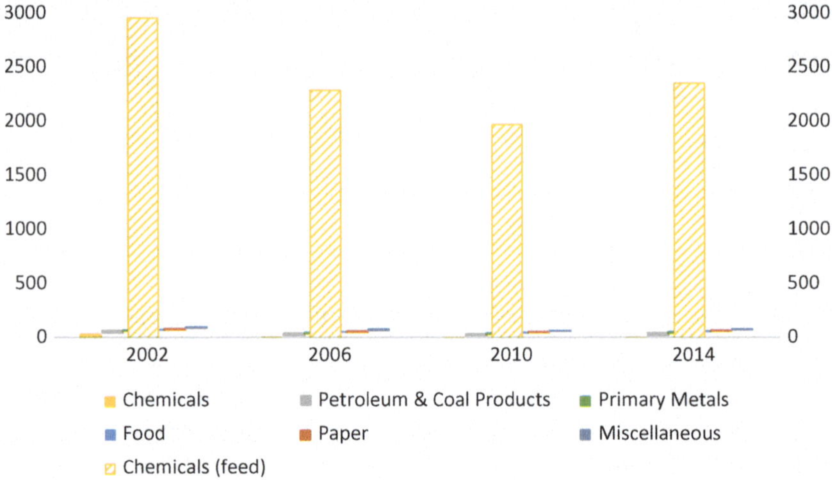

Fig. 3.3 U.S. consumption of NGLs for fuel and feedstock by manufacturing industry (trillion Btu). (Source: Authors' calculations using data from MECS 2002, 2006, 2010, and 2014 (EIA 1991–2014). Note that, as before, we separate feedstock use for chemicals. Excludes natural gasoline; includes ethane, ethylene, propane, propylene, normal butane, butylene, ethane–propane mixtures, propane–butane mixtures, and isobutane produced at refineries or natural gas processing plants, including plants that fractionate raw NGLs)

chemical sector will be the only one increasing its share because the increase in natural gas use in this sector dwarfs increases in all other sectors. Looking year-year (Fig. 3.4, bottom), the surge in natural gas use for chemicals reflects the aggressive build-out that we describe later. Beyond 2025, the EIA outlook suggests a much smaller "echo" or second wave of added capacity could be possible. Any continued expansion will be highly contingent upon economic recovery from Covid-19 along with the complex commodity market dynamics and project economics that we discuss. The longer the economic disruption, the longer the aftermath, and the more difficult it will be to launch new and meaningful capacity expansions.

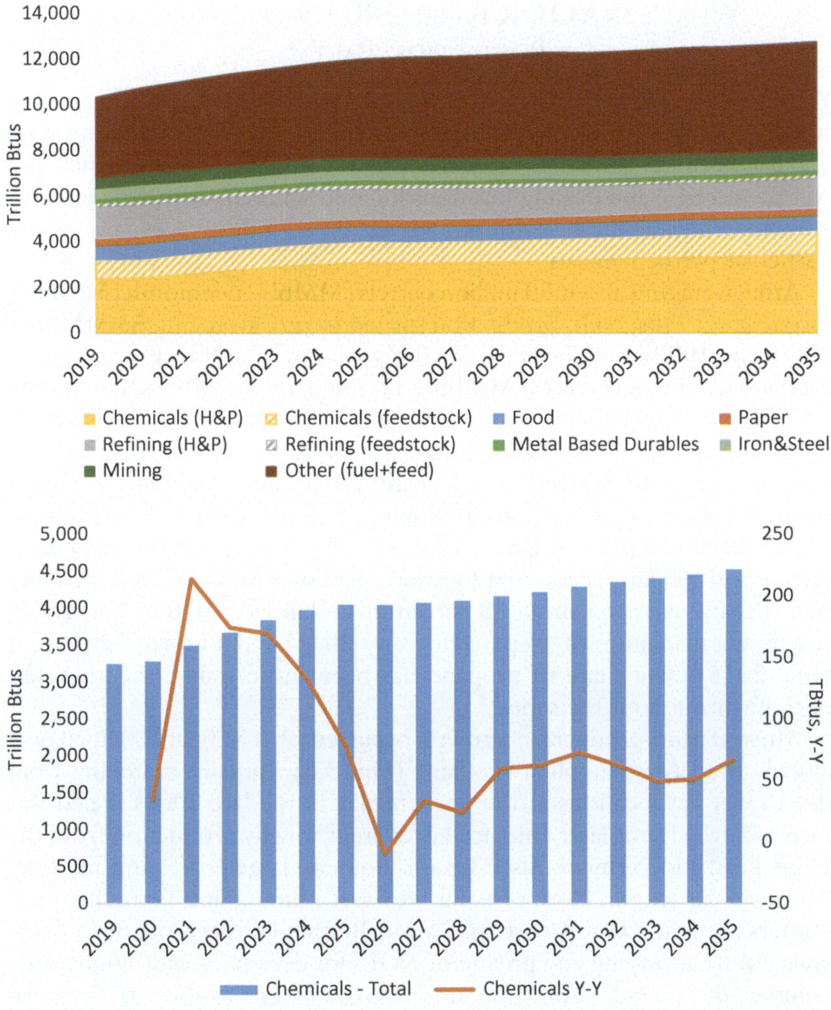

Fig. 3.4 Long-term outlook for U.S. total natural gas consumption for fuel and feedstock in major industrial sectors (top) and chemicals fuel and feedstock (bottom). (Source: Authors' calculations based on AEO reference case projections tables, specifically Tables 25–34 (EIA 2019b). H&P = heat and power)

What's in YOUR Barrel? Retooling Company Portfolios, Part 2

What's in YOUR Barrel, Part 1, in Chap. 1 provides a detailed analysis of how domestic oil and gas production portfolios evolved with shifting oil and gas price signals. The change in focus as companies targeted oilier and wet-gas acreage and drilling locations focused on NGL capture, a monetization strategy at the heart of natural gas based industrial expansion—in particular petrochemicals.

After averaging about 50 million barrels (MMbbl) per month (MMbbl/mo) in the 1980s, NGL production started to rise, averaging 53 MMbbl/mo in the 1990s and about 55 MMbbl/mo in the 2000s. Production of NGLs started to surpass 60 MMbbl/mo regularly in 2009, when drilling started to shift to liquid-rich parts of the Barnett Shale play and elsewhere in the face of low natural gas and high oil prices. By late 2011, production was more than 70 MMbbl/mo. In early 2019, more than 140 MMbbl/mo was produced, with output peaking at more than 162 MMbbl in March 2020 just prior to Covid-19 onset (Fig. 3.5). From the early days, ethane and propane accounted for more than two-thirds of NGL production. Ethane averaged about 38 percent from January 2016 to May 2020, reaching a maximum of 44 percent (early 2011) and a low of 32 percent (July 2015). The share of propane has been more stable, averaging 31 percent throughout the series.

Most ethane production growth occurred at TX Inland, which was already the largest supplier of ethane (Fig. 3.6). Initially, switching from dry to wet gas locations in the Barnett play in the late 2000s fueled this increase, which was later enhanced in a larger way by production from the Eagle Ford and Permian. Also, Texas is home to large processing and fractionation capacity in close proximity to vast refining and petrochemicals clusters along the Gulf Coast, and Mont Belvieu has been the main reference point for trading and pricing of NGLs for decades. Accordingly, large volumes of "y-grade," or "raw mix" NGLs,[6] began to flow to Texas for processing from as far away as the Marcellus Shale after pipeline-capacity expansion, including flow reversals.

Ethane supply in the Marcellus region increased significantly after 2013, once new processing capacity began to come online in West Virginia, Ohio, and southwest Pennsylvania (Appalachian No. 1). The volume of natural gas processed in Texas increased from about 3.8 Tcf in 2005 to 4.8 Tcf in 2011, when Marcellus production was rising fast, although still

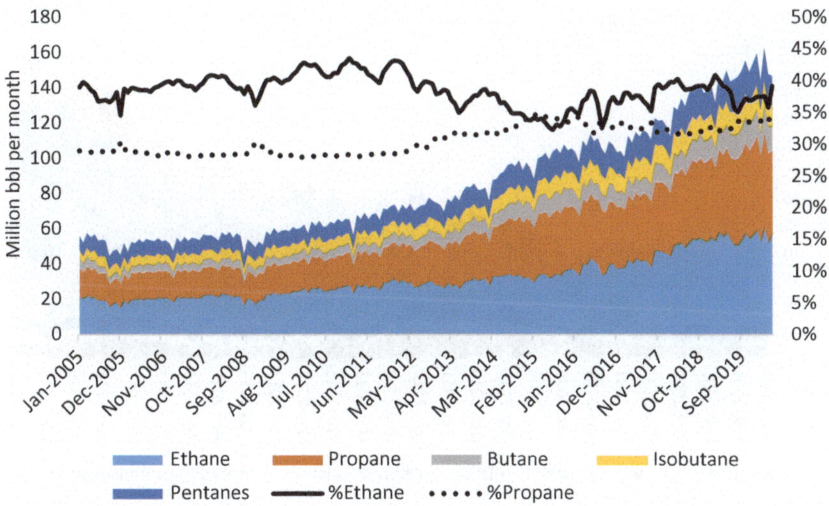

Fig. 3.5 NGL production (MMbbl/mo). (Source: Authors' calculations based on EIA data on natural gas plant field production EIA 2020)

less than 5 Bcf/d. Texas processing peaked around 6.8 Tcf in 2014, by which time 0.9 Tcf was being processed in West Virginia and 0.3 Tcf in Pennsylvania and Ohio each. In 2017, plants in West Virginia and Pennsylvania processed about 1.5 and 0.5 Tcf, respectively, as Texas processing fell to 6.3 Tcf. Texas plant supply has since surged, a consequence of both field production as well as shipments of rich gas from the Appalachians with natural gas pipeline reversals and as producers sought better Gulf Coast pricing and processing capacity. Some increased production has occurred in North Dakota, driven by Bakken drilling activity, more in Oklahoma, driven by activity in the STACK/SCOOP play.

Regional evolution of propane production is similar to that of ethane (Fig. 3.7). However, propane production increase has been continuous since early 2009, although it picked up speed in early 2014. In contrast, ethane production stagnated after its initial rise in 2009 and picked up after 2014, when more supplies from the Marcellus region and Texas began to find their way to the growing market rather than being rejected. Expansion of processing, fractionation, and pipeline capacities helped with these increases by completing the value chains to steam crackers. Relief also came from ethane exports to Canada and as a liquefied product first

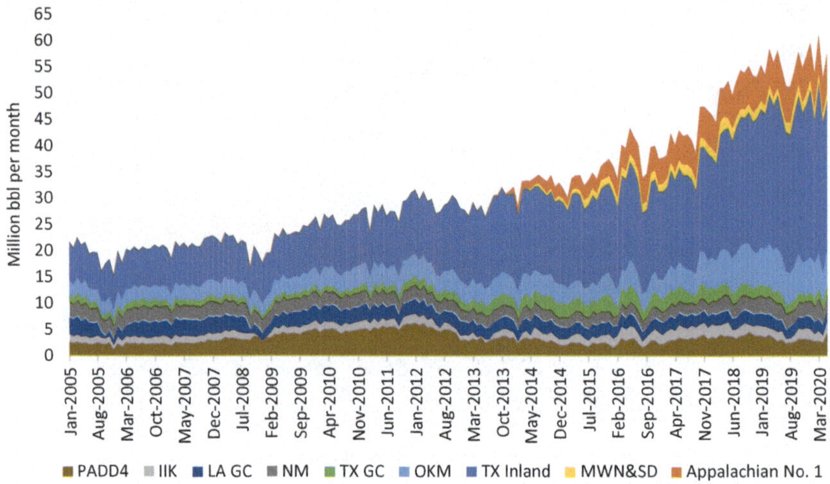

Fig. 3.6 Ethane production by region. (Source: Authors' calculations based on EIA data on natural gas plant field production (EIA 2020). Appalachian No. 1 is the only Petroleum Administration for Defense Districts (PADD) 1 area included, and no East Coast ethane production is reported. All three PADD 2 areas are included: Oklahoma, Kansas, Missouri (OKM); Indiana, Illinois, Kentucky (IIK); and Minnesota, Wisconsin, North and South Dakotas (MWN&SD). Four PADD 3 areas are included: Texas (TX) Inland, TX Gulf Coast (GC), Louisiana (LA) GC, and New Mexico (NM). North Louisiana and Arkansas and PADD 5 ethane productions are negligible and not reported)

to Europe, from the Marcus Hook terminal in Pennsylvania, and then to global markets from terminals along the Gulf Coast. Propane also is exported as LPG.

Impact on Producer Economics

Increased NGL production helped producers who were able to switch their capital spending from dry-gas to liquid-rich areas because of the higher value of NGLs other than ethane, with their prices following the oil price (Fig. 3.8). However, NGLs values and spreads[7] have been volatile because a variety of constraints affect prices of high-molecular-weight (C_{3+}) gases, including infrastructure bottlenecks (pipelines, fractionation capacity) between emerging production regions and key markets. For

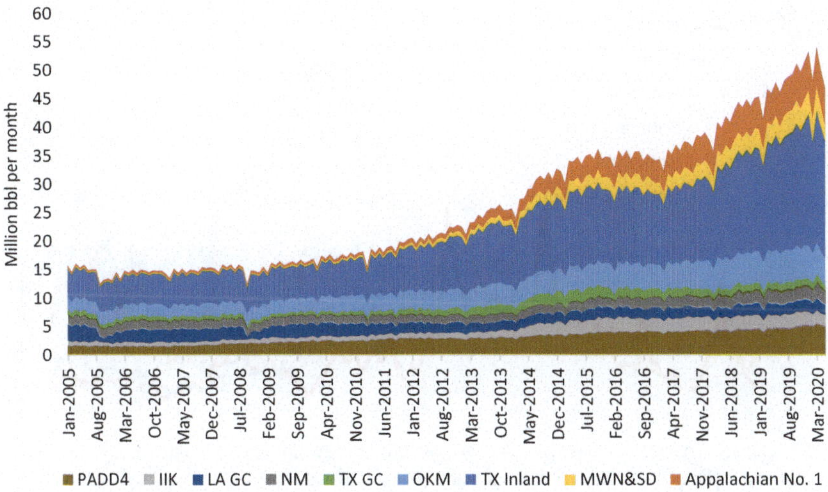

Fig. 3.7 Propane production by region. (Source: Authors' calculations based on EIA data on natural gas plant field production (EIA 2020). Appalachian No. 1 is the only Petroleum Administration for Defense Districts (PADD) 1 area included, and East Coast ethane production is negligible and not reported. All three PADD 2 areas are included: Oklahoma, Kansas, Missouri (OKM); Indiana, Illinois, Kentucky (IIK); and Minnesota, Wisconsin, North and South Dakotas (MWN&SD). Four PADD 3 areas are included: Texas (TX) Inland, TX Gulf Coast (GC), Louisiana (LA) GC, and New Mexico (NM). North Louisiana and Arkansas and PADD 5 ethane productions are negligible and not reported)

example, propane prices in Conway and Mont Belvieu hubs at times diverged from their historically high correlation. Divergence can be due to cold weather increasing heating demand for LPG (e.g., early 2014). Or, it can be the result of variations in product purity from Conway to Mont Belvieu, which also suffered from y-grade volumes exceeding fractionation capacity (e.g., in 2018). Excess propane supplies from Marcellus and Utica production flooding the Conway hub worsened the situation.

Nevertheless, after the collapse of the price of methane in late 2009, C_{3+} prices remained significantly higher than the methane price. For example, demand for propane exports continued to increase as the United States gradually became a net LPG exporter. Even the price of ethane was much higher than that of methane until increased production began to cause rejection and methane began to set the ethane price in early 2013.

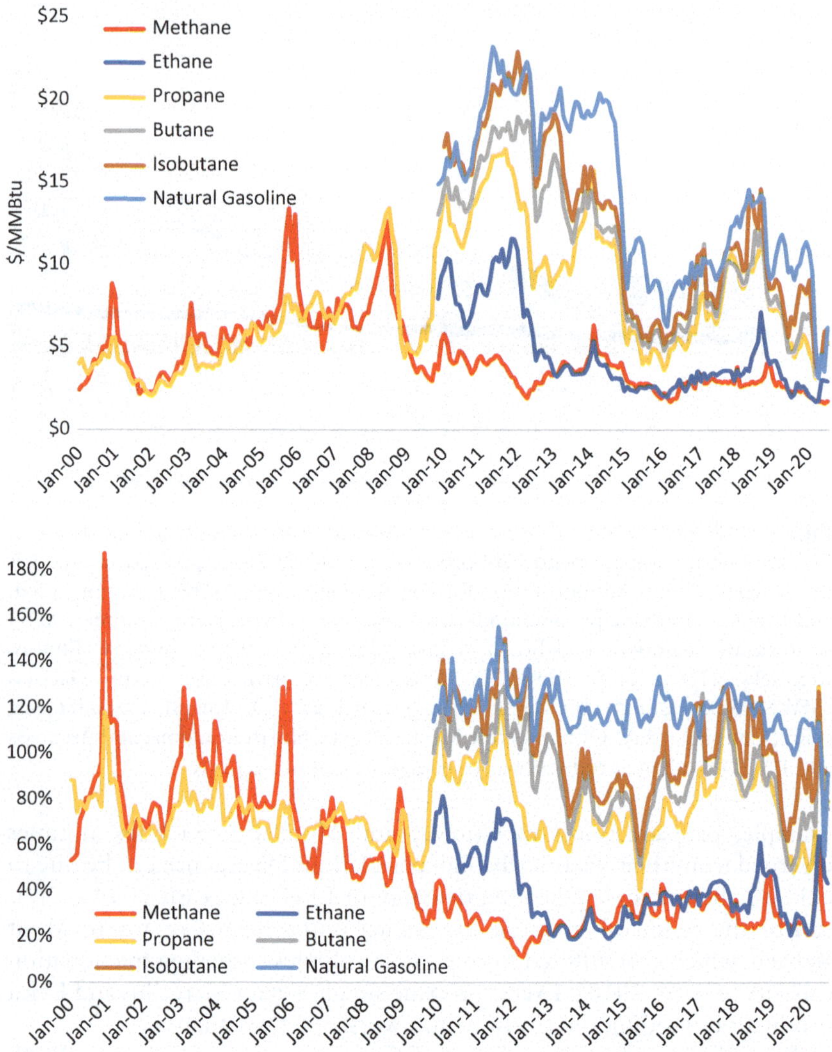

Fig. 3.8 Methane and natural gas liquid prices (top) and as percent of oil price (bottom). (Sources: EIA and CME/NYMEX for natural gas (methane), CME/NYMEX prompt-month Mont Belvieu contract prices, as provided by Quandl)

Although infrastructure bottlenecks, as well as constraints in downstream capacity development and export markets, also created downward pressure on the prices of heavier molecules, their prices remained significantly above those of methane and ethane until the oil-price collapse of 2015 and 2016.

A common metric for tracking incremental value of NGLs is the *frac spread*, the difference between the weighted average price of NGLs and that of methane (Fig. 3.9). This positive spread provides a boost to producers who were able to switch their drilling to high-Btu regions (Fig. 3.10). Potential NGL boost is calculated as a weighted-average price of production stream, assuming that 85 percent of it is marketed methane and 15 percent of it is marketed NGLs. As discussed before, these proportions will depend on the Btu content of the gas stream produced at any given location. Also, not all operators will receive the Henry Hub price or the NGL boost (Fig. 3.10) because basis differentials are significant across the plays demonstrating considerable volatility over the years. Nevertheless,

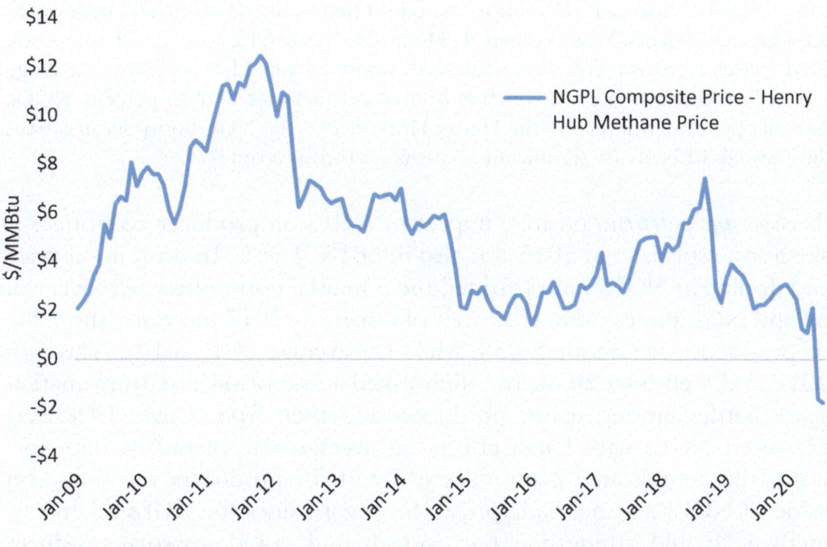

Fig. 3.9 Frac spread. (Sources: EIA, author analysis. Natural gas liquids (NGL) composite price is derived from daily Bloomberg spot-price data for natural gas liquids at Mont Belvieu, Texas, weighted by gas-processing-plant production volumes of each product as reported on Form EIA-816, "Monthly Natural Gas Liquids Report")

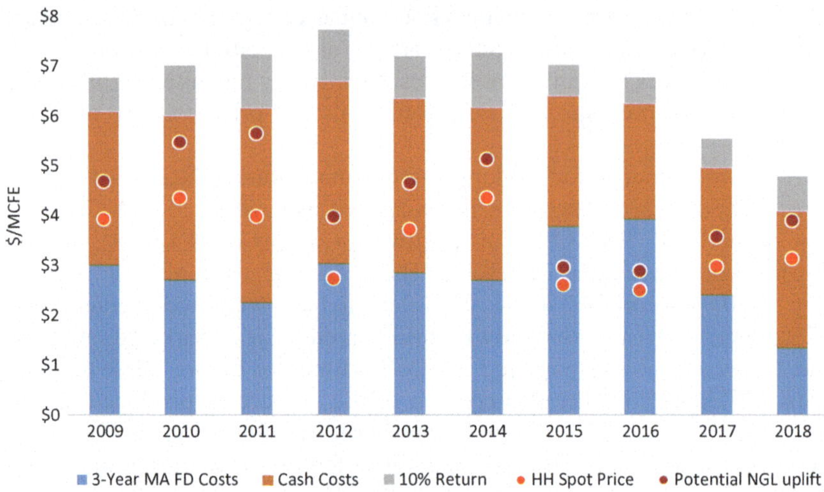

Fig. 3.10 Upstream economics and potential NGL boost (average of 16 operators). (Source: Authors' calculations based on financial analysis of 16 operators as presented by Michot Foss in Chap. 1. Henry Hub natural gas price and composite NGL prices are from EIA. Potential NGL boost calculated as a weighted average price of production stream, which is 85 percent methane and 15 percent NGLs. Not all operators will receive the Henry Hub price or the NGL boost because basis differentials of both are significant across plays through time)

the *average potential* positive impact of NGLs on producer economics is apparent, especially in 2011 but also in 2018. The 2015 drop in oil price and decline in NGLs values eroded the potential boost effect. Recovery of oil and NGL prices other than that of ethane in 2017 increased the value of production to about $3.58/Mcfe on average (Fig. 3.10). Through 2019 and well into 2020, the diminished value of oil first from market share battles among major producers and then from Covid-19 effects pressured NGLs with harsh effects on average frac spreads. Going forward, the complicated economics of uplift for producers will hinge on value of NGLs and methane prices. Stronger values for NGLs relative to methane would strengthen frac spreads and could improve producer returns as well as those for midstream and downstream processing, fractionation, and refining. Methane pricing would need to remain suppressed, a distinct question given the drop off in drilling for oil in U.S. onshore plays and thus the potential impact on associated gas output (refer to Chap. 1). Otherwise, oil would need to appreciate considerably with commensurate improvements in NGLs prices (or NGLs output reduced relative to demand). Finally, all of these conditions have bearing for the profitability of petrochemicals.

Note that the value of NGLs is realized *only* if the necessary infrastructure for separating them from production streams and delivering them to their best value-add markets is developed in a timely manner. As already discussed, bottlenecks and delays in such infrastructure caused basis blowouts across hubs and undermined value realization by producers. Master limited partnerships (MLPs) were the main vehicles for developing these crucial midstream infrastructure facilities, and the lure of MLPs for investors and MLPs as a form of business organization spurred many formerly integrated domestic producers to convert their midstream businesses into MLPs. Any number of tax and other benefits can be derived from MLPs, which have demonstrated continued success in accessing capital markets for funding. But new pressures are lurking in the lower-commodity-price world. Drops in production, which should increase as producers rationalize to cut cost and improve profitability, affect throughput in midstream pipelines, processing, and fractionation. During the low oil prices of 2015 and 2016, the frac spread diminished as an indicator of midstream value added and margin (Fig. 3.9). Midstream businesses are once again challenged in the slack industry context prevailing at time of writing. Ultimately, any capacity reductions, investment deferrals, consolidation, or other actions to reconcile midstream business prospects with business conditions will improve profitability later on.[8]

Economics of a Renewed Petrochemical Industry

As noted, the natural gas production stream is used in various processes, including methane as fuel to generate power and steam (often in combined heat and power or *cogeneration systems*) and NGLs as feedstock to the petrochemical industry, which produces the necessary ingredients for ubiquitous products of our daily lives (Fig. 3.11). For example, ethylene, which can be produced by cracking ethane and some other hydrocarbon molecules, and other olefins produced from the steam-cracking process, are building blocks for many intermediate products used in manufacturing familiar consumer products. Many facilities are flexible in using various feedstocks to optimize their operations in response to feedstock costs and prices of their final products. As such, ethane-only crackers in

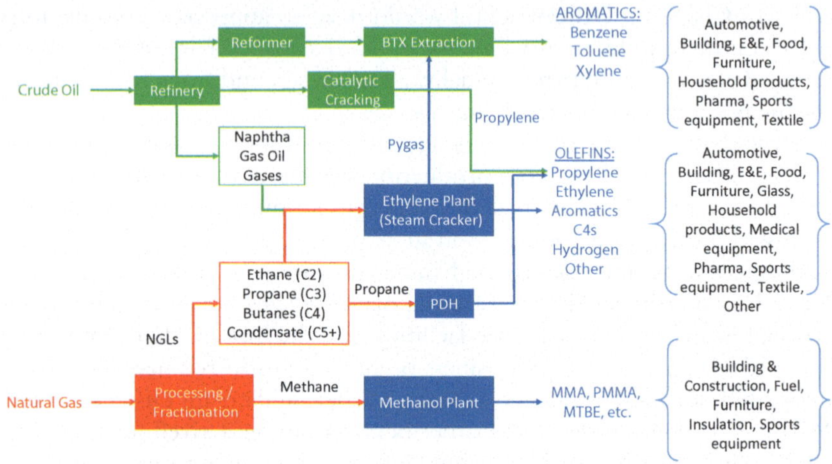

Fig. 3.11 Hydrocarbon use in petrochemicals. (Source: Authors' depiction. E&E = electric and electronics, including consumer products. MMA = methyl methacrylate. PMMA = polymethyl methacrylate. MTBE = methyl tertiary butyl ether)

the United States may be less competitive in an environment of lower oil prices because some crackers, especially elsewhere in the world, may switch to naphtha or other hydrocarbons that are cheaper inputs and that yield more byproducts such as pyrolysis gasoline (pygas). Also, ethane-only crackers yield small amounts of propylene (Table 3.1), the demand for which has increased for producing polypropylene, a plastic in increasing demand. As a result, investment has increased in propane dehydrogenation (PDH) facilities. On the other hand, ethane cracking's chief byproduct, hydrogen, is readily marketed on the U.S. Gulf Coast, where a multitude of refineries find this supply attractive (Fig. 3.11). In short, operators of downstream facilities, including refineries and various petrochemical plants, pursue continuous optimization of their operations, exploiting byproduct synergies with other facilities in close proximity and responding to price signals from markets for a wide range of products. Such optimization necessitates operational flexibility in terms of feedstock and output yield configurations.

Increased ethane production has been the key driver for most investments because ethane has been the largest component of NGL supply and the domestic demand for it has been limited, lowering its price relative to other feedstocks. Whereas ethylene can be produced from propane,

Table 3.1 Typical steam-cracking yields by feedstock (percent of weight)

	Ethane	*Propane*	*Butane*	*Naphtha*
Ethylene	78–80%	42–45%	35–40%	25–34%
Propylene	2–5%	15–18%	17–22%	13–16%
C4s	3–4%	4–5%	10%	10–17%
Aromatics	2–3%	7–8%	7%	11–20%
Hydrogen	5–10%	2%	1–2%	1%
Fuel or methane	6–9%	27–30%	19–22%	11–15%

Sources: Various industry trade publications, including RBN Energy and Platts Analytics. Ethylene, propylene, and C4s collectively are known as olefins. C4s include butadiene, isobutylene, and higher olefins. Aromatics include benzene, toluene, and xylenes

butane, or naphtha, the highest yield of ethylene results from ethane. At the same time, as feedstock gets heavier, cracking yields more propylene, C4s, and aromatics (Table 3.1). Accordingly, the profitability of each cracker depends not only on the cost of feedstock, but also on prices of products obtained from the cracking process. As such, a naphtha-based cracker in the Middle East may be more profitable than an ethane-based cracker in the United States if naphtha is cheap and the prices of propylene, C4s, and aromatics are high (even with the low ethane prices of recent times). Prices of heavier hydrocarbons also fell in 2012, although they stabilized at a higher level between 2012 and 2014, with occasional spikes. Even when the oil price collapsed in late 2014, pulling down prices of propane, butanes, and natural gasoline, the values of these NGLs remained higher, recovered faster, and are still above the price of ethane for 2020 to date (Fig. 3.8).

These diverging price fluctuations of alternative feedstocks across a global market create uncertainty for developers of petrochemical projects, given their long-lead project-development timelines and high capital requirements. Polyethylene production is the largest ethylene-derivative market and accounts for over 60 percent of global ethylene consumption, and the interdependency among some of the facilities is another complicating factor. For example, ethane crackers need either sufficient polyethylene capacity to take the ethylene they produce or large ethylene export capabilities. Polyethylene is produced in three main forms: low density (LDPE), linear low density (LLDPE), and high density (HDPE). Markets include film, packaging, containers and articles for the home, and light industrial use.

Propylene is widely used in downstream petrochemical processes to make film, packaging, and synthetic fiber and is a byproduct of oil refining and petrochemical steam cracking. Both of these byproduct processes are producing less propylene right now for a couple of reasons: (1) refineries have had to adjust feedstocks to accommodate lighter hydrocarbons that have become available in abundance and at attractive prices; (2) similarly, lighter feedstock, such as ethane, is replacing heavier feedstock, such as propane, normal butane, and naphtha in chemical plants. As discussed earlier, this situation led to the development of new PDH facilities. The existence of some of this infrastructure in the Gulf Coast, some of which has not been fully utilized, was a big advantage to companies developing facilities in that region, as compared to southwest Pennsylvania, Ohio, or West Virginia, where NGL production also increased.

Investments and End Use

Between 2013 and 2018, we maintained an in-house industrial-project database to track changes in the industrial sector's use of natural gas. We focused on gas-intensive industries, especially the petrochemical sector. Hence, the database includes nearly 300 plants, although we focused only on estimated natural gas consumption and investment numbers for a subset of 126 projects in the petrochemical sector.[9] About 30 facilities had already been completed at the time of writing. Another 20 projects remain under consideration or in early planning (refer to Table 3.2 for project-status definitions). Plant types include ethylene, polyethylene, propylene, methanol, nitrogen fertilizer, and fuels from gas-to-liquids (GTL) and methanol-to-gasoline (MTG) processes.

Table 3.2 Definitions of project status

Completed	Project is finished and operating
In progress	Project is under either project procurement or construction
Permits	Project has some permits, is filing permits, or is awaiting permits
FEED	Project owner retains engineering firm to take holistic approach to stage-gate model for evaluating development of projects. Substantial capital outlay may occur
Planning	Project is declared and consultant may be hired to define budget, risk, and schedule of project
Under consideration	Project is under internal discussion with preliminary announcements. May still look for partners

Estimated Natural Gas Demand

Natural gas use in each type of facility in our database is a function of multiple factors, including need for methane as feedstock and/or heat and power, and capacity utilization. Information on these variables is not readily available and changes from plant to plant, year to year, especially if plants have some feedstock flexibility. Given these caveats, natural gas use estimates are based on assumptions of three key sectors (Table 3.3). We present capacity utilization as an average percentage ratio of actual output to the potential output by industry and the economy. The G17 form released by the Federal Reserve Bank (FRB) reports industrial production and capacity-utilization indexes monthly. Long-term average-capacity utilization for the chemical sector is 76 percent.

Using the assumptions in Table 3.3, we estimate that incremental natural gas demand from projects that were completed in 2016 and 2017, in front-end engineering design (FEED), in pursuit of permits, or otherwise in progress will amount to about 3.1 Bcf/d by 2022 (Fig. 3.12). This estimate is consistent with the *Annual Energy Outlook 2020* reference case, which predicts roughly a 3.5 Bcf/d increase between 2015 and 2022 in the chemical sector's use of natural gas as fuel and feedstock (Fig. 3.4). Note that the increase in industrial-sector gas use is significantly less than the possible increase in the power sector. The analysis in Fig. 2.13 suggests up to about 7.5 Bcf/d incremental gas burn in power generation between 2015 and 2022. The AEO 2020 reference case projects about 4.7 Bcf/d, which is closer to our lower bound in Fig. 2.13. But other AEO 2020 cases indicate higher incremental gas demand for power generation as depicted in Fig. 2.13.

Our estimate of gas consumption, based on facilities in our database that were completed before 2016, is included in the existing natural gas demand of about 21.5 Bcf/d. Tallying projects under consideration or in early planning (vertical bars in Fig. 3.12) adds about 0.6 Bcf/d by 2022 and about 1.5 Bcf/d in the future (because many projects did not announce a target startup date). These volumes are an early indication of what a second wave of petrochemical-capacity expansion might entail.

Table 3.3 Unit natural gas consumption ranges of various industries (MMBtu/t)

Ethylene	19.3
Methanol	32.0
Nitrogen fertilizer	30.9

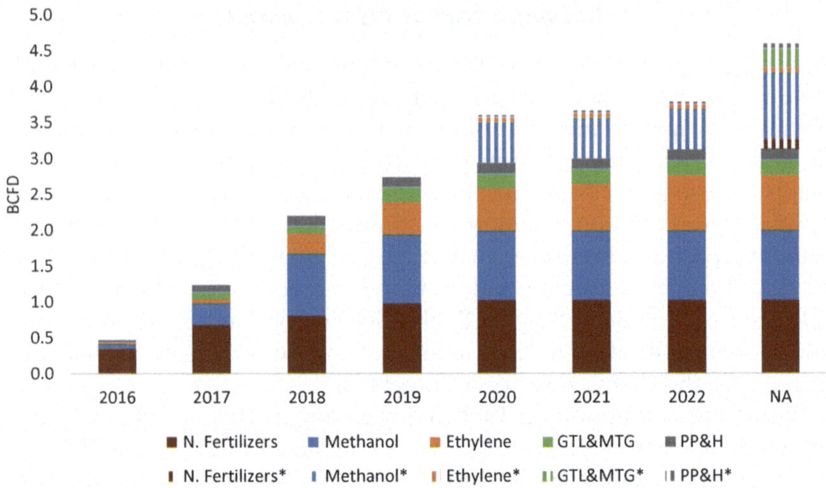

Fig. 3.12 Incremental gas demand (cumulative Bcf/d) from key petrochemicals projects. (Source: Authors' calculations from proprietary petrochemical-projects database, last updated in December 2017. Authors' depiction based upon petrochemical database as described. Solid bars represent expected incremental natural gas consumption, both as fuel and feedstock from projects that are completed, in FEED, in pursuit of permits, or otherwise in progress. Note that some projects may come online later owing to schedule delays. Bars with vertical lines reflect estimated natural gas consumption from projects announced as in planning or under consideration (marked with *). Most had no date associated with them, hence the NA category. Industrial gas demand in the United States, including nonpetrochemical sectors, in 2016 was about 21.5 Bcf/d)

We expected fertilizer and methanol plants to contribute about 1 Bcf/d each by 2020, followed by ethylene plants, with about 0.6 Bcf/d. With less certain projects included, the methanol sector's natural gas needs may increase from about 0.6 Bcf/d by 2022 to about 1 Bcf/d on some unannounced date in the future. Some expect a resurgence of the industrial renaissance by the mid-2020s. Plants currently in the early planning stages can be early movers in the second wave anticipated by some industry observers.

Capital Investment

Although methanol and nitrogen fertilizer plants are leaders in terms of estimated natural gas consumption, ethylene plants have been attracting the most investment (Fig. 3.13). The olefin complex, with the addition of propylene and polyethylene plants, accounts for even a larger share. Note that we assigned the total investment of each project to the year in which it was finished or announced to be finished. As such, some of the investment seen in 2018, for example, has already been occurring as plants have gone under construction. Accordingly, at the time of writing, more than $50 billion will have probably been spent just on the 60–70 projects that have been making progress. If we were to include chlor-alkali and other chemical projects built before 2017, total investment would surpass $60 billion. Importantly, our database reflects a snapshot of project planning and execution before Covid-19. Capacity additions denoted by vertical

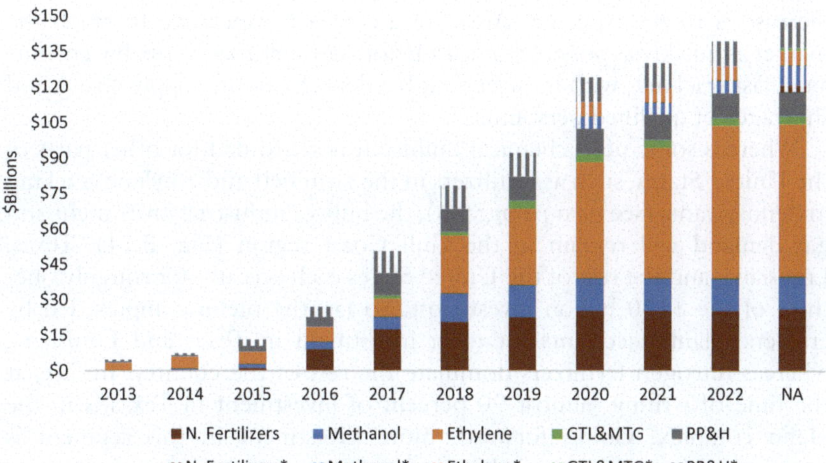

Fig. 3.13 Incremental cumulative investment in key petrochemical projects. (Source: Authors' calculations from proprietary petrochemical-projects database, last updated in December 2017. Solid bars represent expected incremental investment in projects that are completed, in FEED, in pursuit of permits, or otherwise in progress. Note that some projects may be pushed to future years owing to schedule and other delays. Bars with vertical lines reflect estimated investment in projects announced as in planning or under consideration (marked with *). Most had no date associated with them, hence the NA category)

bars in Fig. 3.13 are particularly vulnerable to delays or cancellations. Even projects under construction are affected, as we observe in various references throughout this chapter.

About 41 percent of this investment went to ethylene projects; 29 percent to nitrogen fertilizer projects; 17 percent to polyethylene, propylene, and hydrogen (PP&H) projects; 11 percent to methanol projects; and the remainder to GTL and MTG projects.[10] Another 30–40 projects in our database are making progress (FEED, obtaining permits) and are expected to come online by 2022. Their investments add up to another $70 billion, distributed as follows: 49 percent ethylene, 21 percent in nitrogen fertilizer, 15 percent methanol, 12 percent PP&H, and 3 percent in GTL and MTG facilities. These estimates are based on company announcements of project costs and industry reporting. At least some of these projects most likely cost more than these initial estimates. Note that the number of petrochemicals, refining, and LNG projects increased globally and that a limited number of EPC firms are best qualified to build such projects, so cost increase is to be expected. Also, the perceived imperative to reach the market as quickly as possible (at least before competitors) probably encouraged fast tracking, with its attendant bottlenecks across supply chains and shortages of qualified personnel.

Whereas some petrochemical build-out is scheduled for other parts of the United States, such as fertilizers in the farm belt and ethylene cracking in Pennsylvania (see next paragraph), the bulk of industrial investment and gas demand will remain in the Gulf Coast region (Fig. 3.14). Texas, Louisiana, and the rest of the United States each account for roughly one-third of the $120 billion investment. So far, the olefin complex, led by ethylene plants, accounts for most investment in Texas and Louisiana, whereas nitrogen fertilizers dominate the rest of the country. In fact, at the time of writing, almost 90 percent of investment in Texas is in the olefin complex. Going forward, more investment in this segment is expected, although some sizable methanol investment is also planned for Texas, and Louisiana attracted the most investment in methanol plants. Anticipated investments in Louisiana are much lower than in Texas and the rest of the country.

Outside the Gulf Coast, only Shell's $6-billion ethane cracker with associated polyethylene units is under construction in Pennsylvania. As discussed earlier, the Gulf Coast has many advantages over locations in Pennsylvania, West Virginia, or Ohio. Despite their proximity to Marcellus and Utica production, which is expected to supply enough NGLs

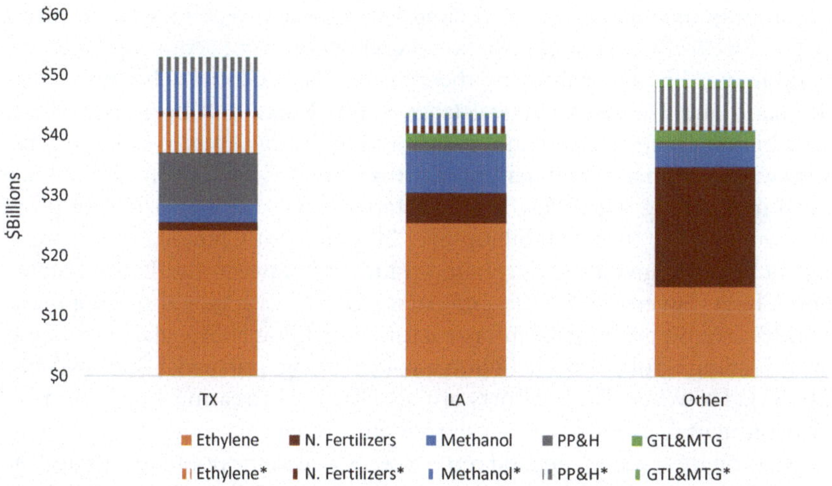

Fig. 3.14 Total investment by industry by region in key petrochemical projects (2012–2017 realized; 2018 and beyond, under way or planned). (Source: Authors' calculations from proprietary petrochemical-project database, last updated December 2017. Solid bars represent expected incremental investment in projects that are completed, in FEED, in pursuit of permits, or otherwise in progress. Note that some projects may be pushed to future years owing to schedule delays. Bars with vertical lines reflect estimated investment in projects announced as in planning or under consideration (marked with *). Most had no date associated with them, hence the NA category)

(particularly ethane) for several more cracker and derivative facilities, these locations, unlike their Gulf Coast counterparts, are not in proximity to a large conglomeration of other downstream and midstream assets, nor do they have easy access to export routes. Shortages of NGL and chemicals storage continually hamper project developers. Although a valuable export outlet, the Marcus Hook port facility near Philadelphia is capacity constrained. Access to another outlet, the Canadian downstream sector, is limited by pipeline capacity. In any case, the Canadian market is small and faces challenges similar to those of U.S. inland locations. As we concluded our research, alternatives were being pursued (e.g., port facilities in Charleston, South Carolina).

Nevertheless, the ACC has posited that $36 billion in petrochemicals and plastics can be invested in the Appalachian region if infrastructure constraints such as NGL and chemical storage and pipelines are resolved (ACC 2019c).[11] Several international companies were acquiring land and conducting FEED analysis in the region. PTT Global Chemical from Thailand and Daelim Chemical from South Korea had been assessing a $10-billion complex of ethane cracker and derivative units in Ohio, but no FID was announced.[12] China Energy Investment Corporation Limited has been negotiating with West Virginia state officials for a portfolio of projects worth more than $80 billion over 20 years, but Chinese investment is facing hurdles, given the deepening trade war between the United States and China (Silverstein 2020). Industry groups and regional-development entities are also pushing for infrastructure, including an Appalachia Storage and Trading Hub, a $3.4-billion project being pursued (BusinessWire 2018a). However, these efforts are also facing increasing opposition by environmental groups and local residents regarding potential negative impacts on local water and land resources, as well as the population's health.

At the same time, there are some concerns that the traditional Gulf Coast locations with proximity to existing downstream complexes and easy access to ports are becoming scarcer, and traffic at ports more congested. Ironically, Covid-19 will provide some relief as activity slows. Shortages of locally available qualified labor and higher cost of transported labor also were concerns, in light of the intense construction activity throughout the Gulf Coast region. As well, there is the ever-present tropical storm season threat, with the potential to disrupt and incur real damage on facilities and shipping. Regardless, the Texas and Louisiana coastlines offer more opportunities, in particular for market price signals (more robust given the critical mass of regional hydrocarbon processing) and shipping for international trade, than the Appalachia region, as indicated by the large portfolio of projects under development.

Risks and Uncertainties Facing the Industrial Renaissance

The fundamental driver of risks facing the U.S. petrochemical sector is the need for most products from the new plants to be exported. Global demand for various products depends on economic growth, especially in key emerging markets such as China and India. Many economists expect petrochemical demand growth to be strong, driven by GDP growth expectations of 6–7 percent in China, 7–8 percent in India, and similar rates in other emerging markets, but there is no consensus. Other economists and country experts expect a sizable slowdown in chemical demand.[13]

On the other hand, industrial policies in such major importers, as well as hydrocarbon powerhouses, such as Saudi Arabia and Qatar, signal stiff competition. Unlike in the United States and Europe, many facilities in these countries are built by state companies using state funding and subsidized feedstocks as part of a large state-economic strategy and planning, such as the expensive coal-to-olefin and methanol-to-olefin plants in China. China is also allowing international companies to develop projects there, and some, including ExxonMobil and BASF, have already responded.

Low NGL prices, especially for ethane, have contributed to the industrial renaissance in the United States more than the low price of methane. Methanol and fertilizer plants that use methane as feedstock accounted for about 36 percent of total investment (>$40 billion) from 2012 through 2017. The remainder is mostly for steam crackers, most of which are ethane only. Their continued competitiveness depends on not only the evolution of global balance of supply and demand but also the comparative cost of feedstocks and the overall economics of the plants. For example, many expected the price of ethane to increase further as the new ethane-only crackers came online in 2018 and 2019 (e.g., Lippe 2018). Indeed, we observed the price of ethane rising during the second half of 2018, but only to drop back in line with that of methane by mid-2019 (Fig. 3.8). The price of ethane may recover, but global crude oil and United States ethane price expectations continue to indicate cheaper ethane per Btu. And yet, as discussed earlier, cracking economics is more complex. The profitability and, hence, competitiveness of crackers depend on not only the cost of feedstock but also the price of byproducts such as propylene, aromatics, and C4s. Naphtha and other heavier molecules yield more of these byproducts than ethane (Table 3.1), and depending on demand for various products, different feedstocks may be profitable for a cracker even if it costs more than others.

Finally, the cost of methane and NGLs as feedstock in the United States also depends on upstream economics and domestic demand for methane, which we discuss next.

Global Demand and Competitiveness of U.S. Petrochemicals: The Case of Ethylene

Global ethylene capacity increased from about 113 million metric tons per year (mtpa) in 2005 to almost 144 mtpa in 2015 and is expected to reach 160 mtpa, if not by the end of 2018, then certainly before 2020. The big wave of expected U.S. completions in 2018 (and possibly with delays in 2019) will be responsible for the significant jump in the near future. However, to date, the most significant increase has occurred in the Middle East, led by Saudi Arabia, Iran, UAE, and Qatar (Fig. 3.15). The Middle East's share increased from under 10 percent in 2005 to about 19 percent in 2015. China nearly tripled its ethylene capacity from 2005 to

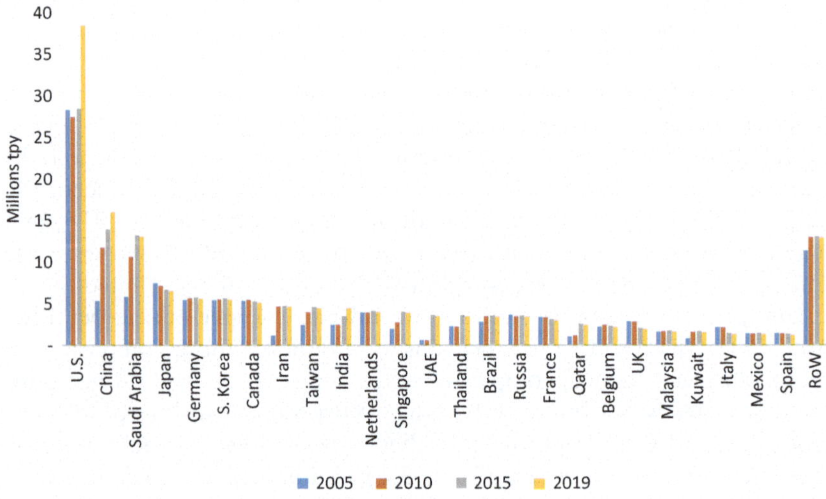

Fig. 3.15 Ethylene capacity (million metric tons per year, mtpa). (Source: Authors' calculations based on various issues of *Oil & Gas Journal* ethylene capacity and construction surveys. Numbers represent installed capacity as of January 1st of each year. Data for 2005, 2010, and 2015 are directly from *Oil & Gas Journal* ethylene surveys. 2019 estimate based on *Oil & Gas Journal* construction surveys and includes facilities expected to come online in 2016 through 2018, except for the United States, which is based on our database and reflects expected incremental investment in projects that are completed, in progress, in FEED, or in pursuit of permits with a target date of completion between 2016 and 2018. Note that some projects may be delayed to 2020 and beyond)

2015, raising its share from less than 5 percent to 10 percent. The U.S. share declined from 25 percent in 2005 to below 20 percent in 2015, still the largest share of any single country. The share of U.S. capacity may increase again, as the projects continue to come online, but other countries are expected to continue adding capacity as well. For example, ADNOC has a $45-billion plan to build a petrochemical complex by 2025 (BusinessWire 2018b). Similarly, Saudi Aramco and SABIC have several projects across the globe (Saudi Arabia, India, South Korea, and the United States) worth tens of billions of dollars, including crude oil-to-chemical (COTC) plants (OGJ 2018). Charlesworth (2017) suggested that COTC plants can be profitable, depending on relative pricing of crude oil and naphtha and the quality of the crude.

In contrast, capacity has been flat or declining in most European countries, including former Eastern Bloc members. The shares of Western and Eastern Europe have fallen from roughly 24 percent and 5 percent to 16 and 3 percent since 2005. However, according to WoodMackenzie (2018), the decline in Western Europe may have ended with ethane imported from the United States helping the economics of some facilities and capacity expansion plans for the early 2020s. India almost doubled its capacity to nearly 5 mtpa, but its share of the world remains below 3 percent.

Although more crackers pursue lighter feedstock, such as ethane, propane, and butanes, the existing capacity continues to rely on naphtha for more than 40 percent of its feedstock (Charlesworth 2017). Ethane accounted for 36 percent of ethylene feedstock in 2016 but is expected to increase its share as ethane-only U.S. facilities come online. China is expected to add new methanol-to-olefin (MTO) plants and coal-to-olefin (CTO) capacity by 2025, although these accounted for only 1 percent each in 2016. For example, Alvarado (2017) posited that in the early 2020s, about 20 percent of methanol will be used in MTO operations, led by China. There is probably a limit to how much of the capacity can shift to lighter feedstock, especially ethane, because the global economy will continue to need C4s, aromatics, and other products obtained from cracking hydrocarbon molecules heavier than ethane (Table 3.1).

More than 3 mtpa of capacity has been lost in Europe since 2010. As a result, utilization of existing plants has been near 90 percent in recent years (e.g., WoodMackenzie 2018). Facilities that came online in 2018 and in succeeding years, especially in the United States, are well placed to take advantage of demand growth (assuming that growth continues strong). Pre-onset of Covid-19, IHS Markit predicted a tight market through 2022, not only owing to strong demand growth, but also because of supply-side issues in China related to feed switching. Chinese demand for ethylene imports could also rise if the country shuts down its unprofitable MTO plants and CTO plants owing to environmental reasons[14] (e.g., see Boswell 2018).

However, WoodMackenzie (2018) reported that China continues to, or plans to, add MTO and CTO capacity in addition to 10 mtpa of new steam-cracker capacity by 2025, and *Oil & Gas Journal* construction surveys confirmed roughly 10 mtpa of ethylene and MTO capacity in China, including several projects either under construction or in engineering phase to be completed by the early 2020s. In addition, investments in other countries will provide about 8 mtpa of cracking capacity by the end of the decade. Considering projects in planning with target dates beyond 2020 across 14 countries, about 13 mtpa of additional capacity is possible by mid-2020s, according to *Oil & Gas Journal* construction surveys. Other estimates are more bullish (Fig. 3.16).

Demand growth has been strong, with more than 30 mtpa of additional demand between 2011 and 2017, for an average annual growth of about 3.6 percent. Budde and others (2017) estimated that demand growth for petrochemicals "may go down by between 0.5 and 2 percent over the next 10 years," from an average annual growth of 3.6 percent experienced in the previous decade. Cetinkaya and others (2018) narrowed the range somewhat by raising the lower limit to 2 percent, and these papers by McKinsey & Company experts offered several reasons for the change:

- First, many chemical products are becoming commoditized, and new entrants, primarily from China but also elsewhere, create overcapacity for many products, as well as the advantage of offering valuable inputs to their manufacturing sectors domestically. A possible counterpoint to this argument is whether or how long China will be willing to continue supporting the sector as the cost of imported feedstocks, whether they are ethane, naphtha, or methanol, become challenging to their economics. CTO avoids import costs and yet remains one of the costliest processes. A consolidation of the Chinese industry is probably long overdue, but its impact on the global scene is not clear.

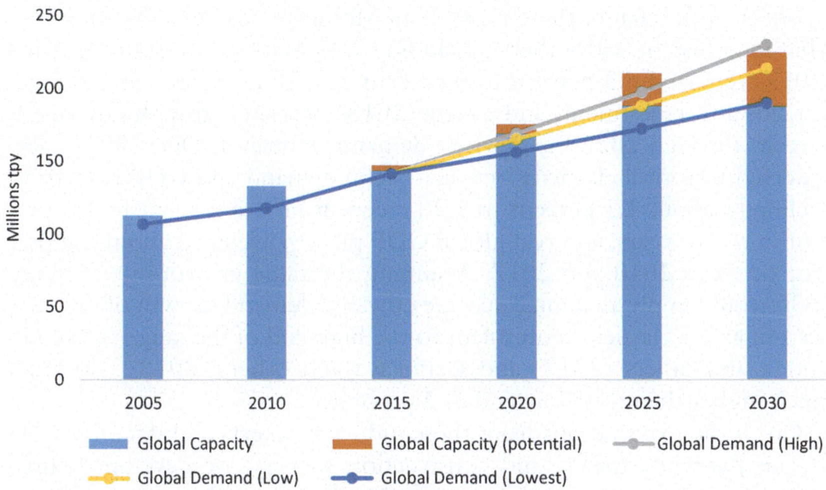

Fig. 3.16 Global ethylene scenarios (mtpa). (Source: Authors' calculations based on various issues of *Oil & Gas Journal* ethylene capacity and construction surveys and assumptions offered in Budde and others (2017), Cetinkaya and others (2018), Dina (2017), Eskew (2018), and WoodMackenzie (2018). Numbers represent installed capacity as of January 1st of each year. Data for 2005, 2010, and 2015 are directly from *Oil & Gas Journal* ethylene surveys. 2020 and 2025 estimates are based on *Oil & Gas Journal* construction surveys and include facilities expected to come online, except for the United States, which is based on our database)

- Second, the link between economic growth and demand for chemical products is not as strong as it used to be. The slowing GDP growth in China and elsewhere is expected to reduce demand, but also, because many Chinese have already achieved middle-class status, their contribution to demand growth will be limited.
- Finally, McKinsey analysts pointed to increased recycling of plastics as a factor that could reduce the need for chemical products produced by traditional routes. Given that much value creation in the last 10–15 years has been due to demand growth in emerging economies, slower growth will be a challenge, especially to new plants that do not have access to cheap feedstock such as ethane in the United States and natural gas in the Middle East.

On the other hand, these views from McKinsey & Company are somewhat inconsistent with others', including IHS Markit. For example, Dina (2017) reported 3.5 percent to 4 percent growth in olefin demand as an attraction to investment, and Eskew (2018) implied a growth rate of 3.9 percent through 2022 for ethylene demand. However, Dina (2017) also expected historical elasticity between olefin demand and GDP growth to decline to about 1.1 percent to 1.2 percent from 1.3 percent to 1.5 percent in recent years, and real global GDP growth averaged about 2.8 percent between 2010 and 2017. Assuming the same growth rate through 2030 would imply an annual average ethylene demand growth of only 3.1 percent at 1.1 elasticity, equivalent to the high end of the range offered in Budde and others (2017) and Cetinkaya and others (2018), although much higher than their low end of 2 percent.

Given the expectations from these industry experts and data from *Oil & Gas Journal* ethylene and construction surveys, we developed three potential pathways for ethylene demand and contrasted them to ethylene capacity, shown in Fig. 3.16. Blue columns reflect capacity already in operation and those in various stages of development and expected to come online by the early 2020s; orange columns reflect potential projects. For 2015, a potential capacity of about 3.7 mtpa reflects the difference between the total global capacity reported in the *Oil & Gas Journal* ethylene survey and the capacity from other sources. For 2020, the difference is 6 mtpa, reflecting the difference between the IHS Markit estimate and projects reported in *Oil & Gas Journal* construction surveys and our database for the United States. For 2025, we added 16 mtpa to capture expected projects in China, including steam crackers, as well as CTO and MTO plants. For example, WoodMackenzie (2018) reported more than 10 mtpa of steam crackers and more than 4 mtpa of CTO projects, in addition to an unspecified number of MTO plants. Eskew (2018) reported over 9 mtpa of announced projects. For 2030, we added 15 mtpa of announced projects for the United States, *the second wave*, per Eskew (2018).

On the basis of Fig. 3.16, we can confirm the high utilization rates reported for ethylene capacity around the world over the last decade and a half. The strong demand growth and high utilization would also support high profitability reported by many chemical companies. Looking ahead, ethane-only U.S. crackers that will be coming online by 2020 are well positioned to take advantage of the low cost of ethane as feedstock in a strong demand environment. But there are scenarios in which global build-out may lead to significant overcapacity if demand growth slows significantly. In this scheme, the U.S. ethylene industry may remain competitive, as long as the price of ethane stays low relative to the oil price. Any rationalization in noncommercial practices in China and the Middle East would also help the U.S. industry. Finally, the continued retirement of older, economically challenged plants around the world, such as the European naphtha crackers, will also render crackers in the United States more competitive.

And yet, whether the market opportunity will remain for a second wave of U.S. ethane-based crackers beyond the early 2020s is speculative especially because these uncertainties may delay investment decisions. Capital costs have increased, not only with the general global economic recovery, but also with the increased activity along the Gulf Coast, which is the preferred location but where appropriate locations for greenfield plants and export facilities are increasingly in short supply and demand premium prices. The plants that are about to begin construction are expected to cost significantly more than plants built five or six years ago (e.g., Kelley 2018). Ethane crackers in our database that have been completed or are in progress have an average cost of about $2600/t, according to company announcements, and, in some cases, reported cost after completion. Without expansion projects, the average increases to nearly $3000/t, and capital costs around the world can be much lower. The U.S. ethane price advantage will have to overcome this capital-cost disadvantage, perhaps with the help of synergistic opportunities available along the Gulf Coast that allow for integration across the value chain. Interestingly, China (as well as other countries) can import cheap U.S. ethane to be used as feedstock in crackers that can be built at a lower capital cost. Such developments and resulting cost competitiveness of alternative approaches deserve tracking over the next several years.

Considerations from Other Uses of Natural Gas

Methane supplies for methanol, fertilizer, and other industries such as feedstock have to compete with two sectors: U.S. power generation and LNG exporters. As discussed in Chap. 2, although the upside to gas burn for power generation is significant, it depends on many factors, including large amounts of coal, nuclear, and older gas-unit retirement in the near future. Without such retirement, gas-burn growth, albeit still notable, will be constrained by an increasing share of renewables. In this scenario, the power-sector gas burn may not lift the price of natural gas noticeably.

Before Covid-19, we expected U.S. LNG exports to increase by the early 2020s because the world seemed to be working through excess-liquefaction capacity faster than predicted.[15] As Andy Flower concludes in Chap. 4:

> the much talked about second wave of U.S. LNG exports has stalled as the developers of 176 mtpa of capacity, which has regulatory approval from the DOE and FERC, struggle to secure commitments from LNG buyers and off-takers, who are reluctant to make new long-term commitments in the aftermath of Covid-19, which has increased the uncertainty in the demand for natural gas in downstream power and natural gas markets.

Price sensitivity of many of the new importers (and risky credit ratings of some) and the flexibility introduced with floating storage regasification units and spot trading can easily undermine expectations. If oil prices recover and stabilize around $70/bbl, any increase in Henry Hub much above $3/MMBtu could render U.S. LNG less competitive, although most projections do not foresee such prices for natural gas in the future.[16] Finally, as discussed in Chap. 5, the future growth of natural gas demand in China and India, as well as other countries, depends heavily on their ability to build infrastructure and rationalize pricing. Otherwise, the main consumer of natural gas in many importing countries—power generation—will be under continuous pressure from nuclear, coal, and renewables. In the pre-Covid context, analysts' opinions were that U.S. LNG exports could increase significantly without triggering any repercussions for U.S. natural gas prices (examples are Bernstein et al. 2016; ICF 2017).[17] In the post-Covid context, slack demand for energy, including for LNG, could offset any price effects associated with competing demand for U.S. production and a rising Henry Hub marker.

Last, there are considerations arising from exports of NGLs, an alternative monetization pathway to U.S. downstream offtake. We point to capacity expansions for NGLs exports in earlier sections of this chapter. Export capacity expansions are recent and so facilities and shipping logistics are new, with imperatives for owners to maximize use of these assets. For instance, even with economic malaise from Covid-19, current outlooks are calling for robust demand from new ethane crackers in China as that country's industrial base recovers. Relative to anticipated flat ethane output (per the following section on upstream caveats) and in light of cost and timing for adjustments (to reduce ethane rejection, to substitute propane and naphtha for feedstocks or other solutions), the result is likely to be higher prices for ethane (Braziel 2020). If similar stories play out across other NGLs exports, the U.S. chemicals businesses could face margin squeezes if the prices for their products (ethylene, propylene, etc) do not keep up.

Upstream Considerations

As presented in Chap. 1, how much natural gas and NGLs can be supplied by U.S. producers, at what price, and over what timeframe, is worth considering further. As noted in that chapter, oil price is a key determinant for upstream drilling decisions, in particular to sustain the yield of low cost associated natural gas that is the byproduct of liquids. Although the resource base is large, low oil prices of 2015–2016 and from early 2019 to present, combined with persistently low natural gas prices since 2007, along with the extreme disruptions to the upstream segment posed by the pandemic, including bankruptcies and other threats, have undermined drilling activity not only in the United States but globally. While the cost of oilfield services has declined significantly in response, pulling down drilling and completion (D&C) costs, bankruptcies, and reductions in oil field service providers will eventually impact D&C expense. A persistent low-interest-rate environment provides some relief for heavily burdened U.S. producers but the underlying and deep economic recession is a harbinger of disarray in demand for fuels and feedstocks worldwide.

Pre pandemic, lenders began to demand capital discipline and some sign that U.S. producers could be profitable. In particular, investors wanted to see evidence of free cash flow available for drilling and that upstream operators would be less dependent upon external funding sources. As documented in Chap. 1, U.S. producers face enormous pressures to try to reduce spending on underperforming wells—not easy in tight oil and shale plays. Since 2014, oil price volatility and a suppressed Henry Hub forced upstream operators to focus on their best acreage and to hone acreage portfolios. Until early 2019, high grading helped to sustain and, in some locations, even grow liquid production. Going forward, the disarray across the upstream businesses encumbers heavily predictions of future incremental supply available for additional chemicals expansions and LNG exports.

Associated gas from liquid-rich locations has been, and most likely would remain, the cheapest and thus main increment of marketed natural gas available for industrial customers. As the best tight oil and liquids rich acreage becomes exhausted, operators will need to return to drilling locations in lower quality geology and dry gas areas. As such, going forward, the ability of the operators to control unit costs will be critical in supporting the petrochemical sector's global competitiveness. Although there seems to be sufficient NGLs production to feed the new downstream capacity that has been built and to support new capacity, industrial buyers of natural gas fuel and feedstock could face higher prices and a squeeze on margins if chemicals products remain cheap in a soft global economy. A restructured, consolidated and more disciplined upstream business segment will help secure long-term hydrocarbon supplies needed by various sectors of the economy. At risk could be the large and cheap surplus that resulted from the frenzy of financially unsustainable leasing and drilling.

Conclusion

Owing to increased supply of oil, gas, and NGLs from tight rock formations, the U.S. industrial sector has been going through a rebuilding phase, and investments in the petrochemical sector have been most significant. Ethylene manufacturing facilities, especially ethane-only crackers that are taking advantage of low-cost ethane in the United States, have been attracting the largest investments, especially when combined with derivative units of polyethylene. Methanol and fertilizer facilities that take methane as feedstock follow the ethylene plants in terms of investment. There is also capacity expansion in other facilities, such as chlor-alkali, other chemicals, and plastics. For the most part, these investments have taken advantage of the existing refining and petrochemical clusters along the U.S. Gulf Coast, especially in Texas and Louisiana. Because the U.S. market for production from these facilities is limited, easy access to export facilities is also a big benefit.

Some expect a second wave of expansion in the petrochemicals sector, especially in ethylene and its derivatives and, possibly, methanol. If the global demand for these products remains strong and the United States continues to have a cost advantage in terms of cheap ethane and methane feedstock relative to naphtha and other feeds around the world, the second wave will most likely materialize after 2025. But developers' interest and seriousness should begin appearing much sooner, given the lead time necessary to develop greenfield projects. Although the plants of the first wave, and any that might be built in a second wave, will contribute to natural gas and NGLs demand, there are commerciality risks, especially for later plants. In terms of incremental natural gas demand, an industrial renaissance remains less influential than power and LNG exports, contributing about 3–4 Bcf/d. The importance of the industrial sector in creating and anchoring offtake for NGLs and, hence, supporting U.S. upstream economics, should be acknowledged.

Commentary: A Historical Perspective by Barbara Shook[18]

Only engineers who run them, bankers who finance them, and tax assessors watching municipal revenues climb may get as excited as I do about the construction of a new petrochemical plant. Years of watching jobs in the petrochemical industry go overseas where feedstocks and salaries were cheaper made me wonder if I would ever see the industry swing back to the United States. Or would more plants continue to be dismantled and their jobs disappear?

Then the "shale gale" began blowing through the U.S. oil and gas patch in the early days of the century. The "winds" picked up slowly. The late George Mitchell and his engineers and geoscientists worked for decades to crack the code for extracting natural gas and associated NGLs first from the Barnett Shale region of North Texas. Service companies quickly spread the new processes throughout the industry. The decline in natural production in Texas that began in the early 1970s first slowed, then reversed.

By 2010, the chemical industry was deep into studies of the long-term viability of shale-based resources. Would the newly discovered gas and NGLs finds be large enough and of the necessary quality to support a new round of ethane-cracker construction? An ethane cracker is designed for a 40-year operating life, and depending on its size and configuration a greenfield project could cost between $2 billion and $10 billion. Would the feedstock and fuel meet the cost, quality, and availability criteria?

As press releases began to cross my desk at Energy Intelligence's Houston office around 2011, synapses in my brain that had not been fired in decades began to crackle. I started to focus on memories that had not come to the forefront in about six decades. Fact is, I can't remember when chemical plants, natural gas processing plants, and power plants were not a part of my life. Nonetheless, I hadn't thought about those days in

Hooker, Oklahoma, or Longview, Texas, since I was a small child even though I had worked in or around the industry all my adult life.

During my early days, my electrical engineer father worked for a company that specialized in power plant construction. In those times in the U.S. Midwest and Southwest, many of those projects were in the oil and gas industry. I may not had known exactly what kind of plant it was, but I learned the job probably had something to do with oil and gas.

Those were the days when states began implementing the original no-flaring laws for natural gas. The late Texas Railroad Commissioner William J. Murray led the effort in Texas. He began before World War II while still a young field engineer for the agency. Murray's estimates showed that as much as 2 billion cubic feet of natural gas per day were going up in smoke. Murray saw this as a waste of a natural resource and an economic resource. After his appointment to the Railroad Commission in 1947, he had the force of regulations behind him. Murray said later that producers "cussed me all the way to the bank," but Texas producers eliminate flaring. The recovered ethane and propane became the feedstock for a new industry—petrochemicals—and natural gas fueled the plants. The recovered hydrocarbons also led to the creation of number of natural gas and NGLs pipelines. One small South Texas gas pipeline grew into Coastal Corp., a major national integrated pipeline system. Founder and chairman, Oscar S. Wyatt Jr., once told a journalist that oil producers "would practically give you the gas" if a company would build a pipeline to get it.

The no-flaring laws took our family to Longview in East Texas in 1952. Eastman Chemicals was building an ethane cracker to take NGLs and natural gas then flared from the giant East Texas field. The resulting ethylene would be manufactured into a broad slate of plastics and consumer goods, which the company continues to do in 2018. Longview sat at the north end of the East Texas field, then the largest in the United States. When discovered in 1930, the field contained more than six billion barrels of light, sweet oil and helped the Allied Powers win World War II. How much natural gas it contained may never have been calculated. Billions, if not trillions, of cubic feet likely were flared.

My father was construction superintendent on the power plant at the Eastman project that would be fueled by natural gas from the giant field. He often would take me out to the job site (no Occupational Safety and Health Administration or OSHA in those days). From the seat of our 1948 Chevrolet truck, where he firmly directed me to stay, I watched the plant emerge out of the red East Texas dirt.

When I tell senior executives from major petrochemical companies about my ancient memories, a common reaction is: "Wow! You were there at the creation of the original industry!" And it is starting again.

The mammoth East Texas oil field—the original almost source of fuel and feedstock for Eastman Chemical's Texas Operations—has today almost played out. According to the company's website, Eastman Chemical is connected to its principal supply sources by seven pipelines, some of which are 200 miles long and extend to the Texas Gulf Coast. On average, the company ships nearly 10 million pounds per day of 40 different chemical products to its customers worldwide.

When I entered the oil and gas industry in the early 1970s, U.S. production was peaking and the Arab oil embargo was not far off. The subsequent high prices of the late 1970s and early 1980s brought good times to the U.S. oil patch, but not to the overall economy. And when the oil boom went bust, so did the economies of the producing states. The Texas economy improved sporadically in the 1990s and early part of the new century, but only after recovery from the Great Recession of 2008–09 began did the full impact of shale gas production register.

Texans noticed increased natural gas production first from the Barnett Shale located northwest of Fort Worth. Soon the U.S. was glutted, first with natural gas, then with NGLs. U.S. companies had been planning to import billions of cubic feet of LNG daily. Perhaps most incredibly, companies brought plants out of "mothball", and drew up plans for new facilities. Now, plans were developing for the U.S. to export a like volume. And, the U.S. was becoming the center of action in the global petrochemical world.

The excitement at the IHS Chemical Global Petrochemical Conference in 2012 was palpable. Most industry executives had never experienced such exhilaration and anticipation. By then developers had proposed seven world-scale crackers, six on the Gulf Coast and one in the Marcellus Shale. Upstream operators were producing so much ethane and propane that export terminals were in development. Only a few years earlier, the U.S. had been a major propane importer.

A year later, the excitement at the conference was even greater. Chevron Phillips Chemical was about to begin construction, and Exxon Mobil was awaiting its final permit. OxyChem had made a final investment decision and would be building by the end of 2014. Six other projects were in different points of the design and development process, four on the Gulf Coast, two in the Marcellus. All told, more than \$10 billion in new projects have been proposed for the United States, many by foreign companies keen to take advantage of low feedstock costs.

Not even Hurricane Harvey in 2017 could halt what has become the U.S. petroleum renaissance. Delay, yes, but not destroy. Chevron Phillips was knocked back almost six months, but it is up and running now. Exxon Mobil also suffered damaged that took several months to repair. Downstream derivative plants also suffered extensive damage and require much work to bring back on line.

The 2018 IHS Markit conference had a completely different tone. Times had been good, at least from a market perspective for several years and appeared likely to stay that way well into the future. What "black swan" event could change it? Would the Saudi's crude to chemicals effort be competitive with U.S. NGLs? What about trade issues? Petrochemical executives know that the business always has been cyclical and always will be.

Nothing seems to be slowing the overall U.S. "petrochemical renaissance." (Will the virus pandemic be a temporary setback?) Just a few months ago, Exxon Mobil and Saudi Arabia's Sabic agreed to go ahead with the largest ethane cracker project in the U.S., a 1.8 million pounds per year complex with derivative plants, near Corpus Christi, in South Texas. Cost: $10 billion.

For most people in the oil and gas patch, seeing the birth of any facet of the industry is at best a once in a lifetime experience. I have been lucky. I saw the U.S. petrochemical industry at its creation—and now its re-creation.

Notes

1. Braziel (2020) frames the issue of ethane rejection this way: "Ethane rejection is one of the main market mechanisms that determines the supply/demand balance for ethane. If ethane is worth more as gas at the processing plant, it is rejected from the plant's recovered stream and sold as natural gas. If it is recovered, it moves to a petrochemical plant (steam cracker) or export facility somewhere. Most crackers and the largest ethane export facilities are located along the Gulf Coast. As a general rule, the farther away ethane is from the Gulf Coast, the more it will cost to get it there, and the more expensive that ethane will be."
2. The plant broke ground in September 2019 ahead of the pandemic. See Freeman (2019).

3. Shell's project is an example of Covid-19 disruptions (Litvak 2020).
4. For detailed analyses of the Marcellus and other shale resources and economics, see the Bureau of Economic Geology's shale analysis at http://www.beg.utexas.edu/research/programs/shale
5. The International Monetary Fund (IMF) now calls it a crisis like no other. https://www.imf.org/en/Publications/WEO/Issues/2020/06/24/WEOUpdateJune2020
6. Y-grade or raw mix is the total volume of output from a processing plant, which is further split through refining or fractionation into the distinct NGLs products. A good public domain source for definitions and background is https://www.energy.gov/sites/prod/files/2017/12/f46/NGL%20Primer.pdf
7. Spreads, often referred to as basis differences or differentials, can be locational, between production and processing; financial, between spot and futures; or between co-products, such as methane and NGLs commodities ("frac" or fractionation spreads). Domestic operators have faced all of these risks at various times.
8. Background on the midstream segment can be found at https://www.beg.utexas.edu/files/cee/legacy/2016/CEE_Research_Snapshot_IsMidstreaminCrisis_Apr16.pdf
9. American Chemistry Council provides a more complete list of industrial projects that are advantaged by shale gas. As of the end of 2018, ACC reported more than 330 projects, with an announced value of more than $200 billion. See https://www.americanchemistry.com/Policy/Energy/Shale-Gas/Infographic-Shale-Gas-and-New-US-Chemical-Industry-Investment.pdf
10. These projects came under considerable stress with collapsing oil prices in 2015 and again in 2019. None of the projects captured in our database have moved forward. Proposed projects have been suspended or cancelled.
11. See https://www.americanchemistry.com/Infographic-Appalachian-Region-Hub.pdf
12. Daelim backed out of the project in July 2020 casting doubt on the endeavor (Burger 2020).
13. Blake Eskew, IHSMarkit, noted that petrochemicals demand typically grows in excess of GDP, since because they are used across the consumer and commercial sectors and are still continuing to benefiting from substitution for metals, paper, and other materials. As markets mature, growth is likely to decline back to the GDP level. "The major uncertainty now is the impact of new policies to address the plastic waste problem, which could reduce the overall demand growth and reduce feedstock growth due to recovery and recycling."
14. Comments from Steve Lewandowski, global business director of light olefins at IHS Markit.

15. Comments from Chap. 4 author, Andy Flower, during draft preparation.
16. As noted in Chap. 1, Chap. 2, and elsewhere in the book, traded natural gas (methane) at Henry Hub will be influenced by tight oil drilling and incremental supply of associated gas available to the market. The lower the level of tight oil drilling activity, especially in the Permian, the greater the propensity for HH prices to rise as the abundance of available natural gas for export diminishes. As well, natural gas-directed drilling in a less robust oil price environment will require a stronger HH price signal even in prolific areas like the Haynesville. Pipeline bottlenecks in Appalachia will continue to constrain supply from that region. Any/all of these conditions challenge LNG spreads relative to competing fuel oil and coal options and methane prices in receiving markets.
17. The U.S. Department of Energy, which issues LNG export permits including those to non-free trade agreement countries, also took this view. See https://www.energy.gov/sites/prod/files/2015/12/f27/20151113_macro_impact_of_lng_exports_0.pdf
18. Written on June 29, 2018.

References

Alvarado, M. 2017. Methanol industry overview: Stanford University natural gas initiative opportunities and challenges for methanol as a global liquid energy carrier meeting, Stanford, CA, July 31–August 1, 46 p. https://ngi.stanford.edu/sites/default/files/Alvarado_Stanford_Methanol_Meeting_2017.pdf

American Chemistry Council (ACC). 2019a. U.S. chemicals trade by the numbers. AmericanChemistry.com. https://www.americanchemistry.com/Policy/Trade/US-Chemicals-Trade-by-the-Numbers.pdf. Accessed 12 Dec 2019.

———. 2019b. ACC joins USMCA coalition with commitment to promote manufacturing growth. AmericanChemistry.com. https://www.americanchemistry.com/Media/PressReleasesTranscripts/ACC-news-releases/ACC-Joins-USMCA-Coalition-with-Commitment-to-Promote-Manufacturing-Growth.html. Accessed 12 Dec 2019.

———. 2019c. Appalachian region could become a petrochemicals & plastics manufacturing hub. AmericanChemistry.com. https://www.americanchemistry.com/Infographic-Appalachian-Region-Hub.pdf. Accessed 9 Jan 2020.

Bernstein, P., S.D. Tuladhar, and M. Yuan. 2016. Economics of U.S. natural gas exports: Should regulators limit U.S. LNG exports? *Energy Economics* 60: 427–437. https://doi.org/10.1016/j.eneco.2016.06.010.

Boswell, C. 2018. IHS Markit WPC 2018: Global ethylene capacity maxed-out through 2022. *Chemical Week*. https://chemweek.com/CW/Document/94489/IHS-Markit-WPC-2018-Global-ethylene-capacity-maxed-out-through-2022. Accessed 6 Dec 2019.

Braziel, D. 2020. Till you use me up—Ethane recovery must increase to meet demand. RBN Energy Daily Blog, August 10. Subscription or other access required. https://rbnenergy.com/til-you-use-me-up-ethane-recovery-must-increase-to-meet-demand. Accessed 1 Sept 2020.

Budde, F., O. Ezekoye, T. Hundertmark, M. Prieto, and T.J. Simons. 2017. Chemicals 2025: Will the industry be dancing to a very different tune? McKinsey & Company. https://www.mckinsey.com/industries/chemicals/our-insights/chemicals-2025-will-the-industry-be-dancing-to-a-very-different-tune. Accessed 6 Dec 2019.

Burger, B. 2020. Deputy U.S. energy secretary to visit, push petrochemical plant. *The Columbus Dispatch*, August 11. https://www.dispatch.com/news/20200811/deputy-us-energy-secretary-to-visit-push-petrochemical-plant

BusinessWire. 2018a. Appalachia development group announces engineering, procurement and construction partner for appalachia storage and trading hub. BusinessWire.com. https://www.businesswire.com/news/home/20180829005106/en/Appalachia-Development-Group-Announces-Engineering-Procurement-Construction. Accessed 9 Jan 2020.

———. 2018b. ADNOC announces US $45 billion investment plan to become leading global downstream player. BusinessWire.com. https://www.businesswire.com/news/home/20180513005054/en/ADNOC-Announces-45-Billion-Investment-Plan-Leading. Accessed 9 Jan 2020.

Cetinkaya, E., N. Liu, T.J. Simons, and J. Wallach. 2018. Petrochemicals 2030: Reinventing the way to win in a changing industry. McKinsey & Company. https://www.mckinsey.com/industries/chemicals/our-insights/petrochemicals-2030-reinventing-the-way-to-win-in-a-changing-industry. Accessed 6 Dec 2019.

Charlesworth, R. 2017. Direct oil and gas to ethylene—The search for the holy grail. In *Middle east refining technologies conference annual meeting*, Manama, Bahrain, January, 36 p. http://www.wraconferences.com/wp-content/uploads/2017/01/Direct-Oil-Gas-to-Ethylene-Advantageous-Technologies-or-False-Dawns-draft.pdf

Dina, T. 2017. North American petrochemical competitiveness: How long does the light olefins gravy train last? Pittsburgh Chemical Day, Pittsburgh, PA, October 3, 30 p. http://www.pittchemday.com/pdf/IHS%20Markit%20PittChem%20Day%20presentation%202017.pdf

Eskew, B. 2018. U.S. petrochemicals: The growing importance of export markets. In *EIA energy conference*, Washington, DC, June 4, 20 p. https://www.eia.gov/conference/2018/pdf/presentations/blake_eskew.pdf

Freeman, S. 2019. Exxon Mobil plant breaks ground. *Corpus Christi Business News*, September 19. https://www.ccbiznews.com/news/exxonmobil-plant-breaks-ground

ICF. 2017. Impact of LNG exports on the U.S. economy. A brief update: Report prepared for American Petroleum Institute, Washington, DC, 58 p. https://www.api.org/~/media/Files/Policy/LNG-Exports/API-LNG-Update-Report-20171003.pdf

Kelley, L. 2018. U.S. methanol boom in billion dollar investment phase. Independent Commodity Intelligence Services. https://www.icis.com/resources/news/2018/05/17/10222821/us-methanol-boom-in-billion-dollar-investment-phase/. Accessed 12 Dec 2019.

Lippe, D. 2018. U.S. ethane demand finally surges. *Oil & Gas Journal* 116 (6). https://www.ogj.com/refining-processing/petrochemicals/article/17232384/us-ethane-demand-finally-surges

Litvak, A. 2020. Shell to temporarily suspend construction at ethane cracker plant after days of pressure amid COVID-19. *Pittsburg Post-Gazette*, March 18. https://www.post-gazette.com/business/powersource/2020/03/18/Shell-reset-construction-ethane-cracker-plant-covid-19-contractors-unemployment-health-coronavirus/stories/202003180106. Accessed 25 Aug 2020.

Oil & Gas Journal (OGJ). 2018. Aramco, SABIC select location for crude-to-chemicals complex. OGJ.com. https://www.ogj.com/refining-processing/refining/capacities/article/17296221/aramco-sabic-select-location-for-crudetochemicals-complex. Accessed 9 Jan 2020.

Silverstein, K. 2020. Tensions with China are wounding West Virginia—The one state the president wanted to save. *Forbes*, June 1. https://www.forbes.com/sites/kensilverstein/2020/06/01/tensions-with-china-are-wounding-west-virginia%2D%2D-the-one-state-the-president-wanted-to-save/#2cd693567bc1. Accessed 25 Aug 2020.

U.S. Department of Energy (DOE). 2018. *Natural gas liquids primer with a focus on the Appalachian region*. Washington, DC: U.S. Department of Energy, 48 p. https://www.energy.gov/sites/prod/files/2018/06/f53/NGL_Primer.pdf

U.S. Energy Information Administration (EIA). 1991–2014. Manufacturing Energy Consumption Survey (MECS). EIA.gov. https://www.eia.gov/consumption/manufacturing/index.php. Accessed 12 Dec 2019.

———. 2019a. *Annual energy outlook 2019 with projections to 2050*. Washington, DC: U.S. Department of Energy, 165 p. https://www.eia.gov/outlooks/aeo/

———. 2019b. Reference case projections tables. EIA.gov. https://www.eia.gov/outlooks/aeo/tables_ref.php. Accessed 9 Jan 2020.

———. 2020. Petroleum & other liquids—Natural gas plant field production. EIA.gov. https://www.eia.gov/dnav/pet/pet_pnp_gp_a_EPL2_FPF_mbbl_m.htm. Accessed 18 Aug 2020.

WoodMackenzie. 2018. The emergence of new ethylene powerhouses. WoodMackenzie. https://www.woodmac.com/news/editorial/the-emergence-of-new-ethylene-powerhouses. Accessed 12 Dec 2019.

CHAPTER 4

LNG in the Global Context

Andy Flower

Introduction

The 2000s has seen the U.S. play an important role in the global liquefied natural gas (LNG) market. In the first decade, the U.S. was expected to be the main growth market for LNG imports. Forecasts of growing demand for imported LNG in the U.S. were based on expectations that domestic natural gas production would decline, and imports by pipeline from Canada would fall as more of its production was used to meet growing domestic demand. Observers thought that the U.S. could potentially overtake Japan as the world's largest importer in the 2015–2020 time frame.

Natural gas pipeline companies and utilities had built four receiving terminals in the 1970s and early 1980s in response to earlier outlooks for LNG imports (see the Appendix for a flavor of the U.S. gas policy and politics during this era). With gas production growth in the early to mid-1990s, two of the legacy facilities (Cove Point in Maryland and Elba Island in Georgia) were mothballed from the early 1980s until 2001, and Lake Charles in Louisiana had operated well below capacity. The fourth and

A. Flower (✉)
Independent Consultant, Surrey, UK

M. Michot Foss et al. (eds.), *Monetizing Natural Gas in the New "New Deal" Economy*,
https://doi.org/10.1007/978-3-030-59983-6_4

oldest, in Everett, Massachusetts, had been in continuous service to provide peaking fuel for the New England winters.

By the end of the 1990s, stronger economic growth and diminished gas supply—because low oil and gas prices discouraged drilling—began to show up in higher prices and price shocks (see Chap. 1). In the early 2000s, plans to expand three of the existing U.S. terminals and to develop greenfield import terminals were supported by the expected increase in new LNG supply in the Atlantic Basin and the Middle East. The U.S. had become a target market for much of this proposed new liquefaction capacity. By 2005–2006, proposals had been made for around 50 new terminals. Eight were built, including three offshore facilities using ships to store and regasify LNG.

However, the same natural gas price events during the early 2000s that spurred new LNG receiving capacity development also encouraged new drilling, in particular from the major shale plays. By 2008, as new receiving terminal capacity began to be commissioned, gas supply growth had gathered pace. It became clear that the U.S. not only did not need imported LNG but also would soon have surplus natural gas production available for export. By the end of the first decade, the additive effect of higher oil prices and migration of the U.S. domestic industry to liquids-rich plays induced a burst of associated natural gas production. These tranches of prolific supply growth cemented views that the industry needed to position strategically for exports.

The owners of the import terminals that had been built or were under construction were left with stranded assets, which were no longer required for LNG imports. Cheniere Energy was the first to see the opportunity to convert the import terminals into export plants, using existing storage tanks, jetties, and berths and adding liquefaction trains. The owners of all the LNG import terminals—with the exception of those using ships as floating storage and regasification units (FSRUs, which can be redeployed to other markets) and the terminal in Everett, Massachusetts—have converted, or are planning to convert, their facilities to liquefaction plants. Roughly as many proposals have been made for the development of greenfield liquefaction plants as were for new receiving capacity. Some are on sites previously planned for receiving terminals.

The impact of U.S. LNG derives not only from the amount of product supplied into the global market. U.S. LNG developers also are transforming LNG business models. The pricing structures and contractual arrangements being used for U.S. projects differ greatly from those that have been used for projects elsewhere in the world. For many buyers or off-takers, the price of U.S. LNG loaded onto a ship at the liquefaction plant comprises the cost of natural gas supplied to the plant and a liquefaction fee. As a result, the price of LNG is linked to the cost of natural gas delivered to the liquefaction plant (in many cases the Henry Hub price is used) rather than to oil prices. Furthermore, there are no restrictions on destinations to which U.S. LNG can be delivered, giving buyers and off-takers greater flexibility to manage demand uncertainty than they would have got under traditional sale and purchase agreements (SPAs). The contracts also provide for buyers and off-takers to cancel cargoes at relatively short notice (two months or less); the buyer or off-taker has to pay the liquefaction fee, but not the cost of natural gas that would have been supplied to the plant.

After an initial surge of interest from buyers between 2011 and 2013,[1] when high oil prices made the U.S. appear to be a significantly lower-priced source of LNG supply than oil-indexed product, commitments to U.S. output slowed. The start-up of projects that took FID between 2012 and 2015 has contributed to an oversupplied LNG market. U.S. developers, needing to secure commitments to planned output (required to underpin investment), have faced strong competition from planned developments in other countries including Canada, Mozambique, Papua New Guinea, Russia, and Australia.

In 2020, the Covid-19 pandemic, along with lockdowns imposed by governments to control the spread of the virus and associated economic dislocation, has increased uncertainty for LNG importers. Many are unwilling to make commitments to new supply until natural gas demand recovers for power generation and in downstream markets. Buyers and off-takers also have opted to cancel large numbers of U.S. cargoes, slowing down the growth of U.S. LNG production in 2020.

The impact of the Covid-19 pandemic on global LNG demand and prices led to the U.S. becoming a swing LNG producer in 2020. Companies committed to purchase or off-take U.S. LNG have used the terms of their SPAs and tolling agreements to cancel large numbers of cargoes because spot prices in Asia and Europe do not cover short-run marginal costs. Uncertainties about LNG demand also have put on hold final investment decisions (FIDs) for over 170 Mtpa of U.S. LNG projects, which have export permits from the U.S. Department of Energy (DOE)[2] and regulatory approvals from the Federal Energy Regulatory Commission (FERC). All but one of the FIDs targeted for U.S. projects in 2020 have been delayed to 2021 or later.[3] These delays will slow what is often referred to as the "second wave" of U.S. LNG export capacity.

With six export plants in operation as of August 2020, the U.S. had become the world's third-largest LNG producer. As production from the plants in operation builds up to full capacity and projects under construction are commissioned, and barring countervailing events, the U.S. could be on course to overtake Qatar and Australia to become the world's largest LNG producer and exporter by the mid-2020s. The question going forward is whether the U.S. LNG export businesses can remain on that fast track.

LNG Supply in August 2020

Projects in Operation

In August 2020, a total of 20 countries were exporting LNG. The number excludes Yemen, where liquefaction has been offline since April 2015 because of the civil war in the country. The total installed capacity in these 20 countries is an estimated 435.3 Mtpa. The Pacific Basin region had the most plants in operation and largest installed capacity in August 2020, with 170.1 Mtpa, followed by the Atlantic Basin, with 154.2 Mtpa (excluding the 5 Mtpa capacity SEGAS plant in Egypt, which has been out of action since December 2012 because of a lack of natural gas supply); the Middle East has 95.3 Mtpa in operation, and the Arctic region, where three-train Yamal LNG plant is in operation in Russia, has 17.5 Mtpa of capacity in operation.

However, with production from plants commissioned in late 2019 and the first seven months of 2020 building up to full capacity and natural gas supply shortfalls constraining production at plants in Algeria, Trinidad and Tobago, and Indonesia, available capacity was around 400 Mtpa in mid-2020. Global LNG production was 357.2 mt in 2019, which represented an 85% utilization of the capacity available during the year.

Qatar, which has installed capacity of 77.5 Mtpa at its Qatargas and RasGas plants, was the largest LNG producer in the world in 2019, with exports of 79.5 mt. Australia, which has 11 liquefaction plants in operation and a total capacity of 83.3 Mtpa, followed Qatar with 76.0 mt of production, an increase of 8.6 mt (12.8%) over 2018, attributable to production build-up from newly commissioned trains.

The U.S. was the third-largest LNG producer in 2019, with output of 35 mt. At the end of 2019, the U.S. had six LNG export plants in operation: Sabine Pass in Louisiana (five trains in operation), Corpus Christi in Texas (two trains), the single-train Cove Point plant in Maryland, Freeport LNG in Texas (two trains), Cameron LNG in Louisiana (one train), and two small-scale (0.25 Mtpa capacity) trains at Elba Island in Georgia. In the first seven months of 2020, two trains at Cameron LNG and one train at Freeport LNG, plus six more small-scale trains at Elba Island, were commissioned, taking the U.S. liquefaction capacity in operation to 69.4 Mtpa at the end of July 2020.

Argentina became the world's newest LNG exporter in 2019, when the Tango LNG floating liquefaction barge, which has been chartered by YPF from the Belgian shipping company, Exmar, for ten years, produced a first partial cargo in June of that year.[4] The barge, which has a capacity of 0.5 Mtpa and can store 16,100 m^3 of LNG, was originally built for an export project in Colombia, which was abandoned before the barge left the yard. It was moored at a berth in the port of Bahia Blanca, which was previously used by an FSRU importing LNG. Shale gas production from Argentina's Vaca Muerta region had led to the country having surplus natural gas production, especially during the summer months when demand is low. However, in June 2020, YPF sent a force majeure notice to the owner of Exmar, stating that is was unable to pay for the charter of the barge because of Covid-19. Exmar responded that the declaration of force majeure was "unlawful", but operations have ceased.[5]

Forecast Supply 2020–2035 from Projects in Operation in August 2020

At the end of 2019, before Covid-19 became a global pandemic, LNG supply was expected to increase by around 34 mt in 2020 taking it to 390 mt, as the production from projects commissioned in 2019 built up to full capacity and more projects were commissioned in 2020. It was assumed that the main growth markets for the additional output would be in China, South Asia, and Southeast Asia, while Europe would continue to act as the balancing market for any LNG not required by these markets or by markets in the Middle East and North Africa (MENA) and the Americas.

However, the outlook has dramatically changed as a result of the Covid-19 pandemic. Lower demand in key markets, where there have been lockdowns to control the spread of the virus, has slowed down the economic activity and has put downward pressure on prices, which, in mid-2020, fell to levels that no longer covered the short-run marginal costs of producing and transporting LNG to market, resulting in the cancellation of U.S. cargoes and producers in other parts of the world shutting-in capacity. Forecasts of production from liquefaction projects have had to be revised downward for 2020 and 2021. I have assumed that projects now in operation will return to operating at full capacity by 2022, provided the virus is under control by then. On this basis, production from projects in operation in August 2020 is forecast to increase from 357 mt in 2019 to 362 mt in 2020 and to 396 mt in 2024. Thereafter, output from these projects is forecast to decline steadily to 393 mt in 2025, 367 mt in 2030, and 338 mt in 2035 as liquefaction plants are shut down because facilities reach the age where continued production is no longer economic or as production is reduced because of a shortage of natural gas supply.

Liquefaction Capacity Under Construction in August 2020

In August 2020, a total of 102.4 Mtpa of liquefaction capacity was under construction globally. Table 4.1 lists these projects and shows when they are expected to start up. There are 14 large-scale onshore trains with

Table 4.1 Liquefaction capacity under construction in August 2020

Country	*Project*	*Capacity in Mtpa*	*Expected start-up*
Malaysia	Floating LNG Unit 2	1.5	4Q20
U.S.	Elba Island Trains 9–10	0.5	Oct-20
U.S.	Corpus Christi Train 3	4.8	1H21
U.S.	Sabine Pass Train 6	4.8	2H22
U.S.	Calcasieu Pass	10.0	1H23
U.S.	Golden Pass Trains 1–3	15.6	2024
Russia	Yamal Train 4	1.0	End-20
Russia	Arctic 2 LNG Trains 1–3	19.8	2H23
Canada	LNG Canada	14.0	Mid-24
Indonesia	Tangguh Train 3	3.8	1H22
Mozambique	Coral FLNG	3.4	2H22
Mozambique	Mozambique LNG Trains 1 and 2	13.1	mid-24
Mauritania/Senegal	Tortue LNG	2.5	1H23
Nigeria	Nigeria LNG Train 7	7.6	2H25
	Total	**102.4**	

Source: Author's proprietary database

capacities between 3.8 Mtpa and 7 Mtpa, 21 small-scale onshore trains with capacities ranging from 0.25 Mtpa (at Elba Island, Georgia, in the U.S.) to 1 Mtpa (Yamal LNG Train 4 in Russia), and three FLNG units with capacities between 1.5 Mtpa and 3.4 Mtpa.

The U.S. has 35.7 Mtpa of capacity under construction, which is 35% of the global total; Russia has 20.8 Mtpa (20%), and Mozambique has 16.5 Mtpa (16%). During the last four months of 2020, only 3 Mtpa of capacity (Russia's Yamal Train 4, the final two trains at Elba Island and Malaysia's second FLNG unit) is scheduled to start-up. Cheniere Energy's Corpus Christi Train 3 is the only project scheduled to start in 2021, but the commissioning of new capacity will gather pace from 2022. All the capacity under construction is scheduled to be in operation by the end of 2026, and full production of 102.4 Mtpa should be reached by 2027 or 2028.

Over the five-year period 2011–2015, FIDs were taken on an average of 25.4 Mtpa per year (Fig. 4.1). The fall in oil and LNG prices in mid-2014 led to a slowdown in new FIDs in 2016 and 2017, when commitments were made to only three projects with a total capacity of 9.7 Mtpa. For many of the planned projects, a barrier to taking FID was the failure to secure the new long-term commitments for the output that were needed to underpin the financing of the capacity.

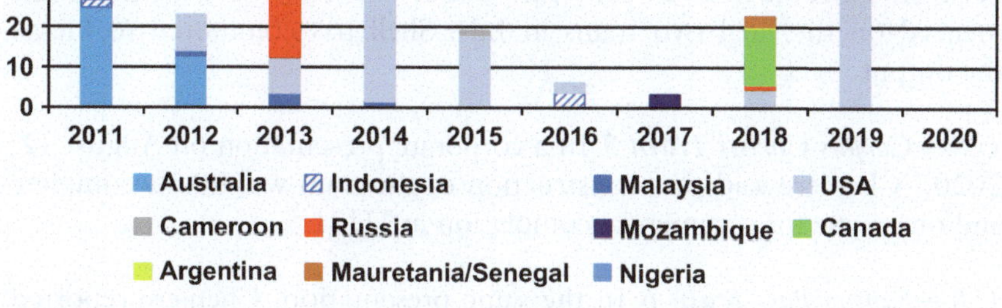

Fig. 4.1 Final investment decisions (FIDs) on liquefaction capacity, 2011–August 2020. (Source: Author's estimates)

In 2018, FIDs were taken on five new projects, with a total capacity of 22.8 Mtpa: small-scale units in Russia (Yamal LNG Train 4) and Argentina (Tango LNG unit), a third train at Cheniere's Corpus Christi plant, the Tortue FLNG on the maritime border between Mauritania and Senegal, and LNG Canada. In 2019, FIDs were taken on 71.1 Mtpa of capacity, a record for a single year, surpassing the total in 2005 when decisions were made on 50 Mtpa of capacity, including four 7.8 Mtpa mega-trains in Qatar.

The decisions taken in 2019 included 30.4 Mtpa of capacity in the U.S., through the sixth train at Sabine Pass (4.8 Mtpa) in Louisiana, Golden Pass LNG in Texas (15.6 Mtpa), and Calcasieu Pass in Louisiana (10 Mtpa). Commitments were also made to Mozambique LNG (13.1 Mtpa) and to Arctic 2 LNG in Russia (19.8 Mtpa), Novatek's second major project in the Arctic region. In December 2019, Nigeria LNG announced the go-ahead for its Train 7 project, which includes the debottlenecking of the existing six trains. No FIDs were taken in the first eight months of 2020.

Progress of Projects Under Construction

Malaysia—Floating Liquefaction Unit 2 Petronas's second floating liquefaction unit left the Samsung yard in South Korea in February 2020 and is now on location at the Rotan field, offshore Sabah.[6] In its first quarter 2020 results announcement, Petronas said that start-up is expected by the end of 2020. The output will be marketed by Petronas as part of its LNG sales portfolio.

U.S.—Elba Island The first eight 0.25 Mtpa trains were commissioned between November 2019 and July 2020, and start-up activities commenced on the final two trains in July. Shell has committed to lift all the output.

U.S.—Corpus Christi Train 3 In a corporate presentation on August 12, 2020,[7] Cheniere said that construction of the train was 90.5% complete and on course for commercial completion in 1H21.

U.S.—Sabine Pass Train 6 In the same presentation, Cheniere reported that construction was 63.9% complete, with commercial completion expected in 2H22.

U.S.—Golden Pass Qatar Petroleum (QP) (70%) and ExxonMobil (30%) took FID in February 2019 on the conversion of their Golden Pass receiving terminal to a liquefaction plant, which will have three 5.2-Mtpa trains. The output is being marketed by Ocean LNG, a joint venture LNG marketing company owned by the project partners.

U.S.—Calcasieu Pass In August 2019, Venture Global took FID on the 10 Mtpa Calcasieu Pass project in Louisiana.[8] Contracts have been secured for 8 Mtpa of output: from Shell (2 Mtpa), BP (2 Mtpa), Italy's Edison (1 Mtpa), Portugal's GALP (1 Mtpa), Poland's PGNiG (1 Mtpa), and Spain's Repsol (1 Mtpa). The plant will have eighteen 0.626 Mtpa trains arranged in nine blocks of two trains each, giving it a total capacity of 11.27 Mtpa, which means that there is clearly the potential for it to operate significantly above the nominal capacity. The trains are being built in a Baker Hughes facility near Florence in Italy and will be shipped to the site. Speaking at CWC/dmg's Japan LNG and Gas Summit in early July, Venture Global's Chief Commercial Officer, Tom Earl, said that construction had not been affected by Covid-19 and was on schedule for start-up in late 2022. The roof has been raised on the two storage tanks, and the first two cold boxes were delivered to the site by Chart Industries, four months ahead of schedule. He added that construction of the first of the trains had been completed in Italy.

Russia—Yamal LNG Train 4 When Novatek took FID on the 1 Mtpa train, which will test a Russian liquefaction technology called "Arctic Cascade", start-up was expected by the end of 2019. However, it has been delayed until "around the end of 2020", because of "technical problems with pipelines that are not designed for the extreme temperatures in the area".[9]

Russia—Arctic 2 LNG The 19.8 Mtpa Arctic 2 liquefaction project will have three liquefaction trains on gravity-based structures that are being constructed in a purpose-built yard in the Murmansk region. Start-up of the trains is scheduled in 2023, 2024, and 2026, respectively.[10] There have been cases of Covid-19 at the construction site, but, in June 2002, Novatek said that the outbreak has been brought under control and has not affected the schedule. Novatek has a 60% share in the project, and its partners, each with a 10% share, are Total, CNPC, CNOOC, and Japan Arctic LNG (Mitsui and JOGMEC). The partners will lift and market their equity shares of the output.

Indonesia—Tangguh Train 3 When FID was taken in mid-2016, the start-up was scheduled for mid-2020. However, in July 2019, it was announced that start-up had been delayed by 12 months, to 3Q21, because natural disasters across Indonesia had delayed shipments of materials and financial difficulties faced by a contractor had also hampered progress. Start-up has been further delayed because of Covid-19 and is now scheduled in the first half of 2022.[11]

Mozambique—Coral LNG Construction of the 3.4 Mtpa FLNG unit, which will be supplied with natural gas from the Eni-operated Block 4 offshore Mozambique, is reported to be still progressing on schedule for it to leave the Samsung yard in South Korea, as planned, in 2021 and for production to commence in mid-2022.[12] The hull was launched in January 2020, and work on installing the modules has started. BP has contracted to lift and market all the output from the unit.

Mozambique LNG FID was taken on the $20 billion, 13.1 Mtpa Mozambique LNG project in June 2020.[13] In the months leading up to the decision, Anadarko, the operator, was the target in a takeover battle between Chevron and Occidental. It was eventually won by Occidental, which was mainly interested in Anadarko's upstream assets in the U.S. It did a deal for Total to acquire Anadarko's African assets, including its 26.5% share in Mozambique LNG, and Total is now the operator of the project. Total announced in mid-July 2020 that it had signed loan agreements for US$14.9 billion for the project.[14] The loans are from 8 export credit agencies (ECAs), 19 commercial banks, and the African Development Bank. Start of production is targeted in 2024.

Total had to quarantine the site because of cases of Covid-19 in April 2020, and Islamic insurgency in Cabo Delgado province, where the plant is located, is a potential threat to the progress of construction. In August 2020, Total signed an agreement with the Government of Mozambique for security to be increased at the site.

Total's partners in the project are ENH, Mozambique's national oil company, (15%); Japan's Mitsui (20%); Indian companies ONGC (10%), Oil India (10%), and Bharat Petroleum (10%); and Thailand's PTTEP (8.5%). Eight LNG SPAs have been signed with buyers in Japan, China, India, Indonesia, Taiwan, and the UK, with Shell and with EDF Trading. The duration of contracts is reported to be from 13 years to 20 years, and several ways of pricing the LNG have been used—JLC (Japanese LNG

Cocktail—the average price of LNG imported into Japan), oil indexation with Brent, the UK's NBP, and the Netherlands' TTF. Two of the contracts are with joint buyers from different countries. This will allow cargoes to be switched between destinations depending on demand. The joint contract with Tokyo Gas and the UK's Centrica is unique since it involves buyers from Europe and Asia, who can take advantage of the project's location approximately equidistant from both markets.

Canada—LNG Canada When it announced FID in October 2018, Shell said the project was expected to be in operation by 2025.[15] This suggested a construction period of six to seven years, which was longer than would normally be expected for a liquefaction project, even in the relatively remote location in Kitimat in northwest British Columbia. However, the number of workers on the site was reduced by 65% after cases of Covid-19 were found on the site. Shell said that only non-time critical work was affected. TC Energy, which is constructing the 670 km Coastal Link pipeline from the reserves on the British Columbia/Alberta border, has reported that construction is on schedule. Agreement has been reached with all the First Nations on the route, some of whom had objected to construction.

The joint venture, partners Shell (40%), Petronas (25%), PetroChina (15%), Korea Gas (5%), and Mitsubishi (15%), will lift and market their equity shares of the output. Petronas and Mitsubishi have announced preliminary contracts for the sale of part of their share of the output.

Mauritania/Senegal—Tortue LNG In December 2018, FID was taken on the project, which will be supplied with natural gas from deep-water reserves in the Greater Tortue–Ahmeyim fields that straddle the maritime border between Mauritania and Senegal in West Africa. A Golar LNG ship, which came into service in 1976, is being converted to an FLNG unit, using the same design as the unit now in operation in Cameroon. The unit will have a capacity of 2.5 Mtpa and will moor at a purpose-built berth close to shore. First gas was targeted for the first half of 2022, but in April 2020, BP issued a force majeure notice to Golar, because Covid-19 had slowed work on the construction of a breakwater during the 2020 time-critical weather window, delaying the start-up of the project by around 12 months.[16] BP has committed to purchasing the entire output from the project on a free-on-board (FOB) basis.

Nigeria LNG Train 7 The final FID in 2019 was in the last days of December when commitment was announced to a 7.6 Mtpa expansion of the 22.2 Mtpa plant.[17] The additional capacity will be from a 4 Mtpa seventh train, with the other 3.6 Mtpa through debottlenecking the existing six trains. The announcement in December appears to have been premature since it was not until May 2020 that Shell announced that it had taken FID.[18] A consortium of Saipem, Chiyoda, and Daewoo has been awarded the Engineer, Procure and Construct (EPC) contract for project, which is referred to as "train 7" despite it being partially a debottlenecking of existing trains. Production is scheduled to commence in 2025, but the start of work is reported to have been delayed, so the schedule may slip.[19] The project's foreign partners, Shell, Total, and Eni, are expected to lift and market the output.

Forecast of Incremental Supply 2020–2035 from Liquefaction Capacity in Operation and Under Construction

Growth in LNG supply over the period to the mid-2020s will be mainly from the 102.4 Mtpa of liquefaction capacity under construction in August 2020, because it typically takes around four years to construct new liquefaction trains, plus a further 6–12 months for production to build up to full capacity. However, there is additional uncertainty over the build-up of production from these projects because of the impact of Covid-19 on the progress of construction. Several sites have had cases of Covid-19 in the first half of 2020, which has required the number of workers on site to be reduced.

Operators have to institute health checks and modify work practices, such as deep-cleaning equipment between shifts, to ensure the safety of their workforce. In addition, the virus will also have an impact on the transfer workers to and from sites, especially in remote locations, because of travel restrictions and fewer flights operating. Two projects under construction have already announced delays of up to 12 months in start-up because of Covid-19 (Fig. 4.2).

Pre-Covid LNG supply was forecast to increase by 34 mt in 2020, as output from trains commissioned in 2019 built up to full capacity and more trains were commissioned. The increase in supply was expected to slow to 14 mt in 2021 and 4.9 mt in 2022, because commitments were

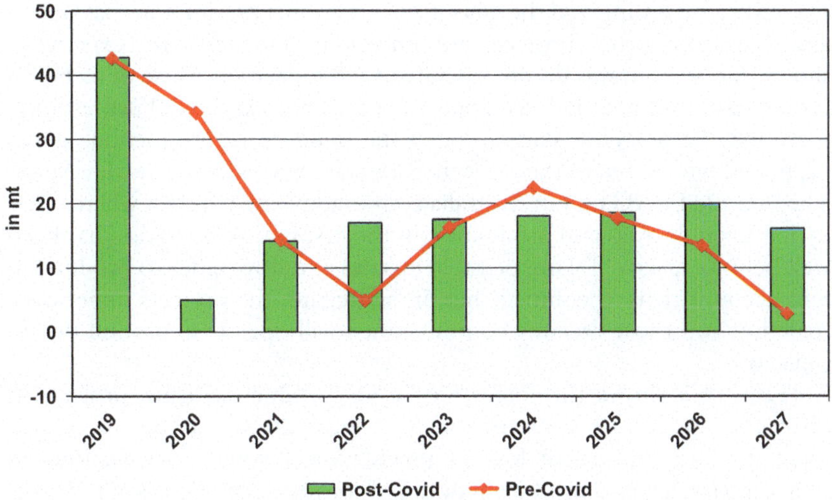

Fig. 4.2 Incremental LNG supply in the period 2019–2027 from projects in operation and under construction in August 2020; pre-Covid and post-Covid forecasts. (Source: Author's estimates)

made to a total of only 9.3 Mtpa of capacity in 2016 and 2017. Incremental supply growth was expected to accelerate from 2023 as projects on which FID was taken in late 2018 and in 2019 come on stream.

The post-Covid supply profile is very different. Low prices, slower demand growth, and U.S. cancellations will restrict the increase in incremental supply to a forecast 5 mt in 2020, but, on the assumption that the pandemic is brought under control in 2021 and the global economy returns to growth, LNG supply is forecast to increase by between 14 and 20 mt each year between 2021 and 2026.

Some of the new trains may operate above their design capacities, and output could, in some projects, be further increased through debottlenecking. This could add up to 20 Mtpa to output by the late 2020s, if it is assumed that all the new projects under construction and those commissioned in 2018, 2019, and the first six months of 2020 operate at 10% above design capacity. This has been achieved by some projects in recent years, including Cheniere which has increased the "run rate" capacity on its trains from the original 4.3–4.6 Mtpa to the current 4.7–5.0 Mtpa.[20]

However, the timing and the amount of additional production that will be available from other projects are uncertain. Furthermore, experience shows that some trains do not operate at full capacity because of technical problems or lower natural gas supply than had been expected. Furthermore, there may be delays in start-up or in the build-up of production, as has happened with some of the projects commissioned over the last few years. The Prelude FLNG unit in Australia is an example of a project where start-up has been delayed and production in the first year of operation has been well below capacity. Taking possible upsides and downsides to production into account, I have assumed that, in aggregate, the projects under construction and those recently commissioned will operate at around design capacity.

Figure 4.3 shows the forecast of LNG production from projects in operation and under construction in August 2020 and the pre-Covid forecast. The cumulative loss of production through cancellations of U.S. cargoes, lower output from non-U.S. projects, and delays in the projects under construction is approximately 160 mt.

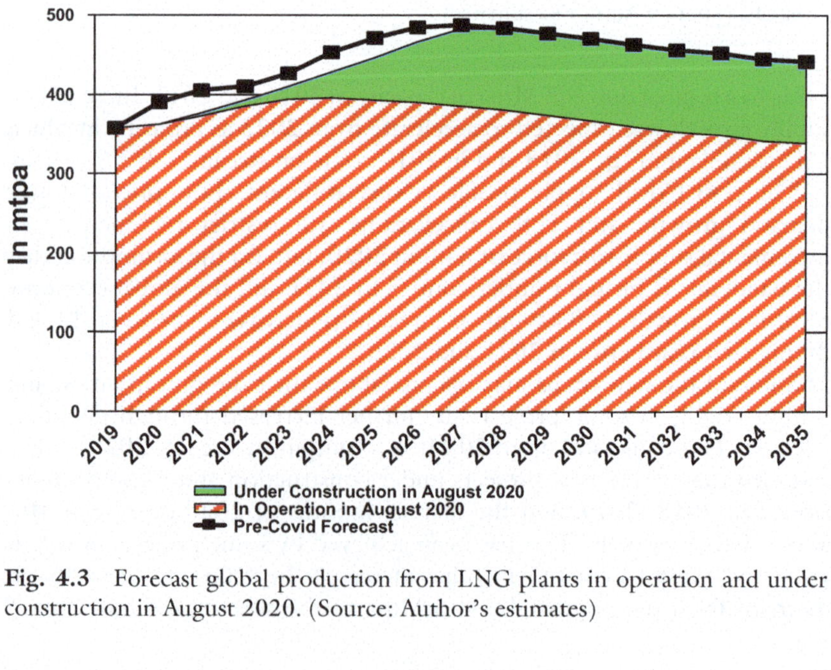

Fig. 4.3 Forecast global production from LNG plants in operation and under construction in August 2020. (Source: Author's estimates)

LNG Production from Projects in Operation and Under Construction in the U.S.

Six projects were operating in the U.S. in August 2020—five trains at Cheniere Energy's Sabine Pass plant in Louisiana, Dominion's 5.3 Mtpa, single-train plant at Cove Point in Maryland, two trains at Cheniere's Corpus Christi plant in Texas, three trains at both Cameron LNG in Louisiana and Freeport LNG in Texas, and eight small-scale trains at Elba Island. In 2019, a total of 35 mt was delivered to markets around the world from these projects, an increase of 14.5 mt over 2018. The expansion of U.S. liquefaction was, before Covid, expected to gather pace in 2020 and 2021 as output built up from newly commissioned trains. However, the cancellations of cargoes by buyers and off-takers, which started in April 2020, mean that the increase in output in 2020 will be significantly lower than originally expected. It is estimated that around 60 cargoes (3.9 mt) were cancelled in the second quarter of the year, with around 125 cargoes (8.2 mt) cancelled in the third quarter. The number of cancellations is expected to be lower in the fourth quarter as spot prices in Europe and Asia increase but, overall, U.S. exports are expected to increase by 6.8 mt in 2020 (Fig. 4.4), compared with forecast 24 mt at the start of the year.

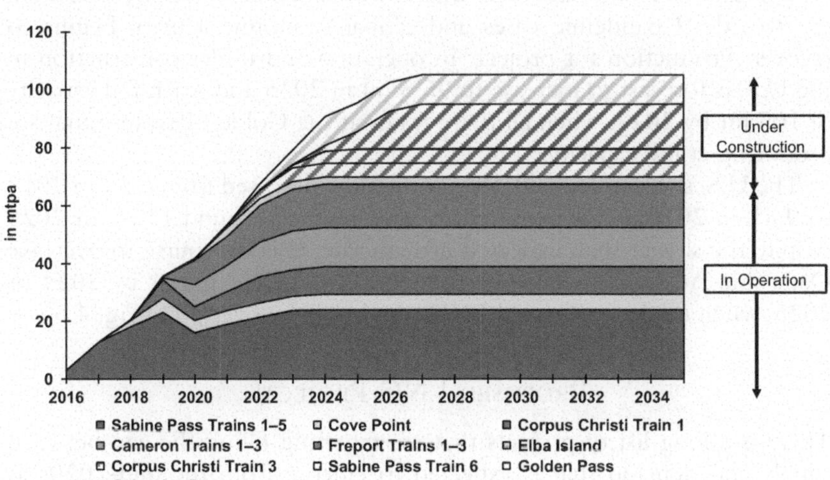

Fig. 4.4 Forecast production from U.S. LNG plants in operation and under construction in August 2020. (Source: Author's estimates)

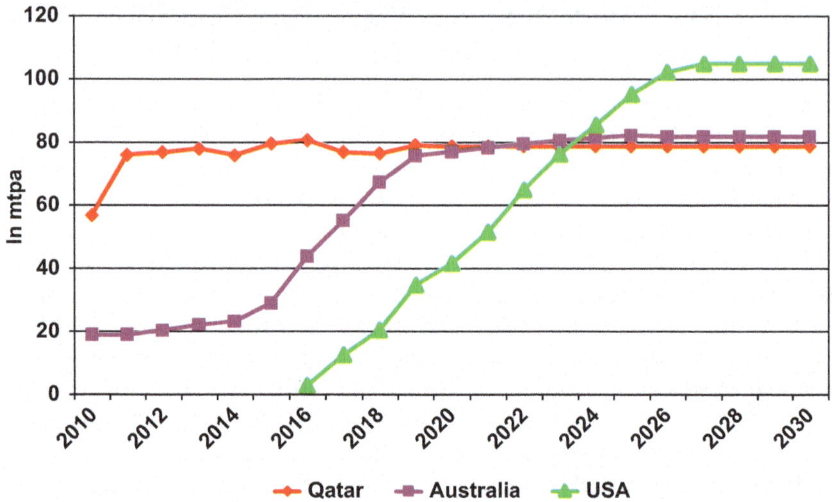

Fig. 4.5 LNG exports from Qatar, Australia, and the U.S., 2010–2030. (Source: Author's estimates)

The growth in U.S. LNG production will accelerate in 2021, provided the Covid-19 pandemic eases and global economic activity begins to recover. Production for projects in operation and under construction in the U.S. is forecast to increase to 95.5 mt in 2025 and reach full capacity of 105 mt by 2027, when all three trains at the Golden Pass terminal are producing at full capacity.

The U.S. share of global LNG production increased from 6.5% in 2018 to 9.8% in 2019 and is expected to have reached around 11.5% in 2020 despite the slower than expected growth rate. It is on course to overtake Qatar and Australia to become the world's largest exporter by 2024 or 2025, when its share of world LNG supply will be over 20% (Fig. 4.5).

Proposed LNG Projects

There is a long list of projects that are targeting filling the gap between supply and demand that is expected to emerge from the mid-2020s as LNG demand grows. In August 2020, proposals had been made for the development of projects with an estimated total capacity of 484 Mtpa (Table 4.2), of which just over 50% is in the U.S.

Table 4.2 Global liquefaction capacity, August 2020

	Capacity in Mtpa		
Country	*In operation*	*Under construction*	*Proposed*
USA	69.4	35.7	245
Canada	–	14.0	52
Mexico	–	–	25
East Africa	–	16.5	50
Australia	87.3	–	5
Qatar	77.0	–	49
Russia	28.5	20.8	30
Rest of Atlantic Basin	84.8	10.1	10
Rest of Pacific Basin	71.8	5.3	18
Rest of the Middle East	16.5	–	–
Total	**435.3**	**102.4**	**484**

Source: Author's proprietary database

The status of the proposed projects ranges from those with most of the requirements to take FID in place, including completion of front-end engineering design (FEED) and having secured regulatory approvals, to those at an early stage in the planning process. Consequently, the aggregate proposed capacity of 484 Mtpa should be considered indicative of intent rather than a forecast of the liquefaction capacity that will eventually be built.

At the beginning of 2020, the developers of 202.1 Mtpa of proposed capacity, 42% of the total shown in Table 4.2, said they are targeting FID in 2020. It was always unlikely that all the targeted FIDs will be achieved, given the success rate over the last decade when, on average, FID had been taken on around 30% of the targeted volume. In 2019, FID was taken on 71 Mtpa of capacity out of the targeted volume of 213 Mpta at the beginning of the year. A similar 30% success rate in 2020 would have added a further 60 Mtpa of capacity under construction, but with only three of the projects listed in Table 4.3 not having announced a delay in the first 8 months of the year, the outcome for the year could be no FIDs being taken.

In August 2020, the developers of three projects on which LNG had been targeted in 2020 had not ruled out a decision by the end of the year:

- Mexico—Sempra's Costa Azul conversion (2.5 Mtpa);
- U.S.—Venture Global's Plaquemines (20 Mtpa); and
- Qatar—Qatargas expansion phase 1 (33 Mtpa).

Table 4.3 Developers' targets for FID in 2020

Country	*Project*	*Operator*	*Capacity in Mtpa*
U.S.	Plaquemines	Venture Global	20.0
	Magnolia LNG	LNG Ltd	8.8
	Rio Grande LNG	Next Decade	9.0*
	Driftwood LNG	Tellurian	16.6*
	Port Arthur	Sempra LNG	11.0
	Freeport Train 4	Freeport LNG	5.0
	Texas LNG	Texas LNG	2.0
	Annova	Annova LNG	6.0
	Delfin LNG	Delfin LNG	3.0*
	Corpus Christi LNG Phase 3	Cheniere	9.5
	Lake Charles	Energy Transfer	16.5
	Total USA		***107.4***
Mexico	Costa Azul Phase 1	Sempra LNG	2.5
Qatar	Qatargas Expansion	Qatargas	33.0
Mozambique	Rovuma LNG	ExxonMobil	15.2
PNG	PNG LNG Expansion	ExxonMobil	2.7
	Papua LNG	Total	5.4
Russia	Ob LNG	Novatek	4.8
Canada	Woodfibre LNG	Pacific Oil and Gas	2.1
	Goldboro LNG	Pieridae	10.0
	LNG Canada Expansion	Shell	14.0
Australia	Pluto Train 2	Woodside	5.0
	Total non-USA		***94.7***
	Total		**202.1**

*Assumes partial FID on full project scope

Source: Author's proprietary database

Mexico—Costa Azul Conversion Sempra plans to convert the little used Costa Azul receiving terminal in the Baja California region of Mexico to a liquefaction plant to be supplied with natural gas from the U.S. It is on the West Coast and will be able to take advantage of the shorter shipping time to Asian markets. The first phase is the construction of a 2.5 Mtpa train, and there is the potential to add two 5.5 Mtpa trains in the future. In November 2018, Total, Tokyo Gas, and Mitsui signed Heads of Agreements for 0.8 Mtpa each from the project. In May 2020, Sempra said that binding SPAs had been signed with Total and Mitsui, and FID was expected by the end of the second quarter.[21] However, in July 2020, Sempra's Mexican subsidiary, IEnova, said they were waiting for a final permit from the Mexican government, which had been delayed due to Covid-19.[22]

U.S.—Plaquemines Venture Global is planning to build a 20 Mtpa plant on the right bank of the Mississippi in southern Louisiana. It will use the same technology as the company's Calcasieu Pass project. The company has ordered thirty-six 0.626 Mtpa trains from the Baker Hughes plant in Italy for this and its Calcasieu Pass project. In June 2020, FERC gave approval for Venture Global to proceed with an initial mobilization and limited site preparation. Venture Global had previously said that it intended to start work on the site in mid-2020 before financial close (FID) in late 2020.[23] It currently has 20-year SPAs for output from the plant, with Poland's PGNiG for 2.5 Mtpa and with EDF Trading for 1 Mtpa.

Qatar—Qatargas Expansion In November 2019, Qatar Petroleum (QP) announced it will add two 8 Mtpa mega-trains to its originally planned expansion of four mega-trains, taking Qatar's total liquefaction capacity to 126 Mtpa (from 77 Mtpa currently) by 2027.[24] The expansion is being planned in two phases. Work is underway offshore for the first phase, North Field East, which will supply the first four of the new trains. The second phase, North Field South, will supply natural gas to the two additional trains. There have been some delays, including in the selection of foreign partners for the first four trains and in the awarding of EPC contracts.

Qatar is negotiating with partners in the existing trains, ExxonMobil, Total, Shell, and ConocoPhillips, along with Eni, Equinor, and Chevron. Russian and Chinese companies and buyers of the output are also possible partners. However, Saad Al-Kaabi, the chairman and CEO of Qatar Petroleum, has said that Qatar does not need partners and will go ahead with the development on its own if it does not receive acceptable offers. He has also said that QP is prepared to take the market risk and so does not need long-term contracts with buyers, although Qatargas is active in the market seeking commitments from buyers, and is thought to be prepared to offer competitive prices. The discussions are taking place in parallel with negotiations with Japanese and Korean buyers over the extension of existing long-term contracts for around 11 Mtpa that expire between the end of 2021 and 2024.

A decision on foreign partners was expected by late 2019 or early 2020, but it is still awaited. In April 2020, Saad Al-Kaabi said that Qatar is fully committed to the expansion despite the Covid-19 crisis.[25] However, the start of production has been deferred from 2024 to 2025, following a delay in the EPC bidding process, with the final train expected to start-up in 2027.

Qatar has signaled its intent to proceed with the expansion by signing ship-building agreements with Chinese and Korean yards. The first, in April 2020, was with the Hudong yard in China for eight firms and eight options for ships with a capacity of 175,000 cubic meters (cm).[26] The orders are subject to Chinese buyers committing to purchase the output from the expansion trains and, of course, FID on the expansion. A few weeks later, Qatar signed contracts for the supply of more than 100 ships at a cost of US $19.1Bn from Korea's three major shipbuilders—Daewoo, Hyundai, and Samsung—for delivery between 2024 and 2027.[27] No details have been released on the split of the orders between the yards or how many ships will be for the expansion, how many will replace older steam ships currently in operation, and how many will be for QP's 70% share in the 15.6 Mtpa Golden Pass project in the U.S.

Qatar's approach to the expansion appears to be to continue to progress the development without formally announcing FID. The key decision will be the awarding of the EPC contract for the first four trains, which I expect to happen in early 2021, with an award on the additional two trains probably delayed until 2022 or even 2023.

Deferred FIDs on U.S. LNG Projects

The remaining projects listed in Table 4.3 have announced delays in FID into 2021 or in some cases an indefinite delay. No project has been abandoned, although the reality is that the prospects for some of them are poor, as they run low on funds or find it impossible to secure commitments for the output. There is, however, a surprising level of optimism from developers, especially in the U.S., over the prospects for their projects. There have been changes in the plans for some of the projects, including redesigning of the facilities and changes of ownership.

Magnolia LNG LNG Ltd., the Australian listed company developing the planned 8.8 Mtpa project in Lake Charles, Louisiana, ran out of money to continue the development, and it was put up for sale in early 2020. The project and LNG Ltd.'s Optimized Single Mixed Refrigerant (OSMR) liquefaction technology were finally acquired by Glenfarne,[28] a privately owned energy and infrastructure development and management company, for US$2 million, after deals with two other companies fell through. Glenfarne has not said what its plans for the project are. LNG Ltd. has retained its second project, Bear Head LNG, in eastern Canada, and the rights to use the OSMR technology there, but the probability of the project being developed is low.

Rio Grande LNG In the last 12 months, Next Decade has not secured any more commitments from buyers to add to the 2 Mtpa agreement with Shell for output from the 27 Mtpa plant that it plans to build in Brownsville, Texas. It has reengineered the design to reduce the number of trains from six to five while maintaining the capacity at around 27 Mtpa. It claims that the redesign will reduce CO_2 emissions. It has also sold the planned Rio Bravo pipeline, which will supply natural gas to the plant, to Enbridge. In May 2020, it said that it had sufficient capital resources to sustain operation through to the end of 2021, by which time it expects to have taken FID.[29] Next Decade's strategy of using large-scale liquefaction trains differentiates it from other U.S. developers including Venture Global, Tellurian, and Cheniere, who are planning smaller-scale trains (0.6–2 Mtpa), which they say give more flexibility in scheduling construction in line with the requirements of buyers.

Driftwood LNG Tellurian's novel business model for its 27 Mtpa Driftwood LNG project in Louisiana requires buyer to invest \$0.5 billion and agree to service \$1 billion of debt to secure the right to 1 Mtpa of LNG for the life of the project. The investments plus loans will be used to purchase natural gas in the ground, to develop production and pipelines to transport gas to the plant, and to construct the plant. Investors pay the cost of servicing the loans, the operating costs of producing and piping the natural gas to the plant, and the cost of liquefying LNG that they lift. Tellurian estimates that operating costs will be between \$3 and \$4/MMBtu.[30] In October 2019, Tellurian signed a Memorandum of Understanding (MOU) with Petronet for the investment of \$2.5 billion in Driftwood LNG to lift 5 Mtpa from the plant. This added to the preliminary agreements with Total for 1 Mtpa of capacity and 1.5 Mtpa of purchases and with Vitol for the purchase of 1.5 Mtpa. It appeared that Tellurian had secured sufficient commitments to support first-phase investment in 11 Mtpa of capacity, provided, of course, the preliminary agreements were turned into binding contracts. It was agreed that Tellurian and Petronet would target a final contract by the end of March 2020, which was extended by two months, but, at the end of May, Petronet allowed the MOU to expire. The prospects for the Driftwood project appeared to have improved in July when Petronet agreed to restart negotiations to turn the MOU into a binding commitment, but Petronet warned in August that it is re-evaluating its plans and would come up with a fresh decision soon. Tellurian has also decided to remove three of the four pipelines it originally planned to build to supply natural gas to the plant, because of the need to reduce costs.

Sempra's 11 Mtpa **Port Arthur** project in Texas has appeared to be in a stronger position to take FID than many of its competitors in the U.S. It has an HOA (Heads of Agreement) with Saudi Arabia's Aramco to purchase 5 Mtpa of LNG and to negotiate the acquisition of a 25% share in the project, and a definitive SPA with Poland's PGNiG for 2 Mtpa. In early January 2020, Sempra and Aramco announced the signing of an interim project participation agreement. Sempra said at the time that it intended to take FID in 3Q20, but in May, it accepted that FID that year was no longer realistic and the decision had been delayed to 2021, "because of the market uncertainty caused by the coronavirus pandemic".

Freeport LNG (5 Mtpa) has FERC and DOE approval for a proposed 5 Mtpa fourth train and a binding HOA with Sumitomo for 2.2 Mtpa of capacity in the plant on a tolling basis. However, market uncertainty means FID has been delayed. Freeport LNG has been given approval by FERC for a delay of three years, until May 2026, in the date by which it has to start production from the train. As an expansion of an operating project, it should be well placed to take FID when the market improves.

Annova (6 Mtpa), Texas LNG (2 Mtpa), and Delfin LNG (3 Mtpa) are three U.S. projects with regulatory approvals in place but no commitments from buyers or off-takers for the output. They are all now targeting FID in 2021.

Corpus Christi Phase 3 (10 Mtpa) In November 2019, Cheniere received FERC approval for phase 3 of the development of its Corpus Christi plant, which will consist of seven mid-scale liquefaction trains with a total capacity of approximately 10 Mtpa. At the time it said that FID, which was planned for 2020, was contingent on clinching an EPC contract and acquiring essential financing and contracts for the output. During the presentation of the company's 1Q20 results, Jack Fusco, the CEO, said: "because of all the issues – coronavirus, the warm winter – the whole urgency among customers to sign long-term contracts has dropped. It will be tough to continue to get our fair share of contracts and continue to commercialise phase 3 at this point".[31] However, as an expansion of an operating project by a company with a track record of performance, it should be in a strong position to secure the contracts it needs when buyers decide to commit to new supplies.

Lake Charles (16.5 Mtpa) In March 2019, Shell and Energy Transfer (the owner of the Lake Charles receiving terminal) signed a Project Framework Agreement to advance the Lake Charles liquefaction project jointly. It brought Shell back into active participation in a project for which they appeared to have given low priority after becoming a partner through the acquisition of the BG Group in 2016. Twelve months later, in May 2020, Shell announced it would not go ahead with equity involvement in the project,[32] presumably as part of its program to reduce capital expenditure. Energy Transfer said it would take over the role of lead project developer and evaluate various options for the project, including the possibility of bringing in one or more equity partners and reducing the size of the project from three (16.5 Mtpa) to two trains (11 Mtpa).

Deferred FIDs on Non-U.S. LNG Projects

Mozambique—Rovuma LNG In October 2019, ExxonMobil (25%) and its partners Eni (25%), CNPC (20%), Portugal's GALP (10%), Korea Gas (10%), and ENH (10%) said they planned to invest US $500 m in the initial construction plans for the 15.2 Mtpa project, but a full FID, which ExxonMobil had earlier said would be by the end of the year, was delayed to the first half of 2020. A consortium of JGC, Technip, and Fluor was awarded the EPC contract for the project. ExxonMobil has now said that FID has been delayed "until market conditions are right".[33]

PNG LNG and Papua LNG (8.1 Mtpa) Negotiations between the government of PNG and ExxonMobil over the terms for the development of the P'nyang broke down in January 2020, which halted progress on the joint development of 8.1 Mtpa of capacity through the construction of three identical 2.7 Mtpa trains: a third train at PNG LNG supplied from the P'nyang field and two trains at Papua LNG supplied from the Elk and Antelope fields in the Southern Highlands region. In its 2Q results announcement in July 2020, Oil Search, a partner in both projects, reported that exploratory talks with the PNG government had continued, and in May, the government and ExxonMobil had restarted discussions on the P'nyang agreement. However, because of Covid-19, ExxonMobil and Total, the operators of PNG LNG and Papua LNG, respectively, demobilized the majority of their LNG technical and commercial staff, which means there is likely to be an extended delay to the expansion. In August, Oil Search's CEO said that he was confident that the PNG expansion and

Papua LNG projects would go ahead in time to meet a window of demand for new LNG in 2027.[34]

Russia Ob LNG (4.8 Mtpa) Novatek's plans for a third project in the Arctic have been put on hold because of Covid-19. It is determined to go ahead with the project and is probably prepared to take FID without firm commitments from buyers. Consequently, FID in 2021 is possible.

Canada Woodfibre LNG (2.1 Mtpa) In March 2020, Woodfibre LNG announced a delay of a year to FID because a fabrication yard in China had been shut down due to Covid-19 and the preferred U.S. construction contractor for the marine facilities had filed for Chapter 11 bankruptcy and was not able to start work as expected.[35] It is now three years since Sakunto Tanoto, the billionaire owner of Singapore's Royal Eagle Group, of which Woodfibre is a subsidiary, released the funds for the project.

LNG Canada Expansion (14 Mtpa) FID in 2020 seemed to be more of an aspiration for Shell (40%) and its partners, Petronas (25%), PetroChina (15%), Mitsubishi (15%), and Korea Gas (5%), than an expectation, so a delay is not a surprise.

Canada—Goldboro LNG (10 Mtpa) Goldboro LNG is the only LNG export project still being actively progressed in eastern Canada. The operator, Pieridae LNG, has managed to keep alive the agreement for 5 Mtpa from the first of the two trains with Germany's Uniper, which was signed in 2013. The agreement also means that the project is eligible for $4.5 billion of loan guarantees from the German government. However, it suffered a setback when its deal to acquire Shell's reserves in Alberta to supply the plant was blocked by the province's regulator. Pieridae had selected KBR as the EPC contract, but KBR had said it will no longer carry out the work under a fixed price contract; hence, Pieridae is now looking for a new contractor.

Australia—Pluto LNG Train 2 (5 Mtpa) In July 2020, Woodside, facing a fall in revenues because of low oil and LNG prices, said that it was delaying a decision on its two largest projects, Scarborough and Browse, until the second half of 2021 and 2023, respectively, at the earliest.[36] The development of the offshore Scarborough field, in which Woodside has a 75% share that it acquired from ExxonMobil, with BHP owning the other

25%, is planned to supply a second train at the Pluto plant, to be owned 100% by the company. The Browse development is intended to backfill the North West Shelf project, which is expected to run short of natural gas supply, as reserves in the fields currently supplying the plant are depleted.

Woodside has not been able to secure commitments from buyers for output from Pluto Train 2 in the current environment. It has also failed to receive support from its partners in Browse for the development of the reserves to supply the North West Shelf project. We could see some changes to the NWS Joint Venture following Chevron's decision to sell its 16.7% share. It is also possible that Scarborough could be a supply source for the North West Shelf plant rather than for a second train at Pluto.

The Status of Other Proposed Projects

The earlier section focused on projects that were targeting FID in 2020. They account for 42% of the proposed capacity. The projects making up the other 58% are at an earlier stage in the planning process and face the challenges of securing commitments from buyers, reducing costs, gaining regulatory approval, and raising finance.

Covid-19 and the collapse in oil demand have led many organizations to lower their forecast of oil and natural gas prices, and LNG project developers have responded by looking at the ways to reduce capital costs to ensure the economic viability of proposed investments. Cost reduction is also important in positioning projects to be able to meet LNG buyers' demands for more flexible terms in new contracts. They want lower take-or-pay levels, prices that respond more quickly to changes in their markets, and the removal of destination clauses, which restrict their ability to divert LNG cargoes to terminals other than those they own or use. They need greater contractual flexibility to help them manage increasingly uncertain demand in their downstream power and gas markets.

Aggregators, such as Shell, BP, Chevron, Gazprom and Total, provide one option to manage the disconnect between developers, who require long-term commitments from buyers with a strong credit rating, and buyers who are looking for short-term and more flexible contracts and, in some cases have a lower credit rating and lack LNG experience. Aggregators can commit to purchase or off-take LNG on a long-term basis and market it on a short- or medium-term basis to buyers, who are not prepared to contract on a long-term basis or have low credit ratings. In the process, aggregators take over some of the volume and off-take risk from developers.

BP's commitment to the entire output from the Coral project in Mozambique and from the Tortue project in Mauritania and Senegal exemplifies an aggregator providing the off-take security that a new project requires. BP will take the output from both projects into its supply portfolio, which it markets through a mix of spot, short-, medium-, and long-term contracts. BP and Shell have taken similar roles in Venture Global LNG's Calcasieu Pass project in the U.S., with each committing to purchase 2 Mtpa from the planned 10 Mtpa plant.

The LNG Canada and Golden Pass projects are examples of a new business model where FID is taken with project shareholders taking the responsibility of marketing their equity shares of output rather than the project signing long-term deals with power and gas utilities, the typical business model in the past. However, the impact of Covid-19 and lower prices on major oil and gas companies may make them more cautious about taking on volume and price risks by making new long-term commitments to the output from projects in which they are a partner or to third-party projects.

Proposed LNG Projects in the U.S.

The first wave of U.S. LNG export projects, on which FID was taken between July 2012 and November 2016, was in operation in August 2020, with the exception of two 0.25 Mtpa trains at Elba Island. The anticipated second wave of U.S. projects has struggled to progress. Since the end of 2016, Cheniere has committed to single 4.8 Mtpa train expansions to its Sabine Pass and Corpus Christi projects, ExxonMobil and Qatar Petroleum have committed to the 15.6 Mtpa Golden Pass project, and Venture Global to its 10 Mtpa Calcasieu project, but there is a long list of projects that have full regulatory approval or are seeking that approval where construction has not yet started.

Regulatory Approvals for U.S. LNG Exports

The key approvals developers need at the federal level are from the Department of Energy (DOE) and the Federal Energy Regulatory Commission (FERC). DOE's role is to approve the export of U.S. natural gas to countries with which the U.S. has a Free Trade Agreement and to non-FTA countries. The Natural Gas Act 1938[37] requires DOE to approve applications for exports to FTA countries without modification or delay, which makes approval a formality.

In the case of exports to non-FTA countries, DOE must consider the impact on the U.S. natural gas market and prices in deciding whether to approve the application. When plans for LNG exports from the U.S. were first announced, DOE said it would review applications in the chronological order in which they were submitted. In 2014, as the queue of applications built up, with 24 pending, DOE announced it would only review applications after a project received approval from FERC. This ensured DOE only considered commercially mature projects with environmental and other approvals in place.

Securing FERC approval for the siting, construction, and operation of an LNG export plant is more demanding in terms of time and cost than securing DOE approval. FERC must consider the impact of the project on the environment, consult local communities, and ensure that it can be constructed and operated safely. Project developers must invest in environmental studies and produce a detailed design of the planned facilities. FERC review of an application typically takes up to 18 months, and the cost of preparing the application and responding to FERC requests for additional information and clarification reportedly can reach up to $100 million. The time taken and the financial costs of the FERC approval process ensure that only companies with access to funds and seriously committed to development are likely to reach the stage of preparing and making an application to FERC.

The FERC website lists projects that have received approval but have not yet started construction, have filed an application with FERC, or are in pre-filing stage with FERC; this gives an indication of the projects in which developers are prepared to invest the necessary funds to advance them to a stage where they are positioned to take FID. Table 4.4 summarizes the status of proposed U.S. LNG projects on May 29, 2020, according to the FERC website.

Fourteen projects (including Alaska LNG), with a total design capacity of 163 Mtpa, had been approved by FERC by May 2020 for the siting, construction, and operation of the planned liquefaction plant and by DOE for the export of the output to both FTA and non-FTA countries. In addition, the 13 Mtpa capacity Delfin project, which will use four floating liquefaction (FLNG) units, has completed permitting with the Coast Guard and the U.S. Department of Transportation's Maritime Administration (MARAD) and has DOE approval for exports to FTA and non-FTA countries. From the regulatory standpoint, these projects are in position to take FID, but they still need to secure commitments from buyers or off-takers for the planned output to support the financing of the investment. Table 4.5 lists the projects that are at this stage.

Table 4.4 Planned U.S. LNG export projects

	Capacity	
	FERC application in Bcf/d	*Design in Mtpa*
Approved construction not yet started	24.16	143.0
Approved by MARAD Construction but not yet started	1.80	13.0
Alaska LNG (approved by FERC construction but not yet started)	2.63	20.0
Proposed to FERC	3.04	19.4
Projects in pre-filing with FERC	5.51	49.5
Total	**37.14**	**244.9**

Source: FERC Website dated May 29, 2020

For Table 4.4 through Table 4.6, https://www.ferc.gov/industries-data/natural-gas/overview/lng

Table 4.5 U.S. export projects with full regulatory approval not yet under construction

Project	*Location*	*Developer*	*Capacity in Mtpa*
Lake Charles LNG	Lake Charles, Louisiana	Energy Transfer	16.5
Magnolia LNG	Lake Charles, Louisiana	LNG Limited	8.8
Cameron LNG Trains 4 & 5	Hackberry, Louisiana	Sempra	10.0
Port Arthur LNG	Port Arthur, Texas	Sempra	11.0
Driftwood LNG	Calcasieu, Louisiana	Tellurian	27.6
Freeport LNG Train 4	Freeport, Texas	Freeport LNG	5.0
Gulf LNG	Pascagoula, Mississippi	Kinder Morgan	10.0
Texas LNG	Brownsville, Texas	Texas LNG	4.0
Rio Grande LNG	Brownsville, Texas	NextDecade	27.0
Annova LNG	Brownsville, Texas	Annova LNG	6.0
Corpus Christi Phase 3	Corpus Christi, Texas	Cheniere	9.5
Jordan Cove	Coos Bay, Oregon	Pembina	7.6
Alaska LNG	Nikiski, Alaska	Alaska Gas Line	20.0
Delfin LNG	Offshore Louisiana	Delfin LNG	13.0
	Total		**176.0**

Source: From table on FERC website dated May 29, 2020

All the projects are in Louisiana and Texas, except for Jordan Cove, which is in Oregon on the West Coast, and Alaska LNG. The list includes three expansions of operating plants plus one offshore project using FLNG units.

There were two projects that were being reviewed by FERC in August 2020 and four projects in pre-filing (Table 4.6).

Table 4.6 Applications to FERC for LNG Exports

Project	*Location*	*Developer*	*Capacity in Mtpa*
Filed			
Commonwealth LNG	Cameron, Louisiana	Commonwealth LNG	9.0
Port Arthur LNG	Port Arthur, Texas	Sempra	11.0
	Total Filed		**20.0**
In pre-filing			
Port Fourchon LNG	Lafourche, Louisiana	Energy World Corp	5.0
Galveston Bay LNG	Galveston, Texas	NextDecade	16.5
Pointe LNG	Plaquemines, Louisiana	Pointe LNG	8.0
Delta LNG	Plaquemines, Louisiana	Venture Global	20.0
	Total in pre-filing		**49.5**

U.S. LNG Export Business Models

Three basic business models are being used for U.S. LNG projects:

Free-On-Board Sales

In this model, the project developer is responsible for arranging the supply of natural gas, piping it to the liquefaction plant, liquefying it, and loading it onto buyers' ships. The buyers are responsible for arranging the shipping to transport the cargo to market. Provided the project developer has obtained approval from DOE to export LNG to non-FTA countries, there are no restrictions on the destinations to which the buyer can transport cargoes. Cheniere Energy chose the free-on-board (FOB) sales model for its Sabine Pass and Corpus Christi projects, and it has also been chosen by Venture Global for its Calcasieu Pass project, which is under construction, and for its two planned projects in Plaquemines Parish in Louisiana. The FOB price is the sum of the cost of natural gas delivered to the plant and a liquefaction fee.

The buyer contracts to purchase and lift LNG on a long-term basis. However, in the case of most of Cheniere's SPAs, the buyer has the right to cancel cargoes by giving notice by the 20th day of the month, two months before a cargo is scheduled to be lifted. When buyers exercise that right, as they have done in 2020, they pay the liquefaction fee but do not have to pay for the natural gas. Liquefaction fees for Cheniere projects range between \$2.25/MMBtu and \$3.50/MMBtu, 85–90% of which is fixed for the life of the contract; the remaining 10–15% escalates with

U.S. inflation and covers the plant operating cost. The majority of liquefaction fees for Cheniere projects are in the public domain because the contracts Cheniere signed with buyers had to be reported to the U.S. Securities and Exchange Commission.

Tolling

In this model, the buyer is responsible for securing natural gas supply and arranging its transport by pipeline to the plant. The plant owner is responsible for building and operating the liquefaction plant and using it to liquefy buyers' natural gas. Off-takers (companies who have entered into tolling contracts) arrange the shipping to transport the LNG to market. They commit to liquefaction capacity in the plant, typically for 20 years, and pay the tolling fee regardless of whether or not they use the capacity. The arrangements for electing not to lift a cargo are written into the contracts, but less notice than for the FOB model is typically required, since it is the off-taker, not the plant owner, who arranges the supply of natural gas to the plant. Tolling fees are not in the public domain, because the companies that have developed projects using this model are either privately owned or owned by large corporations for which LNG is only a part of their business. However, the general view is that, while tolling fees vary between projects, they are similar to the liquefaction fees in the FOB sales model.

Integrated

A small number of the planned projects are being developed using the traditional integrated project structure, in which the natural gas reserves are dedicated to the project and are owned, or natural gas is purchased on a long-term basis from upstream producers, by the project developers. ExxonMobil and QP have structured their Golden Pass project this way. ExxonMobil has invested heavily in shale gas reserves and production in the U.S., while, in June 2018, Saad Al-Kaabi, CEO of QP, announced plans to invest $20 billion in U.S. oil and natural gas, some of which would go to lining up supply for the Golden Pass plant.[38]

Tellurian has announced a novel integrated structure for its planned 27 Mtpa Driftwood LNG project (see "Deferred FIDs on U.S. LNG Projects" section). Alaska Gasline Development Corporation's planned Alaska LNG project will also use an integrated project structure, with reserves on the North Slope dedicated to supply the plant, and it will build a pipeline from the north of the state to the plant site at Nikiski on the Cook Inlet in the south.

How Competitive Is U.S. LNG?

U.S. LNG developers offer LNG buyers and off-takers several alternative project structures, giving them the opportunity to be involved in parts of the LNG chain, from arranging natural gas supply and investment in the plant in the tolling model to all parts of the LNG chain in the Tellurian model. The ability to deliver cargoes to any destination without the requirement to seek the permission of the seller or to share extra revenues that may be generated by the diversion of cargoes is important to many buyers, who have complained for many years about the unfairness of restrictive destination clauses in LNG contracts.

The ability to cancel cargoes at relatively short notice has been described as an advantage to the buyer because it helps them balance supply with demand in their downstream markets. However, it comes at a price, because the liquefaction or tolling fee has to be paid regardless of whether or not the cargoes are lifted. The liquefaction fee will, in most circumstances, be lower than a take-or-pay payment under the terms of a traditional sales and purchase agreement, which required payment at the prevailing contract price if the buyer takes less than the annual contract quantity minus any downward quantity tolerance (DQT) allowed under the terms of the contract. However, the payment for a cargo not taken can be offset against the cost of the cargo when it is taken as make-up at a later date. U.S. sales and tolling contracts do not have any DQT provisions, which are 10% each year, subject to a cumulative cap, in many Asian contracts. Furthermore, the liquefaction fee for a cancelled U.S. cargo cannot be recovered. There are very few cases of a payment being made for cargoes not taken in traditional take-or-pay contracts in Asia over the long history of the LNG business, but, as is discussed later, cancellation fees for U.S. cargoes that have not been lifted in 2020 already amount to well over $1 billion.

A key consideration for buyers deciding whether to buy U.S. LNG or LNG from other sources is how price competitive U.S. LNG will be over the life of the contract. According to the 2020 edition of the International Gas Union's *Wholesale Gas Price Survey*, which was published in June 2020, the price of 59% of the LNG sold in 2019 was indexed to crude oil or oil products. This compares with 72% in 2017. The share of U.S. LNG exports, which under the FOB sales model or the tolling model are indexed to U.S. natural gas prices, increased from 4.4% in 2017 to 9.8% in 2019. Making a long-term commitment to LNG indexed to U.S. natural gas prices presents both an opportunity and a risk for buyers as U.S. gas prices and crude oil prices now move independently of each other.

U.S. LNG prices are essentially cost-based rather than indexed to another commodity. The FOB price under a sales or tolling contract is the sum of the cost of the natural gas supplied to the plant and the liquefaction or tolling fee. In the case of Cheniere projects, the cost of natural gas is 15% uplift on the Henry Hub price. The uplift covers the cost of natural gas used in the liquefaction plant and other costs incurred in purchasing the natural gas and delivering it to the plant. The liquefaction fee is between \$2.25/MMBtu and \$3.50/MMBtu in the contracts Cheniere signed between 2011 and 2016. The FOB prices in tolling contracts for other U.S. LNG projects are not in the public domain. However, they are thought to have a similar structure to the Cheniere contracts, but the percentage of the natural gas consumed in the plant may be different—for example, the Freeport LNG plant uses electric motors rather than gas turbines to drive the compressors, and as a result, significantly less natural gas is consumed. However, power supply to the plant has to be purchased.

The cost of natural gas supplied to plants by companies with tolling contracts depends on how they procure the supply and where it is produced. Consequently, it is probably linked to the price at a different U.S. natural gas trading hub rather than directly to the price at Henry Hub. However, in the analysis later in the chapter of the competitivity of U.S. LNG exports, the Cheniere price formula has been used.

Shipping costs depend on the distance to market, the charter rate for the LNG ship, the cost of fuel (boil-off gas and fuel or marine diesel), port costs, and the transit fee, if the Panama Canal is used. Assuming a modern diesel-engine ship with a capacity of 170,000 m^3 using the Panama Canal, shipping costs for delivery of LNG from the Gulf of Mexico to Northeast Asia (Japan, South Korea, China, and Taiwan) range between \$1.40/MMBtu and \$1.80/MMBtu. Thus, an indicative price of U.S. LNG delivered to Northeast Asia $P(LNG)_{nea}$ is expressed by the equation:

$$P(LNG)_{nea} = 1.15 \times P(HH) + B \tag{4.1}$$

Where P(HH) is the Henry Hub natural gas price
And B is between \$3.65/MMBtu and \$5.30/MMBtu.

For deliveries to Europe, the shipping cost is estimated to range from \$0.70/MMBtu to \$0.90/MMBtu, setting the Europe-specific constant B in an equation analogous to Eq. 4.1 within the range \$2.95–\$4.40/MMBtu.

Figure 4.6 shows the notional price of U.S. LNG delivered to Northeast Asia from January 2016 to July 2020 based on average monthly Henry Hub prices and compares it with the average price of LNG imported into Japan based on the monthly data from the country's Ministry of Finance. The average monthly prices of LNG imported into China, South Korea, and Taiwan over the same period were similar to those for Japan. Figure 4.6 also shows the average Japan Korea Marker (JKM) price over the same period.

From February 2016, when LNG production at Sabine Pass commenced, until the end of 2017, the price of U.S. LNG delivered to Japan

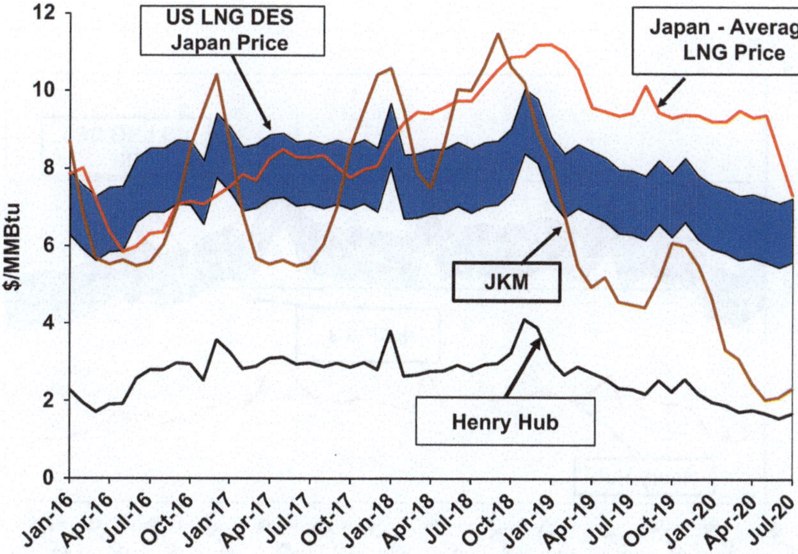

Fig. 4.6 Notional U.S. export price versus average LNG import price in Japan and JKM, January 2016–July 2020. (Source: Japan LNG prices from Ministry of Finance monthly data on LNG imports, JKM from S&P Global Platts, and Henry Hub prices from Enerfax Daily)

was at a similar level to the average price of all the LNG imported into Japan during the same month. However, from the beginning of 2018 until early 2020, the U.S. LNG price was lower than the average price of Japan's LNG imports as crude oil prices strengthened, averaging between $60 and $70/bbl. The gap between the price of U.S. and average LNG imports had, however, narrowed by July 2020, as the fall in crude oil prices in March 2020 fed through to oil-indexed LNG prices, which in Asia are typically indexed to crude oil prices with a lag of up to three months.

From early 2016 to the end of 2018, U.S. LNG prices delivered to Asia were generally lower than JKM in the winter months and higher in the summer months. However, JKM has been on a downward trend since early 2019, and the fully built-up price of U.S. LNG delivered to Asia has been at a premium to JKM.

Figure 4.7 compares the notional prices of U.S. LNG delivered to the UK from January 2016 to July 2020 with the United Kingdom (UK) National Balancing Point (NBP) price minus $0.30/MMBtu (the estimated cost of receiving and regasifying LNG at a UK receiving

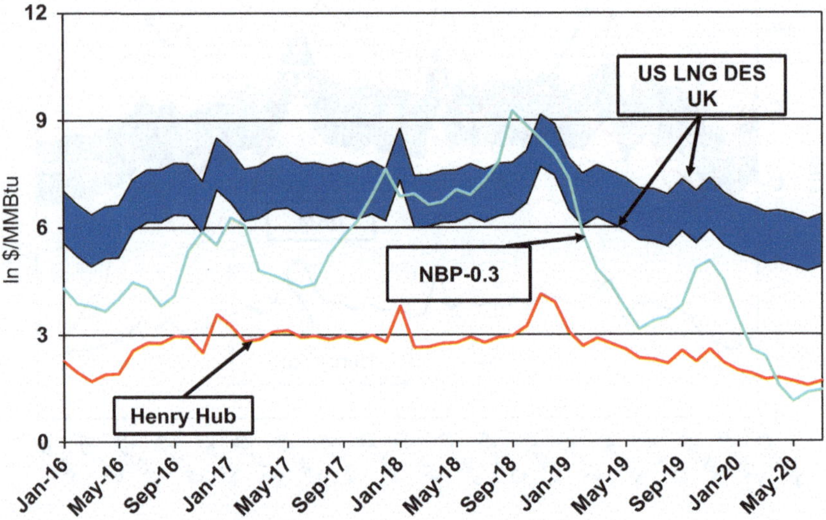

Fig. 4.7 Notional U.S. LNG export prices and UK NBP prices, January 2016–July 2020. (Source: NBP prices from ICIS LNG Daily and Henry Hub prices from Enerfax Daily)

terminal). It shows that the fully built-up cost of U.S. LNG delivered to the UK was higher than NBP minus the regas cost throughout the period except for late 2017 to the beginning of 2019. In May and June 2020, NBP was below the Henry Hub price, so the revenues from delivering U.S. LNG to the UK did not cover the cost of natural gas supplied to a U.S. LNG plant.

U.S. Cargo Cancellations

Low spot prices in Asia and Europe in 2020 left buyers and off-takers of the U.S. with little choice but to cancel cargo liftings under the terms of their long-term SPAs, unless they had contracts to sell cargoes at oil-indexed prices or a price based on the cost of U.S. LNG. Figure 4.8 shows the economics of U.S. LNG for a buyer or off-taker lifting a cargo for delivery to Northeast Asia on a spot basis.

The three solid lines show the fully built-up cost of the cargo, that is

$$P(\text{LNG}) = 1.15 * \text{HH} + \text{liquefactionfee} + \text{shippingcost}$$

at three different liquefaction fees:

- $2.25/MMBtu, Shell's fee for LNG from Sabine Pass (Cheniere's lowest)
- $3/MMBtu, the fee paid by most of the other buyers from Sabine Pass
- $3.50/MMBtu, the fee for LNG from Corpus Christi

The dashed line shows the cost on a short-run marginal cost basis,

$$1.15 * \text{HH} + 0.50$$

Under the terms of long-terms SPAs or tolling agreements, the liquefaction fee is a sunk cost, since it has to be paid even if a cargo is not lifted. The charter rate for the ship is also a sunk cost if the buyer or off-taker has entered into a term charter—an alternative approach in this analysis would be to assume that a ship is chartered on a spot basis, which would increase the marginal costs. If the ship is chartered under a term charter, the marginal shipping cost is the cost of fuel used on the voyage (boil-off gas and any fuel oil or marine diesel) and the port costs at the loading and unloading terminals.

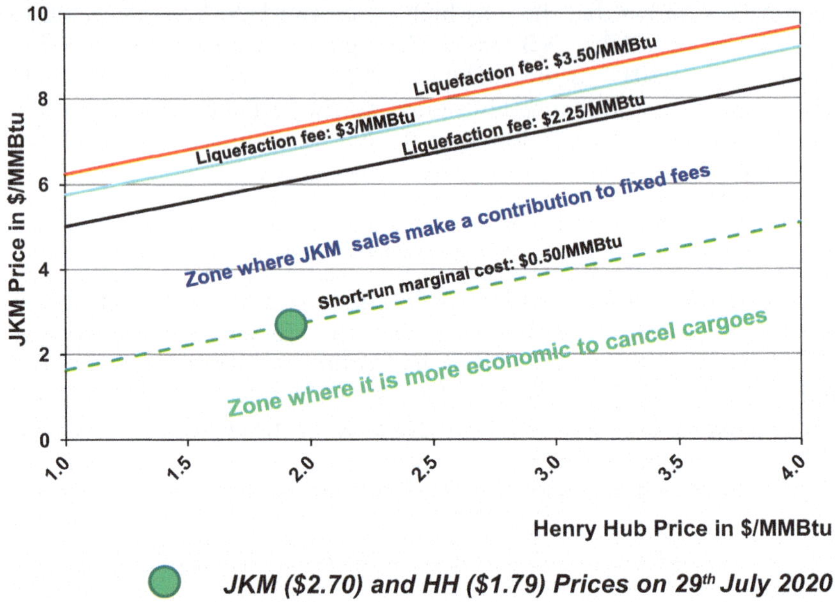

Fig. 4.8 U.S. breakeven economics for LNG sales to Northeast Asia

The vertical axis in Fig. 4.8 is the JKM price that would be needed to cover the costs at Henry Hub prices ranging from $1 to $4/MMBtu. The gap between the short-run marginal cost and the fully built-up cost is the zone where buyers and off-takers would be expected to lift cargoes, since the JKM price covers the marginal costs and makes a contribution to the fixed costs (liquefaction fee and ship charter). Above the solid lines is the zone where the buyer or off-taker makes a profit on the cargo. Below the dotted line is the zone where it is more economical to cancel cargoes since lifting them would add to the losses the buyer or off-taker incurs in paying the liquefaction fee and the ship charter. For much of the second quarter of 2020, JKM and Henry Hub prices put the economics in the zone where it is more economical to cancel cargoes. Figure 4.8 shows that, on July 29, 2020, the marginal costs would just be covered, so a decision on whether or not to cancel a cargo could go either way.

Figure 4.9 shows the same analysis for cargoes for delivery to Northwest Europe. At TTF and Henry Hub prices in 2Q20 and on July 29, 2020,

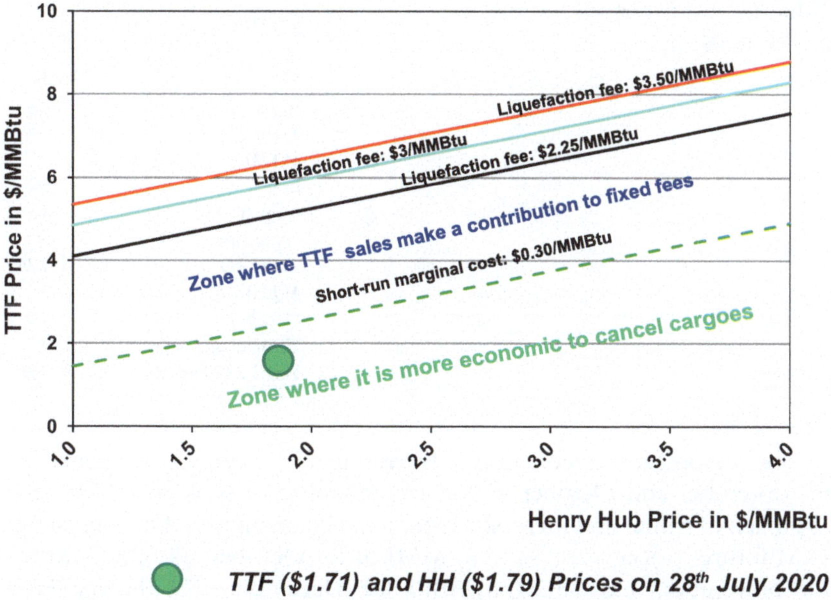

Fig. 4.9 U.S. breakeven economics for LNG sales to Northwest Europe

the decision on whether to cancel was clear with the potential revenues for a sale not covering short-run marginal costs.

Under the terms of Cheniere's contracts, buyers have to give notice of the cancellation of cargoes by the 20th of the month, two months before the month of lifting, that is, a cargo scheduled to be lifted in October 2020 should be cancelled by August 20, 2020. Under tolling contracts, the tollers or off-takers can cancel cargoes closer to the date of lifting.

Buyers, tollers, and producers have been reluctant to give firm details of the numbers of cancellations, so we have to rely on estimates of cancellations from the U.S. Energy Information Administration[39] and other sources[40], which are shown in Table 4.7.

The total volume of LNG cancelled in the 195 cargoes between April and October 2020 is around 12.7 mt. The average liquefaction fee for the cargo loaded onto a 165,000 m^3 ship is \$10–12 million, so the total cost of liquefaction fees for cancelled cargoes over a six-month period is between \$1.3 and \$1.52 billion.

Table 4.7 U.S. cargo cancellations

2Q20	
April	2
May	12
June	46
Total 2Q	*60*
3Q20	
July	50
August	45
September	30
Total 3Q	*125*
4Q20	
October	10
Total to date 4Q	*10*
Total 2020 to date	*195*

The reason for the reduction in the number of cargoes being cancelled in September and October is the strengthening of spot prices with the approach of winter and increased natural gas consumption. On August 28, JKM futures prices were $3.975/MMBtu for October, $4.625/MMBtu for November, and $5.20/MMBtu for December. The Henry Hub futures price for October was $2.71/MMBtu. In August 2020, a trader would have been able to lock in the JKM price in November or December, agree to lift a cargo in October based on a Henry Hub price of $2.71/MMBtu (so the cost of gas supplied to the plant would be $3.12/MMBtu), and lock in the profit by lifting the cargo and delivering it to a buyer in Asia in November or December.

U.S. LNG Exports from February 2016 to July 2020

Exports of LNG from Sabine Pass commenced in February 2016, with Cove Point following in March 2018, Corpus Christi in December 2018, and Elba Island, Freeport, and Cameron in 2019. In 2016, when oil-indexed prices in Asia were low, the main destinations for U.S. LNG were in the Americas. However, as Asian prices strengthened and long-term contracts for Sabine Pass LNG with buyers in South Korea and India came into operation, the share of U.S. LNG delivered to Asia increased (Fig. 4.10).

In 2018, Asia's share of U.S. exports was 53.2%, with 27.4% being delivered to the Americas, 6.4% to the Middle East and North Africa (MENA), and 13% to Europe. However, in the last three months of 2018,

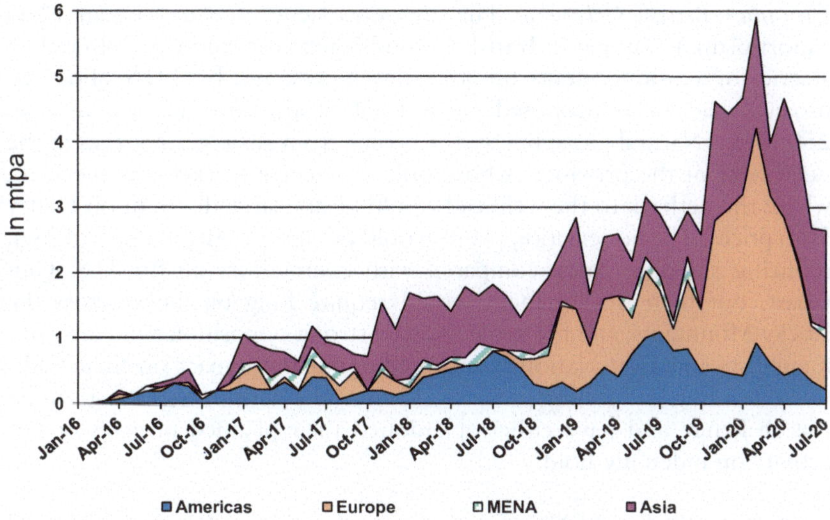

Fig. 4.10 U.S. LNG exports, February 2016–July 2020. (Source: Author's estimates)

the share of U.S. exports delivered to Europe began to increase, and in 2019, Europe replaced Asia as the main destination for U.S. exports, with a share of 38.5% compared with 36.8% being delivered to Asia. In the first 7 months of 2020, the share of U.S. LNG exports going to Europe increased further to 49.9%, with Asia's share at 36.9%. The changing shares of LNG delivered to regional markets demonstrate how the destination flexibility of U.S. LNG is enabling buyers and off-takers to switch cargoes between markets in response to changes in demand and movements in prices.

Competition from Outside the U.S.

The developers of proposed U.S. export projects face strong competition in securing commitments to the planned capacity from developers in other countries seeking to build LNG export plants to monetize stranded natural gas or natural gas surplus to the requirements of the host country. LNG buyers, especially in countries where LNG is the main or only source of natural gas supply, often want to encourage competition among suppliers to avoid overdependence on any one source of supply.

Canada—British Columbia The announcement of plans for an LNG export plant at Kitimat in British Columbia ten years ago was followed by a series of announcements by other developers, and by 2016, about 20 projects had been proposed, with total production capacity of over 250 Mtpa. Natural gas supply was to come from shale gas reserves in the northwest of the province, whose only alternative market was the U.S., where the netback to the wellhead would be at a large discount on Henry Hub prices. The liquefaction plants would be closer to the markets of Asia, reducing shipping costs, compared with competitors on the U.S. Gulf Coast, but their development would require long pipelines across the Rocky Mountains, and the projects faced strong opposition from environmentalists and First Nations concerned about the impact on their traditional hunting and fishing grounds. Most of the developers have given up the challenge and have either abandoned their planned projects or put activity on indefinite hold.

Only the Shell-led LNG Canada project has taken FID. Pacific Oil and Gas, a subsidiary of the Royal Golden Eagle (RGE) group based in Singapore, continues to progress its 2.1 Mtpa Woodfibre LNG project at Squamish, north of Vancouver, but FID has been deferred until 2021. Chevron and Woodside Energy have suspended work on their planned Kitimat LNG project, and Chevron has said it is looking to sell its 50%.

Eastern Canada At one time, five projects had been announced for Eastern Canada, with Europe the main target market. Only one, Pieridae's Goldboro LNG is still being actively pursued. LNG Ltd.'s 8 Mtpa Bearhead LNG project was not part of the deal that saw its Magnolia LNG project acquired by Glenfarne, but the probability of it being developed is low.

Mexico In addition to Sempra Energy's plan to convert its Costa Azul receiving terminal in Baja California into a liquefaction plant, which is discussed earlier, Mexico Pacific LNG is planning a 12 Mtpa LNG at Puerto Libertad in Sonora state on the West Coast. It is controlled by AVAIO, a U.S. infrastructure investment firm which says FID on the first 4 Mtpa is expected in 2021, with the start of production in 2024.

Australia Ambitious plans once existed for Australia to continue the expansion of the country's LNG capacity beyond the seven projects for which developers took FID between 2009 and 2012. These plans included adding new trains at plants in operation and under construction and developing new greenfield projects. As costs escalated, most of those plans were abandoned or put on indefinite hold. The focus now is on developing proven gas reserves to backfill the North West Shelf and Darwin LNG plants as reserves decline in the fields currently supplying the plants. It is possible that the Scarborough field, which Woodside has been planning to develop to supply a second train at Pluto, could supply the North West Shelf plant.

Papua New Guinea The plans to increase capacity by 8.1 Mtpa though the construction of three 2.7 Mtpa trains are on hold, and unless the government and ExxonMobil are able to reach agreement soon on the development of the P'nyang field to supply one of the trains, the expansion could lose out to projects elsewhere in the world.

Indonesia The most recent news on the 9.5 Mtpa Abadi project has been Shell's decision to sell it 35% share of the project[41] as part of the actions it is taking to reduce capital expenditure in response to the Covid-19 pandemic and low oil prices. Inpex, the operator, has said it will continue to develop the project and is targeting production start-up in the late 2020s.[42]

Russia Plans for a third train with a capacity of around 5.5 Mtpa at the operating Sakhalin 2 project were put on hold in November 2019 because of lack of natural gas resources, U.S. sanctions, and Gazprom giving priority to increasing pipeline natural gas supply to China. The decision to put Sakhalin 2 expansion on hold means that the Sakhalin 1 consortium led by ExxonMobil with Russia's Rosneft, India's ONGC Videsh, and Japan's SODECO is now focusing on developing a 6.2 Mtpa LNG plant.

In June 2020, Gazprom signed agreements for the feedgas supply and construction of petrochemicals facilities at its planned integrated petrochemicals and LNG development in the Baltic Sea port of Ust-Luga. There was no mention of the planned 13 Mtpa Baltic LNG plant in Gazprom's announcement of the agreements, which suggests it is seen as a future option rather than a priority.

Novatek has ambitious plans to add more liquefaction capacity in the Arctic in addition to Ob LNG, to develop large-scale reserves discovered in the Yamal region.

Tanzania There appears to have been no progress in discussions between the government and Shell, Equinor, ExxonMobil, Ophir Energy, and Pavilion Energy on "host government agreements" for the development of the LNG project, which restarted in 2019. The project is effectively on hold, with no prospect of production starting before the late 2020s at the earliest.

How Much New Liquefaction Capacity Is Needed to Meet Demand Growth?

A critical issue for companies planning to develop new liquefaction capacity is how much supply from new projects will the global market require, and when. Owners and financiers are generally only prepared to make the funds available for capital-intensive LNG projects if the volume risk is mitigated through long-term commitments to a major share of the proposed output by buyers or off-takers with a strong credit rating. The share of the output that needs to be covered varies among projects, but typically shareholders and financiers are looking for at least a 70% share.

The appetite of buyers and off-takers to make new long-term commitments varies as markets and prices change. According to Shell's 2020 LNG Outlook, commitments were made in aggregate to an average of around 800 Mt per year of LNG supply between 2011 and 2014, including commitments to output from the first wave of U.S. export projects. Some established buyers found themselves overcommitted to supply, and between 2015 and 2017, new contracted volumes averaged only 300 Mt per year. However, the strong growth in LNG demand in 2017 and 2018, led by China, gave more confidence to buyers, and 600 Mt of LNG was contracted in 2018 and around 350 Mt in 2019, supporting the surge in FIDs on new liquefaction capacity between October 2018 and December 2019.

At the beginning of 2020, before Covid-19 was declared a global pandemic, buyers appeared to be prepared to make further new long-term commitments as LNG demand continued to grow. The developers of 200 Mtpa of planned new liquefaction plants lined up to take FID in 2020 in response to what was expected to be a buoyant market. However, Covid-19 has added to the uncertainty over how demand will grow in the countries that currently import LNG and which countries will emerge as importers.

Countries import LNG for many reasons:

- It is the only source of natural gas supply, as in Japan, South Korea, and Taiwan.
- To supplement declining domestic production, as in Thailand, Argentina, Pakistan, and Bangladesh
- To create competition for the dominant supplier of natural gas, as in Poland and Lithuania
- As a cleaner alternative fuel for power generation, as in Jamaica, Colombia, Dominican Republic, and Malta
- To diversify sources of natural gas supply, as in China, India, Singapore, Spain, France, Greece, and Italy
- To move natural gas from remote domestic reserves to centers of population, as in Indonesia and Malaysia
- To meet seasonal natural gas demand, as in northern China, Kuwait, UAE, and Argentina

In Northwest Europe, not only demand drives LNG imports; the terminals in the region also provide a "market of last resort" for LNG producers and sellers who have cargoes surplus to the requirements of other, more-highly valued markets. Consequently, the balance of supply and demand in the global LNG market will have an impact on the level of European imports.

I have developed forecasts of LNG demand under three scenarios for the period to 2035:

Base Demand Case: It is assumed that global economic growth begins to recover in 2021 and reaches the pre-Covid level by the mid-2020s. In Japan, only a small number of the mothballed nuclear plants are brought back into operation, and in the rest of the world, few new nuclear plants are built and older plants are shut down. Renewables continue to grow strongly, but the targets of many governments prove to be over-optimistic. Switching from coal to natural gas in the power and industrial sectors is the main source of natural gas demand growth. New LNG importers around the world are a source of LNG demand growth together with demand from the transport sector (mainly ship bunkers and heavy-duty road vehicles and buses).

High Demand Case: It is assumed that there will be a stronger and more rapid return to growth for the global economy as Covid-19 is brought under control. The use of natural gas will be supported by governments and consumers to reduce air pollution and carbon emissions. Governments will speed up the development of LNG imports by accelerating the permitting of new terminals. The use of LNG in the transport sector will increase more rapidly than in the base case scenario.

Low Demand Case: In this scenario, it is assumed that natural gas will be widely treated as "just another carbon emitting fossil fuel", slowing the growth in demand as the development of renewables increases rapidly. LNG will come under pressure from environmentalists highlighting whole chain carbon and methane emissions.

On the base case, global demand is forecast to increase from 357 mt in 2019 to 475 mt in 2025, 575 mt in 2030, and 610 mt in 2035 (Fig. 4.11). The average annual growth rate is 4.9% from 2019 to 2025, slowing to 3.4% from 2025 to 2030 and 1.2% from 2030 to 2035. The average over the period from 2019 to 2035 is 3.4%, around half the historic growth rate of approximately 7% pa. Asia remains the main market for LNG as demand grows in China and South and Southeast Asia. However, demand

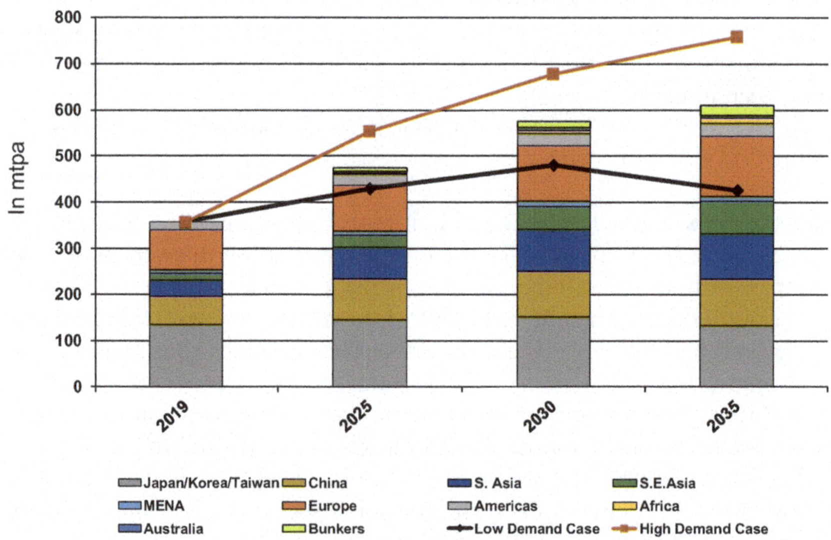

Fig. 4.11 Global LNG demand and supply, 2019–2035. (Source: Author's forecasts)

grows slowly in the established markets of Japan, South Korea, and Taiwan over the period to 2030 and declines over the following five years.

In the high case, demand is forecast to grow to 555 mt in 2025, 680 mt in 2030, and 760 mt in 2035, an average annual growth rate of 4.8% between 2019 and 2035, which is lower than the historic growth rate. In the low case, demand is forecast to increase to 430 mt in 2025, 480 mt in 2030, and decline to 425 mt in 2035.

Figure 4.12 compares the demand cases with the expected production from projects in operation and under construction in August 2020. The gap between supply and demand on the base case is 28 mt in 2025, increasing to 105 mt in 2030 and 170 mt in 2035. In this case, the requirement for output from projects currently at the planning stage only begins to emerge in 2025, which is the earliest significant production from which planned projects could be available, given that few, if any, FIDs are expected in 2020. The requirement for 105 Mtpa of new liquefaction capacity by 2030 is around 50% of the capacity on which developers were targeting FID in 2020, and even in 2035 only 85% of that capacity would be required.

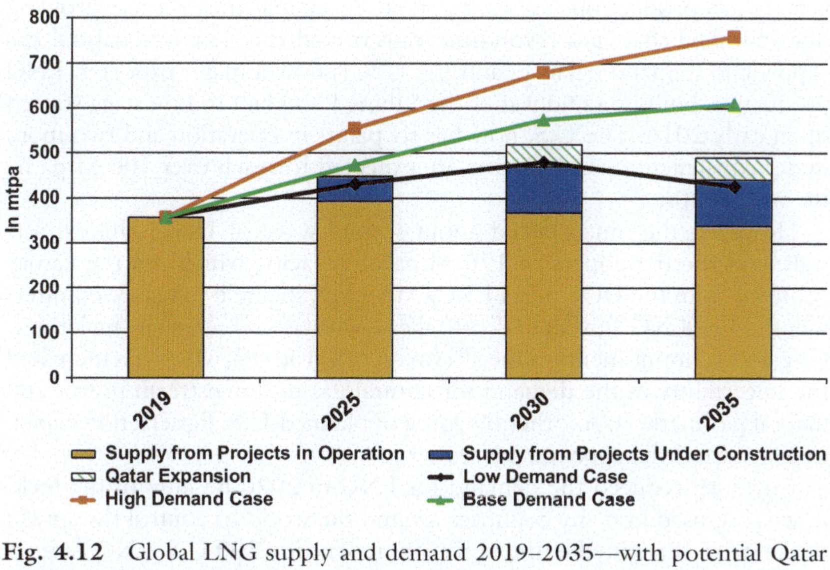

Fig. 4.12 Global LNG supply and demand 2019–2035—with potential Qatar expansion volumes added to supply from projects in operation and under construction in August 2020. (Source: Author's proprietary database)

The low demand case would mean a limited requirement for the output from planned plants, because demand can be largely met by the capacity in operation and under construction in August 2020. The high demand case is one that developers must be hoping for, with 108 Mtpa of new capacity needed by 2025 increasing to 210 Mtpa by 2030 and 320 Mtpa by 2035.

Qatar appears to be determined to go ahead with the construction of a six-train expansion to its current capacity, which will add 49 Mtpa to production by the late 2020s. As Fig. 4.12 shows, the output from these trains would meet around 50% of the additional capacity required in 2030 on the base demand case.

Conclusion: A Challenging Time for the Developers of New Liquefaction Projects

It is often forgotten that the U.S. was the second country to start exporting LNG, with the Kenai project in Alaska sending its first cargo to Japan in October 1969. For most of the next 50 years, it has been an importer rather than an exporter, and twice, in the 1970s and in the early 2000s, it was forecast to become the world's largest importer because domestic natural gas production was expected to be unable to meet the growing demand. The shale gas revolution transformed the domestic natural gas supply and demand balance, and the U.S. is now a major exporter. LNG production built up rapidly after the Sabine Pass plant in Louisiana started up in early 2016. The U.S. now has six plants in operation and two more under construction, and exports are expected to reach over 100 Mtpa by the mid-2020s.

However, the much talked about second wave of U.S. LNG exports stalled as the developers of 176 Mtpa of capacity, which has regulatory approval from the DOE and FERC/MARAD, struggle to secure commitments from LNG buyers and off-takers, who are reluctant to make new long-term commitments in the aftermath of Covid-19, which has increased the uncertainty in the demand for natural gas in downstream power and natural gas markets. Another 69 Mtpa of planned U.S. liquefaction capacity has started the approval process.

Covid-19 reduced the demand for LNG in 2020 because of the lockdowns imposed in many countries around the world to control the spread of the virus. It resulted in the cancellation of nearly 200 U.S. LNG cargoes in 2020 as well as adding to the uncertainty of future demand growth for

LNG. Importantly, as our book went to press, after falling to a pandemic low of about 2.6 Mtpa in July 2020 (Fig. 4.10) U.S. exports surged so that January 2021 volumes exceeded the pre-pandemic peak in January 2020.

LNG demand is expected to return to growth as the pandemic is brought under control and the global economy recovers. When it does, proposed U.S. projects, which account for just over 50% of proposed projects globally, will face strong competition to secure commitments from buyers, who are likely to be more demanding of sellers in the negotiation of new contracts. Buyers and off-takers will seek lower prices that respond to changes in supply and demand in their power and natural gas markets, and they will want increased volume and off-take flexibility.

Developers are looking for ways to reduce costs to position their projects to respond to the requirements of buyers and off-takers and to ensure that their projects are economic in the lower price world that is now forecast as a result of Covid-19 and following the collapse in crude oil prices in 2020. They also need to be able to give buyers and off-takers confidence that their project will be a safe, reliable, and competitive source of supply and that the schedule for the start of production will be met. Relationships will, as always in the LNG business, be important in building the trust between buyer and seller required for the commitment to a long-term sale and purchase agreement.

The most formidable competition for U.S. projects will come from Qatar, which is determined to develop its enormous natural gas reserves and expand its liquefaction capacity by 49 Mtpa. Its costs are amongst the lowest, if not the lowest, in the world; geographically it is midway between the markets of Asia and Europe; it has a track record of safe and reliable supply, and having supplied LNG to most of the world's buyers, it has well-established relationships. Proposed projects in other countries including Russia, Mozambique and Canada want to develop reserves as quickly as possible to minimize the risk of being left with stranded assets if targets for reducing carbon emissions lead to declining demand for natural gas.

Even if LNG demand recovers quickly from the impact of Covid-19 and grows strongly, it is unlikely that there will be a market for all the close to 500 Mtpa of proposed capacity, making it inevitable that many of the projects will eventually be abandoned. The challenge for the developers of planned U.S. capacity is to develop a commercial tool kit that enables them to make a compelling offer to buyers and off-takers in a challenging and competitive global market.

Notes

1. Off-taker contracts with Sabine Pass, Freeport (first two trains), Cameron and Freeport (third train) were signed between 2011 and 2013. FIDs followed between 2012 and 2014.
2. For background on U.S. LNG and export rules, see https://www.energy.gov/fe/science-innovation/oil-gas/liquefied-natural-gas
3. The project that has not formally announced a delay in FID almost certainly will be, given that, at the time of writing, we are near the end of the year, developers only have commitments to 3 Mtpa of the 10 Mtpa of the planned first phase output and they will need to raise finance.
4. Exmar, 2019, Tango FLNG Fully Commissioned and Accepted by YPF, Exmar News Update, June 6. http://www.exmar.be/sites/default/files/media/tango_flng_fully_commissioned_06062019_0.pdf
5. MarineLink, 2020, Exmar Slams "Unlawful" Tango FLNG Force Majeure by YPF, Marine Link Report, June 26, https://www.marinelink.com/news/exmar-slams-unlawful-tango-flng-force-479692
6. Petronas 2020, Petronas Group Financial Results Announcement Q1 FY2020 Page 9, https://www.petronas.com/sites/default/files/quarterly-report/Financial%20%26%20Operational%20Results%20for%20Quarter%201%20FY2020.pdf
7. Cheniere 2020, Corporate Presentation, August 12, Figures 17 and 18 https://d1io3yog0oux5.cloudfront.net/_d7571489142d1e1767fd8e2c588f7e48/cheniere/db/708/6243/pdf/08+12+2020+Corporate+Presentation+-+vFinal.pdf
8. Venture Global 2020, Venture Global Announces FID and Financial Close for Calcasieu Pass LNG, Press release August 19, https://venturegloballng.com/press/venture-global-announces-final-investment-decision-and-financial-close-for-calcasieu-pass-lng/
9. Arctic Today 2020, The Yamal LNG project's fourth train is off to a troubled start, January 23, https://www.arctictoday.com/the-yamal-lng-projects-fourth-train-is-off-to-a-troubled-start/
10. Novatek 2020, Unblocking Arctic Potential: Expanding Our Global LNG Footprint to 2030, Novatek Presentations http://www.novatek.ru/en/investors/presentations/
11. Energy Voice 2020, Virus Looks Set to Delay BP's Tangguh LNG Expansion, March 20, 2020, https://www.energyvoice.com/oilandgas/asia/231601/virus-looks-set-to-delay-bps-tangguh-lng-expansion-tan/ (accessed August 27, 2020).
12. Club of Mozambique 2020, Mozambique: Coral South FLNG Project on Schedule, June 5, 2020, https://clubofmozambique.com/news/mozambique-coral-south-flng-project-on-schedule-aim-report-162307/ (accessed August 27, 2020).

13. World Oil 2019, Anadarko announces FID on Area 1 Mozambique LNG project, June 19, 2019, https://clubofmozambique.com/news/mozambique-coral-south-flng-project-on-schedule-aim-report-162307/ (accessed August 27, 2020).
14. Bloomberg 2020, Total's Mozambique LNG to Sign Financing in June, May 20, 2020, https://www.bloomberg.com/news/articles/2020-05-20/total-s-mozambique-lng-set-to-sign-15-billion-financing-in-june?sref=PLczA45e
15. Shell 2018, Shell gives green light to invest in LNG Canada, Shell Press Release, Oct 2, 2018, https://www.shell.com/media/news-and-media-releases/2018/shell-gives-green-light-to-invest-in-lng-canada.html#:~:text=Shell%20Canada%20Energy%2C%20an%20affiliate%20of%20Royal%20Dutch,expected%20before%20the%20middle%20of%20the%20next%20decade
16. Reuters 2020, BP issues force majeure notice to Golar LNG Unit of floating facility, April 7, 2020, https://uk.reuters.com/article/uk-golar-lng-lng-bp/bp-issues-force-majeure-notice-to-golar-lng-unit-on-floating-facility-idUKKBN21P2IS
17. Offshore Energy 2019, Nigeria Makes Train 7 FID, December 30, 2019, https://uk.reuters.com/article/uk-golar-lng-lng-bp/bp-issues-force-majeure-notice-to-golar-lng-unit-on-floating-facility-idUKKBN21P2IS
18. Oil and Gas Journal 2020, Shell Takes NLNG Train 7 FID, EPC Contract Signed, May 18, 2020, https://www.ogj.com/pipelines-transportation/lng/article/14176131/shell-takes-nlng-train-7-fid-epc-contracts-signed
19. The Punch 2020, Train 7 project faces delay amid COVID-19 pandemic, June 28, 2020, https://www.msn.com/en-xl/news/other/train-7-project-faces-delay-amid-covid-19-pandemic/ar-BB163bUs
20. Cheniere 2020, Corporate Presentation, Figure 8, August 12, https://d1io3yog0oux5.cloudfront.net/_d7571489142d1e1767fd8e2c588f7e48/cheniere/db/708/6243/pdf/08+12+2020+Corporate+Presentation+-+vFinal.pdf
21. Reuters 2020 "Sempra delays big Texas LNG project as global energy demand slumps" May 4, 2020, https://www.reuters.com/article/us-sempra-usa-results-idU.S.KBN22G1IS
22. Reuters 2020 "Sempra still awaiting for Mexican export permit for Costa Azul", August 5, 2020, https://www.reuters.com/article/sempra-lng-costa-azul-idU.S.L1N2F70M9
23. Offshore Energy 2020 "Venture Global to Start Plaquemines LNG Site Work", June 16, 2020, https://www.offshore-energy.biz/venture-global-to-start-plaquemines-lng-site-work/

24. Reuters 2019 "Qatar Plans to boost LNG production to 126 mln T by 2027", November 25, 2019, https://www.reuters.com/article/qatar-energy-qp-idU.S.L8N2851HI
25. Qatargas 2020 "Qatar Petroleum Announces the Start of Development Drilling Campaign of the North Field East Project" Qatargas Press Release, April 15, 2020, http://www.qatargas.com/english/MediaCenter/Pages/Press%20Releases/Qatar-Petroleum-Announce-the-Start-of-the-Development-Drilling-Campaign-of-the-North-Field-East-Project.aspx
26. MarineLog 2020, "Qatar LNG carrier agreement hailed as China's largest shipbuilding export deal yet" April 22, 2020, https://www.marinelog.com/news/qatar-lng-carrier-agreement-hailed-as-chinas-largest-shipbuilding-export-deal-yet/
27. Bloomberg 2020, "Korean Shipyards Draw $20 Billion of Work from Qatar", June 1, 2020, https://www.bloomberg.com/news/articles/2020-06-01/qatar-looks-to-boost-global-lng-lead-with-19-billion-ship-deal?sref=PLczA45e
28. LNG Global 2020, "Magnolia LNG Acquired by Glenfarne", June 9, 2020, https://www.lngglobal.com/magnolia-lng-acquired-by-glenfarne
29. Yahoo Finance 2020, "NextDecade Provides Corporate Update, Confirms Capital Resources Sufficient to Sustain Operations Through Year-End 2021", May 18, 2020, https://sg.finance.yahoo.com/news/nextdecade-provides-corporate-confirms-capital-103000547.html?guccounter=1&guce_referrer=aHR0cHM6Ly93d3cuYmluZy5jb20v&guce_referrer_sig=AQAAALh4uNrVT1rbGfNXnChy8hBn6XcPwOe-lDujjyfcduWThjUGcsj4Jf8M3M33FpVzZZ9eUBtzkp2VfN3q37P9j8QN-PeTN0ZkUL12vQU2Fr4xpT9PXJMnLhQNpTngd4luFloTQf06e-3zL7lcRo8oJ27oT6hahuYxBMviJwyUEwTZXS
30. Tellurian 2020, Corporate Presentation May 2020, https://d1io3yog0oux5.cloudfront.net/_c1a48f073edeffd8b97b2e48c8f165d2/tellurianinc/db/284/2098/pdf/Corporate+presentation_Tellurian_May+2020.pdf
31. Seeking Alpha 2020, "Cheniere could delay export project amid tough long-term LNG market", February 25, 2020, https://seekingalpha.com/news/3545613-cheniere-delay-export-project-amid-tough-long-term-lng-market
32. Shell 2020, "Shell exits proposed Lake Charles LNG project" Shell Media Release, March 30, 2020, https://www.shell.com/media/news-and-media-releases/2020/shell-exits-proposed-lake-charles-lng-project.html
33. S&P Global Platts 2020, "Delay to Rovuma LNG latest setback for Mozambique LNG sector" April 9, 2020, https://www.shell.com/media/news-and-media-releases/2020/shell-exits-proposed-lake-charles-lng-project.html

34. Reuters 2020, "Oil Search slashes costs to position itself for growth from 2025", August 25, 2020, https://www.reuters.com/article/oil-search-results/update-2-oil-search-slashes-costs-to-position-itself-for-growth-from-2025-idU.S.L4N2FQ4CV
35. CBC 2020, "COVID-19 pandemic leads to delay of Woodfibre LNG project", March 25, 2020.
36. Woodside 2020, Half Year Report, August 13, 2020, https://files.woodside/docs/default-source/asx-announcements/2020-asx/half-year-2020-report.pdf?sfvrsn=6ec651a9_4
37. U.S. Office of Fossil Energy, Division of Natural Gas Regulation, https://www.energy.gov/fe/services/natural-gas-regulation
38. Hydrocarbons Technology 2018, "Qatar Petroleum to invest $20Bn in U.S. oil and gas fields", June 27, 2020, https://www.hydrocarbons-technology.com/news/qatar-petroleum-invest-20bn-us-oil-gas-fields/#:~:text=Qatar%20Petroleum%20is%20reportedly%20planning%20to%20invest%20%2420bn,developing%20in%20partnership%20with%20Exxon%20Mobil%20and%20ConocoPhillips
39. U.S. Energy Information Administration 2020, Today in Energy, June 23, 2020, https://www.eia.gov/todayinenergy/detail.php?id=44196
40. S&P Global Platts 2020, "Fewer cargo cancellations for October to aid continuing U.S. LNG output recovery" August 21, 2020, https://www.spglobal.com/platts/en/market-insights/latest-news/natural-gas/082120-fewer-cargo-cancellations-for-october-to-aid-continuing-us-lng-output-recovery
41. Offshore Energy 2020, "Indonesian regulator confirms Shell Abadi LNG exit talks", July 8, 2020, https://www.offshore-energy.biz/indonesian-regulator-confirms-shell-abadi-lng-exit-talks/#:~:text=Indonesian%20upstream%20regulator%20SKK%20Migas%20has%20confirmed%20Shell,Masela%20offshore%20block%20involved%20a%20floating%20LNG%20plant
42. INPEX Corporation 2020, Financial Results for the six months ended June 30, 2020, Page 11, August 7, 2020.

References

International Gas Union. 2020. *Wholesale gas price survey 2020 edition—A global review of price formation mechanisms 2005 to 2019*. Barcelona: International Gas Union, 68 p.

Royal Dutch Shell. 2020. *Shell LNG outlook 2020*. The Hague: Royal Dutch Shell, 37 p.

CHAPTER 5

Between the Old and New Worlds of Natural Gas Demand

Anna Mikulska and Gürcan Gülen

Introduction

Over the last 20 years, the natural gas industry landscape has been transforming from regional enclaves to a more global market. The long-distance transportation and storage of gas and the need to connect many customers via pipeline networks are not as straightforward as transporting, storing, and consuming liquids such as crude oil and refined products, or solids such as coal. Profitable investment in natural gas midstream and downstream infrastructure also benefits from a mix of customers (households, commercial and industrial facilities, and power plants) who can pay the full cost of delivering natural gas to their facilities.

A. Mikulska (✉)
Baker Institute for Public Policy, Rice University, Houston, TX, USA
e-mail: anna.b.mikulska@rice.edu

G. Gülen
Independent Consultant, West Brookfield, MA, USA
e-mail: gurcan@g2eis.com

M. Michot Foss et al. (eds.), *Monetizing Natural Gas in the New "New Deal" Economy*,
https://doi.org/10.1007/978-3-030-59983-6_5

Hence, natural gas traditionally has been consumed within the region where it was produced, as long as someone invested in the gas infrastructure. That someone was often a state company dominating the gas value chain, that is, production and/or import of gas, pipeline networks, and delivery to end-users. Otherwise, private companies, mainly in the U.S., Canada, and Western Europe, were incentivized via regulatory constructs to build and operate midstream and downstream infrastructure. Many natural gas discoveries or even gas-heavy oil discoveries around the world were not developed because their monetization was very difficult, if not impossible, given the absence of state-owned or regulated private companies to develop the necessary—but very costly—midstream infrastructure (see Chap. 6 for a detailed discussion of commercial frameworks necessary for gas monetization).

The liberalization efforts in electricity and gas sectors across the world since the 1980s, albeit only partially successful in most cases, allowed for development of more gas resources and infrastructure, and induced competitive procurement of gas from competing producers but also via imports. Many countries became first-time producers, exporters, or importers of natural gas. In 2019, about 30 percent of global gas consumption was traded internationally as compared to about 23 percent in 2000 (BP 2020 Annual Statistical Review of Energy). There is a much larger number of exporters and importers across a wider geography. Although pipelines continue to account for more than half of global gas trade, the share of liquefied natural gas (LNG) has increased considerably in the twenty-first century; in 2019, the shares were roughly 62 percent pipeline and 38 percent LNG. Much LNG trade resolved regional dilemmas associated with pipelines (geopolitical or terrain). Longer pipelines can quickly become more expensive than LNG options. The growth in LNG trade has been at least partially driven by efforts to monetize "stranded" natural gas resources across the world, but most prominently in Qatar, Australia (coal-seam and conventional), and more recently the U.S. (shale gas). This strong supply-push has come at an opportune time: persistent high economic growth, especially in Asia-Pacific, led by China and followed by India and others.

High rates of economic growth driven by industrialization and the need to improve the standard of living of more than 3 billion low-income denizens of the world need strong support of reliable and affordable energy sources. While population growth, higher in lower-income countries, adds to this challenge constantly, energy needs of growing middle and upper classes are higher. After all, with more disposable income, people live in homes consuming more energy, travel more, and buy more energy-intensive products. Middle classes also demand lower pollution.

Natural gas has become an important option owing to several factors: (1) increased availability of abundant global natural gas resources via new discoveries and growth in LNG trade, (2) cleaner burning qualities of the fuel when compared to coal and some liquids, and (3) energy security enhancement of adding another fuel, from different providers than those supplying oil or coal to the energy portfolio of a growing economy. Still, the addition of natural gas to a country's energy portfolio and, in particular, growing its consumption has not been without issues.

This context inspired us to organize our chapter by pointing to a distinction between the Old World and New World of gas demand. The most obvious criterion is the evolution of gas demand centers. All analysts and observers expect most future demand for natural gas to come from faster growing economies in Asia-Pacific and, to a lesser extent but in aggregate potentially as significant, the Middle East, Africa, and Latin America (New World) rather than the U.S., Canada, and Western Europe (Old World) in the geographic sense. Obviously, this dichotomous approach is a simplification of the spectrum of countries that differ in terms of gas demand growth potential, gas market structures and liquidity, and role of government. Many fall in between the Old and New "extremes."[1] For example, while Russia can be easily classified as Old World in terms of established gas demand (since the 1960s) that is not expected to grow significantly, in terms of the dominant role of government and importance of gas exports to the Russian economy, it gravitates to our New World classification. In contrast, post-Soviet EU countries will likely see gas demand growth, and although the role of government will remain important, it will be tempered by EU membership requirements. In Asia-Pacific, Japan, and South Korea, although OECD members, will continue to have high government involvement to ensure energy security while decarbonizing. Accordingly, gas demand growth is still possible. Even in Australia, another OECD member, government policy may lead to gas demand growth to replace coal and as part of a pandemic-recovery stimulus program. To unravel our Old-New classification's multidimensional nature, we proceed in three distinct steps.

First, we look at the changes in geoeconomics of gas demand in recent years and in the future. We start with a comparison of major outlooks to identify commonalities and differences in assumptions that lead to significantly divergent scenarios. We then contrast historical and future policy and regulatory and infrastructure development trends across the world. This comparison highlights the rationale for our "Old World" versus "New World" classification. Within the latter, China is on its way to becoming the world's largest gas importer. India remains a laggard (only one-fifth of China's consumption), but it has large potential, somewhat supported by the growing investment in gas infrastructure. The post-Soviet bloc provides a great illustration of geopolitical implications of gas trade. The Middle East, a larger consumer of gas than Russia, will likely expand its consumption as part of industrial policies of key countries in the region, but perhaps at a much slower pace than the region experienced in the last decade. Latin America and Africa already consume nearly three times as much gas as India, but a few countries dominate consumption. In addition, there are significant differences across the countries in each region, including a variety of geopolitical and governance challenges. At the same time, gas demand growth everywhere—even in the Middle East—faces competition from renewable energy, coal, and nuclear. Finally, all of these considerations are influenced by the struggle for power among world's largest economies, which also present different visions of political organization and societal priorities.

Second, we look at changes in the commercial underpinnings of gas trade. We point to an increasing availability of LNG from a growing number of suppliers and rising interest of a growing number of countries in importing LNG, which has been made easier and cheaper by floating storage and regasification units (FSRUs). Contracts are more flexible in terms of length, ability to divert cargoes, pricing formulas, and more. Although these changes point to emergence of a global gas market, these conditions are not yet universal. A mix of practices coexists. In the New World, powerful state-owned enterprises (SOEs) and their governments are shaping these practices, raising questions about how liquid the global gas market really can become.

Third, we look at the importance of SOEs, which are instrumental to construction of sufficient natural gas infrastructure to support gas demand growth subject to energy security considerations. We see similarities between the role of SOEs and state in the New World and the beginnings of gas market development in North America and Western Europe where the state, if not SOEs, played an important role in developing the policy and regulatory conditions to facilitate gas infrastructure development. After all, a liquid gas market cannot exist in the absence of widespread gas pipeline and storage networks with sufficient spare capacity to balance regional and seasonal fluctuations in demand and supply. Although higher liquidity in the global LNG market has been inducing efforts to liberalize the gas sector in many countries, including China, India, and Central and Eastern European countries, SOEs remain important particularly where expensive domestic gas infrastructure still needs to be built to ensure sufficient and secure supply. Many of these markets are not attractive to private investors because the dominant role of SOEs and state's socioeconomic pricing policies undermine liberalization efforts.

In this sense, the trajectory of gas demand in the New World is likely to be a reflection of geoeconomic considerations on the part of both gas suppliers and consumers within the context of rising international competition for political power. This is why energy security and, in case of natural gas, security of supply have grown in importance. Countries will use different strategies to achieve their preferred energy mix. For natural gas, these strategies range from free-market alternatives to state-led, centrally planned undertakings and have a bearing on short- and long-term gas demand.

Where Are We and Where Are We Going: What Energy Outlooks Tell Us

Our distinction between the Old World and New World of gas demand lies at the intersection of energy consumption and access to gas resources. In the twenty-first century, the vast majority of economic growth has and will come from the New World. Natural gas has become an important part of the energy mix in many New World countries; and others are adding natural gas into their energy mix.

In Fig. 5.1, we graph future gas demand for different regions under a variety of scenarios produced by various entities. Our goal is to underline the trends and divergences across scenarios as inputs to our analysis. In particular, we want to question implicit assumptions behind some of these scenarios. Are countries capable of investing? Do they have sufficient access to funds? Do their SOEs have technical and managerial capabilities necessary to develop natural gas infrastructure? Can their market and institutional arrangements attract private investment? Can their consumers across various sectors pay the full cost of natural gas delivered to their premises? What are their energy security and environmental priorities? What alternatives do they have? Can renewables, coal, and/or nuclear meet their needs? What are their geopolitical considerations? And many more.

In recent years, there has been a transition in energy scenarios, including scenarios presented by oil and gas companies such as BP. It has become more common to see scenarios where global natural gas consumption peaks by 2030. The BP Energy Outlook released on September 15, 2020, is particularly interesting in terms of its significant shift from the company's 2019 Outlook. Most strikingly, the BP 2020 Net Zero scenario approaches the Greenpeace scenarios Stern describes in the Foreword to this book. Nevertheless, scenarios in Fig. 5.1, a mix of business-as-usual and climate scenarios, corroborate Stern's conclusions that natural gas demand will continue to rise in the New World, led by China and non-OECD Asia, while it remains flat (the U.S. and Russia) or declines in the Old World. In China and India, even BP 2020 and the Equinor Renewal scenarios call for higher gas consumption in 2050 than in 2020.

Still the difference between BP 2019 Rapid Transition and BP 2020 (Rapid) scenarios for India is striking. After all, India has been investing in long-term projects such as LNG import terminals and pipeline networks and pursuing policies to switch industries and cities to gas and to encourage domestic exploration and production (E&P). Importantly, scenarios such as the BP 2020 Net Zero represent what needs to happen in order to achieve a climate target rather than the lack of natural gas' cost competitiveness, which often drives reference scenarios. As such, the value various governments attach to their energy security and economic and human development versus the value they attach to complying with international climate agreements is a critical consideration.

In this context, of interest is the relatively more bullish outlook of the Institute for Energy Economics of Japan (IEEJ). Given Japan's dependence on imports for majority of its energy needs, it is instructive to observe this industrialized economy seeking its energy security in nuclear and imported gas and coal rather than relying on renewables exclusively. The IEEJ scenarios probably reflect this experience. IEEJ expects gas demand to rise significantly in Africa, the Middle East, and Latin America (not shown in Fig. 5.1) as well. Under certain scenarios, aggregate gas demand growth in the Middle East, Africa, Latin America, and Eastern Europe and Eurasia can be as high as demand growth in Asia-Pacific. We tend to lean toward these more bullish outlooks driven by energy-secure economic and human development goals of most New World countries. Importantly, there will be many willing suppliers of gas within the New

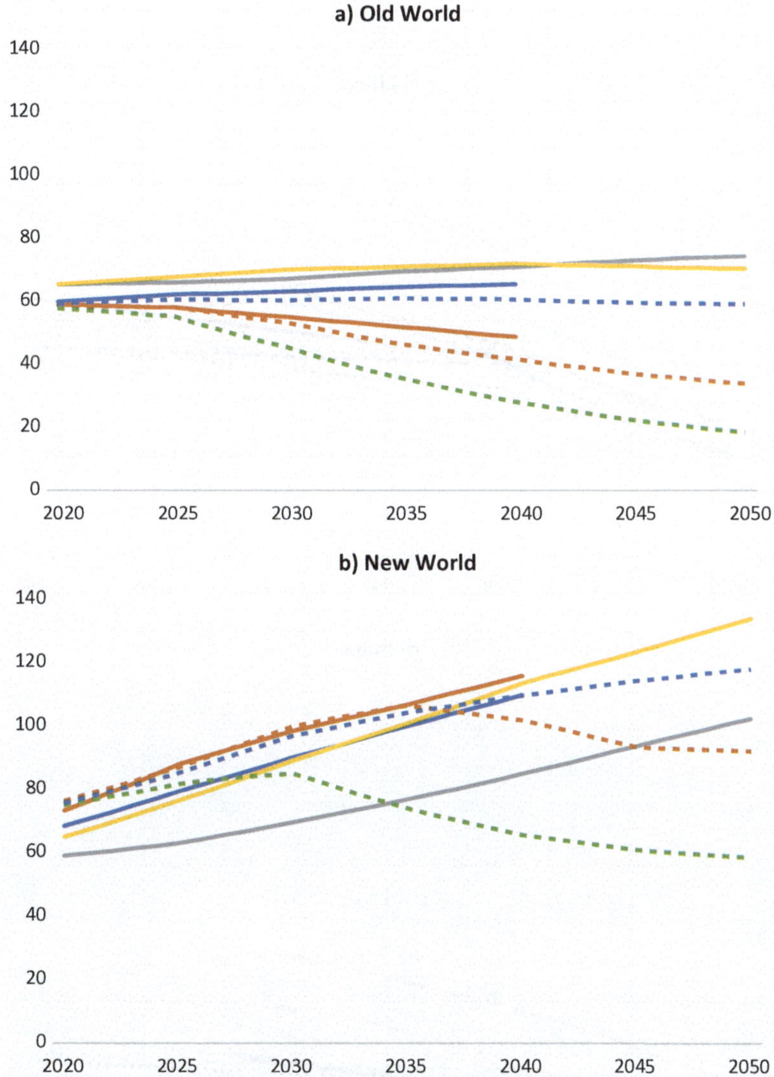

Fig. 5.1 Natural gas consumption scenarios (Quadrillion Btu, 2020–2050). (Sources: Compiled by the authors using data from RFF Global Energy Outlook 2020 and BP Energy Outlook 2020. Quadrillion Btu is roughly equivalent to a trillion cubic feet. The regional coverage of various outlooks varies and is not granular at a country level. Still, we are able to approximate our Old World as the U.S., Europe, and Eurasia/Russia and New World as the rest of the world). Since no scenario envisions gas demand growth in Russia, its inclusion in the Old World does not influence the contrast between Old and New Worlds. In addition to variation of regional definitions, 2020 values differ across scenarios also because different base years lead to different 2020 forecasts)

(*continued*)

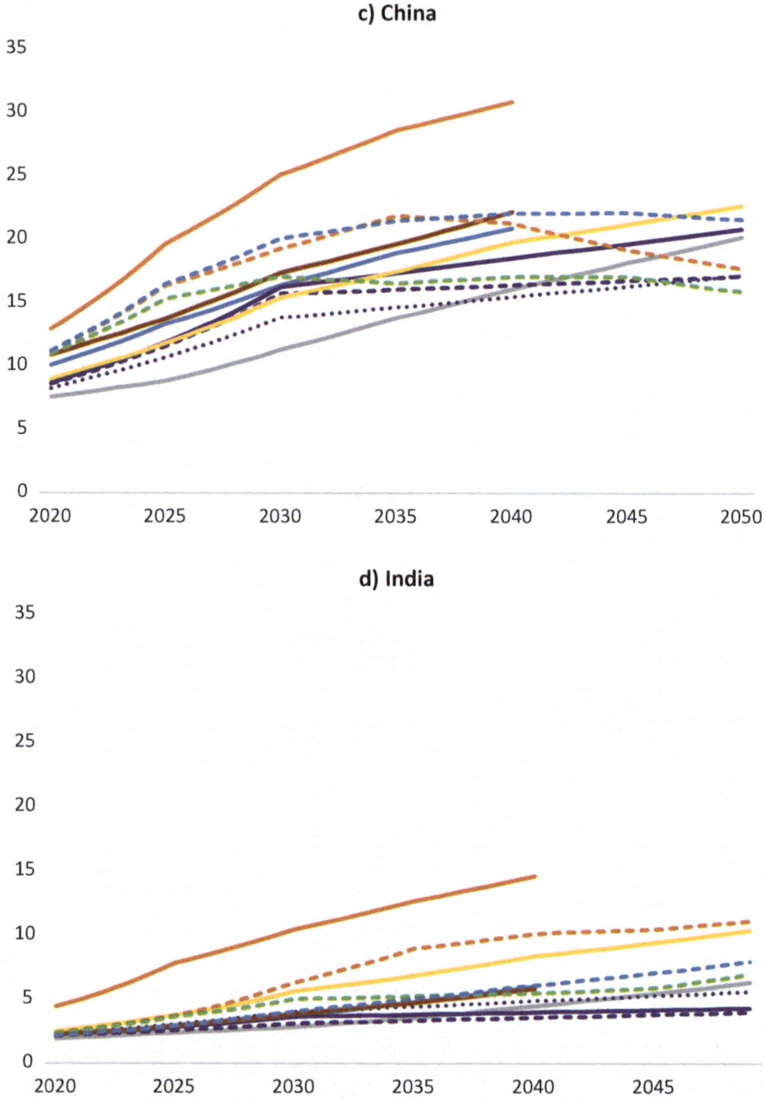

Fig. 5.1 (continued)

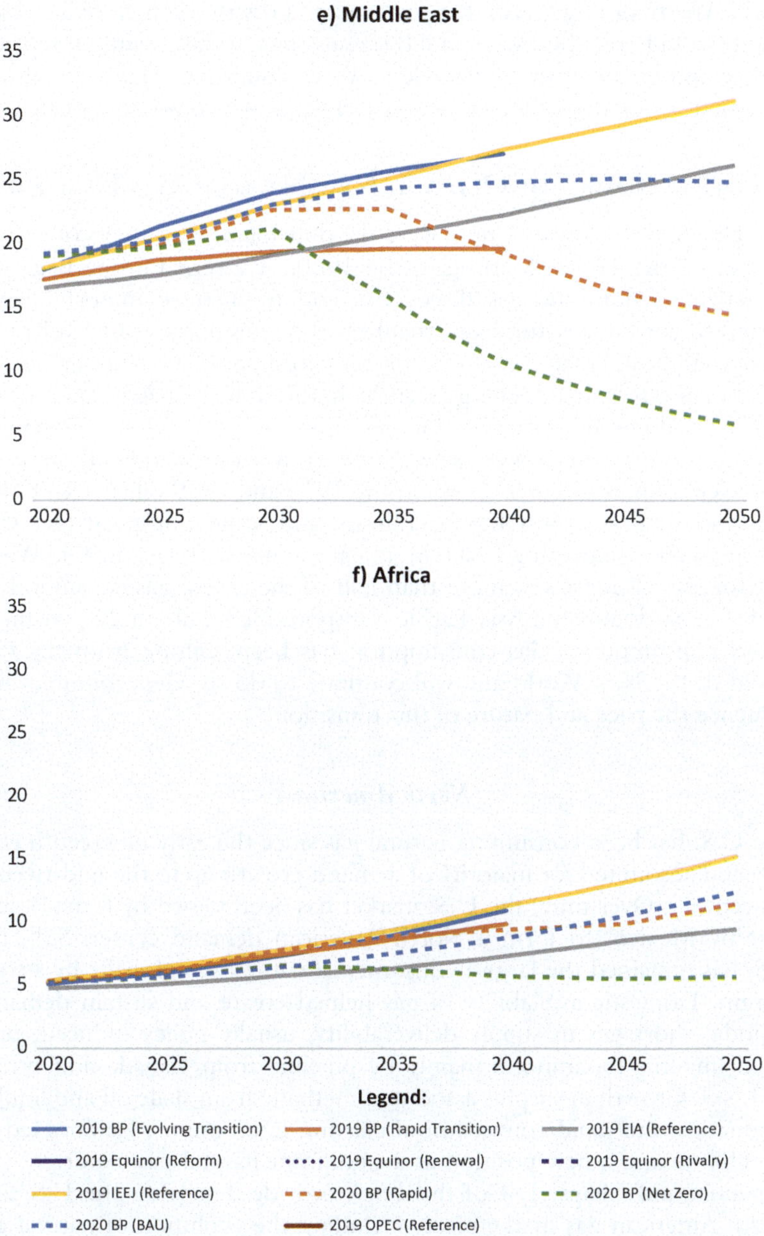

Fig. 5.1 (continued)

World. Worth noting is also that gas demand growth will help reduce local pollution and greenhouse gas (GHG) emissions to the extent gas replaces coal, common in most of the New World countries. This view also is informed by the discussion of energy trends, to which we now turn.

Geoeconomics of Old and New Natural Gas Demand

The U.S. and the Soviet Union were the only major consumers of natural gas before the 1970s. Starting in the 1960s, Western Europe began to monetize its domestic gas discoveries and to increase imports. Japan started to consume natural gas, thanks to LNG imports from Alaska that started in 1969. Japan's goal was not only to support the country's economy but also to enhance energy security in this industrialized island nation that lacks domestic natural resources. LNG imports allowed Japan to diversify—mostly in power generation—away from Middle Eastern oil perceived as increasingly risky given the 1973 and 1979 oil shocks. Other countries such as South Korea, Taiwan, and some European countries joined Japan in importing LNG on similar premises. Today, the Old World and Russia still represent more than half of the global gas consumption, while China-dominated Asia-Pacific is responsible for about 22 percent of global consumption. Gas consumption has been shifting from the Old World to the New World and will continue to do so. Geoeconomics will influence the pace and nature of this transition.

North America

The U.S. has been consuming natural gas since the early nineteenth century and accounted for majority of demand growth up to the mid-twentieth century. Over time, the U.S. market has been joined by Canada, and later by Mexico, to form a North American demand center. Still, the U.S. has remained the largest consumer of natural gas globally by a wide margin. Domestic availability of gas helped create and sustain demand. Periodic shortages in supply deliverability, usually policy induced, provided impetus for imports mainly by pipeline from Canada and briefly via LNG. Growth in surplus associated methane from shale oil and liquids production and rapid conversion of existing LNG import facilities led to the U.S. taking a new position as a significant natural gas exporter. The Appendix and Chaps. 1–4 of this book provide details on the U.S. and North American gas marketplace, including the evolution of natural gas supply and impact of shale plays, gas use in power generation (40 percent of total gas delivered to consumers), industrial sector (30 percent), and LNG exports, as well as policy and regulatory shifts.

Russia and Two Europes

Russia (and earlier the Soviet Union) is world's second largest gas consumer with more than half as much consumption as the U.S. In 2019, gas constituted approximately 53 percent of total energy consumption in Russia, used mostly for power generation (46 percent share of total generation), space heating, and industry (BP Statistical Review of World Energy 2020). Given low, regulated prices, domestic gas has been competitive against coal.

As in the U.S., the origin of gas demand in Russia is rooted in the availability of domestic supply, initially as a byproduct of oil. However, for the Soviet Union, natural gas development did not start until the mid-twentieth century. Afterward, production soared, bringing natural gas to major Soviet cities, including Moscow and Leningrad. Just slightly later, gas reached Nizhniy Novgorod or Cherepovets as well as the Baltic Republics.

The centrally planned economy of the Soviet Union has not allowed for development of a gas market. Moreover, development of gas fields remained secondary to both development of crude oil and military goals of the Soviet Union. Despite high resource endowment, the natural gas industry lagged behind in its ability to provide sufficient supply until supported by a strong demand-pull from Western Europe associated with transfer of technology and pipelines. After the collapse of the Soviet Union, a newly created company, Gazprom, took over the role of the Soviet Gas Ministry. The close connection between Gazprom and the Russian state was formalized in 2005, when the Russian state became majority shareholder.

Gazprom still controls the majority of Russian gas reserves and the entire Russian gas pipeline infrastructure, known as Unified Gas Supply System (UGSS). Until recently, the company had monopoly over all gas exports. It still continues to control all Russian gas exports via pipeline. However, privileges rarely come without a price. In case of Gazprom, the price is in the company's domestic obligations, with gas considered a societal rather than a market good. Within this framework, Gazprom's role is to support Russia's economy and government's social policies rather than making a profit. The company has been obligated to sell gas to domestic consumers at regulated prices that only recently have become closer to export netback prices.[2] In addition, Gazprom is considered a supplier of last resort in situations where consumers (private, institutional, or industrial) are unable to pay their bills.[3] Take, for example, the 2009–2010 worldwide economic recession when many Russian natural gas users were unable to cover costs of gas use. Gazprom effectively financed these customers, which propped the Russian economy by contributing to ability of companies to survive the crisis (Loe 2019).

Attempts at liberalizing Russian gas market have not been successful due to strong pushback against deregulated prices (OIES 2020). Trading gas at the Saint Petersburg International Mercantile Exchange (SPIMEX) has had limited impact because there are significant limits to secondary trading of purchased gas (Henderson 2011). In addition, companies that fail to consume the volumes of gas they purchased on SPIMEX face contractual penalties from Gazprom. Importantly, the latter continues to own the UGSS with only limited third-party access.[4]

Given these constraints, domestic Russian gas consumption, while sizable, has not resulted in substantial monetization of gas within the domestic market. Moreover, while the track record on monetization via gas exports has been better, the history of trade with Europe points to important non-monetary goals of this trade.

Here it is useful to make a distinction related to European demand. We have become accustomed to treating most members of the European Union (EU) similarly. However, when it comes to natural gas demand and Russian gas imports, a significant distinction persists between Western European countries and their counterparts from the former Soviet bloc.

Western European demand has been incentivized by domestically available supplies (predominantly North Sea and the Groningen field) and expanded on the heels of the 1970s oil shocks and concerns about energy security. By that time, the Soviet gas industry already was invested in promoting Russian natural gas exports to Europe. This supply-push was predicated upon significant discoveries of gas in Western Siberia. In this case, however, the motivation for exports has been amplified by the shortcomings of the Soviet industrial system. To develop its gas and expand its reach (even domestically), the Soviet Union needed significant additions of high-quality pipeline and compression. As a result, the first Soviet gas exports were effectively structured as more or less a "barter deal" in which natural gas was exchanged for pipeline and technology. The gas price was oil-indexed to reflect gas value as a substitute for fuel oil in the European economy.

Despite the Cold War, Western Europe has seen gas trade with the Soviet Union as less of a danger to energy security than reliance on Middle East oil. The underlying reason: a gas pipeline between points A and B creates interdependency between the supplier and the consumer. As European gas development stagnated and fell behind demand growth, Soviet gas became an increasingly important part of the West European energy consumption. For the Soviet Union and later for Russia, Europe has become an important export market: oil and gas export revenues constituted just over 40 percent of Russia's federal budget revenues in 2019 and closer to 50 percent in years prior (Yermakov and Henderson 2020). Oil indexation of gas exports contributed to the growing importance of gas as a source of Russia's income but also exposed the risks associated with oil price collapses in 2015–16 and 2020.

Common dependency made for rather uneventful, commercially driven relationship where Western European gas and utility companies collaborated with Gazprom on a variety of projects. Significant geopolitical issues and breaks in gas supply have not occurred until after the Iron Curtain fell, exposing the rifts in policy goals between Russia and the post-Soviet world and underlining the differences in motivations behind Russian gas exports to Western Europe versus those flowing to the post-Soviet bloc.[5]

Only Ukraine and Romania have had significant domestic natural gas supply. Ukraine's reserves were exploited to a large degree during the Soviet era: Ukraine was the initial source of Soviet gas supply before the center of gas development moved to Western Siberia. As noted by Mikulska and Kosinski (2020), despite attempts to revive Ukrainian gas production to produce more gas, including for export, there is not much to show for it at this time. Domestic gas production in 2019 reached 20.7 billion cubic meters (bcm) supporting approximately 70 percent of Ukraine's total gas demand that year (29.8 bcm). Romanian gas still satisfies most of that country's domestic demand, and new developments are under way, though admittedly not without challenges (Visenesc and Bartelet 2017; Reuters 2020a). Gas demand in other post-Soviet states was developed because of their communist relationship with the Soviet Union. Russia would be a source of majority, if not entire, supply of gas to those territories. The gas was often provided as barter for other products (industrial, agricultural) or was supplied at a very low price (compared to gas exported to Western Europe) to reflect the communist bond.

As such, gas was a tool of geopolitics in the region from the beginning. Post-1990 Russia has used this tool to influence politics in Eastern Europe and the Caucasus region. The 2006 and 2009 spats with Ukraine were most severe and resulted in disruptions to gas supply to Western Europe. Gas also was important in Russia's relations with Armenia and Georgia, and the latter's support for oil and gas pipelines from Azerbaijan to Turkey to avoid Armenia as a transit country. The Trans-Anatolian pipeline plays an important role in diversifying gas supplies for Turkey but also Southeast Europe via the recent Trans-Adriatic pipeline.

Diversification has become an important element of gas market strategy in that region (Hinchey and Mikulska 2017; Swora and Mikulska 2017) as Gazprom has been known to take advantage of its dominant position in post-Soviet gas markets. Gazprom has done so both, in terms of geopolitical influence and economically (by setting high prices) (Michot Foss and Palmer-Huggins 2016; Collins 2017; Newnham 2011). Many countries, including but not limited to Poland, Lithuania, and Croatia, have been investing, with the help of the EU, considerable resources to build LNG import terminals and new pipelines to improve connectivity and allow for better balancing of the gas market domestically and at the regional level.

Changing realities of natural gas trade combined with diversification efforts and EU competition authorities looking into specific trade agreements also have caused Gazprom to take a more market-oriented stance in the region by amending many of its long-term contracts and introducing lower pricing, hub-indexing, and lower take-or-pay commitments. Given a troubled past and lack of mutual trust, energy security and geopolitical risk play important roles in post-Soviet calculus when it comes to Russian gas supplies. As a result, some countries seem to be willing to pay a premium for non-Russian gas, with Poland being an extreme example as it seeks to eliminate long-term contracts with Russia altogether.

These developments have implications for monetization of non-Russian gas. Many of the long-term contracts between Russia and post-Soviet countries are slated to expire in the 2020s. As such, these countries present an opportunity for non-Russian suppliers to enter the market where Russian gas would be otherwise too competitive to push out. In a way, this avenue signifies new and growing demand source for non-Russian supplies, even if gas demand in those countries holds steady or declines. On the other hand, Russian gas reaching the European market via existing and new pipelines such as the Turkish Stream and Nord Stream 2 (as this book was completed, Nord Stream 2 was still not finished) may still find its way to these markets. Landlocked countries such as Hungary, Slovakia, Serbia, and the Czech Republic cannot import LNG directly. Direct LNG imports are also difficult for Romania, Bulgaria, or Ukraine due to the need for LNG ships to go through the Turkish Straits, possibility of which has been keenly rejected by Turkey. But as long as Russian gas is pooled in a liquid European market with access to a wide range of global resources and well-connected pipeline network, energy security of importers will be enhanced as compared to sole dependence on Russian gas from a direct pipeline (Collins and Mikulska 2018; Collins and Mikulska 2020).

From the perspective of gas monetization, it is worth noting that many of the post-Soviet countries are experiencing high levels of economic growth relative to developed economies in Western Europe. This is likely to incentivize higher energy demand, including higher demand for natural gas. The latter, actually, could be a result of EU decarbonization policies. Even though in Western European countries those policies also target natural gas as a fossil fuel and source of greenhouse gas (GHG) emissions, in Eastern Europe the same policies can actually enable natural gas demand as the most viable alternative to coal, which supplies a good portion of domestic energy demand.[6]

Asia-Pacific

Japan used to dominate discussions about Asia-Pacific natural gas, even though in the 1970s, China consumed nearly as much. Unlike Japan, Chinese consumption was satisfied with domestically produced natural gas. During the 1980s, Australia, Indonesia, Pakistan, Malaysia, Thailand, and Bangladesh either increased or started producing and consuming significant amounts of natural gas, with some of these countries becoming large exporters. By the mid-1990s, Indonesia and Malaysia were responsible for half of global LNG exports, with Australia representing more than 10 percent. Around the same time, Japan accounted for about two-thirds of global LNG imports. At the time, global LNG trade was about one-fifth of what it is today.

Japan's initiation of LNG imports from Alaska, Brunei, and Indonesia in the 1970s was driven by that country's desire to improve its energy security and to reduce air pollution. Home to one of the world's largest economies, Japan has always depended on energy imports because the country lacks oil, natural gas, and coal resource endowments. Switching power generation from imported (mostly Middle Eastern) oil to natural gas (LNG) helped Japan's energy security by diversifying its energy portfolio in terms of both type of fuel used and countries of origin. LNG facilities were built mostly by Japanese utilities since the 1960s. Government policy, financial assistance (e.g., to power companies to switch to gas), and price regulation allowed for cost recovery.

Energy security considerations have also been important for Japan's decision to heavily invest in nuclear power. After the closure of nuclear plants following the Fukushima disaster, LNG imports, enabled by the existence of import terminals, prevented a major energy shortage. This demonstrated the option value of these assets. To increase its options further, Japan also increased subsidies for solar generation that reached 7.5 percent of total generation, roughly equal to hydropower. At the same time, coal-fired generation still provided about 30 percent of country's electricity needs, which underlines the importance of cost for global competitiveness, even for a highly developed economy. After Fukushima, coal often provided a cheaper alternative to nuclear power than LNG. To avoid potential overreliance on coal and/or LNG, Japan is in the process of restarting its nuclear power fleet, albeit slowly, as it continues to consider nuclear as the cheapest option to provide the reliable energy its industrial economy needs. Increasing nuclear generation also helps with lowering emissions and improving its trade balance. Nuclear is also central to new ambitions for hydrogen production. A recent pledge by Japan to be carbon neutral by 2050 may instigate early retirement of certain coal plants, which may benefit gas and renewables (e.g., McCracken 2020).

Today, Japan remains the world's largest LNG importer accounting for roughly 22 percent of LNG imports, followed by China (17 percent), South Korea (11 percent), India (7 percent), and Taiwan (5 percent). In other words, the Pacific Basin still dominates global LNG trade and is likely to do so, given the projections for gas demand growth in the region.

In South Korea, growth in gas demand will most likely come from phasing out coal-fired power plants, which currently generate more than 40 percent of electricity. In early 2019, the government reduced the LNG fuel tax by 75 percent while increasing the coal fuel tax 28 percent, resulting in the coal fuel tax being twice as large (Global Gas Report 2020). Assuming that LNG prices remain cheap relative to substitutes, this will encourage more coal-to-gas switching. However, long-term sustainability of switching will remain dependent on various factors, including (1) government policies on further taxation of pollution (coal), (2) the price of oil (to which most LNG coming to South Korea is indexed), and (3) LNG import arrangement (share of short-term and spot cargoes relative to long-term oil-indexed supply). Nuclear power could also be a significant competitor to natural gas, as South Korea is a leading nuclear technology developer and exporter. The share of nuclear generation has been increasing, supplying 26 percent of electricity in 2019. There are four plants under construction. In 2017, the new president announced plans to phase nuclear out by 2060 or so, which contributed to cancellation of plans for several new nuclear plants. Combined with policies to improve air quality, a moratorium on new nuclear capacity will likely increase LNG demand further over the next couple of decades.

As opposed to natural gas-poor Japan and South Korea, Indonesia and Malaysia used to be the major LNG exporters. Even today, they account for only about 16 percent of global LNG exports. More strikingly, they also import LNG due to declining reserves, increasing domestic demand, and difficulty of connecting different regions of these countries given the numerous islands and challenging terrain.[7] In these countries, power generation, industrial (fertilizer), and, to a lesser extent, transport sectors drive natural gas demand. Similar forces are pushing self-sufficient consumers of the past such as Pakistan, Bangladesh, and Thailand to become LNG importers. Power generation is often the key driver of demand, but fertilizer and light industries, as well as widespread use of compressed natural gas (CNG) in transport, also are important. Vietnam and other small economies in the region are following suit.

The single biggest player in Asia-Pacific is, of course, China. The country is currently consuming nearly 8 percent of global gas (compared to 22 percent for the U.S., 14 percent for Europe, and 11 percent for Russia) while producing more than 4 percent (still, more than Australia, the second largest producer in the region). China's natural gas infrastructure mostly has been shaped by long-term policies rooted primarily in energy security considerations. Industrial sector (mainly petrochemicals) drives demand growth, but power generation, city distribution networks to serve smaller customers, and the transport sector also contribute. Today, however, pressures from China's growing middle class to reduce urban air pollution are propelling coal-to-gas and liquids-to-gas switching. China has the world's largest LNG-fueled truck fleet, while the country prefers electric drive for smaller vehicles. Since 2010, Chinese gas demand grew at an annual average of 12 percent, while domestic production grew only at 7 percent. The expanding gap was balanced with pipeline and LNG imports, which grew at 34 percent per year since 2015 as compared to a steady 18 percent for pipelines.

China built a dual gas pipeline from Turkmenistan via Uzbekistan and Kazakhstan to the Chinese border (each about 1800 km) and then invested in pipelines for delivering that gas to the consumption centers in the east. Private companies could not commercially justify such a pipeline, especially given the geopolitical risks. Similarly, pipelines from Myanmar and Russia (Power of Siberia) would have not been built without state (SOE) involvement and public funds. China's national oil companies (NOCs) have built most of the 22 LNG terminals currently operating, and more are under construction, with private companies starting to play a more dominant role. Overall, the country has substantial capacity across the natural gas value chain, albeit still insufficient to balance growing demand and supply smoothly across the country throughout the year. Thus, investment in gas infrastructure continues to be needed. In essence, China, via its SOEs (some owned by local governments), has been investing in real options that give the country flexibility to switch between fuels and suppliers to meet its energy needs at lowest cost, essential for energy and economic security. Increasingly, private companies are entering the fray by building LNG import terminals and trading gas, encouraged by some reforms such as the creation of an independent midstream company that will provide open access to pipelines.

India has the potential to be a second China in terms of fast-growing natural gas demand. Growing population, hazardous air pollution in major cities, and increasing demands of a growing middle class for less pollution are pushing the country toward gas use in industry (India's largest consumer of gas in 2019), transportation, and buildings (commercial and residential). Unlike China, however, Indian public funding and SOEs are not as capable of building gas infrastructure capacity. Pricing and regulatory frameworks have not been conducive to private investment in domestic E&P or midstream. As such, insufficient domestic infrastructure has been more of a constraint on gas demand growth in India than in China. There are only six LNG import terminals and about 17,000 km of transmission pipelines. There also are external challenges to pipeline gas imports. The geography and geopolitics of the South Asian region has prevented several pipeline projects (from Iran and Turkmenistan via Pakistan and Afghanistan), and high cost has been a handicap for others (underwater pipeline from the Middle East).

Therefore, when it comes to gas as India's energy security enhancement, much will depend on LNG imports, which currently meet more than half of India's gas consumption. India's government plans to add more than ten LNG terminals (including FSRUs). It will also expand its pipeline infrastructure from 17,000 to approximately 32,000 km in the next few years, per India's oil minister Dharmendra Pradhan (Srivastava 2020). Most important, affordability of natural gas remains a major challenge in India, especially for the fertilizer industry and urban users, which historically used cheaper, often subsidized, fuels.

It is significant that gas-fired generation has not been able to reduce the role of coal in Indian power generation. In fact, gas-fired generation peaked at less than 120 terawatt-hours (TWh) in 2010 and has been stable at about 70 TWh since 2011. In contrast, coal-fired generation increased from 640 TWh in 2010 to 1170 TWh in 2018. India has plans to gasify 100 million tons of thermal coal (roughly 14 percent of 2019 production). Although details are unclear at this time, Coal India Ltd. is indicating up to $55 billion investment in gasification and liquefaction (for fertilizer production) by 2030. Given the importance of coal to local communities and Indian economy, these plans cannot be ruled out as too expensive or inconsistent with environmental goals. Still, gas is promoted by the Indian government among other alternatives, especially in fertilizer, city distribution networks, and transportation (CNG), with a goal of 15 percent share of the energy mix for gas in 2030. In November 2020, Prime Minister Modi increased this target to 25 percent. A great deal depends on the implementation of reforms the Indian government announced in 2020, which, besides development of midstream infrastructure, also promise market-driven gas pricing to encourage domestic and foreign investment along the gas supply chain (Srivastava 2020).

Middle East

Gas consumption in the Middle East has been increasing pursuant to a strategy of oil-to-gas switching and industrialization over the 2010s, but demand growth may slow within a decade. Mills (2020) predicts "improved efficiency, higher gas prices, slower economic growth and alternative generation" to drive this slowdown.

The region consumes about 14 percent of global gas (similar to Europe or Russia, and nearly ten times as much as India), but 40 percent of this consumption occurs in Iran and another 20 percent in Saudi Arabia. Due to years of sanctions, Iran has not been able to export much gas, except to Turkey and Iraq, via pipelines. The use of gas instead of oil or refined products also allows the country to export more liquids and generate more hard currency. Similar strategies are being followed by other major oil exporters in the region, including Saudi Arabia and UAE.

With significant gas reserves in the region (roughly 20 percent of global proved reserves) and demand expected to grow further (Fig. 5.1), more upstream, midstream, and downstream gas investment is already under way or planned to increase both domestic consumption and exports. That being said, difficult relations between Qatar, region's largest LNG exporters, and Saudi Arabia (and other Gulf Cooperation Council, or GCC, countries), have so far resulted in very sparse intraregional pipeline infrastructure. Indeed, regional tensions and rivalries have prevented pipeline gas trade in a region that should be one of the more conducive to cross-border exchanges (a similar pattern is in place in South America, as we note later). In addition, gas faces competition from renewable energy, nuclear, and coal. (The BP scenarios in Fig. 5.1 reflect the potential impact of this competition.) For example, the UAE, where gas used to provide all power generation in the past, plans to reduce the share of gas to 38 percent of installed capacity by 2050. Renewables are forecast to constitute 44 percent, nuclear 6 percent, and coal 12 percent of power generation. The first nuclear plant of nearly 6 GW of capacity in the UAE started generating from one completed unit in August 2020, while the construction of other units continues. Surprisingly, Dubai is building the second-largest coal-fired power plant in the region (3.6 GW of planned capacity). These choices reflect energy security concerns within the context of difficult relations with Qatar and Iran (Krane 2020).

Another challenge is the potential increase in the cost of gas. Historically, most gas in the region has been associated with oil (hence very low cost), and consumers have been paying very low prices set by governments. Low oil prices since 2015 have strained government budgets and subsidies have been cut, though not fully eliminated. Gas prices also have been rising partially to justify new gas resource development (e.g., see Mills 2020). Higher prices raise concerns about economic competitiveness, but governments seem to be focused on improving efficiency (e.g., switching to combined-cycle power generation from combustion turbines) rather than reinstating significant end-user subsidies. Instead, governments focus on developing major petrochemical and other industrial capabilities (e.g., see Benali and Al-Ashmawy 2020).

Latin America

Latin America is not a major consumer of natural gas (only 4 percent of global total). The region is home to significant resources that remain mostly underdeveloped. Long-standing regional tensions and rivalries, including territorial conflicts, have limited the growth of cross-border pipelines for natural gas trade. For example, Bolivia, a landlocked country with sizable reserves, has been exporting gas to Argentina and Brazil, but the volumes fluctuated, depending on the performance of the volatile economies of Argentina and, to a lesser extent, Brazil. More importantly, those countries' ability to meet their energy needs from alternative resources undermined Bolivian exports. For instance, high hydroelectricity (wet) years in Brazil reduce the need for gas-fired generation. Also, both Brazil and Argentina have their own gas resources and ability to import LNG. Argentina, already the largest consumer of gas in the region, likely will increase its self-sufficiency with the development of unconventional resources in Vaca Muerta, which is being targeted by the government as part of a stimulus plan (e.g., see Braga 2020), but high cost of production and transportation from remote location of resources remains a challenge.

Argentina resumed exports to Chile after cutting them during the economic crisis of the mid-2000s to provide subsidize gas to its citizens, which reduced upstream development. Today, domestic demand once again trumps exports to Chile, which is encouraged to expand its LNG import capacity to enhance its energy security. Brazil also could achieve self-sufficiency with associated gas from its giant pre-salt fields. With solutions to technical challenges, Brazil could satisfy domestic demand as well as export LNG.[8] The historical animosity between Bolivia and Chile prevented Bolivian gas exports to Chile as well as Bolivian gas being exported to other countries via a liquefaction facility in Chile. Peru LNG was the catalyst that allowed the development of the Camisea field and eliminated the Peru option for Bolivian exports. This long history of unstable exports to Brazil and Argentina and the lack of upstream investment in Bolivia due to unattractive fiscal regime, high political risk, and low domestic demand led to a decline in reserves and production in Bolivia.

Peru and Colombia, though smaller consumers, are the only two countries that have seen stable growth in gas demand since the Great Recession of 2008. In both countries, use of natural gas in vehicles has been significant. Bolivia, already doing the same, may increase gasification of its transport sector as its export volumes to Argentina and Brazil decline. Although there are many uncertainties in this historically volatile—politically and economically—region, availability of large natural gas resources and production history induces us to favor outlooks that foresee at least 50 percent increase in gas demand over the next 20 years.

Africa

Africa, as ever, is promising. With nearly a billion people, mostly in sub-Saharan Africa (SSA), the continent has the largest concentration of people without access to modern energy, which makes elimination of massive poverty with all the attendant ills even more difficult. This situation is paradoxical since many countries have large oil and gas resources: Nigeria, Angola, Egypt, and Algeria. Africa is also home to emerging producers such as Cameroon, Mauritania, Senegal, Mozambique, Tanzania, and Ghana. Only a few countries such as Algeria and Egypt have been able to monetize their resources via pipeline and LNG exports as well as domestic use, mainly for power generation.

In contrast, Nigeria has the largest gas reserves in Africa. However, the only monetization occurs through LNG exports, which is set to expand as *Nigeria LNG* decided to add a seventh liquefaction train and has plans to add more trains. Otherwise, the country has not been able to develop most of its gas. Notably, Nigeria has been unable to monetize associated gas, which ends up being flared. There are many reasons for this failure, including the terms of legacy upstream contracts that do not ban flaring, incumbent interests in the power generation sector, and other, mostly political, considerations. Importantly, the gas-power value chain is broken; electricity prices are set by the government, often below cost; and many customers do not pay their bills, which creates a domino effect: distribution utilities cannot pay the transmission company, which, in turn, cannot pay private generators, which, then, are unwilling to commit to long-term contracts with gas suppliers.

Ultimately, the inability to finance and develop domestic gas and electric power infrastructure has been a major impediment. Nigeria, with a population of roughly 200 million, has less than 15 GW of installed generation capacity and only a fraction of this capacity is able to dispatch consistently due to infrastructure bottlenecks. Over 80 percent of Nigeria's estimated peak electricity demand is met by off-grid electricity generation, often fueled by diesel. The long-awaited Petroleum Industry Bill, which was submitted to Nigeria's National Assembly at the end of September 2020, may address some of the legal and regulatory gaps when it is finally enacted. There are parallel initiatives in the power sector to increase generation and transmission capacity (Goodrich 2020). In the meantime, smaller-scale projects of delivering gas by private investors are moving forward despite the difficulties, driven by the desire to replace expensive diesel. They include expansion of local gas distribution systems, small-scale LNG distribution to business and industrial customers, and CNG projects. Although important, these initiatives only add up to several hundred miles of pipelines and several hundred million cubic feet a day of gas consumption. Much more is needed for Nigeria to use its natural gas to lift its population out of poverty.

Corruption has been the main culprit in SSA, causing massive deficiencies in institutional and governance infrastructure. Nevertheless, there is a renewed hope and homegrown movements to improve the politics and institutions to allow for better governance. A key target of these efforts is to develop continent's natural gas resources for domestic use in power generation and industry to create value added for the economies in the region. Many outlooks predict gas demand to double by 2040, but we must acknowledge significant upside and downside to this scenario, dependent on African countries' performance in eliminating institutional and governance inadequacies and both internal and regional political risks.

Between Coal and a Sunny Place

Given the growing focus on energy transition around the world, it is worth expanding on the energy mix considerations in various geographies and, in particular, how natural gas fits into this transition.

Coal has been prevalent in many of the New World countries. For example, coal consumption nearly tripled in China between the late 1990s and mid-2010s, before stabilizing. Similarly, coal consumption in India tripled between the late 1990s and 2019. Other countries, mostly in Asia-Pacific, also increased their coal consumption. As a result, despite the declining consumption in the Old World, world coal consumption has remained stable since the early 2010s. Coal is used primarily to generate electricity and in heat-intensive industries such as steel. Over the years, these heavy industries migrated to the New World. In particular, metallurgical coal is difficult to eliminate in heavy industries because of its high heat content. In contrast, very little coal is used for space heating, mostly in China, which is expanding gas distribution networks to eliminate household and commercial use of coal and, in doing so, improve urban air quality.

In general, two factors are responsible for coal's decline in the Old World: (1) increasing availability of natural gas and renewables, and (2) policy. The ability of people to pay for potentially more expensive but less polluting energy sources can affect both of these factors. Indeed, as discussed in Chap. 2, the retail cost of electricity has been rising across the U.S., most visibly in states with highest renewables mandates. Although the U.S. consumers, on average, have been able to afford more expensive electricity, millions of households receive assistance from the federal Low-Income Home Energy Assistance Program and many more from state or local programs. For some consumer groups, rising energy costs is a growing concern in the U.S. Other wealthy Old World countries also face the same issue. Per the European Commission, in 2018, approximately 34 million households in Europe were unable to afford indoor thermal comfort (EC 2020). Hence, even countries in the Old World may not be totally free to pursue their clean energy initiatives without consideration of lower-income populations. Lack of such consideration could result in societal dissatisfaction that can be reflected in either electoral results or protests. The "Yellow Jackets" protests in France in 2018, which started in response to additional fuel taxes, were reminiscent of many past protests in New World countries when their governments tried to eliminate their fuel subsidies. This affordability of energy provides important context to coal's resilience.

Coal often is more than a mere energy source in the New World. Where it is available domestically, coal also constitutes a major source of economic activity and employment, which makes weaning off coal more difficult. We know this phenomenon to be the case in the two largest consumers of coal, China and India, mining safety concerns notwithstanding. The economic dominance of coal exists elsewhere too. For example, in Poland, the strong political power of mining communities makes it extremely difficult for policy-makers across the political spectrum to move the country away from coal (Mikulska and Kosinski 2018). Such a shift would endanger livelihoods of thousands of miners and their families, who then, thanks to set of electoral factors, could effectively vote the entire government out of office.[9] Note that while coal-fired power generation in Poland has been falling, it has done so at much slower levels than what would be suggested by Poland's membership in the EU. In fact, Poland is the only EU member that has not signed the European Green Deal and, ironically, Poland is a target for new, energy-intense manufacturing of linchpin green deal technologies, such as lithium batteries for energy storage. While the EU can definitely express its disappointment and even impose fines on its members for not following EU rules, it cannot vote the Polish government out of office (Mikulska and Kosinski 2018).

That being said, advances in power generation have made natural gas a formidable competitor, particularly where prices are low and access is assured (Fig. 5.2). This has been the case in the U.S., where precipitous increase of gas production from low-permeability resources has knocked down prices from the 2005 high point and kept gas near or below $3 per million Btu (MMBtu) for several years (see Chap. 1 for extensive treatment). The U.S. LNG exports directly transmit the low Henry Hub price (see Chap. 4; coal exports transmit the Henry Hub price indirectly). The U.S. exports of light oil also have helped reduce the cost of oil-indexed

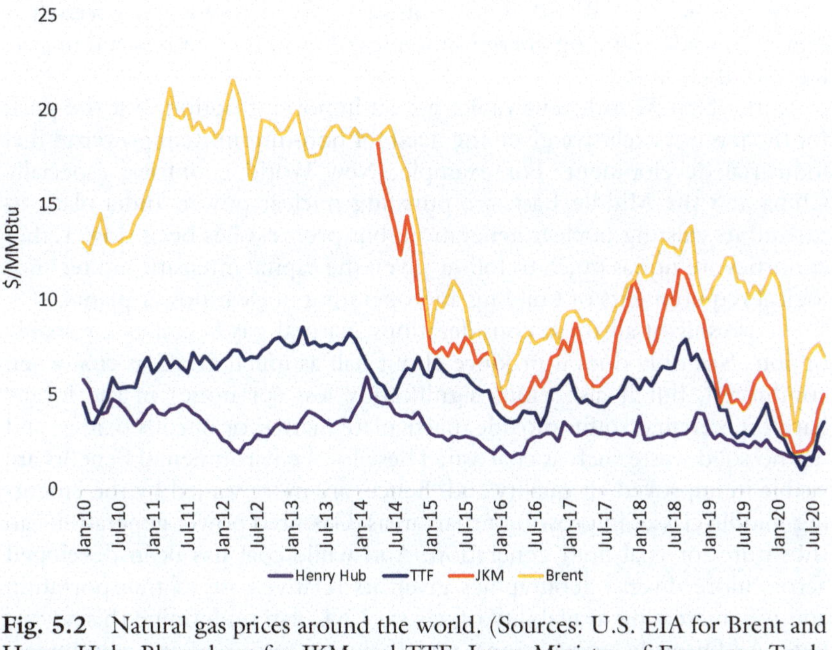

Fig. 5.2 Natural gas prices around the world. (Sources: U.S. EIA for Brent and Henry Hub, Bloomberg for JKM and TTF. Japan Ministry of Economy, Trade and Industry Spot LNG Prices to fill the gaps in Bloomberg JKM data)

LNG. Policy and regulatory actions have accelerated coal-to-gas switch as well. For example, several environmental regulations hastened the exit of many coal plants in an environment of low electricity prices, thanks to cheap natural gas (see Chap. 2). The EU's decarbonization policies have also been successful in pushing out coal to make space for less carbon-intensive fuels.[10]

Political pressure on fossil fuels, reflecting climate activism, increasingly targets drilling and, especially, midstream infrastructure such as pipelines and gas-fired power plants (see Chap. 2 for the U.S. case). Instead, activists promote renewable energy, especially in Old World countries and sub-jurisdictions characterized by wealthier populations. In these locations, government-incentivized investment in alternative energy capacity is almost purely for economic development and/or technology transition. In the New World, by contrast, new energy capacity is needed to meet the basic energy needs of billions of low-income people and new demand from growing populations with more disposable income. Concerns about air quality rather than GHG emissions typically drive the push for cleaner energy in the New World. This contrast between ***choice*** and ***necessity*** is crucial to understanding energy strategies of various countries and importance of their SOEs.

In the New World, renewables are an important option, but the push for them is not exclusive given the need for non-intermittent power to fuel industrial development. For example, New World countries, especially China and the Middle East, are pursuing nuclear power. India plans to expand its existing nuclear generation, but progress has been slow. Other countries are not as quick to follow given the capital intensity and technological requirements of building and operating nuclear power plants.

As a result of all these considerations, natural gas becomes a valuable option. Not only does it produce about half as much GHG as coal when combusted, but it also emits significantly less (or none) of the locally harmful mercury, sulfur dioxide, particulate matter, or nitrous oxides, and has no solid waste such as coal ash. These local environmental benefits are visible in improved air quality and, hence, are more valued by the emerging middle classes in growing urban areas. Gas-fired power generation can substitute for coal-fired generation. And while coal has been developed across more diverse geographies given its relative ease of transportation and use, increasing availability of gas via LNG can undermine this advantage. Additionally, conventional and shale gas resources are now understood to be available across wider geographies. For example, China has been growing its shale production, albeit slowly, given the difficult geology (e.g., see Jacobs 2019). If these resources can be developed at scale, they can provide an alternative to the domestic coal industry when it comes to employment and economic benefits. Nevertheless, the resilience of coal production in many countries around the world suggests that this substitution is not easy, and any movement away from coal and toward natural gas and renewables will be gradual.

New World Order?

A detailed discussion is beyond the scope of this chapter, but the realignment of world powers, which we can crudely simplify as Russia and China relative to the U.S., is a very relevant context for global gas trade. This realignment reveals itself in trade wars, new partnerships around the world, territorial claims, sanctions, and so on. For example, China's Belt and Road Initiative (BRI; or "Belt and Road Strategy" as the Chinese leadership views it) is part of China's expansion of its sphere of influence. China also launched the Asian Infrastructure Investment Bank (AIIB), an alternative to the World Bank and its affiliates such as the Asian Development Bank. The AIIB reports about $100 billion in commitments from its members.[11]

As part of BRI, or to pursue other strategic interests, China has invested more than $2 trillion ***outside of its borders*** since 2005, averaging $180 billion a year in the 2010s. More than $725 billion was invested in energy, averaging $60 billion in the 2010s (American Enterprise Institute). In contrast, total global energy investment averaged about $1.6 trillion a year in the 2010s according to IEA (2020a), with roughly 20–30 percent of investment taking place in China. In other words, China has been investing in other countries' energy sector an amount equivalent to about one-fifth of its domestic energy investment. Although much of the investment has been in resource-rich countries, significant investment has been in countries mostly ignored by Western lenders or donor agencies (e.g., nearly $106 billion in SSA). Notably, Chinese investment does not come with the same conditions with respect to democratic reforms, social norms, or climate change as Western donors often impose.

Without doubt, energy, without secure and affordable supply of which economic power cannot be established or manifest, is critical to this geostrategic game. Natural gas is certainly an important consideration. For example, Russia's "pivot to the east," which was exemplified in the Power of Siberia pipeline to China as well as Arctic LNG, can be seen as part of this realignment. It is also a reaction to energy transition themes in Western Europe. The U.S. LNG exports, although not controlled by the U.S. government, have become an influence tool in this new "cold war." In response to the U.S. trade war, China stopped importing the U.S. LNG, a decision made very easy given the availability of other low-cost LNG supplies. On the other hand, the U.S. LNG is providing Europeans, especially some post-Soviet countries, with an alternative to Russia being the sole supplier of gas. The U.S. sanctions on Nord Stream 2 should also be seen within the same cold war context, although they also strain relations between the U.S. and European allies such as Germany. Also, if anti-gas efforts around the U.S. (see Chaps. 1 and 2) continue to succeed in blocking gas development, the U.S. LNG may not be delivered to Europe in sufficient quantities, further straining the U.S.–EU relations. A market-based strategy could be a better way to support U.S. energy exports while building geoeconomic advantage (Collins and Mikulska 2020).

Old and New Commercial Arrangements

The U.S. gas market is the most liquid market in the world and has been so for a long time. The Canadian gas market is closely linked to the U.S. market with major pipeline connections. Since the 1990s, the Western European gas market has become more competitive as a result of a series of reforms and increased capability of procuring gas supplies from diverse sources. We refer readers to Chap. 1 and Appendix for a detailed discussion of the U.S. gas market.

Liquidity does not come easily. In fact, the dependence of a competitive and well-diversified natural gas market on expansive midstream and downstream infrastructure—somewhat counterintuitively—often requires significant government involvement as regulators in the Old World but often more prominently in the New World through their SOEs and non-market policies. We refer readers to the "Characteristics of Liquid Gas Markets" section in Chap. 6 for a more detailed discussion of gas market liquidity and cross-country comparisons.

The proclivity of New World countries to government-led gas sector regimes is strong, especially where gas imports are significant. In the early days of gas market development, local distribution companies (LDCs) were often part of the SOE that built the import pipelines or LNG facilities as well as the transmission backbone within the country. Alternatively, the

Electrification Versus Gasification

Electrification of all activity in the Old World targets reduction of fossil fuel use, whereas electrification in the New World targets fueling of economic and human development. In much of the New World, the cost of T&D and storage infrastructure needed for increasing natural gas demand can be a serious disadvantage against both coal and renewables. This is particularly visible for countries with a strong electrification agenda. Although Sustainable Development Goals, SDG 7, reporting (ESMAP 2020) suggests less than one billion people without access to electricity, mostly in South and Southeast Asia, Africa, and, to a lesser extent, Latin America, this number is misleading. This is because SDG 7 is a binary metric that defines access as having grid connection or some form of distributed energy source. Ayaburi et al. (2020), in contrast, report roughly 3.5 billion people without "reasonably reliable" access to electricity services. We find the latter number a more accurate depiction of energy poverty. In 2018, global average electricity consumption per person per year was about 3700 kWh. This number should not be confused with average residential consumption. It includes electricity consumed across the economy. After all, an economy cannot modernize without businesses and industries that provide the jobs and services the society needs. Our rough estimates of one-time capital investment necessary to increase electricity consumption of every global denizen to 3700 kWh ranges from $4 trillion (all combined cycle gas) to $12 trillion (all rooftop solar).

Electricity from sources other than gas-fired power plants can provide the modern energy needs for economic and human development, and the country can avoid constructing gas infrastructure. Utilizing the cheapest domestic fuel source, which is coal in India, China, and other Southeast Asian nations, for power generation and deploying renewables where feasible are indeed what has been going on in many countries with electrification goals. Midstream infrastructure investment in the coal-to-power supply chain is significantly less capital-intensive than the gas-to-power supply chain (40 percent of total costs for gas vs. 10 percent for coal according to IEA, 2016). The scenario is, perhaps, oversimplistic but without policy mandates (such as the legal requirement in China that resi-

(*continued*)

(continued)
dential and designated industrial customers switch from coal to gas by a date certain) and/or financial penalties like effective carbon taxes, countries may well seek fuel alternatives that do not bear the transport cost which comes with gas usage. On the other hand, electrification can be pursued with gas-fired power as well. The need for gas infrastructure investment to fuel power plants can be kept to a minimum by placing power plants near gas transmission pipelines and LNG import terminals. Increasing utilization of gas-fired plants would reduce unit cost of electricity, rendering gas more competitive. And, in fact, investment in gas-fired power plants has been averaging about $50 billion in recent years (IEA 2020a), roughly the same as coal-fired plants and about a fourth of solar and wind investments. Importantly, given the low capacity factor of wind and solar due to their intermittency and often lower capital cost of gas-fired plants, these investments result in equivalent or larger gas-fired generation capability than wind and solar.

state may not directly own LDCs, but establish them as monopolies with direct state backing and control. This has been the case in many European countries until privatization efforts in the energy industry began in the 1990s. The regulated, private, investor-owned LDC model adopted since the 2000s in Europe and elsewhere around the world (with some state ownership remaining in some cases) has been the norm in the U.S. since the late 19th century. Regulators of these naturally monopolistic companies are public servants, usually appointed, and thus not always free of influence.[12]

We must acknowledge the ability of consumers to pay mostly unsubsidized prices for competing fuels in developed economies of Western Europe as a key ingredient of the successful formula for developing a well-functioning, competitive natural gas market. Netback pricing, initiated in the Netherlands to monetize the Groningen discovery in 1959, set the price of gas delivered to various groups of customers (households, commercial businesses, industrial facilities) relative to other fuels (e.g., fuel oil) they were consuming. Luckily, the prices of those fuels were high enough to allow gas prices charged to customers to cover the full cost of producing and delivering natural gas, including an acceptable rate of return on capital invested in the transmission and distribution (T&D) infrastructure.

This ability to pay lacks in most countries that are trying to develop their internal gas markets. This is partially due to a history of consuming subsidized or domestically available cheap fuels. We also must note that the ability to pay and the willingness to pay are not always the same. The latter can be undermined if customers are used to paying subsidized prices for other fuels even if they can afford to pay the full cost of delivered gas. Building import infrastructure (pipelines or LNG), developing domestic resources, and using gas for power generation, methanol and fertilizer production are relatively straightforward, albeit costly, but they are insufficient to create a liquid market. Developing a deeper gas market requires a variety of customers that can afford the cost of gas plus the cost of new T&D infrastructure consisting of different diameter pipelines and storage (preferably some large underground capacity). This infrastructure must be geographically dispersed and must have sufficient capacity to balance demand and supply that vary across customer classes and different time frames (within a day, across days of the week, and, perhaps most importantly, seasons).

From these main points of risk inherent in natural gas value chain infrastructure, cultural preferences for balancing market and government strategies to manage and mitigate risk and affordability, we turn to four aspects of liquidity growth today and going forward: anchor customers for large capital projects, price formation patterns and trends, typical price-setting methodologies (traditional oil indexation and leanings toward gas), and the impact of LNG. We will funnel all of these through our Old/New World treatment in order to better understand future prospects for natural gas.

Anchor Customers

To initiate a gas market, power generation and feedstock use (e.g., fertilizer and methanol) have been anchor customers in many countries. These facilities can consume large volumes and be sited in proximity to gas-producing regions, LNG import terminals, or major pipelines. SOEs often develop these facilities. If developers are private, they often obtain state-guaranteed prices and volumes, through contracts with SOE buyers that are government-backed and/or contractual terms such as take-or-pay (TOP). Additional de-risking for private investors may come as part of financing (for instance, backing from multilateral institutions that supports obligations of SOE buyers). Some anchor customers can afford to pay the cost of gas and still be profitable.

The power and industrial sectors can create their own value chain challenges. For example, the ability of customers to pay for electricity from gas-fired plants is often questioned. Many countries that subsidize liquid fuels also subsidize electricity. Even if it is the state-owned utility (national or subnational) that buys the gas or the electricity from the gas-fired plant, its financial credit is often low and government guarantees on power purchase agreements (PPAs) are needed. There are many examples around the world demonstrating how the breakdown of the electric power value chain undermines financial viability of merchant power plants, which, in turn, risks cash flow waterfalls of gas suppliers (e.g., Nigeria, India, and Peru). We discuss these gas-power value chain issues in more detail in Chap. 6. Similar issues exist for fertilizer plants, which are preferred by governments because they can supply subsidized fertilizer to farmers. These subsidies to final products obtained from the use of natural gas necessitate some guarantees from the government for the gas supply agreement. Finally, the electrification trends in the Old and New Worlds have different meanings and, as such, will likely imply different outcomes for gas (see the "Electrification Versus Gasification" box).

Price Formation

There has been much hype about the globalization of natural gas. Prevailing argument is that increasing LNG trade will bring historically unrelated regional markets together. Indeed, LNG trade has been growing much faster than gas traded via pipelines, but it still only accounts for less than 15 percent of global gas consumption.

As compared to the 1990s, when four countries supplied more than 80 percent of LNG and Japan, Korea, and Taiwan purchased more than 70 percent of that supply, there are now a much larger number of LNG suppliers and importers (Fig. 5.3). Moreover, global gas consumption has doubled since 1990. A combination of supply-push and demand-pull encouraged the monetization of more gas resources via LNG. At the same time, growing economies, declining domestic gas production, energy security, and environmental drivers encouraged more countries to become importers. More recently, FSRUs made it easier for many countries to import LNG with shorter-term commitments. Finally, in recent years,

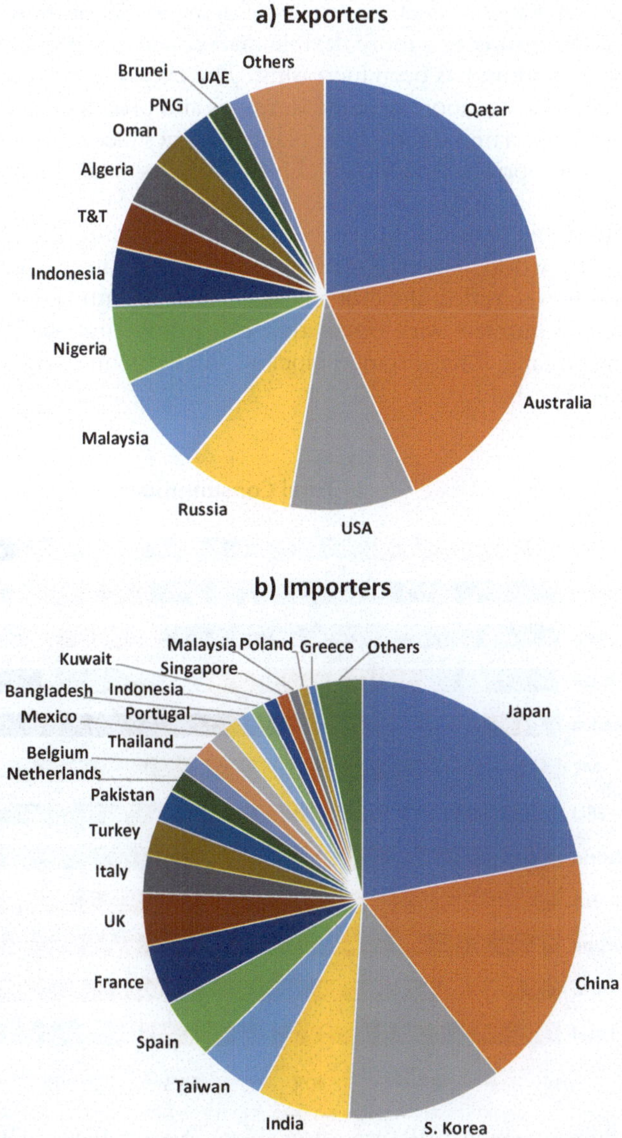

Fig. 5.3 LNG exporters and importers 2019. (Source: IGU (2020a))

liquefaction capacity has been in surplus of demand. All of these developments are contributing to a more flexible market where the share of short-term and spot trading has been increasing. The excess supply condition is probably temporary as more demand develops and production from existing fields and associated liquefaction plants declines (see Chap. 4). In the meantime, low prices encourage LNG imports and increased gas consumption.

Still, significant regional differences persist. Excluding the largest gas markets of the world, North America and Western Europe, gas pricing largely continues to reflect the fundamental reality of natural gas: the need for long-term contracts with prices that can justify large capital investments in upstream, long-distance pipeline infrastructure and the LNG value chains (Fig. 5.4).

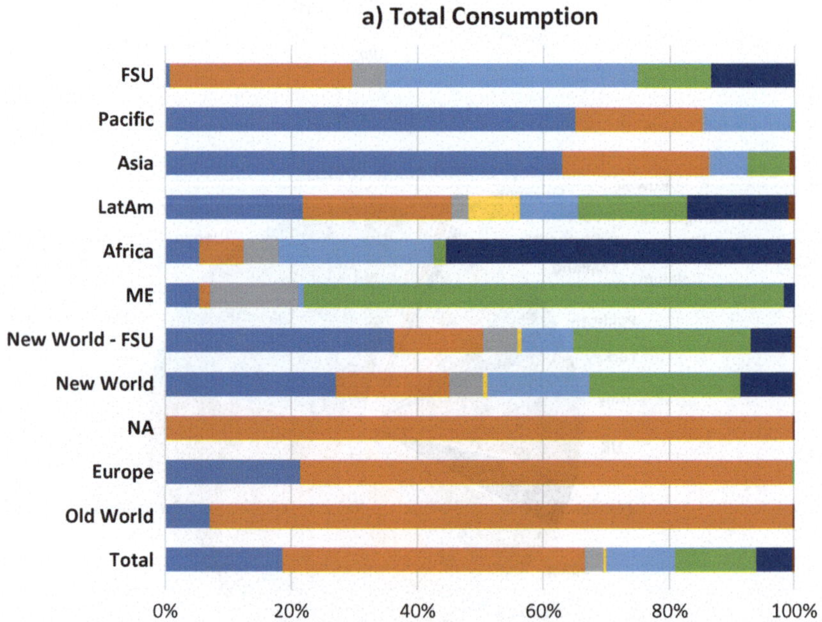

Fig. 5.4 Price formation 2019 (percentage share). (Source: IGU (2020b). OPE: oil price escalation; GOG: gas-on-gas competition; BIM: bilateral monopoly; NET: netback from final product; RCS: cost-of-service regulation; RSP: social and political regulation; RBC: below-cost regulation; NP: no price (free gas))

(*continued*)

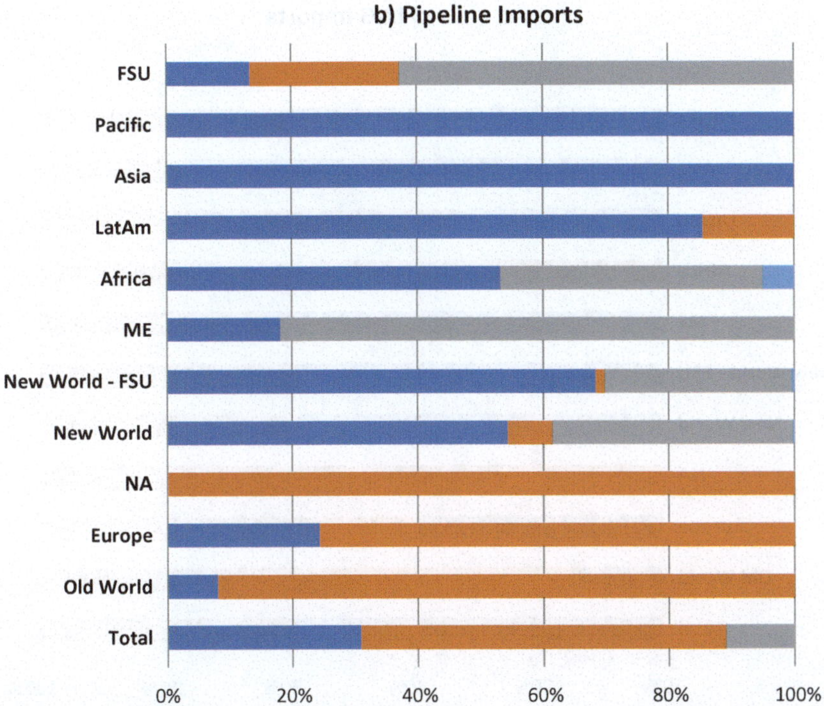

Fig. 5.4 (continued)

Western Europe and Central Europe are the main importing regions where there has been a shift from oil indexing, or oil price escalation (OPE), toward gas-on-gas (GOG) pricing within a regional gas hub. The trend has persisted since the 2000s as a result of declining domestic production, expiring oil-indexed pipeline import contracts, and development of a large number of LNG import terminals. Years of gas use and the push for liberalization of the EU gas market allowed for development of a competitive, relatively liquid market, with National Balancing Point (NBP) in the UK and Title Transfer Facility (TTF) in the Netherlands acting as hub prices. Today, TTF is the main pricing hub in Europe. TTF's share in over-the-counter (OTC) markets has been growing and accounted for more than 60 percent in 2019 according to S&P Platts. Increasing LNG imports and new or renegotiated pipeline contracts have used these hub prices.

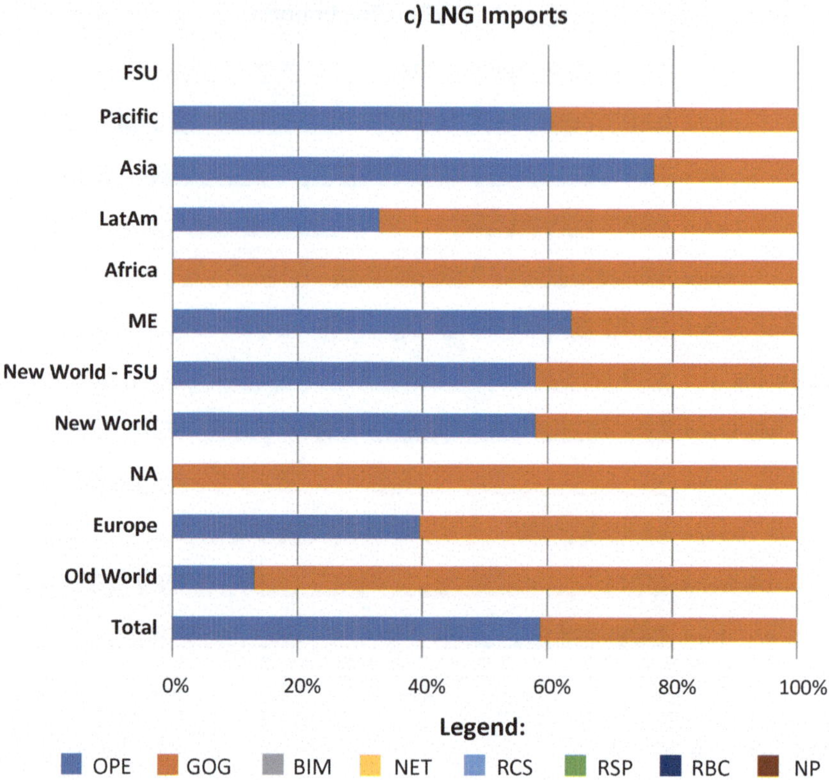

Fig. 5.4 (continued)

Details show that only "large" customers competing for suppliers were able to secure pure GOG pricing. In addition, some pricing reported as GOG in Fig. 5.4 had hybrid pricing: oil indexation within a band set often by hub prices.

In contrast, OPE gained ground and has persisted over the years in Asia-Pacific. In fact, prices set by governments for social and political reasons, often below the cost of service (RSP, or social and political regulation, and RBC, or below-cost regulation), accounted for more than 60 percent of volumes consumed in the 2000s. These have been mostly replaced by OPE and cost-of-service regulation (RCS) in the 2010s. Also, some contracts were switched from pricing based on bilateral negotiation (BIM) to OPE in the late 2000s.

Pricing policies in China are of particular importance. Historically, China's natural gas prices have been a hodgepodge of government-controlled prices for gas produced domestically and end-users. China's National Development and Reform Commission (NDRC) has set the prices with a cross-subsidy from power, industrial, and transport gas users to residential, agricultural, and fertilizer plant users. Domestic gas producers have been paid the city gate price less a pipeline transmission tariff, which is also determined by the NDRC based on construction and operating costs, distance from gas source to city gate, taxes, and an "appropriate margin." This approach often led to a gap between domestic prices and cost of imports based on global markets. Since the three major gas producers (PetroChina, Sinopec, and CNOOC) are also the major gas importers, the losses they incurred on imports reduced the capital available for gas exploration and production. In response, China has been reforming its gas pricing. LNG importers and producers of shale gas and coal bed methane are able to negotiate directly with large industries and power producers. The Turkmenistan–China pipeline started delivering OPE gas in the early 2010s. Chinese domestic production pricing also moved toward OPE. Overall, China has been moving away from RSP, first to RCS and later to OPE, for all sectors except fertilizer to prevent value leakage along the gas value chain and to encourage more investment along the gas supply chain. The unbundling of natural gas infrastructure and creation of an independent midstream company also are expected to encourage domestic production and market-based price creation.

India has been pursuing GOG pricing, but the formula that links the Indian gas price to a weighted average of prices from Henry Hub in the U.S., Alberta Hub in Canada, NBP in the UK, and Russian exports has been questioned by market observers. Since it was enacted, prices in hubs included in the formula have been lower than gas pricing mechanisms using the Japan Korea Marker (JKM) or Japanese Custom Clearing (JCC) that are common in LNG trade in closer geographic proximity to India. Although low prices in formula hubs kept Indian gas prices low and may have encouraged some gas demand in the country, they have been too low to encourage investment in exploration and production of domestic gas resources and have led to increasing LNG imports. India has a "Gas Utilization Policy" that governs the rationing of cheaper domestic gas. First-tier customer classes, in order of priority access to domestic gas, are city gas for households, fertilizer plants, LPG plants, and gas-fired power plants that provide power to distribution utilities. If there is any domestic gas left over after satisfying Tier 1 demand, it goes to steel mills, refineries, petrochemical plants, city gas for industrial and commercial customers, captive and merchant power plants, and others. If LNG has to be allocated to Tier 1 customers, subsidies are provided for them (Sen 2017). As a result, India is struggling with aligning prices of imported gas with delivered prices to end-users because LNG import prices are set based on OPE or increasingly in the spot market.

Resilience of Oil-Indexation in Asia

There are many reasons for the resilience of oil-indexed pricing in Asia. Fundamentally, they all contribute to a lack of liquid gas markets in importing countries. For example, Japan, still the largest LNG importer in the world, has historically used JCC almost exclusively. Other importers in the Pacific Basin have been using JCC as well. In recent years, rising imports from the spot market or based on short-term deals (especially after the Fukushima-induced shutdown of nuclear power plants) increased the share of non-JCC pricing. The JCC formulation still dominates in terms of volumes. The ability of Japanese utilities to pass any increase in LNG import prices to gas consumers via fuel-cost adjustment and customers' ability to pay higher prices undermine the incentive of utilities to seek cheaper supplies. Utilities' dominance in their franchise territories is a result of the lack of domestic competition, which is difficult to establish in the absence of supplies other than LNG imports.

Third-party access to LNG import terminals by competing businesses is an option. Such a strategy has been difficult to implement not only in Japan but also across the world because either SOEs or politically powerful utilities have built and operated import pipelines and LNG terminals, often carrying the responsibility of long-term commitments made to develop those facilities (e.g., Brazil, China, India, Japan, South Korea, and Turkey).[13] Often suppliers are not willing to renegotiate contracts in the absence of commercially viable options. Western Europe, as discussed, has been able to beat this impasse, thanks to a combination of (1) domestic production from the North Sea, (2) access to LNG imports from global sources and pipelines from North Africa, and (3) introduction of a legal regime progressively moving all EU countries toward gas market liberalization via subsequent Energy Packages. Other countries continue to struggle with developing sufficient infrastructure and liquidity, and, even if they are successful, they struggle with market reforms such as regulated third-party access (TPA) with cost-plus tariffs and trading hubs.

One obstacle in creating gas markets, absent in Japan and Western Europe for the most part but quite common in emerging economies, is preferential pricing of gas for specific customers. Governments often pursue these policies for socioeconomic reasons or industrial development purposes. They are necessary when gas replaces cheaper fuels, for example to reduce pollution associated with those fuels. Regardless of the rationale for administered pricing, the broken value chains across gas supply and end-users (including power and industrial sector) ultimately undermine cash flow and financial ability of companies to maintain and expand infrastructure. Specifically, these conditions deter private investment, which perpetuates the importance of public funds and SOEs to create and grow gas demand.

In short, outside of North America and Western Europe, countries are still struggling with meeting the conditions for creating liquid markets. There is no price transparency because geography often prevents sufficient diversity in terms of suppliers and consumers of natural gas in any given region. Sometimes, geopolitics prevents collaboration among the neighbors. In such an environment, energy security often drives natural gas (and other energy) procurement with governments and their SOEs, playing important roles in signing and guaranteeing sale and purchase agreements (SPAs), building and operating infrastructure, and internalizing the cost of administered pricing. These conditions prevent the establishment of physical or virtual pricing references such as Henry Hub in the U.S. and TTF in Europe, along with standardized contracts. Nevertheless, challenges to oil-indexation are emerging. And they are mostly due to growing LNG trade and changing commercial terms of that trade.

The Influence of Growing LNG Trade and Changing Commercial Terms

Large LNG projects for either import or export (including associated facilities for feed gas and upstream production) represent lumpy capacity that are imbued with risk and uncertainty. Thus, although LNG trade has grown, and grown in influence, we still see evidence of strategies forged to distribute risks that rest on government support in various forms, especially the involvement of some of the largest SOEs in existence. A distinct irony exists in that it is Old World, market-led, highly competitive U.S. incremental supply and pricing that are challenging traditions in global LNG trade. This raises a distinct question, as dealt with in Chap. 1, about the longevity of U.S. participation and impact.

In the past, the development of LNG supply projects has been underpinned by long-term SPAs (20–25 years, and some longer) with creditworthy buyers and large enough volumes for only one or two contracts sufficient to support the investment decision on a 4–5 million tons per annum (MTPA) liquefaction train. Today, contracts longer than 20 years are hard to find even for greenfield liquefaction plants. The average duration of LNG contracts has fallen from around 18 years in 2008 to 6 years in 2017, and the average contracted volume is down from 2.3 MTPA to 0.6 MTPA over the same period, though 2019 saw an increase to nearly 13 years and 1 MTPA (Fig. 5.5).

In recent years, long-term SPAs are being signed for terms of 15 years or longer. With more volumes, suppliers, ships, and liquefaction and

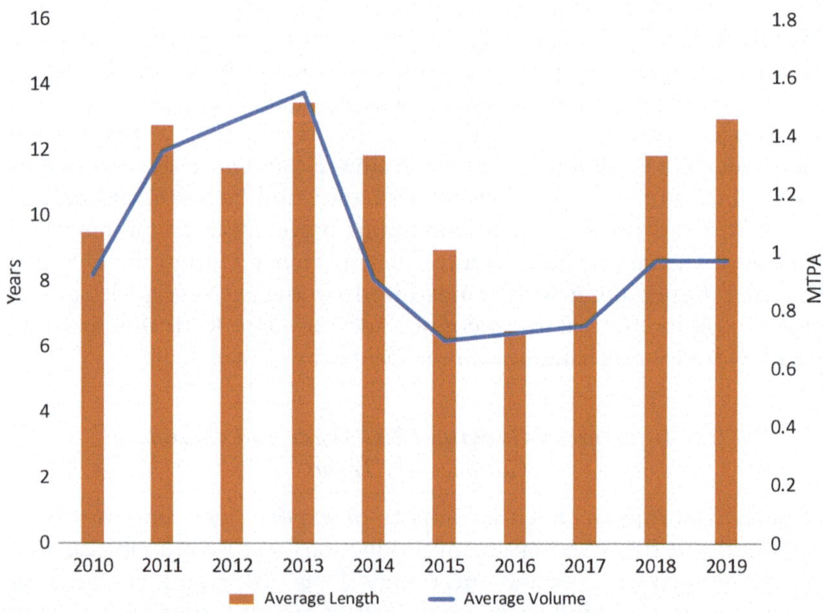

Fig. 5.5 LNG contract durations and volumes. (Source: Based on data from Shell LNG Outlook 2020)

regasification (including FSRUs) infrastructure available, the market also sees significant amount of short- (less than 5 years) and medium-term (5–15 years) trades because the needs of customers vary and shorter contract terms decrease the risk of stranded cargoes. In mid-2020, there were 24 FSRU terminals with more than 100 MTPA of capacity operating worldwide in diverse geographies, including Latin America, South Asia and the Mediterranean. Eight are expected to become operational by the end of 2020 or early 2021 (IGU 2020a).[14]

Spot cargoes, often defined as delivered within three months of transaction date, reached about 25 percent of total LNG volumes in 2018 (Fig. 5.6 reports more than 30 percent for 2019 while defining spot as one year). In 2019, China was the largest spot LNG buyer, closely followed by Japan. Together with India, Spain, South Korea, France, and Turkey, these seven countries accounted for 83 percent of spot LNG trade (IGU 2020a). Shorter-term contracts and spot volumes are based on GOG pricing,

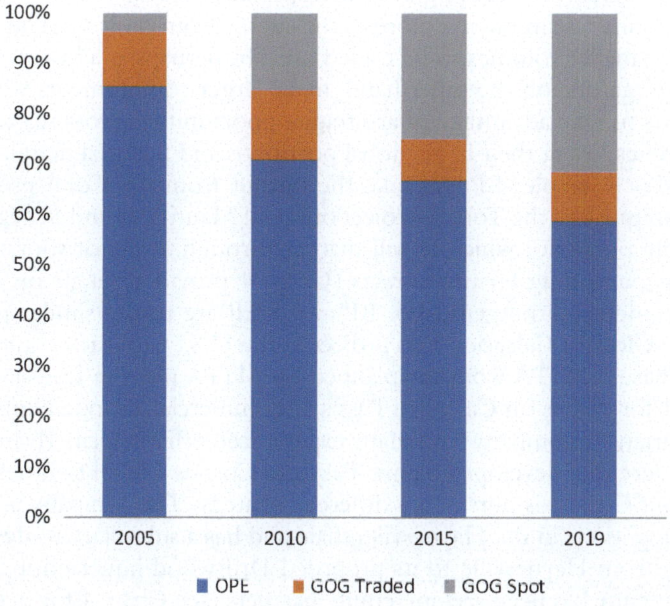

Fig. 5.6 LNG price formation. (Source: Based on data from IGU (2020b). Spot LNG is less than one year. In other studies, "spot" includes short-term contracts (1–4 years). In others, "spot" is defined as 90 days)

hastening the transition from OPE to GOG in LNG markets, although OPE still accounts for about 60 percent of LNG volumes traded (Fig. 5.6).

Legacy contracts for LNG and pipeline imports are starting to expire. Based on data from GIIGNL 2019 Annual Report, more than 115 (190) MTPA of contracts in force in 2018 will expire by the end of 2025 (2030). Asian and, gradually, other buyers are expected to follow the example of Western European importers that gradually switched to GOG pricing, albeit with hybrid formulations in some cases.

These trends suggest that there is differentiation between contracts for the output from new projects versus renewal of expiring contracts and sale of uncontracted LNG from operating facilities. Sellers in the latter group can accept shorter-term commitments because the investment in the facilities has been mostly, if not fully, amortized. Developers of new projects, however, need more traditional long-term contracts (20–25 years) to finance the investment.[15]

Aggregators, or portfolio companies (e.g., Shell, BP, and Total), and, to a lesser extent, traders (e.g., Glencore, Trafigura, and Vitol) are playing an important role in buying more of the supply from projects. The traders focus on smaller volumes to be traded quickly, perhaps at a lower margin. The aggregators, on the other hand, make larger commitments with longer terms to take advantage of arbitrage opportunities across seasons and geographies, using their large global portfolios and financial hedging programs. For example, BP will take the output from the Coral project in Mozambique and the Tortue project offshore Mauritania and Senegal into its supply portfolio, which it will market through a mix of spot, short-, medium-, and long-term contracts (Chap. 4 provides details on Tortue and commercial arrangements). BP and Shell are taking similar roles in Venture Global's Calcasieu Pass project in the U.S., with each committing to purchase 2 MTPA from the planned 10-MTPA plant in Louisiana (see Chap. 4 for details on Calcasieu Pass and commercial arrangements).

Tellurian—a company with many experienced officers formerly involved in Cheniere that developed Sabine Pass and Corpus Christi facilities in the U.S. Gulf Coast—is pursuing a different strategy. The company acquired producing assets in the Haynesville shale and has a subsidiary to develop a pipeline from Haynesville to its proposed Driftwood liquefaction facility. The company has been seeking equity partners (see Chap. 4 for details on Driftwood and commercial arrangements).

In other approaches, global oil majors and state-owned or controlled entities are using their own balance sheets to finance the investment and add the volumes to their supply portfolios, creating an alternative to traditional development approach of using project finance. Several projects—LNG Canada (a joint venture between Shell, Petronas, PetroChina, Mitsubishi, and KOGAS, which combines equity off-take and Shell's aggregator approach; see Chap. 4) and Golden Pass LNG (joint marketing by ExxonMobil and Qatar Petroleum; see Chap. 4)—went ahead without the support of long-term contracts.

Oil-Indexed LNG Pricing

$$P_{LNG} = A \cdot P_{Oil} + B$$

Where P_{LNG} is the price of LNG in \$/MMBtu; P_{Oil} is the price of reference oil in \$/barrel; A is the "slope" term; and B reflects the freight cost.

For most Asian trades, the reference price has been JCC, and for European cargoes, Brent. There is often a lag of one to three months in the oil price used to calculate LNG price. A is either negotiated or bid. Historically, it has been as high as 0.18 and as low as 0.05 (buyer's market of the early 2000s). For LNG price to be equivalent to oil price, A needs to be about 0.165 (based on energy content). The freight cost, B, is negotiated and can be FOB, DES/DAP. The price can be reviewed at regular intervals (e.g., five years).

Even oil indexation itself is undergoing changes (see box). Historically, the price of LNG was indexed to alternative fuels, mostly crude oil (JCC). As discussed before, JCC still dominates in Asia, but as old contracts expire, indexation to natural gas hub prices (Henry Hub, TTF) has been more common in spot and short-term trading. Henry Hub's importance grew with the shale-induced construction of liquefaction capacity in the United States. Although, with the exception of Sabine Pass contracts, the Henry Hub price is not explicit, the threat of cheap US exports indexed to Henry Hub influenced many renegotiations of pricing in existing contracts and new contract negotiations across the world. However, indexation of LNG trade in Asia to natural gas hub prices in North America or Western Europe can be a double-edged sword. On the one hand, such indexation will provide access to financial hedging via trading of futures and derivatives based on these hubs. On the other hand, it exposes buyers to the volatility of these hub prices that reflect demand-supply conditions of those hubs' home markets (i.e., the U.S. and Western Europe; see Chap. 1 for extensive treatment of Henry Hub price history) and, worse, vagaries of financial trading. These have very little to do with conditions in importing markets.

An alternative to gas hub pricing is indexation to Brent, a benchmark crude oil heavily traded at multiple exchanges (Intercontinental Exchange, ICE, and Chicago Mercantile Exchange, CME) and OTC markets. Brent has been popular in recent LNG contracts. Given the LNG surplus in the global market, made worse by the COVID pandemic, slopes of oil indexation formulas have been under pressure as well, staying below 11 percent. This has been the case in European pipeline contracts since 2010. The indexation to Brent also allows LNG importers to use a large portfolio of financial hedging tools. Since the oil market is global and buyers are familiar with oil price volatility from their oil-indexed contracts, indexation to Brent might be preferable to indexation to Henry Hub or TTF.

Lastly, there is the JKM LNG futures contract at ICE and CME offered by S&P Platts as an emerging pricing alternative for gas despite the failure of Asian gas markets to meet many of the traditional prerequisites for a liquid market. The trading of JKM derivatives increased from less than 10,000 lots in late 2017 to more than 70,000 lots in late 2019.[16] Total volume traded in 2019 was nearly 600,000 lots (Ang 2019).

Other changes have evolved in LNG commercial terms that help improve gas market liquidity. Historically, volume commitments were stringent with associated TOP clauses. Justifying billions of dollars in upstream and LNG supply chain development still requires commitments from buyers, but there is a great deal more flexibility in annual and short-term delivery programs, allowances for cargo diversion and less than 100-percent TOP. Both buyers and sellers feel more comfortable with new flexibility given the deeper market with many more buyers, traders, and aggregators. The spot market is an important option for diverted cargoes. Take-or-pay and deliver-or-pay (DOP) arrangements are tied to the spot market. This is especially true for short-term trading. With TOP, if the spot market price is less than the contract formula price, the buyer may compensate the seller for the difference (contract formula price–spot resale revenues–resale cost). With DOP, the seller pays the buyer the difference (cost of replacement–value of contracted cargo).

Increased flexibility is also seen in the transfer of title and risk, which shifts to the buyer when LNG loaded onto a ship free-on-board (FOB) but remains with the seller until LNG is unloaded with delivered ex-ship (DES).[17] Historically, diversion restrictions were the norm in LNG SPAs. The European Union in the 2000s and Japan in the late 2010s declared such restrictions anti-competitive. Destination flexibility is becoming more common. Buyers should be able to divert FOB cargoes with no restrictions. Since the seller carries the title and risk with DES cargoes until delivery, DES cargo diversions still require seller agreement.[18] If the seller agrees, any profits from diversion can be shared between the seller and buyer. Importantly, the U.S. LNG exports are FOB and add to the increased flexibility in the global market. The U.S. LNG contracts are also relatively easy to cancel by either party typically with a notice, two months in advance. The buyer has to pay the liquefaction fees ranging from \$2.25 to \$3.50/MMBtu (see Chap. 4 for more details on the U.S. LNG projects and key commercial terms).

Still, there are limits to the changes that increase liquidity. For example, LNG vessels are still very closely linked to projects, which reduces the availability of ships for spot trading. Tightness in the shipping market becomes visible during winter when demand rises and day rates for ships increase to over \$100,000 per day, dipping in the spring to well below \$50,000 a day (e.g., Wong 2019). Also, the reality of high cost of LNG supply chains and associated upstream development remains. And, as historical data demonstrate, when industry activity picks up, higher demand for services of a limited number of qualified EPC contractors and supply chain subcontractors raises costs.[19] For these reasons, as discussed, SPAs longer than 20 years may be making a comeback. Aggregators and traders are more likely to sign contracts than utilities, IOCs, or NOCs, which may become equity partners in some liquefaction projects. Importantly, although the LNG market is currently awash with supply, growing global demand, declining reserves, and aging liquefaction facilities will eventually necessitate new investments. In this environment, buyers that need certainty of supply will be more willing to sign contracts longer than 20 years. They will also have the opportunity to commit to smaller volumes from each project in large portfolios to enhance their energy security via diversified sources of supply.

Another wrinkle that needs to be ironed out for short-term trading to become truly liquid is contract standardization. There are a number of master SPAs with significant differences. Confirmation notices that set the commercial terms based on the master SPAs can therefore be different as well. Accordingly, several entities (BP, Trafigura, the International Group of Liquefied Natural Gas Importers or GIIGNL, the Association of International Petroleum Negotiators or AIPN) have developed model master SPAs.

Lastly, although the large increase in the number of LNG importers is welcome from the perspective of achieving a deeper market, many of the new importers have low credit ratings. In their World LNG Outlook 2018, Shell reported the share of non-investment-grade buyers (often SOEs and/or their governments) by volume was nearly 50 percent in 2017. Until 2010 or so, a great majority of all volumes under long-term contract were with A-rated buyers, with the remaining having a B-rating. This new mix of buyers raises the risk of long-term contracts, the mitigation of which may require government guarantees. Alternatively, companies willing to take and manage risks better in a portfolio (e.g., aggregators and traders) will fill the void.

Government Involvement: New World, Same Old?

As already discussed, regulated private sector entities dominate the natural gas industry in the Old World. Policy and regulation can boost or impede natural gas investments. This is least pronounced for the U.S. demand, which is mostly market-driven.[20] In Europe, however, governments are much more involved in shaping energy markets influencing demand for natural gas. For example, EU rules allow for third-party access (TPA) exemptions for new large investments such as LNG terminals or pipelines for imports.[21] That being said, project developers rarely need direct public funding—a good thing given that public support of the industry is waning in Western Europe.

However, state involvement continues to be the norm in other parts of the world, including post-Soviet EU countries. State-owned Gazprom exemplifies the dominant role of state in Russia. In South Korea, state-owned KOGAS imports all LNG. Japan's government plays a significant role in energy security via SOEs, regulation of private utilities, and international negotiations.

Several reasons exist for states' dominant role, including political context, need for large investments, and energy security. Hence, there is a wide variety of flavors when it comes to the role of state within the natural gas sector. In Fig. 5.7, we offer a spectrum with our interpretation of some

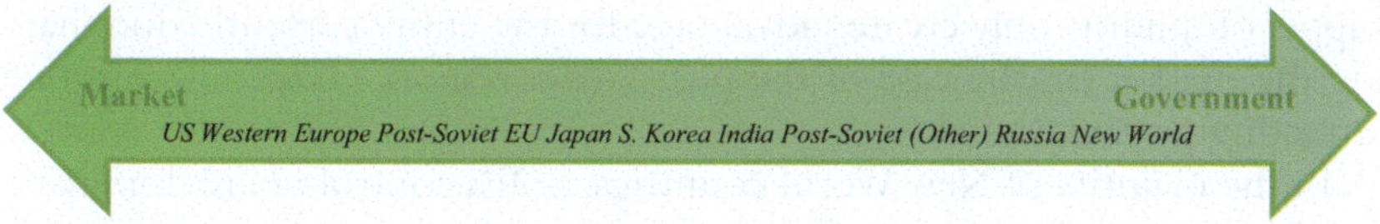

Fig. 5.7 Significance of market versus government across the world of gas

countries' relative positioning at the time of writing. Clearly, these positions can change as markets evolve and governments implement new policies such as deregulation.

The majority of Old World countries historically had been in relatively convenient situations where security of supply has been quite robust. The U.S. domestic supply and Canadian gas supply have been sufficient to meet regional demand, with periodic hiccups mainly due to policy or regulatory miscalculations. Western Europe's barter deal with the Soviet Union, availability of domestic production (North Sea), and access to pipelines from North Africa and to global LNG via numerous entry points into the continent allowed for a diversified supply portfolio. The Soviet Union's ample resources were also sufficient to meet its own and its peripheral countries' needs.

This has not been the case for industrialized economies such as Japan, South Korea, or Taiwan, which launched LNG imports in the 1970s and 1980s and had to rely exclusively on only a few LNG suppliers until the late 2000s. Accordingly, governments and/or SOEs have played, and many continue to play, roles that are more prominent. Similarly, today, governments of post-Soviet countries and, in some cases, their SOEs play important roles in securing a diverse supply of gas (to reduce dependence on Russia) as well as achieve other energy objectives. The dominant role of the state also reflects the historical political context in these countries. As a result, the integration of post-Soviet countries with the much more liberalized market system in Western Europe has been difficult.

In many cases, even if the ownership of natural gas and gas transmission belongs to separate companies, each of them is either controlled or owned by state. Large SOEs also discourage small, private competitors from entering the market. This trend is well visible in Poland, where state-controlled oil and gas enterprises currently are being consolidated into a large conglomerate with the goal of competing globally. The lack of a functioning market is another reason for keeping relatively centralized government control. Liberalization, if pursued before infrastructure can support liquidity, only creates advantage for the entity currently dominating the market (in the case of the post-Soviet region: Gazprom) without attracting private capital.

In the majority of New World countries, SOEs control or are dominant in all segments of the gas value chain. Often third-party participation is explicitly prohibited or limited. Where domestic production of oil and gas exists, NOCs control or dominate access. In countries that decided to import gas, new SOEs are formed for that purpose. Where TPA is permitted, investors are often confronted by frequent government interventions focused on achieving social or political goals unrelated to the economics of gas sector investments.

Government interventions often include below-market gas prices, which allow demand to increase without a corresponding increase in gas supplies and infrastructure unless SOEs and public funding fill the void. In many countries, the costs of below-market gas prices also are borne by SOEs that are the major gas suppliers resulting in decreased capital available for expanding gas infrastructure. Such broken value chains discourage private investment.

Below-cost gas pricing is sometimes necessitated by price subsidies provided to competing fuels if, for example, the government wants consumers to switch to gas or renewables from polluting fuels. For example, in China, gas industry participants complain about central government subsidies to renewables, which they claim have been much higher than any financial support provided to natural gas. While China had been reducing its renewable subsidies until 2020, a recent budget increase seemed to favor solar developers. While the impact of subsidy policy seems somewhat uncertain,[22] subsidies encourage more solar development. Even in the absence of subsidies, wherever renewable costs continue to decline, the price pressure on gas will persist. Subsidies to alternative heating fuels can also render gas less competitive, especially when infrastructure investment is needed to deliver gas (e.g., coal vs. gas in China). For example, China's coal-to-gas switching policy hit some roadblocks in the winter of 2017–18 because midstream bottlenecks created gas shortages and the government had to allow coal use.

Most New World countries need third-party investment because their energy SOEs and government budgets are already burdened with many subsidy programs, and due to low credit ratings (partially as a result of their poor balance of payments), their access to capital is limited. Even in China, there are constraints on the ability of both sovereign and provincial jurisdictions to continue investing in gas infrastructure as cash reserves are earmarked across a wide range of industries and social programs. During tough economic times, governments have fewer resources to allocate across various areas. Expanding gas infrastructure may not always rank high enough given the existence of alternative energy sources. Stimulus packages to help with the recovery from the COVID pandemic envision large infrastructure investments. In the Old World, the focus is on clean energy.[23] In the New World, stimulus packages are more modest and priorities often are different. These stimulus packages as well as legacy energy policies and subsidies cause energy sector investors to assess a variety of long-term risks (see "Investor's Dilemma" box).

Investor's Dilemma

At the risk of oversimplifying, companies investing in the energy industry have two choices:

1. Invest in clean energy in the Old World
2. Invest in gas in the New World

Both options need government support in various forms (tax credits, direct public funding). Where can shareholders expect the highest return? Where are market and political risks highest?

Low credit ratings of many New World countries and histories of subsidized energy pricing raise the risk of investing in those locations. Their need for energy to sustain their economic and human development often leads them to prioritize energy projects and offer guarantees for cost-recovery prices. In spite of these actions, guarantees have not always secured cash flow growth.

Growing debt burdens of Old World countries raise the likelihood that governments will cut subsidies to clean energy as they reprioritize needs such as health. Since wind and solar are now commonly presented as cheaper than conventional technologies, it may be easier to justify ending public support. Meanwhile, renewables' low operating cost and intermittency undermine their profitability. Also, even "clean" energy projects, especially if they are relatively new such as hydrogen infrastructure, may fall victim to "not-in-my-backyard" inclinations, or "NIMBYism" in the Old World.

(*continued*)

(continued)

To us, given the demand growth in growing economies of the New World and their ability to site projects relatively easier, risks for gas as well as other energy projects seem to be more manageable in the New World. Most outlooks agree on where demand growth will occur. Time will tell where profitable energy infrastructure will be developed ...

Still, many New World countries may like to see gas play a bigger role in their fuel mix given its flexibility as a power plant fuel, importance as industrial feedstock, and immense local environmental benefits, especially as alternative to coal or diesel.[24] Many undertake efforts to improve gas sector commercial frameworks. However, untangling the knots in existing arrangements, including the dominant role of incumbent SOEs as well as price and subsidy policies for alternative fuels, is a lengthy process prone to bumps and unintended consequences along the way. The political difficulty of wresting power from SOEs that were tasked to build infrastructure and often secure supply (via production and/or imports) is made more difficult if the same SOEs also carry the burden of subsidies. For example, in China, the NDRC has been trying to transfer control of the gas pipeline network away from its NOCs to an independent entity since 2013. It made little progress until December 2019 when it finally launched the National Oil and Gas Pipeline Company (PipeChina). It took several more months to transfer control of major pipeline infrastructure and ten LNG import terminals to PipeChina from China's NOCs, including PetroChina and Sinopec. In May of 2020, PipeChina also announced that it started building another LNG import terminal in the Shandong province. In the meantime, other infrastructure transfers will likely be identified and TPA rules should be developed. These steps toward establishing a gas market are promising, but their success depends on PipeChina's performance and Chinese government's commitment to promoting competition (e.g., see Downs and Yan 2020).

Even in Japan, where regulated private utilities have been importing LNG, reforming the gas sector to allow for TPA has been challenging. Japan has been moving forward with price deregulation, unbundling, and TPA to LNG terminals and pipelines. Competitive suppliers now serve most of the customers in major markets, but TPA is not commonly available. In South Korea, Korea Gas Corporation is the exclusive wholesaler of gas to 34 retailers. Large consumers can arrange with LNG terminals to import LNG for self-use but only if KGC-committed volumes leave room.

These snapshots of global experience suggest that it is naïve to think that natural gas can become a significant part of any country's energy portfolio in relatively quick fashion solely based on private sector participation. At the same time, these experiences demonstrate the difficulties faced by most countries and their SOEs to develop the infrastructure necessary for a robust gas market. We now turn our attention to defining those difficulties.

The Critical Junction: Pipeline and Storage Infrastructure

The insufficiency of midstream and downstream gas infrastructure is a critical impediment to most New World countries introducing natural gas into their energy mix beyond anchor customers (Table 5.1). For example, the most successful so far, China, is about the same size as the U.S. in terms of land area, but its gas consumption is about a third of the U.S. gas consumption and its gas pipeline network is a fraction (about 4 percent) of the U.S. pipeline network. The deficits in storage infrastructure are even more striking. In the Old World, underground storage (UGS) capacity is critically important and typically accounts for 15–30 percent of annual consumption in a country. In addition, most countries have large tanks at LNG import terminals and small LNG storage near their distribution networks for balancing demand and supply during daily fluctuations, especially during winter. For example, the U.S. has about 110 small LNG storage and peak shaving facilities. India has no reported UGS capacity and relies on tank capacity at its LNG regasification terminals. China has been expanding its UGS capacity, but 26 facilities currently operating cover 4 percent of gas consumption. China has 17 UGS facilities under construction, and the country's 22 LNG terminals provide significant storage capacity, albeit only near where these facilities are located.

The lower energy density of gas increases transportation cost and, as such, is an inherent disadvantage for natural gas affordability, particularly in developing countries that have limited gas T&D infrastructure. The experience from more liquid gas markets demonstrates the need for all kinds of storage, including geologic, LNG, and linepack (to sustain pipeline throughput), to balance supply and demand. Imbalances derive from swings in gas demand (e.g., winter heating demand, summer air conditioning demand, the need to provide peaking and load balancing services

Table 5.1 Gas infrastructure density

	Pipelines (km)	*Km of pipe per km²*	*Km of pipe per million population*	*UGS*
United States	2,600,000	0.32	7,855	386/1/16%
Russia	177,700	0.01	1,217	28/4/17%
China	104,000	0.011	72	26/17/4%
Iran	20,794	0.014	248	3/3/3%
Canada	500,000	0.05	13,263	53/1/23%
Saudi Arabia	2,940	0.001	85	NA
Japan	4,456	0.01	35	5/–/<1%
Mexico	18,074	<0.01	140	NA
Germany	26,985	0.08	322	47/2/27%
UK	28,603	0.12	421	14/2/2%
UAE	3,277	0.04	331	NA
Italy	20,223	0.07	334	3/6/25%
India	16,800	<0.01	12	NA
Egypt	7,986	<0.01	78	NA
S. Korea	3,790	0.04	74	NA
Australia	30,054	<0.01	1,179	9/–/13%
Thailand	5,900	0.01	85	NA
Argentina	29,930	0.01	662	1/–/<1%
Pakistan	12,984	0.02	59	NA
Algeria	16,415	<0.01	374	NA
Indonesia	11,702	<0.01	43	NA
France	15,322	0.03	235	6/–/27%
Uzbekistan	10,341	0.02	308	2/1/9%
Turkey	14,666	0.02	174	4/3/8%
Malaysia	6,439	0.02	199	NA

Sources: Countries with a share of 2019 global gas consumption higher than 1 percent according to BP Statistical Review of Energy. Ranked from largest consumer down. UGS = underground storage. Numbers in the storage column represent UGS facilities operating, UGS facilities under construction, and operating UGS capacity as percentage of total annual gas consumption. Gas pipeline mileage is from CIA World Factbook, https://www.cia.gov/library/publications/the-world-factbook/ except for the U.S. (https://www.phmsa.dot.gov/data-and-statistics/pipeline/annual-report-mileage-gas-distribution-systems), Canada (https://www.nrcan.gc.ca/our-natural-resources/energy-sources-distribution/clean-fossil-fuels/pipelines/pipelines-across-canada/18856 and https://www.cer-rec.gc.ca/en/safety-environment/industry-performance/interactive-pipeline/index.html—~50,000 miles of gas transmission and ~450,000 km are gas distribution lines), and China and India (Global Gas Report 2020). Storage data are from CEDIGAZ UGS database (https://www.cedigaz.org/databases/)

to the power sector) as well as disruptions in supply (e.g., pipeline outages, cycles in upstream investment, and lags in drilling).

For now, in most of the New World, gas penetration in buildings (heating) sectors is low due to the widespread usage of traditional biomass, coal, or fuel oil. But if New World countries are to increase their natural gas consumption by expanding service to residential and commercial customers, not only pipeline but also storage infrastructure will become critical. This is especially true for inland areas; coastal regions may benefit from the storage tanks of LNG import terminals or FSRU access.

Who Is Investing in Energy Infrastructure and Where?[25]

Since many New World countries do not have an investment-grade credit rating (Table 5.2), there is less international capital available to them from traditional sources, and what is available is often more expensive. Others, in particular China, may fill the void in realignment of global power structure (see the section "New World Order?").

China stands out with a high credit rating. Assuming that China is willing to reduce the role of SOEs and allow international private investors, this rating should facilitate private investment once reforms under way at the time of this writing signal the opportunity to create value across the

Table 5.2 Sovereign credit ratings of selected New World countries

	Investment grade
China	High
India	Lowest investment grade
Egypt	Highly speculative
Thailand	Nearly upper medium
Argentina	In default
Pakistan	Highly speculative
Indonesia	Lower medium
Turkey	Highly speculative
Malaysia	Upper medium
Brazil	Speculative
Bangladesh	Highly speculative
Venezuela	In default
Colombia	Lower medium
Vietnam	Speculative
Peru	Lower/Upper
Chile	Upper medium

Source: https://countryeconomy.com/ratings

gas supply chain. One of the reasons for China's high credit rating is its strong balance of payments, which allowed the country to undertake much gas infrastructure investment via public funds or SOEs' ability to borrow, which is positively influenced by China's sovereign rating. In contrast, India's barely investment-grade rating is a handicap for a country that needs international private investment to speed up the expansion of its gas and other energy infrastructure.

Many South and Southeast Asian countries have speculative (below investment-grade) ratings. It is very difficult for them to attract international capital without strong government guarantees in contracts. Even such guarantees may not be sufficient for internal pipeline or LDC projects. The ability to move FSRUs in case of non-payment is attractive to suppliers. SSA countries, though not included in Table 5.2 due to low levels of gas consumption at this time, have below investment-grade ratings as well and have faced the same challenges for years (e.g., see the discussion on Nigeria in the "Africa" section earlier).

In many of the same countries, domestic capital formation is also limited, and local financial institutions are not equipped to deal with large levels of funding and risk management capabilities required to develop the natural gas infrastructure. The natural gas sector must compete for scarce public funding (central or local governments, multilateral donor agencies) not only with other energy segments but also with a host of public services and infrastructure (health, education, transportation, water).

Often public funding comes from bilateral and multilateral donor agencies, including AIIB, or directly from China. The Organization of Petroleum Exporting Countries (OPEC) Fund, with $25 billion in commitments, is becoming another option especially in Africa. According to the Public-Private Infrastructure Advisory Facility (PPIAF) (2019), in 2017 about $250 billion was invested globally in electricity and gas infrastructure, nearly 80 percent of which was financed by SOEs or other public entities. Most of the investment was in electricity generation and grid. Gas grids received little funding. Private sector investors have pursued renewables projects because of their fast turnaround time and subsidies provided by governments. Importantly, most of their financing was also provided by public banks, bilateral or multilateral donor agencies. SOEs carried the burden of investing in thermal generation, electricity, and gas grids. The IEA (2019) estimates that only about $50 billion a year was invested in lower-middle-income and low-income countries (including many from Asia-Pacific).

It is possible to observe the manifestation of trends discussed so far in energy investment data (Table 5.3). Global investment in gas supply (including upstream, midstream, and downstream) has been consistently around 15 percent of total energy investment between 2015 and 2019 as

Table 5.3 Investment in gas supply, gas-fired power, oil and gas upstream, oil and gas midstream and downstream, billion of 2019 USD (percent share of global total)

	2015	*2016*	*2017*	*2018*	*2019*	*2020*
North America	87, 17, 183, 64 (26, 23, 29, 24)	77, 19, 129, 78 (26, 24, 28, 28)	90, 17, 157, 84 (31, 23, 34, 29)	86, 15, 173, 73 (30, 21, 36, 26)	82, 13, 173, 61 (29, 18, 36, 22)	55, 10, 109, 44 (30, 17, 34, 23)
Latin America	11, 3, 51, 9 (3, 4, 8, 3)	10, 4, 38, 8 (3, 5, 8, 3)	9, 4, 38, 8 (3, 5, 8, 3)	8, 4, 43, 8 (3, 6, 9, 3)	8, 4, 45, 9 (3, 6, 9, 3)	7, 3, 29, 8 (4, 6, 9, 4)
Europe	43, 7, 66, 26 (13, 10, 11, 10)	37, 7, 46, 26 (13, 9, 10, 9)	31, 7, 40, 28 (11, 9, 9, 10)	24, 8, 38, 25 (8, 11, 8, 9)	26, 10, 42, 24 (9, 13, 9, 9)	18, 7, 30, 16 (10, 12, 9, 8)
Africa	18, 9, 68, 10 (5, 12, 11, 4)	17, 10, 55, 11 (6, 13, 12, 4)	15, 9, 57, 11 (5, 13, 12, 4)	13, 7, 54, 9 (5, 10, 11, 3)	14, 9, 50, 10 (5, 12, 10, 4)	10, 6, 33, 10 5, 10, 10, 5)
Middle East	26, 10, 74, 40 (8, 13, 12, 15)	21, 10, 54, 34 (7, 13, 12, 12)	19, 10, 48, 31 (6, 13, 10, 11)	13, 9, 45, 25 (5, 13, 9, 9)	13, 9, 47, 26 (5, 12, 10, 9)	10, 7, 36, 18 (5, 12, 11, 10)
Eurasia	62, 6, 90, 28 (18, 9, 14, 10)	55, 7, 70, 28 (19, 9, 15, 10)	53, 9, 65, 31 (18, 11, 14, 11)	46, 10, 61, 25 (16, 14, 13, 9)	44, 12, 61, 19 (15, 16, 13, 7)	23, 8, 36, 12 (12, 13, 11, 6)
Asia-Pacific	86, 22, 93, 69 (25, 29, 15, 26)	73, 21, 69, 71 (25, 27, 15, 26)	64, 19, 62, 71 (22, 26, 13, 24)	67, 17, 65, 78 (23, 25, 14, 27)	68, 18, 65, 79 (24, 24, 13, 29)	48, 19, 49, 52 (26, 31, 15, 28)

Author calculations based on data from IEA (2020a, b). The 2020 numbers are IEA estimates. Gas supply includes upstream, midstream, and downstream. Percentage is the share of gas supply in total energy investment in that region. Gas-fired power may include some oil-fired generation as IEA (2020a) reports them together. Oil and gas midstream includes refining and petrochemicals in addition to oil and gas pipelines and storage. It is provided as a comparison to total gas supply. LNG investment is part of the gas supply. LNG in Eurasia is Russia; LNG in Asia-Pacific is Australia; other LNG investments not included in the table add up to nearly $8 billion across the years.

reported by the IEA (2020a, b). This share has been only about 10 percent in Asia-Pacific, which is expected to see the largest gas demand growth in the coming decades. And, only 3 percent of total energy investment in Asia-Pacific has been in gas-fired power as compared to 4 percent worldwide. On the other hand, the region accounted for about 24 percent of global gas supply investment and 26 percent of global gas-fired power plant investment.[26] Although IEA data do not allow distinguishing between oil and gas, given that Asia-Pacific accounted for only 14 percent of upstream investment but 27 percent of oil and gas midstream and downstream investment, it seems safe to deduce that more of the gas supply investment in the region has been in midstream and downstream. In addition, upstream investment has been declining, while midstream and downstream investment has been rising. It is not hard to conclude that LNG terminals and pipeline developments, majority in China and some in India, have accounted for most of this investment. IEA (2019) reports that China and the rest of South and Southeast Asia accounted for about nearly 50 and 30 percent, respectively, of oil and gas downstream and infrastructure investment in Asia-Pacific.

Overall, however, gas does not seem to be central to energy policy in Asia-Pacific. Coal supply investment in the region has been relatively stable, with its share rising from 79 percent of world total in 2015 to 87 percent in 2019. Coal, renewables, and nuclear attracted significant investments and are alternatives to gas-fired power generation. Coal-fired power plant investment has been declining in dollars and share in total world coal-fired power plant investment (from 86 percent to 71 percent), while renewables investment increased their share of global investment (from 47 percent to 52 percent). Importantly, dollars invested in renewables have increased from 167 percent of coal and gas-fired generation investment in 2015 to 279 percent in 2019. Nuclear investment in the region (mainly China and South Korea) accounted for 41 percent of total global nuclear investment.

Among the other regions where gas demand is likely to grow, Middle Eastern countries have invested 16 percent of their total energy funding in gas supply. Slightly above the global average, this level of investment is driven by the continued policy of oil-to-gas switching in the region. Africa and Latin America are not seeing the investment levels necessary for high gas demand growth scenarios in Fig. 5.1. Investment shortfall also is visible in oil and gas upstream in these regions despite their abundant resource potential. Upstream investment is dominated by North America, hosting a third of global upstream investment, followed by Eurasia (about two-thirds in Russia) and Asia-Pacific (nearly half in China) accounting for 14 percent each.

The data in Table 5.3 and associated discussion provide a backdrop for a general story of gas pipeline and LDC investment, which seems very limited and mostly concentrated in China and India. Pipeline networks, albeit not as extensive as in the Old World, already exist in many countries with a history of domestic gas production, such as Indonesia, Malaysia, Bangladesh, Pakistan, and Thailand. For these countries and others (Vietnam, the Philippines), LNG imports seem to be sufficient to introduce or increase the share of gas-fired power generation in their energy mix as well as industrial and transport sector use. However, competition from coal remains a threat in some of these countries, including Indonesia, Malaysia, Thailand, Vietnam, and the Philippines. Outside Asia-Pacific, Turkey, Poland, Brazil, and smaller economies in Central America are also pursuing LNG imports, many via FSRUs, to enhance their energy security by diversifying their gas suppliers or introducing gas as a new fuel to their energy mix.

China

The winter of 2017–18 sharply exposed the shortcomings of the gas delivery system in China. China's gas consumption increased by 15 percent in 2017, and a large component of that growth has been attributed to a strong coal-to-gas switching program in the residential and industrial sectors (e.g., Lee 2018a) in order to meet 2017 deadlines for achieving air pollution goals. The gas demand resulting from this program and winter weather in northern China led to gas supply shortages in several regions. The government had to allow affected residential consumers as well as schools, hospitals, and other necessary public services to return to coal-fired heating. Gas deliveries to industries, many of whom had just converted from coal to gas-fired boilers, were cut causing production interruptions in some cases.

These shortages were mainly due to deliverability failures because of pipeline constraints between LNG terminals and northern demand centers and insufficient storage capacity to balance significant seasonal swing in gas demand in northern China. In Beijing alone, 2017–18 winter gas demand was 11 times higher than summer demand.[27] China used its LNG tanker truck fleet (largest in the world) to alleviate the shortages. In 2017, trucks delivered 12 percent of China's gas consumption (e.g., Graeber

2018). Trucking LNG may be a viable option when there is not enough time and/or it is too costly to build or expand pipelines to uncovered areas. It is also a way to build a market and customer base for future pipeline development to happen when critical customer mass is achieved. Nevertheless, the China National Petroleum Corporation's Economics and Technology Research Institute (ETRI) acknowledged that "inadequate gas peak shaving capacity is becoming a prominent problem" (e.g., Zhaofang 2017).

In April 2018, the NDRC "requested" that gas suppliers should boost storage to at least 10 percent of their supplies. This request does not have the force of law, but it shows the government's awareness of the natural gas storage challenge. However, despite several years of price reforms, prices to some consumers (e.g., residential) remain politically very sensitive and are administered by local governments that may not have agendas consistent with those of the central government. As Lee (2018b) reports, full deregulation of city gate gas prices has been delayed until 2020. If gas prices lack incentives to deliver, the government's environmental priorities could be undermined.

Currently, China has approximately 10 bcm of storage capacity that it expects to increase to 13 bcm in 2020, 20 bcm by 2023, and over 40 bcm in 2030.[28] It is hoped that seasonal arbitrage opportunities created by pricing reforms, if they are sustained, could spur investment in gas storage. In addition, there is a chance for PipeChina, newly established midstream company, to push for development of gas infrastructure. China hopes that this will incentivize not only domestic gas production but also investment in China's gas market (Shi 2020). Establishment of an independent midstream company is a step toward liberalizing the Chinese gas market via eventual TPA to the pipeline and storage infrastructure.

China was mostly self-sufficient in gas until the end of the 2000s. Since then, consumption grew much faster than domestic production. As discussed in the "Price Formation" section, a big challenge was that domestic producers (major NOCs) did not always receive a cost-recovery price for their production and transmission while they carried the higher cost of importing gas and delivering that gas to end-users at a price often lower than the cost. Pricing reforms partially targeted aligning the price received by domestic producers with import prices. As a result, domestic production growth picked up pace since 2016, although it is still growing less than demand. Nevertheless, some NOCs predict the majority of Chinese gas consumption to be supplied domestically by 2035, with significant volumes expected to come from coal bed methane (CBM) and coal-derived synthetic natural gas (SNG) (e.g., see Weijun 2020). Given the high economic and environmental cost of CBM and SNG and challenges such as access to water, these predictions appear suspect. In addition, geology of Chinese shale gas is "chaotic" as put by Jacobs (2019), who discusses difficulties with drilling and completion due to challenging geology. As such, Chinese shale gas production may not expand as much as expected nor would it be cost-effective. China does not seem to be putting all of its gas eggs in the domestic production basket as manifested in expanding import capacity. Accordingly, we would expect imports to increase their share as long as global LNG prices remain competitive.

India

India's gas infrastructure is even less extensive than that of China. There is no pipeline network per se but rather long-distance transmission lines that connect production zones and LNG import terminals to major demand centers. The Indian government had a plan to spend $8 billion beginning in 2012 to develop a National Gas Grid and expand gas pipeline market delivery capacity to about 18 billion cubic feet per day (Bcf/d) by April 2017. However, there were only 16,800 kilometers of pipeline in India in early 2020, with another 14,200 under construction or proposed. India consumed less than 6 Bcf/d in 2019. Nevertheless, gas expansion is moving forward. India had its rounds 9 and 10 to award licenses for LDC development. Like in China, reducing urban air pollution has been a major driver for developing gas networks, with CNG as transportation fuel playing an important role. When all LDCs and connecting transmission pipeline capacity are developed, about 70 percent of India's population will have access to gas (Global Gas Report 2020).

Today, the large regional imbalance in gas pipeline location remains, with the northwestern part of the country hosting most of the pipelines (40 percent in Gujarat and Maharashtra, home to first LNG import terminals and LDCs in major cities). With LNG import terminals and associated pipelines under construction or planned, gas is expected to reach most major cities in south and eastern half of the country. However, it is difficult to extend the gas delivery infrastructure in India and build new import terminals due to limited access to capital, dominance of SOEs, and significant land acquisition problems as well as the myriad of bureaucratic problems afflicting the expansion of any industrial activity in India. To address the issue and potentially inspire new demand growth, Shell, Petronet, and other companies are considering LNG trucking option in India, but it is highly unlikely for LNG trucking in India to reach the levels seen in China, given the constraints in road infrastructure and bureaucratic and sociopolitical dynamics of the country. The regulator is also pursuing to replace the existing distance-based transportation tariff with a unified tariff (postage stamp) to reduce the total cost of delivered gas at locations farther away from production or LNG import zones. Although gas demand may increase in those locations, it may decline in locations closer to supply zones since they would have to pay a higher transportation tariff than their current rate.[29]

The Gas Authority of India Ltd. (GAIL), an SOE, owns nearly three quarters of India's gas transmission capacity, imports about a fourth of the LNG, and sells about 55 percent of the gas consumed in the country. GAIL also owns about two-thirds of CNG stations in the country and has plans to expand its CNG and LNG capabilities to increase the use of gas in transport and industrial sectors. There is talk of unbundling the company, but until it is implemented with TPA, GAIL's dominance will continue.

India's domestic gas production declined 40 percent between 2010 and 2017 in part due to a lack of investment in the upstream sector. It increased but only slightly (by 2.3 percent) in the fiscal year 2017/18 and stabilized at that level for 2018/19 fiscal year, only to fall by almost 4 percent in 2019/20 according to the Petroleum Planning and Analysis (PPA) Cell of the Ministry of Petroleum and Natural Gas. The decline is partly due to a government-administered natural gas pricing which works directly against the 2016 reform (so-called HELP) that was supposed to attract domestic and foreign investors in the sector (IEA 2020b, p. 288). Domestic gas producers said they needed prices of at least $6–7/MMBtu and sometimes $10/MMBtu to revive gas production. In response, the central government approved a special pricing policy for existing but undeveloped discoveries and new discoveries in deepwater, ultra deepwater, and high pressure–high temperature fields in March 2016. Producers can negotiate prices for production from those fields subject to a price cap tied to the lowest of import prices for fuel oil, coal, naphtha, and LNG. The initial cap was $6.61/MMBtu but went as high as $9.32 in early 2019, before falling back to $5.61 in mid-2020 (Indian Oil & Gas 2020). In lower oil price periods, the special prices have been too low for upstream development. More importantly, volatility of this administered ceiling undermines investor confidence around future cash flows. The government has been promising freeing of domestic prices to induce domestic

E&P activity, but balancing consumer concerns seems to be preventing a final decision.

Energy Security

One overarching theme emanating from our survey of gas demand growth around the world is the importance of energy security in guiding energy strategy, including the role of natural gas, and investments. Of course, energy security has always been a key driver for all countries, but it gains further significance and some nuances in the New World where public funding and SOEs dominate the energy sector and new alignments among global powers are influenced by access to energy. So, it is worth discussing a bit further.

Energy security can be defined in the most basic form by a "4 As" approach: available, affordable, accessible, and acceptable access to energy supply.[30] In the past, the regional nature of natural gas put the suppliers and consumers of gas in a position of more or less equivalent dependency on each other. Today, natural gas is a more global commodity with a larger and growing number of producers, exporters, and consumers, mainly thanks to LNG.

A larger number of suppliers encourage competition and allow for supply diversification. Under competitive conditions, consumers can achieve lowest possible prices and possibly most advantageous contractual obligations. As Jonathan Stern notes in his Foreword to our book (and expanded relative to the role of competitive U.S. supply in Chap. 1), affordability is an important component of future of energy security and can determine the level of penetration gas can achieve in any given market. The consideration is particularly salient in less developed markets where governments may be constrained in ability to subsidize gas and hence may be more likely to keep coal as a major fuel. However, "lowest possible price" does not always mean lowest cost. For example, when countries want to avoid dependence on one supplier, they may invest in infrastructure necessary for supply diversification with redundancy. As we noted earlier, these expensive investments cannot always be achieved with purely commercial motive. We see a mix of market and government strategies and approaches worldwide.

For example, post-Soviet countries rejected at least some volumes of potentially lower-priced option (Russian gas) by investing in LNG import terminals and pipelines. This new infrastructure not only is able to bring gas from new supply sources like the U.S., Qatar, or Norway but also can efficiently distribute them within the region to better balance the market, preventing local shortages and/or price hikes. Much of the new infrastructure was not physically needed. The capacity of existing pipelines that bring Russian gas to Europe is large and could have been enhanced with compressors and interconnections. This investment would have been less than the cost of what has been built and/or is currently planned. Why the expense?

To begin, lack of competition from other suppliers in post-Soviet countries enabled Russia to charge higher prices than in Western Europe where Gazprom competes with other suppliers and interconnections exist to balance the market. In addition, gas has been a bargaining chip geopolitically as Russia used either price hikes or breaks in supply to influence policies of post-Soviet countries (Collins 2017). Availability of alternative supply (even simply as a credible threat of entry) prevents such behavior. For this availability, the marketplace needs large infrastructure investment. Thanks to this new capacity, Russia now is forced to price competitively. A good example here is Lithuania, where a new FSRU terminal pushed Russia to offer a 25 percent discount (Hinchey 2018). Access to LNG supplies via Greece has been a factor in 40 percent drop in prices of Russian gas in Bulgaria. Increasing bargaining power of post-Soviet countries also allowed them to secure more flexible terms in new Russian gas contracts.

China has been implementing a similar strategy of diversification that is visible in its gas import infrastructure that allows access to numerous LNG suppliers from around the world and pipeline gas from Russia as well as Central Asia (Turkmenistan, Kazakhstan, and Uzbekistan) (Pirani 2019). China is also making sure that its bargaining position vis-à-vis its suppliers is strong. Hence, when China negotiated the Power of Siberia pipeline to bring Russian gas, it made sure that the pipeline would not be directly connected to the same gas resources that currently serve the European market. Instead, an eastern route was designated. Though it needs new gas fields to be developed, it serves no other market but China. Such a situation precludes possible arbitrage opportunity on the side of Russia and hence makes the newly contracted deliveries more secure.

At the same time, Russia's own energy security considerations induce the country with the largest proved gas reserves in the world (19 percent of total; see Chap. 7) to diversify its export markets away from Europe. As such, the Power of Siberia appears to be a mutually beneficial project, although China may have the upper hand in terms of cost of gas at this time. It is suggested that Russia (Gazprom) built the pipeline as an incentive for China to agree on another pipeline Power of Siberia 2, which would bring Russian gas to China from Western Siberia, where gas is already developed and is currently supplying European demand (Pipeline & Gas Journal 2020). If the second pipeline is built, Russia could accrue substantial geopolitical influence as well as ability to arbitrage between European and Chinese demand.

To minimize situations where it needs to compete for natural gas with other centers of demand, China has been developing its own gas reserves, including in shale formations. Coal, nuclear, and renewable power are also attracting significant investment and are domestic alternatives to gas imports. Not only does China build coal-fired generation domestically, it also invests in coal power in other countries generating additional competition to natural gas demand there, including in Turkey, Vietnam, Indonesia, Bangladesh, Egypt, and the Philippines (NPR 2020; Li et al. 2020, pp. 1–9). "All of the above" seems to be the principle for ensuring China's energy security even if some options are more expensive than others (domestic gas, nuclear), less able to serve base, especially industrial, load (renewables), or more polluting (coal).[31]

The redundant infrastructure needed for energy security is suboptimal from a commercial perspective and may be a money-losing proposition, especially in many New World countries with illiquid markets distorted by administered pricing policies. Thus, state involvement becomes a needed element in developing that infrastructure. This is not unlike other public infrastructure that is beneficial for economic activity but not profitable enough to attract private investment, or for which a public interface is needed for assignment of property rights and coordinate common use (e.g., road, air, and water transportation infrastructure, water and sewage systems).

An important consideration for the scope and duration of state involvement is the political system. The more independent government is from the public, the more it can do, to support or hurt natural gas demand. In particular, governments with more central authority may have longer-term horizons in their strategic goals when compared to democracies, where election results often depend on economic performance and other public concerns. In democracies, executive branches (ministries and agencies) can develop long-range plans, but execution is subject to political cycles for appropriations. Short election cycles prevent politicians—often predominantly focused on getting reelected—from focusing on long-term priorities. A distinct question is how concerns about environment and climate figure into the complex picture of political systems and regimes, and with what implications for energy and economic priorities and development. In the Old World, public attitudes toward environment and climate deviate from those in the New World where economic development imperatives are stronger (Fig. 5.8). It is important to underscore that even in the Old World, 20–30 percent of randomly sampled respondents also consider the effects of climate change to be too far into the future to worry about, with another 10–15 percent not sure.

If a government with more central power sees natural gas as an important part of the country's energy mix, it could direct state-led investment toward gas infrastructure even if other societal needs have to be met at a

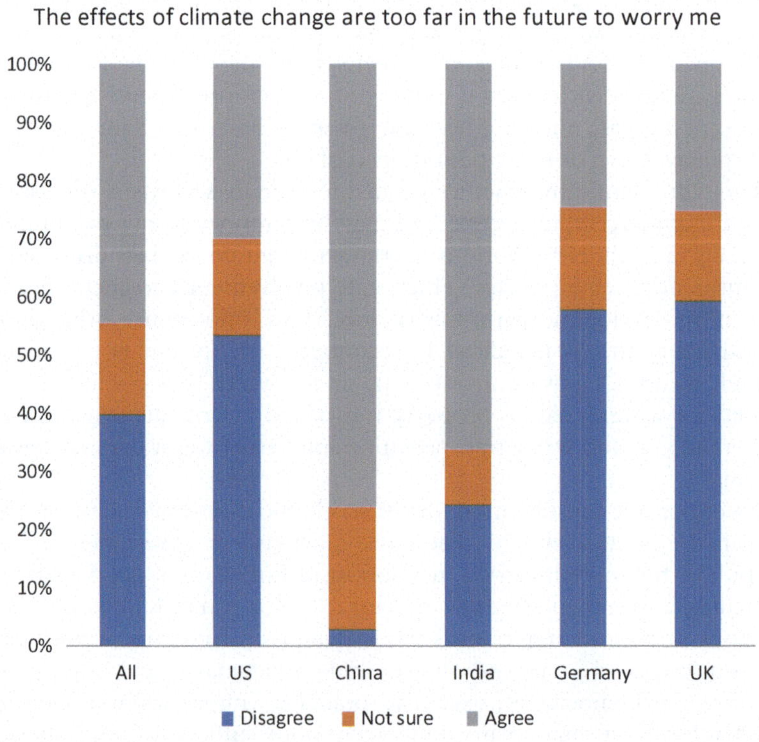

Fig. 5.8 Importance of climate change across the world. (Source: Khan 2020)

lower level. It can also direct investment to other energy infrastructure. China is an oft-quoted example of how a centrally planned economy could be a catalyst to rapid development in energy and other industrial imperatives, often via its SOEs. This includes building of LNG terminals, gas pipelines, and other gas infrastructure as well as coal, nuclear, wind, solar, and hydro facilities. In contrast, the politics in India (the largest democracy with a federal system, and which has to focus on immediate and complex needs of a multicultural society) might contribute to slower pace at which the country is able to move more decisively from coal to alternatives, including natural gas, and/or implement a long-term energy plan. Being a democracy does not mean SOEs are not important or corruption is not a problem. Indian SOEs are dominant in the energy sector, including the gas industry, as we discussed before. China and India have the same poor score in 2019 corruption perception index (Transparency International 2019). So, energy investments in both countries are likely to be inefficient from a commercial perspective.

Our goal is not to write a political thesis. Ultimately, how governments are organized and their ability to implement policies depend on a complex set of historical, cultural, and geographical factors that created today's legal and political systems. We do acknowledge, however, that the current political system in any country matters for gas suppliers and their ability to make decisions based on long-term goals such as energy security and climate change commitments, even under difficult times. From this perspective, China might instill more confidence in global gas suppliers than India, because it has been able to sustain investment in natural gas infrastructure and, of great importance, honor its long-term agreements. We must also acknowledge that, since the early 2000s, China has had significant current account surpluses, while India experienced large deficits. It is reasonable to see China's surplus as a result of country's consistent pursuit of its long-term economic and trade strategies. Ultimately, policy consistency and infrastructure built by public funds are expected to lay the foundation for private investors to develop projects by raising funding in global capital markets to the extent they reduce or eliminate various risks to projects. At the same time, we must follow closely the dynamic forces of global geopolitics, China's macroeconomic status, and the feedback loop between the two, which we discuss in some detail in Chap. 7.

A related observation concerns the investment decisions across the spectrum of countries in Fig. 5.7. For example, the U.S. companies hurt by difficult market conditions (see Chap. 1) were already consolidating or cutting back investment in the upstream, and new U.S. LNG projects were struggling to get financing. A convergence of factors was at play—slowing economic activity and energy demand in early 2019, which induced lower crude oil prices, and low U.S. natural gas prices with persistent surpluses, which induced lower LNG prices in receiving markets, squeezed LNG margins. Saturated buyers, who had rushed into LNG contracts following the Fukushima Daiichi accident in Japan in 2011, were under pressure to adjust. The pandemic exposed these weaknesses and sped up consolidation in the U.S. upstream and project deferments or cancellations in liquefaction.

By comparison, despite the pandemic, Russia and Qatar have been supporting their companies in strong natural gas development. These countries have few options for revenues and hard currency than to support their champion industries. For example, in Russia, Novatek, a nominally private company, continues with Arctic LNG expansion with significant support from the Russian government, including tax holidays and critical infrastructure buildup in the Arctic (e.g., Port of Sabetta). Gazprom has been benefiting from Russian government's support in building Power of Siberia (Mikulska and Jakubowski 2020). Qatar Petroleum has announced the expansion of its LNG fleet by up to 100 new vessels to support its aggressive liquefaction capacity expansion and signed preliminary agreements with Chinese and Korean shipbuilders. Qatar Petroleum is capable of financing these projects mostly from its equity, reducing the need for securing long-term contracts with creditworthy buyers (e.g., see Benali and Al-Ashmawy 2020).

Overall, in the New World, a convergence of energy security imperatives among resource-rich countries that have few other options for sustaining export revenues and those of emerging economies that see gas as a valuable alternative for their growing energy mix sustain and probably enlarge the role of governments. Also, the increasing regulatory burden in the Old World (especially Western Europe and possibly ahead for the U.S. and Canada) renders pragmatic New World countries more attractive markets for resource exporters. The fact that most of these suppliers and importers have political systems that concentrate power more centrally than democracies is an important determinant not only for natural gas but also for all energy investments and, indeed, many other aspects of economic and sociopolitical life.

Lessons Learned

1. In the Old World, primary energy consumption is decreasing, while it continues to increase in the New World. The challenges faced by gas in a declining energy demand world are much higher than in a growing one.
2. There seems to be little doubt that gas demand will grow in the New World, most significantly in Asia-Pacific led by China. Post-Soviet countries, including EU members, have been growing faster than Western Europe, and their energy transition favors coal-to-gas switching even when complying with EU targets. Although much hyped given its size, Indian gas demand growth may not be as significant as growth in the Middle East. Even the resource-rich SSA and Latin America may increase their gas consumption more than India if perennial governance problems of those continents can be solved.
3. Natural gas is facing competition from alternative fuels, most prominently from coal (New World) and renewables (Old World and New World). Coal is most competitive against gas in Asia-Pacific, mostly due to its reliability and affordability but also the long history of local coal-based economies. Alternative energy will be most competitive based on the criterion of acceptability (i.e., environmental benefits) as emerging middle classes want cleaner air, water, and land, especially in growing urban areas, and consider coal and most polluting liquid fuels unacceptable. We must allow for risk and uncertainty on this front as environmental and affordability impacts associated with alternative energy technologies come under greater scrutiny (true as well for Old World countries).
4. Given the limitations of intermittent and difficult-to-scale renewables, gas will likely benefit from the same socioeconomic trends related to local pollution in the New World. In the Old World, gas demand growth is at risk because of public's fear of climate change. Western Europe and parts of the U.S. will continue reducing their gas consumption.
5. Declining demand for gas in Old World countries that have been net importers could mean less competition for supply among New World buyers. To that extent, New World economies probably welcome declining gas consumption in the Old World. More gas, likely at lower

cost, especially from New World suppliers, could be available for their energy needs. Their bargaining power as importers might also increase.

6. The New World is characterized by strong roles for sovereigns, including regulation and involvement via state-owned or state-dependent companies. Even in the Old World, the role of government is potentially forceful and expanding in terms of energy policies, including mandates and subsidies, and regulations that favor alternative energy technologies over fossil fuels. In this sense, most "clean energy" companies are state-dependent in the Old World as well. As countries continue to fail to achieve climate-related targets based on economic calculus, there is a risk of some Old World countries' energy policies becoming more command-and-control than most New World countries.
7. The extent of state involvement may be related to the level of gas market development a country is currently exhibiting. Less developed markets may need more government intervention to help them grow to a point where they can be a host to competitive and liquid supply. Even in China, there are efforts to deregulate gas pricing and allow for private participation in gas delivery as the country continues to expand its gas infrastructure. In contrast, India exemplifies the fundamental challenge of most growing economies: balancing noble intentions to offer subsidized energy to the poor and their need for energy. Subsidy policies, however, are often quickly corrupted and undermine investment in energy supply chains. As such, expecting a gas market à la Western Europe (let alone the U.S.) in most New World countries is unwarranted.
8. State involvement also is related to the political system in a country. Most New World countries have political systems that do not follow Western models. Even democracies have different organization and style shaped by geography, historical and cultural underpinnings, and legal systems, among other factors.
9. Moreover, realignment of world powers with Russia and China as counterbalance to the U.S. also influences gas infrastructure development around the world.
10. Energy security is an important part of the calculus that fuels extensive government involvement. Historical policies of subsidizing cost of energy, and control of existing infrastructure by legacy SOEs, influence gas pricing and development of gas infrastructure.

Notes

1. Although imprecise and simple, to a great extent, our definition of Old and New World overlaps with OECD and non-OECD. Comparisons of the latter two have been the norm in most energy outlooks and similar discussions. As we discuss in this chapter, however, there are significant differences across OECD members, and some have more in common with the non-OECD countries when it comes to natural gas demand and markets.
2. Export netback prices relate to the price of gas exported by Gazprom minus transportation cost (usually taken from Moscow), minus export tax. For more see Henderson (2011) and OIES (2020).
3. For example, when prices of gas for industrial customers rose in 1997, Gazprom received only 29 percent of payments (only 12 percent in cash). For more, see Henderson (2011).
4. Since 2012, the company has to award access to third-party purchases via SPIMEX.
5. The post-Soviet-bloc designation relates to countries, which used to be either part of the Soviet Union or part of the Soviet influence sphere. For the purposes of this chapter, post-Soviet bloc includes Latvia, Lithuania, Estonia, Ukraine, Belarus, Poland, Czech Republic, Slovakia, Hungary, Romania, Bulgaria, Moldova, and republics of former Yugoslavia.
6. Even Poland, the EU country that has been highly dependent on coal for power generation and that has been persistent in allowing coal mining and coal power to operate, has now committed to eliminating coal from power generation by 2050–2060. See, for example, Reuters (2020b).
7. This issue is not limited to Asia. For example, several LNG import terminals have been under consideration in Australia—world's second largest LNG exporter—as the country struggles with uneven distribution of gas within its territory and opposition to development of new gas supplies and pipeline infrastructure. On issues around Australia's natural gas, see Maher and Mikulska (2017).
8. The dominant role of Petrobras (Brazilian NOC) across the gas supply chain and gas-fired power generation still handicaps gas market development in the most populous country in the continent.
9. Note that state initiatives to save some nuclear plants in the U.S. were also driven, at least partially, by political concerns around whole towns near a plant losing their economic raison d'être. Local economic and job impacts have also been key ingredients of successful renewable policies in the U.S. and elsewhere. Unsurprisingly, the stimulus packages to mitigate the impacts of the COVID pandemic focus on creating jobs, especially in the clean energy and general infrastructure sectors. It is useful to keep these

observations from the Old World in mind when we discuss the role of state in developing natural gas infrastructure in the "Government" section.

10. Important exception here is Germany. As the country expanded its push for renewables and banned nuclear power generation, it was unable to wean itself from coal. In fact, even recently a new coal-fired power plant was opened there, despite an almost concurrent stipulation to end coal use by 2038.
11. Members include major economies from Asia-Pacific, including Australia and South Korea (but not Japan), Central Asia, the Caucasus region, Russia, richest resource countries from the Middle East, Canada, and largest economies of Europe (including the UK, Germany, France, Italy). The U.S. opposed AIIB.
12. In the U.S. and Canada, LDCs are overseen by subnational, state, and provincial/territorial regulatory authorities, a reflection of constitutional norms that assign and protect the rights of these subjurisdictions. In the U.S., a handful of state regulators are elected.
13. In the U.S., an important ruling by the U.S. Federal Energy Regulatory Commission in 2002, the "Hackberry Decision," waived third-party open access requirements for LNG import terminals in order to encourage risk-taking development. In effect, the FERC agreed with the Hackberry receiving terminal developer, Dynegy, that LNG storage could be treated akin to producing fields, that is, regasified LNG would be dispatched into the U.S. pipeline system in competition with field production, alleviating the need for the FERC to set tariffs and rate schedules as part of certifying new facilities. See Hollis (2007).
14. We note that Chap. 4 mainly covers large-scale onshore LNG projects, which account for the overwhelming majority of LNG capacity.
15. For example, CPC and Cheniere signed a 25-year SPA (2 MTPA). Mozambique LNG has a 20-year SPA with Centrica LNG and Tokyo Gas (2.6 MTPA). Venture Global has 20-year SPAs with PGNiG (2.5 MTPA) and EDF Trading (1 MTPA) for its Plaquemines (Louisiana) project.
16. One lot = 10,000 MMBtu or ~195 metric tons.
17. Incoterms by the International Chamber of Commerce (ICC) now calls this delivered at place (DAP).
18. Re-exporting of a delivered cargo does not qualify as diversion.
19. According to Bresciani et al. (2020), the cost of liquefaction increased to about $2000 per ton in 2012, before declining to $900 in 2017. Some companies are pursuing smaller liquefaction trains and a modular approach to reduce and/or manage capital expenditure.
20. The main exception for market-driven natural gas demand in the U.S. derives from air quality actions that affected and reduced coal-fired power, stimulating increased use of methane.

21. This is equivalent to the Hackberry decision by the U.S. FERC, allowing the risk-taking LNG project developers to retain control over capacity in the same way they would control producing fields; see book Appendix.
22. However, the government has not been able to pay all the developers and is trying to reduce the number of projects eligible to receive subsidies. Most developers are SOEs, but publicly traded firms are hurt in the absence of subsidy cash flows from the government (e.g., Energy Voice 2020).
23. Australia is focusing on natural gas as part of its recovery (e.g., Kemp 2020).
24. For example, in South Asia, switching of smaller vehicles to CNG has been promoted since the 2000s to reduce urban air pollution. More recently, many Chinese cities have been switching from coal to natural gas in residential and industrial applications.
25. Portions of the text in this section were drawn from an earlier version of this chapter prepared by Miranda Wainberg, and reflect previous work.
26. IEA (2020a) reports gas and oil power generation investment together. Given that there is little investment in oil-fired power generation in most of the world, we treat the reported numbers as gas-fired power plants.
27. See Wainberg et al. (2017) for discussions of gas infrastructure bottlenecks.
28. China lifted underground gas storage capacity to 10.2 bcm in 2019 (Reuters 2020c).
29. For example, see https://www.spglobal.com/platts/en/market-insights/latest-news/oil/110320-interview-india-seeks-to-plug-energy-gap-though-gas-reforms-transition-fuels.
30. The traditional approach of 4 As has been recently challenged by some to include climate change and local pollution concerns (e.g., see Czerp and Jewell 2014).
31. As we were writing this chapter in September 2020, President Xi Jinping pledged net zero carbon by 2060. Like many such pledges, details are lacking. China's current energy mix and large investments in new coal-fired capacity and energy-intensive industries and infrastructure do not bode well for China meeting this pledge, but it does suggest a bigger role for gas along with renewables and nuclear to replace coal.

References

American Enterprise Institute. China global investment tracker. https://www.aei.org/china-global-investment-tracker/

Ang, S. 2019. JKM LNG derivatives volume up 56% on month in September. S&P Global, Platts. https://www.spglobal.com/platts/en/market-insights/latest-news/natural-gas/100119-jkm-lng-derivatives-volume-up-56-on-month-in-september

Ayaburi, J., Morgan Bazilian, J. K., and Todd Moss, 2020. Measuring "Reasonably Reliable" access to electricity services. *The Electricity Journal*, 33 (7). https://doi.org/10.1016/j.tej.2020.106828.

Benali, L.R., and R. Al-Ashmawy. 2020. *MENA gas & petrochemicals investment outlook 2020–2024*. APICORP.

Braga, B. 2020. Argentina's stranded asset. *Natural Gas World Magazine* 5 (20). https://www.naturalgasworld.com/argentinas-stranded-asset-ngw-magazine-82895. Last accessed 11 June 2020.

Bresciani, G., S. Heiligtag, P. Lambert, and M. Rogers. 2020. The future of liquefied natural gas: Opportunities for growth. McKinsey & Company. https://www.mckinsey.com/industries/oil-and-gas/our-insights/the-future-of-liquefied-natural-gas-opportunities-for-growth

Collins, G. 2017. Russia's use of the "energy weapon" in Europe. Baker Institute for Public Policy. https://www.bakerinstitute.org/research/russias-use-energy-weapon-europe/

Collins, G., and A. Mikulska. 2018. Gas geoeconomics in Europe. Baker Institute for Public Policy. https://www.bakerinstitute.org/research/egas-geoeconomics-europe/

———. 2020. Trans-Atlantic gas diplomacy. Baker Institute for Public Policy. https://www.bakerinstitute.org/research/molecule-indifferent-gas-geoeconomics-not-energy-sanctions-are-best-option-harden-europe-against-rus/

Czerp, A., and J. Jewell. 2014. The concept of energy security beyond the four as. *Energy Policy* 75: 415–421.

Downs, E., and S. Yan. 2020. Reform is in the pipelines: PipeChina and the restructuring of China's natural gas market. Center on Global Energy Policy, Columbia University. https://www.energypolicy.columbia.edu/sites/default/files/file-uploads/PipeChina_CGEP_Commentary_091420.pdf

Energy Voice. 2020. China increases renewable subsidies 7.5% to 13 billion. https://www.energyvoice.com/otherenergy/246746/china-increases-renewable-subsidies-7-5-to-13-billion/

ESMAP. 2020. Tracking SDG7. *The energy progress report*. https://trackingsdg7.esmap.org/

European Commission. 2020. Commission recommendation on energy poverty (C(2020) 9600). https://ec.europa.eu/energy/sites/ener/files/recommendation_on_energy_poverty_c2020_9600.pdf

Global Gas Report. 2020. https://www.igu.org/resources/global-gas-report-2020/

Goodrich, G. 2020. Bringing it home: The emerging role of Nigerian gas for domestic use. Africa Oil & Power. https://www.africaoilandpower.com/2020/09/11/bringing-it-home-the-emerging-role-of-nigerian-gas-for-domestic-use/

Graeber, D.J. 2018. Trucks fill Chinese gaps in LNG market, June 4. https://www.upi.com/Trucks-fill-Chinese-gaps-in-LNG-market/

Henderson, J. 2011. Domestic gas priced in Russia – Towards export netback? Oxford Institute for Energy Studies. https://www.oxfordenergy.org/wpcms/wp-content/uploads/2011/11/NG_57.pdf. Last accessed 10 Dec 2020.

Hinchey, N. 2018. The impact of securing alternative energy sources on Russian-European natural gas pricing. *The Energy Journal* 39 (2): 173–196.

Hinchey, N., and A. Mikulska. 2017. LNG versus Russian gas in Central and Eastern Europe: Playing poker on a continental scale. *Forbes*. https://www.forbes.com/sites/thebakersinstitute/2017/08/24/lng-versus-russian-gas-in-central-and-eastern-europe-playing-poker-on-a-continental-scale/?sh=5d9666062c3a

Hollis, S.S. 2007. Liquefied natural gas: "the big picture" for future development in North America. *Environmental & Energy Law & Policy Journal* 2 (1). University of Houston Law Center. http://www.law.uh.edu/eelpj/publications/2-1/02Hollis.pdf

Indian Oil & Gas. 2020. Freeing up gas price: Agreed but Reluctant to Act. Vol. 27(11), September 10.

International Energy Agency. 2016. World energy investment 2016.

———. 2019. World energy investment 2019.

———. 2020a. World energy investment 2020. https://www.iea.org/reports/world-energy-investment-2020

———. 2020b. India 2020, Energy policy review 2020.

International Gas Union. 2020a. 2020 world LNG report. https://www.igu.org/resources/2020-world-lng-report/

———. 2020b. Wholesale gas price survey, 2020 edition. https://www.igu.org/resources/wholesale-price-survey-2020-edition/

Jacobs, T. 2019. China's shale dream rests atop chaotic geology. *Journal of Petroleum Technology* 71 (6): 36–40. https://doi.org/10.2118/0619-0036-JPT.

Kemp, A. 2020. Australia relies on its gas. *Natural Gas World Magazine* 5 (18). https://www.naturalgasworld.com/australia-relies-on-its-gas-ngw-magazine-82190

Khan, Mehreen. 2020.Europe's climate ambitions meet reality. *Financial Times*. September 15. https://www.ft.com/content/bc4952be-f9eb-4eaa-a8db-53c5cd585a24

Krane, J. 2020. Dubai's coal push upends Abu Dhabi's clean energy strategy. MEES, Issue 63/35. https://www.mees.com/2020/8/28/op-ed-documents/dubais-coal-push-upends-abu-dhabis-clean-energy-strategy/a5986ad0-e92d-11ea-82e9-bf5bb5670a2d

Lee, D. 2018a. China revs up coal-to-gas switching. World Gas Intelligence, June 20. http://www.energyintel.com/pages/eig_article.aspx?DocID=1001740

———. 2018b. China to delay city gate gas price deregulation. LNG Intelligence, June 14. http://www.energyintel.com/pages/eig_article.aspx?DocID=1001747

Li, Zhonhsu, K.P. Gallagher, and D. Mauzerall. 2020. China's global power: Estimating Chinse foreign direct investment in the electric power sector. *Energy Policy* 136: 1–9.

Loe, J.S.P. 2019. But it is our duty! Exploring Gazprom's reluctance to Russian gas sector reform. *Post-Soviet Affairs* 35 (1): 63–76.

Maher, M., and A. Mikulska. 2017. Australia's conflicting natural gas policies. *Forbes*. https://www.forbes.com/sites/thebakersinstitute/2017/07/05/australias-conflicting-natural-gas-policies/#684511b87741

McCracken, R. 2020. Japan slow to tackle coal. *Natural Gas World Magazine* 5 (20). https://www.naturalgasworld.com/japan-slow-to-tackle-coal-ngw-magazine-82906. Last accessed 11 June 2020.

Michot Foss, M., and D. Palmer-Huggins. 2016. European and Asian natural gas market developments-swamped by the present? In *Managing energy price risk*, ed. V. Kaminski. London: Risk Books.

Mikulska, A., and P. Jakubowski 2020. The future of Russian gas: A tale of two cities. Baker Institute for Public Policy.

Mikulska, A., and E. Kosinski. 2018. Explaining Poland's coal paradox. *Forbes*. https://www.forbes.com/sites/thebakersinstitute/2018/03/28/explaining-polands-coal-paradox/

———. 2020. What's next for natural gas in Ukraine? Baker Institute for Public Policy. https://www.bakerinstitute.org/media/files/files/6754d0f0/ces-wp-ukraine-050720.pdf

Mills, R. 2020. Under a cloud: The future of Middle East gas demand. Center on Global Energy Policy, Columbia University.

Newnham, R. 2011. Oil, carrots, and sticks: Russia's energy resources as a foreign policy tool. *Journal of Eurasian Studies* 2 (2): 134–143.

NPR. 2020. Why is China placing a global bet on coal. https://www.npr.org/2019/04/29/716347646/why-is-china-placing-a-global-bet-on-coal

Oxford Institute for Energy Studies (OIES). 2020. Sponsor meeting spring 2020, Webinar 7: "Russia and CIS gas." https://www.oxfordenergy.org/wpcms/wp-content/uploads/2020/04/Session-7-Russia-CIS-Gas.pdf

Pirani, S. 2019. Central Asian gas: Prospects for the 2020s. Oxford Institute for Energy Studies. https://www.oxfordenergy.org/wpcms/wp-content/uploads/2019/12/Central-Asian-Gas-NG-155.pdf

Public-Private Infrastructure Advisory Facility (PPIAF). 2019. Who sponsors infrastructure projects? Disentangling public and private contributions (with World Bank). https://ppi.worldbank.org/content/dam/PPI/documents/SPIReport_2017_small_interactive.pdf

Reuters. 2020a. Exxon Mobil confirms may exit Romanian offshore gas project. https://www.reuters.com/article/us-romania-energy-exxon/exxon-mobil-confirms-may-exit-romanian-offshore-gas-project-idUSKBN1Z70XP

———. 2020b. Poland plans to merge utilities, carve out coal: minister. https://www.reuters.com/article/us-poland-energy-coal/poland-plans-to-merge-utilities-carve-out-coal-minister-idUSKBN24Z0SE

———. 2020c. China lifted underground gas storage capacity to 10.2 bcm in 2019 – state TV. https://www.reuters.com/article/china-gas-storage-idAFL4N29S2CA.

Sen, A., 2017, India's gas market post-COP21. The Oxford Institute for Energy Studies. OIES paper: NG 120. https://www.oxfordenergy.org/wpcms/wp-content/uploads/2017/06/Indias-Gas-Market-Post-COP21-NG-120.pdf

Shi, W. 2020. Letter from China: Pipeline reform heats up. *Petroleum Economist.* https://www.petroleum-economist.com/articles/midstream-downstream/pipelines/2020/letter-from-china-pipeline-reform-heats-up

Srivastava, S. 2020. India sets out multi-faceted reform to support gas. *Petroleum Economist.* https://www.petroleum-economist.com/articles/midstream-downstream/pipelines/2020/india-sets-out-multi-faceted-reform-to-support-gas

Swora, M., and A. Mikulska. 2017. U.S. LNG in central and eastern Europe – Taking diversification seriously. *Forbes.* https://www.forbes.com/sites/thebakersinstitute/2017/07/11/u-s-lng-in-cee-diversification/

Transparency International. 2019. Corruption perceptions index. https://www.transparency.org/en/cpi#

Visenesc, R., and H. Bartelet. 2017. How Romania can become a key player in the European gas market. *Energypost.eu.* https://energypost.eu/romania-key-player-gas-eu/

Wainberg, M., M. Michot Foss, G. Gülen, and D. Quijano. 2017. Current and future natural gas demand in China and India. The University of Texas at Austin-Bureau of Economic Geology, April. https://www.beg.utexas.edu/files/cee/legacy/2017/CEE_Research_Paper-China_and_India_Current_Future_Natural_Gas_Demand-Apr17.pdf

Weijun, S. 2020. China's gas demand growth. *Natural Gas World Magazine* 5 (21).

Wong, W. 2019. LNG shipping rates rise in Atlantic Pacific basins to $100,000/day amid low spot vessel supply. S&P Global, Platts. https://www.spglobal.com/platts/en/market-insights/latest-news/shipping/101119-lng-shipping-rates-rise-in-both-basins-to-100000-day-amid-low-spot-vessel-supply

Yermakov, V., and J. Henderson. 2020. The new deal for oil markets, energy insight L67. The Oxford Institute for Energy Studies. https://www.oxfordenergy.org/wpcms/wp-content/uploads/2020/04/Insight-67-The-New-Deal-for-Oil-Markets-implications-for-Russias-short-term-tactics-and-long-term-strategy.pdf

Zhaofang, D. 2017. China natural gas market status and outlook. CNPC Economics & Technology Research Institute. https://eneken.ieej.or.jp/data/7693.pdf

CHAPTER 6

Building Sustainable Natural Gas Markets

Michelle Michot Foss and Gürcan Gülen

Introduction

Most long views incorporate increased global natural gas consumption for decades ahead (see our Foreword and Chaps. 1 and 5). Hundreds of billions of dollars invested in gas and liquefied natural gas (LNG) supply chains and gas-consuming infrastructure every year, backed by long-term contracts, support these expectations. As noted by other authors throughout this book, there are few good, cost-effective options for balancing electricity provided by intermittent renewable energy sources. However, much less is said about the use of natural gas as "a," or perhaps "the," baseload fuel for electric power generation although at one time it was almost a generic assumption. For that matter, not much is said about natural gas as "a," or "the," key baseload fuel source for other applications, like transport, or even petrochemicals, in spite of the tremendous advantage

M. Michot Foss (✉)
Baker Institute for Public Policy, Rice University, Houston, TX, USA
e-mail: michelle.m.foss@rice.edu

G. Gülen
Independent Consultant, West Brookfield, MA, USA
e-mail: gurcan@g2eis.com

M. Michot Foss et al. (eds.), *Monetizing Natural Gas in the New "New Deal" Economy*,
https://doi.org/10.1007/978-3-030-59983-6_6

natural gas molecular feedstocks have in the U.S. and the importance of materials to the global economy. Notwithstanding relative abundance and low cost, and regardless of its critical importance as a primary heating fuel in colder climates, natural gas is most often discussed as an incremental fuel source, one that ultimately would be replaced by vast additions of renewable energy capacity, hydrogen, and electrification.

Expanding the role of natural gas even as a vital incremental fuel source faces many challenges, more so in regions and locations where infrastructure is weak and "rules of the game" do not provide clarity for risky investment. Value creation across the natural gas supply chain requires expansive networks of pipelines of different sizes and specifications to transport natural gas from production areas to consumption centers. As detailed in Chap. 1 and the Appendix (reference to the natural gas system flow chart, Fig. A.1), effective natural gas systems need production gathering at the field level and processing to separate out various molecules so that mostly methane can be supplied to pipeline networks and other molecules (natural gas liquids) can be monetized. All natural gas markets benefit from storage facilities for methane and natural gas liquids (NGLs) to balance daily and seasonal fluctuations in demand. For direct use of gas, effective natural gas systems incorporate local distribution companies to move methane to factories, businesses, and homes via smaller diameter pipelines. All direct methane and liquid petroleum gas (LPG) consumers need appropriate appliances. If customers will receive natural gas as imports via pipelines or as liquefied natural gas (LNG), they will need pipelines and LNG receiving terminals (along with supporting LNG supply chains). Natural gas infrastructure is expensive to build, maintain, and operate. Connecting customers of different sizes and metering their consumption can represent a large portion of end-user prices. For example, in the U.S., more than half of the unit cost of natural gas for a small customer (residential or commercial) is associated with the local distribution utilities (see Appendix).

In large, open, liquid natural gas markets such as the U.S., basis differentials inform the producers regarding bottlenecks across geographies and midstream investment needs. Producers can either be satisfied with discounted wellhead prices if their assets are behind bottlenecks or decide to invest in those midstream assets themselves if the higher netback pricing allows them fast recovery of that investment. In the U.S., Canada, and some other locations, independent midstream companies will detect opportunities to generate value by responding to differentials and making those investments (albeit often with producer commitments, as addressed in Chap. 1). In general, in openly competitive liquid markets, upstream, midstream, and downstream companies will react to market prices and basis differentials by building necessary infrastructure. Their investment responses can come under different arrangements that can change over time with market conditions and as consumers adjust their demand for natural gas.

Energy and environmental policies shape consumer behavior in ways that alter the competitiveness of and access to natural gas resources and supply. The more mature natural gas markets also teach us that three uses primarily drive demand for natural gas: space and water heating in residential, commercial, and industrial facilities; feedstock and fuel for industrial manufacturing, especially for the petrochemicals sector (including fertilizers); and power generation. In the absence of sizeable industrial and heating load (e.g., in temperate climates), the only alternative to create a substantial market for natural gas relatively quickly is power generation. Using natural gas only for power generation avoids (or at least, postpones) much of the large gas infrastructure investment. However, power sector conditions can create uncertainty about future natural gas use. In many countries, electricity grid operations are in the hands of state-owned enterprises (SOEs) that act as monopolies. Often, power grids provide unreliable service with frequent outages. Subsidies for end-user prices are very common and governments can change, sometimes capriciously, such prices unfavorably for power plant investors. This is the result of electricity being primarily a politicized commodity in most countries.

Without domestic resources, many countries are dependent on imports of natural gas via pipelines or LNG. Government funding has been the usual solution for overcoming upfront capital investment obstacles. During early phases of natural gas market development SOEs typically manage or at least oversee and certainly are gatekeepers for investment. They assume control and often ownership of the resulting facilities. Many pipelines span long distances of difficult terrain and multiple jurisdictions, incurring cost and geopolitical challenges. Many countries have become LNG importers in recent years largely owing to floating storage and regasification units (FSRUs) that bypassed the need to spend several billion dollars in onshore regasification terminals. Nevertheless, importing LNG remains expensive in many countries, especially when customers compare the cost of LNG to fuels it would replace. For example, in China and India, both domestic and imported coal remain cheaper than natural gas for power generation. Similarly, gas delivered via local distribution networks is more expensive than low-grade coal, subsidized LPG or kerosene, and non-commercial biomass for most residential and commercial customers. With new gas-fired power generation, the cost-reflective price of gas-fired electricity exceeds that of electricity generated from existing coal or hydro. Governments often heavily subsidize end-user prices, especially for low-income customers. Subsidies always invite the consequence of discouraging investment in the very energy supply and services that these populations desperately need, exacerbating energy poverty around the world.

Although government support and direct investment by SOEs may be necessary in initial phases of developing natural gas infrastructure, the cost-effective expansion of the system requires a well-functioning market with many private participants and large doses of transparency for pricing. In most countries, SOEs and their governments do not have the financial wherewithal to expand the gas infrastructure sufficiently. Often, governments have other priorities for their budgets. International development assistance funding for natural gas infrastructure development has been immaterial since the 2000s with the exception of some interregional pipelines. Much of that funding has been flowing to power generation, including gas-fired power plants but mostly renewable energy projects. Building and overseeing expansive networks also is challenging from an institutional capacity perspective. The natural gas marketplace requires proper regulatory oversight for tariff-setting and safe operations. Many countries lack the experienced regulatory personnel and institutions. In the absence of commercial frameworks that facilitate proficiently regulated private investment, it will take even longer, if ever, to develop natural gas markets or, for that matter, any energy market with sufficient depth and breadth. Inefficient SOE investment can induce a waste of scarce public capital. Such has been the case for most of Latin America and nearly all of Africa as noted in Chap. 1 and illustrated in Fig. 1.1.

Commercial Frameworks

What investors may need to develop a commercially successful project is not necessarily the same as what a well-functioning marketplace needs to develop and induce efficient investment for the long term. Developers can sanction projects anchored by long-term bilateral contracts with

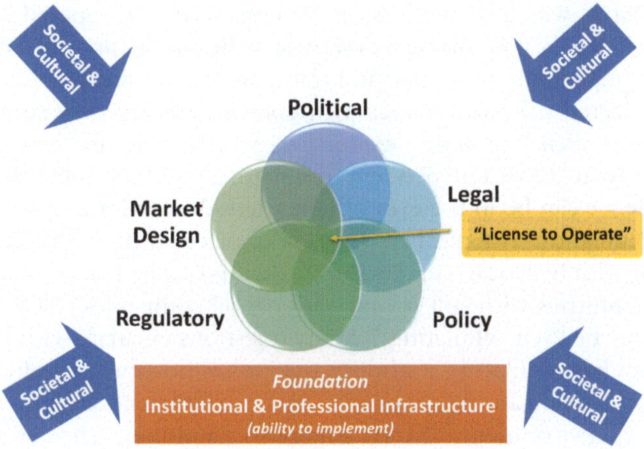

Fig. 6.1 Conceptual space for commercial frameworks. (Source: Developed by authors)

government guarantees. They face the distinct risk that policies of subsequent government administrations could undermine the investment. To capture the range of possibilities we offer Fig. 6.1 as an illustration of the "conceptual space" within which commercial frameworks exist, along with associated dynamics.

How governments work and how projects are designed, in a commercial sense, are subject to the underlying *law* of the land, the legal system of a jurisdiction. Civil and common law are typical forms, but particular legal systems, such as Islamic law, can have considerable consequences for investment. Everything from how projects are financed, to how contracts are written and executed, to procurement, hiring and immigration rules for expatriate workers and customs for goods are affected by the underlying legal system. An important part of due diligence by investors is *politics*, the political organization, and style of a host country. Democracy or something else? Party system with competitive elections, or not? How do citizens vote? Coups, nationalizations, including "creeping expropriation" (the tendency for governments to exert control or even ownership shares in projects and/or subsidiaries through changes in taxes and other rules) are political events, vetted as part of political risk. *Policy* does not happen in a vacuum. Policies shape legal and regulatory choices which determine market design outcomes, all of which can be influenced by technological developments, which themselves can be enhanced or hampered by policy, regulatory, legal, and market design specifics. The process of policymaking is important—is it open and transparent, how are laws formulated, how do elected officials interact with constituents are only some of the questions. Policies underlie *regulation*, which can take many forms. Countries may have independent regulators; even in these situations, independence can be in the eyes of beholders. Ministries can develop and enforce regulation. A typical approach is to place authority for regulation associated with hydrocarbons laws in the hands of a hydrocarbon ministry. In some countries with still strong national oil companies (NOCs), these entities may be "self-regulating." Many questions emanate with regard to what body has regulatory authority over what portions of value chains, with what organization, processes, and performance. Safety, security, health, and environment (SSHE) imperatives and the particular demands inherent in capital-intensive energy businesses put pressures on abilities of regulators to develop and enforce appropriate guidance and rules. *Market design*, how buyers and sellers ultimately interact, is the outcome of all of these forces. Our main concern is access to markets by either producers or customers, whether they can engage in transactions directly with their counterparties, whether governments intervene in transactions (for instance, regulating prices), and whether monopolies exist and with what implications. Even a country strongly identified with open, competitive markets, like the U.S., is usually a mixed economy, with distinct roles for government at different levels. The more open a market, the more important are standards—understandings about typical terms and conditions for buying and selling energy fuels and services.

All of these spheres of influence are under constant pressure from mutually reinforcing sociocultural forces. These forces can cut across jurisdictional boundaries. It is common to find non-governmental organizations (NGOs) exerting influence on proposed projects far from the NGO's home country. A distinct quandary is that civil societies are symbolic of democratization including the right to intervene adding to risk and uncertainty surrounding energy resource and infrastructure development. Of course, these are challenges even in mature markets today. In Chap. 2, we demonstrated how policies at state, city, and federal levels undermine electricity markets in the U.S. They also are challenges beyond legacy fuels and systems. Publics routinely oppose large grid-scale renewable energy projects including hydropower, offshore wind, and high-voltage electric power transmission including facilities specifically needed to link alternative energy sources with markets. As their "footprint" continues to rise, we should expect more opposition. "License to operate," loaded terminology in light of competing agendas among and within governments and societies over who should have the final say on project approvals, is ephemeral. We also can think of "license to operate" as the combination of variables leading to "workable, bankable" investment conditions. By that, we mean a context that enables "de-risking" projects sufficiently so that they can achieve financing and sanctioning. "Above ground risk" is widely acknowledged as a leading factor in capital project delays and overspending. Once achieved, shifts in any of the spheres often with swings in public perception and opinion can undermine the license to operate, diminishing bankability.

Over the years, we have examined natural gas and electric power commercial frameworks across numerous jurisdictions around the world (see the box in the section). Overall, we have found a high degree of variability in approaches even for countries that have moved very strongly in tandem with their reform approaches across the two sectors. This variability reflects relative conditions in these sectors as well as political culture and attributes. Electricity sector infrastructure is similar in all jurisdictions we have studied but there are relevant distinctions. The condition, reliability, and density of existing infrastructure and customers' ability to pay create uncertainties across the electric power value chain. The mix of generation technologies, often determined by availability of local resources such as hydro, coal, oil, or natural gas influence cost of electricity. Increasingly, environmental and energy security concerns induce policies for supporting wind, solar, and other renewables. These policies, in turn, guide the need for investment in generation, transmission, and distribution segments, and associated pricing and subsidy policies, which influence prospects for gas market growth.

All jurisdictions we investigated would like to grow their electric power systems to sustain economic development and connect populations who remain off-grid. Natural gas is not consumed everywhere. Countries with natural gas resources differ from those without. In many countries where the state is an owner and participant in upstream, oil production influence natural gas supplies. Oil and gas exports yield hard currency returns, and these sales may be the major source of financial balancing in energy sectors where electric power pricing is heavily subsidized. Often, however, associated natural gas is flared because oil is the main source of revenues and investment in capturing associated gas is difficult to justify in the absence of a domestic market based on cost-reflective prices and/or enough volumes to export. State oil companies are, in general, strong entities, protected by constitutions in many cases.

Many countries without natural gas resources import natural gas to enhance energy security by diversifying their energy options and/or to improve environmental quality. Their needs in terms of sector reforms are often different than those in countries with a history of natural gas consumption, hence with some level of natural gas infrastructure. In some cases, state companies that were instrumental in developing natural gas import infrastructure and managing those imports for years have become as powerful as state oil companies or electric power utilities (e.g., KOGAS in South Korea and BOTAŞ in Turkey).

Given the differences between the two sectors, their stage of evolution in each jurisdiction and political drivers of energy and economic policies, it is not possible to come up with one-size-fits-all recipes for coordinated development of natural gas and electric power markets. We cannot universally apply even the basic principles of liquid natural gas markets such as those of the U.S. and Western Europe. For example, allowing private participation along the value chain with third-party, or open, access for gas pipelines and power grids for fair competition can stand in the way of developing sufficiently wide-reaching infrastructure. The development of a new field may require upstream operator(s) to build dedicated pipeline and processing facilities. In a setting such as the U.S., open-access rules would immediately apply. Indeed, the U.S. Federal Energy Regulatory Commission (FERC) along with other U.S. government agencies and some state jurisdictions have consistently settled disputes that reinforce FERC's open-access rules even for high-risk facilities such as deep-water subsea pipelines. Similarly, it may be necessary for upstream operators to invest in anchor gas consumers such as large power plants and industrial facilities. For example, after the discovery of the Groningen field in the late 1950s, Shell and Exxon, in cooperation with the Dutch government, developed a natural gas market in the Netherlands by developing transmission and distribution networks to connect even residential and commercial customers and helping them switch from other fuels to natural gas. Although power generation and large industrial and export market customers were key to justifying such large investments, providing access to smaller customers created additional value.

Establishing brand-new independent regulators before a sufficient number of competitive players emerge can delay market development. Bureaucratic processes implemented by inexperienced agencies and their staff, who are often easily influenced by political forces, can be impediments even though they are essential for long-term viability of the marketplace. One of the most politically charged issues is the removal of subsidies to allow for cost-recovery rates, especially for electricity. In the case of natural gas, the early challenge is often to formulate prices for different customer classes that allow for cost recovery and reasonable rate of return yet are affordable to customers. In the Dutch natural gas market example mentioned in previous paragraph, netback market value pricing that set the price of natural gas to different customer classes at a level equivalent to the cost of alternative fuels plus delivery costs was critical. This level of price was high enough for commercially viable development of the Groningen resources.

Government and industry participants have followed the netback value principle in establishing other natural gas markets since the 1960s. In many cases, customers were paying high prices for alternative fuels (e.g., imported oil products, which, in some cases, also were heavily taxed by governments) so that savings could be identified early on. Today, in many countries where natural gas suppliers are trying to gain footholds, the netback price may not be high enough to cover the cost of natural gas procurement and delivery. For example, if a residential customer in China/India burns cheap coal/kerosene for heating, can a gas distribution network be built to deliver gas to that customer at or slightly below the same cost? In many countries, such fuels are subsidized, especially to small consumers. In other words, the majority of customers may not be able to afford cost-recovery levels of natural gas prices.[1]

Given all of these potential differences, it is necessary to look at the conditions at each jurisdiction in order to assess the commercial viability of natural gas market development. We offer a decision analysis schematic for the scenario of monetizing natural gas resources (Fig. 6.2). There are many examples around the world, some of which we summarize in the nearby box.

Examples of Natural Gas Monetization

Across seven diverse countries (Argentina, Australia, Colombia, South Korea, Taiwan, Thailand, and U.K.), similar steps were taken during the mid- to late 1990s to restructure their natural gas and electric power sectors. In all cases, goals included fostering private investment. Steps taken for electric power commonly included dismantling state monopolies. Varying approaches across the countries included efforts to instill competition in electricity generation, supply, and pricing, including creation of power pools. For natural gas, where NOCs existed and controlled gas supply, including imports, and infrastructure the most common strategies encouraged partnerships with rules for private investment. Third-party access to pipelines was pursued in the U.K., Argentina, Australia, and Colombia. With the qualified exception of Australia and the U.K., state entities in the rest of the countries in this sample continue to play important roles in electricity and, especially, gas industries in at least price regulation and controlling access to infrastructure.

In landlocked Bolivia, with a small internal market for natural gas, large gas resources of the country would not have been developed in the absence of, first, the pipeline to Argentina that was developed in the 1970s, and, then, the Bolivia-to-Brazil (BTB) pipeline that was developed in the late 1990s. The main market for the gas in Brazil was power generation that was expected to grow significantly, as Brazil tried to diversify away from hydroelectricity. However, this pipeline project was a case of supply push as much as demand pull. Exports to Argentina represented 80 percent of Bolivia's total gas production. When gas discoveries in Argentina decreased the demand for Bolivian gas, Bolivia needed an alternative export market. The BTB pipeline attracted private investment to the upstream sector in Bolivia. Between 1997 and 2001, 14 international companies invested about $2.5 billion in oil and gas upstream activities in Bolivia, which raised proven plus probable gas reserves by 700 percent. The support from the World Bank as well as the Brazilian government and Petrobras, national oil company of Brazil, was crucial for the pipeline project's development in addition to involvement of Shell and Enron. The World Bank also supported the pipeline from Bolivia to Argentina in the 1970s. Today, Bolivia is once again look-

(*continued*)

(continued)
ing for markets for its gas as Argentina and Brazil have access to new domestic supplies as well as competitively priced LNG imports. In the absence of exports to Chile and to the world via a Chile-based liquefaction facility, domestic market seems to be the only option. Bolivian gas infrastructure remains sparse and ability to pay for gas remains low for most of its citizens.

In Peru, a 300-mile pipeline was needed to bring natural gas from the Camisea field in Peru's remote rainforests, east of the Andes. The Royal Dutch Shell discovered the Camisea in the early 1980s, with estimated reserves of about 15 trillion cubic feet (Tcf) of gas in multiple blocks. Shell and Mobil formed a consortium to develop the resources; but the consortium withdrew in July 1998 owing to poor economics and financing difficulties in the absence of domestic gas demand. In September 1999, Peru passed the Law for the Promotion and Development of the Natural Gas Industry and associated regulations to facilitate Camisea's development. The regulations guaranteed pipelines "a real annual profitability of 12 percent" and end-user prices were set to encourage consumption by different types of end-users. In addition, the Peruvian government encouraged investment in distribution networks in Lima and elsewhere to increase gas consumption in the country, including natural gas vehicles and small consumers. However, these markets represented small volumes that would take time to build up. The government also created incentives for gas-fired generation, a much larger immediate consumer of natural gas, but these distorted the competitive electricity generation sector, and were challenged by coal and hydro generators. Finally, a new liquefaction facility (Peru LNG) to export gas was also needed to justify the upstream and pipeline investments.

For years after the break-up of the Soviet Union, the landlocked Turkmenistan explored alternative export routes to monetize its rich gas resources, including a Trans-Caspian pipeline. Although this pipeline made economic sense (e.g., Shenoy et al. 1999a and 1999b; Michot Foss et al. 2000a and 2000b), it never materialized partially because legal and regulatory frameworks were not transparent and geopolitics were complicated (e.g., see Michot Foss et al. 2000a). However, China, driven by its desire to diversify its energy sources in

(*continued*)

(continued)
terms of both fuel variety and supply region, financed a long-distance pipeline from Turkmenistan via Uzbekistan and Kazakhstan.

The West African Gas Pipeline (WAGP) was, in addition to LNG projects, one of the outcomes of Nigeria's efforts to reduce flaring of natural gas produced in association with crude oil in country's prolific offshore fields. It was also a sign of regional cooperation as the pipeline was designed to deliver natural gas to Nigeria's neighbors Ghana, Benin, and Togo. Essandoh-Yeddu et al. (2007) demonstrate the economic competitiveness of the WAGP gas against liquid fuels in Ghana. Although the pipeline was built, it has been operating at very low capacity utilization owing to numerous reasons, including interruptions in upstream and transport operations in Nigeria, unresolved gas supply and pricing policies within Nigeria's own natural gas market, and the supply of associated gas from the Jubilee field in Ghana.

Observations from Gas-Power Decision Analysis

Our simplified decision analysis tool for natural gas resource monetization is informative. Note that we also can use our tool to assess whether imported natural gas is a good fit for the domestic power sector or can be a substitute for other fuels in order to develop domestic natural gas markets.

Domestic market potential is often the starting point. If the potential for direct sales to residential, commercial, and/or industrial customers in a domestic market is medium to high, there likely is at least some existing infrastructure and consumption creating potential for growth. Jurisdictions still would need to affirm rules governing the natural gas value chain. Can private entities build new pipelines, if necessary, including for exclusive use even if for a limited time horizon? Is there a well-established midstream sector, or prospects for fostering one, that can develop pipelines and storage with fair and reasonable access rules, including take/deliver-or-pay to address capacity risk, and tariffs? These conditions imply an established and experienced legal and regulatory framework or the need to create one. Can private producers/suppliers sell natural gas directly to customers? In short, is there a natural gas market where the price information flows from

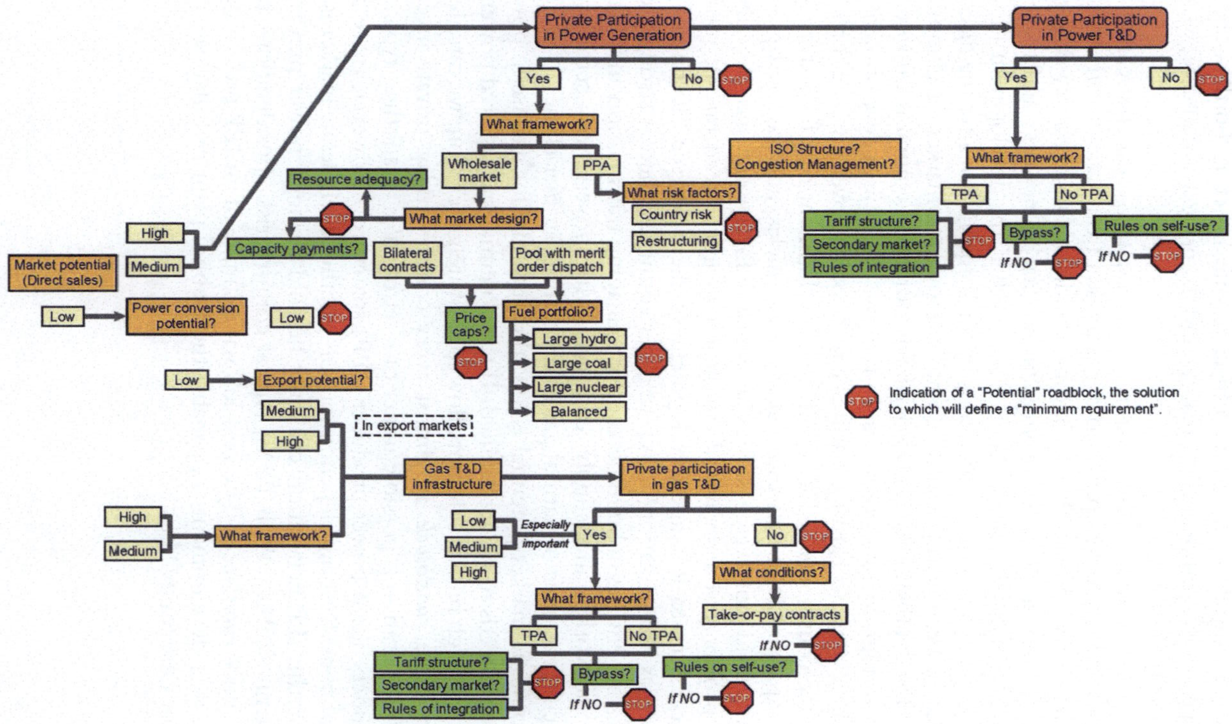

Fig. 6.2 A decision analysis approach to natural gas value creation

demand and supply interactions subject to infrastructure bottlenecks? If not, what are the prospects for creating and fostering a sustainable, workable marketplace?

Even when existing infrastructure is not expansive and the extent of demand is limited, development of a gas market from scratch with private investment may be possible if economic conditions in a country or jurisdiction of interest allow for proper commercial frameworks and there is potential for natural gas use. As discussed earlier, the development of the natural gas market in the Netherlands by Shell and Exxon after the discovery of Groningen field is a good example. However, market development such as the Netherlands experienced has not been common outside of middle- to high-income countries. In the case of Camisea development in Peru, there was no existing natural gas market. Government efforts to incentivize consumers in Lima with the development of a local distribution company (LDC) network, natural gas vehicles, and gas-fired power generation did not create sufficient demand for natural gas. An LNG export project and a dedicated pipeline with guaranteed rate of return were necessary to leverage development of the field (see "Examples of Natural Gas Monetization" box). In other countries, there is strong presence of state entities in building and/or managing transmission and distribution networks, and supply contracts with government setting or influencing the price of natural gas to different customer classes.

If domestic market potential is low, the potential for gas use in power generation needs to be determined. If the potential for gas-fired power is medium to high but laws do not allow for private generation, we can identify a possible ***roadblock***. In almost every country today, private investment in generation is possible under one set of rules or another, typically using independent power producer (IPP) structures. However, there are different considerations depending upon whether a wholesale market is in place or the IPP generation can only be sold through power purchase agreements (PPAs). With PPAs, typical country risk considerations can help identify ***roadblocks***. The best-known example of an IPP project collapsing after development is probably the Dabhol plant in India (see the "Dabhol Case Study" box).

Dabhol Case Study

This power generation project faced problems from early on. In April 1993, the World Bank found that the project was too large for baseload operation in Maharashtra and that the plant's gas-fired electricity would cost much more than coal-fired power available in the region. Under the proposed arrangements, the plant's generation would displace lower cost power, raising average cost of electricity. The conclusion was that the project was not economically viable, and thus could not be financed by the World Bank.

The Indian government also commissioned a report on the project in 1995. The report found that the initial MOU was rushed and "one-sided" (citing a letter from the World Bank), condemned the absence of competitive bids and lack of transparency in the process, critiqued subsequent changes to the project design as addressing "only the concerns of Enron," and found that Enron was given undue favors and concessions. The report also found that capital costs for the project were inflated; that the rates for the power would be much higher than justified, in part because the contract was based on U.S. dollars (placing the risk of currency fluctuations on the state); that there were outstanding environmental questions; and that the project would adversely affect the state of Maharashtra.

The Dabhol project is an example of a project financing deal that failed to appreciate the level of market and political risk in a host country. The PPA (negotiated under a previous government) and its arbitration clause were not sufficient to protect the company when the price differentials were unpopular. The investors were clearly too optimistic about the prospects of selling electricity in India, where many consumers are accustomed to receiving practically free electricity. There was no solid political support for reform in India and the country's populist politicians had always been eager to use electricity as a political tool; the history of electricity restructuring in India as well as privatization efforts in other sectors of the Indian economy should have provided plenty of warning to investors. Moreover, there was neither a clear legal framework nor an independent regulator in Maharashtra. At the same time, the project demonstrates a fundamental conflict in most emerging countries where investment in electricity is vital to support economic growth and millions of poor have no access to electricity.

If there is a wholesale electricity market, the risk assessment is more complex. For example, price caps present a ***roadblock*** if they are too low to provide cost-recovery. Even price caps at the retail level or lack of payment by end-users can have ripple effects up the value chain to the power plant if distribution companies are in financial distress and cannot pay wholesale prices.

The dominance of the generation fleet by hydro, nuclear, or domestically available coal can present a serious *roadblock* to gas-fired generation in economic dispatch because the cost of a megawatt-hour (MWh) from a new gas-fired plant will be higher than these established facilities that use cheaper domestic resources (see the "Dabhol Case Study" box). Then, a *minimum requirement* may be a system of stable incentives for gas-fired power, such as capacity payments, which are also controversial in many jurisdictions trying to create markets. There also is the generally accepted inconsistency of "discriminatory incentives" with open markets. For example, we discussed the Camisea case in our "Natural Gas Monetization" box. The efforts of the Peruvian government to create capacity incentives for gas-fired generation facilities in order to foster a market for Camisea gas was resisted by owners of the coal-fired and hydro plants as a violation of competitive wholesale electricity market principles in the country.

The rules for private participation in power transmission and distribution (T&D) also need consideration. Electricity T&D is a monopoly in almost every jurisdiction around the world because there is no need to duplicate an electron highway that many market participants can all utilize. However, in many countries, an SOE manages the T&D grid. Access can be complicated if the SOE also has its own generation assets and IPPs have to compete with them, especially if there are constraints in parts of the grid during peak periods. Increasingly, location-specific resources such as wind and utility-scale solar farms require long-distance transmission investment. In addition, there are other system integration costs to wind and solar. Many systems do not follow cost-causation principles when assigning transmission or other costs. Instead, governments socialize these costs across the marketplace, with all customers connected to the grid paying a share of the new costs. This approach may delay development of long-distance transmission capacity needed to connect remote resources, especially if financially constrained SOEs are involved. The cost of electricity delivered to end-users has to increase, which may be politically undesirable, or subsidies have to be increased, which may be difficult to accommodate by SOEs or government budgets. Accordingly, private

T&D investment can be preferable in some situations but remains a limited practice.

Similar considerations exist for natural gas T&D networks. Among the most important is the ability to build dedicated self-use pipelines without the obligation to allow third-party, or open, access at least for some time to allow for recovery of resource development costs. Resource owners of newly discovered gas supplies in regions without established natural gas markets would likely support this approach. In deep liquid markets such as the U.S., a large number of private players across the natural gas value chain make investment decisions based on market price signals and an established regulatory framework. Many countries between these extremes where well-intentioned rules and regulations to emulate liquid markets can hamper infrastructure development and delay the establishment of a liquid market.

Finally, importantly, if investors pursue gas-fired power generation as the best or only option for monetizing natural gas, the electricity price must support wellhead economics. This means that either PPA pricing provides sufficient cost recovery and returns to the wellhead (often through gas supply purchase agreements (SPAs)) or electric power market conditions are robust enough to support competitive wholesale delivery of gas-fired power. In many locations, resource-owning host governments have come to expect natural gas producers to engage in helping to develop gas-fired power generation as part of their "license to operate," meaning licensed access to natural gas resources that investors can produce and monetize. Often, gas reserves sanctioned by sovereign owners for LNG export projects will bear the caveat of domestic gas-fired power generation (and sometimes LPG for domestic use) as part of the transaction.[2]

History of Private Investment in Electric Power and Natural Gas

In Chap. 5, we discussed that the global energy investment, especially in the electricity sector, has been much less than what was needed to eliminate energy poverty. We have also provided data to demonstrate that a large majority of investment in electricity and gas sectors, especially T&D networks, have been by state entities and public funding. Now we discuss private sector investment in these sectors in more detail to demonstrate the impact of roadblocks discussed in the previous section.

In the 1990s, many countries pursued restructuring of their electric power industries, often unbundling and at least partially privatizing their state-owned, vertically integrated utilities. The main driver was often to attract private investment in the generation segment. Many countries could not afford to invest in new generation capacity as well as updating their T&D infrastructure due to lack of revenues, often caused by heavily subsidized electricity prices and failure to collect payments.

However, in many countries, despite efforts to restructure or reform electric power systems, they remain inefficient, subject to political meddling, and plagued by subsidies to end-users and increasingly to renewables. Many IPP projects fell short of expected returns and others failed outright despite government guarantees.

State utilities continued to provide the transmission and, often, distribution services. Some also owned generation assets, which sometimes were unbundled from the T&D operations. This significant presence of SOEs presented a challenge to IPPs in terms of open-access dispatching of their generation and selling their generation to customers via bilateral arrangements at profitable rates. Long-term PPAs backed by government guarantees were often the solution to these challenges. A state entity is the off-taker of electricity in PPAs. In some countries, there was a parallel reform in the natural gas sector, albeit mostly trailing the restructuring of the electricity sector.

Private investment started to flow but it collapsed after 1997, partially owing to the financial crisis in East Asia (Fig. 6.3). Nearly two-thirds of the cumulative investment since 1993 occurred in upper-middle-income countries. Although the share of lower-middle-income countries in private investment in their energy sector increased after the Great Recession, low-income countries failed to attract private dollars. Except for Latin America, other regions struggled to maintain investment inflows until the mid-2000s (Fig. 6.4). The boom between 2007 and 2012 occurred mostly in South Asia, Europe, and Central Asia. Investment in sub-Saharan Africa (SSA) started to become noticeable in the 2010s but it still represents a small share of the total in many years. Importantly, private energy investment in SSA is minuscule relative to the needs of the continent to eliminate energy poverty.

The inadequacy of new frameworks to satisfy private investors also caused some project failures and loss of interest by private investors. Even long-term PPAs with government guarantees did not always provide sufficient protection. Albeit relatively small percentage of total investment, many high-profile projects failed during this period, contributing to investors losing interest by the late 1990s.

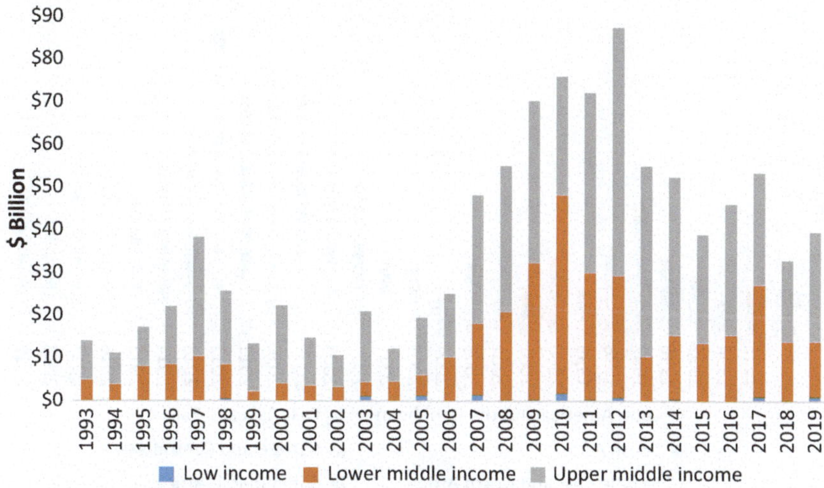

Fig. 6.3 Distribution of private energy investment across income groups. (Source: Authors' analysis of the World Bank's private participation in infrastructure database (http://ppi.worldbank.org/data). Projects include electricity generation, transmission, and distribution, and natural gas transmission and distribution. Low-, lower-, and upper-middle-income countries included. Canceled projects are excluded)

Over the years, a great deal of information has entered the public domain regarding major roadblocks for project success and reforms needed to attract private capital once again. Top investor requirements include adequacy of retail prices and collection discipline to meet cash flow needs; minimizing government interference (with operations and management of assets in particular); governments honoring all commitments related to state-enterprise performance and exchange conversion; enforcement of laws and contracts (e.g., disconnections, payment by counterparties); and independence of regulatory bodies. Requirements for investing in natural gas transmission and distribution are similar. The increase in private investment and lower share of canceled or distressed projects since the late 2000s may be an indication of countries having learned the lessons of the past decades to develop attractive commercial frameworks and companies having learned to conduct better due diligence and choosing their locations more carefully.

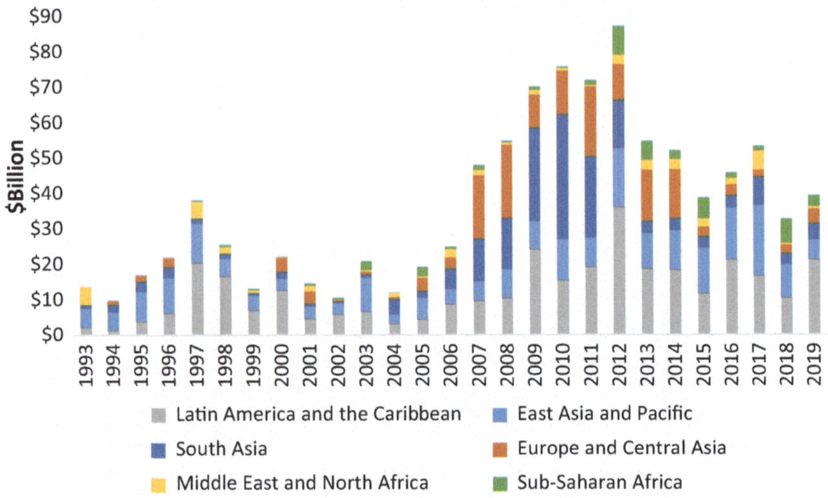

Fig. 6.4 Investment in energy projects in developing countries with private participation. (Source: See Fig. 6.3)

However, there is also growing concentration of investment in generation (Fig. 6.5). Private investment in electricity and natural gas networks (T&D) remains relatively small. As discussed in Chap. 5, SOEs continue to dominate network investments. Commercial frameworks necessary to attract private investment in T&D networks have been difficult to implement because of governments' desire to provide energy to their population at low cost. This handicap has been particularly challenging for increasing the share of natural gas in many countries beyond the anchor customers such as power generation and fertilizer production. Often, the issue is the lower cost of fuels that are targeted to be replaced by natural gas (e.g., coal for power generation and heating, petroleum liquids for industrial processes), especially when natural gas is imported at oil-indexed prices and/or domestic prices are subsidized.

Importantly, generation investment focused on renewable energy, including hydro, wind, and solar in the 2010s (Fig. 6.6). Given the low capacity factor of intermittent wind and solar and weather-dependent hydro generation, these investments will not provide as much MWh for the dollar as thermal plants that can run 24x7. The capacity factor may even be lower if wind and solar facilities developed in best resource locations are not well connected to demand centers. Private sector's lack of

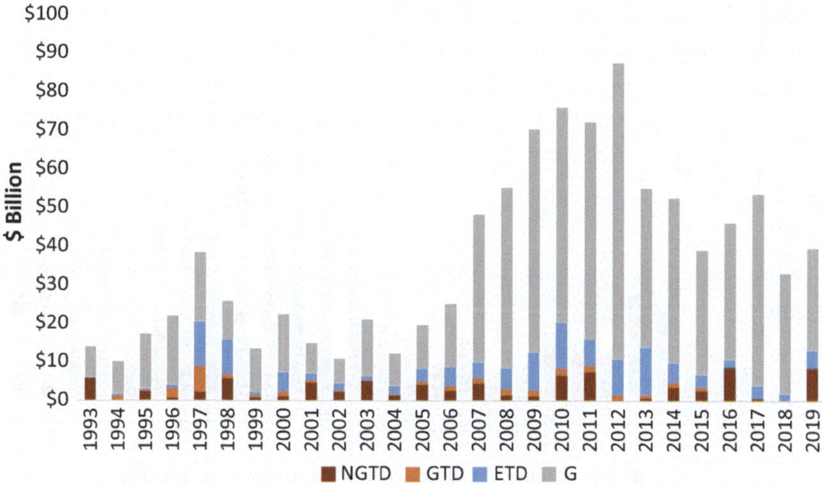

Fig. 6.5 Distribution of private investment across energy segments. (Source: Authors' analysis of the World Bank's private participation in infrastructure database (http://ppi.worldbank.org/data). G generation, GTD generation, transmission and distribution, ETD transmission and distribution, NGTD natural gas transmission and distribution. Canceled projects are excluded)

interest in building transmission lines (or its inability due to local laws and regulations) reinforces the dependence on SOEs to build the transmission capacity necessary to maximize generation from wind and solar.

Also worth noting, investment in coal-fired plants remained significant until 2018. The other category dominated in the 1990s, with diesel-fired generation accounting for most of the investment. The share of other averaged 8 percent since the Great Recession, but this time around, geothermal, biofuels, and waste were dominant technologies.

Although gas-fired plants attracted private dollars fairly consistently, their share averaged 12 percent since the Great Recession. In the absence of SOEs developing natural gas networks, including storage facilities, gas-fired generation will remain constrained to locations near LNG import terminals or along major pipelines. In that case, their dispatchability will depend on SOEs building sufficient electricity T&D capacity.

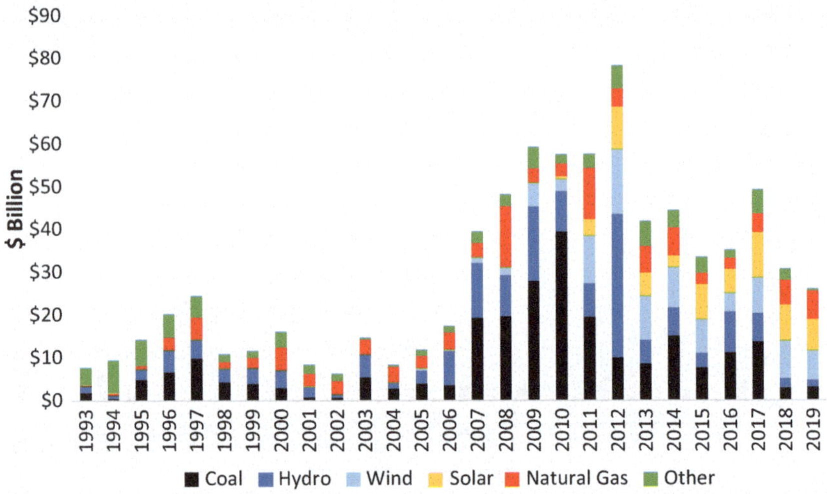

Fig. 6.6 Private investment in generation projects. (Source: Authors' analysis of the World Bank's private participation in infrastructure database (http://ppi.worldbank.org/data). Some projects included more than one type of generation (e.g., coal and diesel, hydro and diesel). We aggregated those projects based on their primary fuel/technology. Canceled projects are excluded)

Challenges Facing Natural Gas Market Development

We have established in our book that demand for natural gas is increasing globally but with differences across countries and regions. Countries ranging from industrialized nations (such as the U.S., Japan, South Korea, and European economies) to the large growing economies of Asia-Pacific (led by China and India) continue to invest hundreds of billions of dollars in natural gas infrastructure. These investments include import pipelines and LNG facilities as well as internal T&D networks and large consumers of natural gas such as power plants and industrial facilities. SOEs play a dominant role in building critical infrastructure in many of the markets with largest growth potential. Natural gas enhances energy security and offers a cleaner alternative. For example, China and India pursue gas distribution networks to reduce urban air pollution by replacing coal, liquid fuels, and biomass in homes, businesses, and vehicles. Despite rapidly increasing investment levels, wind and solar are not seen as viable alternatives capable of meeting these economies' large and growing energy needs in sufficient scale and desired pace. The versatility of natural gas, from power generation to industrial, and from residential/commercial to transportation uses further advantages it against wind and solar that only generate electricity intermittently (see Chap. 2 for system integration costs of renewables).

Natural gas (methane) is becoming a more globalized commodity, with the increasing LNG and, to a lesser extent, pipeline trade. In the early 1990s, Indonesia, Malaysia, and Algeria accounted for 70 percent of the LNG supply with only a few other suppliers. In 2019, 20 countries exported LNG according to the International Gas Union (IGU) (2020). Qatar, which did not start exporting until 1997, was the leading exporter with almost 22 percent of the market, followed closely by Australia (21 percent) and the U.S. (10 percent). New supplies from existing exporters such as Australia and new exporters from East Africa, Eastern Mediterranean, and North America will continue to change the make-up of the exporters club in the next decade and beyond although they are causing the liquefaction capacity to increase much faster than demand in the short term. (See Chap. 4 for a detailed discussion of global LNG market developments and Michot Foss and Gülen, 2016 for example of competitive constraints for U.S. LNG.)

Similarly, there were only a handful of major importers in the early 1990s with Japan dominating the market. According to IGU (2020), more than 40 countries imported some amount of LNG in 2019, including via FSRUs. The number of importing countries is likely to increase in the future. FSRUs accounted for about 15 percent of the total LNG volumes in 2019. They are expected to increase in importance, given their lower initial capital cost and flexibility to move from one location to another.

Most natural gas still is consumed within the region where it is produced with North America and Europe (Old World in Chap. 5 parlance) accounting for the bulk of "domestic" consumption. Commercial frameworks and physical infrastructure are well established in these regions and allow for expansion relatively easily with the exception of Western Europe and parts of the U.S. where energy transition is undermining ability to develop new gas infrastructure. In many of the emerging import markets, power generation has been the driver as well as seasonal balancing, especially for short-term trades, and energy security via diversification of import sources. However, going forward, expansion of natural gas consumption in new LNG importers and other countries, some yet to become consumers of natural gas, will depend on commercial frameworks discussed so far, with special focus on LNG value chain development.

Historically, the LNG supply chain (liquefaction-shipping-regasification) has been financed as a whole with almost all of the capacity tied via long-term contracts, in which the LNG price has been indexed to oil price. A short-term market has been emerging and accounted for 20 percent of the total market before the Fukushima accident, after which the short-term market's share increased to about 30 percent. Given the current supply and demand conditions, one might expect the short-term trade to remain vibrant or, possibly, to grow. Also, there are efforts to reduce the role of oil-indexed pricing, which is helped with the expectation of U.S. LNG exports that will be based on Henry Hub natural gas price (see Chaps. 4 and 5).

The share of short-term contracts, including spot trading, appears to have stabilized at about 30 percent and the efforts to create natural gas or LNG pricing hubs have not succeeded so far (see Michot Foss and Palmer-Huggins 2016), but a new S&P Platts JKM LNG futures contract traded at established exchanges seems to be getting traction. The average duration of LNG sales and purchase agreements was down to 6 years in 2016 versus 19 years in 2006, but bounced back to 13 years in 2019 according to Shell LNG Outlook 2020. LNG value chain investments remain expensive despite the savings offered by FSRUs. If the costs of upstream development, necessary to monetize new discoveries in many locations, are included, the capital expenditures multiply. Long-term contracts with some formula to guarantee sufficiently high prices (hence, cash flows) facilitate financing of such large projects. Some partnerships are pursuing equity-based liquefaction projects, but there are only a few examples in Canada and the U.S. with the backing of large companies such as ExxonMobil and Shell and national champions such as Qatar Petroleum, Petronas, and KOGAS. These projects may not need long-term contracts because they involve member companies that are integrated globally with widespread marketing operations and/or that represent large buyers in their home countries. Aggregators, or portfolio companies, along with traders also provide liquidity that may help project developers secure sufficient commitments from creditworthy counterparties. (See the section "Old and New Commercial Arrangements" in Chap. 5 for a detailed discussion of price formation and changing trends in the global gas market.)

Independent from the upstream and liquefaction investment frameworks, the question of developing liquid natural gas markets in an increasing number of countries that are importing LNG remains of great importance. Can countries/regions develop natural gas markets that will be trusted by investors to replace such long-term contracting needs or the need for state involvement in spot imports?

Investors can trust the price signals coming from a liquid natural gas market and make investments as long as policy environment is stable and regulations are efficient and transparent. Because these prices, including the regulated tariffs for monopolistic infrastructure such as transmission pipelines and distribution networks, will allow for cost recovery plus a reasonable rate of return on capital invested. The North American market is the best demonstration of these principles although policy environment has been increasingly uncertain for the industry in recent years mainly due to growing anti-gas feeling in parts of the U.S. (see Chaps. 1 and 2). Western Europe is getting close to a competitive gas market but the high share of oil-indexed import volumes and national champions in Eastern and Southern Europe (especially, post-Soviet countries in Chap. 5) undermine the progress toward a truly competitive gas market across the EU. Although the EU Gas Directive and related documents set the road map for a natural gas market years ago, there are exemptions. For example, risky investments such as international import pipelines and LNG terminals can be built bypassing open access regulations and with more government involvement. Also, energy transition has been dominating energy policy in the EU, especially in some of the leading economies such as Germany, which targets the elimination of all fossil fuels, including natural gas. The EU experience in creating competitive gas and electricity markets exposes the limitations of such efforts when many sovereign governments are involved. As such, it offers useful lessons for similar efforts in other regions (e.g., efforts of creating gas-trading hubs; see Michot Foss and Palmer-Huggins 2016).

Characteristics of Liquid Gas Markets

Liquidity—the ability to engage quickly in transactions for assets at prices that reflect underlying values—does not come easily. In general, the larger the number of market participants, the more money brought to the table, the more liquid a market. For natural gas, and many other goods, supply and infrastructure are imperative. Consequently, we often see trade-offs made between conditions that foster liquidity with those that reduce investment risk for expensive gas import infrastructure, domestic T&D networks, and the like. Private, profit-seeking enterprises focus on shareholder returns. We tend to assume that governments support long-term, socioeconomic goals through net social welfare gains. Often, in fact typically, private market actors (suppliers and/or buyers) seek government intervention to protect competitive advantage. Plenty of evidence exists, in particular through the very long, deeply researched U.S. history of regulated investor-owned monopolies, that government actors also will seek control of markets and private interests for political reasons or convenience. This certainly is true in economies that tend to be state-led, many of which fall into our New World scheme.

The regimes that emerge for commercial arrangements, commercial frameworks in our parlance, tend to reflect sociocultural biases toward private (market) or public (state or government) outcomes. Regimes can range from fully state-owned and/or state-controlled approaches (the state, typically the national sovereign, absorbing all of the investment risk to provide essential value chain components as public goods) to hybrid approaches. The latter typically occur in mixed economies where private investment is "de-risked" through institutional arrangements that ensure returns of capital and returns on investment to those providing financing. The most common hybrid arrangements entail various methods for providing *regulated returns* to private entities. In project development, the regulated returns represent secure cash flow waterfalls that make projects "bankable." We can find long-term contractual engagements in almost any regime as a supplemental or alternative approach for de-risking. Bilateral contracts are usually inflexible (a classic is fixed destination for LNG cargo deliveries), usually incorporate "take-or-pay" (TOP) or other penalties, and often bear sovereign or other guarantees, all to protect the sacrosanct cash flow waterfall. Long-term contracts remain vital for attaining financing and sanctioning major new capital investments, such as those associated with LNG.

Any and all of these approaches inhibit liquidity in calculated trade-offs to de-risk substantial investments. The issue then becomes whether, and how best, to liberalize in order to improve conditions for liquidity, including transfer and mitigation of price and capacity/volume risks. More competitive, diversified, and thus liquid natural gas markets depend upon common rules, standards, and understandings of commercial terms for continued build-out and use of infrastructure and procuring and pricing supply. In open, mixed economies characterized by competitive markets with separate ownership of different business segments, attaining coordination can be difficult. A key question is how to draw lines around government-led, as opposed to market-led, coordination.

The U.S. and North American Stories

The Appendix to our book (underlying references will lead readers to more details) affords a brief look at the U.S. as an example of early industry (mid-1800s) agitation for government ordering of natural gas and electric power businesses. The United States has a long history of regulatory capture (of both regulators and regulated industry) and associated distortions. Intense competition in the initial phases of local natural gas and electric power generation and delivery depleted profit margins, destabilizing the pioneer holding companies. The well-documented debates surrounding the decisions to legally define "public utilities," certify or otherwise accept franchised monopolies and create regulatory oversight captured all views and a considerable thought regarding potential consequences. The Natural Gas Act of 1938 was strongly argued—records of congressional debate make clear that many felt long-distance pipelines could operate as common carriers. Beginning in the mid-1980s, the natural gas industry embarked on restructuring itself, with the U.S. government (the Federal Energy Regulatory Commission) implementing key actions, largely because new market entrants pushed for entry into businesses dominated by regulated franchise monopolies. Pipelines had regulated tariffs and acted as merchants, holding long-term contracts that locked in suppliers (producers) and buyers (utilities) with TOP clauses. Gas utilities (local distribution companies) had regulated tariffs for distribution on networks that included large industrial and power-generation customers, who typically cross-subsidized smaller consumers. Information technologies supporting common platforms for accessing and trading pipeline capacity and market centers and hubs enabling price discovery eroded long-held defenses of pipeline monopolies over capacity and commodity supply. In coordination with the FERC, the industry chose a market-led approach to coordination through the Gas Industry Standards Board (GISB, now the North American Energy Standards Board, or NAESB, with inclusion of electric power and both wholesale and retail segments for both industries). The transformed U.S. gas market became the most liquid in the world (see Chap. 1).

Canada, which led the U.S. in liberalizing sales and pricing (see book Appendix), connects with U.S. regional markets via major

(*continued*)

(continued)

pipeline connections. Canada's main natural gas hub in Alberta (AECO, formed in the 1990s under the Alberta Energy Company) reflects supply-demand conditions in Canada. U.S. gas market conditions have bearing on AECO depending upon internal balances in Canada. For many years, AECO has reflected a substantial discount to Henry Hub as domestic supply grew in the Lower 48, edging out Canadian production including new supply from Canada's own shale basins and plays.

North American continental integration further enhanced industry performance, responsiveness, and resilience, including both financial and operational sustainability. It largely has been an organic process but issues remain, especially when it comes to energy relations with Mexico.

For many years, the Canada-U.S. border has been "seamless" with respect to physical infrastructure and deliveries of natural gas as well as flows of investment and human talent. Canadian and U.S. policy makers and regulators have tended to respond in kind to shifts in industry activity and development patterns. They acted mostly in unison to advance (from 1988 in Canada and 1992 in the U.S.) "light-handed," non-discriminatory open access for pipeline systems, maintaining a "hands-off" approach to allow market-based pricing to flow from wellhead to end-user. Importantly, the Canada-U.S. cross-border natural gas system incorporates principles of reciprocity. This has been a vital ingredient as fundamental changes in natural gas supply sources occurred. With the expansion of gas deliveries from Canada's giant Western Sedimentary Basin (WCSB) through the 1990s, flows were directed south to customers in the U.S. Lower 48 (L48). Canadian gas sales were mainly to the large heating markets in the U.S. Northeast and Upper Midwest. Once disputes over contracting and pricing were resolved, Canada became a major supplier to the West Coast (Michot Foss et al. 1998). Resurgence of L48 gas production in this century, in particular in Appalachia, upended that pattern. Flows now are more complex and generally counterclockwise. Natural gas moves north from the huge U.S. Marcellus region fields into Eastern Canada, while Western Canada production flows south into the U.S. Pacific Northwest and West Coast locales.

(*continued*)

(continued)

The U.S.-Mexico arrangement is more complicated. Much about Mexico is complementary to what we see across Latin America and the broader global geography of developing-country energy demand. Mexico is characterized by heavy-handed state intervention and thus more closely aligns with the New World patterns of strong government roles in energy (see Chap. 5). Mexico relies heavily on pipeline imports given inability to achieve meaningful upstream investment even though the country has a robust oil and natural gas resource endowment. The government indexes gas prices to Henry Hub, a consequence of the lack of independent, domestic price signals in Mexico. Substantial inadequacies and risks persist in Mexico's own commercial framework, in particular resumption of dominance of its SOEs and especially its NOC, Pemex, which built and owned the nation's T&D network until efforts to liberalize emerged in the mid-1990s.

Mexico was not at the same point of gas market development as its northern neighbors when the original North American Free Trade Agreement (NAFTA) negotiations took place during 1992–1993. Mexico did not have an independent regulator to match Canada's National Energy Board (NEB, now the Canadian Energy Regulator or CER) or the U.S. Federal Energy Regulatory Commission (FERC). There was no oversight of critical infrastructure like oil and gas pipelines, high-voltage electric power grids, and LNG import and export terminals. Mexico's Comisión Reguladora de Energía (CRE) had no real power to enforce internal market rules. More fundamentally, the Mexican states do not have the independent, and legally sacrosanct, authorities on par with Canada's provincial tribunals and the U.S. public service or utility commissions, many of which date to the 1800s and all of which pre-date their national institutions. The U.S. PSCs and Canada's tribunals have retained the upper hand on infrastructure and commercial gas businesses within the respective provinces and states, while at the same time coordinating with NEB/CER and FERC on often-contentious interstate commerce issues.

Most important, until 1995, Mexico's national oil company, Petroleos Mexicanos or Pemex dominated the country's natural gas system. Pemex not only held the sole right to develop sovereign sub-soil resources but also owned and operated Mexico's natural gas

(*continued*)

(continued)

pipeline system, save for an industry-owned local network in Monterrey, Nuevo Leon (see Johnson and Michot Foss 1991; Michot Foss et al. 1993). With no open, or third-party, access to pipeline capacity and with no authority for the regulatory body to implement and enforce such access, it was not feasible for Mexico to provide the kind of reciprocal trade treatment that Canada and the U.S. could accept. Thus, along with many other aspects of Mexico's energy sector, NAFTA was silent on natural gas market conditions and integration vis-à-vis Mexico. Evolution and passage of Mexico's 1995 "regulamento" separated Pemex from local distribution of natural gas, attempted to mimic Canada and U.S. open-access conditions on pipelines, and formalized CRE as a regulatory body more comparable to NEB and FERC. Mexico took its most ambitious steps in 2014 to formalize in law a deeper restructuring of its energy sector, adding upstream liberalization, subject to oversight mainly by Comisión Nacional de Hidrocarburos (CNH) and a national gas pipeline and storage network manager, Cenagás or Centro Nacional de Control del Gas Natural. As this book neared completion, apart from awarded upstream blocks that brought foreign direct and indigenous investment to Mexico's energy sector and oil and gas debottlenecking, substantial portions of the reform are only just unfolding. Or, more properly stated, they would have been unfolding had political support remained in place. Uncertainty about Mexico's path forward is holding back investment in hydrocarbons as well as electric power, also a target of the reform effort. At the time of publication, a major question is whether the current regime of Andrés Manuel López Obrador will roll back or, worse, upend by constitutional action the hard-won 2014 reforms. The hard work of building Mexico's institutions—CRE and CNH and other bodies charged with environmental and safety oversight—and the erosion of confidence with the undermining of their authority have raised the bar on commercial risk.

Increasing reliance on U.S. natural gas (and petroleum fuels) imports has been noticeable and has garnered a variety of reactions within Mexico, many of them negative. With reference back to Chap. 1, the U.S. supplies an astonishing two-thirds of Mexico's natural gas consumption, to great consternation within and beyond the political regime but with no relief in sight for restoring Mexico's capacity to regain self-determination.

Today's liquid gas markets suggest the following conditions for "liquidity": a large and deep market, supported with expansive, open, or third-party, access (TPA) infrastructure (pipelines, storage) with different types of customers (residential, commercial, industrial, power generation) and consumption varying across time (a day, weekdays, seasons). Sizeable heating loads in residential and commercial sectors have historically anchored demand, necessary for development of LDC networks. Power-generation customers and large industrial consumers can bypass distribution networks, buy wholesale gas, and have it delivered via large-diameter transmission pipelines. The size and diversity of the market and geographically distributed storage are critical to balancing demand and supply efficiently. Only in such a market, price transparency can be achieved via physical and financial trading based on standard contracts between a large number of players (consumers, producers, midstream companies, financial players). Price-reporting agencies collect and report data. Basis differentials between prices at different locations relative to a high-volume trading hub signal the need for new investment or consumer response. We depict these building blocks of a liquid gas market in Fig. 6.7.

With these requirements, one can conduct a gap analysis for potential gas markets. In Table 6.1, we present a high-level assessment of natural

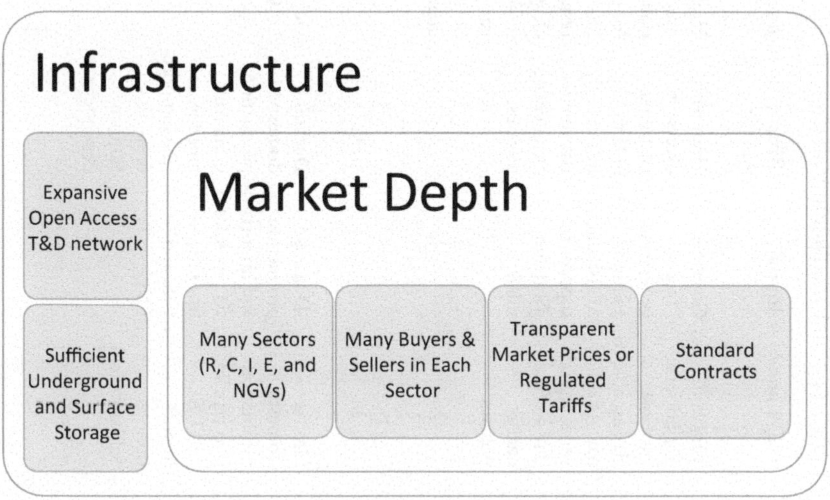

Fig. 6.7 Necessary conditions for a liquid natural gas market

Table 6.1 Features of liquid and illiquid markets

	U.S./Canada	*Mexico*	*Western Europe*	*Japan*	*South Korea*	*China*	*India*
Demand	Very high. Very diverse customer classes; able to pay. At risk in some regions due to clean energy policies.	Growing. Power generation and industrial. At risk due to support to wind and solar.	High with diverse customers able to pay; but at high risk due to clean energy policies.	High but not much opportunity for growth. Nuclear restarts and clean energy policies reduce gas burn for power generation.	High but limited opportunity for growth. Coal cheaper. Large nuclear capacity. Anti-coal and anti-nuclear policies may help but at risk due to rising support for renewables.	Fast growing to replace coal in urban areas. Industry, power generation, transport. Small consumers emerging but ability to pay a challenge. Support for nuclear, wind, solar, coal (energy security).	Slow growth. Power generation, fertilizer industries account for most. Ability and willingness to pay major challenge for consumers. Subsidies to LPG, kerosene, solar.
Supply	Diverse domestic production plus pipeline and LNG import options. Self-sufficient.	Domestic production and imports via pipelines from the U.S. and LNG.	Declining domestic production; numerous pipeline and LNG import options. Import dependent.	Dependent on LNG imports.	Dependent on LNG imports.	Domestic production meets ~60 percent of demand and growing but demand growing faster. Large and expanding pipeline and LNG imports.	Domestic production meets less than half of demand and struggling to grow. Increasing LNG imports.

	U.S./Canada	*Mexico*	*Western Europe*	*Japan*	*South Korea*	*China*	*India*
T&D infrastructure	Largest T&D network in the world. Private upstream, midstream, and downstream companies. New pipelines increasingly challenged.	Growing T&D network but inconsistent investment.	Large T&D network but cross-boundary issues. SOEs still play a role in some countries.	Constraining. LDCs only in Tokyo and a few other cities. Power and industrial users near import terminals account for >75 percent of gas use.	Constraining.	Growing but insufficient. SOEs developing LDC and NGV networks in addition to upstream, import, and transmission capacity.	Growing but even more constraining than in China. SOEs dominate LNG imports and transmission.
Storage	Most expansive in the world. Mix of underground and LNG.	Limited.	Large. Mix of underground and LNG.	LNG terminals.	LNG terminals.	Growing but limited. Underground and LNG.	LNG terminals.

(*continued*)

Table 6.1 (continued)

	U.S./Canada	*Mexico*	*Western Europe*	*Japan*	*South Korea*	*China*	*India*
Commercial frameworks	Hub pricing (HH). Basis differentials. TPA, unbundled. Well-established federal and state regulation but anti-gas movement impacting regulatory practices.	Hybrid of hub pricing (HH) and administered. Immature regulatory framework. SOEs important.	Hub pricing now dominant but oil-indexed imports continue. TPA (new pipeline and LNG import may be exempted), unbundled. State regulation.	LT oil-indexed contracts for LNG imports dominate but ST and spot purchases increasing. Large buyers joining forces to raise bargaining power. Domestic network and LNG terminals unbundled and TPA by 2022. Price deregulation happening.	Korea Gas Corporation dominates the wholesale market. Large consumers have limited access to LNG terminals.	SOE dominated. Administered city-gate pricing and some deregulation toward cost-plus. Subsidized for fertilizer and residential. Exemptions for LNG importers and shale gas producers. Unbundling and TPA expected with new PipeChina. No independent regulator.	Competitive bidding for private LDCs. Administered netback pricing (fuel oil, coal, naphtha) across consumer segments. Subsidized for fertilizer, power plants, LPG extraction, residential, and vehicles. Price controls discourage E&P. Immature and inconsistent regulation.

Source: Developed by the authors based on numerous case studies and direct project experience gas markets across a wide range from the least liquid market (India) to the most liquid (the U.S.). We list some of the gaps below each country/region. Our list under the U.S./Canada heading includes the benchmark characteristics of a liquid market.

Achieving a liquid natural gas market à la the North American marketplace appears very difficult for many countries. Mexico could get there via its integration to the North American market (e.g., increasing pipeline imports from the U.S.). Already, Mexico uses the Henry Hub price to a certain extent. Domestic natural gas pipeline network expansion remains a challenge in Mexico. Pricing natural gas to different customers in a way to allow for cost recovery and reasonable rate of return also is a challenge given the history of fuel subsidies. As such, power generation and industrial users are the target customers. A great deal of political risk resides in Mexico, at the time of publication and as noted in the Appendix, as the current government has undermined reforms undertaken over many years and may take even stronger actions to roll back newly structured markets and regulators

Liquid markets remain distant possibilities among growing consumer countries with the largest potential such as China and India. As discussed in Chap. 5, in these countries and many other New World economies, it is very difficult for private capital to develop the gas infrastructure (T&D networks and storage facilities) that will allow natural gas to replace many inefficient fuels across residential, commercial, and small industrial sectors. Private investment in power plants and large industrial facilities can occur but represent a small percentage of what these countries require in both the power and gas sectors. As discussed before profitability of gas and power investments remains dependent upon agreements with guarantees such as PPAs. SOEs carry out most investment. This raises numerous questions about credit ratings of SOEs and their governments.

Historically speaking, and as we noted earlier, it is common to see sovereign money and companies, SOEs, building most of the infrastructure (import pipelines and regasification terminals, domestic T&D networks) in the early stages of natural gas market evolution. As markets evolve, private sector investment may enter for additional infrastructure and especially new LDC networks, LNG import terminals, and/or power plants to burn gas and pipelines to connect resources or larger customers to the network. Sovereign company interests can become entrenched, threatening private participation. SOEs can be politically powerful. At the same time, since these companies (and their governments by way of guarantees) are often on the hook for long-term import contracts, it can be difficult to achieve meaningful reforms. BOTAŞ in Turkey and KOGAS in South Korea exemplify this situation. Even in the EU, national champions (partially or fully state-owned) and their smaller brethren elsewhere continue to play an outsized role in the gas sector.

Concluding Remarks

The principles of liquid natural gas markets are well established. North American and Western European gas markets embody those principles. Establishing such markets elsewhere in the world remains difficult for a variety of fundamental reasons.

First among these reasons are capital intensity of natural gas supply chains and affordability of natural gas. Physical infrastructure necessary to provide access to large populations is extensive: long-distance transmission pipelines, dense local distribution networks, and storage facilities are all necessary for a well-functioning market. Building such vast networks requires large sums of investment. The catch is that end-user prices that would allow for private financing of this infrastructure are often higher than what most consumers pay for their current energy options. Natural gas imported at oil-indexed prices and subsidized pricing of current energy options add to this already large challenge. As seen before, private investment in natural gas infrastructure has been very limited.

Creditworthiness becomes the logical next challenge. In the absence of private investment, the government, often via SOEs, must step up to the plate. Capital intensity limits development to the largest companies, governments, and customers. Although China and many of the Chinese SOEs have investment-grade credit ratings and may actually build much infrastructure via equity (i.e., with no borrowing), many other governments and their SOEs do not have the necessary financial resources and depend on international capital markets. Nor does the donor community seem to be helping much in natural gas infrastructure. Even the shortest route to bringing natural gas into the energy mix via gas-fired power generation faces high infrastructure costs and inability of customers to pay electricity prices that allow for cost recovery.

The inability to develop large-scale infrastructure limits the number and diversity of customers who can afford to pay. Lower-income countries cannot support state-of-the-art, costly systems. This *lack of market liquidity* constrains funding and capital flows. There is a bit of chicken-or-egg problem. Governments hesitate to liberalize natural gas markets, and, generally, energy markets due to importance of energy services to sections of the population that cannot afford these services. Instead, they often provide these services at subsidized prices. Subsidized prices discourage risky investment. Without liberalization, the flow of funds is constrained to SOEs, which often have to carry the burden of subsidies as well. Governments invoke other reasons for delaying reforms: energy security is often the rationale for longevity of oil-linked long-term LNG contracts. Geopolitics often constrains sensible regional pipeline trade.

Finally, increasingly, the *policy-supported expansion of renewable generation and resilience of coal in many countries* create a large range of uncertainty for the future role of natural gas in power generation. This distinct trend could also discourage natural gas supply development and jeopardize gas trade, with serious and fundamental global economic consequences. Investment in large amounts of gas-fired power generation does not guarantee large consumption of natural gas in electricity generation neither in the short term nor in the long term. As discussed in Chaps. 2 and 5, gas-fired plant utilization may remain quite low in both the U.S. and China, for somewhat different reasons.

Notes

1. We can point to substantial evidence that customers are very willing to pay for cleaner fuels and better service. The main issue is developing energy sources and infrastructure that are compatible with income levels in various locations. Mohan Munasinghe is probably most responsible for encouraging consideration of price for both market and economic development and demand rationing (Munasinghe 1983).
2. The authors worked on a number of projects in a variety of countries in which host governments and investors were combining power generation with upstream negotiations and agreements. In most cases, development of assets for domestic use, such as power gen and LPG, was either sought by the host government or offered by competing investors as part of their own risk-mitigation strategies for upstream and/or LNG licensing. Some countries have made power generation a priority to cure gas flaring. Seldom did we see sound electric power market design implemented. Most often, governments and investors implemented SPAs and PPAs to lock in gas supply and power pricing and win financial support (bankability).

References

Essandoh-Yeddu, J., G. Gülen, and F. Asante. 2007. Net WAGP economic benefit requires Ghana development. *Oil & Gas Journal* 105 (32): 68–73.

International Gas Union. 2020. 2020 World LNG Report. https://www.igu.org/resources/2020-world-lng-report/

Johnson, W. A., and Michot Foss, M. 1991. The economics of natural gas in Mexico, in Proceedings of the IAEE 13th Annual North American Conference, November.

Michot Foss, M., and G. Gülen. 2016. Is U.S. LNG competitive? IAEE Energy Forum, Third Quarter. https://www.iaee.org/en/publications/newsletterdl.aspx?id=342

Michot Foss, M., and D. Palmer-Huggins. 2016. European and Asian natural gas market developments – Swamped by the present? Chapter 6. In *Managing energy price risk*, ed. V. Kaminski, 4th ed. London: Risk Books.

Michot Foss, M., F. H. Garcia, and W. A. Johnson. 1993. The economics of natural gas in Mexico—revisited. The Energy Journal. Special Edition: North American energy after free trade, September.

Michot Foss, M., G. Gülen, and B. Shenoy. 2000a. Caspian pipeline prospects hinge on transparent, logical regulatory frameworks. *Oil & Gas Journal* 98 (34): 68–72.

Michot Foss, M., B. Shenoy, and G. Gülen. 2000b. "Monetizing" stranded gas: The case of Turkmenistan and considerations for explorationists. In *International oil and gas exploration: A business perspective*. Tulsa: American Association of Petroleum Geologists.

Munasinghe, M. 1983. Third world energy policies. *Energy Policy* 11 (March): 4–18.

Shenoy, B., G. Gülen, and M. Michot Foss. 1999a. Caspian oil export choices clouded by geopolitics, project economics. *Oil & Gas Journal* 97 (16): 29–35.

———. 1999b. Analysis suggests economic viability of Trans-Caspian Sea gas line. *Oil & Gas Journal* 97 (46): 51–58.

CHAPTER 7

Conclusions and Path Forward

Michelle Michot Foss, Anna Mikulska, and Gürcan Gülen

Natural Gas Monetization and the New "New Deal" Economies

Natural gas—the general combination of hydrocarbon molecules varying in number of carbon atoms up to C_5 and sometimes higher, but especially C_1, methane—is a critical fuel and feedstock. That natural gas will play an important role in global energy mix at least for several decades seems certain. Yet, divergent positions across geographies around resource wealth and need for energy to grow economies impact investment flows. Differences in energy and environmental policies and attitudes also influence commercial frameworks and investments. We cover a great many of these considerations in our book around the core challenge of natural gas monetization across global value chains.

M. Michot Foss (✉) • A. Mikulska
Baker Institute for Public Policy, Rice University, Houston, TX, USA
e-mail: michelle.m.foss@rice.edu; anna.b.mikulska@rice.edu

G. Gülen
Independent Consultant, West Brookfield, MA, USA
e-mail: gurcan@g2eis.com

M. Michot Foss et al. (eds.), *Monetizing Natural Gas in the New "New Deal" Economy*,
https://doi.org/10.1007/978-3-030-59983-6_7

- Chapter 1 progresses from the broad acknowledgment of oil and gas industry resilience, rooted in the technology pathway that defines industry advances over roughly two centuries and continues to unfold. Chapter 1 combines a quest to "understand the present" with a more nuanced view of upstream, using a ten-year history of producer benchmarks, at a time when the U.S. shale plays dominated perceptions and perspectives. The chapter points to the midstream field-to-market dilemmas, repercussions in commodity markets (eroding returns of and on capital inherent in "Frankelnomics" persistent surpluses), and influence on regional and global trade that play out through the remainder of the book, implicitly and explicitly.
- Chapter 2 tackles the role of natural gas in the U.S. electric power generation drawing on experience with long-term dispatch modeling and analysis of organized market designs. Lower-cost natural gas has undermined coal (and nuclear) but encountered competition from alternative energy sources that are rooted in sociopolitical preferences and declining cost of equipment. We capture the conundrums of politicized choice of generation technologies undermining electricity markets across the U.S. and the resulting wide uncertainties surrounding future gas use in the power generation mix.
- Chapter 3 captures the story of the petrochemicals expansion in the U.S. as downstream investment, described from a project database, mobilized to respond to low-cost natural gas liquids (NGLs). The "renaissance" in petrochemicals and the emergence of new NGL exports reside in a context of petrochemical expansions worldwide and in uncertainties emanating from lower oil prices, which reduce the cost of competing feedstocks. But low oil prices also raise questions about supply and pricing of NGLs given the sensitivity of drilling in liquids rich plays in the U.S. to the oil price.
- Chapter 4 sets ambitions of the U.S. exporters within a global liquefied natural gas (LNG) supply picture that stands to gain from large project expansions and new competing sources, keeping the world well stocked. The dominance of trade patterns toward emerging markets, especially in the Asia-Pacific region, and the influence of commercial strategies and practices emanating from the U.S. projects set the tone for LNG transactions ahead.
- Chapter 5 turns to worldwide demand and delineates strategic differences between emerging market, "New World", and established "Old World" customers. We pick up directly the themes of decarbonization and affordability laid out in the Foreward to our book and incorporate

them into the New World and Old World characterization. Mature, stable, and even declining natural gas demand in the Old World, where decarbonization is a stronger political driver, will impact global balances and could influence Old World members that are net exporters. New World suppliers and buyers are connecting in ways that deepen trade and liquidity but, given economic development imperatives and dominance of sovereign interests and control, do not necessarily expand market-based approaches and commercial practices.

- Chapter 6 points to the challenges for mobilizing investment to build natural gas supply chains to create value for participants and deepen gas market liquidity. We use a decision tool for identifying roadblocks to infrastructure investment. These are rooted in systemic proclivities toward sovereign dominance and, thus, implications for institutional capacity, transparency, and market-based pricing. We highlight the problem of building and implementing commercial frameworks within the complex sociopolitical and sociocultural milieu of any country or jurisdiction (the task of achieving sufficient convergence for "license to operate").

Now we come to the hard part of translating observation and analysis throughout our book into a path forward.

As noted in the Preface, our choice of book title reflects perceptions and realities that are currently in the state of play. Public sentiment and a long-established predilection for the "next new thing"[1] have set up a Rorschach test for natural gas in which its merits or demerits are all in the eyes of beholders. Chapter 1 closes with the prevailing bottom line problem statement—valuations of technology enterprises, including "clean tech" and "green tech" (all generally non-fossil fuel businesses) swamp those of traditional oil and gas issues (see The Patch and Money section and accompanying Fig. 1.37). Longer-term returns for clean/green tech suggest a more complicated, less rosy picture, especially when the backdrop of government support for alternative energy projects and businesses is considered. It could be that improved energy demand will lift oil and gas prices and asset values sufficiently to salve investor wounds. No matter, the perception that fossil fuel industries are a dying breed is firmly in place, with serious implications for investment in the legacy natural gas businesses and, crucially, underlying oil and gas resource development and delivery. Opinions are driven by climate activism and heightened sensibilities stemming from the political correctness that surrounds climate and the push for environment, social, governance (ESG) disclosures, especially vis-à-vis legacy oil and gas operations and businesses. Pandemic-induced economic dislocation, including a historic collapse in oil price amid demand erosion, is spurring notions of combining clean/green tech with post-pandemic economic recovery for an extra boost of stimulus in ways that have broad consequences for energy choices and markets.

As we describe later in detail, all of this is much more complex than pundits, and a good many energy and equities analysts and researchers, make it out to be. Efforts to accelerate an energy transition also will expose environmental footprints of substitute fuels and technologies, which are sizeable, along with labor, trade, and geopolitical conundrums for which there are no easy solutions. ESG risks for clean/green tech are largely unexplored and widely ignored.

Scaling up alternative energy, electrifying transportation, and many other ideas will draw more attention to costs, about which proponents have revealed very little to customers. There are few options for expanding clean/green tech, including all supporting infrastructure requirements, without extensive government and, thus, public support. This means socializing costs through rates paid by consumers, or by the state (the sovereign), which may mean taxpayers and voters will pick up the tab as it has been happening all over the world. Realities of cost and financial risk lead to the notion of "socialized energy", with the role of government enlarging as investors seek protections and guarantees, and to growing pressures to "pick winners" among intensely competing clean/green technologies. How these conditions play out against hard-won gains for greater transparency in energy goods and services, including price discovery, is an open question. So is the cost-benefit accounting of current policies versus externalities they are supposed to mitigate. Strategies that help to "de-risk" projects, such as bilateral contracts, also reduce liquidity and thus diminish price discovery.

The various "energy transition" stakeholders rarely debate the market-government tradeoffs. It is important to recognize that all of these dynamics are unfolding in a world in which pandemic economics are encumbering societies deeply affected by and still in recovery from the 2007–2008 recession, mostly Old World countries. The 2007–2008 recession cycle left an indelible, negative mark, especially in the U.S. and Western Europe, on public psyches about markets and capitalism. Public psyches in New World countries, never fully comfortable with the Western market capitalism, suffered a similar experience following the Asian financial crisis in 1997–1998. These pre-existing conditions are matched by arguments that "climate" is a global emergency, which can only be addressed through international cooperation led by governments.

Altogether, open markets and capitalism have taken serious hits during the past two decades. Historic and crucial accomplishments by Old World natural gas industries to embrace competition, provide nondiscriminatory access and common carriage on pipelines, foster price discovery, and invent and spread compelling commercial practices risk getting trampled upon in the scramble toward new "new deal" economies. This is nothing short of ironic, considering the hopes and beliefs that markets and strategies honed for natural gas could inform how we think about electric power, the single largest focus of energy transition.

The Climate Crux of the Matter

Methane, the main component of natural gas that garners concern, constitutes about 17 percent of total greenhouse gases (GHGs).[2] Estimates put oil and natural gas operations, all together, at about 25 percent of industrial emissions of methane and about 15 percent of total methane releases, including natural sources.[3] Combustion of methane produces other gases—including carbon dioxide (CO_2), nitrogen oxide (NO_x)—that are targets for both climate and urban air quality (NO_x is a precursor to ground-level ozone). Methane flaring during the height of oil and gas upstream industry activity pre-pandemic was a visible sore point. Opinions are that thermal properties of methane in the atmosphere are stronger than CO_2, but neither one is the most potent component of GHG. That honor goes to SF_6, sulfur hexafluoride, one of the class of fluorinated gases, and one with global warming potential that is orders of magnitude beyond CO_2 and methane.[4] Unlike other gases, SF_6 can be directly toxic with exposure to electrical switchgear. This last is tremendously inconvenient given that SF_6 is a widely used insulator for electrical equipment. With expansion of electrical systems, SF_6 and other fluorinated gases already have escalated in emissions and have increased in atmospheric concentration. Although still considerably lower than other GHGs in the atmosphere, the much greater potency of SF_6 suggests that any growth in emissions should be unacceptable. With electrification promoted to displace fossil fuels, SF_6 will increase dramatically in emissions and atmospheric concentrations. Various calls to ban SF_6 have emerged with little or no attention to tradeoffs and new risks, uncertainties, and unintended consequences. Substitutes do exist, although, as usual, with greater cost and far less attractive properties

(De La Fuente et al. 2021).[5] Policy and regulatory treatment to limit or ban SF_6 would threaten the semiconductor industry, where the gas is used in manufacturing, and so considerable resistance exists. When it comes to electric power equipment (switchgear and other components) there is little enthusiasm for the known substitutes. A great deal of risk and uncertainty exists for customers if large orders are placed for existing equipment using SF_6 that would need to be phased out and replaced well before end of life. Such is the complex, haphazard, uncertain realm of climate politics and policy that SF_6 largely is missing from topical discussions. It illustrates the pervasive problem of too little "bandwidth" for big picture considerations and tradeoffs as well as all-too-common silo effects (see next section).

Pre-Covid-19 pandemic, calls for climate action were escalating as gaps between promised and actual emissions reductions were scrutinized.[6] The EU in particular has announced extremely ambitious plans for decarbonizing its economy. Since 2004, EU GHG emissions declined about 13 percent (with some members more successful than others).[7] For the same time period, the U.S. reductions were about 11 percent in spite of fugitive methane as oil and gas industry activity grew.[8]

As pointed out in Chap. 5, randomized surveys indicate higher levels of public concern about climate change in the U.S., Germany, and the UK than in China and India. All attempts to analyze attitudes toward climate and environment are heavily nuanced depending upon how questions are framed, proximity to elections, and contextual factors such as economic status and geopolitical risks. Coupled with these trends are those regarding confidence in science and institutions.[9] Overall, climate concerns and support for action tend to be linked positively to education, youth, and moderate-to-liberal political stance, more common among women than among men, and higher in developed economies than in developing ones.

Politics and ultimately policy in any given country will be influenced by the complex interplay of views and how these translate into political support—or lack thereof—for specific actions and how drastic those actions should be. A test, of sorts, is occurring in the wake of the Covid-19 experience. With the onset of the pandemic and tremendous economic dislocations, post-pandemic economic recovery stimulus and climate action have converged into an assortment of green new deal schemes. As we completed our book, of roughly $11 trillion in various post-pandemic recovery stimulus proposals and plans, only about 2 percent constituted actual, funded commitments for climate-related policies and programs.[10] Importantly, and as discussed in Chap. 5, for some governments, including those in Australia and Argentina, their country's natural gas resources and infrastructure are targets for post-pandemic economic stimulus. The natural gas industry is an obvious stimulus vehicle for major exporters such as Qatar and Russia, but that stimulus only works because there are many willing importers (see Chap. 5).

How can we elucidate the incredibly convoluted politics regarding earth's climate?[11] Given the wide range of uncertainties associated with climate modeling outputs and the distinct dilemma in accommodating dynamic socioeconomic factors—that constantly alter emissions trajectories and thus potential future outcomes—a probabilistic approach based on decision science seems promising. Hausfather and Peters (2020) suggest a risk-based scenario approach that can help policy-makers to focus on likely scenarios and hence allocate funds and develop policies to maximize the benefits at the least cost (Fig. 7.1).

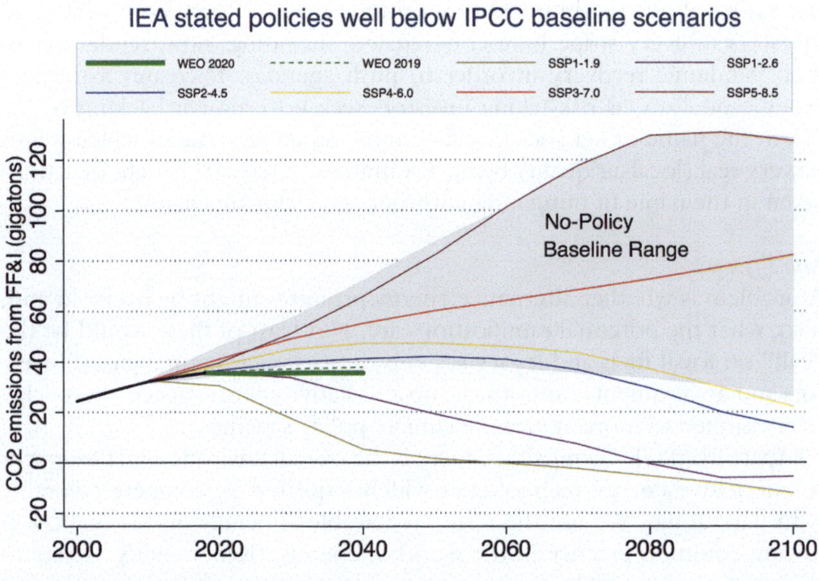

Fig. 7.1 Possible emissions in future and theorized climate responses. (Source: Provided by Zeke Hausfather. FF&I fossil fuels and non-fossil fuels industry, SSP shared socioeconomic pathway. Each SSP represents different potential scenarios of global temperature response with SSP5 being the worst case, considered highly unlikely. See Hausfather and Peters (2020) for excellent treatment of decision-making disparities related to climate policies)

In the end, politicians must make promises (or shed policy-making, for instance, to courts, in order to avoid having to meet voter expectations). Policies that address climate bear a particular burden: that effort undertaken sooner will result, at some point in the future, in an outcome in atmospheric chemistry and physics such that responses in the natural environment could be different from what we might imagine otherwise. That is a tough proposition, especially for elected bodies that depend upon popular votes and thus govern, by design, on short-term objectives. This makes "climate", in so many respects, the poster child for broader discontents regarding societies (the intrusion of economic and social justice being emblematic) and politics (everything from organization of political systems to the markets and government schisms). It also makes "climate" a perfect foil for promoting an array of ideas that can only exist with alignment of interests between politicians and financiers. In everyday positioning, it has never been about "climate", per se, even including broader discontents, but rather about the business propositions around which companies and investors of every stripe have congregated, including, now, tendencies to grab pandemic recovery in order to push agendas. It creates a form of crony capitalism, as risk-taking investors seek government backing to de-risk in the name of net social welfare improvements, some of which might be very real (local air quality being a commonly cited side benefit of actions taken in the name of mitigating anthropogenic climate change).

Silo Effects?

A problem is whether alternative energy promises might be oversold and, if so, what the potential ramifications are. Not least of these would be the "call" on fossil fuels and legacy systems, in particular natural gas, if investors and governments cannot scale up alternative energy capacity as quickly as envisioned in more aggressive climate policy schemes.

Apart from GHG emissions, there is the overall environmental footprint of alternative energy technologies widely expected to compete favorably with natural gas. We use the term "renewable" liberally in this book, following common practice in the world of energy. "Renewability" refers to the energy source such as wind, solar, water (hydroelectric dams), marine (tidal and wave), and biofuels (with replenishment of crops). Crucially, the components we use to mechanically, and/or chemically, convert these potential sources of energy to perform work are not renewable.

In fact, alternative energy involves large-scale industrial projects and equipment, including large supply chains to mine, process, and transport raw materials and transform them into equipment such as windmills, solar panels, and batteries. These footprints will only grow with the expansion of alternative energy installations around the world. Alternative energy also entails substantial new infrastructure such as long distance, high-voltage transmission lines to move produced energy from often-remote locations to market centers (see Chap. 2). Public opposition to infrastructure such as gas pipelines is mentioned in Chap. 1 and addressed in a later section, and extends well beyond the U.S. and North America. This opposition also extends to electric power systems and the difficulty of winning public support for high-voltage transmission to carry electricity from new generation sources, regardless of what they may be. Raw material requirements for renewable energy and battery storage—to displace foregone storage inherent in natural gas, other fossil fuels, and uranium—are considerable.[12] *Materials intensity for alternative energy, including electrification of transport, exceeds that of legacy fuels and systems.*[13] Battery manufacturing is a process that is particularly energy- and emission-intensive.[14] *Renewable energy and battery life cycles incorporate end of life management challenges on par with other industrial systems, including legacy fuels.*[15]

Growing awareness of stresses imposed on critical minerals is raising new questions about strategies for decarbonization. The ESG dilemmas range from environmental and societal impacts of mining and mineral processing to access and control of resources and associated geopolitical security and supply chain risks.[16] The decline in cost of solar panels and battery storage derives mostly from the vast scale-up of and market power associated with Chinese capacity. Chinese manufacturing growth and dominance of energy and sensitive information technologies, Chinese control of critical minerals supply chains (FP Analytics 2019; Braw 2017; CEMAC 2017), including positioning in frontier minerals resources such as seabed extraction (Reuters 2019), and its capture of intellectual property are all complicating trade and geopolitical balances. By many accounts, manufacturing in China comprises 60 of global capacity for wind and 70 percent for solar, while battery manufacturing (electronics and EVs) is upward of 80 percent (Yergin 2020).[17] To finance aggressive build-out of manufacturing as well as to support domestic wind and solar installations, the national government has provided generous subsidies, and some provincial governments and funds, and banks have supported with low-cost debt what many consider to be an overt national strategy to establish Chinese dominance in alternative energy and electric vehicles.[18]

While China is the emerging power in "new" energy technologies, it remains the largest single coal-consuming country, with nearly 52 percent of global coal consumption.[19] These facts are related. As we note earlier, battery manufacturing is one of the more energy-intensive undertakings and as such contributes considerably to industrial GHG emissions (Frith 2019). While many believe that China can re-jig its economy to rely more on renewable energy, maintaining and growing its position in critical manufacturing for advanced technologies clearly is a high priority. It remains to be seen whether the competitive pressures inherent in "new" energy supply and value chains can accommodate fundamental realignments in old ones. China is also one of the magnets for oil and natural gas monetization. Nearly every large LNG exporter strategy has China as the cornerstone for robust Asia-Pacific sales (see Chaps. 4 and 5). China could use more natural gas to balance emissions from its energy-intensive industries—that much is obvious. As noted in Wainberg et al. (2017), however, the evolving wealthier coastal urban enclaves are better able to absorb the cost of LNG imports or pipeline gas delivered from Russia and Central Asia. Interior locations are likely to remain wedded to baseload coal generation. Nuclear power additions could represent a "ringer".

Reverberations for Natural Gas

All of these facts should cloud views of energy transition. At the core of the conundrum in which the natural gas industry finds itself is whether natural gas use in key applications such as electric power should or can be discouraged and, if so, in which geographies.

Twin phenomena exacerbated debates about the role of natural gas in power generation in recent years. One is tenaciously low methane prices that have made gas-generated electricity cheap and raised the bar for other power generation sources, including coal and nuclear, while making renewables difficult without extensive public support. Can natural gas (methane) remain as cheap as it has been? As detailed in Chap. 1, pre-pandemic, the clear link between relatively high oil prices and oil-directed drilling yielded the huge volumes of associated gas that U.S. industry players have been striving to monetize. Drilling levels toward the close of 2020 are insufficient to sustain these volumes. Coincidentally, the persistently low Henry Hub price signal has discouraged drilling in locations that are less attractive for liquids. The long-run Henry Hub average of $3 per MMBtu and long-run median of close to $4 are indicative of price adjustments that could occur. Appreciation in natural gas prices would translate into higher wholesale electricity prices, improving revenues for gas-fired generators as well as competitors in the alternative energy space along with coal and nuclear. Customers would be less enthralled.

The other phenomenon is the falling costs for renewable energy components and chemical energy storage—wind, solar photovoltaics (PV), and mainly lithium-based batteries. However, declining costs of equipment do not always translate into cheaper electricity to end users. Most important, the levelized cost of energy (LCOE), the common measure used to compare different power generation technologies, is highly misleading when the inputs of the LCOE formula are not adjusted for local conditions and, more importantly, represent only the tip of the iceberg of system integration costs. These costs can be very high for intermittent and variable wind and solar technologies, especially if the best resources are located away from load centers or capacities are installed in poor-resource locations (see Chap. 2 and Gülen 2019). In a nutshell, the scope and scale requirements of "new" energy technology supply and value chains are not being scrutinized nearly enough.[20]

Fitting subsidized intermittent energy sources into competitive markets with their legacy coal, nuclear and natural gas generation has led to numerous market design conflicts (see Gülen 2019 for the US case). Although gas-fired generation is often seen as the most dispatchable and cleanest complement to intermittent renewables, this load-following use of gas-fired plants is probably unsustainable for operators under current market designs that do not always provide sufficient revenues. There is a growing movement, strongest in Western Europe and parts of the U.S., away from markets toward planning of electricity systems, inclusive of generation portfolios, distributed resources and energy efficiency, with decarbonization as a key objective. All generation fuels and technologies bring distinct pros and cons. The issue is how best to build level playing fields, which many assume can happen with carbon policies. ***On that point, it is not clear, at all, that the natural gas industry is advantaged by climate-related policies, and in particular carbon pricing or taxation.*** When it comes to the cost of adapting to these, or other, approaches, the affordability question plays a large role. Although carbon reduction is a distinct industry strategy, there are many, and very good, reasons to expect that decarb policies would not be friendly to natural gas use. Indeed, the industry's advertising of the lower CO_2 benefits of natural gas combustion and the even smaller GHG contribution when methane is used as feedstock for hydrogen seem to have whiplashed in the politics of methane emissions.[21]

When it comes to decarbonization, the natural gas industry system sits squarely in a conundrum with divergent geographical characteristics. That natural gas provides a lower emissions alternative to many other fuel and feedstock options is well established and ensconced in hallmark publications such as the International Energy Agency's (IEA's) "Golden Age of Gas" (IEA 2011). Natural gas is now helping China and India, among others, to clean their urban environments (Chap. 5). However, the major component of natural gas delivered to customers is methane, a GHG. Methane came under greater scrutiny as climate evolved to dominate conversations about environment rather than local air quality. Fugitive methane emissions and GHG emissions from flaring are estimated to negate lower CO_2 benefits of combusting gas rather than coal to generate electricity (about 50 percent less).[22] Perceptions have shifted accordingly and, along with these, agitation to regulate or even prevent natural gas drilling, transportation, and distribution. These trends underscore another IEA effort to outline best practices in drilling, completions, and production of gas, especially from unconventional plays (IEA 2012).[23] Already, fugitive methane emissions and flaring are targets for regulatory control. The industry is also motivated because any methane molecule that is not sold at the market represents financial leakages. Upstream and midstream operators can and do retrofit their facilities to reduce and eliminate emissions. A distinct hurdle to preventing field production losses is pipeline connectivity. If the cost of reducing or capturing fugitive methane associated with drilling operations exceeds the cost of other options, reducing methane losses can be difficult to achieve.

More obvious than fugitive emissions is flaring, the occasional combustion of natural gas at drill sites as wells are being tested or in locations where there are no pipeline connections to exit gas from leaseholds. Nevertheless, even when pipelines may be present, there are issues. Why would operators flare if gathering and pipeline access is available? In simplest terms, if flaring is cheaper than the costs to connect and the shipping tariff charged by the midstream operator—even after the producer pays royalties owed to minerals owners!—then flaring becomes the more economic choice. A crucial question, at the interface between field production and pipelines to markets, is how pipeline capacity risk and financing are allocated between producers and pipeline operators. It may seem simple to resolve, but there are no easy answers.[24] Adversity attracts inventors, and so a growing and increasingly diverse array of options for capturing leasehold gas are entering the marketplace. Concepts range from power generation for field operations, including to support new electrified pressure pumping, to established concepts for converting natural gas to liquids (GTL; Jacobs 2020). These best practices are likely to spread around the world driven by a desire to create greater value from the resources as well as to reduce environmental footprint.

More problematic is the opposition to pipeline projects, a tactic that has emerged as a means of prohibiting natural gas resource extraction and consumption. Although safety has often been presented as a primary concern, as Wang and Duncan (2014a, b), among others, have shown, methane pipeline incidents are relatively rare. However, when they do occur, they garner deserved attention and can complicate approvals for new projects. The U.S. Government Accountability Office, GAO, investigations regarding pipeline safety, such as the aftermath of the Pacific Gas & Electric pipeline explosion in San Bruno, California, in 2010 (GAO 2017a, 2018a, b), are representative.[25] There is no doubt that pipelines and natural gas storage facilities have functioned, and will continue to function, safely, not only in the U.S. but also around the world. Hundreds of thousands of miles of transmission and distribution pipelines have been operating for decades with minimal incidents wherever competent regulatory oversight is provided.

Finally, we must acknowledge the importance of oil price as a driver for hydrocarbon exploitation, including methane. The direct link is gas that is associated with oil; as explained in Chap. 1, the pursuit of oil targets that yield associated gas results in natural gas supply that is oil price sensitive. Even non-associated gas production can benefit if oil-directed exploration efforts result in gas discoveries (wet gas with NGLs; or dry gas, which may include other components). Over the course of the long history of the oil and gas industries, we have seen repeated cycles in which more valuable crude oil, on a barrel equivalent basis, has been key to at least initial developments for natural gas as a by-product of oil production, with monetization usually as LNG and traditionally on an oil-indexed basis. As value chains mature, it is easier to find the business case for expansion and new opportunities that are rooted in the value of the natural gas content and gas-based pricing. As discussed in Chap. 5, most gas still is traded indexed to oil, especially in Asia-Pacific where gas demand is expected to grow the most. Energy outlooks released in 2020 tend to depress the role of oil worldwide and among regions while emphasizing continued supply of and demand for natural gas. Thus, a crucial question is what the consequences for gas resource development and monetization could be if investment in crude oil exploration and production decreases over the next decades.

New "New Deal" Solutions?

Flowing from the previous section, we can boil down challenges faced by the natural gas industry into two interrelated areas. One is the public and political acceptance of the aggressive carbon taxing approaches that would be needed to garner meaningful GHG emission reductions not just for natural gas or energy, but all industrial, and many non-industrial, activities. The second and more difficult to measure is public perception of natural gas as a fossil fuel harmful to climate, ignoring all of the local air, water, land, and environmental benefits when replacing coal and liquids or even relative to alternatives.

For customers already challenged by affordability of natural gas, carbon costs on top of already expensive value chains are not a happy mix. Technological solutions to decarbonize natural gas include “green LNG”, “blue hydrogen”, and carbon capture and sequestration (CCS), among others. Pipeline and local distribution system owners and operators often see biogas as a solution, albeit a competitor to natural gas but one that enables continued use of legacy pipeline and local distribution systems. All will add to the cost of energy delivered to consumers, but the specifics can favor one over the other in different locales.

The simple proposition for **green LNG** is to reduce GHG emissions or offset them as part of LNG project and value chain development (Medlock et al. 2020). Reductions can come from using alternative energy sources for LNG processes, deploying CCS or other measures. In addition, emissions can be offset with certified carbon credits from other projects. Steam reformation of natural gas to obtain **gray (blue if CCS is used) hydrogen** currently is the most practical way to move toward the “hydrogen economy” because hydrogen already is produced in many refining and petrochemicals complexes. Since hydrogen is an energy carrier and not an energy source, leveraging existing operations that yield hydrogen routinely bypasses significant cost of hydrogen production.[26] Repurposing existing natural gas facilities such as pipelines for hydrogen makes hydrogen an attractive energy carrier, but it also needs refurbishment of pipelines and other equipment to make them suitable for safe handling of hydrogen. Many see the most attainable on-ramp for hydrogen as a blend with existing delivered natural gas (blends of 20 percent or more would require changes to infrastructure and end-use equipment such as turbines for power generation to address gas quality issues; see K&L Gates 2020 for abundant examples, opportunities, and caveats). The use of hydrogen for vehicle transportation requires appropriate hydrogen fuel cell vehicle (HFCV) designs. These currently encompass platinum catalysts, which encumber HFCV commercialization due to high cost and critical minerals’ ESG risks. **CCS** could enter natural gas value chains in a number of ways, but gas-fired power generation is probably the best-known route, as coal-fired power plants are key targets of CCS. Few experimentations exist for CCS associated with natural gas-fired generation.

The lack of data and published information from actual commercial deployment introduces large uncertainties into outlooks such as those presented in the Foreword. Neither coal nor natural gas CCS is considered to be commercially attractive with the rare exceptions when captured CO_2 found customers willing to pay for it and its transportation in operators of oil fields who wanted to enhance oil recovery.

These and many other schemes are highly dependent upon assumptions about prices of oil, gas, electricity, as well as carbon or other policy measures including outright government support that would induce people to internalize the posited GHG externalities (e.g., tax incentives for wind, solar, and CCS). Nor has massive scale-up of other "low carbon" or "zero carbon" technologies, including those proposed for vehicle transport, been fully exposed to commercial tests and due diligence for costs, net decarbonization benefits, and economic impacts, including affordability. This lack of market-based commerciality proof makes typical growth

Commercial Framework Uncertainties

All of the options we touch on are burdened by the usual complications. These include:

- High cost (with government support as an enabler for financing and de-risking).
- The need to win approvals for resource development and delivery infrastructure (decarbonization strategies, including alternative energy projects and their infrastructure requirements such as high-voltage transmission, are not assured of public acceptance or regulatory approvals).
- Lack of markets to support pricing and to establish values of credits for offsets, with implications for bankability and financing.
- Lack of common standards and practices for certifying and guaranteeing the ESG benefits that would be valued.
- Lack of common policies on carbon taxing.
- Lack of clarity on "firmness" of commitments to carbon reductions in target markets. While related to the previous risks and uncertainties on policies, the underlying firmness reflects shifting public attitudes and thus political support that would be essential for large scale investments.
- Lack of common approaches and metrics for monitoring and enforcement.

trajectories for alternative energy sources seem fragile and raises the risk of perpetual state support to either project developers or consumers or both. Nevertheless, perception trumps reality any day, and the natural gas industry finds itself in the most difficult messaging environment it has faced since the 1976 supply curtailments that led to the tangle of Carter administration laws and policies (see the Appendix).

All of the options are, therefore, fully exposed to the set of "license to operate" conditions—the conceptual space for commercial frameworks—explored in Chap. 6 and illustrated in Fig. 6.1. The bottom line is that there can be no certainty that political and/or public backing can or will exist even for options that move natural gas into compliance with climate politics-directed perceptions and expectations. The picture is more complicated once we overlay it with divergent country resources, political cultures, economic needs, and societal perceptions. The acceptance of natural gas grows in most of the growing economies of the world, although its affordability and competitiveness against coal, nuclear, and renewables remain in doubt in some.

Divergence of "New Deal" Economies Across Geographies

We can summarize the major themes and findings in our book by exploring the natural gas chessboard—the distribution of resource endowments, supply, and demand across political boundaries, and how these distributions play into attitudes, positions, potential conflicts, and room for cooperation. The divergence in viewpoints regarding the role of natural gas, and their non-random assignments across jurisdictions, have important implications for monetization of natural gas on many levels. To begin, they amplify the growing misalignments in the geographies of global natural gas supply and demand.

Supply derives from reserves, a small portion of the resource base that, at the time of reporting, producers can deliver with current technologies and market prices. Over the past two decades the proved reserves increased about 2100 trillion cubic feet (Tcf), or 43 percent, despite global consumption of about 2200 Tcf. Figure 7.2, panels (a) and (b), shows the proportional split of proved gas reserves between the OECD and non-OECD worlds remained the same between 2000 and 2019 (10 and 90 percent, respectively). As panel (c) shows reserves increased in traditional areas such as Russia, Turkmenistan, some other Commonwealth of Independent States (CIS) countries, Qatar, and Iran. Reserves growth in China and the U.S., roughly equivalent in Tcf, increased the share of China

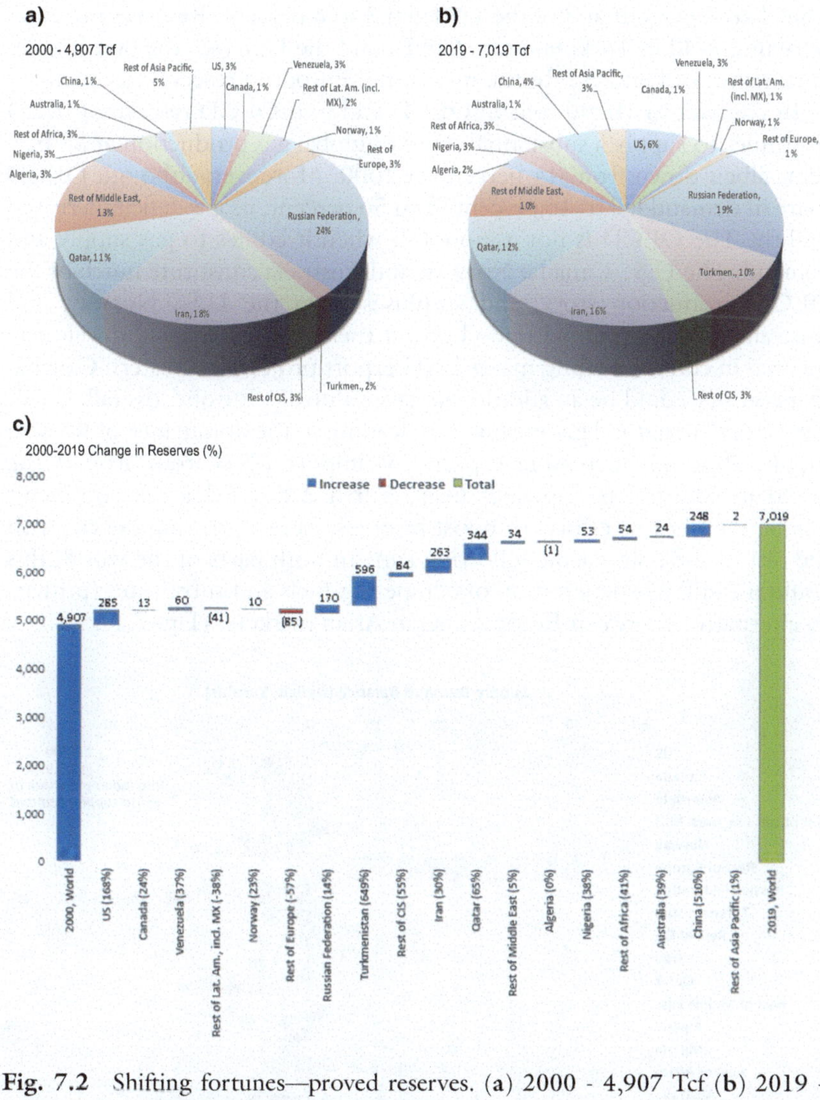

Fig. 7.2 Shifting fortunes—proved reserves. (**a**) 2000 - 4,907 Tcf (**b**) 2019 - 7,019 Tcf (**c**) 2000-2019 Change in Reserves (%) (Source: For all panels, authors' depiction based on BP Annual Statistical Review of Energy 2020, www.bp.com)

from 1 to 4 percent and of the US from 3 to 6 percent. Reserves increases were multifold in Turkmenistan, China, and the U.S. (see the percentages in panel (c) of Fig. 7.2). In the meantime, European reserves declined.

In contrast to 10–90 split of OECD and non-OECD reserves, OECD continues to supply a substantial share of global gas production at 38 percent, albeit down from 44 percent in 2000. Moreover, although OECD share of demand fell to 46 percent from 56 percent, its gas deficit increased slightly. The OECD is not a monolith when it comes to gas supply and demand. The U.S., Canada, Norway, and Australia constitute much of the OECD production story, and surpluses from the U.S., Norway, and Australia feed into global trade beyond their regions. Should developers succeed in commissioning major LNG export projects in Western Canada, that country could be an additional player globally. Europe, overall, is falling "short" in natural gas production, leading to the dominance of Russian supply, although increasing capacity to import LNG from around the world in addition to pipelines from North Africa helps the continent. China, for all of its efforts to boost reserves, faces a growing deficit, with the rest of the Asia-Pacific following suit. In both parts of the world, this could mean faster penetration of competing fuels and substitutes (primarily alternative energy in Europe, coal in Asian markets) (Fig. 7.3).

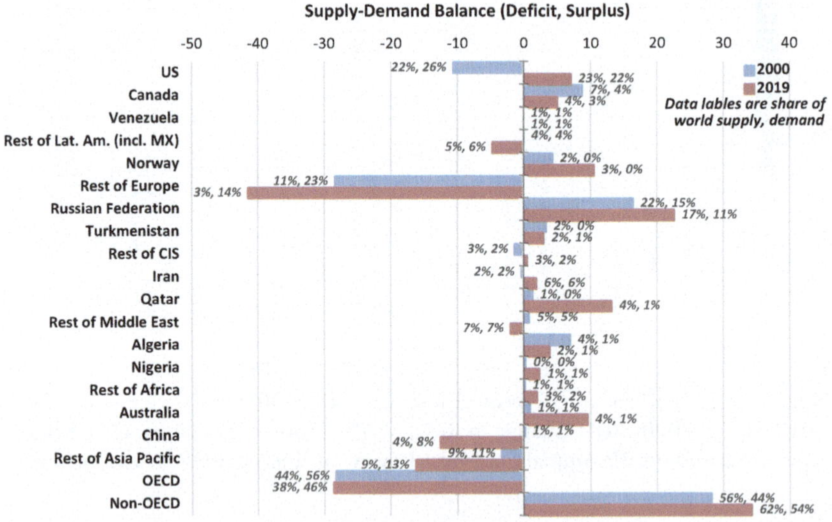

Fig. 7.3 Supply–demand balance, 2000 and 2019 deficits and surpluses. (Percentages represent shares of world supply and demand)

Among the contiguous, nationwide natural gas industry systems in existence, the U.S. industry and marketplace persist as the world's largest, at roughly 30 Tcf, comprising about 22 percent of global gas consumption. The extent of the U.S. natural gas infrastructure network supports natural gas electric, industrial, and local distribution systems for end users, including from the largest to the smallest. Russia's internal market is just over half that size at 16 Tcf and about 11 percent of global gas use. China's is just over one-third the size at 11 Tcf, with about an 8 percent market share.[27]

The North American continent, in particular Canada and the U.S., represents the largest, openly competitive, free-flowing volume of international natural gas sales across a single border globally. Canada-U.S. exchanges constitute about 12 percent of global gas pipeline (methane) trade. When the U.S. exports to Mexico are included, the North American share of global gas pipeline trade bumps up to about 18 percent. While Russian exports account for nearly 28 percent of global gas pipeline trade, they involve many more receiving countries in Europe and myriad complex and often fraught relationships with transit countries like Ukraine.[28]

In sum, between 2000 and 2019, the balance of natural gas demand and supply shifted toward non-OECD countries even as the huge global natural gas reserves expanded 43 percent and production and consumption grew more than two-thirds.

These realities, the positions of pieces on the chessboard, raise several interrelated issues. One is the obvious question of how some OECD governments (most part of the Old World in Chap. 5 parlance) could influence gas supply should they impose decarbonization ("decarb" in common parlance) policies. Output from those countries would become more expensive and could be curtailed. Chapter 1 touches on vulnerabilities in the U.S., but producers in other OECD countries, especially in Europe, are under varying degrees of stress. It is also possible that these pressures could impact international operations of companies based in these countries as exemplified by announcements of Shell, BP, and to a lesser extent Statoil and Total, although all of them seem to emphasize the future role of gas in their decarbonization efforts, given their large investments in gas resource development and LNG supply chains.

The current layout of the natural gas chessboard also affects the energy security dilemma, discussed in Chap. 5, which plagues all countries that are not self-sufficient in energy, but particularly those in the New World (including some OECD countries), as their energy needs are and will be growing into the future. Customers and governments do not take decisions lightly to move toward natural gas, given the serious infrastructure investment shortcomings in these geographies. Developing countries not only lack funds but also have trouble with attracting investment from outside, as noted in Chaps. 5 and 6. Suboptimal choices, when it comes to slating energy sources and infrastructure, can negatively affect economic growth while also increasing geopolitical risk, in particular if natural gas suppliers become less diverse. A smaller pool of suppliers could use natural gas exports to influence domestic policies of import-dependent customers.[29]

Scenario Games

So: what if the major producers in OECD (the U.S., Norway, Australia) took actions that significantly reduced or completely exited their natural gas output, potentially removing 30 percent of global supply?

With their massive surpluses, it is quite imaginable that more could come from non-OECD countries, particularly where natural gas production already exists. This includes mainly the big players like Russia and Qatar, who could be the winners in the gas monetization game. Much less swayed by issues of climate and relatively insulated (in the short term at least) from societal moods and preferences, they can invest in development of new gas resources and the needed infrastructure. As documented in Chaps. 4 and 5, they have been doing so already, even during the COVID-19-related slump in demand to ensure their market share now and in the future. Qatar could be, in fact, the big winner if politics and policies in developed countries played out in the worst case. The country houses some of the cheapest gas to develop, largely a consequence of condensate and natural gas plant liquids production that comes as by-products. With all of its exports as LNG, Qatar seems to have more flexibility in terms of accessing markets around the world than Russia, which is still heavily dependent on pipeline exports to Europe.

Russia also has been forging ahead to ramp up its flexibility when it comes to deliveries and ability to access new markets. As described in Chap. 5, strong decarbonization policies among large European customers, along with diversification via alternative pipeline and LNG supplies, are challenging Russia's Gazprom. In addition, geopolitical considerations are pushing many countries in Central and Eastern Europe (CEE) and Southeastern Europe (SEE) toward non-Russian sources of gas even if that implies higher prices featuring what some call a "security premium".[30]

The Russian government recognizes these issues, and it has long worked to diversify its own customer base. China, in particular, is the market that Russia has been keen to win for decades. Until recently, Russia had great difficulty convincing Chinese leaderships to build pipeline connections.

Historically, Russia (previously the Union of Soviet Socialist Republics (USSR)) and China have not seen eye to eye. Within the international realm, these countries have always occupied very different positions and pursued diverse strategies and tactics. Today their relative status has pretty much flipped, with China being a leading economic power and Russia diminished by loss of geopolitical influence and generally slow economic growth. Both countries have been vying for greater international influence. Under the leadership of Vladimir Putin, the Russian government has pursued two strategies. In the "Near Abroad" region, the Putin regime has used typical "hard power" instruments ranging from geopolitical influence to direct aggression to reestablish control (e.g., the invasion of Ukraine and annexation of Crimea). Elsewhere, the regime has deployed campaigns of disinformation and/or interference in elections. Both strategies are generating increasing backlash from the international community, including multilateral and unilateral sanctions and general distrust toward Russia.

Under Xi Jinping, China has increasingly relied on its economic prowess and its position as center of both supply and demand as a way to position itself in the world, particularly vis-à-vis the U.S. and other developed countries. China's increasingly significant geo economic position, along with harder approaches toward smaller governments in China's orbit, has been a worry for other international players for some time. Xi's Belt and Road Initiative, touched on in Chap. 5, has only worsened concerns, as Chinese outbound investments, especially in weak and fragile countries, are more widely reported. These developments underscore the recent US–China trade war and the EU's caution when it comes to allowing Chinese direct investment in the community. Tensions have become even more vivid during the COVID-19 crisis as supply chain dependencies on China for everything from critical minerals to pharmaceuticals and healthcare equipment receive greater scrutiny. There has been an economic backlash for China as countries move, at least partially, toward shifting supply chains to domestic markets or diversifying supply chains. However, a joint survey of 25 companies by AmCham China and PwC in March 2020 suggests that, rather than pulling out from China, companies may pursue a "China+1" strategy (Forde 2020). In the face of these tensions, China could pull back to focus more on its domestic economy. Pre-pandemic, the Xi regime began placing more emphasis on domestic consumption and on industrial sectors like services, which includes information technology, that are less dependent upon exports for economic growth.[31] China is not likely to pull back fully from its engagement in South and Southeast Asia and Africa, although digital technology may gain prominence over more expensive projects such as energy infrastructure (e.g., Blanchette and Hillman 2020). Importantly, however, we must acknowledge the real dangers facing the Chinese economy: an aging population, large debt, intractability of banking system and SOEs, the communist party dynamics (e.g., central versus local power balance), and so on. Magnus (2018) and McMahon (2018) provide detailed analyses of these and other risks facing the Chinese economy. Fundamentally, the challenge seems to be the deficiency of stable economic and political institutions as aptly demonstrated in Acemoglu and Robinson (2012). These analyses suggest that opaque and non-inclusive communist party regime is a risk in China. None of this should be taken as evidence of Chinese economy imploding in the near future, but a more inward-looking economy growing much more slowly should be seen as a real possibility.

The increasingly evident lack of trust among many countries toward both Russia and China has fostered, ironically, a platform for collaboration between these rivals. We already see this in the energy sphere where the U.S. and EU stance regarding Russian territorial grabs spurred Chinese investment in new gas ventures such as the Yamal LNG project. Chinese financing and its involvement as a shareholder have been extremely useful given sanctions imposed on Russia. Chinese entities hold 29.9 percent of shares in the project (with China National Petroleum Corporation (CNPC) owning 20 percent and the Silk Road Fund 9.9 percent). China National Offshore Oil Corporation (CNOOC) and CNPC will each take 10 percent of shares in the Arctic LNG, the next project of Russian private company, Novatek.[32] For China, this engagement is consistent with its push for the so-called Silk Road on Ice, trading along the Arctic route, including in winter with massive new icebreakers (Roston 2018) and its strategy of diversification of energy sources. Russian LNG provides an alternative to LNG coming from Australia, Qatar, or the US as well as pipeline gas from Central Asia or Myanmar.

In addition, after decades of negotiations and lobbying by Russia, China agreed to a new integrated pipeline project, Power of Siberia, which has been transporting Russian gas to China since year-end 2019. China was able to leverage Russia's desire to find new markets for its gas and negotiated extremely beneficial terms. Russia hopes that Chinese participation will lead to Power of Siberia 2, which would connect China to the same gas resources that currently supply Europe. Such a move would give Russia arbitrage opportunities and strengthen its position against European governments and customers. All in all, the practical bonds between the two countries have been growing, encouraged by developments in international relations. The COVID-19 pandemic may propel further collaboration between the two countries. This could include subsequent arrangements for natural gas trade, as the EU pursues decarbonization policy and both the EU and the U.S. move to protect their respective interests relative to Chinese dominance and influence on myriad fronts.

Iran could be another candidate to fill the potential void in natural gas supply, but also must first contend with sanctions. The country increased its production nearly fivefold since 2000 although its proved reserves increased only 30 percent. Almost all of the production is consumed domestically. The country needs to prove up more reserves to meet its domestic needs, let alone to become a major exporter. As long as the sanctions limit foreign investment in Iran, the country's ailing economy is not likely to corral the financial resources necessary to prove up gas reserves, especially if oil prices remain low. Even without sanctions, exploration and development would take numerous years, given the need to develop new fields (including its share of offshore South Pars or North Field as Qatar calls it).

As described in Chap. 5, countries in Africa and Latin America could grow gas supply but pervasive above-ground issues related to political stability, corruption, and regulatory regimes are ongoing burdens for both domestic and foreign investors. These regions also face prospects for growing demand and a broad range of geographic and political barriers to achieving internal, regional trade. Both regions represent sources of ESG risks and uncertainties to investors. Also, decarbonization policies of the traditional donor countries and institutions limit investment in developing domestic gas resources for local economies. The influx of Asian, in particular Chinese, capital in recent years has filled some gaps, albeit with trade offs such as loan obligations and external influence on weak and fragile governments. Inbound investment from Asia could expand under certain conditions, especially to support export-oriented projects, and especially in raw materials. Investment to support internal consumption growth and energy security needs in Africa and Latin America will hinge on sustained, high-quality commercial frameworks, as presented in Chap. 6, and ability to mobilize domestic capital and entrepreneurship.

To sum up, geographical misalignments of supply and demand create opportunities for natural gas monetization, but with, at times extreme, complexity. Demand increasingly derives from relatively resource-scarce locations in the developing world. The risks and uncertainties along the energy transition front are substantial. In spite of treaties, no unity exists among governments in their approaches, and countries are moving toward "decarb" mandates at quite different speeds and with considerable variation in commitment among their polities. Even within the European Union, disunity exists between the West and the rest. Non-OECD natural gas supply, already dominating worldwide natural gas consumption and trade, is poised to become even more important with interesting new geographical alignments that could test established international mores and alliances.

All of these suggest higher gas consumption and trade volumes (i.e., a continuation of the past trend, perhaps even picking up speed), but profound geographical misalignments could also undermine gas monetization as governments react to various signals. These include security of supply considerations on the part of the New World that would keep coal in play and/or hasten introduction of competing new energy alternatives. Supply security fears could be minimized, however, given proven natural gas endowments present in the developing world and the extent to which creative, innovative solutions could be implemented for de-risking large-scale exploitation and monetization. The winning parties would be those that can ramp up investment and production, are minimally constrained by societal pressures, and can be seen as reliable suppliers capable of minimizing energy security concerns.

Commercial Frameworks and Natural Gas Value Chains

The expectation of market-driven supply responding to demand that is ever more price sensitive within an increasingly liquid global marketplace has become a hallmark of developments over the last decade or so. As we show throughout this book, these developments have been related to increased depth of the market, with growing numbers of both suppliers and consumers. The natural gas industry is now host to new market structures and commercial practices that include shorter, more flexible contracts, increasing reliance on gas-on-gas pricing, and expanding use of spot transactions. The entrance of the U.S. as a major natural gas exporter, carrying with it influence stemming from the organization of North American gas market, has propelled many of these advances.

The U.S. participation as a global supplier has neither shielded the U.S. gas producers and LNG exporters from challenges nor pushed non-U.S. suppliers to transform themselves to look and function more like the U.S. producers. As such, while international gas transactions become more market-based, many of the participants in those transactions are state-owned and do not rely on market principles in their organization and functioning. Hence, those producers stay insulated, while reliance of U.S. companies on market forces exposes them to sometimes-punishing market fluctuations such as those experienced during the COVID-19 pandemic, and uncertainties associated with decarbonization politics.

Yet, crucially, it is also reliance upon and the degree of sophistication in using market-based approaches and commercial practices for risk management and mitigation that so strongly define the U.S. oil and gas industry resilience even when individual companies fail, as mapped in Chap. 1. Low level of governmental involvement in the U.S. oil and gas sector often makes those companies more desirable as business partners since geopolitical risk is minimal, even if the U.S. mixed economy style fosters the presence of federal and state governments in the U.S. oil and gas business affairs. Also, again discussed in Chaps. 4, 5, 6, and elsewhere, the U.S. companies will seek partners and anchor customers who benefit from support of their sovereigns in order to de-risk and achieve bankability for large-scale capital projects such as LNG value chains. All of that said, the separation of business and government when it comes to market-based pricing and commercial transactions and practices are fundamental to the U.S. model. Many countries may never reach nor want to reach the size and scope of market openness and financial liquidity of the U.S., but the U.S. model is the biggest influence as countries develop their commercial frameworks for a natural gas market.

The U.S.

In the US, recognition of the increasing reliance on natural gas and its attractiveness underscored the push to modernize and to reconsider how natural gas markets might function. For sure, there were plenty of commercial interests at stake, but there also were visionary moments. Since the 1970s, the federal government with an agglomeration of industry and customer groups and some help from academics restructured the natural gas industry from wellhead to end-user marketplace in ways that:

- Increased competitiveness and thus efficiencies
- Improved deliverability (pipeline, storage, and associated infrastructure)
- Provided greater market access for both suppliers and customers
- Increased the transparency of price signals
- Streamlined policy and regulatory oversight

This process was not without its "bumps", but the payoff was substantial. More importantly, as legislators and regulators were making crucial decisions and implementing the open access regime, the marketplace did not collapse. Nor were there many, or even very serious, attempts to roll back or weaken the commitment to a more open, competitive landscape.

The U.S. natural gas industry remains the best funded (based on IEA 2019), the most diverse in terms of market participants from upstream to downstream, and the best equipped in oil and gas field services capacity. The U.S. hosts a robust, still growing field-to-market midstream segment. Money and market participants together are measures of "liquidity" and indicative of the ease of "doing business". The U.S. natural gas marketplace is emblematic of organizational structures in which "the whole" truly is more than"the sum of its parts," all of which must cooperate, often across intensely competing interests.

The market evolution within the U.S. is set within a context of periods of historic supply abundance with every progression along the oil and gas technology pathway yielding favorable pricing for customers but diminishing returns upstream. After topping records set during 2018, the U.S. natural gas-marketed production during 2019 hit a new high, averaging 100 Bcf/d (EIA data). Henry Hub, the main natural gas price index, sits well below the $3/MMBtu depicted in the Chap. 1 gas price thermostat (Fig. 1.4). As 2020 opened, Henry Hub had fallen below a pronounced psychological barrier of $2. Traded U.S. light crude oil has remained firmly in the mid $50s until pandemic lockdowns, and then firmly entered the low $40s. These prices are well below hurdle rates that lured investors first to "shale gas" ($8 with views to $15 and a rush to imported liquefied natural gas, LNG) and then to "shale oil" ($80 with views to $120 and the rush to export LNG).[33] In light of the long history of natural gas as by-product to oil, these price relationships matter. Frankelnomics rules. The "ignorance of sunk costs" and tendency to surplus hasten the erosion of commodity prices. Drilling activity has been flat to declining across the U.S. Valuations for publicly traded oil and gas companies have pushed them off investors' radars. Credit stress across independent producers has complicated exit strategies. Oil field suppliers are in doldrums, and some midstream operators are under scrutiny mainly where producer commitments are in question given the shaky upstream finances.

Against a backdrop of natural gas supply robustness, natural gas has entered a prolonged "buyers' market". A takeaway from the U.S. experience, which applies to many other situations (in particular where natural gas is "stranded"), is that most of the time monetization comes with "supply push". That means, mainly producers put up the necessary guarantees for field-to-market linkages. This is a much more frequent state of affairs than "demand pull", which often means someone else willing to fund those vital connections. In this book, we discuss monetization strategies in power generation (Chap. 2), petrochemicals (Chap. 3), and LNG (Chap. 4). Altogether, expansions and greenfield projects in these segments account for all of the additional roughly 42 Bcf/d of production as it doubled from 2005. Along the way, with gas exports rising and oil and refined product imports declining, the U.S. reached a status in which, on a barrel of oil equivalent basis, it exports about as much natural gas as it imports crude oil and oil products. Notably, this change in hydrocarbon trade balance helped to narrow the U.S. trade deficit, an accomplishment that, as we went to press, was highlighted by pandemic-induced widening of the trade deficit.

The U.S. has been the fastest growing new supply source for LNG. This is due entirely to the large volumes of associated gas production in excess of domestic consumption, and a vigorous supply-push to export these volumes. LNG was the favored strategy. Mexico, by contrast, represents demand-pull, conveniently located just south of the border from major liquids-driven developments in Eagle Ford and Permian, with large volumes of associated gas and an extreme deficit in internal supply relative to consumption (as noted, the US is Mexico's largest supplier via piped gas exports; see Chap. 6 on The U.S. and North American Stories). The attraction for LNG export monetization was the headroom associated with oil-indexed supply and purchase agreements. We raised numerous caveats in our book regarding the pace and ultimate extent of gas-on-gas pricing, gas-indexed contracting, liquidity deepening, and other facets of globalizing gas trade. One of the most important considerations is the industry's ability to finance high cost of LNG supply chains and upstream gas resource development in a liquid global gas market without oil-indexed long-term contracts or another commercial arrangement that would secure sufficient future cash flows to create value. All of these realities have ramifications for the geographies and misalignments between supply sources and customers, strategies for both producers and buyers, and regional and global trade, with implications for natural gas monetization.

Beyond the US

The Canada-U.S. border has been "seamless" with respect to physical infrastructure and deliveries of natural gas as well as flows of investment and human talent. Canadian and the U.S. policy-makers and regulators have tended to respond in kind to shifts in industry activity and development patterns. They acted mostly in unison to advance (from 1988 in Canada and 1992 in the U.S.) "light-handed", nondiscriminatory open access for pipeline systems, maintaining a "hands off" approach to allow market-based pricing to flow from wellhead to end user. The UK and, for the most part, Australian business models are quite sympathetic with these core principles. Western Europe has also been moving toward competitive natural gas markets with TPA and gas pricing hubs, but there are many exceptions–perhaps due to energy security concerns driven by large import dependence—but the legacy of powerful state companies is still strong in some countries (see Chap. 5).

These more or less open market models stand in contrast to most other suppliers of natural gas where sovereign interests take much more involved positions, including through direct ownership, infrastructure buildup, or other subsidies. Mexico, though becoming increasingly integrated to the North American market, remains dominated by Pemex (Petroleos Mexicanos, the country's long-established national oil company) and CFE (Comisión Federal de Electricidad, the national electricity organization), with unclear support for and direction of regulatory reforms implemented in 2012 (see Chap. 6 and the Appendix). As discussed in Chap. 5 in detail and summarized earlier, both major exporters such as Russia and Qatar and major importers such as China, India, South Korea, and Japan depend heavily on their state entities managing their energy needs, including natural gas, and public funding to develop the necessary infrastructure. Even when private companies are involved, their investments are grounded on either direct or indirect state support and sanctioning. This can be seen as a transition from a pure statist approach to crony capitalism, but in the absence of liquid, competitive markets with independent and competent regulation, these approaches offer a way of de-risking multibillion-dollar investments in energy infrastructure.

The challenge, of course, is that public money at risk has been increasing. It is not clear that even China can sustain the levels of investment seen in the past, given, as discussed earlier, the growing geopolitical tensions that we, and others, expect to lead to at least some de-globalization and the high cost of recovering from the pandemic around the world. Importantly, crony capitalism has been increasing in the Old World as well, often driven in the energy sector by decarbonization policies that de-risk alternative energy projects for investors and developers via tax credits, surcharges in customer bills, and direct public funding. Of course, one can easily argue that crony capitalism has been the dominant form of capitalism in the energy sector given the importance of government policy and regulation across oil, gas, and electric power value chains. The share of investments, returns of which are dependent on explicit state incentives, has been rising, especially in the electric power sector, and, in some cases, has overcome market-based investments (see Gülen 2019 for the case of the US electricity markets). Since power generation is a large market for natural gas, a question then arises on whether market-based investments along the natural gas supply chain can be maintained. So far, gas replacing coal in power generation and exports has sustained demand in the US, but the future remains uncertain (Chap. 2).

Finally, as we made clear in our suggested scenario (see earlier section on Scenario Games), a distinct paradox is that strong pressures for climate action in the Old World can attain the same outcome of favoring coal in the New World if natural gas supplies from the Old World (especially the US and Australia) become too expensive. An all-inclusive pursuit of energy sources and technologies certainly seems to be the strategy in China that has been investing large sums in coal, nuclear, hydro, gas, and renewable energy infrastructure. Chinese exports of wind, solar, and battery equipment, especially to Old World countries with strong incentives, certainly help with China's trade surplus.

Overall, despite all the increase in global natural gas trade and the share of market-based trading, we can see likely limits to the expansion of commercial frameworks conducive to creating liquid gas markets from two sources. First is the tendency of governments, in those markets expected to grow the most, to manage energy needs in their economies. This means direct government incursion in a variety of ways, directly through public investments or indirectly through financing and guarantees. Second is the expansion of decarbonization policies with somewhat uncertain paths in terms of energy options. Again, we see the tendency for sovereigns and, in federalized countries, lower jurisdictions like states, provinces, territories to step into the decarbonization fray with policy and regulatory or other inducements that circumvent competitive markets to achieve comparative advantage or other goals and objectives.

Gestalt or Entropy?

As we tried to summarize earlier, the existential "issue du jour" of decarbonization and the bottom-line problem of affordability underlie much of what influences the industry and marketplace today. Policy-makers, analysts, and citizenry increasingly recognize local environmental benefits in burgeoning markets such as China and India, as they use natural gas, to the extent they can develop the necessary infrastructure, to replace coal, liquids used in transportation, and traditional biomass. At the same time, as installed capacities rise and some reach retirement age, we are starting to realize the full ESG impact of supply chains for raw materials inputs used in wind and solar components and batteries, as well as their development, operation, and end-of-life treatment.

Within this very messy milieu, natural gas monetization proceeds. A realistic view is that "modern, successful gas exploitation requires opportunities to maximize the value of the resource to the end of the value chain, whether it [is] high-efficiency power generation, combustion in high value non-substitutable applications, or feedstock use".[34] How can we build the "resource to opportunity" path for monetizing a resource that is abundant worldwide? That global resource endowment enlarges even more when subsea methane hydrates, a "hydrogen economy" that could emerge with natural gas as an accessible feedstock, and other frontier resources are included. How does the industry deal with persistent uncertainties emanating from decarbonization debates while communicating the immense local environmental benefits of the fuel?

The structure and the interdependence of typical natural gas system value chain segments, in a country or globally, have a great deal to do with underlying economics and affordability. Supply and infrastructure costs define affordability, which is harder to achieve with expensive decarb measures. *Understanding the value chain, that is, how participants create and distribute value, and separating powerful endogenous dynamics from exogenous factors is key to analysis of natural gas market systems. Otherwise, distinct risks and uncertainties underlie both business and government approaches to effective natural gas development and use.* Conflicting goals and ambitions continuously buffet natural gas commercial frameworks. Investment flows by private companies are returns-sensitive. Many actions taken in the name of improving affordability work directly against profitability. These include social engineering of electric power markets and the overall proclivity of governments to interfere in response to political interests and agendas, especially in the New World where gas demand is expected to grow the most.

How these debates play out, and whether realized net benefits for the environment will meet expectations, presents enormous incremental risks and uncertainties to businesses, governments, and societies. This introduces the possibility of inertia in decision-making, commitments of scarce public resources, and even ambivalence among the public—especially voting publics in countries where policy-making is subject to open elections.

In the end, our essential question is this: *How can we best achieve routine accessibility to and affordability of natural gas while also ensuring financial sustainability and durability of natural gas supply and value chains given the uncertainty around future paths? Will we see a new order managed primarily by states, but with sufficient market flavor, or will we continue in growing disorder with divergent energy and environment policies around the world amid growing geopolitical tensions?*

Notes

1. Phrases such as "next new thing" and "next big thing" are linked to the Silicon Valley information technology cluster as depicted by Michael Lewis in his iconic 1999 book, *The New New Thing: A Silicon Valley Story*, published by W.W. Norton. Slogans like "new green deal" clearly are a throwback to the original New Deal platform carried forward by then US president Franklin D. Roosevelt which was not without many critics and detractors, still today. We couple these sentiments in our book title.
2. Among many sources, Our World in Data, https://ourworldindata.org/, is convenient for published information.
3. Based on the International Energy Agency, IEA, methane tracker, https://www.iea.org/reports/methane-tracker-2020
4. See the EPA GHG site for information, https://www.epa.gov/ghgemissions/overview-greenhouse-gases#methane

5. See the BBC coverage at https://www.bbc.com/news/science-environment-49567197. See Ottersbach (2018) for a synopsis of SF_6 characteristics.
6. See the United Nations Environment Programme Gap Report 2019, https://wedocs.unep.org/bitstream/handle/20.500.11822/30797/EGR2019.pdf?sequence=1&isAllowed=y
7. See the EU reporting page, https://ec.europa.eu/eurostat/cache/infographs/energy/bloc-4a.html
8. See the US Environmental Protection Agency's tracking of US GHG emissions, https://www.epa.gov/ghgemissions/overview-greenhouse-gases#methane
9. Good examples of extensive survey research on attitudes can be found at the Pew Research Center. For instance, worldwide views on whether climate is a major "threat" vary hugely, https://www.pewresearch.org/fact-tank/2019/04/18/a-look-at-how-people-around-the-world-view-climate-change/ (notably, China and India are not included in this survey). Confidence in science and elected officials, who ostensibly would design and execute climate-related policies, is low in the US, https://www.pewresearch.org/science/2016/10/04/the-politics-of-climate/. Public attitudes differ strongly across partisan, age, gender, income, and educational divides, https://www.pewresearch.org/science/2019/11/25/u-s-public-views-on-climate-and-energy/
10. Based on the proprietary Carbon Tracker maintained by Bloomberg New Energy Finance, as of September 2020.
11. At heart is the sheer difficulty of modeling earth's climate, combining what is known (realizing that there are vast unknowns) regarding natural variability; the carbon cycle; whether changes in atmospheric chemistry precede, follow, or are coincident with climate shifts (requiring a level of granularity in paleoclimate data that simply does not exist); how human (anthropogenic) emissions from all sources (with reliable measurements worldwide) figure into the picture; and, worse, the role of human behavior. We recommend two recent views that pull together the abundant and varied critiques and unease with the state of understanding and modeling: Lindzen (2020) and Brady (2020).
12. Underpinnings for content in this section include a scoping workshop on energy and minerals held by Rice University and Imperial College-London, *Framing Integration Futures*, September 18–19, 2019 (unpublished materials).
13. Lower energy densities of alternative energy technologies translate to higher materials intensity. See p. 390 of the US Department of Energy's Quadrennial Technology Review, 2015, for a comparison across different electric power generation technologies in tons per terawatt hours (TWh),

https://www.energy.gov/sites/prod/files/2017/03/f34/quadrennial-technology-review-2015_1.pdf. For batteries, research on alternative vehicle designs sheds light on energy storage dilemmas. A number of sources provide inferences for materials intensity in light of specific energy and specific power tradeoffs, measured as watthours per kilogram (Wh/kg) and vehicle performance criteria such as weight. See Thomas (2009), Schlachter (2012), Vijayagopal (2016) and Vijayagopal et al. (2016) and USDRIVE (2017).

14. See endnote 12. Also based on proprietary reports by Bloomberg New Energy Finance (BNEF). From BNEF data and published life cycle analysis (see Michot Foss and Zoellmer 2020), energy requirements are roughly 400 to 1 of battery energy capacity with substantial GHG emissions as a possible outcome, depending upon where battery manufacturing is located.
15. Based on unpublished research in progress by Rachel A. Meidl and Michelle Michot Foss at Rice University's Baker Institute for Public Policy, Center for Energy Studies. For example, see presentation by Meidl at the 2020 MIT A+B Applied Energy Symposium, August 13–14, 2020, https://www.bakerinstitute.org/media/files/files/94dfa360/mit-harvard-applied-energy-symposium-2020.pdf. See Michot Foss et al. (2020) for additional comments and sources on battery end-of-life challenges and related research and development.
16. Since release of the World Bank's June 2017 report, *The Growing Role of Minerals and Metals for a Low Carbon Future*, http://documents1.worldbank.org/curated/en/207371500386458722/pdf/117581-WP-P159838-PUBLIC-ClimateSmartMiningJuly.pdf, numerous publications and research documents are accumulating knowledge on an assortment of challenges underpinning the push for alternative energy capacity. Mining and minerals processing are attracting significant attention in light of raw materials inputs. See Lee et al. (2020) for a broad view on mining-related risks, and Sonter et al. (2020) on biodiversity impacts. Energy intensity of mining and minerals processing encumbers materials intense technologies (previous endnote 13) by worsening both GHG emission potential and broader sustainability criteria. Declining grades for many critical minerals ores means increasing energy inputs and emissions outputs. See Michot Foss et al. (2020) for a review of mining and minerals considerations for G20 briefing materials including background references on critical minerals, battery chemistries and performance, life cycle analysis results on batteries, and other aspects. See congressional testimony by Michot Foss (2020) on minerals and materials inputs for energy transition for public comments and resource links including life cycle aspects.
17. BNEF proprietary reports indicate these rough shares for wind and solar.

18. Based on BNEF proprietary reports on Chinese renewable energy transactions. The financial exposure associated with subsidies paid to developers and sellers of internal wind and solar power has soared, so much so that proposals have been made for a bond issue, likely through China's State Grid, to cover the roughly $158 billion subsidy burden at its estimated peak in 2032. Various sources, including BNEF, report on plans to phase out subsidies, but similar announcements have been made in the past, to little effect.
19. Based on BP's Statistical Review of World Energy 2019 (BP 2019), https://www.bp.com/en/global/corporate/energy-economics/statistical-review-of-world-energy.html. China has commanded more than half of world coal use since 2011 and has ramped up coal generation capacity steadily over the past 50 or so years, fluctuating around business cycles and key events like the 2008 Olympics buildout. From BNEF data, it is clear that battery manufacturing emissions in China are worsened by coal-fired power generation. See ongoing research at Rice University's Baker Institute on China's energy infrastructure, including electric vehicle battery production for illustration, https://www.bakerinstitute.org/chinas-energy-infrastructure/ and for details and sources https://www.bakerinstitute.org/opensource-mapping-of-chinas-energy-infrastructure/. Other locations for expanding battery making, such as Poland, would face similar hurdles.
20. See presentation by Michot Foss to the Federation of Scientists-Energy Permanent Monitoring Panel, August 19, 2019, Erice, Italy, as posted, https://www.bakerinstitute.org/research/energy-transition/
21. This observation is drawn from extensive interactions [by the lead editor] with leaders of natural gas industry trade associations, senior managements, and boards. For one meeting, a request was made to not use the term "methane" in presentation materials for a trade association audience, given heightened sensitivities.
22. "Fugitive" emission is natural gas that escapes during drilling, extraction, and/or pipeline transportation. Industry typically is able to avoid fugitive emissions by deploying proactive measures. Flaring and venting are intentional in nature. As noted by the US DOE, "both of these activities routinely occur during oil and natural gas development as part of drilling, production, gathering, processing, and transportation operations. The reasons behind both flaring and venting may be related to safety, economics, operational expediency, or a combination of all three". Delays and other problems that prevent development of midstream field-to-market linkages in timely fashion can prolong flaring (see Chap. 1 on the US midstream with analogies for Canada).

23. Throughout this book, we use the term "unconventional" following the simple US EIA definition for hydrocarbon production that does not flow readily to a wellbore.
24. In many countries where natural gas is produced as a by-product of oil, insufficient capacity and market exist to capture associated gas, and flaring can be persistent. Nigeria represents a classic case of difficulty in building internal markets, especially to support gas-fired power generation, or other export strategies to reduce flaring. Many countries have penalties for flaring that are not enforced. The Global Gas Flaring Reduction Partnership (GGFR) was formed in recognition of this problem and the need for solutions, https://www.worldbank.org/en/programs/gasflaringreduction. Not everyone agrees that anti-flaring initiatives get the intended results. See Calel and Mahdavi (2020) for a recent review.
25. While it involved a natural gas storage facility, the GAO and Interagency Task Force reports on the Aliso Canyon leak near Los Angeles in 2015 (GAO 2017b and ITF 2016) also make for useful reading. The US Department of Transportation's Pipeline and Hazardous Materials Safety Administration (PHMSA) posted its final rules on Aliso Canyon at https://primis.phmsa.dot.gov/ung/index.htm
26. Electrolysis of water using alternative energy sources such as wind and solar would supplant natural gas and provide green hydrogen as the ultimate solution, but high capital cost of dedicating wind and solar capacity to electrolysis would lead to more expensive hydrogen.
27. All from BP's Annual Statistical Review of World Energy, June 2019, https://www.bp.com/en/global/corporate/energy-economics.html
28. Ibid.
29. The GEFC (Gas Exporting Countries Forum), established in 2001, is a good example of how the multiplicity of suppliers makes cartelization difficult, if not impossible. Both natural gas supply and demand expanded significantly in recent years, making cartelization of gas production even more difficult. Expansion of exports from countries where governments leave decisions on contracted volumes to private operators based on commercial imperatives (the US and Australia) is a major obstacle. While the link to oil pricing has been weakened, it has not been because of cartel influence but rather because of liberalization and deepening of the global natural gas market.
30. A question is reliability of the US as an LNG supplier to European buyers, should the American natural gas industry face strong decarbonization or related constraints, as noted earlier and in Chap. 1. As we completed our book, French utility Engie suspended negotiations on a $7 billion contract to purchase LNG from the proposed Rio Grande project in Texas. It is not clear whether the action was a harbinger of things to come or a reflection

of pandemic-induced impacts on demand and budgets to support transactions. See Eaton and McFarlane (2020), among many other news sources.
31. Observation of trends based on data from Statista, www.statista.com, that draws from various Chinese national data sources and reports.
32. From company web sites: http://yamallng.ru/en/project/about/ and http://www.novatek.ru/en/business/yamal-lng/. Last accessed November 19, 2020.
33. Apparently in PA and Permian gas production is currently pretty much back to 2019 levels "as if 2020 never happened".
34. Observation from a reviewer for this book, Blake Eskew, IHSMarkit, September 2019.

References

Acemoglu, Daron, and James A Robinson. 2012. Why Nations Fail: The Origins of Power, Prosperity and Poverty (1st). 1st ed. New York: Crown, 529.

Blanchette, J., and J.E. Hillman. 2020. China's digital silk road after the coronavirus, Center for Strategic & International Studies. https://www.csis.org/analysis/chinas-digital-silk-road-after-coronavirus. Last accessed on 11 May 2020.

Brady, H.T. 2020. Problems in climate science from the viewpoint of an historical geologist. ACDE seminar -October 6th, the Arnt-Corden Department of Economics, Crawford School of Public Policy, ANU College of Asia and the Pacific. https://s3.amazonaws.com/jo.nova/guest/usa/brady-howard/anu-seminar-final.pdf

Braw, E. 2017. China needs to spell out its arctic ambitions, to ease suspicions. *South China Morning Post*, November 21. https://www.scmp.com/comment/insight-opinion/article/2120850/china-needs-spell-out-its-arctic-ambitions-ease-suspicions

Calel, R., and P. Mahdavi. 2020. Opinion: The unintended consequences of anti-flaring policies—And measures for mitigation. *Proceedings of the National Academy of Sciences* 117 (23): 12503–12507. https://www.pnas.org/content/pnas/117/23/12503.full.pdf

Clean Energy Manufacturing Analysis Center (CEMAC), 2017, Benchmarks of Global Clean Energy Manufacturing, NREL/TP-6A50-65619, January. https://www.nrel.gov/docs/fy17osti/65619.pdf

De La Fuente, Diego, R. A. Meidl, and M. Michot Foss. 2021. SF_6: The Little Gas That Could… Make Global Warming Worse. Forbes. https://www.forbes.com/sites/thebakersinstitute/2021/03/25/sf6-the-little-gas-that-could-make-global-warming-worse/?sh=39c0796522ad

Eaton, C., and S. McFarlane. 2020. France's Engie backs out of U.S. LNG Deal. *Wall Street Journal*, November 3 (updated). https://www.wsj.com/articles/frances-engie-backs-out-of-u-s-lng-deal-11604435609. Subscription or other access required.

Forde, M. 2020. PwC, AmCham China predict companies will pursue a 'China+1' strategy after COVID-19. *Supply Chain Dive.* https://www.supplychaindive.com/news/coronavirus-companies-expect-china-operations-normalize-under-3-months-pwc/576355/. Last accessed on 11 May 2020.

FP Analytics. 2019. Mining the future – Foreign policy, special report on China, May 1. https://foreignpolicy.com/2019/05/01/mining-the-future-china-critical-minerals-metals/. Subscription access required.

Frith, J. 2019. Lithium-ion battery manufacturing emissions, Bloomberg New Energy Finance (BNEF), June 27. Proprietary report.

Gülen, S.G. 2019. Net social cost of electricity: Policy smog and waning competitive markets, lack of consumer participation, importance of the grid, and scalability challenge, The University of Texas at Austin-Bureau of Economic Geology Udden Series, 86 p. https://store.beg.utexas.edu/special-books/3777-us0007-net-social-cost-of-electricity.html

Hausfather, Z., and G.P. Peters. 2020. Emissions – The 'business as usual' story is misleading. *Nature* 577 (January): 618–620. https://www.nature.com/articles/d41586-020-00177-3. Subscription or other access may be required.

IEA. 2011. *World energy outlook special report: Are we entering a golden age of gas?* 130 p. Paris: IEA/OECD. https://webstore.iea.org/weo-2011-special-report-are-we-entering-a-golden-age

———. 2019. *World energy investment*, 176 p. Paris: IEA/OECD. https://webstore.iea.org/world-energy-investment-2019

International Energy Agency (IEA). 2012. *World energy outlook special report: Golden rules for the golden age of gas*, 155 p. Paris: IEA/OECD. https://webstore.iea.org/weo-2012-special-report-golden-rules-for-a-golden-age-of-gas

Jacobs, T. 2020. Innovators seek to transform flaring into money and power. *Journal of Petroleum Technology.* Society of Petroleum Engineers, March 1. SPE membership or subscription or other access required.

K&L Gates. 2020. The H_2 handbook. https://www.klgates.com/epubs/h2-handbook/index.html

Lee, J., M. Bazilian, B. Sovacool, and S. Greene. 2020. Responsible or reckless? A critical review of the environmental and climate assessments of mineral supply chains. *Environmental Research Letters* 15 (10), October 13. https://iopscience.iop.org/article/10.1088/1748-9326/ab9f8c. Subscription or other access may be required.

Lindzen, R.S. 2020. An oversimplified picture of the climate behavior based on a single process can lead to distorted conclusions. *The European Physical Journal – Plus* 135 (462). https://doi.org/10.1140/epjp/s13360-020-00471-z. Access required.

Magnus, G., 2018, Red Flags: Why Xi's China is in Jeopardy, 1st Edition, Yale University Press, 248 p.

McMahon, Dinny, 2018, China's Great Wall of Debt: Shadow Banks, Ghost Cities, Massive Loans, and the End of the Chinese Miracle, Houghton Mifflin Harcourt, 288 p.

Medlock, K.B. III, S.R. Miles, and M. Hook. 2020. "Green LNG" – A pathway for natural gas in an ESG future?. *Forbes*, October 26. https://www.forbes.com/sites/thebakersinstitute/2020/10/26/green-lng%2D%2Da-pathway-for-natural-gas-in-an-esg-future/?sh=4757b1a566e9

Michot Foss, M. 2020. Critical minerals considerations for energy transitions, testimony before the Subcommitte on environment and climate, U.S. House Energy & Commerce Committee. Hearing on "Building a 100 Percent Clean Economy: Opportunities for an Equitable, Low-Carbon Recovery", September 16. https://energycommerce.house.gov/committee-activity/hearings/hearing-on-building-a-100-percent-clean-economy-opportunities-for-an-0

Michot Foss, M., and K. Zoellmer. 2020. Will electric vehicles transform distribution networks? Only time will tell. IAEE Energy Forum, Second quarter, 19–21, 28. https://www.iaee.org/en/publications/fullnewsletter.aspx?id=103. IAEE membership required.

Michot Foss, M., M.S. Moats, and K. Awuah-Offei. 2020. Framing energy and minerals for future pathways, policy brief for Task force 10, sustainable energy, water and food systems. G20 Saudi Arabia. https://t20saudiarabia.org.sa/en/briefs/Pages/Policy-Brief.aspx?pb=TF10_PB12

Ottersbach, N. 2018. Why the EU should ban SF6, Energypost.EU, May 21. https://energypost.eu/why-the-eu-should-ban-sf6/

Reuters. 2019. China leads the race to exploit deep sea minerals: U.N. body, U.S. News and world report, October 23. https://money.usnews.com/investing/news/articles/2019-10-23/china-leads-the-race-to-exploit-deep-sea-minerals-un-body

Roston, E. 2018. Russia is building $320 million icebreakers to carve new arctic routes. *Bloomberg Businessweek*, July 9. https://www.bloomberg.com/news/articles/2018-07-09/russia-is-building-320-million-icebreakers-to-carve-new-arctic-routes?sref=QKlHH2Pn. Subscription or other access required.

Schlachter, F. 2012. The back page – Has the battery bubble burst? *APS News* 21 (8), August/September. https://www.aps.org/publications/apsnews/201208/backpage.cfm

Sonter, L.J., M.C. Dade, J.E.M. Watson, R.K. Valenta. 2020. Renewable energy production will exacerbate mining threats to biodiversity. *Nature Communications* 11(4174), September 1. https://www.nature.com/articles/s41467-020-17928-5. Subscription or other access may be required.

Thomas, C.E. 2009. Fuel cell and battery electric vehicles compared. *International Journal of Hydrogen Energy* 34 (15): 6005–6020. https://doi.org/10.1016/j.ijhydene.2009.06.003. Subscription or other access required.

U.S. Department of Energy (U.S. DOE). 2015. Quadrennial technology review. https://www.energy.gov/sites/prod/files/2017/03/f34/quadrennial-technology-review-2015_1.pdf

U.S. Government Accountability Office (GAO). 2017a. Pipeline safety: Additional actions could improve federal use of data on pipeline materials and corrosion, August, 55 p. https://www.gao.gov/assets/690/686390.pdf

———. 2017b. Natural gas storage: Department of Transportation could take additional steps to improve safety enforcement planning, November, 44 p. https://www.gao.gov/assets/690/688553.pdf

———. 2018a. Gas pipeline safety: Stakeholders' and officials' views on federal odorizing requirements, April, 27 p. https://www.gao.gov/assets/700/691319.pdf

———. 2018b. Interstate pipeline inspections: Additional planning could help DOT determine appropriate level of state participation, May, 25 p. https://www.gao.gov/assets/700/692059.pdf

U.S. Interagency Task Force (ITF). 2016. Ensuring safe and reliable underground natural gas storage, October, 92 p. https://www.energy.gov/sites/prod/files/2016/10/f33/Ensuring%20Safe%20and%20Reliable%20Underground%20Natural%20Gas%20Storage%20-%20Final%20Report.pdf

USDRIVE. 2017. Electrochemical energy storage technical team roadmap, U.S. DOE. https://www.energy.gov/sites/prod/files/2017/11/f39/EESTT%20roadmap%202017-10-16%20Final.pdf

Vijayagopal, R. 2016. Comparing the powertrain energy and power densities of electric and gasoline vehicles, Argonne National Laboratory. Presentation at the University of Michigan Transportation Research Institute, July 20. http://www.umtri.umich.edu/sites/default/files/Ram.Vijayagopal.ANL_.PTS21.2016.pdf

Vijayagopal, R., K. Gallagher, D. Lee, and A. Rousseau. 2016. Comparing the powertrain energy densities of electric and gasoline vehicles. SAE technical paper 2016-01-0903, https://doi.org/10.4271/2016-01-0903.

Wainberg, M., M. Michot Foss, G. Gülen, D. Quijano, 2017. Current and future natural gas demand in China and India. The University of Texas at Austin, Bureau of Economic Geology's Center for Energy Economics, April 2017. https://www.beg.utexas.edu/files/cee/legacy/2017/CEE_Research_Paper-China_and_India_Current_Future_Natural_Gas_Demand-Apr17.pdf

Wang, H., and I.J. Duncan. 2014a. Understanding the nature of risks associated with onshore natural gas gathering pipelines. *Journal of Loss Prevention in the Process Industries* 29: 49–55. https://doi.org/10.1016/j.jlp.2014.01.007.

———. 2014b. Likelihood, causes, and consequences of focused leakage and rupture of U.S. natural gas transmission pipelines. *Journal of Loss Prevention in the Process Industries* 30: 177–187. https://doi.org/10.1016/j.jlp.2014.05.009.

Yergin, D. 2020. The new geopolitics of energy. *Wall Street Journal* September 11. https://www.wsj.com/articles/the-new-geopolitics-of-energy-11599836521?mod=searchresults&page=1&pos=1. Subscription or other access required.

Appendix: All of the "Pre-reading" You Could Ever Want

Michelle Michot Foss

Overview

This appendix provides essential information for the reader. It offers a broad overview of the U.S. natural gas industry system and components; the regulatory landscape with a brief, relevant historical context; and a snapshot of natural gas system pricing using public domain information (U.S. Energy Information Administration).

Natural Gas System Value Chain

Structure, Organization and Interactions

As with any industry, typical natural gas system supply and value chains can be substantial in scale and scope (Tussing and Barlow 1984 and Tussing and Tippee 1995 remain the starting points for mapping the U.S. natural gas industry pre- and post-restructuring; see later section on Regulatory Oversight and History). Even a cursory review of Fig. A.1, the U.S. system in a nutshell, should provide a sense of the richness and complexity. We think of "richness" in terms of "liquidity", in both participants and

M. Michot Foss
Baker Institute for Public Policy, Rice University, Houston, TX, USA

M. Michot Foss et al. (eds.), *Monetizing Natural Gas in the New "New Deal" Economy*,
https://doi.org/10.1007/978-3-030-59983-6

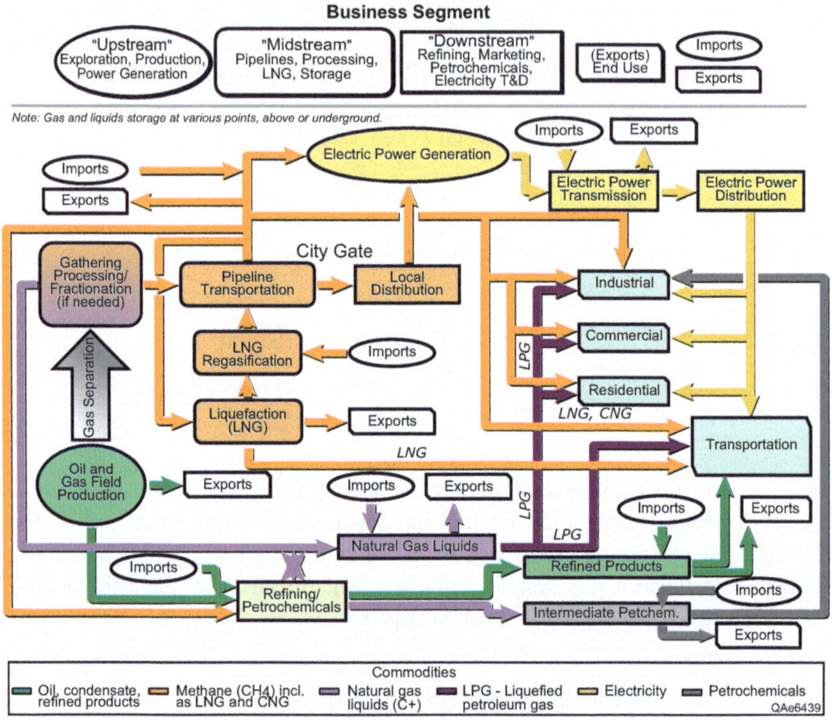

Fig. A.1 Natural gas system value chain. (Source: Developed by the author. Notes: Natural gas liquids (NGLs) may also be termed natural gas plant liquids (NGPLs) after processing. For other specific terms, refer to list of acronyms for this book. The U.S. EIA glossary, https://www.eia.gov/tools/glossary/, and PetroWiki, created and maintained by the SPE, also is useful for terminology, https://www.petrowiki.org/PetroWiki)

financial backing, potential interactions and linkages. The U.S. system is notable for the sheer number of opportunities for transactions with associated multiples and, not least, government intervention. In practice, the more open and accessible a system value chain, the more liquid but also more complicated it becomes. An annual review of natural gas transactions reported to the U.S. Federal Energy Regulatory Commission (FERC) indicates that, on average during 2018, a natural gas molecule was traded about 2.4 times from point of production to point of end use (Leonard et al. 2019).

Numerous innovations have been devised to deal with systemic complexity, and associated risk and uncertainty ranging from: new sources of supply (resource plays in the United States and Canada); contracting to manage specific customer needs; financial market outlets for mitigating price and other risk; engineering, procurement and construction (EPC) project management approaches to gain control over the myriad infrastructure development risks and uncertainties. While the depiction shown in Fig. A.1 is most representative of the United States and Canada, the main physical elements exist in every location that accommodates natural gas as piped methane, liquefied natural gas (LNG) and natural gas liquids (NGLs) and use of methane for electric power generation. The more significant differences across countries lie in political oversight of the industry. Many countries continue to engage in active forms of economic regulation or outright sovereign control including ownership of: the resource as well as system supply; network access or the network itself; and pricing for both supply and system services. How government jurisdictions interact with their natural gas industries and the methods chosen to impose oversight or control can create any number of tensions and conflicts across the entire system and, in too many situations, lost efficiencies and efficacies. (See Chaps. 5 and 6 for a full treatment of these dilemmas.) The United States has afforded many lessons in this regard, as mentioned in various places through this chapter and book.

In simplest terms, Fig. A.1 separates the functional boundaries of:

- "Upstream", exploration, development and production of resources.
- "Midstream", including gathering or aggregating wellhead production, along with processing to separate gaseous from liquid fractions of the production stream and treatment to remove impurities. Liquefaction and the LNG global shipping and trading businesses are included in midstream. Storage, both above (as LNG) and below ground, also is considered a midstream function.
- "Downstream". For natural gas, downstream incorporates lower-pressure local distribution of methane as well as the commonly recognized downstream businesses of oil refining and petrochemicals and products marketing. Downstream also encompasses refining and petrochemical uses of the various components of natural gas, which include methane and NGLs. NGLs are gases heavier than methane that become liquid under pressure: ethane (C_2), propane (C_3), butane (C_4) and isobutane, and pentane (C_5; a common reference is to "pentanes plus" or natural gasoline, which includes molecules heavier than pentane). Distribution of liquid petroleum gas (LPG, a mixture of propane and butane) also belongs to this category.

The disposition of dry natural gas (methane) across the huge US system is depicted in Fig. A.2 to provide physical context for the reader. Growth in natural gas use as the U.S. economy recovered from the December 2007–June 2009 recession also has been spurred by shifts away from coal for power generation, including retirements (as discussed in Chap. 2), the boost in demand for petrochemicals (addressed in Chap. 3) and North American pipeline and LNG exports (Chaps. 1 and 4). At time of publication, 2020 gas production (and exports) had fallen sharply but also recovered sharply by early 2021. Methane delivered to customers barely registered pandemic effects.

Overall, considerable overlap exists between oil and natural gas midstream and downstream functions as molecules are separated, isolated, recombined, marketed and sold for value capture in countless ways. Electric power is a natural gas end user with its own value chain. In Fig. A.1, electric power generation is shown as an upstream function given how natural gas generation has emerged as a distinct business (see more extensive

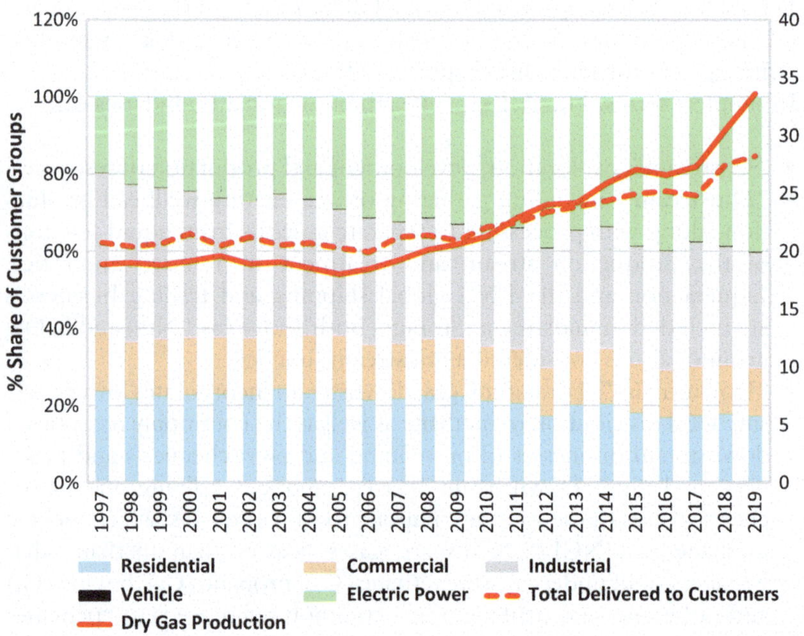

Fig. A.2 Shares of customer groups and total consumption. (Source: EIA author calculations and depiction)

discussion below). The wholesale price of electricity is driven by, and nets back to, the wellhead value of gas production plus transportation cost. “Spark spread” (see later Fig. A.4) captures that value creation, the difference between the price paid to the generator for electricity and the cost the generator paid for natural gas fuel. Transmission and distribution of electrons are downstream of the electric power “burner tip”.

The LNG portion of the system value chain resides in the middle of Fig. A.1. Importantly, LNG plays a role in domestic gas transactions. In the United States, Canada, Europe and other locations, piped gas is often liquefied and stored in above-ground tanks for seasonal peaks. In the United States, imported LNG is usually regasified and may be re-liquefied at peak shaving storage locations. In some locations, such as New England, imported LNG is distributed via truck to satellite storage locations for peak seasonal use in local distribution systems. LNG also provides options for use of natural gas, such as vehicle transport. More is said later on all of these. When it comes to LNG and its place within the Fig. A.1 scheme, the main emphasis for this book is on the large, growing, global LNG supply and value chain which offers access to international trade beyond the reach of large diameter, long-distance pipelines.

The liquefaction and regasification portions of the LNG value chain segment are annotated with a dashed upstream symbol. The “upstream” connotation of midstream-positioned assets relates to a 2002 decision by the FERC, which has regulatory jurisdiction over LNG import and export facilities, to allow operators of these facilities to control capacity as if the facilities were equivalent to producing fields, the alternative sources of supply. In other words, the FERC maintains no regulatory oversight over pricing of LNG facility capacity or the commodity. The FERC allows owners and other capacity holders to utilize all of the capacity as they see fit and at market prices. The FERC’s concurrence with industry arguments reflected an acknowledgment of the risks of developing large-scale LNG import/export facilities, even though for many the FERC judgment seemed to fly in the face of the transformation to open access for pipelines (see Knowles 2003). This jurisdictional boundary, as illustrated in Fig. A.1, is associated with cryogenic tanks that store LNG, regasification capacity for send out of imported LNG via pipelines and liquefaction capacity—the large “trains” that liquefy pipeline gas for sale abroad.

Apart from large-scale LNG import/export facilities, LNG storage that exists across the United States may be part of interstate pipelines under FERC jurisdiction, or large intrastate pipelines and gas distribution companies/utilities that are overseen by state public utility commissions (PUCs).[1]

In the case of either, LNG storage would be part of the pipeline and distribution rate base, the fixed capital upon which operators earn regulated returns, with the molecules or commodity subject to market prices. While the FERC tends to allow interstate pipelines to charge market-based rates or equivalent, rules for intrastate pipelines and utilities vary across states.

Economic Drivers
A number of observations can be drawn about the natural gas system value chain economic drivers. These are dealt with throughout the book.

Upstream Matters!
As I made clear in Chap. 1, all value chains begin upstream and are influenced by upstream cost structures. Components of the price of gas that customers pay begin with the cost of production, wherever it is located. Apart from US federal, state and tribal lands, hydrocarbon resources are privately owned. Outside of the United States, resources are sovereign owned, with varying degrees of access when it comes to exploration drilling and development rights. In a large number of countries, national oil companies, commonly referred to as NOCs, retain control over hydrocarbon resources.

Within the United States and worldwide, upstream costs vary considerably across basins and plays; across countries and fiscal systems; and across operating companies, and service and equipment suppliers. As a general rule, and as demonstrated throughout this book, natural gas supply will be more competitive and attractively priced:

- The more liberal and competitive the access to mineral resources and the rights to develop them.
- The more enabling the terms of participation, regardless of public or private ownership of resources.
- The more adept the operating company.
- The better equipped and staffed the service industry.
- As dealt with extensively in Chap. 1, the more that methane output can be leveraged by production of higher value, larger molecules, in particular black oil.

Beyond upstream conditions, the cost of delivered supply becomes a matter of distance to market. More remote customers must be willing (and able) to pay a price that can attract supplies and/or domestic upstream activity and/or substitutes. Too many customer nations do not have the wherewithal, or the creditworthiness (perhaps even more crucial, as explained in Chaps. 5 and 6), to attract LNG or expensive pipeline imports. Too many countries, overall, have fiscal regimes that are unfriendly to resource development. Too many countries have inadequate "commercial frameworks", in our parlance, to support natural gas market development on the whole. And, in too many countries this is the case even when domestic resources exist and could be exploited for economic benefits and quality of life improvements.

Midstream Transportation Is Key

For natural gas, in particular methane destined for consumer end use, pipeline networks are key. Liquid fuels have an advantage in the many modes of transportation that can be used. Crude oil and petroleum products can be moved via truck or an array of waterborne options and more easily stored until transported. Methane transport beyond pipelines requires compression or liquefaction for favorable economics; both options are discussed later. With pipelines, as with other infrastructure, scale is important to keeping unit costs low and meeting revenue targets. The more robust the demand for piped methane, the easier it is to justify costs for and development of large, dense pipeline networks. While industrial and power generation offtake helps to underpin pipeline costs, the best examples of large, dense methane pipeline networks are those in locations with distinct winter heating demand. The long history of long-distance methane pipelines in the United States and Canada illustrates these points well. Tremendous volumes of methane in the US southwest and Gulf Coast, including the first shallow water offshore production, and in western Canada supported the cost to convert oil pipelines and/or build new, state-of-the-art, large-diameter, high-compression methane pipelines. These investments enabled delivery of volumes for industrial use (World War II was a driver) and to the large receiving markets with substantial winter heating load. Produced methane was substituted for "town gas" manufactured from coal in these urban markets and in other municipal locations where methane was beginning to compete with energy sources like wood and coal. Seasonal premium prices for winter heating fuel, in effect, helped to amortize much of the U.S. and Canadian natural gas pipeline and distribution system.

In the United States, Canada and some other countries such as the UK and Australia, most pipeline operators do not own the methane they carry. They rely on tariffs to amortize and earn returns on pipeline investment.

Tariffs represent a midstream claim on the spread between what the producer collects for methane at the wellhead and what the end user pays. The ability to collect tariffs represents the value of connecting, with transportation service, methane supply and consumption. The adequacy of methane reserves and prospective consumption is thus crucial to the economics of pipeline construction.

The later section on regulation recaps U.S. pipeline industry development and touches on the shift in thinking about the sanctity of interstate (cross-state), federally regulated pipeline capacity. Canada experienced similar revisionist thinking and indeed led the United States in experimenting with rules governing how gas pipelines were developed and operated. In short, the typical arrangement was for long-distance carriage of methane to be bundled, with the pipeline operator providing both gas and transportation. Pipelines held supply contracts with producers and sales contracts with local gas distributors, with stiff take-or-pay (TOP) terms if contracted gas supply or transportation volumes were not met. In effect, pipelines operated as merchants. The drive to "unbundle" the pipeline transportation system enabling anyone who needed access to pipeline capacity to get it, and to remove potential or real discriminatory conflicts of interest embedded in the control pipeline operators had over their facilities, all underline the open, competitive Canada-U.S. markets that are in effect today.

In many countries, NOCs control the major value chain system components (midstream to downstream) in addition to hydrocarbon resources, with varying models for foreign and indigenous investment and/or equity ownership. These ownership and control structures, while they may have political appeal, introduce numerous constraints to innovation and efficiency and impinge on capital investment flows for pipeline transportation. Many of these market locations do not have seasonal premiums for natural gas use and thus depend on other end users—industrial and especially electric power generation—to serve as impetus for pipeline investments. Chapter 6 provides more coverage on these topics.

LNG "Fuels" Global Ambitions

Beyond some distance, movement of natural gas (methane) from field to market becomes problematic. Unlike liquid fuels, methane cannot be shipped overseas without changing phase. The most typical approach is cryogenic liquefaction (chilling natural gas to minus 256 degrees F). The phase change shrinks gas volume by a factor of 600 and makes ship transport potentially economic. Clearly, the cost of liquefaction and shipping must be absorbed in the receiving market. This typically has been done by charging an LNG price linked to a crude oil index or a basket of crude oil prices, with an adjustment mechanism that balances gains and losses between suppliers and buyers as oil prices fluctuate. Receiving customers that have been willing to enter into such arrangements are most commonly those with limited or no domestic natural gas resource endowments and high supply security sensitivity. As a group, industrialized Japan, South Korea and Taiwan are still the largest buyers of LNG in the world today at more than twice the volume of China and India.[2] As documented in Chap. 4, widely held expectations are that LNG demand growth will center in the latter two countries.

As noted in the Foreward, Chaps. 1 and 4 and elsewhere in the book, numerous attempts are being made to convert at least some portion of international LNG sales to a "natural gas price", with the U.S. price index (Henry Hub) most often the candidate. A consideration is whether gyrations within U.S. natural gas markets could disrupt customer comfort levels with contracts linked to the Henry Hub price index. Current low prices and lower volatility are muffling these concerns. Paralleling the trend toward natural gas price–indexed LNG contracts is a desire among both sellers and buyers for more flexibility to change destinations and engage in other market clearing tactics such as swaps, short-term sales and ship-to-ship transfers. As noted in Chap. 4, however, contract terms during 2018 lengthened, highlighting the differences in contracting practices between new projects with debt and equity financing and thus sensitive cash flow waterfalls and established locations, in particular those with uncommitted spare capacity.

A host of dilemmas, from good (how best to capture potential new opportunities) to bad (reduced revenues to LNG project developers, for instance), can arise with such a profound strategy shift. At issue is whether more competitive LNG prices, an artifact of a cheaper US Henry Hub price, along with shorter contract durations, elimination of restrictive TOP clauses and the ability to change (at a cost) LNG ship manifests can support LNG value chain cost and development as effectively as traditional oil-linked contract transactions. The bottom line in these debates will hinge on what financiers may be willing to accept given the perceived riskiness of any proposed LNG project.

Storage Makes Markets

Liquefaction can also help to solve a crucial problem in natural gas systems—storage. In the United States, Canada and Europe storage for natural gas is primarily underground (depleted producing fields or salt caverns). Above-ground (LNG tank) capacity can be used for satellite storage and peak shaving. Any or all forms of storage can be part of pipeline and/or local distribution networks or operated independently. Natural gas use invariably will reflect seasonal and cyclical patterns of demand. Countries with strong seasonal heating and cooling swings require storage to balance the system. (Per above, countries without strong seasonal swings may face a different problem stemming from insufficient core demand to support pipeline and distribution infrastructure investment.)

In the United States and Canada, it is typical to find LNG satellite facilities. In some locations, like New England, imported LNG provides crucial supply for winter heating. As noted, imported LNG is distributed via truck to satellite storage locations, and then ultimately regasified and delivered to customers via pipeline. In countries with sizeable LNG import tank storage, those terminal bases can be used for seasonal peak management.

Around the world, prospects for underground storage capacity vary widely, but one thing is for sure—it is tough to beat the U.S. portfolio of underground storage assets, clocking in at about 9260 Bcf of capacity with roughly half of that available for "working gas" in the form of seasonal methane injections and withdrawals. The natural gas, oil and petrochemicals industries have made effective use of the rich abundance of salt dome features scattered along the U.S. Gulf Coast, a unique geological occurrence in size and extent of salt layers. Salt cavern storage for methane, about 716 Bcf of total capacity of which about 500 Bcf is working gas, is more expensive to develop but can provide a faster response with higher recovery of stored volumes during extreme seasonal swings. Storage in depleted fields tends to be cheaper, but with more investment in unrecoverable "cushion gas". Stored natural gas in depleted fields also is slower to drawdown but generally better integrated with the pipeline grid. Similar conditions would manifest in other countries and regions.

In countries like the United States and Canada, with distinct and price-sensitive winter consumer heating markets, the ability to release natural gas from storage to meet peak seasonal needs is crucial to offsetting pressure on prices and ensuring reliability throughout the natural gas system. Storage assets are more attractive to investors and more easily financed with seasonal volatility that provides intrinsic value, the difference between seasonal lows that facilitate acquisition of gas supply cheaply and the seasonal highs that provide price premiums for capital recovery and profitability. Outside of countries with seasonal swings, storage can still be crucial for balancing variations in demand with economic activity or because of energy system disruptions. Japan's experience following the 2011 tsunami, damage to the Fukushima nuclear base and suspension of nuclear energy generation in the country demonstrated the usefulness of LNG storage (and how LNG storage could be quickly cycled). Storage adds to liquidity in a natural gas market system with capacity, participants and mechanisms of exchange. Can effective, efficient natural gas markets evolve and be sustained without ample storage endowments or options?

All Natural Gas "Politics is Local"

That wonderful phrase, commonly associated with then Speaker of the U.S. House of Representatives Tip O'Neill, perfectly captures natural gas industry political dynamics. As shown in Fig. A.1, natural gas is transferred often, but not always, through a "city gate", the metering system operated by lower-pressure local distribution networks that take gas from higher-pressure pipelines. The local networks are often referred to as local distribution companies, or LDCs. These tend to be regulated, investor-owned gas utilities, standalone or combined with electricity and/or water delivery, regulated at the state and/or municipal levels (some are part of municipally owned and operated utilities). LDCs have long been the touchstone for U.S. natural gas industry political interactions. For decades LDCs were the primary buyers, acting as the "offtakers" for supply agreements that interstate pipeline companies held with producers in the old pipeline merchant business model. Those supply contracts along with pipeline capacity rights for delivery were, at times, contentious in many states and locales. Where LDC systems were poorly served by pipelines, market power was the source of conflict. LDC mileage is the larger component of overall natural gas system mileage. Maintenance costs and safety considerations follow accordingly.

The significant liberalizing credo in Canada and the United States, emulated in many other countries, was to operationalize the widespread acknowledgment that pipeline capacity could be auctioned and allocated through transparent platforms among competing users. Restructuring took away the ability for pipelines to control their own capacity but, ironically, hastened the transition away from reliance on LDCs as the major pipeline customers. This shift away from LDCs has been true especially for larger, steadier volume customers like industrials and electric power generators. Almost any of these larger-volume customers can bypass LDC fees and take gas directly from pipelines, and they have done so. The long-established stance among regulators has been to allow "economic bypass" for the benefits conferred across the economy. It is no surprise that the rapid growth in gas-fired power generation mostly has been along pipeline routes and where generators can also tap directly into power transmission grids. However, bypass and direct pipeline interconnections for larger customers leave the political problem of allocating the higher marginal costs of LDC systems to higher marginal cost, smaller volume, more erratic, mainly residential consumers.

Based on industry data, gas supply cost is the larger portion of typical LDC customer bills. LDC maintenance and operations (M&O) costs have come to the forefront as systems age, shifts in demographics and U.S. building stock occur, and economic fortunes in LDC service areas grow or sag. Gas utilities have struggled with these trends, arguing for regulatory treatment of LDC capacity and systems that would provide consistent revenues.

Gas delivery via the LDC once formed the main point of state public utility regulatory oversight for the U.S. industry. Regulators across the U.S. states, and Canadian provinces, now commonly allow gas commodity price changes to pass through directly to LDC customers, albeit usually with review periods. It was once thought that the adoption of nondiscriminatory open access for pipelines would extend to LDC systems, pushing the liberalization process down to smaller retail consumers such as commercial businesses and even households. The idea was to provide a form of retail choice for gas supply with competing suppliers able to access LDC systems to serve customers. Gas retail choice has had very limited success in the United States. More success with retail choice has been achieved in Canada. Other examples include Great Britain[3] and the European Union.[4]

A final consideration for LDC economics has been the pervasive penetration of electric power devices, displacing delivered gas for what had been many base load applications. The affinity of home owners and buyers for electric appliances, rather than direct use of gas for heating buildings and water and for cooking, has deeply challenged LDC economics. This created new tensions around how best to cover and allocate LDC costs if systems are to remain viable. LDC gas systems are dense and urban development over the years has complicated system maintenance and safety. At some point, the difficulty and cost of sustaining LDC systems in the face of competition from electricity could force substantial tradeoffs, potentially altering the core, residential and commercial baseload of direct use of natural gas. LDCs still provide a valuable hedge against risks from weather and natural hazards, as distribution piping is buried. In most locations around the U.S., electric power distribution wires are above ground and exposed.

Natural Gas for Vehicle Transport Is Always the Future
Besides pipeline delivery and direct use, a number of other applications push natural gas into diverse transportation customer sectors. Natural gas vehicle transportation remains ambitious.

Methane in its densest phase as LNG can be deployed in a number of applications. Its cryogenic properties also can be creatively captured, for instance, for power plant cooling and for electronics. The 600-to-one improvement in energy density most often attracts interest for transportation. LNG ship operators have long captured "boil off" from tanks to supplement tanker operations. LNG can be siphoned from either export or import terminals and distributed for trucking. Or, methane can be withdrawn from pipelines, liquefied and dispensed for on-highway and regional truck refueling or even railroad locomotives. For land-based transport, LNG trucking has seemed most doable, with estimates[5] of about 5000 refueling locations needed for successful regional and interstate market penetration. LNG displacement of petroleum marine bunker fuels offers the most promise of late as a consequence of International Maritime Organization (IMO) rules and regulations to reduce sulfur and GHG emissions associated with shipping activities and to improve air quality in ports and harbors worldwide (Palmer-Huggins and Michot Foss 2016).

Costly liquefaction is not always needed to deploy methane in vehicle transport. Methane can be compressed; compressed natural gas, or CNG, allows about 300 times the molecules per unit of volume. This improved energy density enables CNG to compete effectively in some applications. An often-discussed value addition for LDC business portfolios is CNG refueling. LDC systems are a natural conduit for CNG businesses and many LDC fleets are run on CNG drawn from the LDC systems. A substantial barrier to entry for light-duty, passenger vehicle refueling is the sheer number of locations that would be needed. As many as 50,000 or more CNG retail locations would be required for sufficient refueling convenience. By comparison, roughly 160,000 retail gasoline outlets exist across the continental United States.[6] Many LDCs also own and operate LNG satellite storage and peaking facilities, and could engage in LNG vehicle solutions. For marine transport, CNG carriers have long been pursued mainly for shorter-distance, smaller cargo regional trade but commercialization has been slow. The first classified CNG ship was launched in 2016 for use in Indonesia.[7] One of the more interesting concepts is the use of CNG to transport gas supply within the contentious Eastern Mediterranean region, where pipeline projects and costs face huge hurdles (Sukkarieh 2019). Cost for development of a CNG shipping fleet relative to landed prices of natural gas in receiving locations is a primary consideration. CNG also has been under consideration for offshore gas production handling.

Most alluring, but most expensive, "gas-to-liquids", or GTL, offers the possibility of pushing natural gas into direct competition with refined oil products for transportation fuels. The Qatar Airways demonstration of GTL use to fuel a London to Doha flight is one of the more notable examples.[8] Nirvana for the natural gas industry would be reforming natural gas, typically using steam, to extract hydrogen which can be used to power vehicles—or many other things—via fuel cells and other technologies. Toyota Motor Company is perhaps the best-known backer of hydrogen fuel cell vehicle (HFCV) transport, with pilot programs and consumer rollouts in Japan and the United States of their flagship model, the Mirai. Toyota is pushing to lower costs to achieve a viable strategic alternative to electric vehicles and their associated battery supply chains (Tajitsu and Shiraki 2018). As noted in Chap. 7, hydrogen extracted from natural gas or water can be blended with methane to reduce carbon intensity of piped and delivered gas supply. A great deal still is needed to commercialize these approaches.

The attractiveness of methane, GTL or methane-derived hydrogen for any road or waterborne transportation is contingent upon the price of established, higher-density petroleum fuels along with the cost of converting existing vehicles or manufacturing new vehicle engines and model designs. Suffice to say, the incursion of natural gas into transport fuels markets has been uneven, at best. Short of a regulatory or policy "push", for which many are looking to the IMO rules, or green field opportunities in developing countries, with attendant risks, the challenge of amortizing large-scale investments in established markets remains substantial given the enormous presence of legacy petroleum fuels.

NGLs Can Provide Upstream Uplift

Natural gas liquids, extracted in processing plants or in refining and chemical facilities (refining gas liquids), afford distinct value-enhancing revenue streams. Crucially, upstream hydrocarbon rights agreements in countries where these apply would need to include natural gas liquids. Marketed natural gas is an input to petroleum refining; combined refining and chemical operations yield a wide array of intermediate products that are essential to countless industrial and consumer applications. Chapter 3 details this portion of the natural gas system. The distinct values for individual natural gas liquids are driven by relative demand for these molecules as feedstock (see Chap. 3 for details). This has placed a premium on the field-to-market transportation interface. While NGLs are often moved via pipeline, because they are liquids they are amenable to many other modes of transportation for internal and international trade.

Domestic liquid petroleum gas (LPG) distributors can be crucial for energy distribution to more remote or rural locations. In many countries, LPG constitutes the main domestic energy source for cooking and water and building heating. Some LPG distributors have ventured into LPG deployment for transportation. While not so common in the United States or North America, LPG for vehicle transport is often used in places like South Asia because of lower cost and lack of retail infrastructure for gasoline and diesel.

Along with offtake within the United States and North America, opportunities exist to export NGLs. LPG has well-established international markets. Demand for ethane is growing, including opportunities abroad. Ethane now is exported by ship in addition to pipeline transport. Nearly every final consumer product we use around the world today incorporates some components of plastics, waxes, advanced composites and other materials that derive from natural gas liquids and other hydrocarbons. As noted in Chap. 3, NGLs in trade increasingly will compete with refinery naphtha in petrochemical manufacture. The crux for the downstream businesses has always been profit margins, which are rapidly depleted once price spreads are detected, capital is mobilized and enormous tranches of new petrochemical capacity are commissioned to operate. As of this writing, the current cycle of investment and expansion to monetize comparatively cheap NGLs from U.S. production faces that same, historical, cyclical risk.

Electric Power Provides Base Load Offtake

Electric power offers an elegant solution for creating value from natural gas production. "Monetizing" natural gas supply via electric power generation, with the sale of electricity providing the price netback to the wellhead, is an increasingly common strategy worldwide. As noted elsewhere in this book, it is at the "electric power burner tip" where some of the more pressing challenges for the natural gas industry have come to rest.

The bottom-line issue, hotly contested, is continued reliance on a fossil fuel to generate electric power in an increasingly electrified new, "new" economy driven by renewable energy sources. A host of alternatives for electric power generation can exist, depending upon location. However, not all sources of energy for power generation are created equal when it comes to fixed and variable costs, time frame for cost recovery, system integration costs and, most vividly, public sensibilities and attendant political responses.

Natural gas–fueled power generation has evolved toward an economic business model akin to upstream, with unregulated, risk-taking independent power producers (IPPs) competing heavily for the most attractive real estate (access to gas pipeline connections, power grid interconnections, water for steam and cooling, low air quality risks for plant emissions and robust wholesale prices). When natural gas is cheap, as it has been, that low-cost fuel translates into cheaper electricity undermining profitability not only among gas IPPs themselves but also other generation sources (see Chap. 2). Nuclear, coal, hydroelectric and renewables were not built under competitive models. Nuclear and coal were developed under the regulated cost of service model implemented by state PUCs. Nuclear, coal and hydroelectric have long benefited from myriad sources of federal support. Federal and state subsidies and credits in various forms have fostered rapid build-out of renewable generation capacity. In most cases, nuclear and coal plants are fully amortized and are pressured when wholesale electricity prices are low, as explained in Chap. 2. Although renewables can survive owing to tax credits and long-term power purchase agreements (PPAs) in the short term, sustained low electricity prices threaten their commercial viability in the absence of subsidies.

As alluded to in other sections and chapters, the resulting clash of visions, realities and proposed solutions for how to keep the various power generation options alive and healthy has been harsh. These include the prospect of regulatory intervention (already underway to some extent) and a roll back toward integrated utility control of generation (also already underway in many cases) as well as a return to integrated resource planning (IRP), long a popular preference for balancing competing interests.

Crucial to value chain realization is recognition of how useful electric power can be as a conduit between the natural gas field and end user markets. Industry participants often speak of "gas by wire" with conversion of natural gas to electricity and the value of electricity sold providing the return value to wellhead production. As such, electric power will remain critical to natural gas resource development in U.S. and global energy, no matter how the game plays out. A further consideration is that electric power must be dispatched from the generation unit and sold, which requires transmission and distribution networks. High-voltage transmission and low-voltage distribution networks bear many of the same constraints that gas pipeline and distribution networks do. To wit: it is much cheaper, on a marginal cost basis, to serve larger, steadier load customers, such as factories than to serve variable loads from households.

Shifts in demand present ongoing challenges. For power generation sourced from traditional fuels and hydro (water) reservoirs and, to some extent, pumped storage, storage of energy can be embodied in the fuel. This trait has emerged as an underlying philosophy for efforts to preserve fossil fuel and nuclear generation capacity. The U.S. Department of Energy proposed a controversial rule supporting nuclear and coal on the basis of energy security and resilience related to stored fuels. The natural gas industry strongly opposed the DOE proposal, because natural gas was absent, and the FERC rejected it.[9] All of this is no small matter, given that renewable energy storage must be solved in some way, through backup and balancing provided by conventional generators, or from batteries or other solutions, none of which are cheap and all of which would have to be paid for (see Chap. 2 of this book as well as Gülen 2019 and Gülen et al. 2017, 2018 for exhaustive and exhausting treatments of this conundrum).

Lastly, LDCs that operate local electric power networks face the same challenges of increasing M&O costs as gas LDCs as systems age, demographics and building stock shift, economic fortunes in the LDC service area grow or sag. As with retail gas (methane), retail electric choice also has had limited penetration and many states that have adopted retail electric choice experience little turnover by customers and few competing providers (Tsai and Tsai 2018).[10]

Within the United States, much of the electric power value chain is owned and operated by investor-owned utilities (IOUs), subject to state PUC regulatory oversight. As mentioned in Chap. 1 and noted below in the overview of regulation, a considerable amount of experimentation, with varying degrees of success, has been undertaken. Power generation may still be in the hands of IOUs, or provided by competitive independent power producers or IPPs. Where electric power has been most strongly reorganized—Texas and the PJM market area—IOUs have been unbundled to separate generation from "T&D" in order to instill competition at least at the wholesale level and, in Texas, both wholesale and retail (Chap. 2 provides treatment of these and other regional examples). The FERC exerts regulatory oversight of high-voltage transmission that serves the interstate "bulk" market. Some independent entities exist for independent power transmission project development but with few, if any, results. Local distribution is generally the purview of state PUCs, sometimes with municipal authority or with municipal rights abrogated to state PUCs. Many integrated IOUs remain in place in the United States, with ownership of generation, transmission and distribution and regulated rates and prices determined through public utility cost of service ratemaking approaches. Even regulated IOUs may have access to wholesale power that is generated by IPPs. The United States remains populated by rural power cooperatives, and a number of large municipally owned and operated power utilities, often combined with water services. Outside of the United States, in too many countries, electric power remains sovereign owned and/or controlled. Even in Canada, "crown corporations" continue to provide the majority of power generation and service. Mexico's CFE is typical of strongly controlled sovereign electric power organizations worldwide, with full ownership by the national government while allowing purchases of power from IPPs. These power purchase agreements can be sources of patronage, undermining the intended benefits of competition.

Regulatory Oversight and History

Organization

With respect to how natural gas facilities are treated in a regulatory sense, Michot Foss (2012) incorporated an extensive appendix on U.S., Canada and Mexico policy and regulatory oversight of natural gas and electric power. To aid those readers not familiar with the long and complex path toward the natural gas regimes seen today in the United States and North America, this appendix provides an updated summary. Table A.1 offers an updated snapshot of North American natural gas and electric power industry organization and ownership, while Table A.2 summarizes regulatory oversight. In North America energy industry ownership and organization have a great influence on the character of the respective energy sectors and the extent of reliance on markets. The variation in resource ownership is the most obvious. The United States is unique in both North America and worldwide for the extent of private ownership of energy and non-fuel mineral resources. At one time, Canada and Mexico were more closely aligned with public ownership of resources and strong tendencies to reserve the benefits of resource wealth for the needs of domestic populations. While

Table A.1 North American natural gas and electricity organization

Segment	*Private*	*Public*
Natural gas		
Resource ownership	US ("fee" minerals, see Chap. 1)	*Canada (provincial and federal Crown lands) United States (state and federal lands) Mexico (national patrimony)
Resource development	**Canada (Petro-Canada is no longer a Crown corporation) United States	Mexico—Petroleos Mexicanos (Pemex); 2013 upstream reforms enable private investment via competitive bid rounds conducted by Mexico's CNH with exploration and development undertaken through a combination of contract forms (licenses and production sharing arrangements; see Table A.2)[a]
Pipelines	Canada United States Mexico (under 1995 regulatory reform, private investment in pipelines allowed)	Mexico (Pemex retains ownership of some pipelines but no LDCs)
Distribution	Canada (majority of utilities are investor owned) United States (majority of utilities are investor owned) Mexico (under 1995 reform, Pemex franchises converted to private ownership)	Canada (municipal-owned utilities, or "munis") United States (municipal-owned utilities)
Electricity		
Generation	Canada (investor-owned utilities or IOUs, cooperatives or co-ops, private producers) United States (IOUs, co-ops and private producers) Mexico (under 1992 reform, IPPs with sales to customers other than CFE initially restricted; 2013 reforms fully liberalized sales but CFE remains the major power purchaser)	Canada (provincial-owned Crown utilities, some munis) United States (federal power authorities, munis) Mexico (CFE)

(*continued*)

Table A.1 (continued)

Segment	*Private*	*Public*
Transmission	Canada (investor owned, co-ops) United States (investor owned, co-ops)	Canada (provincial grids and Crown corporations) United States (federal authorities) Mexico (CFE)
Distribution	Canada (investor owned, co-ops) United States (investor owned, some co-ops)	Canada (provincial utilities, municipals) United States (municipals) Mexico (CFE)

Source: Adapted and updated from Michot Foss et al. (1998, 2012)

Notes: *Approximately 90 percent of Canada's natural gas resource base is owned by federal (about 41 percent) or provincial (about 48 percent) Crown governments. Some private lands and fee minerals exist in southern Alberta.[b] **Merged with Suncor in 2009[c]

[a]Following the 2016 election of President Andrés Manuel López Obrador new bid rounds for upstream licenses were suspended. An array of issues are affecting Mexico's upstream and energy sector overall. See Grunstein and Michot Foss (2020), Grunstein (2019), Leiss and Duhalt (2019)

[b]See The Canadian Encyclopedia, https://www.thecanadianencyclopedia.ca/en/article/crown-land

[c]Petro-Canada merged with Suncor Energy in 2009 and operates as a Suncor brand for wholesale and retail gasoline and diesel outlets, marine fuels, and other products and services. See https://www.suncor.com/en-ca/about-us/products-and-services/petro-canada and https://www.petro-canada.ca/en/personal?_ga=2.26162365.1832860818.1580671890-1596691156.1580671890

hydrocarbons are firmly a public sector domain in Canada, the upstream businesses are intensively competitive (exclusive of Canada's giant oil sands operations). Likewise, Canadian midstream and downstream enterprises, to include new and expanding international LNG projects, are as lively as in the Lower 48. Many hope that Mexico, which needs energy to serve its young economy, will join its North American partners. Since the early 1990s, Mexico's energy sector reforms have progressed in fits and starts, still with little agreement as to disposition of the primary state-owned enterprises (SOEs) or Mexico's role as an oil and possibly gas exporter (the former still a major contributor to Mexico's treasury).

Regulation in Historical Context[11]

Natural gas policy and regulation in the United States has been a long and winding journey as summarized and updated in Table A.3.

The references to historical events made thus far should hint at the importance of signature actions and decisions and their impact on the shape and performance of the U.S. natural gas industry value chain system. For anyone new to the long history of the U.S. natural gas industry, it is nothing, if not multifaceted (Fig. A.3).

Table A.2 General regulatory oversight in North America

Segment	*Canada*	*United States*	*Mexico*
Natural gas			
Resource access and development:			
Privately owned minerals	Provincial energy utility boards (EUBs) and energy ministries	State conservation commissions	n/a
Under state/ provincial lands	EUBs and ministries	State conservation commissions (or other state entities for leasing)	n/a
Under national lands	n/a (national government ministries coordinate with provincial governments petroleum boards including for Eastern Canada offshore)	Federal agencies with specific authority: Onshore—Department of Interior, Bureau of Land Management; Department of Agriculture, Forest Service Offshore—DOI Bureau of Ocean Energy Management (BOEM), bid rounds and licensing; Bureau of Safety and Environmental Enforcement (BSEE), safety and environmental regulatory oversight)	*Comisión Nacional de Hidrocarburos (CNH), bid rounds and licensing Agencia de Seguridad, Energía y Ambiente (ASEA), safety and environmental oversight Pemex for retained acreage and operations National committee of ministries, including Secretaría de Energía or SE (chair and chair of Pemex board), Hacienda (finance), and office of the President[a] *National energy advisory council
Pipelines			
National	n/a	n/a	**Comisión Reguladora de Energía (CRE) Centro Nacional de Control del Gas Natural (CENAGAS), independent gas pipeline operator
Intraprovincial, intrastate	EUBs	State public utility commissions (PUCs)	n/a

(*continued*)

Table A.2 (continued)

Segment	*Canada*	*United States*	*Mexico*
Interprovincial, interstate	National Energy Board, Canada (NEB)[b]	Federal Energy Regulatory Commission (FERC)	n/a
Local distribution	EUBs	PUCs	CRE
International trade			
Exports	NEB (sales and facility licenses)	Department of Energy (sales to non-Free Trade Agreement or FTA countries), FERC (licenses)	n/a
Imports	NEB (receipts and licenses)	DOE (receipts), FERC (licenses)	CRE (licenses, including private projects), Pemex (self-regulated pipeline receipts using first-hand sales formula based on Houston Ship Channel), CFE (liquefied natural gas or LNG trade with negotiated supply purchase agreements using Henry Hub basis)
Other safety and environment	Industries must comply with national and, in Canada and the United States, provincial and state safety and environmental laws and regulations for occupational, air, water, hazardous materials and other safety, security, health and environment (SSHE) requirements.		
Electricity			
Generation	EUBs (for utilities only)	PUCs (for utilities only)	CRE CFE National committee of ministries, including SE (chair and chair of CFE board), Hacienda, and President National energy advisory council

(*continued*)

Table A.2 (continued)

Segment	*Canada*	*United States*	*Mexico*
****Transmission*			
Provincial, state grids (wholesale)	EUBs	PUCs	CRE, CFE Centro Nacional de Control de Energía (CENACE), national wholesale market and grid manager
Interprovincial, interstate (wholesale)	NEB; participation in reliability councils	FERC; participation in reliability councils	CRE, CFE
Distribution (retail)	EUBs	PUCs	CRE, CFE
****International trade*			
Exports	NEB	FERC (DOE presidential certificates for DC ties)	n/a
Imports	NEB	DOE (receipts), FERC (licenses)	CRE, CFE
Other safety and environment	Industries must comply with national and, in Canada and the United States, provincial and state safety and environmental laws and regulations for occupational, air, water, hazardous materials and other SSHE requirements.		

Sources: Adapted and updated from Michot Foss et al. (1998, 2012). See Serra and Escobedo (2019a, b), for an overview of Mexico's regulatory regimes. See Manning and Tamura-O'Connor (2019) for Canadian oil and gas regulatory regimes and Christian and Shipley (2019), for Canadian electricity regulation

Notes: *Created in 2009 energy reforms. **Created in 1994 with limited authority in electric power, formalized and expanded in 1995 natural gas reform and 2009 reforms. ***All three countries coordinate electric power grid reliability by cooperating in the North American Electric Reliability Corporation (NERC) and Energy Working Group (ministerial). Countries also coordinate through border state commissions and electric power grid operators

[a]Prior to the election of the current president of Mexico, Manuel Andres Lopez Obrador, the official residence of Mexico's leaders was "Los Pinos", with the name extended to represent the office of the president. The Mexico "White House", controversial throughout its history, is now a public space. This development is a useful analogy for Mexico politics as of the current Lopez Obrador "sexenio" and probably beyond

[b]Bill C-69 requires the NEB to become the Canadian Energy Regulator. The "CER Act" does not yet have an in force date. See Manning and Tamura-O'Connor (2019)

Table A.3 US natural gas industry restructuring

Time period	*Era*	*Characterization*
Pre-1920s	"Market raiding"	Competitive LDC industry
1800s–1927	*State public utility regulation*	Formation of Massachusetts Gas Commission in 1885 through regulation of intrastate pipelines in all 48 states by 1927.
1928–1938	*Natural Gas Act (NGA)*	Development of, and federal regulation of, interstate pipeline transportation. Congress at the time debated the wisdom of granting monopoly franchise certificates to pipelines, with some arguing for common carriage (Michot Foss, 1995).
1935		Public Utility Holding Company Act, PUHCA
1938		Creation of Federal Power Commission (FPC); natural gas industry now comprehensively regulated from the burnertip to intrastate transmission to interstate transmission, by state and federal jurisdictions.
1940–1970s	*Wellhead regulation under the NGA*	1940, to the *Phillips* decision in 1954, to 1970s gas curtailments.
1954		Federal regulation of wellhead prices in interstate markets by FPC as result of Supreme Court decision *Phillips Petroleum Co. v. Wisconsin* (347 U.S. 672); natural gas producers selling to interstate pipelines were deemed "natural gas companies" under the NGA and subject to regulatory oversight by the FPC. Federal Power Commission's failure to adequately raise price ceilings led to the beginning of deregulation.
1970s	*Managed deregulation*	Energy crisis–spawned "Carter Doctrine". Phased decontrol of wellhead prices with restrictions on use.
1978		Natural Gas Policy Act (NGPA) extended wellhead price ceilings to the intrastate market by implementing complex vintaging of gas production by depth and age, and reformed FPC into the FERC; introduced the process of deregulation by loosening certification requirements to facilitate gas flows. Powerplant and Industrial Fuel Use Act (PIFUA) outlawed natural gas consumption for boilers. Public Utility Regulatory Policies Act (PURPA) enabled natural gas use for cogeneration sold to utilities at avoided cost.
1980s–1992	*Mandatory contract carriage*	"Phased decontrol" (full wellhead price decontrol achieved in 1989) created surplus conditions. Need for flexible pricing and transportation led to special marketing programs that released gas from long-term contracts into price-discounted supply pools.

(*continued*)

Table A.3 (continued)

Time period	*Era*	*Characterization*
1985		FERC Order 436 created the open access era, provided some resolution for take-or-pay (TOP) liabilities.
1990		Clean Air Act Amendments (CAAA), policy boost for natural gas as a cleaner burning fuel.
1992		Energy Policy Act of 1992 (EPAct 1992), PUHCA reform with the possibility of a restructured electric power industry that both competes with and is a market for natural gas. Preceded by DOE's National Energy Strategy (NES), which promoted open access and a more competitive natural gas industry, and incorporated provision on new interstate pipeline certifications that directly questioned the monopoly status of interstate pipelines (but stopped short of making specific recommendations for state PUC reform of local distribution).
1992		FERC Order 636 final open access order Full wholesale, bulk market created; continued separation of "merchant" and transportation functions of interstate pipelines. Market hubs and centers encouraged Trading viewed as best means for price discovery and transfer
1992–present	*Post-open access*	"Second free market era", with flexibility extending to LDCs. Light-handed regulation, gas price pass-through, incentive rate making and other features. Comparable service, private contracting, regulatory bypass.
1995		Deep Water Royalty Relief Act (DWRRA) spurred deep water drilling in US Gulf of Mexico.
1996	*Bulk electric market*	FERC Order 888, wholesale competition, non-discriminatory open access on public utility transmission grids with stranded cost recovery. FERC acts to implement EPAct 1992.
2000		FERC Order 2000, establishment of Regional Transmission Organizations (RTOs).
Post-2000		Following final Order 2000 a series of orders to address standards of conduct, reliability and deal with myriad issues related to wholesale and retail pricing and market competition for natural gas and electric power. An attempt to "harmonize" gas and power markets and operations was not consummated.

Sources: Based on Michot Foss (1995) after Bradley (1993), and Michot Foss (2012). A large number of orders and refinements on rulemakings followed FERC's Order 2000. Information on all of FERC's major actions since 1994 can be found at https://www.ferc.gov/legal/maj-ord-reg.asp. Background and intent going forward is detailed in FERC's strategic plan, https://www.ferc.gov/about/strat-docs/strat-plan.asp, for most recent as of this writing. In particular, the FERC has issued a number of rulemakings as the agency attempts to address transmission needs and system demands stemming from growth of variable energy sources (renewables), the associated strains placed on grids and markets and tensions between federal and state jurisdictions

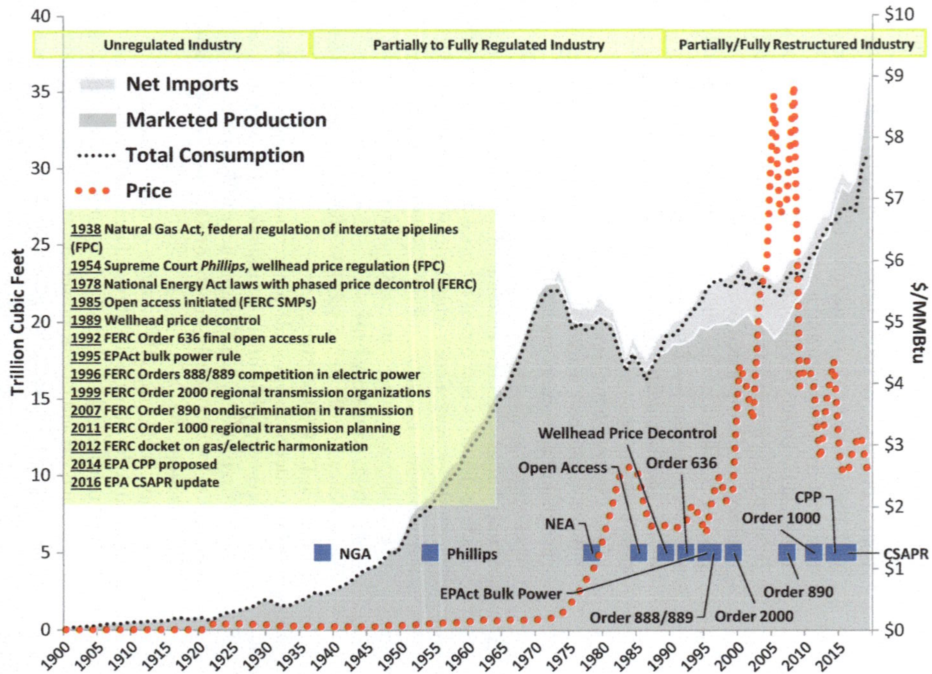

Fig. A.3 The long view of U.S. gas market balances, price and policy/regulatory events. (Sources: U.S. EIA, National Oceanographic and Atmospheric Administration (NOAA), FERC, EPA. Note: the 1978 Carter Administration National Energy Act (NEA) laws included the Natural Gas Policy Act (NGPA), which included phased decontrol; the Powerplant and Industrial Fuel Use Act (PIFUA), which restricted natural gas use in power and industrial boilers; and, by contrast, the Public Utilities Resources Policy Act (PURPA), which incentivized natural gas generation at qualifying facilities. See Michot Foss (2012) for details)

The various stages or "eras" of industry progression in Table A.3 are distinct, with distinct ramifications for suppliers, customers and intermediaries. A great deal of work has been done over the years to identify, analyze and interpret the evolution of government oversight over time, not only of natural gas but of other industries viewed (at the time) to have monopoly/market power attributes (see Michot Foss 2012, previously cited). Importantly, the industry originated with competitive supply of methane (as "town gas" from coal) provided by local distribution businesses that emerged in the mid-1800s. Early network industries were viewed to exhibit either destructive competition, depleting profitability for early investors, or monopoly market power that was unacceptable. From grain elevators and railroads to early natural gas and electric power systems, problems stemming from rapid growth of these vital businesses, and disagreements about how to price capacity, to fear of powerful trusts and other corporate interests led first to regulatory oversight at the state level (state public utility commissions and other entities) and later to federal intervention. The U.S. approach was unique, with creation of "independent" regulatory bodies that were to be free of political interference (although officials were and are appointed by governors and presidents and approved by legislatures and Congress). Regulators were charged with rule making but also imbued with administrative judicial powers based on precedent that complemented the common law tradition embraced as the United States was formed. Early industrialists were not blameless in seeking government oversight in order to exclude competition and ensure returns to investors. The tradeoffs were thought to be manageable because, for many, government oversight was viewed to be short-lived and only to support the establishment and expansion of essential infrastructure networks.

The advent of large-scale natural gas production first in the Appalachians and later in Texas and the southwestern states, along with advances in pipeline construction, fostered construction of interstate natural gas transmission and associated sales. As noted above, the Natural Gas Act (NGA) of 1938 established federal regulation of interstate pipeline transportation capacity and service along with the natural gas commodity as a bundled, certificated franchise monopoly under jurisdiction of the FPC. [Alternative views, and supporting evidence, exist on the origin of and drivers for the NGA and whether there was full agreement on bundling transportation and the gas commodity (Michot Foss 1995).]

A crucial Supreme Court decision (*Phillips*, Table A.3) in the 1950s led to federal government regulation over the price of natural gas in interstate markets. Legal wrangling over natural gas pricing in interstate markets resulted in the Court's action that put the original, 1930s established Federal Power Commission (FPC) in control of regulating the price of methane at the wellhead. The case in question was *Phillips Petroleum Company v. Wisconsin*, with the State of Wisconsin arguing that producers sold natural gas to pipelines at unregulated prices and seeking to close the NGA loophole in order to ensure low prices to consumers.

Applying federal price-setting to millions of natural gas wellheads operated by thousands of producers (the outcome of the *Phillips* decision) proved an impossible task. By the mid- to late 1970s, the United States experienced severe shortages in the interstate system during below-normal winters while gas supply remained plentiful in producer state unregulated intrastate systems. The Federal Power Commission (or FPC), precursor to the current Federal Energy Regulatory Commission (FERC), could not act quickly enough to adjust prices in interstate markets to meet demand. Meanwhile, prices for natural gas sold in intrastate markets reflected supply–demand conditions. This made intrastate sales much more appealing for producers. Supply interruptions during cold winters, in actual fact a consequence of gas being held out of interstate transactions, hastened action on some of the most ill-advised legislation taken in the US energy sector.

What followed were a series of actions by the Carter administration, already struggling with oil supply shocks and other energy disruptions, intended to both restrict natural gas use and to re-introduce competition into the industry system. The Carter administration–era laws were rooted in fears that natural gas supplies were chronically short, that the United States was contending with a true resource scarcity. The Carter energy policies thus initiated more market-responsive pricing for natural gas, while also imposing barriers to natural gas consumption. Allowing prices to rise to reflect demand and stimulate supply growth, while also prohibiting industrial boiler use, resulted in loss of baseload consumption, mainly among industrial users who were already impacted by high oil prices. An outcome of the Carter era–initiated phased price decontrol was a surge in production. Later, the supply response fostered by rising prices was accelerated by both the Reagan and Clinton administrations' drilling incentives.

The competing and conflicting, and difficult to implement, National Energy Act objectives hastened eventual experiments with "special marketing programs (or SMPs) under the FERC, which was reconstituted from the old FPC. SMPs enabled FERC-approved third-party access to gas and interstate pipeline capacity outside of the rigid pipeline contracts that linked suppliers with local gas utilities. As pressure for more access grew, and for full wellhead price decontrol to send better signals to producers and customers, FERC proceeded with subsequent actions[12] culminating in the final rule, Order 636, fully unbundling the interstate pipeline system, endorsing price transparency through market centers and hubs, encouraging third-party midstream participation (in particular storage) and establishing the modern gas industry system in the United States today.

Also important to note is the impact of other policy and regulatory actions that influence natural gas markets, most notably: CAAA, the 1992 EPAct, 1995 DWRRA and FERC electric power orders. Environmental Protection Agency (EPA) actions under its 1990 Clean Air Act authority have the power to re-order fuel use in the electric power sector, both creating and destroying opportunities. As such, EPA is a powerful, and politically charged, entity when it comes to natural gas market conditions and future outlooks. Strongly debated EPA actions include the agency's recent moves to strengthen National Ambient Air Quality Standards (NAAQS), and its 2009 endangerment finding in response to the 2007 Supreme Court decision that greenhouse gases (GHG) are pollutants covered under the CAA.[13] Most obviously, EPA rules could reduce the role of coal-fired electric power generation. Potential economic impacts and industry and business opposition to stiffer NAAQS led to a court-ordered delay of currently proposed revisions.[14] GHG actions are stymied by the inability of the U.S. Congress to promulgate climate policy legislation. While many in the natural gas industry hope for policy inducements for natural gas utilization, the unintended consequences—in terms of both regulatory oversight of natural gas operations that would result from these rules, and broad implications for the U.S. economy—render net benefits to the industry quite unclear.[15]

While environmental concerns have always been part of the mix, the EPA-proposed Clean Power Plan (CPP) with aggressive targets for GHG emissions and the later Cross-state Air Pollution Rule (CSAPR) for meeting more stringent ambient air quality standards and reduce ozone had good and bad inferences for natural gas use. More important, perhaps, was the boost they would provide to renewable energy sources and therefore the potential for disruption to natural gas value chain system. Renewable energy, mainly wind and solar, already was a factor in the busy landscape and heavily promoted by many states, whether through renewable portfolio standards, RPS, programs or other means, along with federal subsidy backing. It has the potential to displace natural gas generation, with ripple effects on the supply side, while placing sometimes onerous requirements on the entire natural gas system for load following and balancing. At heart of debates about these shifts is cost recovery, a constant theme across many parts of the natural gas system and linked power networks. Cost recovery concerns extend from generation capacity that is needed to ensure reliability, but that may be offline for extended periods, to assuring adequate pipeline line pack so that gas can be delivered reliably, to aforementioned gas LDC system integrity, to replacing the lost value of energy stored in generation fuels if those fuels are no longer used (gas, coal, uranium) and so on. The implications from renewable energy scale up run both wide and deep. It is not clear, as of this writing, how the policy actions already on the table will evolve and with what ultimate impact, but any long view must take into account how this point has been reached.

In recent years, attempts at electric power restructuring provided most of the policy and regulatory adventures. The notional idea was to mimic natural gas reforms—separate the commodity (electrons) from infrastructure (wires), facilitate competitive provision of the first (independent power production, where natural gas sat nicely) and, in more ambitious situations, allow competing power retailers to provide the best deals to customers. The 1995 Energy Policy Act (EPAct) kicked things off by embracing the concept of an open, wholesale or "bulk" market for power. To achieve the full benefit of that bulk market would require a similar approach to that used for gas pipelines of nondiscriminatory access to transmission. A corollary was to take a regional approach and reorganize transmission grids into regional transmission organizations (RTOs) in order to gain benefits of regional scale and pricing from competing generators. The FERC proceeded through a number of key orders between the mid-1990s and 2000s to put these concepts and principles into place. Pushback from states was almost immediate and to date, much of the U.S. market operates outside of RTO structures (all of the southeast and most of the west apart from California's independent system operator ISO, or CAISO).[16] While many state concerns were legitimate a larger problem was the uneven adoption of restructuring within states to unbundle utility control of generation and foster competition, restructure transmission rates to enable the flow of price signals and foster investment where it is most needed to ease system constraints. Many states elected not to proceed with restructuring to provide retail choice. A fundamental challenge is "harmonization" of the gas and power industries in operational terms, to better match daily and monthly logistics for typical gas supply acquisition and pipeline capacity nominations with generation fuel requirements and real-time power dispatch.

In so many respects, the lead up to, and rationale for, the final 1992 pipeline restructuring rule was a "Grand Bargain". As noted in Table A.3, the United States always had a choice of investment framework for long-distance natural gas pipelines. Even during the earliest congressional debates during the 1930s, the possibilities for common carriage were considered (Michot Foss 1995 and Michot Foss et al. 1998). By the mid-1980s, when experiments with unbundled sales began, and certainly by 1992, when the FERC implemented Order 636, it was clear that termination of existing TOP contracts and a full open access regime would entail the transfer of price risk across market segments. The bargain constituted the implicit, and important, realization that both producers and customers could be better served by transparent, non-discriminatory competition for pipeline capacity and the market-clearing benefits that would flow from that regime. Producers would have a greater array of options for marketing and sales. Customers would have better access to competitive supply and pricing. To accomplish all this would also entail more transparency around price risk, as well as a transfer of risk across the natural gas value chain. Thus, opportunities and options for price risk management would need to be provided. Risk-accepting entities emerged, in the form of unregulated energy merchants, along with a host of other market participants, providing liquidity in the form of a larger pool of counterparties, and money through both physical and financial brokering and trading.

Suffice to say, from field to market, the number and combination of government participants in the natural gas marketplace can be as large and dense, in form and function, as industry members. Oversight of the thousands of U.S. oil and gas producers, from the largest international integrated oil companies to the smallest "mom and pop" businesses, is mostly at the state level in the United States regardless of mineral ownership (the same is true in Canada, albeit provincial and territorial).

Functions that cross state boundaries, like longline gas pipelines (interstates), fall within FERC jurisdiction, which includes LNG import and export facilities and interstate electric power transmission in areas where wholesale or "bulk" markets for electric power have been created. The NEB in Canada, slated to become the Canadian Energy Regulator, has similar authority. Currently seven wholesale markets exist in the United States and two in Canada (see https://isorto.org/).

The U.S. state public utility commissions, where the notion of independent regulation of industries bearing public utility characteristics originated, have oversight of gas pipelines that operate within state boundaries, LDCs for gas, and electric power transmission and distribution. Depending upon the state, electric power generation may remain subject to state public utility commission (PUC) oversight. Some states like Texas and the PJM region members[17] have "unbundled" electric power to release the competitive potential of generation in the same way that gas pipeline unbundling released the competitive power of gas supply. In 17 states and the District of Columbia, retail customers choose from among competing retail electric providers with ISOs or RTOs managing delivery of electricity by utility or independent providers to local distribution networks. Power transmission grids are managed by independent system operators, or ISOs. Texas has its own grid, a third interconnect within the United States (operated by ERCOT, and separate from the Eastern and Western interconnects).

State interests can diverge with FERC, and have on many occasions, at the "seams"—for instance, where intrastate gas pipelines intersect with interstates, where state and regional electric power transmission systems intersect (including utility ownership and operation thereof), and in how wholesale pricing of natural gas and electric power is determined within this context. Canada's public utility tribunals and NEB share like conflicts. Many states still utilize forms of traditional "cost-of-service" rate making, to establish costs associated with natural gas and electric power systems (pipelines and grids within states, operated by gas LDC networks and gas and electric utilities to include, in those states, utility generation of electric power). The costs are then allocated to system customers, the domestic end users indicated in Fig. A.1. Large commercial and industrial end users, including industrial concerns core to the natural gas system value chain like refiners and petrochemical plants, have often bargained for, lobbied hard and enjoyed the most competitive positions vis-à-vis natural gas and electric power supplies. In many cases, that competitive positioning means the right to negotiate bilateral contracts to lock in supply at competitive (wholesale and or retail) prices.

In Texas, allowing bilateral contracting was a key bargaining chip in that state's implementation of electric power unbundling and retail choice even though it limited the size and scope of the open market for retail power providers. Texas is the only fully liberalized and unbundled (with utilities, excluding municipal and cooperatives who elected to "opt out" forced to separate generation and common carriage of electricity across both transmission and distribution networks), wholesale to retail, electric power market in the United States. It remains the only fully liberalized electric power market in North America as well as the largest sub-national jurisdiction in natural gas generation capacity. The Texas model is "energy only" as documented in Chap. 2. Issues abound, ranging from resource adequacy—sufficient generation to balance the marketplace to accommodating new intermittent generation sources (renewables, including rooftop solar), building new transmission capacity (Texas is the only state to succeed, at considerable cost and effort, in installing transmission lines mainly for renewable energy resources). The open "laboratory" that Texas provides has offered ample evidence of the impacts of intermittent sources, the costs associated with improving forecasting of available wind resources and the challenges of attracting new investment by allowing extreme price signals to flow through the market (see Gülen 2019).

In addition to all of the complex layers and interactions to this point, there is SSHE—safety, security, health and environment rules and practices—to account for. States are responsible for implementing many directives from the U.S. Environmental Protection Agency, EPA, and Department of Transportation, or DOT (like PHMSA); Department of Labor, DOL (like OSHA [Occupational Safety and Health Administration requirements]); and other agencies to ensure that SSHE best practices are maintained. The costs of SSHE protections and assurance hinge on the approach taken, and both government and industry are in a fairly constant search for ways of ensuring SSHE best practices that are compatible with markets. Gas system incidents like those mentioned earlier and high-profile failures like the 2010 Deep Water Horizon offshore rig catastrophe in the Gulf of Mexico can create setbacks that last years. Eventually, changes in approaches, technologies and practices are absorbed and reflected in prices. Notably, too little renewable and alternative energy installed capacity exists to be able to reflect upon SSHE practices and costs associated with system reliability or other disruptions and incidents that could occur.

U.S. Natural Gas System Pricing

Outside of the United States, Canada, portions of Europe and a few other locations, prices for energy tend to be administered. Chapter 5 includes considerable discussion of administered pricing, including complexities and distortions that can emanate from that approach.

Given the topography of the U.S. natural gas value chain system in physical, operational and policy/regulatory terms, how much does natural gas cost? Or, perhaps more to the point, how much do customers pay? With respect to cost, a detailed analysis of oil and gas midstream investment along with attendant assumptions and scenarios is provided by the Interstate Natural Gas Association of America (INGAA) and INGAA Foundation.[18] INGAA estimates that for the period 2018–2035, more than half of the $791 billion expected to be needed in oil and gas midstream investment will be consumed by natural gas infrastructure. Most of that infrastructure expansion will be dedicated to moving the large tranches of incremental associated gas production out of key producing locations to electric power, industrial and export outlets (per Chaps. 1 through 4). As these large investments of capital expense are diffused across the market, all end user groups are likely to be affected to a greater or lesser extent. Figure A.4 provides an indication of the distribution of prices and price differences across the value chain using mostly U.S. Energy Information Administration (EIA) data (data from Intercontinental Exchange [ICE] provided through the EIA are also used). Going forward,

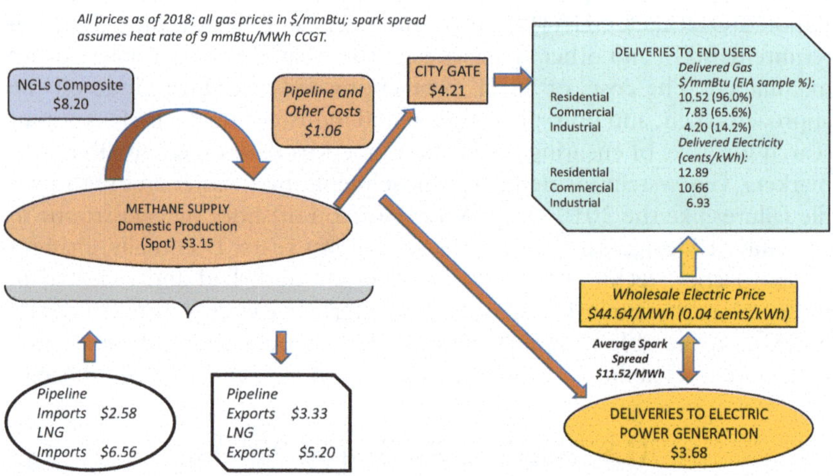

Fig. A.4 U.S. natural gas value chain system 2018 prices. (Source: Developed by author. Price information extracted from EIA and DOE Office of Michot Fossil Energy LNG reports. See https://www.eia.gov/todayinenergy/prices.php for definition of spark spread and formula including heat rate conversion)

it can be expected that the diffusion of cost will roughly follow the long-established patterns of pricing and cost recovery in the U.S. system.

Prices are not costs, of course. As detailed in Chap. 1, the thousands of **upstream operators** must be able to sell their natural gas production at prevailing prices and make sufficient operating earnings and discretionary free cash flow to fund their businesses, much less to reinvest for the future. This often means selling gas production at prevailing discounts relative to producing locations that are underserved by pipelines. Producers try to soften price risk, including locational basis risk, with hedging. In recent years many producers have faced frequent, and frequently wide, discounts. These discounts are artifacts of transportation bottlenecks. In light of these disparities, mostly temporal, success in achieving realized prices with hedging that are close to or better than prevailing market prices is not a given (see Chap. 1 for related discussion).

Nor is pipeline profitability a given, which stymies investment in new capacity. The U.S. gas value chain currently has more than 300,000 miles of pipeline, between and within states.[19] These are run by a diverse set of organizations. Most of the large interstate pipelines were reorganized into master limited partnerships, or MLPs, the typical business structure also used for other midstream activities. On average, **transportation cost** to move natural gas on interstate pipelines in the United States is about $1 per million Btu (MMBtu). Transportation costs are lower or higher the closer or further away from supply, or the less or more congested pipeline capacity may be. Capturing that transportation fee is not assured, although pipeline companies do their best to plan for variation in use. Pipelines live or die on throughput; a drop in carried volumes means that much less revenue for the pipeline company to fund its operations and reinvest. As noted in Chap. 1, to mitigate revenue volatility and hedge against risk, investment in new pipeline capacity increasingly has involved commitments by producers in order to achieve financing for projects. Pipeline companies are more willing to invest their own capital and are more able to obtain external financing when “demand pull” provides the business case for expansion. During times of “supply push”, when producers desperately need to move gas production out of fields to delivery points, producer guarantees are essential.

The cost difference between field and city gate incorporates other midstream charges for the activities shown in Fig. A.1—gathering, processing, dehydrating (water is anathema to pipelines) and so on. The **NGLs composite price** reflects a weighted average of natural gas components that are captured and sold separately (ethane, propane and so on; extensive discussion on trends in these commodities will be found in Chap. 3 on petrochemicals). Some of the value created with NGLs capture and sales will return to producers (and their lessors), should producers have decent market access for processing and fractionation. In recent years and in too many situations producers have effectively had to pay midstream companies to take gas and dispose of NGLs; in other words, the discounted value back to the wellhead after transportation cost is negative.

City gate prices in the United States can vary widely by season. Industry participants typically look to city gate price signals for indication of what customers (LDCs) are willing to pay to sustain service during critical periods, mainly winter heating (wholesale prices for electric power send a similar message). From the city gate, end users pay some portion of the costs of the roughly two million miles of **LDC systems**. Pre–open access restructuring in the United States, the price differences across customer groups in some states were not as stark as today, an indication of tendencies to carry, or cross-subsidize, smaller customers with larger-volume users. Today, industrials and many large commercial customers have more bargaining power, and can make their own supply and pipeline arrangements. As mentioned earlier, industrial customers have bypassed LDC utilities to pay rates that are very close to supply plus pipeline cost, including large intrastate pipelines that are part of LDC corporate holdings. Residential customers typically are captive to LDCs for service and gas supply.

A similar distribution of system costs across end user groups exists for electric power. Again, residential households, with their daily and seasonal variation in use and small volumes at meters, are more expensive to serve than large, steady industrial and commercial users. Local systems are more expensive to maintain and constantly subjected to impacts ranging from digging into natural gas lines to trees and animals interfering with power wires. The difference between the **wholesale cost of electricity** and end user prices includes expenses to transmit power from the generation station to the LDC and end users. Whereas it is difficult for regulators and policy makers to impose additional charges on the more open and competitive U.S. gas system, it remains relatively easy to do so for electric power. Thus, many customers, mainly residential, in many states pay for a variety of "social" costs, such as charges for renewable energy portfolio standards and mandates (see Chap. 2). The **gas cost for electricity generation** is converted to "spark spread". While it is only a very rough guide to profitability, generators must operate facilities successfully within the spark spread, hopefully with positive margins. Spark spread was not high enough to allow for O&M cost recovery before 2018. Wholesale electric prices have been impacted by cheap natural gas, increasing competition from renewable energy sources and other factors, mainly recovery from the 2007–2009 recession. A more vibrant economy, harsher winters, growth in air conditioning demand and many other factors underlie the jump in wholesale prices in 2018. Lack of gas interconnectivity in New England relative to demand and renewable energy policies in New England and California explains much of the regional price patterns (Table A.4).

Given the openness and liquidity in the U.S. natural gas pipeline system, **retail prices for natural gas** move closely with the main price index, Henry Hub. Smaller retail customers—residential and commercial—face higher prices for their delivered natural gas, a consequence of the marginal cost to serve smaller and more erratic customer loads as mentioned earlier. Figure A.5 illustrates **retail electricity prices** during the pronounced cycle in natural gas costs. Certainly, retail power customers and consumers utilize electricity generated from different fuel sources and technologies. However, a persistent question is the rise in retail prices given that natural gas prices have fallen so deeply, and pulled the price of wholesale electricity along with it. All of this happened as a new record for daily natural gas use in power generation was set on July 19, 2019.[20] Any number of explanations have been offered but two stand out—the role of renewables,[21] for which system integration costs can be large (including investment in new transmission lines) and hidden, and the rising costs of maintaining local distribution networks including repair and replacement.[22]

With respect to **international trade**, within North America and externally, **U.S. natural gas imports** are attracted by the spot or cash price at the main Henry Hub (Louisiana) index and traded contract point. Exporters to the United States must be able to discern favorable margins. When it comes to the preponderance of Canadian piped imports, Canadian producers are often as disadvantaged as those U.S. producers operating in basins remote from market centers. Deep discounts revert back to Canadian fields if U.S. demand is slack and/or U.S. supply ample, as it has been. For critical seasonal needs, like those in New England, long-term LNG contracts help to guarantee crucial receipts. Long-term contracts and tolling arrangements were used to backstop new LNG receiving capacity during the construction wave of 2002–2007. That wave resulted in expansions from four original locations (Boston, Cove Point in Maryland, Elba Island in Georgia and Lake Charles, Louisiana, the historical first) to include

Table A.4 Wholesale electricity prices and spark spreads

Location	*Hub*	*2014*	*2015*	*2016*	*2017*	*2018*	*2015*	*2016*	*2017*	*2018*
		$/Megawatt hour ($/MWh)					*Annual percent change (%)*			
Texas	ERCOT North 345KV peak	41.57	29.48	27.16	27.46	30.24	-29	-8	1	10
Indiana	Indiana Hub RT peak	41.36	34.34	34.96	36.74	41.68	-17	2	5	13
Pacific northwest	Mid C peak	36.17	26.06	23.04	26.04	37.42	-28	-12	13	44
New England	Nepool MH DA LMP peak	76.25	49.67	35.57	39.18	49.45	-35	-28	10	26
California	NP15 EZ Gen DA LMP peak	51.11	36.55	33.53	42.14	78.21	-28	-8	26	86
Arizona	Palo Verde peak	40.70	27.18	25.55	32.79	42.44	-33	-6	28	29
Pennsylvania	PJM WH real-time peak	46.50	43.41	34.54	35.00	41.45	-7	-20	1	18
California	SP15 EZ Gen DA LMP peak	50.35	34.15	30.85	39.02	50.62	-32	-10	26	30
Average of weighted average prices ($/MWh)		48.00	35.07	30.31	34.63	44.64	-27	-14	14	29
Cost of methane delivered to electric power customers ($/MMBtu)		5.19	3.38	2.99	3.52	3.68	-35	-12	18	5
Spark spread ($/MWh)		1.29	4.65	3.40	2.95	11.52	261	-27	-13	290

Sources: EIA and ICE; author calculations

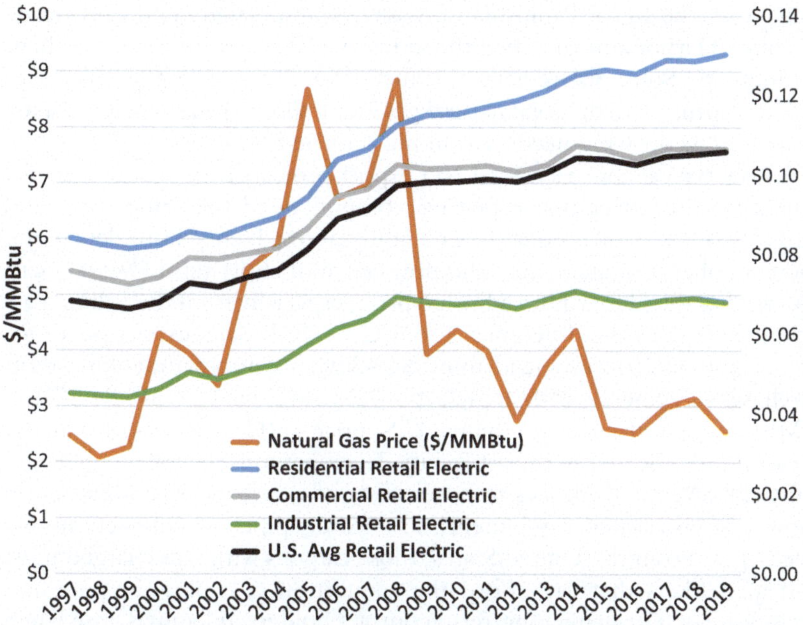

Fig. A.5 Retail electric prices in the United States. (Source: EIA)

Sabine Pass in Louisiana; Golden Pass and Freeport, which uses a tolling model, in Texas; and two floating systems. Countless planned and proposed projects were abandoned as gas prices collapsed in 2007, or retooled or planned for retooling to accommodate exports.

When it comes to **U.S. natural gas exports**, Mexican customers have paid premiums to attract crucial U.S. supply across their border and the costs for both pipeline and LNG infrastructure to support that trade. This contrasts distinctly with the lower prices U.S. customers have paid for Canadian pipeline imports, a result of U.S. gas supply and the ripple effects back to Canadian production. Long-term LNG contracts also have been vital to launching new export projects, anchoring liquefaction and expanded berthing capacity at the existing Sabine Pass facility, the main export point with respect to current cargoes; Cove Point; Elba Island; and Freeport. An export terminal in Corpus Christi, Texas, will join its sister Sabine Pass. Countless planned and proposed LNG export projects are announced and avidly tracked.[23] A future plan for the original LNG export point from the Kenai Peninsula in Alaska, which inaugurated LNG trade to Tokyo Harbor and launched the industry (1969), is conversion to handle imports. Solutions remain ephemeral for the puzzling problems of how to capture North Slope natural gas and build new gas pipeline capacity to address growing needs within the state and for exports.

A now typical approach for LNG export projects is to charge a fee for liquefaction to cover that expensive component of the value chain and natural gas cost that is equal to or slightly above Henry Hub depending upon supplier arrangements. The prevalence of short-term ("spot") cargoes sold at the Henry Hub adjusted price, especially from the Sabine Pass facility, illustrates the difference. From U.S. DOE data, export prices for spot cargoes in 2019 averaged about $4.43 while cargoes under long-term purchase agreements with liquefaction fees averaged about $4.27 per MMBtu, a reflection of prevailing U.S. price (HH) and global demand (weakening). Clearly, an export facility developer must be able to generate sufficient revenue from fees to cover costs of very expensive liquefaction trains and associated equipment, to include pipeline connections for "feed" gas. From the United States, those cargoes with fees charged must land in markets that can afford the acquisition cost plus shipping and regasification. For many long-term contract holders, dilemmas arise when facing obligations to pay these costs should demand drop and LNG and natural gas prices fall in the originally intended receiving markets. For that reason, LNG contracting conventions today are gravitating toward flexibility in destinations to enable cargoes to be delivered where demands (and prices) are best. Long-term contractors must be able to engage in these trades while meeting their obligations to pay liquefaction and other fees at the U.S. export facility, which has proved to be no small challenge in a well-supplied LNG marketplace. These trends are alluded to in the Introduction. Much more discussion is provided in Chap. 4.

Figure A.6 provides a snapshot of **import and export prices** over time, landed prices in the case of LNG exports. Given access to international trade, natural gas suppliers will look to export when external prices appear favorable to the domestic market. The reverse will be true during periods when the domestic market is not balanced. The situation for LNG is most interesting. The era of LNG import expansion is clear during the early to mid-2000s. The surge in export capacity investment as international prices skyrocketed with crude oil has been a fixture in natural gas industry strategy. Of note is the shift in conditions during 2018 as LNG supply capacity worldwide exceeded demand (and New England heating season demand

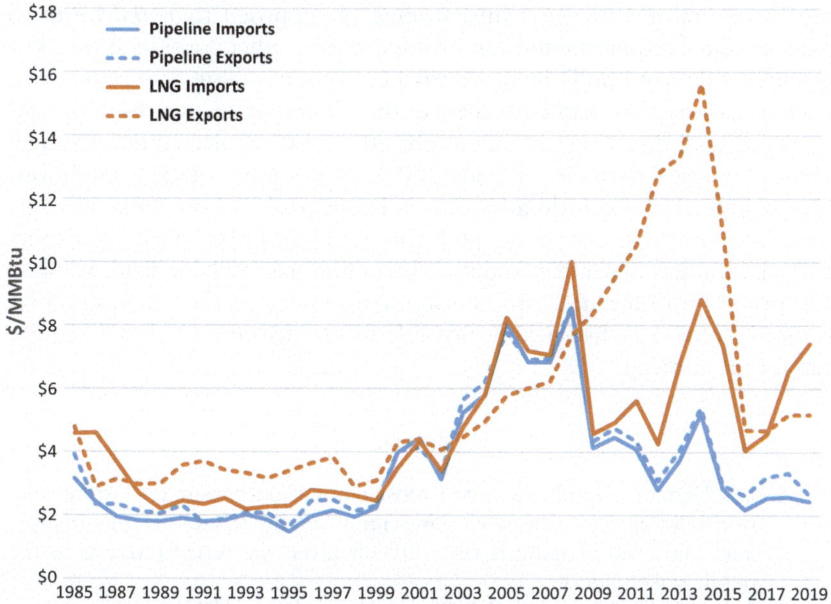

Fig. A.6 Natural gas import and export prices. (Source: EIA)

attracted Russian imports). The tensions going forward for US LNG developers, as presented in Chap. 4, are well illustrated in the Fig. A.6 trends.

Notably, Fig. A.4 does not include a specific estimate of prices associated with **storage**. Natural gas storage is a classic "buy low, sell high" business. Storage, especially the underground salt cavern storage mentioned previously, typically has been built and financed using "intrinsic" and "extrinsic" value. Intrinsic value is derived from seasonal variation in gas use and thus prices. Extrinsic value is derived from reasonable expectations that gas prices will rise in the future, also a function of underlying seasonal variability but also influenced by an overall rising trend in prices that would emanate from views that future gas supply may prove insufficient to meet demand. As such, intrinsic value reflects price volatility while extrinsic value can hinge on change in price level. It should be obvious that a "flat" market with little seasonal variation, for instance a series of warm winters, or a flat market that results from ample supplies of gas, in essence the state of U.S. gas markets since 2007, makes investment in new storage capacity difficult, at best. Decisions about whether, and how much, natural gas to *inject* into storage (as opposed to *withdrawals* to meet seasonal requirements) can be impacted by other considerations. For instance, "demand pull" from external customers willing to pay more for current gas supplies than customers in the United States can result in sales of gas abroad, diverting gas that might otherwise be injected into storage. Here is where international trade and U.S. domestic market conditions may collide. Far too little attention is being paid to how dynamics surrounding international trade and the LNG industry push to export U.S. natural gas may affect supplies, including gas available from storage, and prices for domestic customers and consumers. In the "all gas politics is local" arena, touchstones for possible future disruptions always require careful monitoring.

Notes

1. Les Deman, consultant, noted most natural gas consumers are jurisdictional; for example, they are utilities regulated by PUCs. Investing in pipelines and even hedging is very difficult given the varied interests of the public stakeholders.
2. Using 2018 BP Statistical Review of Energy data, "JKT" accounted for about 138 million tonnes or MT of LNG to the combined total of roughly 58 MT for China and India.
3. See https://www.ofgem.gov.uk/gas/retail-market/gb-gas-retail-market for the British market.
4. See https://ec.europa.eu/eurostat/statistics-explained/pdfscache/8894.pdf for EU details from Eurostat.
5. This target has often been discussed by representatives of Clean Energy Fuels, https://www.cleanenergyfuels.com/
6. Information provided by Clean Energy Fuels.
7. See American Bureau of Shipping (ABS) press release, March 24, 2016, https://ww2.eagle.org/en/news/abs-news/launching-worlds-first-cng-ship.html
8. Qatar Airways, 2009, news release, World's first commercial passenger flight powered by fuel made from natural gas lands in Qatar, October 12, https://www.qatarairways.com/en-gb/press-releases/2009/Oct/PressRelease_12Oct09_2.html
9. See https://www.energy.gov/downloads/notice-proposed-rulemaking-grid-resiliency-pricing-rule. The FERC rejected the notice of proposed rulemaking (NOPR). See https://www.utilitydive.com/news/ferc-rejects-doe-nopr-kicking-resilience-issue-to-grid-operators/514334/ and

https://www.ferc.gov/media/news-releases/2018/2018-1/01-08-18.asp#.W5RChPZFxPY, as the FERC moves to tackle "resilience" more broadly.

10. Also see http://www.beg.utexas.edu/files/energyecon/think-corner/2016/CEE_Snapshot-Retail_Electricity_Connecticut-Sep16.pdf which offers a view of retail electric market structure.
11. Adapted from Michot Foss (2012).
12. Bob Tippee, former editor of the *Oil & Gas Journal* (and peer reviewer for this Appendix), commented that there were almost as many FERC orders unraveling gas regulation as there were price categories in the NGPA. Another telling comment was made by James H. Bailey, "What do you get when you add FERC orders 380, 436, 451, 500, 528, 497, and 636? 3,428!" in a presentation to the International Association for Energy Economics 14th Annual North American Conference, New Orleans, October 26–28, 1992.
13. See the EPA's "Regulatory Actions" (www.epa.gov/pm/actions.html) on NAAQs proposed review and "Endangerment and Cause or Contribute Findings for Greenhouse Gases under Section 202(a) of the Clean Air Act" (http://epa.gov/climatechange/endangerment.html) on GHG endangerment.
14. See "Court Delays EPA Rule on Coal Plants" by Eileen O'Grady, *Reuters*, 30 December 2011, www.reuters.com/article/2011/12/31/us-utilities-epa-idUSTRE7BT17420111231
15. In the Preface to this book, I address GHG concerns relative to natural gas. The main component of natural gas, methane, is considered a greenhouse gas.
16. See https://www.eia.gov/todayinenergy/detail.php?id=790
17. From the original Pennsylvania, New Jersey, Maryland to include all or parts of Delaware, Illinois, Indiana, Kentucky, Michigan, North Carolina, Ohio, Tennessee, Virginia, West Virginia and the District of Columbia.
18. See https://www.ingaa.org/Foundation/FDNreports/Midstream2035.aspx
19. See http://www.pipeline101.com/why-do-we-need-pipelines/natural-gas-pipelines for facts and figures.
20. EIA, August 5, 2019, Today in Energy news release, https://www.eia.gov/todayinenergy/detail.php?id=40753
21. EIA, March 16, 2015, Today in Energy news release, https://www.eia.gov/todayinenergy/detail.php?id=20372
22. Based on comments from industry sources.
23. See https://www.ferc.gov/industries/gas.asp?csrt=4059276950080566368 for all natural gas pipeline, storage and LNG projects.

References

Bradley, R., Jr. 1993. The distortions and dynamics of gas regulation. Paper presented at New Horizons in Natural Gas Deregulation, Cato Institute conference, March 4, Washington, DC.

Christian, J., and L. Shipley. 2019. Electricity regulation in Canada: Overview. Thomson Reuters Practical Law, August. https://content.next.westlaw.com/Document/I915005f065e711e698dc8b09b4f043e0/View/FullText.html?navigationPath=Search%2Fv1%2Fresults%2Fnavigation%2Fi0ad604ad0000016c7dff0064e7aa5126%3FNav%3DKNOWHOW%26fragmentIdentifier%3DI915005f065e711e698dc8b09b4f043e0%26parentRank%3D0%26startIndex%3D1%26contextData%3D%2528sc.Search%2529%26transitionType%3DSearchItem&listSource=Search&listPageSource=7bebf850a496f4a3af792af20e461588&list=KNOWHOW&rank=1&sessionScopeId=75624a566c35f311e2317e923af02cbdb01fbedb2c86d137b1cb2c1bf2f6249e&originationContext=Search%20Result&transitionType=SearchItem&contextData=%28sc.Search%29

Grunstein, M. 2019. Mexico's independent energy regulatory agencies: Institutions at risk, Issue brief December 5. Baker Institute for Public Policy, Rice University. https://www.bakerinstitute.org/media/files/files/862cfb2d/bi-brief-120519-usmx-mexenergy.pdf

Grunstein, M., and M. Michot Foss. 2020. The law of the land – Practices, policies and regulations regarding access to lands for energy projects in Mexico, in Social License to Operate (SLO) in the Extractive and Energy Sectors, Oil, Gas and Energy Law (OGEL) 1, 2020. Subscription required. https://www.ogel.org/journal-browse-issues-toc.asp?key=84

M. Michot Foss et al. (eds.), *Monetizing Natural Gas in the New "New Deal" Economy*,
https://doi.org/10.1007/978-3-030-59983-6

Gülen, G. 2019. Net social cost of electricity. The University of Texas at Austin Bureau of Economic Geology Udden Book Series.

Gülen, G., M. Michot Foss, and C.H. Tsai. 2017. Competitive electricity markets: What future? The University of Texas at Austin, Bureau of Economic Geology, Center for Energy Economics report. http://www.beg.utexas.edu/files/energyecon/think-corner/2017/CEE_Research_Note-What_Future_for_Electricity_Markets-Mar17.pdf

Gülen, G., C.H. Tsai, D. Palmer-Huggins, and M. Michot Foss. 2018. Competitiveness of renewable-generation sources. The University of Texas at Austin, Bureau of Economic Geology, Center for Energy Economics report. http://www.beg.utexas.edu/files/energyecon/CEE_Research_Note_Competitiveness_Generation_Apr18.pdf

Knowles, G.L. 2003. Liquefied natural gas: Regulation in a competitive natural gas market. *Energy Law Journal* 24 (2): 293–319.

Leiss, B.C., and A. Duhalt. 2019. Laying the groundwork for the strengthening of Pemex. Center for Energy Studies, Baker Institute for Public Policy, July. https://www.bakerinstitute.org/media/files/files/ed02a9bf/ces-pub-pemex-071519.pdf

Leonard, G., N.M. Moran, and L. Samuel. 2019. Characteristics of U.S. natural gas transactions, cornerstone research. https://www.cornerstone.com/Publications/Reports/Characteristics-of-U-S-Natural-Gas-Transactions-FERC-Form-552-Submissions-as-of-June-2019

Manning, L., and B. Tamura-O'Connor. 2019. Oil and gas regulation in Canada: Overview. Thomson Reuters Practical Law, August. https://content.next.westlaw.com/Document/Id592f8f2755f11e698dc8b09b4f043e0/View/FullText.html?navigationPath=Search%2Fv1%2Fresults%2Fnavigation%2Fi0ad604ad0000016c7dfa2578e7aa4eef%3FNav%3DKNOWHOW%26fragmentIdentifier%3DId592f8f2755f11e698dc8b09b4f043e0%26parentRank%3D0%26startIndex%3D1%26contextData%3D%2528sc.Search%2529%26transitionType%3DSearchItem&listSource=Search&listPageSource=9d197c520fc1a1b6acbdea0cb9eb83b0&list=KNOWHOW&rank=2&sessionScopeId=75624a566c35f311e2317e923af02cbdb01fbedb2c86d137b1cb2c1bf2f6249e&originationContext=Search%20Result&transitionType=SearchItem&contextData=%28sc.Search%29

Michot Foss, M. 1995. U.S. natural gas in the twenty-first century: Adjusting to the new reality. University of Houston. Ph.D. dissertation, 395 p.

———. 2012. Natural gas pricing in North America, chapter 3. In *The pricing of internationally traded gas*, ed. J.P. Stern, 85–144. Oxford University/Oxford Institute for Energy Studies.

Michot Foss, M., J. Pratt, A. Stone, G. Conine, and B. Keller. 1998. North American energy integration: The prospects for regulatory coordination and seamless transactions of natural gas and electricity. Shell interdisciplinary scholars program report, University of Houston. http://citeseerx.ist.psu.edu/viewdoc/download?doi=10.1.1.151.184&rep=rep1&type=pdf

Palmer-Huggins, D., and M. Michot Foss. 2016. LNG marine fuel applications. The University of Texas at Austin, Bureau of Economic Geology, Center for Energy Economics report, November. http://www.beg.utexas.edu/files/energyecon/think-corner/2016/CEE_Research_Note-LNG_Marine_Fuel_Applications-Nov16.pdf.

Serra, J.C., and J.E. Escobedo. 2019a. Oil and gas regulation in Mexico: Overview. Thomson Reuters Practical Law, June. https://content.next.westlaw.com/Document/Id4af1a831cb511e38578f7ccc38dcbee/View/FullText.html?contextData=(sc.Default)&transitionType=Default&firstPage=true&bhcp=1

———. 2019b. Electricity regulation in Mexico: Overview. Thomson Reuters Practical Law, June. https://content.next.westlaw.com/Document/Ieb49d7bc1cb511e38578f7ccc38dcbee/View/FullText.html?navigationPath=Search%2Fv1%2Fresults%2Fnavigation%2Fi0ad604ad0000016c7decbf75e7aa4c4a%3FNav%3DKNOWHOW%26fragmentIdentifier%3DIeb49d7bc1cb511e38578f7ccc38dcbee%26parentRank%3D0%26startIndex%3D1%26contextData%3D%2528sc.Search%2529%26transitionType%3DSearchItem&listSource=Search&listPageSource=c46b727cbd1872306866ceb685dd31a3&list=KNOWHOW&rank=1&sessionScopeId=75624a566c35f311e2317e923af02cbdb01fbedb2c86d137b1cb2c1bf2f6249e&originationContext=Search%20Result&transitionType=SearchItem&contextData=%28sc.Search%29

Sukkarieh, M. 2019. Gas sector a catalyst for further cooperation between Lebanon and Egypt. *Executive Magazine*, August 7. https://www.executive-magazine.com/economics-policy/gas-sector-a-catalyst-for-further-cooperation-between-lebanon-and-egypt

Tajitsu, N., and M. Shiraki. 2018. Toyota plans to expand production, shrink cost of hydrogen fuel cell vehicles. *Reuters*, July 26. https://www.reuters.com/article/us-toyota-hydrogen/toyota-plans-to-expand-production-shrink-cost-of-hydrogen-fuel-cell-vehicles-idUSKBN1KG0Y0

Tsai, C.H., and Y.L. Tsai. 2018. Competitive retail electricity market under continuous price regulation. *Energy Policy* 114: 274–287. https://doi.org/10.1016/j.enpol.2017.12.012.

Tussing, A.R., and C.C. Barlow. 1984. *The natural gas industry: Evolution, structure and economics*, 284 pages. Pensacola: Ballinger Publishing.

Tussing, A.R., and B. Tippee. 1995. *The natural gas industry: Evolution, structure and economics*. 2nd ed. Pennwell Corporation. 350 pages.

Index[1]

[1] Note: Page numbers followed by 'n' refer to notes.

M. Michot Foss et al. (eds.), *Monetizing Natural Gas in the New "New Deal" Economy*,
https://doi.org/10.1007/978-3-030-59983-6

The manufacturer's authorised representative in the EU is Springer
Nature Customer Service Centre GmbH, Europaplatz 3, 69115 Heidelberg,
Germany. If you have any concerns regarding our products, please
contact ProductSafety@springernature.com

Printed and bound by CPI Group (UK) Ltd, Croydon, CR0 4YY
23/09/2026
02221529-0002